The Handbook
for Managing Change
in Health Care

Also available from ASQ Quality Press

Mentoring Strategic Change in Health Care: An Action Guide
Chip Caldwell

CQI and the Renovation of an American Health Care System: A Culture Under Construction
Sister Mary Jean Ryan, FSM, and William P. Thompson

The Effectiveness of CQI in Health Care: Stories from a Global Perspective
Vahé Kazandjian, editor

How to Lower Health Care Costs by Improving Health Care Quality: Results-Based Continuous Quality Improvement
M. Daniel Sloan

Success Stories on Lowering Health Care Costs by Improving Health Care Quality
M. Daniel Sloan and Jodi B. Torpey

Show Me: The Complete Guide to Storyboarding and Problem Solving
Harry I. Forsha

Show Me: Storyboard Workbook and Template
Harry I. Forsha

The Quality Toolbox
Nancy R. Tague

Measuring Customer Satisfaction: Survey Design, Use, and Statistical Analysis Methods, Second Edition
Bob E. Hayes

Mapping Work Processes
Dianne Galloway

The Reward and Recognition Process in Total Quality Management
Stephen B. Knouse

Staffing the New Workplace: Selecting and Promoting for Quality Improvement
Ronald B. Morgan and Jack E. Smith

Understanding and Applying Value-Added Assessment: Eliminating Business Process Waste
William E. Trischler

The Change Agents' Handbook: A Survival Guide for Quality Improvement Champions
David W. Hutton

To request a complimentary catalog of publications, call 800-248-1946.

The Handbook for Managing Change in Health Care

Chip Caldwell, editor
ASQ Health Care Series

ASQ Quality Press
Milwaukee, Wisconsin

The Handbook for Managing Change in Health Care
Chip Caldwell, editor   ASQ Health Care Series

Library of Congress Cataloging-in-Publication Data
The handbook for managing change in health care / Chip Caldwell,
   editor.
        p.   cm.—(ASQ health care series)
     Includes bibliographical references and index.
     ISBN 0-87389-403-0 (alk. paper)
     1. Medical care—Quality control.   2. Health services
administration.   3. Organizational change.   I. Caldwell, Chip.
II. Series.
     RA399.A1H36   1997
     362.1'068—dc20   97-2861
                                                              CIP

10 9 8 7 6 5 4 3 2 1

ISBN 0-87389-403-0

Acquisitions Editor: Roger Holloway
Project Editor: Kelley Cardinal

ASQ Mission: To facilitate continuous improvement and increase customer satisfaction by identifying, communicating, and promoting the use of quality principles, concepts, and technologies; and thereby be recognized throughout the world as the leading authority on, and champion for, quality.

Attention: Schools and Corporations
ASQ Quality Press books, videotapes, audiotapes, and software are available at quantity discounts with bulk purchases for business, educational, or instructional use. For information, please contact ASQ Quality Press at 800-248-1946, or write to ASQ Quality Press, P.O. Box 3005, Milwaukee, WI 53201-3005.

For a free copy of the ASQ Quality Press Publications Catalog, including ASQ membership information, call 800-248-1946.

Printed in the United States of America

 Printed on acid-free paper

American Society for Quality

Quality Press
611 East Wisconsin Avenue
Milwaukee, Wisconsin 53202

Contents

Foreword

Future historians will look back at the twentieth century as the most productive in the history of health care. During this century the health care industry greatly expanded its attack on communicable diseases and other threats to human well-being, with stunning results. These results included extending the human life span, providing early warning of incipient dangers, improving the quality of life, and reducing pain and suffering. These gains came from continuous improvement in a wide range of health care components: training for health care professionals, diagnostic processes, therapeutic processes, medical equipment and devices, pharmaceuticals, and others. It has been a century without precedent and has earned the respect and gratitude of all mankind.

But human gratitude is fickle. Periodically it raises the bar. In the words of the late Alben Barkley, it asks: "What have you done for me lately?"

During the closing years of this century, the health care industry has been charged with various alleged failings, including the following:

- High and rising costs, with no end in sight
- Long waits for service
- High error rates
- Much unneeded surgery

There is merit to these charges, and the industry is under intense pressure to act on these (and other) failings, while putting stress on value for the entire array of stakeholders. In addition, competition within the industry has intensified, bringing with it the threat inherent in the Darwinian principle of survival of the fittest. During this century we have seen this principle operate with ruthless efficiency in the manufacturing and service industries. It is now clear that the health care industry is not immune from the concept of survival of the fittest. The need for change has become acute, and recognition of this need is now widespread.

In groping for ways to respond, the health care industry has looked sideways at other industries that have faced intensified competition. The most impressive example has been in manufacturing. It suffered great loss of market share from the Japanese quality revolution, resulting in a high mortality rate of companies in some sectors of the industry—a classic demonstration of the ruthless operation of the Darwinian principle. (On the other side of the coin, that revolution became a major factor in making Japan an economic superpower).

There is much to be learned from the experience of the manufacturing industry. At first the industry did nothing—the instrument panel available to the senior managers provided information on financial performance and little else. Then, as the damage mounted, it became clear that to stem the bleeding—the loss in market share—required a revolution in quality. Many companies tried to launch such a revolution, and many strategies were tested out, but most of the efforts fell short of the goal. However, a few companies achieved stunning results and thereby became the role models for the industry. They not only produced stunning results, they also provided the lessons learned—what to do and what not to do in order to get such results.

In their efforts to improve quality, the manufacturing companies demanded better quality from their suppliers, which included service industries of all kinds. At first the service companies contended that the strategies that produced results in manufacturing were irrelevant—"our business is different." However, some venturesome service companies did create successful revolutions in quality, using the lessons learned by the manufacturing role models. They showed that those lessons learned were universally applicable, no matter what the industry.

Currently the health care industry is following a similar scenario. At first there was doubt that the lessons learned in other industries were applicable to health care. That doubt was then resolved, especially by the National Demonstration Project on Quality Improvement in Health Care. That project is described in *Curing Health Care: New Strategies for Quality Improvement* (San Francisco: Jossey-Bass, 1990). In the foreword to that book I identified some of the lessons learned from the role model companies. I venture to repeat them here.

- The upper managers personally directed a new approach to managing for quality through creating and serving on a guiding quality council.

- They applied quality improvement methods to business processes as well as to traditional operating processes, and they attended to the needs of internal customers as well as to those of external customers.

- They adopted the concept of mandated, annual quality improvement. To this end they instituted an infrastructure to identify needed improvements and to assign clear responsibility for making those improvements.

- They adopted the concept that planning for quality should involve participation by those who will be impacted by the plan.

- They adopted a modern, quality-oriented methodology to replace empiricism in quality planning.

- They attempted to train all members of the hierarchy in the modern processes of managing for quality: quality planning, quality control, and quality improvement.

- They provided the workforce with opportunities to receive training and to participate actively in the processes of managing for quality.

- They enlarged their strategic business plans to include quality goals and the means for meeting those goals.

Many health care companies have recently launched efforts to address the quality issue. As was the case in other industries, most of these efforts have produced disappointing results, but a few have produced role models for the industry. (A major contributing factor to the disappointing results, as reported by my colleagues, has been the cultural resistance exhibited by physicians, nurses, and allied health professionals.)

The role models have demonstrated that a revolution in quality is feasible in the health care industry. (The fact that they did it proves that it is doable.) The need is now to scale up—to bring all companies up to the level of the best. Such scaling up requires that all become armed with the essential know-how—the lessons learned from the experience of the role models. This handbook takes a long step toward providing that know-how.

Central to any revolution in quality is the concept of project-by-project improvement. Many chapters of this handbook deal with the methods and tools for carrying out such improvements. The numerous case examples serve to illustrate the application of the improvement concept to various environments: clinical and administrative processes, conventional hospitals, government health care centers, and academic medical centers.

Knowing how to make improvements is necessary but not sufficient. It is also necessary to know how to mobilize company resources to carry out improvements at a revolutionary pace, year after year. This handbook deals extensively with this critical need, again as applied to various environments. An essential ingredient in such mobilization is the role of leadership. Several chapters deal with this sensitive topic.

Relations with stakeholders is another major issue. Much of the current national debate on health care relates to finding an acceptable balance among the competing claims of stakeholders: customers; physicians, nurses, and other licensed professionals; administrative personnel; the community; and still others. Changes proposed to benefit one stakeholder can easily result in unintended damage to others. Striking an acceptable balance requires an understanding of the interrelation among the needs of the various stakeholders. This handbook includes chapters focusing on specific stakeholders.

There is more. The "big picture" of managing for quality (total quality management) includes additional elements: strategic quality planning and deployment, human resource management, national quality awards, and others. It is evident that the editor has made a conscious effort, even for this first edition, to deal with all major topics that relate to managing for quality in health care.

A final impressive feature of this handbook is the list of contributing authors. They consist of hands-on experts from all corners of the industry: CEOs of prestigious companies, practicing physicians and other health care professionals, researchers, and consultants. It is a tribute to the spirit of cooperation in the industry that so many busy people volunteered to contribute to this pioneering handbook.

J. M. Juran
Chairman Emeritus
Juran Institute, Inc.

Preface

Why compile this handbook, and why now?

First, an incredible amount of work has been accomplished in the health care industry since Don Berwick, Paul Batalden, and Blan Godfrey led the National Demonstration Project beginning in 1988. That work is accelerating at an unprecedented rate. Thanks to the work of Jim Roberts, formerly at the Joint Commission on Accreditation of Healthcare Organizations (JCAHO) and now at Voluntary Hospitals of America (VHA), and Dennis O'Leary, president of JCAHO and a chapter author, every hospital in the United States and Canada must document an effective continuous quality improvement program. Add to this mandate the work of visionary leaders like Tom Sawyer and Chris Barnette of General Health System in Baton Rouge, Louisiana; Michael Pugh, formerly of Presbyterian Medical Center in Pueblo, Colorado; Jim Brexler and Jerry Fitzgerald at Oakwood Health System; John Oliver of Oakville-Trafalgar Hospital in Oakville, Ontario; Charles Jacobson of Premier; Brent James at Intermountain Health System; Robert Waller, president of Mayo Foundation; and many, many others, the potential in driving strategic results has been visibly demonstrated. This list is growing far faster than my ability to keep up. Due to mounting results and lessons learned, it seemed that a little cataloging was needed.

Second, while most of the contributing authors are well published, no collective work yet exists to illustrate these vital lessons learned. These authors desire yet one more opportunity to tell us their stories.

The compilation of this handbook has been both an exhilarating and frustrating endeavor. After first laying out the key topics and identifying prospective authors, the real work of researching, reflecting, organizing, and writing began. As I read and reread the material, I was overwhelmed at all that has been done since the other authors and I began our quality journeys in the late 1980s. One cannot help but feel a sense of great accomplishment in the health care industry, in both clinical practice improvements and improvement in administrative processes. We have successfully transformed the most complex industry in the entire world, and not a single corner remains untouched—not regulatory agencies; not providers; not insurers; not employers; not even patients themselves. While some argue that quality is dead and something else is in, it would be hard to deny that fundamental customer needs assessment, process knowledge discovery methods, and measurement and improvement techniques exist in fewer than 90 percent of our health care organizations. They just may not call their activities quality.

It was also disheartening in many ways. We have come so far, but have so far to go. And I cannot help but observe that many organizations that were quality management pioneers have failed to maintain quality performance due to the omission or erosion of basic quality control systems. Many of the very same inquiries written by the first pioneers—Don Berwick, Blan Godfrey, Paul Batalden, and others—remain. Can quality improvement work in health care? From time to time, I am emphatically told that quality is dead. While I respect the need for change agents to pour old wine into new wineskins in order to maintain momentum, I am also troubled that an unintended result may be throwing out the baby with the bath water. Certainly, we need to continuously improve the improvement process itself, but the constructs of Paul Batalden's mandates to remain customer minded, process minded, and statistically minded is perhaps more important than ever before in this era of unprecedented change. We have come so far, but have so far to go.

Therefore, the thematic layout of the handbook centers around a change model in an effort to stimulate our thinking about the continuing challenges that lie ahead.

The authors of this book have come together to document and catalog experiences in an effort to collectively climb yet one more rung up the ladder. Most of us have written about our experiences with an eye toward how we might have approached the task differently, reporting without shame our failures, struggles, and ignorance. It is our hope that readers will accept our reporting in this way. I approached the subject matter in the broadest context, hoping to cover every conceivable topic, yet hopefully not diluting any central themes because of the breadth. I also aimed at a diverse audience. I hope that this handbook is immensely valuable to anyone in health care—senior leaders, clinicians, policy makers, professors, and quality professions in every country around the world. I know the audience and purpose is aggressive, but achieving even 75 percent of this purpose will be gratifying.

Acknowledgments

I am grateful to each and every author who contributed to the handbook. Almost without exception, the compilation of the manuscripts meant great hardship for the authors. They each manage very challenging professional obligations and were already stretched beyond reasonable limits prior to agreeing to contribute. Every one of them gave up nights and weekends to meet the publication requirements (sometimes with more than a little nagging), readily accepted the constructive comments of the reviewing editors, and rewrote segments of their chapters.

All of the authors are grateful to the reviewing editors, whom we probably know, but whose identifies are kept secret to protect the guilty. Each one of them reviewed several chapters and returned constructive comments on how we might make our chapters stronger and more meaningful to the intended audiences.

We would also like to extend our deepest gratitude to Kelley Cardinal, our ASQ Quality Press acquisitions editor. Under normal circumstances, she might simply have been doing her job. But a contributed work with this many authors goes well beyond traditional editing. Not only did she have to keep me on track, she did more than her share in communicating and organizing the work of all contributing authors—an overwhelming task that kept both of us challenged.

Finally, on behalf of all the authors, we would like to extend our appreciation and love to our families for being so understanding of our passion to leave some legacy behind as we progress through life. It is often our families who are the unsung heroes, the ones who tolerate with love and understanding that extra weekend or just one more late night, as we accept yet another commitment that might well have been left for others to fulfill. To you, we all extend a virtual hug and kiss and hope that you love us in spite of ourselves.

Chip Caldwell, editor

Introduction

Could there possibly have been a more exciting time in the history of health care practice evolution than now? Could there possibly have been a more frightening time? I suspect that we are not the first generation to have thought so, but to date I suspect we are the most equipped to gain knowledge for change.

Leadership for Change

A popular Biblical story tells of a difficult question posed to Jesus during one of his sermons: "Rabbi, of all the law, what is the greatest commandment?" Jesus responds, "To love your God with all your heart and to love your neighbor as yourself." In the characteristically enlightened way of all great teachers, he affinitized generations of laws, commandments, and practices into two concise guiding principles, comprehendable by all. I think that, in many ways, an individual or organization attempting the advancement of change utilizing quality management faces the same dilemma. The body of knowledge about quality has grown so large and is growing at such a rewarding rate that it is difficult to keep our arms around it. But if I were asked the question "What are the most important tenets of quality management?" I would respond in this way.

First, find your passion and pursue it with great urgency. As Tom Sawyer, President of General Health System, puts it, "Find your hot button." At the many conferences and client sites I attend, a stark contrast can be observed on the faces of attendees. Some appear bored, wishing they were on the golf course. Others are so intense, with smiles on their faces, and are unable to contain their excitement and enthusiasm; they are eager to return home to try a new technique or concept. This passion can be turned into profound results for us and for our organizations if we use it as the basis for updating our personal learning plans. We can use it to prioritize our calendar activities.

Second, we can serve and mentor each other. The power of having those things about which we are passionate affirmed and understood by our colleagues is immense. Yet so often, in our own excitement, we unwittingly listen half-heartedly to our colleagues, waiting to tell our stories. In reflecting back over all the years I have been mentored in quality management, I remember less and less about the specifics of what Paul Batalden advised me and more and more about how he helped fuel my passion for change. The power of mentoring is perhaps best illustrated by something I observed recently at a conference in Orlando. As a colleague and I approached a friend who was dining with his wife and 10-year-old son, the boy, who was engaged in playing a handheld video game, ignored us when we were introduced. The mother made some unflattering remark to the boy about his manners, to which my colleague responded, "Enjoy him while you can, because he will be in college all too soon." He then turned his attention to the boy and said, "Hey, you're pretty good in school, aren't you?" The boy shrugged a little, and he continued. "You know, I can tell. I can tell by looking at you that when you grow up you are going to be a great man and accomplish great things." The boy stopped what he was doing and looked up. My colleague said, "You know, I can't really tell you what you will great at, I just can tell you will do wonderful things. What do you think you might be good at?" The boy said, "I really like science." The conversation went on for a few minutes more, and I have been struck by it ever since. What a wonderful gift of mentoring this person possesses. Most of us must really work hard at it. But it is a skill worthy of mastery.

The third is to serve society. I so often get wrapped up in the accomplishment of the moment that I forget what is really important about quality management. During a question period at an annual meeting recently, J. M. Juran was asked a question about the relevance of customer knowledge. His response surprised most of us, mostly because of its profound nature. He said, "To serve and benefit society." Only courageous leaders can face this promise. Another colleague was asked the question, "What is the greatest problem facing health care?" I was anticipating something like clinical practice variation or resistance to change. Instead, he suggested that the plethora of mergers and acquisitions in the name of health care reform is draining the available health care resources of our country to serve not the patient, not communities, not society, but investors far removed from the patient. The uncompromising commitment to recognize that society is our most important customer will remain a hallmark of the truly visionary leader.

A Change Model

This handbook chronicles the journey of change—the journey faced by all mentors and leaders passionate about serving their customers and serving the society in which they live and work. In order to properly set the structure of this handbook, it is necessary to create a common model for change on which to build each chapter. This is obviously not the only change model, but it does provide a mental model from which to plunge into the core competencies necessary to master and accelerate change. Contributing authors from world-class organizations producing world-class results were invited to share their notions within a particular facet of change and quality management; many have included discussion questions for governing bodies, senior leaders, and managers at their chapter conclusions.

Any world-class change model requires seven integrated yet distinct processes, as illustrated in Figure I.1.

Strategic Intent

First, the organization must have a widespread passion to achieve a clearly stated, customer-driven strategic intent. A strategic intent follows the organization's mission and can generally be classified as value leadership (or cost leadership), customer loyalty leadership, or technology leadership. Organizations can serve only one master; the concept of strategic intent is vital in this regard. Consider the likely response of a nurse confronted with an elderly patient whose discharge has been delayed by two hours because a transporter and wheelchair could not be found. Strategic intent drives her

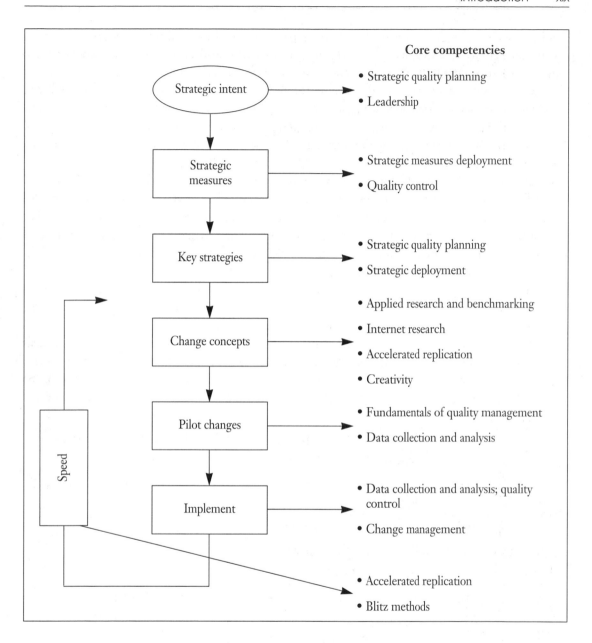

Core competencies

- Strategic quality planning
- Leadership

- Strategic measures deployment
- Quality control

- Strategic quality planning
- Strategic deployment

- Applied research and benchmarking
- Internet research
- Accelerated replication
- Creativity

- Fundamentals of quality management
- Data collection and analysis

- Data collection and analysis; quality control
- Change management

- Accelerated replication
- Blitz methods

Figure I.1. Change model.

mind-set. In a value leadership strategic intent, the unit's quality control contingency plan followed by the nurse and all her colleagues will direct them to do all in their power to pacify the patient—apologizing profusely—but nothing more. In a customer loyalty strategic intent, she would be empowered through the unit's quality control contingency plan to provide free flowers, perhaps call the next day to apologize, or do whatever it takes to recover from the defect. The strategic intent also drives project mission statement construction. Consider a surgical unit wishing to improve the call light response process. In a value leadership strategic intent, the mission statement would read something like, "To reduce the cost of the call light response process by 20 percent while maintaining response time at 16 minutes in 60 days." On the other hand, in a customer loyalty strategic intent, the mission statement might read, "To reduce the call light response time from 16 minutes to 12 minutes without increasing expense in 60 days." The difference in one project is perhaps subtle, but magnified by 80 projects per year over three years, the results shown in strategic measures would be radically different.

It is also important for senior strategists and governing boards to realize that they do not set the strategic intent; the customer does. Several examples inside and outside health care make the point. Consider IBM's mainframe strategy of the mid-1980s. It nearly bankrupted them. Consider a teaching institution insisting that teaching costs be borne by employers in the community. These are tough discussions, but vital in setting the proper customer-driven strategic intent.

The strategic intent must then be expressed in the form of a vision. The vision statement is so crafted that it can inspire others to accomplish whatever it takes to reach the organization's higher purpose. Vision statements should be short so that they can be easily remembered and recited by new employees upon completion of orientation; they should be concise enough to appear on internal billboards and the backs of business cards.

Two core competencies must be mastered and matured in order to excel in the facet of strategic management of quality—strategic quality planning and leadership. Strategic quality planning is the enlargement of traditional quality planning—which includes the environment scan, competitive assessment, regulatory requirements, and medical staff development—to encompass the quality plans and goals of the organization, as well as the strategic goals, technology goals, capital plan, and marketing goals.

After a history of quality management in health care by A. Blanton Godfrey, chairman of the Juran Institute and coauthor of *Curing Healthcare*, several contributors focus on the two competencies of strategic quality planning and leadership.

"Setting a Strategic Course: Juggling Multiple Urgent Priorities" by Maureen A. Bisognano

"Results-Driven Management: Strategic Quality Deployment" by Chip Caldwell

"Leadership in an Emerging Integrated Delivery System" by William C. Mason, Thomas H. Sawyer, and Kimberly E. Sangari

"Strategic Deployment in an Integrated Delivery System" by Sherry Bright

"Managing Quality in PROs" by Vicki S. Davis

"Quality Management in Military Medicine" by Charles B. Mount

"Quality Management in Veterans Health Administration" by Galen L. Barbour

Strategic Measures

Second, it is impossible to determine if our strategic intent is being realized unless we establish a fundamental tracking mechanism in the form of strategic measures. The core competencies needed here are strategic measurement and quality control. Although the chapter on results-driven management reveals a rich body of strategic measurement content and Paul E. Plsek's chapter on fundamentals of quality management later in the handbook addresses quality control, two chapters focus specifically in this area.

"Measuring Clinical Outcomes at the Front Line" by Eugene C. Nelson, Mark E. Splaine, Paul B. Batalden, and Stephen K. Plume

"Measuring Health Care System Quality and Performance" by Eugene C. Nelson, Nancy Mihevc, Mary Gentry, Deborah Kehne, April Levine, Paul B. Batalden, and Stephen K. Plume

Key Strategies

Third, once our strategic intent has been determined, articulated into a vision statement, and a measurement template established, we enter the deployment competencies. Development of key strategies requires basic skills in the areas of strategic quality planning (richly covered in the first section), strategic deployment, and assessment. One of the assessment methodologies perhaps requires a definition before proceeding; the notion of *cost of poor quality* is a fundamental industrial quality planning and control term used to define all the costs incurred by an organization to produce the desired level of quality. Another way to express it is the difference between actual costs and the minimum costs if all processes performed without defect or variation. These costs fall into the categories of appraisal, inspection, internal failure, and external failure costs. It is generally recognized, as is amply demonstrated by the authors, that observed costs of poor quality are a minor fraction of the total costs of poor quality caused by lost referrals, loss of customer loyalty, and suboptimal employee morale as a result of inadequate processes. Obviously, the goal of any quality system is to maintain the cost of poor quality at a minimum, hence the need for assessment. It is this area of management that should capture the attention of chief executive and chief financial officers because reducing the cost of poor quality not only dramatically reduces costs, it increases customer satisfaction and loyalty. In addition to assessments of cost of poor quality and customer loyalty, external accrediting bodies provide a source for key strategies.

Key strategies, as shaped by our strategic intent, drive results. Examples of some key strategies in a value leadership strategic intent might be the following:

- Decrease costs through reduction of process constraints and bottlenecks.

- Increase deployment of multiskilled job positions.

- Decrease rework loops in clinical and administrative processes. (Two companion annual goals might be "reduce diabetic readmissions within six months of discharge from 14 percent to 10 percent" and "decrease managed care rebillings from 15 percent to 10 percent.")

Several chapters in the previous section focus on strategic intent and development of key strategies. The chapters in this section that focus on the use of assessments to deploy key strategies are the following:

"Costs of Poor Quality: An Opportunity in Health Care" by Harvey Dershin and Julie A. Magrath

"Cost-of-Poor-Quality Analysis: The Prescription for Profitable Change Management" by Anthony J. Romagnole

"Process and Organization Structure for JCAHO Accreditation" by Howard B. Nussman

"Using the Malcolm Baldrige National Quality Award Process to Stimulate Organizational Excellence" by Ellen J. Gaucher

"Public Disclosure of Quality and Performance Information in Managed Care" by Cary Sennett and Margaret O'Kane

"The Joint Commission's Agenda for Change and Beyond" by Paul M. Schyve and Dennis S. O'Leary

Change Concepts

Fourth, the change model must excel at uncovering and generating change concepts aimed at achieving the key strategies at the process level. This term has been popularized by Don Berwick, president of the Institute for Healthcare Improvement, when he created the Breakthrough Series, a structured, collaborative process to help organizations improve quality more rapidly.

Following the key strategies in a value leadership strategic intent from the previous discussion, the key strategy "Decrease rework loops in clinical and administrative processes: reduce diabetic readmissions within six months of discharge from 14 percent to 10 percent" was suggested. Two potential change concepts to support this strategy might be "provide a take-home nutrition and exercise video to patients at discharge" and "provide exercise training on the day of discharge." Change concepts are tangible, implementable process improvements. Change concepts are not loose goals like "reduce CABG length of stay to the Academic Medical Center Consortium average of 7.3 days;" this would be classified as an annual goal supporting the key strategy of "reduce waits and delays." A change concept to "reduce CABG length of stay" might be "social services to discuss the discharge plan with the patient and family 48 hours prior to admission."

The core competencies required to excel in uncovering and generating change concepts are applied research and benchmarking (including lessons from past reengineering efforts), Internet research, accelerated replication, and creativity. Although Internet research and accelerated replication have been placed in the section called The Need for Speed, the following chapters are devoted to the other disciplines.

"Reengineering the Surgical Process" by Elizabeth H. Dougherty, William F. Minogue, and Jay B. Mathur

"Reengineering in an Integrated Health System" by Nancy Henley

"Quality Management in Academic Health Centers: Using Peer Institutions to Support Practice Improvement" by Kimberly J. Rask and Jean Livingston

"Community Involvement: The Kingsport Experience" by Rob Johnson and Jim Herbert

"Directed Creativity and the Management of Quality in Health Care" by Paul E. Plsek

Pilot Changes

Fifth, as every experienced project manager and quality professional is well aware, change concepts almost never perform as expected; the skill set to introduce change concepts remains the fundamental building block of a strong quality system and is ably summarized and articulated.

"Techniques for the Management of Quality" by Paul E. Plsek

Implementation

Sixth, the organization must have effective implementation processes that overcome our natural resistance to change. And, following implementation, it must have a workable quality control system in place to ensure that improved processes maintain performance at their new height of achievement and do not slip back into poor performance.

Gaining knowledge, as a result of our competencies in change concept management, is only 50 percent of the process. On discovery of knowledge (that is, uncovering change concepts), process owners must apply it. Our ability to improve is governed by this latter process as much as or more than by knowledge discovery. It is in this dimension that case studies provide the most insight. How have our colleagues implemented new techniques and methods? What methods have been successful in other organizations in generating buy-in and reducing resistance to change? How has resistance thwarted an organization's zeal to increase its rate of improvement? Five chapters, including one on the emerging organizational structure of self-managed work teams, concentrate on the competencies required to master implementation.

"Managing Change in Health Care" by David W. Hutton

"Clinical Path Success Factors" by Robert B. Halder and Jackie Lobien

"Success Factors in Reducing Cost in Hospital Organizations" by Ijaz M. Bokhari and David A. Farson

"Physician Leadership in Developing Systems of Care" by Kimberly E. Sangari and Gene Beyt

"Emerging Concepts: Self-Managed Teams" by Lisa Ethier and Marian Furlong

The Need for Speed

The advent of the Information Age, if indeed we have not evolved to the Cyber Age, equips us to uncover the most recent advances in a nanosecond if we program our Netscape software to alert us to the publication of a new medical advance on the Internet or if the quality resource department or medical library posts Intranet messages. Further, many organizations have innovated new ways to utilize the discipline of quality management at ever-accelerating rates. Two chapters reveal the emerging trends in rapid cycle improvement.

"Accelerated Replication Approaches" by Chip Caldwell

"A Quality Planning Blitz Team: Developing a Medical Record in 15 Days" by Kimberly Blake, Julie O'Shaughnessy, and Peggy Schroeder

Summary

This handbook has been crafted with this comprehensive change management model in mind. It includes theory, application of theory, case studies, and integration of advanced techniques in the topical areas detailed in Figure I.1. Each of these processes operates in an aligned fashion, and erosion of any serves as a constraint to the entire change management effectiveness.

In preparation for maximizing the lessons that can be applied by organizations from the collective knowledge of the contributors to this handbook, the organizational sponsor of this publication should consider organizing a two-hour session of key stakeholders to create the tension for change. The authors of the handbook have come together with a number of personal and collective goals. Chief among them is that we wish for our collective experiences, warts and all, to be of some constructive benefit in the advancement of managing change and improving quality in health care and to expand the depth of understanding—particularly among CEOs, CFOs, COOs, and governing bodies—that quality and costs are not two ends of the same scale, but are inherently intertwined in the optimization of value-adding work. The following introductory questions for senior leaders, clinical and department leaders, quality professionals, and other interested stakeholders are intended to stimulate the necessary tension for change so that the strategic deployment process can be advanced.

1. Strategic intent

   a. What does the organization's mission and vision say about its strategic intent of being the value (cost) leader, customer loyalty leader, or technology leader?

   b. Would interviews of five staff physicians, five employees, or five department managers regarding the organization's strategic intent produce zero variation, 50 percent variation, or 100 percent variation?

   c. Posed with the dilemma of replacing an elderly patient's lost dentures and in concert with the organization's strategic intent of being the value leader, customer loyalty leader, or technology leader, would five staff nurses arrive at the same action plan?

     d. Summarize the intended activities from five department plans for the current year. What percentage of goals and projects align with your strategic intent? Are any goals or projects contraindicated?

2. Strategic measures

     a. Plot and review a run chart of the last 24 months' performance measures for operating cost per adjusted discharge per month, patient overall satisfaction per month (or quarter), and market share per quarter (or net revenue per month). What conclusions can be drawn? Does the trend match your intended direction?

     b. If these measures are not trended for senior leader analysis on a frequent basis, are senior leaders comfortable with the alternative methods of gaining insight into progress toward goal achievement?

     c. Project results: How many total projects were chartered last year? What was the average cycle time per project? How many accomplished results in the category of the organization's strategic intent (value, loyalty, or technology)?

These questions are not intended to be a conclusive analysis, but a stimulant to obtaining agreement among senior leaders regarding top priorities for improvement and for generating the tension for change. Many of the chapters that follow contain a more detailed set of questions for key stakeholders to use in setting action priorities. These readings can be digested in bite-sized increments. If stimulated, readers can organize other leaders to process new knowledge or insights, or to resurface diverted ones and get back on track. It is unlikely, and certainly not intended, for any organization to mobilize efforts to apply each of these concepts simultaneously, but rather to construct a deployment plan consistent with the organization's key issues of today while positioning to apply further concepts over time. The chapters that follow will carry the reader on a journey of sorts—through history, assessment, measures, strategy, methods, and emerging concepts—all with the intended purpose of enhancing knowledge, stimulating action at the individual and organizational levels, and creating the tension for change.

Chapter 1

A Short History of Managing for Quality in Health Care

A. Blanton Godfrey

Not many years ago most people in health care, like in many other industries, were convinced that higher quality meant higher costs. If people wanted better health care, they would have to be willing to spend more. Better quality meant new technologies, new medicines, and more staff.

In many ways these beliefs were similar to those of people in other industries. For many years, people in many different companies and industries thought that higher quality meant higher costs and, therefore, higher prices. And for some aspects of quality, in particular feature quality, this was true. But there is another critical side of quality: the absence of defects. We can almost always reduce costs and improve quality by removing defects. These defects may be real problems such as infections, readmissions, adverse drug reactions or they may simply be non-value-added work. Far too often we have designed processes (or simply let them evolve) that are full of wasted effort, wasted time, and errors. For many hospitals the admissions process in the emergency room is far too notable an example.

Several years ago while writing an article on the evolution of quality management in telecommunications,[1] I also was involved in reviewing a presentation to be made by Shinji Sakai, CEO of Toyota Motor Sales, U.S.A. He was tracing the evolution of quality management in the automotive industry as the foundation of his talk.[2] We were both stunned by the similarities of the evolution of quality management in the automotive and telecommunications industries. Perhaps even more surprising are the strong parallels among quality management in health care and both the automotive and telecommunications industries.

The Evolution of Quality Management in Health Care

In most industries, quality management appears to have evolved through several distinct steps or phases. These phases include a focus on product quality, product process quality, service quality, service process quality, business planning, strategic quality planning, and integrated strategic quality planning (see Figure 1.1).

Product Quality

All organizations began their quality management efforts with a focus on product quality. In health care this focus is on clinical outcomes. Whether this challenge is developing an automobile, inventing

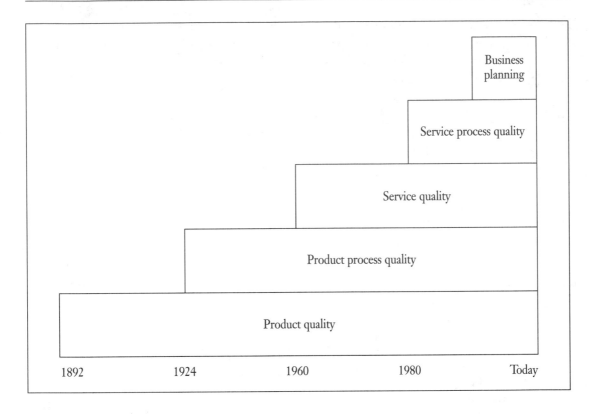

Figure 1.1. The evolution of quality management.

the telephone, or curing a disease, this focus on the basic function is entirely appropriate. Unless we can accomplish the basic task, cost and service quality do not matter. We must first produce something that is desirable and has value.

At the first introduction of a product, say an antibiotic that cures a previously incurable disease, product quality is by necessity defined from the producer's point of view. In medicine, only the pioneers would know what is possible and what can and should be done. The customers (patients) have little contribution to make regarding the definition of quality at this stage. They may know their needs and wants, but in the case of a truly new product their inputs are ambiguous and somewhat vague.

In our study of the evolution of quality in telecommunications, this was clearly the case. The telephone was truly a new product. Potential customers were amazed that it worked at all and had absolutely no idea how it worked. The driving forces for defining quality were the engineers trying to make it work well enough to be a salable product. As early as 1892, the Bell System was developing inspection procedures to ensure that the specifications and requirements developed by the engineers (the company's definitions of quality) were being met by the production personnel.

For many years in modern medicine, the definitions of quality focused on outcomes. These were defined by the medical specialists—the doctors. Elaborate quality assurance procedures, usually based on inspection, were developed to review the outcomes and assign responsibility for less-than-perfect outcomes.

For other industries, service or manufacturing, this also appears to be the case. The early airlines concentrated their entire efforts on product quality—providing quick transportation from point A to point B. This basic definition of product quality—safe, fast, reasonably on-time air travel—occupied all of their efforts for years.

In the health care industry, we should also note that this focus on clinical outcomes has continued up to the present. As quality management evolves, new dimensions of quality do not replace the old dimensions; they become additional dimensions. Much recent work on clinical outcomes would fall in this category. Researchers have extended the traditional definitions of outcome to include patient performance, lack of pain, and ability to work. This carries the traditional definition of outcome quality far beyond the walls of the hospital.

Product Process Quality

The next phase of the quality evolution in manufacturing industries began in the 1920s with the creation of the control chart and other process control tools. For some time it had become evident that controlling product quality through final inspection was quite expensive. In the installation forces of the rapidly growing American Telephone & Telegraph company, the rallying cry had become, "Do it right the first time." Finding the wiring errors in complex switching machines after the machine had been assembled was a time-consuming, costly process. It was far more economical to ensure functioning parts and carefully control the assembly than to go back and try to find the problems.

In health care there were many similarities. Complications after surgery or infections acquired while in the hospital created much waste and additional costs. Many "modern management methods" were adopted and applied in operating room procedures, nursing procedures, and the daily care of patients.

This stage of product process quality—focus on the processes producing the final outcomes—has continued to the present. Many sophisticated methods have been added to the arsenal: process engineering, protocols, patient-focused care, clinical guidelines and care maps, clinical trials, and, more recently, process simplification and reengineering. Any methods that try to improve the outcomes of work through improving the processes by which we create those outcomes are in the product process phase. For the most part, in other industries, these have focused on the cost side of producing the product.

Service Quality

The next phase for some industries began in the early 1960s. I suspect for other industries it had begun much earlier; for others not until the 1980s or even 1990s. This was the expansion of the traditional definition of product quality to include the services surrounding the product. For automobiles this included the service at the dealership and the warranties and extended warranties offered. Today many luxury car dealers are providing 24-hour-a-day roadside service covering all situations. In telecommunications this included repair and maintenance services, order entry, billing, and modular phones that the customer could easily self-install and maintain.

Many health care organizations began offering new features in hospitals including private rooms, televisions, telephones, valet parking, facilities for parents to stay with sick children, outpatient facilities, and new meal services. These are sometimes called features or the salability part of quality.

For many manufacturing companies, the 1960s and 1970s were the wake-up calls for this aspect of quality. Customers were no longer just interested in the quality of the car. Service provided by the dealership, parts availability, roadside assistance, the sales experience, financing, leasing, and many other aspects of the supplier/customer relationship became part of the competitive quality battleground. In the late 1980s we saw this accelerated with the introduction of the Japanese luxury cars (Acura, Infinity, and Lexus) with their special dealerships, new service relationships, and new levels of support. General Motors has taken this down to the basic car lately with its Saturn division.

These changes also started happening rapidly in the health care industry. The costs of running the administrative services, the food services, the housekeeping, and other "hotel-like functions" became targets for efficiency improvements. Quality management became routine in these areas.

Service Process Quality

In the 1980s, a new focus on quality occurred as companies started focusing on the costs of providing the quality of these services: business process quality management or improvement. Many of the same techniques (for the most part, rather standard industrial engineering tools) used in product process quality were applied for the first time to the horizontal processes that cut across organizations and were, for the most part, totally unmanaged.

Some new ideas also emerged. The concept of a process owner and a process team expanded the power of a quality council by continuously examining and identifying opportunities for team interventions in critical business processes. In many ways these process teams acted as focused councils deploying improvement, control, and planning teams to the macroprocess or to microprocesses within the macroprocess.

Many of these processes were found to be so poorly designed, ineffective, and inefficient that an almost manic wave of reengineering swept the United States. This had a major impact in health care. Driven by the myriad rules, regulations, and paperwork requirements forced on them by insurers, government agencies, health plans, and others, many health care organizations' processes had become bureaucratic nightmares. Their processes were ripe for reengineering. Again, the focus was primarily on costs. These reengineering or business process quality improvement efforts were directed at reducing cycle times, reducing numbers of steps or handoffs, and improving efficiency overall. Many of these business process interventions also improved the quality of the output.

We began to see a cycle emerging. The evolutionary process of total quality management seems to alternate between a focus on quality and a focus on the costs to attain that quality.

Business Planning

In the past few years we have observed many companies starting to integrate quality management with their business planning cycles. This integration of quality goals with financial goals has been a major thrust in leading companies. Recently this integration was listed as the major effort currently underway by respondents to the Business Roundtable survey on TQM.

The process of setting quality goals; subdividing the goals into subgoals, annual goals, and projects; and deploying the goals throughout the organization (hoshin kanri, hoshin planning, policy deployment, or strategic quality planning) has become one of the major breakthroughs in total quality management for many companies. Some are actually going beyond the annual business planning cycle and incorporating these methods with their five-year or even longer-term plans.

This naturally leads to the question of what the next steps are in the evolution of TQM. The immediate next step to the pyramid is fairly obvious: strategic quality planning. Some companies are beginning to go even further and have implemented integrated strategic planning, where they are involving customers and suppliers in joint strategic planning.

The Malcolm Baldrige National Quality Award Criteria

During the 1980s there was a growing interest in the United States in promoting what is now called total quality management. Many U.S. leaders believed that a national quality award, similar to the Union of Japanese Scientists and Engineers' Deming Prize, would help stimulate the quality efforts of U.S. companies.

A number of individuals and organizations proposed such an award, leading to a series of hearings before the House of Representatives Subcommittee on Science, Research and Technology. Finally, on January 6, 1987, the Malcolm Baldrige National Quality Improvement Act of 1987 was passed. The act was signed by President Ronald Reagan on August 20, 1987, and became Public Law 100-107. This act provided for the establishment of the Malcolm Baldrige National Quality Award Program. The purpose of this award program was to help improve quality and productivity by

> *(A) helping stimulate American companies to improve quality and productivity for the pride of recognition while obtaining a competitive edge through increased profits,*
>
> *(B) recognizing the achievements of those companies which improve the quality of their goods and services and providing an example to others,*
>
> *(C) establishing guidelines and criteria that can be used by business, industrial, governmental and other organizations in evaluating their own quality improvement efforts, and*
>
> *(D) providing specific guidance for other American organizations that wish to learn how to manage for high quality by making available detailed information on how winning organizations were able to change their cultures and achieve eminence. [H.R. 812]*

The act provided that up to two awards could be presented to companies in each of three categories: small businesses, companies or their subsidiaries, and companies that primarily provide services. The act also stated that companies must apply for the award by submitting a written application. The company must also permit a "rigorous evaluation of the way in which the business and other operations have contributed to improvements in the quality of goods and services."[3]

In 1995, the Baldrige Award process was opened on a trial basis to health care and educational organizations. Forty-six health care organizations participated in the trial by completing full applications for evaluation.

The act also called on the Director of the National Bureau of Standards (now the National Institute of Standards and Technology) to

> *Rely upon an intensive evaluation by a competent board of examiners which shall review the evidence submitted by the organization and, through a site visit, verify the accuracy of the quality improvements claimed. The examination should encompass all aspects of the organization's current quality management in its future goals. The award shall be given only to organizations which have made outstanding improvements in the quality of their goods or services (or both) and which demonstrate effective quality management through the training and involvement of all levels of personnel in quality improvement.*

The Baldrige Award was intended to help organizations compare their performance with that of world-class companies. The elements of the strategy were as follows:

- To create a national value system for quality
- To provide a basis for diagnosis and information transfer
- To create a vehicle for cooperation across organizations
- To provide for a dynamic award system which would evolve through consensus and be continuously improved

The design strategy has been followed carefully. The award criteria have been changed and improved each year. By extending these criteria and the process to health care, this will further expand the sharing of quality methodology among health care organizations and with companies in other industries.

The Baldrige Award criteria are the basis for making awards and giving feedback to the applicants. The criteria also have three other important purposes, all critically important to health care organizations.

- To help raise quality performance standards and expectations
- To facilitate communication and sharing among and within organizations of all types based on a common understanding of key quality and operational performance requirements
- To serve as a working tool for planning, training, assessment, and other uses

There are 10 core values and concepts embodied in the award criteria. These core values and concepts are the following.

1. *Customer-driven quality.* Emphasis here is placed on product and service attributes that contribute value to the customer and lead to customer satisfaction and preference. The concept goes beyond just meeting basic customer requirements, including those that enhance the product and service attributes and differentiate them from competing offerings. Customer-driven quality is thus described as a strategic concept directed toward customer retention and market share gain.

This focus on the customer was emphasized by former U.S. President George Bush.

> *In business, there is only one definition of quality—the customer's definition. With the fierce competition of the international market, quality means survival.*[4]

2. *Leadership.* A key part of the Baldrige Award focus is senior executive leadership. The leaders must create a customer orientation, clear and visible quality values, and high expectations. This concept stresses the personal involvement required of leaders. This involvement extends to areas of public responsibility and corporate citizenship as well as to areas of development of the entire workforce. This concept also emphasizes such activities as planning, communications, review of company quality performance, recognition, and serving as a role model.

3. *Continuous improvement.* This concept includes both incremental and breakthrough improvement activities in every operation, function, and work process in the company. It stresses that improvements may be made through enhancing value to customers; reducing errors, defects, and waste; improving responsiveness and cycle time performance; improving productivity and effectiveness in the use of all resources; and improving the company's performance and leadership position while fulfilling its public responsibilities and corporate citizenship.

4. *Employee participation and development.* This concept stresses the close relationship between employee satisfaction and customer satisfaction. It explains the value of employee satisfaction measurement and how this is an important indicator of the organization's overall performance. There is an increasing awareness in the United States that overall organization performance depends increasingly on workforce quality and employee involvement. Factors that bear on employee safety, health, well-being, and morale need to be part of the company's continuous improvement objectives.

5. *Fast response.* The value of shortening cycle times is also emphasized. Faster and more flexible response to customers is becoming a more critical requirement of business management each year. Improvements in these areas often require redesigning work processes, eliminating unnecessary work steps, and making better use of technology. Measures of time performance should be among the quality indicators used by leading organizations.

6. *Design quality and prevention.* Throughout the criteria, the importance of prevention-based quality systems is highlighted. Design quality is a primary driver of downstream quality. This concept includes fault-tolerant (robust) products and processes. It also includes concept-to-customer times— the entire time for the design, development, production, and delivery to customer of new goods and services.

The concept of continuous improvement and corrective action involving upstream interventions is also covered here. This concept stresses that changes should be made as far upstream as possible for the greatest savings.

7. *Long-range outlook.* This concept stresses the need to take a long-range view of the organization's future and consider all stakeholders, customers, employees, stockholders, and the community. Planning must take into account new technologies, the changing needs of customers and the changing customer mix, new regulatory requirements, community/societal expectations, and competitors' strategies. Emphasis is also placed on long-term development of employees and suppliers and to fulfilling public responsibilities and serving as a corporate citizenship role model.

8. *Management by fact.* This concept stresses the need to make decisions based on reliable data, information, and analyses. These data need to accurately reflect the needs, wants, expectations, and perceptions of customers; to give accurate descriptions of the performance of goods and services sold; to reflect clearly the market situation; to portray accurately the offerings, performance levels, and satisfaction levels of competitors goods' and services; to provide clear findings of employee-rated issues; and to accurately portray cost and financial matters. The role of analysis is stressed. Here, also, emphasis is placed on the role of benchmarking in comparing organizational quality performance with competitors' or best-in-class organizations' performance.

The need for organizationwide performance indicators is also stressed. These indicators are measurable characteristics of goods, services, processes, and company operations. They are used to evaluate, track, and improve performance. They should be clearly linked to show the relationships between strategic goals and all activities of the company.

9. *Partnership development.* The need to develop both internal and external partnerships to accomplish overall goals is also emphasized. These partnerships may include labor–management relationships; relationships with key suppliers; working agreements with technical colleges, community colleges, and universities; and strategic alliances with other organizations.

10. *Corporate responsibility and citizenship.* The core values and concepts also emphasize that an organization's quality system should address corporate responsibility and citizenship. This includes business ethics and protection of public health, public safety, and the environment. The company's day-to-day operations and the entire life cycle of the products sold should be considered as they impact health, safety, and environment. Quality planning should anticipate any adverse effect from facilities management, production, distribution, transportation, and use and disposal of products.

Corporate responsibility also refers to leadership and support of such areas as education; resource conservation; community services; improving industry and business practices; and sharing nonproprietary quality-related information, tools, and concepts.

The foundation for any quality system rests on a few basic concepts. This foundation consists of strategic quality management, executive leadership, and a continual focus on the customer.

At the 30th Anniversary Congress of the Asian Productivity Organization, Hideo Sugiura, former chair of the Honda Motor Company, stated the roles of senior management and strategic quality planning better than anyone I had heard before. Sugiura described four "sacred obligations" of management. The first is a clear vision of where the company is going. This must be clearly stated and communicated to every member of the organization in language that each understands. The second is clearly defining the small number of key objectives that must be achieved if the company is to realize its vision. The third is the translation of the objectives throughout the entire organization so that each person knows how performing his or her job helps the company achieve its objectives. The fourth is a fair and honest appraisal so that each and every employee knows how his or her performance has contributed to the organization's efforts to achieve the key objectives, with guidance on how the individual can improve performance.

In the United States this process of defining the vision, stating the objectives, and translating these objectives throughout the organization has come to be known as strategic quality planning. In other countries it is sometimes known as hoshin kanri, policy deployment, or even hoshin planning. It has become an important management tool for some organizations, allowing the organization to set clear priorities, establish clear target areas for improvement activities, and allocate resources to the most important things that must be done. For other organizations, it has become a bureaucratic nightmare; one more excuse to resume paralysis by analysis and let endless meetings and planning take the place of real action or accomplishment.

To be effective, strategic quality planning must be used as a tool—a means to an end—not as the goal itself. It must be an endeavor that involves people throughout the organization. It must capture existing activities, not just add more activities to already overflowing plates. It must help senior managers face difficult decisions, set priorities, and eliminate many current activities—not just start new ones.

Companies that have implemented strategic quality planning carefully and iterated plans throughout the organization in true catchball fashion are reporting many breakthroughs. For many, it is the first time that everyone has had a clear picture of where the organization is going, why it is going there, and what activities are necessary to get there. For others, it is the first time that people felt their views were important and saw evidence of their ideas incorporated with the priorities of the organization.

Other organizations report that it is the first time they have systematically reviewed each planned project (problem scheduled for solution or new opportunity to be seized). They have forced themselves to know whether they have provided adequate resources, adequate training and skills for the people doing the job, and active supervision and management support. These organizations have discovered the true value of strategic quality planning. It is not just another task; it is a tool for improving how they do the jobs they must do. It is a tool for making sure that they are focusing on the right things and providing the leadership and support to do these things right.

This is the stage at which many health care organizations now find themselves. There are many questions to be answered about the organizations' strategic intent, priorities, and way of operating in the future.

Notes

1. Al C. Endres and A. Blanton Godfrey, "The Evolution of Quality Management Within Telecommunications," *IEEE Communications Society Journal* (October 1994).

2. Shinji Sakai, "Relentless Pursuit of Perfection—The New Dimension of Quality," *IMPRO 94: Juran Institute's Conference on Managing for Total Quality* (Wilton, Conn.: Juran Institute, 1994).

3. National Institute of Standards and Technology, *1993 Application Forms and Instructions: Malcolm Baldrige National Quality Award* (Gaithersburg, Md.: NIST, 1993).

4. National Institute of Standards and Technology, *1993 Award Criteria: Malcolm Baldrige National Quality Award* (Gaithersburg, Md.: NIST, 1993).

A. Blanton Godfrey is chairman and chief executive officer of Juran Institute, Inc. Godfrey has maintained the traditions of leadership and distinguished service of the Institute's founder, Joseph M. Juran, while expanding its range of services and worldwide capabilities.

Godfrey earned M.S. and Ph.D. degrees in statistics from Florida State University and a B.S. degree in physics from Virginia Tech. In 1993 he was named a distinguished graduate from Florida State's School of Arts and Sciences. He is an adjunct professor of Columbia University's School of Engineering and Applied Science, where he teaches a graduate course in quality management and control. He is also an adjunct professor in the School of Textile Engineering and Management at North Carolina State University and a guest lecturer in clinical quality management at Harvard University.

Godfrey is a fellow of the American Statistical Association, American Society for Quality, and the World Academy of Productivity Sciences. He is also a member of Sigma Xi, the New York Academy of Sciences, and an academician of the International Academy for Quality. He is also listed in *Who's Who in America*. He has published more than 80 articles and book chapters and co-authored two books, *Modern Methods for Quality Control and Improvement* and *Curing Health Care: New Strategies for Quality Improvement*.

From 1987 to 1990, Godfrey contributed to the creation of the Malcolm Baldrige National Quality Award and served as a judge for the first three years of the award. He has also served as a judge for the Florida Sterling Award and now serves on the board of directors for the Connecticut Award for Excellence. He has served as a chairman of the judges for the U.S. Air Force Quality Award. He has also been involved in assisting the establishment of other national quality awards based on the Baldrige Award and serves as Executive Advisor for the Australian Organization for Quality.

In 1992, American Society for Quality presented Godfrey the Edwards Medal for his outstanding contributions to the science and practice of quality management.

Section I
Strategic Intent

Chapter 2

Setting a Strategic Course: Juggling Multiple Urgent Priorities

Maureen A. Bisognano

Little improvement is accidental; improvement must be planned and led.

—Don Berwick, M.D.

Here is the challenge: At a time when the pressures to improve seem nearly overwhelming, it is almost impossible to find the time to do it. At every turn, health care leaders are facing the need to make huge improvements in structure and performance. They are scanning the community and the competition and choosing partners to share their future. Nearly every integrated delivery system now faces the challenge of proving that all of its work was worth it to the patients they serve; care, access, and costs must improve, and quickly.

Patient satisfaction results fell 4.1 percent last year.[1] Health care systems have targeted 10 percent to 30 percent expense reductions this year, and new national quality databases are publicly comparing performance on customer-sensitive indicators like access and waiting times. The *Dartmouth Atlas*[2] spells out for purchasers the unexplained and costly variations for the same procedure between delivery sites. Within the same county in Maine, a variation of more than 300 percent exists in hysterectomy rates by age 70. Large corporations such as Ford, GTE, and General Motors are collecting and analyzing data on health care providers toward specific goals of improving care for employees and reducing health insurance costs. General Motors spends more on employee health insurance per car than it does on steel, and the rate of increase, in comparison with other expenditures, has put health care costs high on General Motors' agenda for improvement. Cost reduction has then cascaded to the health care industry as a high priority goal and requires focused waste reduction while maintaining high-quality outcomes and access.

The blurring of professional roles and the years of consecutive labor budget cuts have left their mark on employee morale. Changing from a profession-centric, silo-driven work environment to a cross-functional care team is a challenging evolution, even for those providers committed to patient-focused care.

It's time for new leadership skills. These approaches can make the difference between organizations that adapt and those that stagnate. The skills required, however, are new and are not yet routinely reflected in the curricula of health professional education programs. The challenge is how to master new skills and adopt personal, visible leadership style changes while juggling major organizational transformation.

This chapter will help you to contemplate what new leadership means for you and your organization. You may find a transformational path in these pages that will help you sort the multiple priorities and effectively achieve new performance levels. We know that it can be done. Corporate leaders from other industries have paved the way for us. While he was chairman at Motorola, Bob Galvin balanced personal change and new skills, visibly displayed with an organizational emphasis on customer-defined quality. He describes changing the agendas at meetings he attended to place customer feedback and product performance at the top, ahead of financial reports. Sometimes he left the meeting after these reports generated action plans, quietly making his point: Focus on quality and the finances will follow. Galvin asserts that "the CEO has to embrace quality with intensity and a sense of proprietorship that is very first person, and then, of course, he has to help to engage everyone else along the way.[3]

Roger Milliken, president of Milliken and Company, underwent a personal transformation that was very visible to those managers who worked with him for years to build a highly successful textile business. Although Milliken was always obsessed with product quality, he learned new skills—listening, improvement, planning with customer needs in mind, and aggressively reducing waste to keep prices competitive. As he changed, so did the others at Milliken, paving the way for a major corporate success story. And, of course, we have leaders of this caliber in the making in the health care industry. By and large, though, we need visible leadership more than at any other time in the industry. There are lessons to be borrowed from these leaders, which may help form the basis for your personal plan.

This chapter will outline some best practices in leadership and will focus on both personal and organizational change. New leadership will be defined in several dimensions.

- Setting a strategic course: Juggling multiple urgent priorities
- Building partnerships with staff: Human resources strategies for the future
- Tracking progress and measuring for change

Improvement is difficult. Leaders in health care organizations today must feel like teammates of Willie Mays when he said, "If you turn, hit, run the bases, hit with power, field throw, and do all these things that are part of the game . . . then you're a good ballplayer." And not only must you be good at the basic fundamentals of leading complex groups and institutions, new skills must be added in order to achieve the rapid performance changes necessary to stay in the game.

Achieving balance is the fundamental challenge for leaders today: leaders are setting aims for rapidly accelerated rates of improvement and innovation in a context needing focus, attention to detail, and time for clinicians to practice personalized, thoughtful medicine. The messages leaders send can confound the work at the direct care site—today, are we improving care or saving money, or making new relationships with physician groups, or improving the health of our community? The work of leaders has never been so closely scrutinized, nor has their impact been so widely felt. It is time to take a second look at leadership.

Three elements of health care leadership need strengthening. First, we need more aggressive and clearer aims for improvement. Second, we can benefit from the lessons learned in other industries— customer obsession and lean process design can effectively reshape the care delivery processes in every type of health care setting. Finally, we need a way to manage the resistance to change that is slowing down our efforts at aggressive improvements.

Setting a Strategic Course

On the matter of aim, senior leaders have two critical jobs to do. The first requires that leaders set the rate of improvement. Faster is not always better; many health care organizations are becoming undone by aggressive reengineering efforts without the time to consider the social impacts of the technical changes. In fact, many health care leaders report either disappointing results from these expensive efforts or a failure to hold the gains made over time. This is not to say that we should be patient with the year-long quality teams of days past. The aims should be aggressive but also need to consider organizational tolerance, breadth of impact, and the resources required to carry out such a rate of improvement.

With a focused plan in mind, leaders should set as aggressive a rate of improvement as the organization can tolerate. Stretch goals are key. Bob Galvin understood that overcoming resistance begins with such a stretch goal. Any less invites "tampering" with care systems and minimal change. Galvin called for 10-fold improvement in quality at Motorola in five years and extended the goals to 100-fold improvement in 10 years.[4] Applied to health care, that goal would reduce medication errors in hospitals by the thousands each year, save thousands of frontline nursing positions by achieving waste reduction in process redesign, and increase the throughput in every managed care office without reducing patient/physician time together.

Once the *rate* of improvement is set, leaders need to fulfill the second key responsibility in this area: they must set specific *aims* for improvement. General mandates do not work. Focus is key. The leadership team needs to determine five or six important areas that must be radically improved in the course of the next 12 months. These aims can be widely deployed, with the entire organization working on pieces of the improvement process; but specific aim drives improvement, and little improvement happens in their absence.

In 1994, Don Berwick challenged the industry with "Eleven Worthy Aims for Clinical Leadership of Health System Reform."[5]

> *Aim 1: Increase appropriateness of practice.* Reduce the use of inappropriate surgery, admissions, and tests. Important initial targets may include: management of stage I and II breast cancer, prostatectomy, carotid endarterectomy, coronary artery bypass surgery, low back pain management, hysterectomy, endoscopy, blood transfusion, chest X-rays, and prenatal ultrasound.

> *Aim 2: Increase effective preventive practices.* Improve health status through reduction in "upstream" causes of illness, including especially smoking, handgun violence, preventable injuries in children, and alcohol and cocaine abuse.

> *Aim 3: Reduce cesarean section rates.* Reduce cesarean section rates to below 10%, without compromise in maternal or fetal outcomes.

> *Aim 4: Reduce unwanted care at the end of life.* Reduce the use of unwanted and ineffective medical technologies at the end of life.

> *Aim 5: Rationalize pharmaceutical use.* Adopt simplified formularies and streamline pharmaceutical use, especially for antibiotics and for drug prescriptions for the elderly.

> *Aim 6: Involve patients in decisions.* Increase the frequency with which patients participate actively in decision making about therapeutic options.

Aim 7: Reduce wait states. Decrease uninformative waiting in all its forms.

Aim 8: Reduce, consolidate, and regionalize high-technology services. Reduce the total supply of high-technology medical and surgical care. Consolidate high-technology services into regional and communitywide centers.

Aim 9: Reduce wasteful and duplicative recording. Reduce the frequency of duplicate data entry and of recording of information never used in medical record and administrative systems.

Aim 10: Reduce inventory costs. Reduce inventory levels.

Aim 11: Reduce racial and economic health status inequities. Reduce the racial gap in infant mortality and low birthweight.

These aims may serve as a starting point for some leaders; others may have different organizational priorities. The key, however, is to set and deploy several aims and to focus clearly on accomplishing these changes.

Key Leadership Points

• *Establish an urgent and aggressive rate of improvement.* Understand the resources required for a rapid rate of change; support the organization emotionally and structurally to achieve improvement.

• *Set specific aims that align organizational energy for the upcoming year.* Gain consensus among senior leaders and key medical staff members on four to six strategic areas for improvement. Deploy these aims widely and connect medical staff committee work, departmental and cross-functional goals, and teams to make cumulative, visible progress.

• *Align improvement efforts with organizational strategic plans.* Improvement aims will harness the most energy when it is made clear throughout the medical staff and all areas of the system that improvement in these areas is required for survival. Aligning the aims with specific patient populations, community needs, or key customer requirements is a vital first step.

Customer Focus and Lean Process Design

The second element of health care leadership requiring attention is customer focus and lean design. Health care leaders often say that their leadership teams are customer focused, but observations of their behavior contradict this. Analyze, for example, the last six months of minutes from senior team meetings; it is rare to find the topic of customers on the agenda. Deeply understanding customers' needs and designing care around these needs is required for long-term success and seems so obvious that it shouldn't require saying. Carrying this out is quite a different matter.

It requires time. Bob Galvin responded to a suggestion in the mid-1980s that he should connect with Motorola's customers. He operationalized this by dedicating one day each month to meeting with customers. The results: He came back to Motorola with concrete ideas for improvement that fueled the energy already in play at Motorola. He began to understand the connection between customers' needs and the actual work processes in new ways. At L.L. Bean, you'll hear the same story. The leaders are in contact with customers, know customers' needs and expectations, and have come to connect work processes in a different way. At a recent meeting of senior executives from major, successful manufacturing and service corporations, the leaders were asked whether health care executives could drive major improvements from within the industry without an intimate knowledge of customer needs and work processes. Every leader said no. They believe this to be a fundamental requirement of successful leadership. Yet health care executives generally report a level of distance between senior team focus and action and the voice of the customer linked with daily work.

The learning tasks for leaders include gaining a deep understanding of customer needs. A strategic plan is needed for moving from customer satisfaction to a level of loyalty that produces longer-term relationships. Particularly now in the age of integrated delivery systems, we need to design loyal, lifetime relationships with customers—a giant leap from merely satisfied encounters. Leaders must develop a new ability to conceptualize and deliver care in lean systems—care processes that produce desired results without the 30 percent waste built into virtually every health care process today.

In some ways, leadership in health care is undergoing the same transformation that work systems throughout the country have experienced. We've moved from an era of craftsmanship to mass production in work systems across the United States in response to volume demand. Henry Ford's famous saying, "You can have any color you want, as long as it's black," reflected the system's need to increase throughput, lower cycle times, and reduce defect rates to produce automobiles in growing numbers as market demand increased.

When customers demanded more options, greater reliability, and lower costs, the manufacturing sector moved to lean production methods, which added industrial engineering science to the art of listening to the voice of the customer. Lean methods incorporate 16 system features in the design and production processes (see Figure 2.1). These methods, when integrated with the systems of production as work principles, allow for enormous improvement in space and equipment utilization, worker safety, and product reliability and cost. Once manufacturing methods are lean, the production processes can be segregated to yield mass customization for specific populations of customers.

At Levi Strauss, mass customization means that fewer stores carry thousand of jeans in inventory to ensure that a particular style, size, and color are available for a particular customer. Product segmentation and stratification systems in sales and production are now available to meet needs in a lean but customized way: The customer is fitted for jeans with an electronic tape measure that feeds sizing data to the cutting room. As a fitter "designs" the jeans with customers, they are being produced and readied for shipment. The customers are delighted with jeans that fit perfectly, and Levi Strauss can compete more aggressively by lowering costs and eliminating waste. In a similar vein, the leadership legends of the past have demonstrated skill and agility by responding to marketplace needs and technological capability of their times.

In health care, we've moved from an era of craftsmanship to mass production. Most health care organizations have adopted clinical algorithms or guidelines as tools to standardize care and improve outcomes. Grappling with the challenges of reducing cycle times and costs has stimulated many health care organizations to adopt lean methods. At Sewickly Valley Hospital, operating room delays and long turnover times are almost a thing of the past as managers use pull systems to smooth flow, manage supply and demand in scheduling, and error-proof the supply systems. At Kaiser Permanente, lean principles—including batch scheduling, reducing uninformed waits, eliminating rework, and schedule simplification—produced remarkable results.

- Access for appointments in one clinic setting improved from a wait of three to four weeks to two days.

- High patient satisfaction results were maintained.

- Costs per visit were reduced by 20 percent.[6]

18

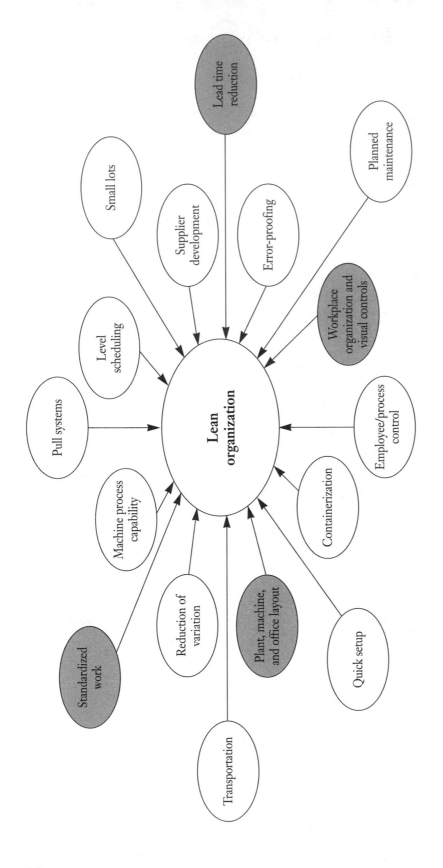

Figure 2.1. Lean production principles.

Although these are nontraditional health care management tools, they are appropriately employed in both clinical and operational settings to produce faster, more efficient systems and as focused tools to reduce waste. The industry now verges on the next transformation: mass customization of care, designed to produce uniquely personal care with the best achievable outcomes at lean-level costs. Imagine a patient with controlled diabetes or another stable chronic disease being admitted for a surgical procedure. A unique path for the patient can be created that will take advantage of the patient's personal strengths and match his or her needs with the appropriate care systems. Patient educational systems can be customized to individual learning styles (visual versus auditory versus tactile learning preferences) and disabilities (hearing or visual impairments). Medications can largely be patient-controlled with technically supported measurement systems. Meals can be designed to meet the typical eating habits of the patient and family with minimal waste, resulting in lower cost with improved nutritional status and satisfaction. Clinical paths can be designed and modified in partnership with patients and measured/adapted at the bedside. Data and plans can be passed on to home care providers to create a smooth path for patients' return to their home for care.

Using mass customization methods, it is possible to design a relatively small number of lean pathways or clinical alternatives that cover the majority of patient conditions. The era of mass customization in patient care relies on several new skills at the senior level, including technical knowledge of lean methods, waste identification and elimination, and using the patients' voice to guide the design process.

These lean systems require a new knowledge and definition of waste. A recent analysis of an operating room process defined 808 steps to move a patient through a typical procedure. Our overly complex systems have evolved over the decades and are now muddied with excessive handoffs and non–value-added steps and delays. Clinical practice variation that does not improve outcomes is wasteful. In a time when virtually every health care organization is reducing expense budgets, leaders need a new definition of waste.

Think of the pressure we place on midlevel managers and physicians. Most often, we provide financial reports detailing full-time equivalent expenses, overtime hours, and supplies. When leaders design budget reduction targets, it is no wonder that we see layoffs, attrition, and lowest-bid supplies as the methods employed to achieve the necessary cuts. Virtually every health care budget has waste built in; 30 percent or more is a common figure upon deep analysis. The skills required for competitive organizations include knowing how to find the waste imbedded in processes and systems and eliminate it; redesign processes; reorganize the physical plants more rationally in light of the newest methods of patient care; and operationalize the best design features to ensure safe, effective, and customer-focused care.

Some organizations set the balance in this way: Specific strategic goals are set for the coming years in each of three areas key to growing competitively.

• Clinical programs, new services, new and updated technological requirements, and plant enhancements are designed to meet the needs of the community served. This requires a clear view of the current health status of the population, an understanding of which needs are being met by the organization or by others, and a listing of priorities to bring excellent clinical care and preventive programs to patients.

• The second area for detailed aim setting is service and access quality. Improvements in this area will speed up appointment/information access and enhance the services provided by decreasing waits, delays, and unnecessary duplication experienced by patients.

• Leaders will then focus on what needs to happen to create an exceptional work environment. Understanding the frustrations in daily work will drive a list of improvements to support staff members at the front line and reduce the stresses and tensions associated with the critical role they serve in support of patients and families.

These leaders design the three years' work, all geared to improve the market/revenue side of the organization by connecting improvement with the real and changing needs of the community. Of course, all of this costs money. At a time when budget cuts of 10 to 20 percent per year are commonplace, leaders may find these dreams placed on the shelf without an internal funding source. New skills in waste identification and process redesign/waste reduction can free up financial resources within the existing budget, and successful leaders then carefully plan phase two.

• A targeted sum is identified for reduction within each of the next three years. Midlevel managers and physician leaders are supported with education and training in the new skills for budget reductions, and feedback loops to demonstrate progress are built. Measurement systems must be designed to ensure that a "push-down, pop-up" phenomenon does not occur, where quality defects rise as budgets are cut.

Leaders then design the uses of budget reductions targeted for each year and typically deploy these savings as follows:

• Some percentage of the savings is earmarked for clinical programs and services or for new/replacement technology required for excellent patient care.

• An additional sum is targeted for vital infrastructure supports such as information system improvements, or training and development for staff—investments that build internal capability for the future.

• A third budget is created to support the organization's bottom line. As revenues shrink with declines in volumes and managed care discounts, financial stability is "budgeted" as a line item on the strategic plan.

Each year the points of emphasis may shift and the priorities might change, but a forward-thinking strategy can help staff to see why waste reductions are important, assure the medical staff and frontline employees that quality will not suffer, and demonstrate the organizational commitment to excellence with its plans for the future of patient care.

Key Leadership Points

• *Develop an aggressive learning plan for the senior team.* Plan leadership benchmarking visits to companies with track records of success; create a plan for learning process-level understanding; acquire deep knowledge of process redesign, waste reduction, and customer input into design.

• *Design a system to actively seek customer feedback and input.* Role model customer obsession at the senior levels of management. Use the voice of the customer as a guide for improvement and system design.

• *Set targets for waste reduction.* Line up appropriate organizational resources to support waste identification and elimination. Educate all levels of managers and physician leaders in these skills. Redeploy cost reduction savings to programs and service that will benefit patient care.

Resistance to Change

One of the greatest challenges leaders face today is organizational resistance to change. It is not that any one individual stands in the way of improvement; rather, organizational behavior thwarts change at every turn. The evidence lies in the abundance of proven best practices detailed in hundreds of journals that sit, ignored, in hospital and managed care offices. Clear evidence abounds on methods to achieve better outcomes at lower costs that are not implemented. Consider the improvement uncovered at Kapiolani Medical Center in Hawaii. Staff members in the neonatal intensive care unit questioned the value of gowning when staff and visitors entered the neonatal intensive care unit. They conducted a literature survey and found that several studies done in past years had shown that gowning added no value for patients and did nothing to protect babies from infection. Reluctant to adopt the new idea even though the research supported the practice of no gowns, the staff undertook a year-long, detailed study to prove that gowning was not necessary for safe practice. Once their study confirmed the acceptability of abandoning the practice, they stopped gowning and saved the hospital $120,000 per year without any increased risk to babies. Given these findings, published widely in the medical literature, imagine the savings the system could accumulate through widespread adoption of this practice!

Improvements such as this are now being published regularly in the medical literature. Part of the barrier to widespread adoption is the difficulty of keeping up with voluminous amounts of work being published. The larger problem, however, is change resistance.

Even within a single hospital or system, it is easy to find isolated pockets of excellence: a nursing unit where registered nurses have achieved an outstanding level of pain control, or a pharmacy team with few errors and fast cycle time in order fulfillment. Why can't these results be transferred easily throughout the rest of the system? Imagine the performance levels of an integrated system in which leaders have a deep understanding of the key processes of patient care, best practices are visible through the measurement data, and leaders facilitate a rapid transfer of best practices to achieve new systems of care.

Studying how this kind of replication is designed and led was the focus of research by Rogers.[7] The diffusion of innovative ideas across various groups within a social system can be designed when leaders understand how people adopt new ideas. One classification of adopters measures innovativeness as a time continuum with categories of different approaches to new ideas (see Figure 2.2). Individuals within each group view change quite differently. Innovators, for example, are adventurous and are able to deal with occasional setbacks when new ideas don't work. Early adopters are generally respected leaders and serve as role models for change. Because others seek their opinions on new ideas, early adopters make considered decisions regarding changes. A key characteristic of the early majority is the deliberateness with which they approach change, "Be not the first by whom the new is tried, nor the last to lay the old aside,"[8] which represents more than one-third of a normal population. This group may serve as an organizational link between the innovative–aggressive and those who wait for every uncertainty to be removed.

The skeptics, the late majority group, are also large in number and tend to change only as a result of proof. Social pressure, concrete case examples, and testimonials may be effective with this group; scientific evidence is generally not as useful. With this group and with the laggards, leaders often need to remove the status quo as an option. Given the choice, the status quo—an immensely powerful pull on any organization's efforts—will prevail.

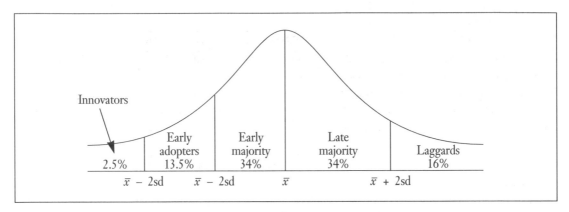

Source: Everett M. Rogers, *Diffusion of Innovation*, 4th ed. (New York: Free Press).

Figure 2.2. Adopter categorization on the basis of innovativeness.

Leaders can study these categories to learn effective strategies for change. Communication about innovation is key. The message can be tailored to each group, and a reasonable expectation for the resources required and the likely time needed to spread innovation can be planned. At a time when leaders report a need for urgent change, these models are helpful for planning the next 12 to 24 months of change and for creating a framework to expeditiously process the transfer of learning throughout the organization. After all, improvement can be accelerated by taking one team's work and replicating the changes throughout—but resistance, the not-invented-here syndrome, can substantially slow progress.

Another change obstacle, often mislabeled as resistance, is apparent when new ideas or improvement projects fail in the implementation phase. When asked why these failures occur or why improvement gains made during the team testing phase decay over time to a prior poor level of performance, leaders will often cite resistance at the level of frontline physicians and staff. David Gustafson and others from the University of Wisconsin have another take. They have identified 24 factors that are key to the successful adoption of a new project. The factors can be viewed as a manager's job description in implementing change (see Figure 2.3).

Designing improvements, guiding diverse staff in testing better methods, including the voice of the customer in all design decisions, and holding gains made over the long haul are the key and non-delegable responsibilities of leaders.

These ideas about managing resistance, when implemented from the top, do produce a new phase of momentum. Think "pull leadership" versus "push management" when you are considering how to move ahead. Resistance will appear to take many forms and shapes, but can be effectively managed.

Key Leadership Points

• *Take a test: Use the model to assess your change management ability.* Create an agenda item for a regular leadership team meeting to review your last 10 team improvement activities. Use the results from the assessment to drive change in management methods—from strengthening the process for mandates, to improving the support structures for teams, to incorporating controls, to the gains.

Factor	Question to answer
Mandate	Have the "powers that be" given you the right to tackle this problem?
Support of key power groups	How strong is the organizational endorsement and support for this new process, including from physicians?
Power group involvement	How much were the influential members of the target group (including physicians) actively involved in exploring the problem and designing the solution?
Supporters and opponents	Who are the supporters and opponents of this project? On balance, which side stands to gain or lose more?
Support from the middle managers	How strong is the support of middle managers for the new process and the implementation strategy?
History with change	To what extent has the target group resisted previous attempts to implement similar kinds of changes in the past?
Change agent commitment	How committed is the change agent to making this project succeed?
Change agent reputation and values	What is the reputation of the person leading the change (change agent) among the affected parties?
Power of the change agent	What power does the change agent have?
Tension for change	How dissatisfied with the current situation are those people most directly affected (e.g., the rank-and-file employees who will need to change)?
Perceived chance of success	Does the target group feel that the change is likely to be successful?
Problem exploration	How carefully was the problem explored before a solution was developed?
External expertise	Were literature reviews and contacts with people outside the organization used to get ideas on how to solve the problem?
Funding	What funds are available to support the development and implementation of the solution?
Alternative solutions	To what extent were several very different ways of solving this problem seriously considered during the problem-solving process?
Radicalness of design	How radical is the proposed solution?
Relative advantages of design	How do the parties involved perceive the relative advantages and disadvantages of the proposed process?
Flexibility of design	Can the proposed process be easily modified to fit the special needs of this organizational unit and still be effective? What aspects can't be changed?
Evidence of effectiveness	What kind of concrete evidence exists that the new process will work?
Complexity of implementation	How difficult will it be to implement the proposed solution?
Target group qualifications	Will the target group be capable of doing the things needed to make this change a success?
Support materials	To what extent are there written materials, videos, etc. that do a good job of explaining why and how the new process is to be implemented and operated?
Feedback	How will the change agent obtain feedback from the target group during implementation?

©David H. Gustafson, University of Wisconsin 1996.

Figure 2.3. Implementation factors.

• *Design strategies for communicating your vision of the future and for replicating innovations to get there.* Substantial changes in performance require a strategic blend of improvement tests followed by replication. No organization has the resources or the energy to improve every process independently. The skill of replication requires that leaders learn how to make and deploy innovation and to manage resistance to the dreaded not-invented-here syndrome.

Building Partnerships With Staff: Human Resources Strategies for the Future

> *The greatest teacher is visualization—seeing others do it and aspiring to their level of performance.*
>
> —Tony Kubik

Perhaps the most powerful leverage in stimulating improvement among all employees is role modeling by leaders. A strategic plan with the key elements described as follows is vital for change, but in the absence of credible leader behavior the best plans fall flat. I learned this lesson the hard way when I served as chief executive officer of a Massachusetts hospital. I thought of myself as an open, friendly, and supportive leader. When I began to uncover the staff's perception of me, I found that even an approachable style could not undo years of built-in fear of authority. "Driving out fear,"[9] as Deming prescribed, is not an easy item to handle on a management agenda and requires the ongoing attention of the senior team. The work begins with a recognition of the amount of fear typically paralyzing staff. When interviewed about innovation and improvement in health care organizations, many clinicians describe a sense of fatality and bureaucratic heaviness that limits ability to change.

Developing an open, trusting culture pays off for the organization. Involved, skilled staff are in the best position to achieve delightful levels of customer service and to offer creative ideas for improving quality and reducing waste in work processes. This kind of involvement and competence in managing process quality is a building block of an effective human resource strategy.

Employment Involvement

Involvement sounds like the warm fuzzy side of quality when, in fact, involvement and empowerment are quite technical as well. Total involvement is key. Learning how to manage quality and achieving a customer focus are prerequisites for every staff member. Many customer complaints in service organizations can be categorized as an inconsistency in approach, process, or outcome. A patient making her way through a physical exam at a clinic encounters 12 staff members on average and runs into dozens of opportunities that will make involvement in quality improvement mandatory in health care organizations; the time for allowing some clinicians and staff to opt out of this learning is past.

Three methods can be used to help gain involvement. The first is empowerment, a word that often raises unpleasant images in managers' minds. Empowerment is not an abandonment of control or an adoption of laissez-faire management. On the contrary, empowerment is a process that requires considerable work on the part of managers in collaboration with frontline staff (see Figure 2.4).

Empowerment requires three related elements. The first is designed and controlled work processes. For a staff member to manage process quality, the work—both clinical and support processes—needs to be designed and monitored. An operating room manager will have little chance of predicting tomorrow's schedule flow without understanding the elements of scheduling and operating room

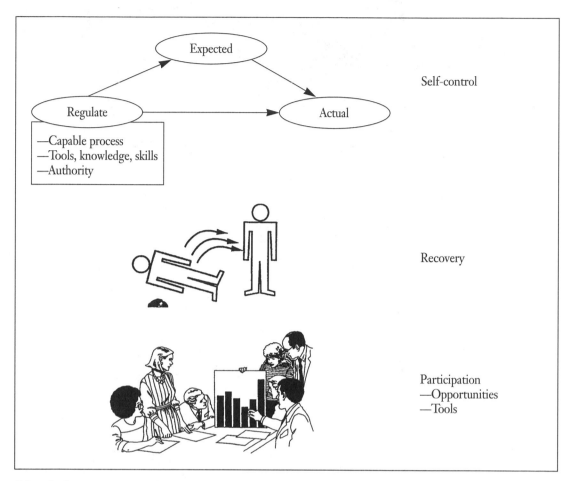

© Juran Institute

Figure 2.4. Empowered employees.

management processes and without a control chart that allows the manager to see routine process times from day to day. These design features represent a substantial investment in education and dedicated time for managers and staff to design and measure the processes of daily work. The plan to monitor and react to process performance, quality control, helps to prevent process decay. The control process takes place by use of feedback loops (see Figure 2.5).

In many health care organizations, direct patient care staff receive little performance feedback. It may happen in an annual review session or by distributing patient/member satisfaction results throughout, but this general feedback is not specific or timely enough to empower staff to link it to a process and to take action in real-time situations or to see what is occurring and prevent a problem entirely.

The feedback loop lets control responsibility be assigned directly to the front line for processes appropriately owned at that level. The important elements of self-control provide employees the following:

- A means of knowing what the organization's goals and standards are.

- A means of knowing what the actual performance is, as timely and as directly as possible.

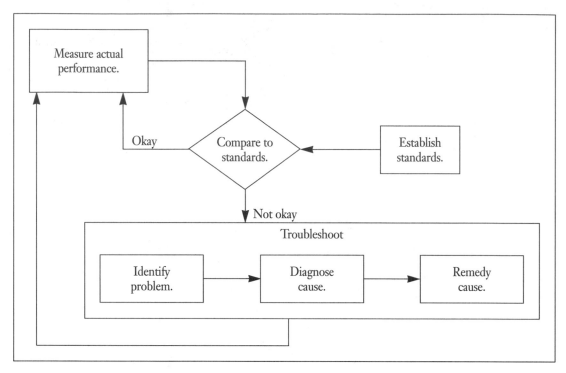

© Juran Institute

Figure 2.5. Feedback loop.

- A means for changing the performance in the event that actual performance does not meet goals and standards.

When problems do occur, a control spreadsheet gives the staff immediate access to a number of measures for regaining process stability (see Figure 2.6). However, simply identifying an assignable cause and remedying it does nothing to allay customer dissatisfaction. The second vital component of empowerment is the concept of service recovery.

Many employee empowerment attempts in health care organizations have failed to include a consistent set of guidelines for employees to implement once a problem has caused an external failure (one recognized by the customer). Simply advising employees to "make it right for the customer" presents several problems. First, customers experience great variation from employee to employee when individuals are left to devise a strategy on their own. Second, employees are at a great disadvantage without some policy guidance regarding management's knowledge of the degree of service recovery appropriate for a given process failure. Many managers equate recovery with "giving away the store" when, in fact, experience shows that most employees take no service recovery action at all without guidelines for fear of over- or undercompensating for a failure.

Studies have demonstrated that a customer who has experienced a service disappointment and who is ably and promptly recovered is your most loyal future customer, even more loyal than a customer who received expected service in the first place. For a managed care organization striving to grow its membership, retaining current customers through a recovery strategy is the most cost-effective marketing investment it can make.

Control subject	Unit of measure	Sensor	Goal	Frequency of measure	Criteria for decision	Who acts?	Does what?
							Quality control
							Service recovery

Figure 2.6. Quality control and service recovery spreadsheet.

The third vital element for empowerment is the opportunity (time and training) to participate in the design, measurement, and improvement of daily work. Health care organizations, under the cost-cutting strain, have been notorious for underinvesting in the infrastructure for quality. Defect reduction is managed directly by empowered teams, resulting in improved quality and reduced costs. General Motors' improvement methodology is now being used by empowered teams in health care organizations and has resulted in substantial improvement in record time—staff at the Deaconess Hospital in Boston, Massachusetts, rearranged the inpatient dialysis unit in four days and increased both patient dialysis time and throughput with fewer overtime hours and less patient travel time. The leaders' commitment to designing the time away from work to learn and improve is repaid with greater customer satisfaction and lower costs.

Key leadership points to consider include the following:

• *Budget senior leaders' time to improve.* Set aside time at leadership meetings to map high-level organizational processes and cascade the process through to the departmental/service line level.

• *Control key processes and feed back the results.* Once processes are mapped, develop measurement and control systems to identify goals and feed back real-time process information to staff. Work with managers to locate departmental and cross-functional vulnerabilities and to develop recovery strategies for defects that may recur.

• *Partner with physicians.* Invest time at medical staff meetings to review performance data, defect rates, recovery strategies, and customer loyalty measures.

Education and Development

The second key human resource strategy requires skill building and development of staff at all levels. The curriculum in professional and technical programs that prepare physicians, clinicians, and technical staff focus on the skills necessary for the job, rarely on the skills necessary to improve the work. World-class organizations have tested a variety of methods for supporting this learning and all agree that a well-designed educational plan is a cornerstone for achieving breakthrough levels of quality.

Leaders, with input from staff development experts and managers, design a strategy that defines these elements.

- The scope of the organization's needs for education, backed up with data and best practices information from various internal groups.

- A design for how to meet these needs.

- A comprehensive understanding of resources, time, and support required, particularly detailing management's roles in achieving the desired effects from the education.

- A set of measures to demonstrate effectiveness, impact, cost–benefit ratio, and satisfaction.

In many health care organizations, the investment for staff education at all levels from the board and medical staff through all frontline workers has been cut or was never adequately funded. A look outside our industry will demonstrate, by comparison, how some leading companies fulfill the need for skill and capability growth. At Motorola, the importance of ongoing education is role modeled from the top; managers at all levels attend the respected Motorola Management Institute for two weeks of extensive training on the challenges of managing change and maintaining world-class quality in a rapidly changing, competitive world. All Motorola employees participate in 40 hours of training per year, nearly 20 of which are devoted to improvement.

At Xerox the cascade approach to training has become the benchmark for effectiveness in quality education.[10] Former chair David Kearns started the learning personally by undertaking a journey of exploration. He visited with many corporate leaders, attended conferences, read books and articles, and conducted benchmarking visits to companies he admires. With a firm grasp of what he wanted to achieve, he personally led a six-day, 48-hour course for his direct reports that emphasized his obsession with customers and outlined the new skills needed to manage at Xerox—technical and interactive people skills. The training then cascaded throughout Xerox in "family groups," led by managers at each successive level. The training accomplished two critical outcomes for Xerox: First, it effectively refocused the company on the customer and provided every employee with the skills needed to improve; and second, it coached the managers at every level in their new roles as teachers and mentors. The most significant effect from cascade training, however, is that it often begins a transformational culture change as it produces improved performance.

Key leadership points to consider include the following:

- *Focus on the customer.* All training, whether clinical or operational, should be designed to support the organization's work with patients and other external customers. The context for learning is key. Improvement methods should be integrated with the curriculum of other subject matter learning as well.

- *Use an educational cascade for best results.* The staff learn as much from the interaction with managers as they do from the subject matter. This important lesson managers are learning and teaching produces positive cultural as well as improvement results. The lessons from the classroom, when taught by managers, can be immediately translated and reinforced in patient care settings.

- *Design the system with adult learning theory in mind.* The learning should be continuous—articles shared weekly from one level to another; book reviews for 15 minutes at the start of a weekly meeting; quarterly field trips to excellent companies for leadership teams—and should respect how different adults learn. The methods should include a variety of media, from self-learning modules to on-the-unit coaching to multimedia classroom experiences.

• *Train for the next job.* The "war room" in the human resource office needs a wall-size map of the strategy to move people from the downsizing units into the upsizing area of these systems. The reactive layoff/attrition method is taking its toll widely on morale, quality, and trust relationships. An aggressive, proactive plan that identifies and prepares staff for new roles in other areas of the system will be key in managing the more transitional workforce of the future.

Performance Feedback and Recognition

As one publication recently summarized the problem, "When employees are urged to cooperate but paid to compete, you've got a little problem."[11] Leaders in most health care settings today are concerned about the toxic effects of their pay systems, but no real industrywide solutions have been crafted. Much has been written about the perverse effects of rewards in the workplace.[12] The evidence is clear: When leaders pay bonuses, give raises, and recognize managers primarily for making budget, the energy for improving quality will lag behind budget-cutting efforts.

Tests in other industries have been underway for years and may be helpful in forging change in health care. At General Motor's Powertrain Division, a redesigned compensation system has been separated from the appraisal system and now supports a structure based on a "maturity curve."[13] The curve—a function of the employee's seniority with GM, expertise and skill, and a competitive market analysis—provides a framework for pay rates and expected growth opportunity. Staff members are "placed" on the curve with input from peers, subordinates, and managers.

The feedback process for GM's Powertrain employees is designed to guide an individual's development plan and is separate from the pay rating system. The combination has proved a positive approach and accomplishes the dual missions of equitable compensation and stimulating employee development and growth.

Other companies such as Xerox and Ford are moving to coaching rather than rating. Several health care systems have experimented in this area, as well as with decoupled performance/payment systems or no approval systems at all. One hospital adapted Peter Scholtes' work[14] by linking improvement with process feedback. Feedback begins with agreement on the six or seven most important processes of work. For example, the chief executive officer defined with the vice president for human resources the most important work in that area, specifically employee relations, hiring and orientation, wage and salary administration, benefit management, education and development, and workplace communication. The human resources owner defined each process and the key suppliers, process coworkers, and customers. Each process is then analyzed with input from the key groups and against process, cost, and outcome measures. The feedback process then generates a very customer-focused improvement plan that becomes the personal plan for the manager. The process is continuous; one of the six processes is studied every other month, and the planned changes begin as the next review cycle is designed.

The value of the process is found in separating the personal judgment of work from the worker. Managers are planning and implementing focused improvement to reduce costs and defects and to add features that delight their customers. Improvement becomes personal and constant. The feedback is direct to the manager and provides a powerful stimulus for change.

Appraisal is currently an area of redesign in many health care organization. Linked with recognition, these processes require the attention of senior leaders to align the messages. Although recognition seems like an easy thing to accomplish, designing a sustained, meaningful recognition system that reinforces the organization's key aims and does not decay into insincere routine is a major challenge. Listening to physicians and staff is a place to begin; amazing differences are charted between the configuration of most recognition systems and what staff members say is most meaningful in their work life.

Key leadership points to consider include the following:

• *Investigate options to linked appraisal/compensation systems.* Leaders can begin with a serious appraisal of the current system, including manager and employee feedback on the messages reinforced by the system, improvements resulting from it, and options for change.

• *Design recognition to meet the real needs of staff.* Employees value support and action from managers; frontline staff can design recognition that really matters. They often suggest

—Managers who know what the staff members are working to improve

—Real listening and aggressive management of the barriers to improvement

—Assurance that their ideas and plans are implemented

—Personal communication of thanks and appreciation

• *Plan an ongoing recognition and celebration process.* This is more difficult than it seems. Having fun at work seems almost unnatural to many health care managers. Leaders need to design and carry out an ongoing plan to break down cross-professional and cross-departmental barriers and to recognize the success of the staff in an open and sincere forum.

Healthy Workplace Development

Tending to the culture is one of the thorniest parts of health care management today. Nearly all senior leaders recently interviewed about the culture and well-being of their organization's staff want improvement. Cultural assessments point out areas that staff say can be improved. And yet, changing the culture seems like an impossible mission.

Creating a healthy workplace environment was a successful starting point for many Baldrige Award–winning companies. These leaders often were silent on their desires to have a more balanced, exciting workplace but, instead, let their actions speak for them. USAA, a major insurance carrier with 14,000 employees, aggressively manages turnover in an industry where this is a costly problem. Flexible schedules mold work and personal lives together, and a focus on the health of all employees and on-site health facilities are visible signs of the commitment.

At the Institute for Healthcare Improvement in Boston, Massachusetts, we use a focus on personal mastery to achieve a sense of balance for staff members who work in a hectic, complex environment juggling travel, demanding schedules, and tight deadlines. The mastery exercise is a focused way to think about a healthy and sensible work/personal balance and represents the Institute's commitment without crossing the line to a paternalistic environment. The exercise, led by the Institute's leaders, supports personal goal-setting in the following areas.

• Personal development

• Professional growth and development

• Financial security

• Health and exercise

• Spiritual health

• Family time and relationships

• Friends and supportive relationships

The goals are supported by tangible evidence of the Institute's commitment to the balance considered to be key to achieving excellence in the workplace. Health assessment is offered with personal fitness planning for each staff member; and financial counseling, employee assistance support, flexible schedules, and professional career planning are designed into the work plan. The Institute's staff convened recently to codify each staff member's commitment to our customers and to each other, the Institute's commitment to the staff, and each staff member's to the workplace. These citizenship guidelines (see Figure 2.7) are the guiding principals we live by, but the staff members together own a plan making the guidelines come to life. This activation process is the difficult part of any cultural change plan and the part that requires monitoring, measuring, and action planning regularly at the senior levels of management.

Key leadership points to consider include the following:

• *Whatever you design, measure and improve it.* Although the cultural side of management presents greater measurement challenges, leaders must chart progress toward their visions of an ideal work culture, or their plans get left in the cloud of employee skepticism.

• *Develop an ongoing and regular method for listening to the staff.* Input from medical staff leaders and managers is vital to the design of the workplace, but must be added to the voice of the physicians and frontline staff members who are in daily contact with patients.

• *Focus on safety.* Senior leaders at many Baldrige Award–winning companies obsess about employee safety. Monitoring and analyzing days lost to work, unsafe conditions and factors, and the costs borne by the institution becomes the regular work of the leadership team. Improvement in this area pays off in decreased costs and positive cultural changes in the workplace.

• *Overcommunicate.* Most health care leaders feel they communicate adequately and list several direct lines to the medical staff and frontline staff. Most of the customers to the communication report feeling adrift in a fast-paced, changing environment. If ever there was a time for a well-designed, multimedia, regular system of communication, that time is now.

Tracking Progress and Measuring for Change

How can we know all of this work is really improving quality? How can leaders decide which improvement opportunity is the most crucial in the short term? The answer to these questions may reside in the data the senior leaders use to steer the organization's path. Often, leadership meeting time is spent reviewing financial performance, acquisitions, and merger plans and responding to the issues of the day. These are critical responsibilities of the team, but often replace a real understanding of the organization's performance in providing clinical care—its major role.

Effective teams drive change based on a full and rather detailed knowledge of the organizational performance. They study the gaps between their goals and the defects and flows of the current state. They study the best achieved performances in the industry and how their performance compares. They direct focused improvement and measure quality in the front office and at the front line.

Paul Batalden and Eugene Nelson at Dartmouth Medical School describe a comprehensive system to inform leaders about the state of the organization's performance. Effective leaders use data in the following ways.

• To assess performance related to the mission and vision of the organization

• To evaluate the success of strategic plans and action such as the integration progress

Preamble

We are the people of the Institute for Healthcare Improvement. We believe that, to build and sustain a successful organization, we must embrace a culture characterized by personal commitment to each other, our customers, and our work. We define commitment as an understanding, acceptance, and active participation in the shared responsibility to meet needs and obligations. We recognize that as individuals and as an organization, this commitment must be supported by clear statements that help us identify how we are each expected to conduct ourselves and how we each would like to be treated. We therefore adopt the following guidelines for our daily work together.

I. Our Commitment to Customers

1. Our customers expect us to provide leadership and vision for the improvement of health care through its products and services, and through its ability to bring people together for a common purpose.

2. Our customers expect to get value for their money, and they expect our products and services to be timely and high quality.

3. Our customers expect to have their needs met by staff that are knowledgeable, courteous, and guided by the principles of quality improvement.

4. Our customers expect to receive information that is accurate, need specific, and consistent. They expect to have to ask only once, and they expect staff to talk to each other and share information about their needs.

5. Our customers expect us to not waste their time and resources with overly complex and extraneous materials or information.

6. Our customers expect us to show interest and concern for their particular situation and are delighted with interactions that are personalized and friendly.

II. How We Treat Each Other

1. We are all individuals, each deserving acknowledgment of his or her value, each deserving respect, each deserving the acceptance and interest of us all. We bring our own distinct viewpoints and talents to the organization, and we welcome the diversity that this adds to the whole of us. We do not pass judgment on personalities and lifestyles.

2. We communicate openly and honestly with each other and keep each other informed on a daily basis. We acknowledge disagreement without fear and address difficult subjects without delay. We seek to understand opinions that differ from our own, and we both give and receive feedback constructively. We resolve personal disagreements with those directly involved. We keep our word, and we keep confidences that are entrusted to us.

3. We listen to each other.

4. We forgive each other, and we are not afraid to say "I'm sorry" and "thank you."

5. We are a team. We depend on and are responsible for each other. We ask for help when we need it, and offer support, both practical and emotional, when we can. Our jobs are intertwined and flexible; we do not allow job descriptions or hierarchy to limit the nature of the work or who does it. We are accountable for the work we agree to do, and we are honest about our capacity to take on more. We are trustworthy and conscientious in our own work and in any work we do on behalf of others.

6. We believe in humor as a means to keep each other grounded. Our mission is serious, but we do not always have to be. We are not afraid to laugh at ourselves and allow ourselves to be teased, but our humor is friendly and fun, never mean-spirited.

7. We celebrate successes together, and we acknowledge and value the individual contributions that make them happen.

8. We show respect for the personal space, property, and privacy of each individual.

III. Our Organization's Support for Us

1. IHI is an organization that values its integrity. Through its commitment to excellence, it fosters a sense of pride, dignity, and professionalism in our work for it. It is in vigorous compliance with all the legal requirements of a nonprofit organization, and it practices the concepts of continuous quality improvement in its policies, actions, and daily work.

Figure 2.7. Institute for Healthcare Improvement: Our guidelines for citizenship.

2. IHI understands and supports our individual needs and aspirations. It provides us, within its utmost capabilities, job security and opportunities for personal growth and professional development. It provides us with positive and constructive feedback for improvement.

3. IHI respects us, acknowledges our contributions, and trusts us.

4. IHI views us as partners, actively seeking our input in a constant review of programs and actions to determine consistency with our mission and long-term goals. It does not dictate policy, but works in collaboration with us to create and maintain operating principles that are clear and specific but also flexible and continuously improved.

5. IHI supports open, solid, and easy communication among and across all levels and committees—including the board of directors—about individual programs and activities and how they relate to each other. It is forthcoming and honest with information regarding the organization's strategic direction and financial condition.

6. IHI is committed to supporting a positive environment in which we feel both physically and emotionally safe, in which our physical work space is pleasant and efficient, in which we each understand our roles and responsibilities, in which needed resources are supplied in a timely manner, and in which celebration is both frequent and joyful.

7. IHI recognizes the importance of a healthy balance between work and personal life and provides adequate support so that people do not feel strained in this regard.

IV. Our Support for the Organization

1. We are each caretakers of IHI's mission and vision, sharing in its commitment to excellence and practice of continuous improvement. We each understand how our individual work supports the organization's goals.

2. We are responsible and accountable for our work. We ensure that it is completed efficiently, with attention to accuracy and quality. We constantly examine our processes and look for opportunities to enhance quality while reducing costs. We are knowledgeable about our work, and we seek opportunities to expand that knowledge and keep it current.

3. We are quick to take initiative, solving problems creatively and working independently to meet the needs of customers and coworkers. We "hit the ground running," at times juggling duties and responsibilities, understanding that some ambiguity is always inevitable and that it need not be paralyzing.

4. We are reliable and trustworthy. The organization can depend on us to show up and do our best for it.

5. We are focused on delighting our customers, anticipating their needs, responding to them promptly, and constantly searching for better ways to serve them.

6. To our customers and to the public, we represent IHI, and we therefore maintain a professional appearance and attitude when working outside of the office.

7. We are responsible and frugal in our use of resources, minimizing the cost of waste to the organization, and maximizing opportunities for recycling and conservation.

8. We accept responsibility for the shared stewardship of the organization, and we participate freely in efforts to improve its management and operations.

Making It Real
This document is a representation of our beliefs as an organization, a reflection of who and what we would like to be. In order to make IHI's guidelines for citizenship a living document that is relevant to all current and future employees and associates, a system must be developed that will provide communication about the content and a method for measuring its effectiveness.

The document will be read twice a year at special event meetings for content and measure of effectiveness. All staff will participate in a review and commentary. In addition, the guidelines for citizenship will be discussed with new IHI employees in their regular orientation sessions.

Figure 2.7. *continued.*

- To monitor the core processes of work
- To identify the drivers of customer satisfaction
- To identify "push down—pop up" effects of change

The executive team members often review the data together and strategize on how to expend the organization's limited improvement resources. This review requires data that are concise (limited to several pages), compelling (pointing out the potential rather then assuring that performance is "acceptable"), and focused (aimed at measuring progress in one of the five categories listed rather than focused at a level of detail more appropriate for different owners). Another important element to consider in the design of senior leaders' measures is a sense of balance in the measures. The balanced scorecard rounds out the traditional financial data reviewed by the senior team with key outcomes and performance measures, an overview of customer satisfaction, and often a measure of the innovativeness or adaptability of the organization.[15] Chip Caldwell also suggests that a balanced scorecard approach can both drive the integration of delivery systems and measure progress along the way.[16]

The vital focal point for leaders, however, is not measuring but improving. The data needed at regular senior meetings need to be compelling to help drive change. It's important to develop a measurement cascade down to the program and service level to ensure that detailed data are driving the improvement efforts of the physician and staff at the frontline level. The most critical analysis will tally the improvements made in results, outcomes, lowering cost, and reducing cycle times, not in the number of guidelines developed.

Key leadership points to consider include the following:

- Evaluate the data that drive the senior leadership's decision making and add components, if necessary, to achieve a balanced sense of performance and a timely assessment of progress toward goals.
- Design the feedback loops and cascades necessary to align the information and measurement throughout the programs, services, and levels in the organization.
- Assess how effective your measurement system is in highlighting areas for improvement and compelling change.
- Track improvements made as a result of regular review.

Senior teams in health care often use data to assure that they are in a safe range with other similar organizations. Leaders in Baldrige Award–winning companies use data to drive improvement. They collect data that are uncomfortable and that compel change to meet even higher performance levels. Review the last 12 months of senior leadership team meeting minutes and quantify the data.

- How often (and how deeply) does the council review the voice-of-the-customer feedback?
- How does the council review quality data (outcomes, processes, cost, and customer satisfaction) on the top 10 DRGs, procedures, or patient types?
- How many improvements (unique changes by department/individuals) were charted by the council?
- How long did the changes take?
- Are the changes being tracked over time? Where?
- Did the council recognize each improvement? How?
- How much time have the council members spent learning together?

- What is the satisfaction level of the council members with the improvement projects and teams they receive from senior management?

- What strategic progress has been made in reducing waste/cost/cycle time?

Conclusion

Health care leaders are at a crossroad. The choices we make now will have much more substantial and lasting consequences than in the past decades and the drive for improved performance has never been more urgent. At the same time, lessons learned from leaders in health care and from other industries show that it can be done.

One thing is sure: No organizational transformations have occurred without a leadership commitment to change. The improvement aims and a dogged pursuit of more excellent care are hallmarks of the most successful health care organizations.

A personal learning plan is a powerful starting place and can serve to add momentum to an organizational strategy when past efforts "hit the wall." Leadership can be defined by how executives acquired and demonstrated the learnings they gained from theory, from other organizations, or from internal experiments to improve within the system. Just as physicians and managers are learning to leapfrog to new performance levels with clinical and operational benchmarking, so can executive teams benchmark leadership practices of the best to learn breakthrough strategies and management techniques for achieving rapid and sustainable rates of change.

Many industries have gained tremendous knowledge about the nature of transformational leadership over the past several decades. Senior executives who visit world-class organizations to study their leadership practices can readily adapt the critical elements to the health care environment. The advantage is a learning cycle that promotes robust, strategic systems of care, leadership, and revolutionary improvement. Such a tour requires some prework. To prepare for the experience, the executive and medical staff leaders should brainstorm a list of learning objectives and accompanying questions. Commonly asked questions include the following:

- How do world-class leaders spend their time?

- How much of their work day is spent alone? With the senior team? In the community? With their key customers?

- What data do they review and how much improvement does that data really compel?

- How much individual learning is occurring? How much learning is done as a team?

- What efforts have succeeded in creating a more effective culture? Which, if any, have failed?

- How does learning happen at all levels of the organization?

- How do these world-class leaders replicate successes across the organization?

- How have they managed resistance to change?

- What bottom-line results have they achieved? Do they believe the results have justified the effort?

- What lessons have they learned about accelerating change?

Once its learning objectives and questions are complete, the team is ready to embark on benchmarking visits. These leadership meetings can be energizing opportunities that produce rich exchanges of benefit to both organizations.[17]

One thing is sure: Transformations do not occur as a result of leadership exhortation. They only begin and are only substantial when leaders demonstrate that they, too, are willing to learn and change.

Notes

1. American Customer Satisfaction Index, co-sponsored by American Society for Quality and the University of Michigan Business School as a national economic indicator.

2. *Dartmouth Atlas.*

3. J. Main, *Quality Wars: The Triumphs and Defeats of American Business* (New York: Free Press, 1994).

4. Ibid.

5. D. M. Berwick, "Eleven Worthy Aims for Clinical Leadership of Health System Reform" JAMA 272 (1994): 797–802.

6. Institute for Healthcare Improvement, Breakthrough Series Project Report on Waits and Delays (Boston: Institute for Healthcare Improvement, 1996).

7. E. M. Rogers, *Diffusion of Innovation*, 4th ed. (New York: Free Press).

8. Alexander Pope, *An Essay on Criticism Part II.*

9. W. E. Deming, *Out of the Crisis* (Cambridge, Mass.: MIT Center for Advanced Engineering Study, 1982).

10. "Batting 1000" is AT&T's total quality approach.

11. J. Main, *Quality Wars.*

12. D. Berwick, "The Toxicity of Pay for Performance," *Quality Management in Health Care* 4 (1) (1995): 27–33.

13. J. Main, *Quality Wars.*

14. Peter Scholtes.

15. R. S. Kaplan and D. P. Norton, "Using the Balanced Scorecard as a Strategic Management System, *Harvard Business Review* (Jan.–Feb. 1996).

16. Chip Caldwell, "Strategic Performance Measurement in an Integrated Healthcare System," *Health System Leader* (September 1994).

17. M. A. Bisognano, "Best Practices in Quality Leadership," *Quality Letter* (July–Aug. 1995).

Maureen A. Bisognano is executive vice president and chief operational officer at the Institute for Healthcare Improvement in Boston, Massachusetts, where she oversees program development, operations, and strategic planning. Prior to joining IHI, she was senior vice president of Juran Institute, Inc., where she consulted with senior management on the implementation of total quality management in health care settings. Prior to joining Juran Institute, she was employed by Quorum Health Resources. She served as chief executive officer of Massachusetts Respiratory Hospital in Braintree, Massachusetts, where, as part of the National Demonstration Project, she introduced total quality management. Bisognano earned a B.S. degree from the University of the State of New York and an M.S. degree from Boston University.

Chapter 3

Results-Driven Management: Strategic Quality Deployment

Chip Caldwell

This may be the most unique of times in health care delivery around the world. Every health care system in every nation is struggling to remove cost without jeopardizing clinical outcomes and patient satisfaction. In fact, one country has mandated a 3 percent budget cut for hospitals of which $1^1/_2$ percent can come from reduction in services. I would estimate that among the health care organizations in the United States, as many as 30 percent have resorted to traditional methods of cost reduction versus a retooling of their quality initiatives to measure outcomes while intensely identifying and driving out non–value-added (NVA) cost. Some organizations, like Henry Ford Health System in Detroit, Michigan, General Health System in Baton Rouge, Louisiana, and Mayo Clinic in Rochester, Minnesota, have been rewarded through the enhancement of total quality management (TQM) tools and methods to drive out NVA cost while systematically reducing the cycle time to generate results.

Strategic Intent

One of the greatest challenges organizations currently face in their TQM deployment initiatives is the generation of the linkage between their strategic plans, financial plans, and their quality plans. So often, companies that I mentor treat the quality plan—if indeed one exists at all—as a document and process entirely separate from the strategic plan and financial plan.

As J. M. Juran has pointed out for years, organizations are very effective in the deployment of financial plans and many are very good at deploying strategic plans.[1] Few, however, have mastered the integration of all three into a cohesive approach based on the quantified needs of customers. He encourages upper managers to think of the construction of the quality plan as a parallel process to the construction of the financial plan. The process to create an integrated quality plan follows the same steps as generating the budget; a greater degree of coordination is required in that, first, customer needs are quantified, then quality goals and objectives are articulated, and these requirements become the framework to compile financial requirements.

Every activity in which an organization embarks should be centered around the achievement of the vision and strategic deployment road map. One of the results of this separation may be the loss of interest by the chief executive officer (CEO) and other senior leaders in the TQM initiative. It becomes quite apparent to everyone in the organization if the CEO is not attending quality council meetings or leading other TQM communications activities. This observation might have the effect of sending a sign that the organization's TQM priorities and the organization's strategic priorities have taken different roads. However, rather than proceed down different paths at ever greater rates of speed, the best advice an organization can follow is to reassess the strategic agenda and the quality agenda, then synchronize the two. If the CEO does not see the TQM agenda as the best vehicle to drive strategic results, if the chief financial officer (CFO) does claim that the TQM program's reduction of NVA cost is the highest rate of return of any of the investments this budget year, if the operations vice presidents (VPs) do not daily recite how TQM teams and other visible evidences of use of TQM tools and techniques are accelerating their divisions' efforts, then basic examination of the focus of the quality council's recent agendas, minutes, and future plans might help assess the degree to which strategic issues are being addressed.

Focus on Results

Often organizations that do not possess an integrated strategic deployment road map—consisting of quality, financial, and strategic imperatives—seem not to have a proper alignment of key priorities, or their priorities appear to focus on strategies unrelated to customers. History provides adequate examples for us to examine, but our own experiences may, in fact, provide a richer pool. Consider from your own experience the organizations that, due to the CEO's own lack of vision or the organization's failure to embrace it, have obviously strayed from a customer-focused mind-set, embracing perhaps financial targets or internal political achievements above a deeper sense of customer commitment. These organizations—at least the ones that come to mind when reflecting on this question—seem to possess no thirst to exceed customer expectations, and employees do not appear to share a common mind-set that the key customers' needs stand above all else. Rather, employees privately remark that senior leaders care only about the bottom line or that customer complaints are not taken seriously. The organizations that come to mind for me have either ceased to do business or have radically revised their cultures.

Consider, on the other extreme, those organizations with which you have enough familiarity to know that, from the CEO to everyone affiliated with the organization, customer needs have become the focal point of all activity and planning. Within those organizations that come to mind as I contemplate this question, an unexplainable vibrancy seems to permeate the workforce. Employees appear confident in their jobs and express delight about working in the organization.

This latter organization is representative of the model for emulation, one that has articulated customer needs into the very fabric of all organizational activity—the strategic plan, the budget, capital allocation, employee rewards and recognition, and the anecdotes that are heard in the cafeteria and at new employee orientation. This organization has introduced processes that uniquely match its own culture, but that focus on results as interpreted from customer needs assessments.

In my experience, organizations that excel do so because they have maintained their attention on measurable results as the focal point of all other activities. These activities seem to fall into one of three categories, as illustrated in Figure 3.1.

Culture. Concentration on the organizational culture might be the most important factor, although I was slow to recognize this important factor. A properly aligned culture leads to a widespread passion of everyone in the organization to achieve the organization's vision. This first became apparent to me when I witnessed a medication adminstration team present its successful 50 percent reduction

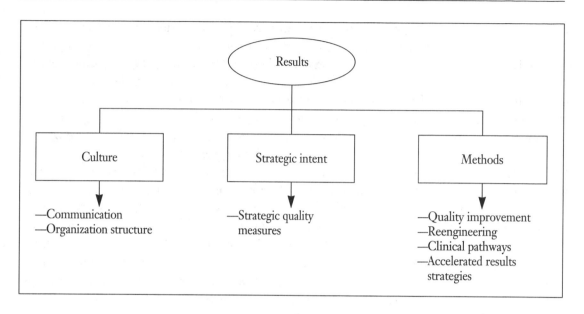

Figure 3.1. Results model.

of turnaround time; one delaying factor in the process was that the pneumatic tube system frequently jammed. The maintenance person responsible for the tube system was added to the team and quickly helped find the root cause of the problem and through brainstorming the team removed it. During the presentation, the maintenance person had tears in his eyes and remarked afterward, "I never knew my job was important to patient care." These kinds of experiences, repeated over and over by project teams, build a passion toward organizational excellence. The second and related factor is fear. As Paul Batalden of Dartmouth Medical School often remarks, "Fear is a major quality thief."[2] For whatever reason, human nature leads us, on examination of a list of suggestions for improvement, to accentuate the negative rather than acknowledging the positive along with the negative. This pattern begins even as early as grade school; just think how the term *below average* makes you feel. The resultant behavioral conditioning is that all of us are terrified of appearing ignorant, and we therefore often miss golden opportunities to build passion within the workforce to make rapid and continuous improvements. Masao Nemoto, the talented Toyota mentor, created a marvelous solution to this pattern for Toyota's project team reviews.[3] He required that reviewers begin their remarks with several observations under the category, "Here is what we can celebrate with this team." Then the reviewer comments on "If we could ask you to do more." The beauty of his system is that the reviewer can have no more items in the do-more category than in the celebrate category.

Several remedies come to mind to ensure alignment of culture-building activities toward results assurance. Are your project teams reviewed on project completion, or have you grown tired of reviews? Are storyboards displayed wherever you look, or have team leaders become complacent over the years? Does the quality council deploy new ways to recognize team and department manager successes on a semiannual basis? Are true champions recognized, both formally and informally, for their measurable achievements? Have policies and procedures been reexamined to ensure that the organization does not create barriers to fast results?

Strategic Intent and Strategic Measures. How might an organization determine the activities and priorities for this year's plan that will guarantee market success in 1999, in 2000, and in 2002? One way to think of the critical success factors common to any organization is to ask, "What must we achieve this year?" Generally, these short-term priorities center around cash flow generation and cost reduction. Therefore, one might reason that to stay in business in 1999 we need to focus current efficiency and select, among other measures, cash flow as a percent of net revenue, accounts receivable days, and labor productivity for our 1999 strategic measurement set. Next we can ask ourselves, "If we wish to ensure success in 2000, at what must we excel?" Generally, organizations conclude that, due to word of mouth and the strength of market reputation, we must manage and improve the perception of current customers in order to assure a steady stream of customers in 2000. That is, if we excel today at customer service, customers will express delight about us publicly and will, therefore, accelerate market share growth. Thus, our year 2000 measurement set might include, among other measures, customer satisfaction scores and customer complaints. Finally, we can ask ourselves, "At what must we excel today in order to assure success in the year 2002?" We might conclude that we must drive up the rate of innovation and drive down the cycle time for new product introduction if we are to surpass our competitors' strategic efforts. Therefore, we could construct measurements for the number of new products and the number of months to develop them, as well as the volume of quality improvement team improvements and the number of days per project team cycle.

After considering market needs, many organizations constructing a strategic plan skip over measurement and jump directly to "What are we going to do?" Are we going to introduce new Product X in 24 months? Construct an outpatient surgery center? Form a physician–hospital organization (PHO)? Merge with another health care organization? Each of these elements falls under the category of tactical plans. These organizations, in an effort to be proactive, fail to ask, "Based on what we believe the market is doing, how might we best measure the impact of our strategic tactical plans?" However, the second stop along the road—after speaking to customers—should be to construct the strategic measurement template to assess the degree of effectiveness of the tactical actions.

Our efforts over the years and the observations from organizations I now mentor have led to the acknowledgment that five key strategic endeavors, followed with the absolute aggressiveness required of all serious strategic thrusts, should form the basis of any organization's strategic deployment plan. They are as follows:

1. Increase the rate of innovation by 20 percent per year.

2. Reduce non–value-added cost by 20 percent per year.

3. Increase customer satisfaction by 20 percent per year.

4. Progressively integrate the organization as a system.

5. Exceed stakeholder cash flow expectations by 20 percent per year.

1. *Increase the rate of innovation by 20 percent per year.* The sustainable growth targets of most businesses require a fundamental understanding of the ideation and introduction of new products and services into the marketplace. We are referring here not only to product breakthroughs, but the entire scope of innovations that can and should be managed in an organization—new products, new markets, employee suggestions, quality improvement team cycle time, and so on. And the dimension of innovation deserving the focus of efforts is not only the value of an individual innovation, but, more importantly, its cycle time compared to our previous innovation work. What is the average number of

months for a quality improvement team to complete a cycle? How many days did this team trim off the cycle compared to its last cycle? What is the rate of increase in the number of customer-driven employee suggestions? How many months does it take us to introduce a new or modified product or service compared to this time last year?

If we can learn anything from historical evidence, increasing the rate of innovation should become the cornerstone of every organization's strategy, as suggested in Figure 3.2.

In the movie *City Slickers*, one scene in particular highlights the critical nature of this strategy. At dusk, after a tough cattle drive throughout the day, the three city boys sat around the campfire with their trusty but frighteningly rugged and asocial guide, sharing stories of awe at their discovery of the peaceful but austere existence enjoyed by the cowboy on the open range surrounded by hundreds of aimless cattle. They had come to respect the cowboy life as one not only filled with adventure, danger, and unpredictability, but of great responsibility. It had occurred to them that the survival of hundreds of animals depended on the cowboy's skill, judgment, and tirelessness over unforgiving natural elements. They came to learn that without these attributes, everyone and everything on the cattle drive would quickly perish. At the conclusion of the scene, Billy Crystal, a "city slicker," turned to the old, wrinkled cowhand, played by Jack Palance, and inquired, "Your life seems so peaceful and full of contentment; how can I achieve the peace of life you have captured?" The old cowhand appeared to reflect for a moment, then remarked simply, "It's just one thing." Crystal inquired further, "What one thing? What do you mean, 'It's just one thing'?" to which the cowhand quietly answered, "That's up to you. But to be truly happy, a person must pursue—just one thing."

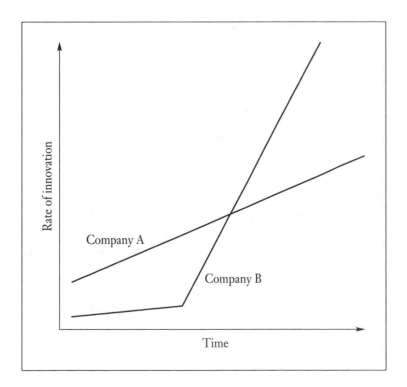

Figure 3.2. Impact of increasing the rate of innovation.

Likewise, if a CEO or senior strategist were to ask me, "To be truly—I mean truly—successful, what must we do?", I would respond, "It's just one thing. Increase your rate of innovation faster than your competitors."

2. *Reduce non–value-added cost by 20 percent per year.* As a measurement of customer dissatisfaction and as a measure of needless cost, most organizations would be best served by radically decreasing their dependence on traditional, vertical budget reporting systems and focusing on the more customer-oriented and revealing horizontal view enabled through NVA cost analysis.

As we will discuss in the next section on measurement, a definitive NVA cost figure should be visibly placed at the highest level of the financial measures hierarchy. To be maximally effective, the fewer strategic measures at the top level, the more scrutiny and activity will be directed toward improving NVA cost. Therefore, it is recommended that CEOs and CFOs subordinate many measures currently located at the highest level, to be reviewed only when they deviate from targeted performance thresholds.

Most financial accounting systems possess inadequate structures to accurately capture NVA cost. Activity-based costing (ABC) systems were created for this purpose. But most organizations might be best served by manually calculating NVA cost once per year for each major division or engaging an outside firm to produce an annual breakdown for them, as opposed to investing millions of dollars of scarce capital on ABC information systems. To wit: One large academic medical center in New England invested heavily to produce reports covering every conceivable category, unfortunately at the expense of leaving resources in the quality department to do anything about NVA cost. They simply invested everything they had in the information systems departments and had nothing left. The result is that more than $10 million of NVA opportunity waits until resources become available to help physicians form project teams; in the meantime, the information system automatically updates the $10 million every month.

Which route the organization takes, however, is not as important as the recognition that NVA cost management is a strategic necessity.

3. *Increase customer satisfaction by 20 percent per year.* If an organization wishes to continually focus on one factor that will drive success three years hence, it is customer satisfaction and market recognition of the value of the organization's goods and services. A lot is written and recorded about the need to achieve customer satisfaction, but most organizations have not gone far enough, as observed by W. Edwards Deming, Juran, and others. They have not engaged an insightful profound knowledge of customers' need or desire for the product or service.

This translation skill set is becoming complex as customers get more sophisticated and production methods permit increased product segmentation. Customer needs are also consistently generalized across industries; that is, customers are experiencing tremendous improvements in convenience and the reduction of waiting times. Supermarkets and airports offer automated teller machines, gasoline stations provide at-the-pump cash payment methods, and almost every industry highlights its time-saving innovations. Customers have come to expect that wait time reductions and greater product options in one industry should be generalized to other industries. Companies have responded to these needs in great order. Market segmentation has become so widespread that we need a new term to accurately label it. Consider, for example, Coca-Cola. In the early 1980s, you bought Coke. By the mid-1980s, you could buy Diet Coke, or Sprite, or Minute Maid Orange. Next, of course, came New Coke (although I still refuse to believe that this admitted error was not a secret market genius). Then you could buy Diet Sprite and Diet Minute Maid Orange. Then you could buy Caffeine-free Coke and Caffeine-free New Coke. Finally, you could buy Diet Caffeine-free Coke and Caffeine-free New Coke. Finally, although I am sure this is not the final segmentation of the soft drink market, consumers were offered the "cherry" option. At the present time, there are 22 varieties! Consumers have come to expect that their needs will be met, and producers respond with market segmentation.

Companies often make the leap from a basic understanding of customer needs to their own interpretation of customer needs. This translation, as Juran refers to it,[4] deserves an entire science devoted to ascertaining the customers' need for the product or service. Don Berwick and A. Blanton Godfrey go to considerable lengths to explore the nature of defined versus perceived customer needs and how best to utilize this customer knowledge as one basis for the chartering and formation of quality improvement teams.[5]

Gene Nelson of Dartmouth and David Fuhrs of NCG Research in Nashville, Tennessee, have devoted their careers to offering guidance identifying which features delight customers and which features repel customers. Two of the 300 questions posed in the patient satisfaction instrument they helped engineer for HCA inquired, "What good surprises did you experience during your stay?" and "What bad surprises did you experience during your stay?" The cumulative responses to these questions can then be affinitized and placed on a storyboard to serve as a portable communication tool throughout the organization. In addition, these responses can serve as one source of ideas for team formation.

No customer research, regardless of how small, is unworthy of communication and scrutiny at each level of the organization in a continuous quest to drive customer satisfaction to higher levels.

4. *Progressively integrate the organization as a system.* Each organization must continually improve its position within the marketplace. The automobile manufacturers are a wonderful example of this. One of the largest markets in the United States is the automobile aftermarket; that is, the installation of accessories into cars after dealer delivery. A major growth strategy for the automobile industry is to track the aftermarket, picking and choosing which portions carry enough margin and volume to meet their investment objectives. Once the aftermarket has matured to a high degree of market acceptance and demand, the automakers move in and offer the aftermarket product as a deluxe option. For example, in the late 1970s and early 1980s, one of the fastest growing automobile aftermarkets was audiotape deck installation; as the market matured, auto manufacturers began offering tape decks during the production phase. Of course, the audiotape market fully recognized the trend and began marketing compact disk players, which, of course, are now a standard auto dealer accessory. Also, in the automobile industry, the growing prevalence of cellular telephones has led manufacturers to offer preinstalled cellular phones, most often hidden in a compartment and equipped with a hidden, hands-free microphone and speaker.

The growth of the superstore model and the tactics of WalMart are further examples of systems integration, but in the opposite direction. Superstores, most common in the personal computer market, sprang up a few years ago to capitalize on a market whose penetration grew to the point that customer-accessible warehousing became possible (see Figures 3.3 and 3.4); availability of options went up while unit costs went down. The consumer wins on both counts. CompUSA and Home Depot are examples of this type of system integration.

The health care industry has gone berserk with both horizontal and vertical integration. PHOs, medical services organizations (MSOs), independent practice associations (IPAs), and integrated delivery systems (IDSs) are all examples of horizontal integration.

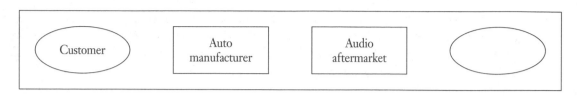

Figure 3.3. Automobile audio aftermarket.

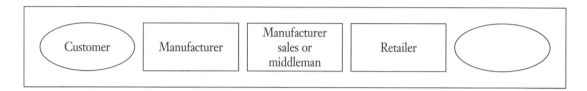

Figure 3.4. Pre-superstore.

The most effective use of systems integration is vertical integration, because the greatest NVA cost and customer dissatisfiers occur as the customer moves longitudinally through the system. The greatest waste occurs at the process handoff points as patients move through the health system. These examples can best be conceptualized through mastery of a mental model like the one in Figure 3.5.

The health care industry, due to the nature of its evolution from a cottage industry of fiercely independent entities, presents many interesting and challenging dilemmas. Should a hospital form a PHO? Can the same objectives be achieved without the expensive legal arrangements necessary for establishing a PHO? Should specialists be permitted an equal vote in the governance to primary care physicians (PCPs)? Should PCPs be organized separately from specialists? Should the organization establish an MSO to manage capitation contracting? If so, should it organize its own or bring in an outside firm? What are the advantages and disadvantages of both options? Will the marketing function of the IDS market to both employers and external HMOs/personal provider options (PPOs)? Should we establish our own HMO? What are the risks and rewards of competing directly against, while trying to contract with, HMOs?

The answers to these questions can best be examined as they relate to each other in the system map. In drawing a map of the organization as a system—or high-level flowchart, as it is sometimes called—the organization gets close to its customers and begins to experience what it is like to be a recipient of the organization's processes.

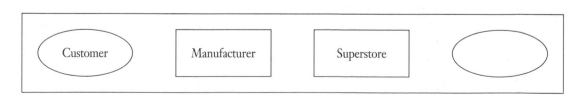

Figure 3.5. Superstore market integration.

The first step is to identify the input, best thought of as the ignition switch that causes the organization to go into action. This input is generally the business the organization is in. For a hospital, for example, it would be "patients with a health care need;" for an HMO, "populations at health risk;" for a computer retail firm, "customers with an automation need;" for a restaurant, "hungry customers." Learning to manage upstream will be a key strategic activity; but for the purposes of the current system it is important to stay focused on the business you are actually in, not the business you would like to be in. For example, a hospital might say it is in the business of maintaining community health, and thus would list as an input, "population at health risk;" unfortunately, this is not what the customers are paying for. They and their proxies, the employers, are paying for hospitals to manage patients with a health care need. Many hospitals provide wonderful community services in the area of preventive care, community education, and the like, but this is no different than IBM facilities funding the arts in their communities or Delta Airlines providing a grant to a local community college. These are higher-order obligations hopefully felt by every organization, but it is not the business they are in.

After identifying the input, construct a high-level flowchart (see Figure 3.6) of how customers move through the organization, from customer awareness of the services you offer, needs identification, product creation, product delivery and follow-up, and ending with a happy customer. Some skill is needed for how detailed to make the high-level flowchart. Too detailed, and users cannot visualize the organization as a system from the 60,000-foot level. Too limited, and users do not benefit from the knowledge of all the necessary handoff points creating NVA cost.

For additional clarification, a hospital high-level flowchart is shown in Figure 3.7, and Figure 3.8 shows the same flowchart with a key business process, treatment and intervention, exploded to reveal additional detail. This latter convention helps reveal details of one particular key business process without adding the confusing detail that would result if all key business processes were exploded.

These smaller systems or collection of processes inside the organization as a whole are referred to as key business processes, and the method by which they are improved is called *business process quality management* (BPQM). It is at this level that most organizations experience the greatest degree of NVA cost and customer dissatisfaction. A fundamental understanding of how the customer experiences the organization is at the heart of TQM strategic deployment.

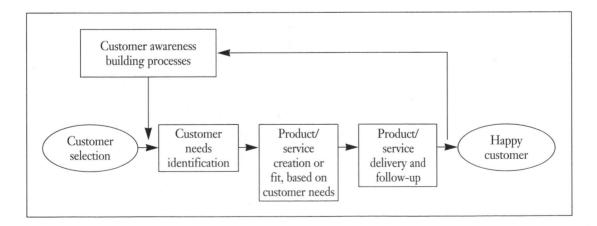

Figure 3.6. Generic customer–product/service development high-level flowchart.

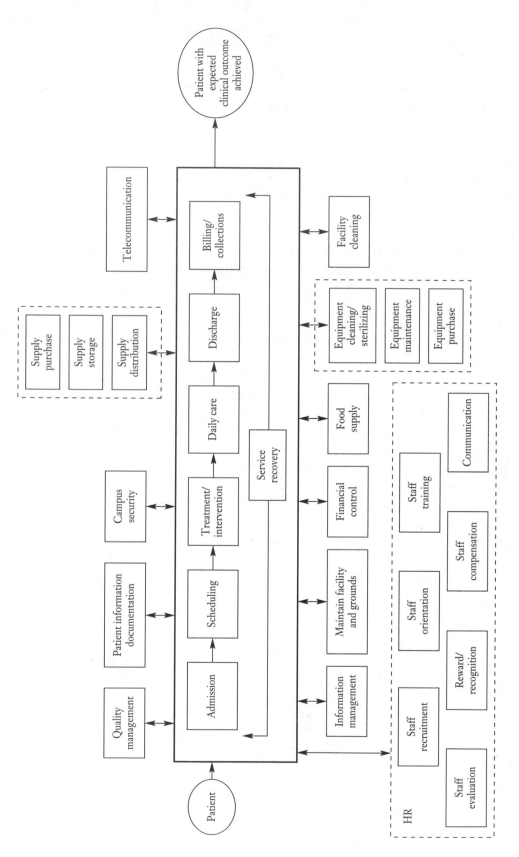

Figure 3.7. Hospital high-level flowchart.

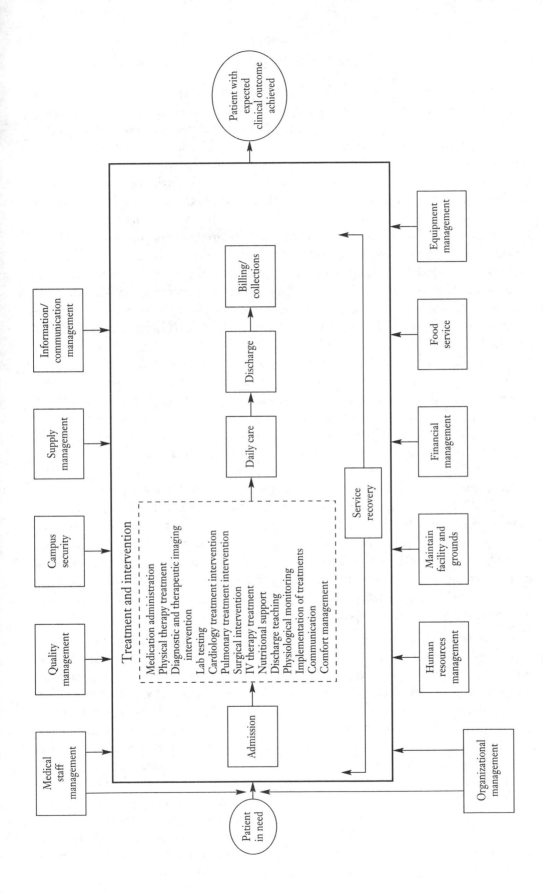

Figure 3.8. Hospital high-level flowchart, with a key business process exploded.

An infrastructure construct suggested earlier in this chapter, BPQM teams, serves as the backbone of most significant breakthroughs in customer service and NVA cost. These teams become marketing teams in the purest sense of the term in that they are very close to the customer, involved daily in the performance of the inclusive processes of the BPQM activity, and, with adequate training and empowerment, can drive market share and margin growth faster and more effectively than any other organizational design vehicle. Some argue that the organization should be totally reorganized around business processes, preferring to dismantle the traditional, stovepipe organizational hierarchy, but this approach requires a significant tolerance for organizational stress. The organization and its culture will be turned upside down, and for this reason I do not recommend to those organizations I mentor to choose this radical alternative without first considering the current organization state.

However, BPQM teams or reorganization is a prerequisite to mastering NVA cost and customer loyalty in any company. BPQM teams can be of two different types: product or service BPQM teams like the clinical teams illustrated here, or functional teams such as information systems or billing. For illustration, Figures 3.9, 3.10, and 3.11 represent the work of BPQM teams. Compare the two clinical BPQM high-level flowcharts for the Center for Mental Health (Figure 3.9) and the Diabetes Treatment Center (Figure 3.10) in relation to Figure 3.7, the hospital as a whole. Where would you visualize these two clinical paths? Which processes within the hospital as a whole are included in the clinical flowcharts? Which are not? In a manufacturing company, these would take the form of key products—like a laptop computer in a computer company, or frozen desserts in a grocery store, or the engineering college at a university. Now examine the support process of the Health Information Department (medical records) in Figure 3.11. Can you locate this department in Figure 3.7, the hospital as a whole?

This exercise of breaking the organization into key business processes will likely reveal a large number of processes. In the case of one medical center, more than 80 key business processes existed, counting both product processes and functional processes. However, an attempt to establish BPQM teams or other elaborate methods to manage each of these processes can overwhelm the organization. I suggest using the familiar Pareto principle[6] to establish 10 or 12 vital few BPQM teams that your quality council believes will drive toward the vision. The processes selected in this example included seven clinical conditions, representing approximately 75 percent of the cost of health care to the community's employers. Some of these teams, then, might logically be obstetrics, mental health, cancer treatment, diabetes treatment, and orthopedic/workers' compensation.

5. *Exceed stakeholder cash flow expectations by 20 percent per year.* Perhaps the need for cash flow as a key strategic imperative is obvious, but what may not be as obvious is the importance of changing the organization's view of cash flow from a key financial indicator to a key quality indicator. Most organizations cannot continue to exist without strong fiscal conservatism. Historically, as discussed earlier, financial needs, strategic needs, and quality needs are rarely, if ever, expressed in recognition of each other. Yet a customer-driven mind-set suggests the importance of integrating all of these needs. Some organizations boldly communicate quality goals to employees, but stop short of educating employees about the organizations' cash flow needs. Presumably the financial plan analyzes expected cash flow, determined from anticipated changes in the balance sheet: Some part of the cash flow budget fuels programs and process changes intended to meet anticipated customer needs, and another part is required to meet debt service requirements and fund either growth needs for nonprofit organizations or investor return for investor-owned organizations. An educated workforce taught to understand the need for cash as well as the need to improve customer satisfaction should also be able to contribute more fully and grow in its contributions toward achieving the organization's vision.

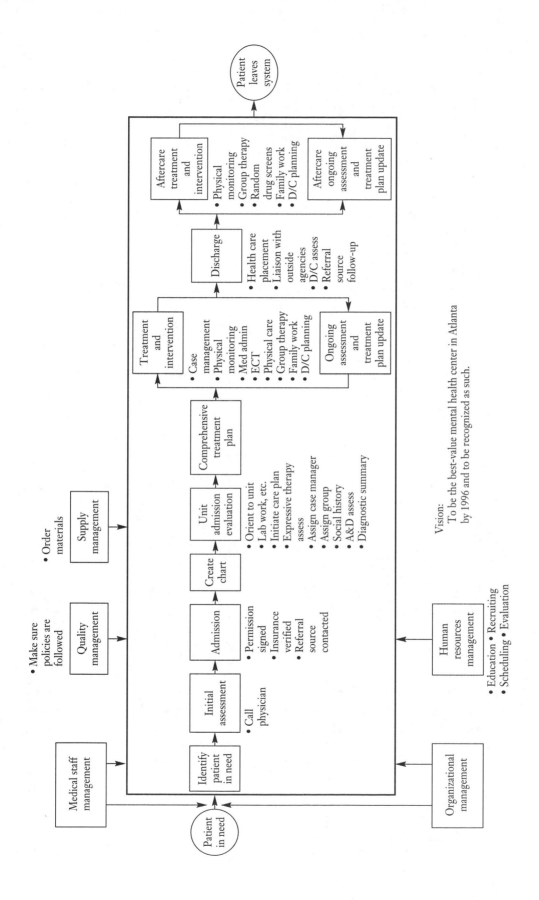

Figure 3.9. Hospital department high-level flowchart—Center for Mental Health.

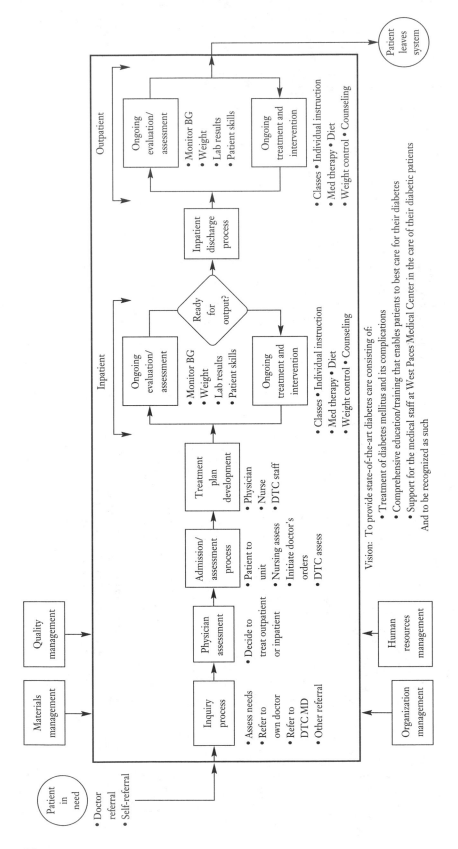

Figure 3.10. Hospital department high-level flowchart—Diabetes Treatment Center.

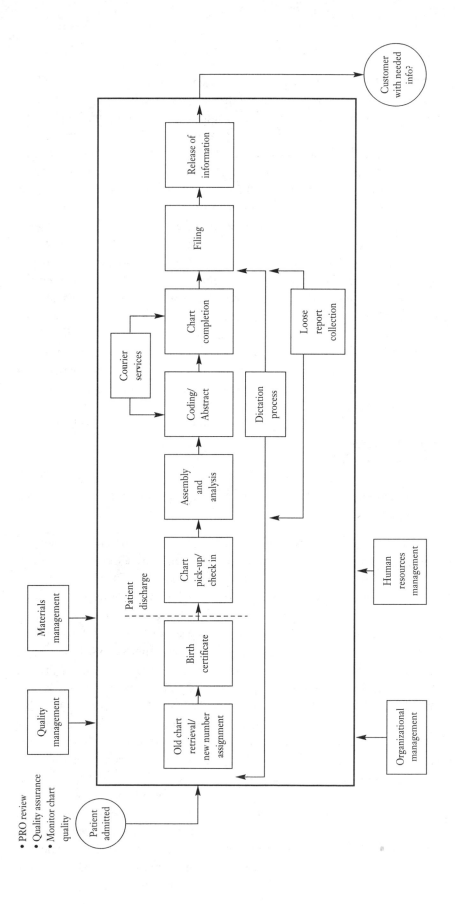

Figure 3.11. Hospital department high-level flowchart—Health Information Department, Medical Records.

51

Methods. The next part of the results model is the proper deployment of methods. While beyond the scope of this chapter and certainly adequately addressed in other chapters, methods are the engine of all strategic results. To date, popular methods include quality improvement teams, quality planning teams, reengineering, clinical paths, accelerated replication, benchmarking, NVA cost analysis, and customer loyalty assessments. Hopefully, the methods available to drive strategic results will continue to develop in the field. One caution about methods, however, is worth addressing. Health care organizations frequently request assistance to "reengineer," deploy "accelerated cost reduction teams," or some other method, often without regard to the results model illustrated in Figure 3.1. These organizations have visited or heard a presentation from an organization that has successfully deployed one or more methods, and they wish to "do it." It seems, however, that the most successful organizations are those that first develop a vision or mission to be achieved during the time frame of the deployed method. I often recommend creating a statement of purpose simply to ensure that everyone on the quality council is in agreement about the strategic intent. I began assisting a rural integrated delivery system in reengineering. After I met with the CEO, several VPs, and the board members, they expressed a target of removing approximately 5 percent of operating expenses. On conclusion of the interviews, I referred to the model in Figure 3.1 and stated that apparently the organization was pursuing a strategic intent of being the community's low-cost provider. Several expressed horror at this suggestion, adamantly maintaining that the strategic intent was to be the customer loyalty leader, not the low-cost leader. Hearing this, I inquired where the reengineering target of 5 percent came from. They told me that they had visited or read of organizations that had recently reengineered toward this strategic intent. After several meetings, the organization concluded that reengineering was indeed in its best interest—not with a cost focus, but with a customer loyalty focus.

In summary, organizations that excel seem to have balanced themselves on a three-legged chair of culture, strategic intent and strategic measures, and methods deployment. Suboptimization of any leg will cause unbalance in strategic results.

Infrastructure. Another part of the results model is infrastructure. This is a good point at which to address one component of infrastructure—the organization chart—and roles and responsibilities of various entities created to support TQM deployment—namely the quality council, BPQM teams (if your organization has embarked on reengineering), cross-functional quality improvement team leaders and members, department quality improvement team leaders and members, and individuals engaged in quality in daily work improvement activities. As Table 3.1 suggests, and as a main tenet of the discussion on the importance of focusing on at least five strategic thrusts, the quality council owns the degree of results achievement and should, thus, invest most of its meeting time to discussing team results and other strategic activities. Many quality councils get trapped into analyzing the type of tools used by teams, the type and construction of TQM education activities, and so on. This is not to suggest that these latter activities are irrelevant, but rather that they are the domain of the quality management department, facilitators, and team leaders. Similarly, the quality council must invest a significant proportion of its time to analyzing and effecting infrastructural change necessary to accelerate the achievement of the organization's vision; this task cannot be delegated to subordinate levels of the organization.

Some observers might question the allocations as less than desirable for their particular organization, and the suggestions in Table 3.1 are certainly not intended to be rigid expectations, but a means by which an organization can conceptualize the various roles and responsibilities involved in carrying out the strategic deployment road map. Others may argue that teams could not possibly contribute to vision achievement by investing only 20 percent of their available time to results; these guidelines, too,

Table 3.1. Time allocation chart.

Time allocation	Results	Methods	Infrastructure
	1. Rate of innovation 2. NVA cost 3. Customer satisfaction 4. Systems integration 5. Cash flow	1. QI teams 2. Quality planning teams 3. BPQM teams 4. NVA cost teams 5. Benchmarking 6. Networking 7. Education	1. Organizational design 2. Compensation 3. Performance appraisal 4. Capital allocation 5. Legal structure 6. Supplier relations 7. Facilities
I. Quality council	50%	10%	40%
II. Quality management director	10%	70%	20%
III. Facilitators	10%	90%	0%
IV. BPQM teams	20%	70%	10%
V. NVA cost teams	20%	70%	10%
VI. Cross-functional teams	20%	70%	10%
VII. Department teams	20%	70%	10%

are always open to debate. However, in keeping with the profound lessons in W. Edwards Deming's teachings that focus on the process, teams should be driven to address process changes through the use of TQM tools in order to achieve results.

Strategic Measures Deployment

The superstructure of any strategy, at least one with any hope of being achieved, is the measurement template. Without focus on quantified results, intentional progress simply does not occur. David Luther, creator of the Corning measurement template, observed, "You get what you measure."[7] Yet in spite of general agreement by most senior leaders of the critical need for a strategic measurement set, some organizations stop short of establishing quantifiable measures of all dimensions of their strategies except financial measures. They are satisfied with simply listing the activities that will occur in the strategic plans and checking off each task as it is accomplished. This approach does not go far enough to quantify the intent of the strategic activity. These organizations might consider mimicking the same logic they follow in their financial accounting system for their strategic requirements.

Further, most organizations do not merge their financial reporting with strategic quality reporting. A failure to integrate the two can have the effect of generating organizational schizophrenia. Leaders do not know which way to turn: toward the budget indicator or the strategic quality indicator. CEOs and CFOs may lose interest with quality initiatives when the two measurement templates are not combined because the financial results, if out of line, require immediate action. Quality initiatives gone astray can be delegated to others to be revisited on another day unless the quality issue generates a quality alarm, like the *Valdez* incident.

I feel obligated to add at this juncture that my experiences have not always supported David Luther's. You do not always "get what you measure." The achievement of results requires a process of its own. Without a ceaseless concentration on regenerative action plans to respond to failure to reach strategic targets, the organization may develop degenerative strategic myopia. It simply has no method to recognize the critical nature of the shortcoming, because the vision is a distant view and the strategic target is only a landmark along the way. The organization has hit this point before, not hitting strategic targets, and everything turned out okay; therefore, this shortcoming will be no different. Leaders may think, "We will make it up in the next six months." The creation of a management feedback process to respond to variation in strategic measures can ensure that you "get what you measure."

This section focuses on the strategic measurement deployment template to measure the effectiveness of the strategic intent activities discussed previously. The purpose of the measurement set is to create a quantified, understandable, manageable, and customer-oriented motion picture of the organization as seen through the eyes of its multiple customers. It is a clairvoyant view of the organization's past, present, and future.

Don Berwick has contributed immensely to advancing our thinking in this vital area. He asserts that measurement is effective when two factors are achieved: expectations are made clear by the measurement itself, and ownership for improvement rests with the measurer.[8] He further goes on to classify measurement into two types: measurement for judgment and measurement for improvement. Both types of measurement are necessary in our society, but Americans tend to drive all measurements toward the judgment type. Perhaps it is because from the time we enter first grade we are ranked by measurement and subconsciously taught that our entire societal worth is dependent on our results.

Of course, measurement for judgment is a good thing if constructively applied, as it often is. Regulators need measurement to communicate to the public the degree to which regulated entities comply with safety requirements or minimal quality standards. This is the role of the EPA, NRC. JCAHO, ISO 9000, OSHA, FDA, CAP, and the like.

Unfortunately, our fear of measurement for judgment immobilizes us from effectively using measurement for improvement. We are so accustomed to being judged by measurement that we experience great anxiety when the same methods are applied to measuring current performance of a process with the stated intent to constantly improve it.

Again, Berwick provides an effective discussion paradigm for measurement theory, to which I added a few of my own, in Table 3.2.[9] Berwick further produces a framework of desired characteristics in Table 3.3.[10]

Table 3.2. Measurement paradigm.

Measurement for judgment	Measurement for improvement
Incentive is to perform	Incentive is for learning
Purpose is for selection and culling	Purpose is to experiment
Mandate is to ensure safety	Mandate is to stabilize and improve
Effect is reward and punishment	Effect is continuous improvement, understanding, and inventing
Outliers search for excuses	Outliers search to benchmark
Process often punishes copying	Process encourages copying
Process produces fear	Process produces self-esteem
Primary user is external	Primary user is internal

Table 3.3. Measurement desired characteristics.

Measurement for judgment	Measurement for improvement
Fairness	Rapid turnaround is more important than accuracy
Objective measurer	Shows change over time
"Correct" is the goal	Locally collected
Easy to interpret	Locally interpreted
Reliable and valid	Reliable and valid
Representative and honest	Complete and honest
Statistically sensitive	Contains lessons about causes
Predictive of the future	Connected to experiments
Elicits fear	Nonaccusatory

It is important for leaders to fully appreciate the differences between measurement for improvement and measurement for judgment if their TQM process improvement work is to be fully optimized. Consider the reaction every hospital and its medical staff has to the annual release of Medicare mortality data. Hours and hours are invested to study each DRG for variations from the expected mortality calculation. For each DRG above the expected mortality figure, medical records are pulled and scrutinized by medical staff members in an effort to explain the variation to the community. Answers such as, "Our patients were sicker and the case mix adjustment protocol possesses too little sensitivity to properly adjust for our sicker patient population" or "Our 50 percent mortality rate for DRG 207 does not fairly represent the quality of our care because we only had two patients with this condition last year and one of them was brought by ambulance in critical condition" are given. This reaction to public release of quality data by a regulatory body is understandable, logical, and in the best interest of clarifying a very confusing analysis.

However, this approach to a quality improvement team database is counterproductive, as Tables 3.2 and 3.3 illustrate. The purpose is to use data in a nonaccusatory manner to learn, experiment, and drive the process to higher performance levels. While the audience for released regulatory data is external, the audience for quality improvement team data is internal. The data are reserved for us.

Unfortunately, we as team members often approach both types of data with the same mind-set. Leaders, facilitators, governing board members, and team leaders equipped with an understanding of how to facilitate the use of quality improvement team data as measurement for improvement can greatly accelerate team results.

Luther also provides insights from Corning's experience as we attempt to refine our strategic measurement panel.[11] One principle established at Corning was that measurement should be constructed to reflect the rate of innovation in each vital process, with a goal of continuous improvement. Second, all process measures should focus on the customer deliverables most vital in driving customer satisfaction; these deliverables, once understood, should be accurately translated into an internally defined operating statistic. Finally, the organization should avoid percentage measures unless using customer survey results; the measurement system should reflect actual results, such as parts per million, reported against performance levels of a world-class performer.

The structure of the strategic measurement panel begins with the CEO-level spider diagram,[12] which represents those measures determined to be most vital to the organization. The total number of upper level measures should not be more than 10, but if your organization's CEO follows the same path I did as CEO of West Paces Medical Center, he or she may not be comfortable with less than 16. One of the organizations I mentored originally came up with 42 CEO-level measures! No organization can stay focused with a measurement panel of this magnitude. Wherever you start, however, it is more important to achieve buy-in from the CEO and CFO than it is to fret over the number of upper-level measures. As the organization and the quality council become more comfortable with the effectiveness of the measurement panel, the number of measures can be reduced. Once complete, the spider diagram is used to cascade the measurement process throughout the organization, through the VP level, key business processes, and departments to the lowest common job function in the organization. A recommended tool to deploy the measurement set is the strategic deployment matrix[13] or tree diagram.

Strategic Spider Diagram

Figure 3.12 illustrates the layout of a typical strategic spider diagram. The diagram reveals several important features of the relationship between the organization's current performance and the expectations of its customers. Try not to become intimately involved with the measures themselves just yet; these will be reviewed in great detail after the spider diagram concepts have been articulated.

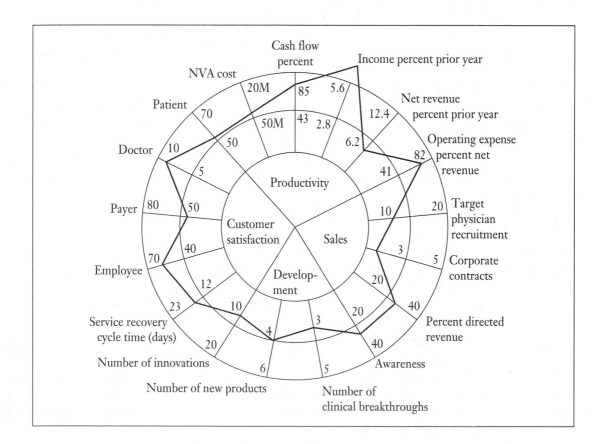

Figure 3.12. Strategic spider diagram.

Take a moment to study the spider diagram. Look at the four categories inside the spider: productivity, sales, development, and customer satisfaction. Look at the 17 labels for each measurement: cash flow percent, income percent of prior year, and so on. Digest the range of performance for each measure through examining the inner circle threshold measure and the outer circle threshold. Prior to any explanation, which will follow, what conclusions can you draw about patient satisfaction in the organization shown? A review of the overall layout, from the 60,000-foot level, indicates that senior strategists see the organization's measures falling into four categories.

1. Productivity

2. Sales

3. Development

4. Customer satisfaction

These dimensions reflect the thinking discussed previously on measuring the strategic critical success factors over a 10-year period. To measure an organization's value today, productivity and sales measures are the best proxies; measuring customer satisfaction today is the best indicator of success in the year 2000; and development, including innovation, serves as the best proxy for 2003.

Again from the 60,000-foot level, another fundamental characteristic of the organization is apparent. The organization is pictured as performing in each of these measures at some level, the thick line, compared to a predefined set of performance thresholds. Most companies when they hit hard times abandon all logic and "slash and burn" without considering the delayed negative impact of key decisions on customer loyalty. Action plans almost always involve an across-the-board reduction in employees and costs by department—that is, each department embarks on a course of action to reduce 5 percent of its workforce and 5 percent of its supply usage. Rarely, if ever, is the impact on customer satisfaction measured. Surely key customers are contacted and persuaded that major cost reductions are necessary, but assured that service levels will remain constant. However, service levels are not measured; therefore, the impact on lost sales in the future is unknown. These programs are often given classy names, like reengineering or right sizing; some companies even veil these actions under the umbrella of outsourcing, even when it is known that outsourcing will result in increased unit costs, but at a decreased total cost because the outsource vendor will drop employees and save the parent company the difficult task of eliminating jobs.

Of course, responding to environmental changes is the essence of good management practice and must be faced rapidly if an organization is to weather the inevitable storms of the corporate world. No one can be criticized for taking decisive action in the midst of changing conditions. However, the enlightened manager will save his or her company millions over the years by constructing scenarios that consider all variables, including future customer loyalty, before choosing the proper course.

The necessity to generate rapid change will become more and more pronounced in the future as technology and entrepreneurs become more closely wed in the race to innovate. These rapid innovations of existing products and the introduction of new products will tend to render others obsolete, and therefore the astute manager will embrace a new paradigm of customer judgments.

It is most instructive to begin any dissertation on customer judgments by examining J. M. Juran's definition of quality: what he calls the "Big Q."[14] Quality must be viewed as the customer views us, and as most of us recognize, this view is not shared by our organizational structure—that is, the customer is almost hidden from us by the nature of the way in which we perform our work. Departments hand customers to each other in an endless stream of often disconnected processes, and the only way we can discern customer satisfaction is to invest large sums of money for customer surveys, focus groups, and the like. Unfortunately, even when we are able to uncover a rough spot, department managers look desperately for the faulty department, responding that "it was not our department's fault." I recall an incident when I was the CEO of West Paces Medical Center that caused my blood to boil. A patient had written a complaint letter to me about being "lost" between the radiology department and labor and delivery (L&D). She indicated that she had been retrieved from radiology by a hospital volunteer after a routine ultrasound and transported back to L&D, where she sat undiscovered for several hours. I am sure the number of hours increased dramatically with each telling of the story; one learns to recognize these patterns and discern that the more probable wait was, in this case, 15 minutes, nevertheless, the complaint was certainly valid, whether exaggerated or not. These customer loyalty issues concerned me most because I knew I would not be the last to hear the story—by the time she went back to work, she had assuredly been left in a damp, dark, dirty corridor for several days without food before being rescued. The point here, however, is that on requesting an investigation, I received a typed letter from the head of radiology indicating that "it was not my fault." This inherent compartmentalization continued to frustrate many of us on the quality council, as well as our customers. This event, too, can be expressed in terms of the paradigm of NVA cost.

In order to construct a framework for managing customer judgments, we found it helpful to utilize Noriaki Kano's levels of customer judgment as a theoretical construct worthy of comprehension and mastery.[15,16] In an effort to help us understand levels of customer needs and expectations, Kano defined customer judgments along three levels.

Level I   Expected; must have

Level II   Requested; nice to have

Level III   Delighted; customers brag about

Kano defined level I as features that a customer would expect. Asked another way, "What features of our processes must be there in order that customers will not be repelled by our services?" It is the understanding of this level of customer need that leads us to understand what features of our products or services must either be in place or customers will reject us. The way to measure achievement of level I satisfiers is through an effective complaint management system.

Level II customer needs are those features of products or services that might be requested by customers. The absence of these features would not repel customers or increase their satsifaction, but these are rather intermediate features that meet intermediate needs. The way an organization measures its level II customer judgments is by asking in customer surveys, "Were you satisfied?"

Level III customer needs are those features that, if present, would cause customers to express delight about our products or services to everyone they meet. The question becomes, "What features of our products, if offered, would cause customers to brag about our services?" Kano suggests that process owners be driven to develop a complete understanding of level III customer needs. Using HCA data, we attempted to uncover level III needs by analyzing underlying answers to the question, "Was the care so good that you would brag about it to your family and friends?" We also affinitized into logical process groupings the responses to the questions, "What good surprises occurred during your stay? What bad surprises occurred during your stay?" The affinitization process allowed us to realize that, among our four customer groups, there were 23 hospitalwide measures of quality. These 23 hospitalwide measures were continuously plotted, studied, and posted for all managers, employees, physicians, and customers to see. In setting the targets for the spider diagram, it is helpful to think of customer judgments along those three dimensions: level I, expected performance; level II, requested performance; and level III, delighted performance. Dropping below level I performance is a signal that customers are being repelled by us, while exceeding level III performance is a signal that customers are expressing delight about us wherever they go. This fundamental construct of customer judgments is vital enough that every organization should constantly struggle with how best to quantify it, even the elusive level III indicators. The spider diagram provides an instant picture of how each measure is performing against customer expectations. The outer circle represents level III performance, the level beyond which we are delighting customers. The inner circle signal level I performance, the level below which customers are being repelled. The level I–level III construct will appear at each layer of the strategic measurement panel, from CEO level through department level.

As pictured in Figures 3.13 and 3.14, a review of the overall layout of the spider diagram further reveals another characteristic: The organization exists in some balance, with one dimension of performance related to another. The notion that performance along productivity, sales, development, and customer satisfaction must be viewed in balance is an important one; it would be foolhardy to consider any dimension in isolation. As exposed in Figure 3.13, this organization has maximized productivity, but at the expense of development and customer loyalty. The organization has seriously suboptimized development and customer satisfaction. This is the picture of an organization that is the cash cow of the moment, but will cease to exist in five years. An unfortunate testimony of the impact of Wall Street on business decision making is that this is the picture of an organization that appeared in *Wall Street Week* as the darling of forecasters.

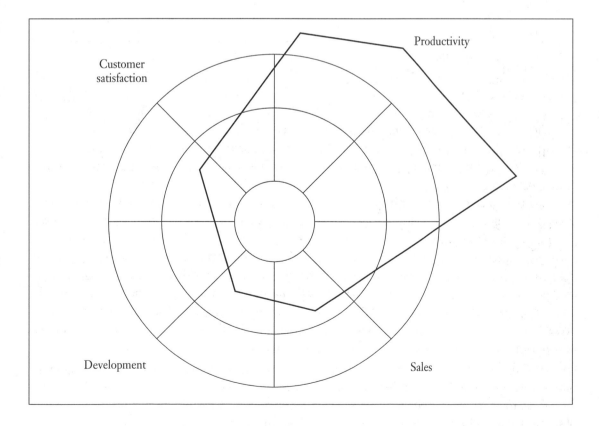

Figure 3.13. Suboptimized customer satisfaction signal.

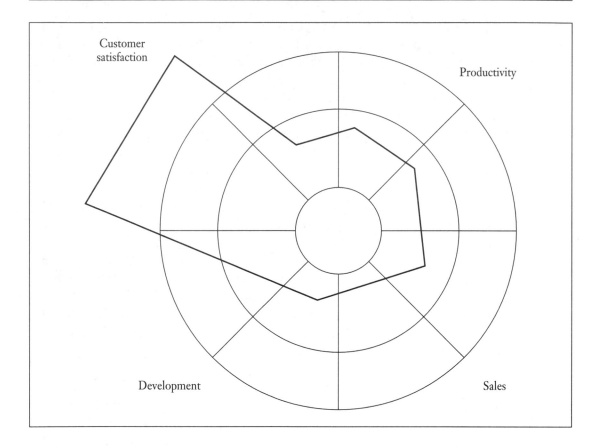

Figure 3.14. Suboptimized productivity signal.

Figure 3.14 exposes the reverse complication. This organization has maximized customer loyalty through the addition of costly product features not yet appreciated by customers. Again, the organization has seriously suboptimized its current cash position. This is the picture of an organization that will cease to exist in a year.

The relevance of the spider diagram's portrayal of organizational performance along all dimensions is that senior strategists and the quality council may view the results of their optimizing efforts. Figure 3.15 illustrates a sample strategic spider diagram for an integrated delivery system (IDS). This particular diagram illustrates yet another dimension: prior year historical performance represented with a thick line, and current-year-to-date performance represented with a dotted line. Again, these are upper-level measures that do not reveal the performance on measures subordinate to them; subordinate measures are determined through the strategic deployment matrix, a subject discussed next. In order to reveal the thinking in establishing this particular spider diagram, the logic of each of the 16 measures, progressing clockwise from 12 o'clock, is as follows.

1. *Cost per member per month.* The price to the marketplace for an IDS is based on a monthly price for each member of a managed care plan or covered by a particular employer. The ability of the sales force to aggressively price the product is, of course, dependent on the cost of providing the service. Subordinate measures would be hospital cost per member per month, further subordinated to

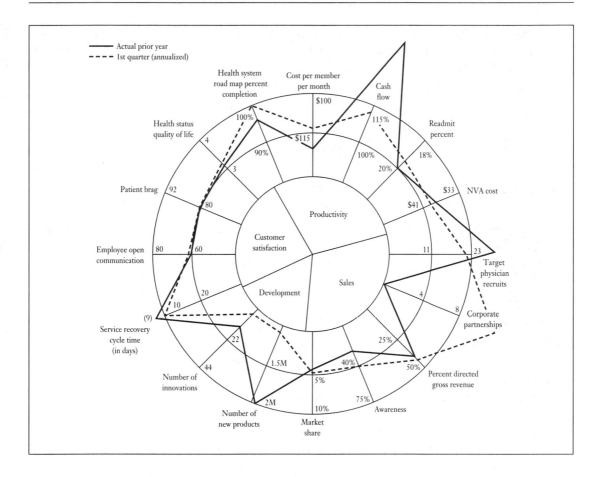

Figure 3.15. Integrated delivery system strategic spider diagram.

admission rate and average length of stay, primary care per member per month, and specialist per member per month. Kano level I, repelling quality, is suggested to be $115 per member per month, believed to be the level above which the IDS would be uncompetitive. Kano level III, delighted quality, is suggested as $100 per member per month, the market's most aggressive performance. Last year's performance (the solid line) fell below the repel point at $117 per member per month, but current performance rests at $114.

2. *Cash flow percent prior year.* This measures the growth rate in cash generation compared to the prior year. Kano level I is set at 100 percent, the level below which the IDS will fail to generate adequate cash to meet strategic objectives and retain stockholder customer loyalty. Currently the IDS is producing 111 percent of prior year, while last year the organization produced a 135 percent growth.

3. *Readmit percent.* The number-one NVA cost indicator in an IDS is the number of patients readmitted to a hospital for the same condition within 12 months of discharge. For example, on average, more than 20 percent of patients treated for substance abuse are readmitted for treatment within the same year, at exorbitant cost to the IDS. Presumably, the readmit rate should be nested inside NVA cost as a subordinate measure, and certainly no error could be charged the IDS Quality Council for

subordinating the measure. But the quality council may feel that certain vital few subordinate measures deserve to be followed on the spider diagram, which is the case here. In this example the readmit rate is 19 percent, with Kano level I at 20 percent and level III at 18 percent.

4. *NVA cost.* NVA cost, the most important productivity indicator, shows level I at $41 million and level III at $33 million. These figures should be determined from an actual NVA cost audit each year. A typical study reveals that up to 30 percent to 40 percent of an organization's costs are NVA costs. The illustrated hypothetical spider diagram suggests $38 million in NVA cost.

5. *Target physician recruits.* A primary sales indicator for an IDS is the number of physicians recruited against the target plan. Level I performance must not fall below 11 physicians, with level III at 23. Last year's performance was 31, with current performance at 21.

6. *Corporate partnerships.* Another primary sales indicator is the number of corporate contracts for IDS services, in this case labeled "partnerships." Level I is set at four contracts, with level III at eight. Last year's performance was zero, a danger signal, but current performance is 12.

7. *Percent directed gross revenue.* One of the greatest threats to IDS or hospital survival at this point in time, due to shifting physician loyalty and financial pressures, are those physicians, contracts, or patient revenues that are not controlled or directed by the organization. For example, physicians in non–managed care arrangements can choose to admit their patients to any hospital they choose, regardless of the reason. Most often physicians choose to admit patients to a hospital on a basis other than quality, like convenience to their offices, the hospital purchasing the type of equipment the physician desires, and so on. In the current competitive health care environment, hospitals must partner with physicians and managed care companies to obtain long-term loyalties. One method to achieve this is for the IDS to jointly control or direct the patient flow through a contractual relationship with payors, or patients, or by recruiting patients through sales and marketing. This measure is an indicator of the degree of control the IDS maintains over hospital admission choice. In this example, level I is set at 25 percent of revenues and level III at 50 percent, with current performance at 41 percent, up from 38 percent last year.

8. *Awareness.* Awareness measures the degree of top-of-mind market awareness, measured annually by a market research firm. Level I is 40 percent and level III is 75 percent, established as the highest top-of-mind competitor in the market. The organization has achieved a 41 percent awareness.

9. *Market share.* No explanation needed.

10. *Number of new products.* The estimated annualized net revenue produced from any new product introduced in the marketplace during the year.

11. *Number of innovations.* The number of quality improvement team cycles completed during the year. As the organization matures in its TQM deployment, innovations include BPQM team cycles, quality-in-daily-work improvements, employee suggestions, and so on. The rate of growth in this indicator is the most important for the organization to master.

12. *Service recovery cycle time.* This is the number of days it takes to resolve a complaint. As the organization becomes more sophisticated in its TQM deployment, quality control and service recovery training should enable the cycle time to be measured in hours.

13. *Employee open communication.* The results of the employee satisfaction survey question on open communication.

14. *Patient brag.* The percentage of patients who indicate that they brag about their care, as a proxy for measuring Kano's level III performance, delight.

15. *Health status quality of life.* The scoring on patients' degree of return to health status after an IDS intervention.

16. *Health system road map percent completion.* A measurement of the degree of accomplishment of each BPQM team and organizational subsidiary road map or action plan.

These measures, in total, are designed to reflect the degree of achievement of the organization's strategic intent. The process to follow to determine which measures are proper for the organization's current status is to

1. Revisit the organization or BPQM system map or high-level flowchart.

2. Define all customers and analyze their needs, both outcome and output.

3. Determine Kano level I and level III requirements for the strategic spider diagram.

4. Locate target level I performance, repel, from competitor data and/or customer surveys. If all else fails, guess. Construct the inner circle of level I using these data. This inner circle represents the point below which the organization's performance must not fall.

5. Locate target level III performance, delight, from competitor data, customer surveys, and/or best-in-class benchmarks from the literature or other information sources. Again, if all else fails, guess. Construct the outer ring of level III milestones using these data. This outer circle represents the target that must be exceeded for the organization to achieve its strategic intent or vision.

6. Identify the organization's current performance for each of the strategic measures and plot the spider diagram data points.

7. Study the picture of the organization as plotted. Examine Figures 3.13 and 3.14 to compare your current performance against a suboptimized profile. Consider any action plans necessary to bring the organization into balance.

8. Establish a method to collect and display the results on at least a quarterly basis.

Strategic Spider Diagram Run Charts

It is my belief that the organization must also examine strategic measures in an analytical format. Plotting and reacting to the spider diagram is a first step in understanding the relationships between the various strategic imperatives facing the organization. However, it is the process of analyzing these process features over time that produces a level of maturity in the management of the organization. Once the strategic targets are established for each of the strategic measures in six-month increments, a chart of performance requirements can be generated. To create these thresholds, begin with the level III target for each measure. Examine the organization's current performance to get some idea of the gap and the work required to achieve the vision. Beginning with the current level of performance, establish in hoshin fashion incremental progress requirements in six-month increments. Following Figure 3.16 as a hypothetical example, it is suggested that patient brag about should serve as the CEO-level patient satisfaction proxy. The hospital plotted data from one question in the hospital's 300-question patient satisfaction survey, "Was the care so good that you have bragged about it to your family and friends?" The percentage of patients who answered "definitely yes" was 64 percent, rising to 65 percent. The ultimate level III achievement to reach the hospital's vision, patient brag, in Figure 3.12 was 70 percent "definitely yes." The organization is performing at 65 percent "definitely yes," but must reach 70 percent to achieve this dimension of the organization's vision. Similarly, Figure 3.17 plots the same strategic process for the employee customer group. To achieve the organization's vision, the strategic spider diagram in Figure 3.12 suggests the need to hit 70 percent "definitely yes" to the question, "Would you work here again?"

Each month, a quality council meeting begins with reviewing the data points from the strategic run charts and the summary level data of the progress of project teams. The combined effect of these strategic targeting processes is to establish firm footing for senior managers to focus on the vital few strategic processes requiring management attention, without allowing for distractions from less vital ones.

Strategic Deployment Matrix

Once the strategic spider diagram and a process to manage performance by the quality council is completed, it is necessary to generate the strategic deployment matrix to move the TQM strategy deployment process to the lowest tier process or subprocess in the organization.

To visualize the deployment process, it has proven helpful to examine the logic of the deployment method, illustrated in Figure 3.18. For each of the 16 CEO-level measures suggested previously, the

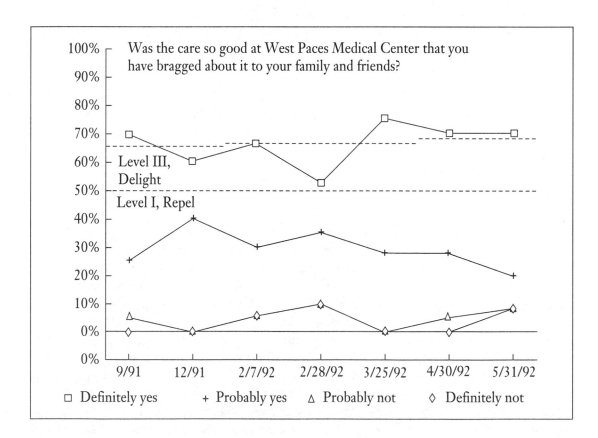

Figure 3.16. Strategic measure run chart—patient brag about.

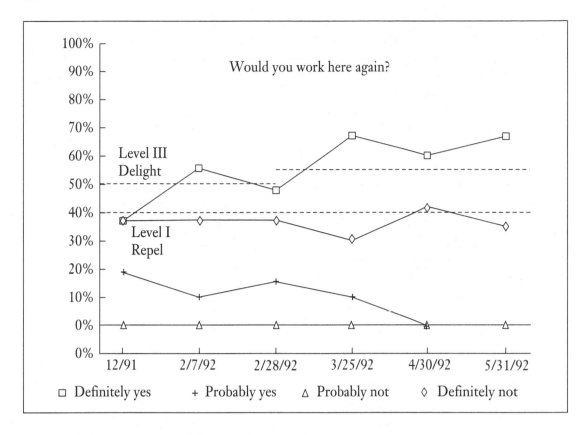

Figure 3.17. Strategic measure run chart—employee brag about.

processes that combine to produce each CEO-level measure must be identified. Generally, three VP-level measures will be identified for each CEO-level measure. At the second tier, the organization does not yet begin to discover BPQM or core processes, defined earlier as the collection of processes that combine to form the macrolevel business processes of the organization. In most cases, the VP-level measures are still management indicators and do not hint at an underlying business process. For example, if the hospital CEO-level measure in question is net revenue as a percent of prior year, then one VP-level indicator might be revenue deductions as a percent of gross revenue. Revenue deductions at the VP-level does not yet suggest a key business process.

The third tier provides key business process identification in most cases. The BPQM processes become manageable collections of processes at this point. Continuing the example, BPQM revenue deductions as a percent of gross revenue cascades to perhaps three BPQM processes: Medicare contractual adjustments as a percent of Medicare revenue, managed care/HMO policy adjustments as a percent of managed care revenue, and bad debts as a percent of patient portion. These three processes combine to form the collections BPQM function in a typical hospital and can be viewed, managed, and measured independently.

A point worth making during this discussion is that CFOs often want to divert away from process measures and cascade measures or derivatives of measures based on product operating margin, rather than focus on the process. This tendency has in the past produced a vital flaw in the

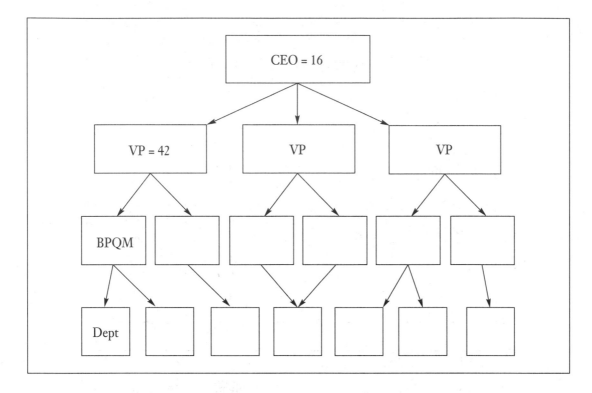

Figure 3.18. Strategic measurement logic.

improvement of processes. Managers simply cannot improve a measure derivative if a process is not the underlying thesis of the measure. This approach only promotes frustration. Managers require process measures in order to manage. This is not to suggest that operating margin does not enjoy a prominent place in the strategic measurement set, but rather that operating margin is used to help an organization understand and advance the product life cycle and does nothing to help managers understand the behavior of a process under their charge. If a product's operating margin dips below expectations, the organization has several choices. It can raise prices. It can cut costs. It can increase market share, building on production economies of scale. Or it can combine all of these, which is usually the approach taken to make sure all the bases are covered. Process measures as suggested Figure 3.18 help managers stay focused on the underlying processes driving cost. Customer pricing measures help sales and marketing personnel manage the sales and marketing processes. Advertising process effectiveness measures and sales process effectiveness measures help the sales personnel evaluate the probability of increasing operating margin given commitment of additional resources. These are three different sets of processes, requiring three different management actions. It is the mixing and production of derivatives of the different process measures that thwarts process managers. Each of these three process measures enjoys a prominent place in the strategic measurement set, but it is important to maintain the discipline to stick to process measures. The best method I have found to ensure that a process measure has been created is to ask, "What subprocess of the superior measure does this measure highlight?" Crossing a measure in violation of process logic is voodoo statistics, and voodoo statistics are not manageable.

It is at the fourth tier that department-level process measures surface. These measures are actually the easiest to derive, because department managers have a closer relationship with the processes they manage and customers' expectations than senior leaders do. It can sometimes create a customer paradigm issue when support departments are asked to identify their customers and claim the external customer instead of the immediate internal customer, but this complexity is easily resolved through analysis of the department high-level flowchart.

Another view of the strategic measurement deployment matrix logic is shown in Figure 3.19. In this view, versus the organizational hierarchy model in Figure 3.18, we can follow process logic. In this example, we have again selected the CEO-level measure of Kano level III, patient brag. The CEO-level measure is one of the 300 questions in the patient satisfaction survey instrument, which asked, "Was the care so good that you have bragged about it to your family and friends?" The multivariate analysis against this question revealed that 19.1 percent of the variation in customer expectations was accountable to promptness. The logic here is that we wished to identify the vital few processes that, if aggressively improved, would likely lead to improved patient satisfaction. Therefore, the second tier was promptness. Upon identifying the key business processes at the third tier, one of which was the medication administration process, the process characteristic of medication administration cycle time was selected because of the importance of promptness at the second tier. In other words, if promptness is the most important patient satisfaction indicator, then the logical process characteristic to track is cycle time. The department level, at tier four, identifies the four department processes that when combined form the key business process of medication administration. They are medication ordering by the nursing unit, drug preparation by the pharmacy, drug dispensing by pharmacy, and finally medication administration to the patient by the nursing unit. We can see, therefore, that the management, measurement, and continuous improvement of each of the four department-level processes making up the key business process of medication administration will lead to improvement of patient satisfaction.

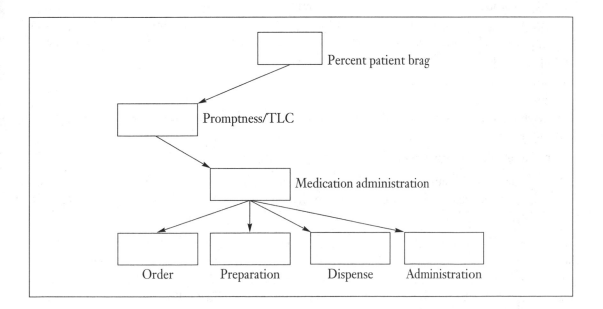

Figure 3.19. Process measurement deployment logic.

Now look at the structure of the strategic deployment matrix in Figure 3.20. This method of measures deployment allows each measure to be viewed in relation to all others. Figure 3.21 provides examples of department-level measures; studying these measures sheds light on how the particular department viewed the relationship of its processes to customer needs.

Finally, Figure 3.22 provides insights into the construction of the strategic deployment matrix for an IDS. Note the relationship between the hospital measures matrix and the IDS matrix. The health system high-level flowchart contains key business processes for primary care physicians, specialist care, hospital care, aftercare, and administration/inspection. The hospital appears as cost under the medical cost per member per month deployment, the NVA cost deployment, and again under member satisfaction.

Department-Level Measures

How does an organization go about discovering the process characteristics most important to customers? One method, illustrated by an education department and shown in Figure 3.23, provides a method for departments to wrestle with those process characteristics vital to improving customer needs. Adapted from the work at Florida Power & Light, the form lists the vital few customer expectations as rows; in this case, physician available time, scheduling, nurses, and so on. The second column asks department managers to identify the impact their department processes have on the customer need. As shown, the physician nurses category has a dark circle, indicating that the education department maintains a heavy impact on this customer expectation. Listed to the right of this indicator are three processes owned by the education department that influence the customer characteristic. By following this process and the department high-level flowchart constructed earlier, department managers are able to articulate in statistical terms for the strategic deployment matrix the vital few process characteristics that must be improved. Figure 3.24 illustrates a typical nursing unit.

Managing, measuring, and improving BPQM and department process measures follows the same method as for CEO-level measures, using run charts. As suggested in Figure 3.25, the environmental services department run chart teaches us that L&D patients express delight about the cleaning process if completed in 25 minutes or less, but are repelled if it takes longer than 32 minutes. With this level of customer information, we can ably manage customer needs.

Pitfalls

No discussion of statistical methods can be considered complete unless it contains a list of pitfalls. Here they are.

- Do not allow anyone to discourage you with pitfalls.

- Ensure that measures are process measures and not derivatives of process measures. To be manageable, managers need information. Information comes in the form of process measures, not voodoo numbers.

- Keep the number of measures manageable—not too many, not too few. For the CEO-level strategic spider diagram and run charts, 10 should be adequate, but more than 15 becomes difficult to manage. Aggregate most current CEO-level measures into a superior-level measure, then include the remainder at the VP level. In this way, the organization can stay focused on the vital few strategic measures.

- Focus on customer measures, not just volume.

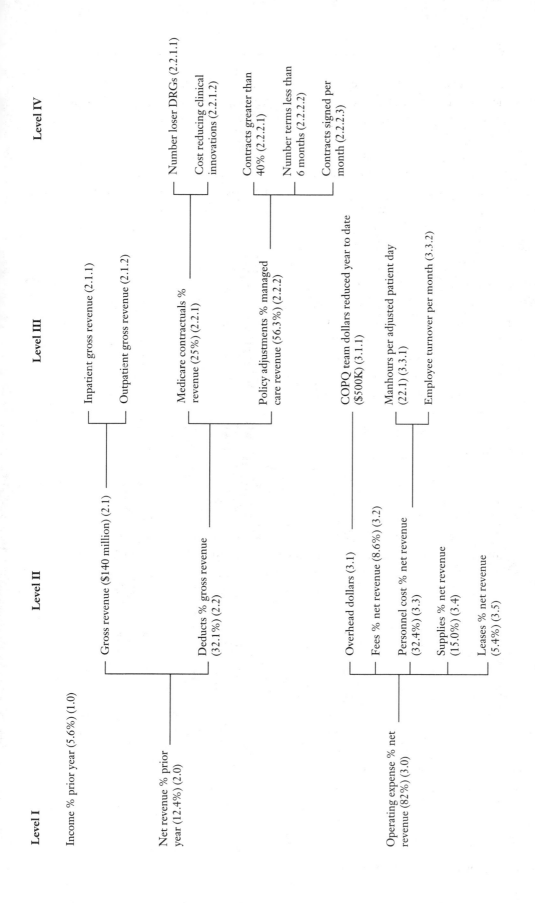

Figure 3.20. Strategic deployment matrix.

69

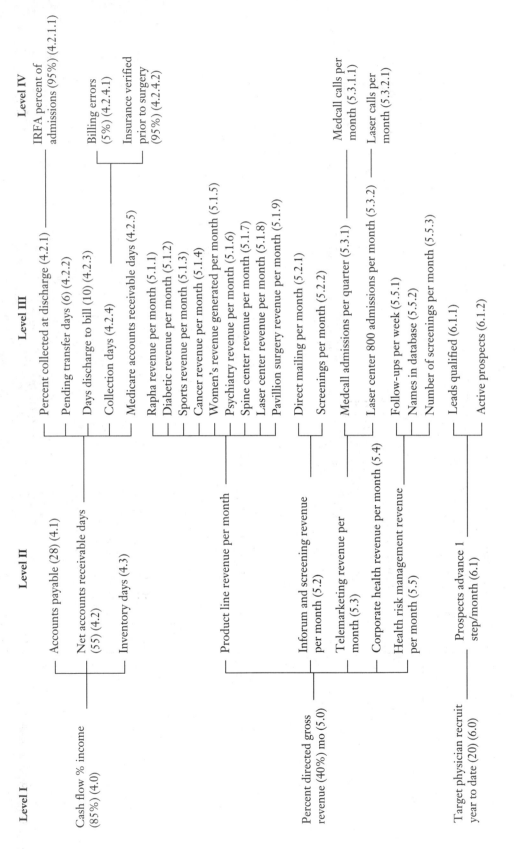

Figure 3.20. *continued.*

Level I	Level II	Level III	Level IV
Corporate contracts (5) (7.0)	Number corporate downloads per month (7.1)	Number active prospects (7.1.1)	
	Number corporate screenings per month (7.2)		
Awareness (40%) (8.0)	Number media exposures per month (8.1)		
	Number advertisements per month (8.2)		
Clinical breakthroughs year to date (5) (9.0)	Number clinical quality improvement teams (7) (9.1)		
	Cycle time per improvement (9.2)	Number clinical team meetings per week (9.2.2)	
New products year to date (6) (10.0)	Number under study (10.1)		
	New product cycle time (10.2)		
Innovations year to date (20) (11.0)	Number quality improvement teams advance 1 step per month (11.1)		
	Number employee quality in daily work (11.2)		

OUTCOMES

Patient "brag" (60%) (12.0)
- "Expected clinical outcome"
- "Responsiveness"
- "Nursing care"
- "Admissions"
- "Discharge"
- "Billing and collections"

BPQM PROCESSES

(See attached process map)

Figure 3.20. *continued.*

Level I	Level II	Level III	Level IV

Doctor "brag" (10%) (13.0)

"Available time maximized"
"Scheduling"
"Nursing care"
"Consultants accessible"
"Reports timely"
"Equipment needs"
"Everyone involved in quality improvement"
"Doctors treated as customers"

Employee "return" (90%) (14.0)

"Departments work together"
"Nursing care"
"Communication and recognition"
"Image for quality"
"New coworkers"
"Staffing"

Payer (15.0)

"Lower premiums and cost"
"Hassle-free paperwork"
"Hire healthier employees"
"One contact person"
"Understandable bill"
"Good value"

Service recovery
cycle time (23 days)
(complaints) (16.0)

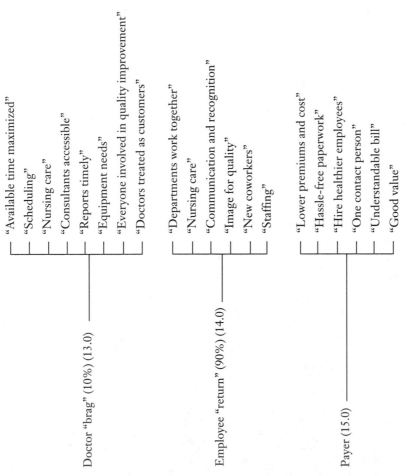

Figure 3.20. *continued.*

Quality Indicators for the Departments

Accounting
1. Days in accounts payable
2. Number of financial statement errors greater than $1000
3. Invoice discrepancy cycle time
4. STAT errors per week
5. Payroll errors per week
6. Medicare remittance posting cycle time
7. Expense per month

Behavior medicine
1. Number of PRN's given daily
2. Patient percent compliance with treatment plan
3. Patient beginning assertiveness training within 24 hours after admission
4. Patients instructed in treatment procedures
5. Documentation cycle time
6. Expense per patient day

Business office
1. Time to complete IR/FA form
2. Billing errors
3. Insurance verification on accounts
4. Files forwarded to billing
5. Expense per admission

Cardiopulmonary
1. Oxygen documentation time
2. Arterial blood gas response time
3. Pulmonary function test report time
4. Electrocardiogram report time
5. Expense per test

Cath lab
1. Cath start time
2. Cath turnaround time
3. Expense per cath

Critical care
1. Number life-threatening conditions per month
2. Lab test ordering/reporting delays
3. Admission assessment within five minutes
4. Monitoring dysrhythmias (telemetry)
5. Medication administration time
6. Expense per patient day

Data processing
1. Generate and distribute daily reports time
2. Data input into distributed system charge data time
3. Data control log balancing errors
4. Master file parameter maintenance behind schedule
5. Expense per month

Education
1. Orientation of patient care employees on schedule
2. Medication administration testing % trained
3. Provision of equipment % requests
4. Education program effectiveness rating
5. Expense per month

Engineering
1. Tube system failures per month
2. Security door checks on schedule
3. Preventive maintenance Bio-Med on schedule
4. Call response time per week
5. Expense per work order

Environmental services
1. Professional building cleaning complaints
2. Patient room discharge cleaning complaints
3. Linen distribution complaints
4. Labor and delivery discharge cleaning complaints
5. Expense per patient day

Food services
1. Nourishment distribution delays
2. Delivery of patient meal trays on schedule
3. Nutritional teaching, instructing, charting, and charging errors
4. Nutritional screening errors
5. Cafeteria serving line average time
6. Expense per meal served

Human resources
1. Number of employees not attending/completing first available orientation
2. Number of payroll action forms received for annual evaluation without proper documentation
3. Number of days from injury before employee incident report received in human resources office
4. Number of payroll action forms returned to department managers for additional information
5. HR expense per employee per month

Lab
1. Turnaround time for charting pathology reports (histology)
2. STAT CBC turnaround time
3. Blood culture contamination rate per week
4. Cardiology blood study delays per week
5. Delayed or incomplete cultures
6. Expense per test

Labor and delivery
1. Delay time for scheduled procedures
2. Change of shift report within 15 minutes
3. Epidural placement errors
4. Expense per patient day
5. Obstetrics anesthesia complaints
6. Cesarean rate

Materials management
1. Stockouts per week
2. Inventory days
3. Mail delivery time
4. Expense per line item filled

Medical records
1. Coding turnaround time per week

Figure 3.21. Sample department strategic measures.

2. STAT chart retrieval time
3. STAT transcription turnaround time
4. Assembly/analysis turnaround time
5. Expense per admission

Neonatal Intensive Care Unit
1. Admission room readiness time per week
2. Admission process culminating in transfer to postnatal unit errors
3. Lab redraws per week
4. Time of physician orders
5. Stabilization of infant's temperature
6. Expense per patient day

Perinatal
1. Change of shift report greater than 15 minutes
2. Call light response time
3. Pediatrician rounds complete on schedule
4. Discharge teaching process errors
5. Expense per patient day

Pharmacy
1. Adverse drug reactions per week
2. Medication delivery turnaround time
3. Medication administration records not reconciled
4. IV waste
5. Order entry request turnaround time
6. Expense per line item filled

Physical therapy
1. Patient procedures delayed
2. Evaluations errors
3. Charges documentation errors
4. Assessments complete within two hours of doctor's order
5. Expense per treatment

Quality management
1. Retrospective reviews demanded by managed care
2. DRG assignment errors
3. Patient stays denied
4. Expense per admission

Radiology
1. Chest X-rays turnaround time
2. Median turnaround time for reports
3. Median turnaround time for transporting patients
4. Median turnaround time for scheduling patients
5. Emergency physicians accuracy of interpretation
6. Appropriateness of exam % total exams (based on clinical indications)
7. Radiologist peer review % total readings (accuracy of interpretation)
8. Expense per exam

Surgical services
1. Scheduling desired time for doctor as % total requests
2. Preadmission visit % complete
3. Discharge teaching within 15 minutes of schedule time
4. Room turnover time for "to follow" cases

5. Procedure starts as scheduled % total cases
6. Expense per case

Volunteer services
1. Escort services time from request until complete
2. Flower delivery in minutes
3. Number volunteers interviewed for vacancies
4. Expense per month

2 North
1. Preoperative teaching complete by 10 min. prior to surgery pickup
2. Discharge process errors
3. Call light response time
4. Expense per patient day

3 East
1. Admission assessment time from admission (minutes) per week
2. Patient request response time
3. Daily sharps procedure errors
4. Expense per patient day

3 West
1. Number times IV team called per week
2. Change of shift report total minutes
3. Responsive time to IV alarms
4. Discharge time from doctor's order
5. Expense per patient day

4 West
1. Change of shift report total minutes
2. Treatment response time (patient with hypoglycemia)
3. Peritoneal dialysis completion time
4. Expense per patient day

6 West
1. Lapsed time for change of shift report
2. Lapsed time for administration of pain medication after request
3. Number of second IV attempts by 6 West nurses per week

23 hour/ER/IV
1. Patient triage time per week
2. Notification of attending physician minutes after intake
3. Peripheral IV starts errors
4. IV team response time
5. Expense per patient

Pavillion surgery center
1. Scheduling requests achieved % total
2. Preadmission visit errors
3. Discharge teaching errors
4. Room turnaround time
5. Procedure starts as scheduled % total cases
6. Expense per case

GI lab
1. Scheduling requests achieved % total
2. Turnaround time
3. Start delays per week
4. Expense per procedure

Figure 3.21. *continued.*

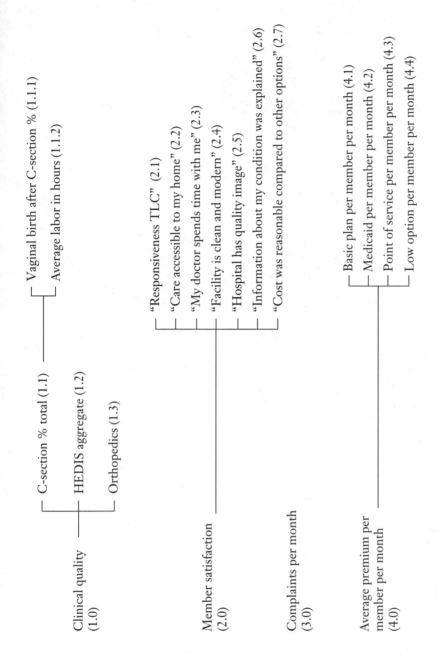

Figure 3.22. Integrated delivery system strategic deployment matrix.

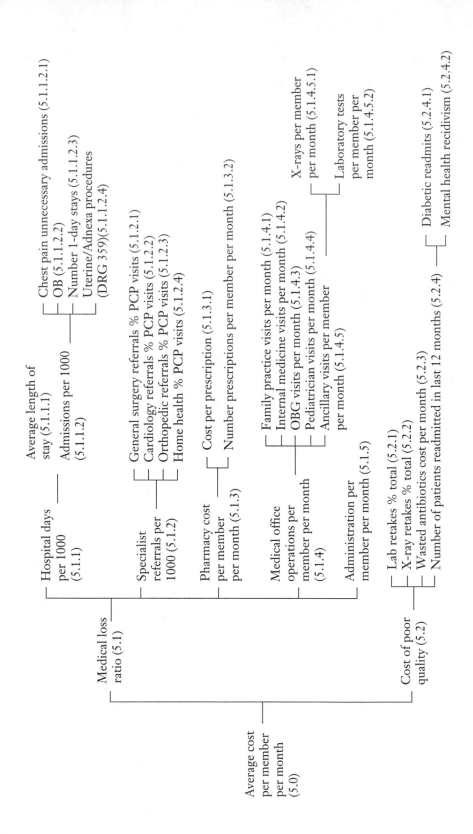

Figure 3.22. *continued.*

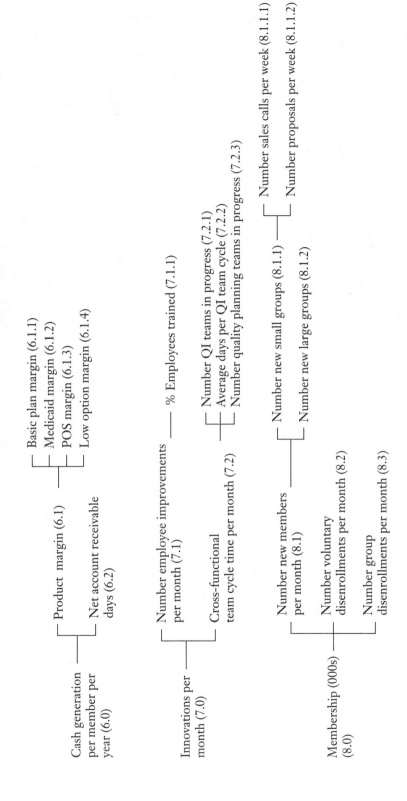

Cash generation per member per year (6.0)
├─ Product margin (6.1)
│ ├─ Basic plan margin (6.1.1)
│ ├─ Medicaid margin (6.1.2)
│ ├─ POS margin (6.1.3)
│ └─ Low option margin (6.1.4)
└─ Net account receivable days (6.2)

Innovations per month (7.0)
├─ Number employee improvements per month (7.1) ─── % Employees trained (7.1.1)
└─ Cross-functional team cycle time per month (7.2)
   ├─ Number QI teams in progress (7.2.1)
   ├─ Average days per QI team cycle (7.2.2)
   └─ Number quality planning teams in progress (7.2.3)

Membership (000s) (8.0)
├─ Number new members per month (8.1)
│ └─ (8.1.1) Number new small groups
│   ├─ Number sales calls per week (8.1.1.1)
│   └─ Number proposals per week (8.1.1.2)
│ └─ Number new large groups (8.1.2)
├─ Number voluntary disenrollments per month (8.2)
└─ Number group disenrollments per month (8.3)

Employee satisfaction (9.0)

Figure 3.22. *continued.*

Departmental matrix   Department: Education

Indicators	Impact	Process 1	Process 2	Process 3	Key quality characteristic
Physician					
Available time	◉	AV support	Patient education resources	CPR training	
Scheduling	◯	AV support	CPR training		
Nurses	●	Orientation	Staff development	Patient education resources	
Timely reports					
Accessible consultants	◉	CPR training	Patient education	Office staff training	
Equipment	◉	AV support	CPR, ACLS		
Employee QI	◉	Orientation	Staff development		
Treated as customers	◉	Orientation	Staff development		
Patient					
Clinical outcome	◉	Staff development	Patient education	CPR training	
Response TLC	◉	Orientation	Staff development	CPR training	
Nurses	●	Orientation	Staff development	Patient education	
Living arrangements					
Billing and collections					
Admission	◯	Staff development			
Discharge	◉	Patient education			

Figure 3.23. Sample education department strategic deployment template.

Indicators	Impact	Process 1	Process 2	Process 3	Key quality characteristic
Employee					
Nurses	●	Orientation	CPR and staff development	Patient education	
Departments work together	◉	Staff development	Division newsletter		
Top leaders understand	◯	Division newsletter	Committee, QIT membership		
Image	◉	Orientation	Staff development	Division newsletter	
Qualified co-workers	◉	Orientation	Staff development	Recruitment, selection, and retention activities	
Efficient processes	●	Orientation	Staff development	Patient education resources	
Payers					
Employees brag	◉	CPR and other community programs	Staff development		
Costs less than competitors					
Reduce costs improve quality					

Key for impact symbol

● Heavy   ◉ Moderate   ◯ Slight   None

Instructions: Review list of hospital quality indicators listed by customer group (physician, patient, employee, and payer). Indicate the degree of impact your department has on each quality indicator by entering the appropriate symbol in the impact column.

List three processes that directly relate to the outcome of customer satisfaction for each indicator. Choose a *total* of three processes that relate to a "heavy" impact indicator from which the QIC will select one as your next opportunity for improvement.

1. Providing employee development opportunities
2. Coordinating patient education resources
3. Orienting new patient care employees

Figure 3.23. *continued.*

Department: 3 West   ● Heavy   ■ Moderate   ▲ Slight

Indicators	Impact	Process 1	Process 2	Process 3
Available time	●	Doctor rounds update	Chart procure	Procedure assistance
Scheduling	▲	Requisition process		
Nurses	●	Doctor rounds update	Procedure assistance	Complications notification
Timely reports	■	Filing	Abnormal result notification	Requisition process
Consultation access	▲	Order notification		
Equipment				
Clinical outcome	●	Acute myocardial infarction	Bronchitis	Heart failure
Response TLC	●	Pain medication	Nourishment	Call light response
Nurses	●	Patient condition information	RN skills assessment	Complaint notification
Living arrangement	■	Complaint notification	Discharge cleaning	Diet order
Admission	▲	DC cleaning		
Discharge	●	Discharge notification	Discharge instructions	

Figure 3.24. Sample nursing department strategic deployment template.

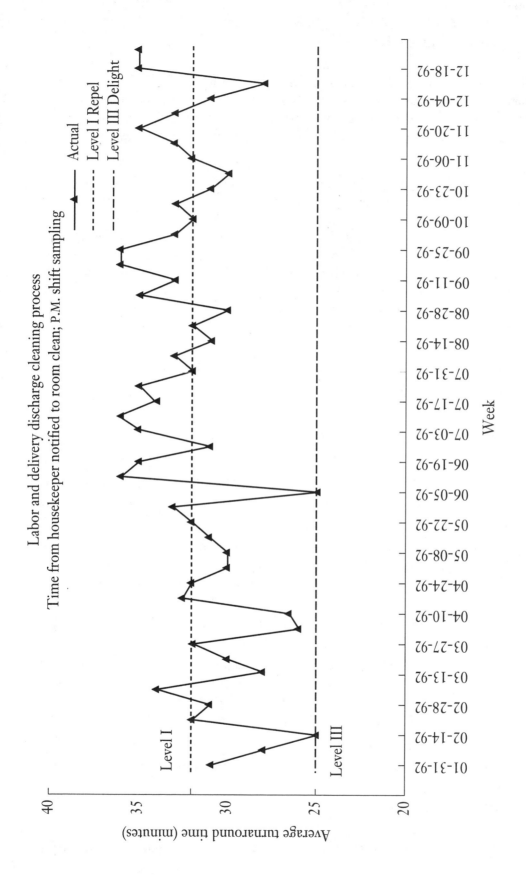

Figure 3.25. Sample run chart for environmental services department.

- Insist that process owners plot their own data and keep run charts in their departments for employees and customers to see. The best place to place customer measures is on the department storyboard that is hung in common corridors.

- Maintain the discipline to utilize the spider diagram, run charts, and a monthly project team tracking worksheet.

Statistical methods are rarely easy to explain and even more difficult to read about and understand. I encourage the use of the quality council and department manager exercises at the end of the chapter to internalize the most important features of the strategic deployment matrix process.

In summary, the results model in Figure 3.1 suggests that organizational success is determined by attention to culture, strategic intent and strategic measures, and methods deployment. Each of these factors requires discipline at all levels of the organization. The reward for those organizations willing to suffer through the first difficult six months of deploying anything new like the strategic measures template will be the satisfying feeling that resources that are deployed to achieve strategic results can be tracked from the CEO level to the clinical and department levels.

Discussion Questions for a One-Hour Quality Council Meeting—Number One

1. Focus on innovation.

    a. What is the average number of months it takes a quality improvement team to complete a cycle?

    b. How many days did this team trim off the cycle time compared to its last cycle?

    c. What is the rate of increase in the number of customer-driven employee suggestions?

    d. How many months does it take us to introduce a new or modified product or service compared to at this time last year?

2. Focus on systems integration: Most organizations are aggressively seeking new relationships with customers and suppliers through reorganization and affiliative arrangements. Systems thinking can go a long way toward helping every organization grasp a more reasonable view of the future of its industry.

    a. Draw on a flipchart the boxes that best represent your industry's system as it exists today in your market. Circle your position in the feeding chain.

    b. Draw your best guess of how these entities will be aligned in five years by drawing a box around affiliated entities with a different color marker. Draw boxes around your view in 10 years. Did you include upstream and downstream entities? Suppliers?

    c. Are types of organizations represented that do not exist today? Will any that exist today cease to exist in five years? Ten years?

    d. How can you integrate your existing TQM framework to drive innovation at key strategic interfaces?

3. What additional training will be necessary to support increased innovation? BPQM teams? NVA cost teams?

4. What additional training will new members of partner IDS entities require to understand your vision, strategic deployment road map, and TQM deployment methods?

Discussion Questions for a One-Hour Quality Council Meeting— Number Two

Focus on Strategy

1. What are your organization's top five strategies for the coming year?

2. Does the strategic plan include increasing the rate of innovation? Decreasing NVA cost? Increasing customer satisfaction? Systems integration? Increasing cash flow?

3. For any of the strategies suggested in item 2 that are not listed, are there any reasons to consider them next year? What are the implications for not including them?

4. Do department managers know the organization's strategy? Vision? Elements of the strategic deployment road map?

5. Do employees and other stakeholders know your strategy? Vision? Elements of the strategic deployment road map?

6. How might your communications plan be modified to ensure the development of a shared vision?

Discussion Questions for a One-Hour Quality Council Meeting for Health Care Systems

Hospitals and medical centers are up to their necks in reorganization and affiliative arrangements. Systems thinking can go a long way toward helping these organizations grasp a more reasonable view of the integrated delivery system's future.

1. Draw on a flipchart the boxes that best represent your health care system as it exists today in your market. Circle your position in the feeding chain.

2. Draw your best guess of how these entities will be aligned in five years by drawing a box around affiliated entities with a different color marker. Draw boxes around your view in 10 years. Did you include PHOs? MSOs? IPAs? HMOs? Public health? Preventive services? Three-day stay surgery centers? Suppliers?

3. Are types of organizations represented that do not exist today? Will any that exist today cease to exist in five years? Ten years?

4. Should a hospital form or reorganize its PHO? Can the same objectives be achieved without the expensive legal arrangements necessary to establish a PHO? Should specialists be permitted an equal vote in the governance to PCPs? Should PCPs be organized separately from specialists?

5. Should the organization establish an MSO to manage capitation contracting? If so, should it organize its own or bring in an outside firm? What are the advantages and disadvantages of each option?

6. Will the marketing function of the IDS market to both employers and external HMOs/PPOs? Should we establish our own HMO? What are the risks and rewards of competing directly against, while trying to contract with, HMOs?

7. How can you integrate your existing TQM framework to drive innovation at key strategic interfaces?

Discussion Exercise for a One-Hour Department Manager/ Team Leader Meeting

One quality council member should serve as a facilitator for this session. The facilitator should give a brief overview of the purpose and construction of a high-level flowchart to introduce the session. As with many other department manager learning sessions, the outcome need not be critiqued; the real application of the learning is when managers begin thinking about NVA cost and customer satisfaction when relating to other departments.

Focus on High-Level Flowcharts (Systems Mapping). It is vital that department managers, as well as the organization's senior leader, learn to think in terms of systems management. The fully mature organization will be the one in which every manager is aggressively seeking new relationships with customers and suppliers through reorganization and affiliative arrangements. Systems thinking can go a long way toward helping every organization grasp a more reasonable view of the future of its industry. For the purposes of this practice exercise, managers should be divided into groups of eight to 10, with one quality council member serving as a sponsor for each group. Select one department manager and his or her department to serve as the guinea pig for the learning exercise.

1. *Getting a hamburger at McDonald's.* On a flipchart, draw a large box, framing almost the entire flipchart page. Draw a circle at the front and at the back. Label the first entry "customer orders hamburger" and the last "customer leaves." Now, with input from the group, draw small boxes inside the larger box to represent the sequential steps taken to get a hamburger. Upon completion, brainstorm as many ideas as possible for why an order might get delayed. Consider hand-off points from one function to the next, supply problems, upstream issues, and so on.

2. *Guinea pig department high-level flowchart.* On a flipchart, draw a large box, framing almost the entire flipchart page. Draw a circle at the front and at the back. Label the first entry "Process begins in my department when _____" and the last "Process is completed in my department when _____." Now, with input from the group, draw small boxes inside the larger box to represent the sequential steps taken to progress through the guinea pig department. Upon completion, brainstorm as many ideas as possible for why an order might get delayed. Consider handoff points from one function to the next, supply problems, upstream issues, and so on.

Discussion Exercise for a Governing Board Meeting

This session should be led by the chairman of the board quality improvement committee or equivalent, or an interested board member. The quality director should assist by recording responses on a flipchart and engaging facilitation when needed. The focus of this session is on strategic imperatives.

1. What are your organization's top five strategies for the coming year?

2. Does the strategic plan include increasing the rate of innovation? Decreasing NVA cost? Increasing customer satisfaction? Systems integration? Increasing cash flow?

3. For any of the strategies suggested in item 2 that are not listed, are there any reasons to consider them next year? What are the implications for not including them?

4. Is there evidence that department managers know the strategy? Vision? Elements of the strategic deployment road map?

5. Is there evidence that employees and other stakeholders know the strategy? Vision? Elements of the strategic deployment road map?

Discussion Questions for a One-Hour Quality Council Meeting— Number Three

1. Create a strategic spider diagram. First, review Figures 3.12, 3.13, 3.14, and 3.15. Then draw a blank spider diagram on a flipchart and post it on the wall in preparation of generating your own rough draft model. Consider this first round a very rough draft and do not be concerned with accuracy at this point.

   a. Using measures generated from other exercises or other activities, identify and list the top three or four measures in each of the following categories.

      1) Productivity

      2) Sales

      3) Development (include rate of innovation/quality improvement team cycle time here)

      4) Customer satisfaction (key customers who drive revenue)

   b. If you are like most organizations, you now have 20 to 40 measures. This is too many. For each category, use nominal group technique to identify two or three measures that can be followed at either the VP level or in some other format. Repeat this process until no more than four measures exist for each category.

   c. For each measure, identify your best guess for level I performance, repel, and level III performance, delight.

2. Plotting the spider diagram.

   a. For the inner circle, level I repel, write the number in the proper location. Note that for some measures the desired direction is ascending while for others it is descending, so the order of level I and level III is reversed.

   b. For the outer circle, level III delight, write the number in the proper location.

   c. Given the range between level I and level III, plot your current performance for each measure.

3. Current status analysis.

   a. Where do you fall below level I? For these dimensions, you are currently repelling customers. For some measures, particularly those that anticipate success five years from today, the impact of this performance may not seem threatening, but do not allow yourself to be lulled into complacency.

   b. Where do you exceed level III? For this dimension, you have achieved your vision. Celebrate!

4. Evaluate the meeting on flipchart paper.

   a. What did you like about this session?

b. What could be improved for future sessions?

Discussion Exercise for a One-Hour Department Manager/ Team Leader Meeting

For this meeting, managers will complete their key process measures, using Figure 3.24 as a guide. Again, a quality council member should facilitate this session. Before this exercise can be conducted, a list of organizationwide customers' needs must be generated to fill the rows of the deployment template. The quality council facilitator, with help from other council members, should complete a sample deployment template to serve as an example. Organize participants in groups of eight. A quality council member should be assigned to each group to assist. Provide enough copies for each department manager and team leader attending.

1. The quality council facilitator should explain that the purpose of the session is to begin thinking about which process measures at the department level are linked to the organization's quality measures. Show the sample deployment template on an overhead projector and ask if participants have questions.

2. Hand out one deployment template for each participant and allow 20 minutes to complete it.

3. With assistance from the quality council member at each group, each member should discuss two or three entries. Allow 20 minutes for this segment.

4. Each group should select one participant to explain two or three entries to the group as a whole, if time allows. Allow 15 minutes for this segment.

5. The quality council member should evaluate the meeting on flipchart paper.

    a. What did you like about this session?

    b. What could be improved for future sessions?

Notes

1. J. M. Juran, "The Quality Trilogy: A Universal Approach to Managing for Quality," *Quality Progress* 19 (August 1986): 19–24.

2. Paul B. Batalden, "Hospital-Wide Quality Improvement" (paper presented at HCA Eastern Group CEOs, Nashville, Tenn., October 29, 1990).

3. Masao Nemoto, *Total Quality Control for Management: Strategies and Techniques from Toyota and Toyoda Gosei*, trans. David Lu (Englewood Cliffs, N.J.: Prentice Hall, 1984), 77–99.

4. J. M. Juran, *Juran on Quality by Design* (New York: Free Press, 1992), 107–114.

5. Donald M. Berwick, A. Blanton Godfrey, and Jane Roessner, *Curing Health Care* (San Francisco: Jossey-Bass, 1990), 35–55.

6. For those interested in the origin of the Pareto principle, this history is reprinted from Juran's book *Managerial Breakthrough*, page 44. Vilfredo Pareto was a nineteenth-century economist who studied the distribution of income among the population. He observed that the majority of the wealth of the country was amassed by a very few people. His observation has been effectively generalized to explain all manner of management and behavioral conditions, having the effect of suggesting action on the "vital few" rather than the "trivial many."

7. David Luther, "Advanced TQM: Measurements, Missteps, and Progress Through Key Result Indicators at Corning," *National Productivity Review* (Winter 1992/93): 25.

8. Donald M. Berwick, "Current Trends" (presentation at George Washington Medical Center conference, Washington, D.C., February 28, 1994).

9. Ibid.

10. Ibid.

11. Luther, "Advanced TQM," 23–36.

12. Takashi Kanatsu, *TQC for Accounting: A New Role in Companywide Improvement* (Cambridge, Mass.: Productivity Press, 1990), 187–192.

13. Ibid., 190–191.

14. Juran, *Juran on Quality by Design*, 11–12.

15. Berwick, Godfrey, and Roessner, *Curing Health Care*, 55.

16. Batalden, "Hospital-Wide Quality Improvement."

Chip Caldwell, FACHE, senior vice president of Premier, specializes in strategic deployment of clinical and systems quality improvement and cost reduction initiatives in medical centers, extended care facilities, integrated health systems, and health plans. He previously served as senior vice president of Juran Institute. He also served as president of the Columbia HCA Atlanta health system, an eight-hospital network with 15 owned family practice centers and more than 250 contracted physicians. He also served as president/CEO, HCA West Paces Medical Center in Atlanta, from June 1986 to July 1993. As an internationally recognized speaker, he was one of two U.S. hospital executives to address a special Congressional committee on quality improvement in health care in March 1990 and again in April 1994. As a published author, he serves on the editorial advisory boards of Aspen's *Quality Management in Healthcare*, *TQM* magazine, *Quality Progress*, and the National Healthcare Forum.

Active in development of business–provider partnerships, Caldwell was selected by the Atlanta Healthcare Alliance to head its metro Atlanta TQM demonstration project in March 1993 and has assisted the Midwest Business Group on Health in Chicago since 1990. He also served as vice chairman of the Atlanta Chamber of Commerce Quality Resource Center from 1993 through 1994. He was selected by the Juran Institute as one of two U.S. health care executives to address the U.S. Chamber of Commerce in a live video conference on TQM in health care in June 1993.

Chapter 4

Leadership in an Emerging Integrated Delivery System

William C. Mason, Thomas H. Sawyer, and Kimberly E. Sangari

Health care leadership has never been more difficult than in the current decade—and the near future looks to be even more demanding. Understanding the evolution that has transpired, and the current transformation in play, provides a frame of reference for creating the future while managing in today's reality. We are maturing as an industry and moving rapidly from the Machine Age and fragmented health care delivery to a new enterprise reality focused on systems of care that promote the health of the community and provide high-quality services in a cost-effective, integrated manner. There are changes, drivers, and industry initiatives that set the platform for the emergence of the integrated delivery system. However, simply constructing the structural elements and developing a strategy does not ensure success and is only a means to an end. The real strength will be realized in the next generation, where we move from structure and strategy to systems, people, and intellectual property.

Just as the industry is transforming, so is the role of the leader. In an industry marked by turbulence and dynamic change, the characteristics and focus of health care executives are increasingly centered on such issues as clarity of purpose, values, change mastery, and systems thinking. This is quite different than the focus of the businesslike era of the 1980s and early 1990s, which are most noted for profits, market share, and competitive strategy. A new kind of health care industry is evolving, not just an improved version of the previous. Creating a new reality, while managing the current reality, translates into operational implications for today's health care executive that provides exciting opportunities (such as creating new models of care that focus on health promotion and prevention) as well as perplexing challenges (for example, balancing between short-term budgetary goals and long-term vision). The fundamental shift is from hospitals as a business to health care systems as a value enterprise for promoting and meeting the health needs of the community. The health care executive's role is to guide the transformation and creation of the future in a manner that restores the higher sense of purpose and enthusiasm that will springboard the industry evolution into the twenty-first century. While the path is not fully defined, there are tools and competencies that will assist today's health care executive with navigation and improved performance.

Reflections from the Field: How Did We Get Here?

Today's problems come from yesterday's solutions.

—Peter Senge, *The Fifth Discipline*

At the predawn of the Medicare era (1950s to 1960s) more than 6000 American hospitals functioned as a cottage entity. The overall characteristics were autonomy and independence. Most hospitals were owned and operated by religious organizations (Catholic, Protestant, and Jewish). Others were owned and operated by public bodies like cities, counties, and states. Some were community teaching hospitals, and still others were federal military and Veterans Administration hospitals. While there were a very few hospitals owned by physicians, of which the majority were small and rural, hospitals were primarily built for community necessity or physician convenience and not primarily for the profit motive. The vast majority of hospitals were voluntary and not for profit.

Graduate education for hospital administrators was a relatively new concept. The curriculum, depending on the program, was based on the fundamentals of internal hospital management. Courses on medical staff bylaws, hospitals' architectural design, nursing staff and patient care, and support services (such as laundry, dietary, and housekeeping management) were required. Hospital accounting and finance were also taught, but the focus was similar to that of a plant manager.

Then, in the 1960s, came Medicare. The entrance of federal money into the practice of medicine revolutionized the health care landscape over the last 35 years of the twentieth century, and with that revolution caused the lives and careers of health care executives to be forever altered.

Medicare for the first time began to reimburse hospitals for returns on equity. That policy was an entirely new concept to hospitals, with a significant emphasis on making a profit. The new investor-owned hospital initiative further began to change the way health care was organized and delivered and has had far-reaching effects on the career requirements for our nation's health care executives.

The Medicare cost-based reimbursement program spawned massive growth in the health care field during the 1970s. Senior citizens fully enjoyed their use of the Medicare program, and the health care system of the country quickly needed more physicians and hospitals. In response to the need for additional physicians, immigration of foreign-trained physicians grew dramatically after Medicare. More than 40 new medical schools sprang up, and the country's graduate medical education programs proliferated. Because the new medicine program provided funds for medical research and development, an enormous explosion of new medical technology occurred at an astonishing rate. The Medicare cost-based reimbursement program was designed to pay physicians and hospitals for procedures performed, and residency programs taught the use of those procedures. Growing numbers of new, highly specialized physicians poured into the field, and hospitals rapidly expanded their size and numbers to accommodate the new physicians, the growing numbers of Medicare patients, and the new technology.

In the 15 years after this inauguration of Medicare, health care expenses in the United States exploded from about 6 percent of the gross national product (GNP) to more than 12 percent. In 1982, the administration in Washington responded to this growth with a new prospective reimbursement system—diagnostic related grouping (DRG)—designed to slow the growth of health care spending. The DRG system was followed by growth of the managed care business. In the mid-1980s, the managed care business began a process that would reverse the oversupply of physicians and hospital facilities and thereby create demands for new skills our health care executives would be required to master.

The decade of the 1990s represents a period during which the U.S.'s physicians and hospitals are required to reform and reshape themselves. Since health care spending had reached 15 percent of the GNP by 1990, the United States was being put at a competitive disadvantage in the global marketplace. The price of health care services increasingly became the most critical determinant. Competition among and between the hospitals for managed care contracts, and therefore for patients, became an increasingly important aspect of daily executive work. The oversupply of hospital beds and facilities was fertile ground for managed care competition. Further, the significant oversupply of physician specialists fueled the increasing competition. The irony is that despite the oversupply of providers, there still remains an estimated 37 million Americans who are uninsured.

Current Reality and Beyond

> *Structures of which we are unaware hold us prisoner.*
>
> —Peter Senge, *The Fifth Discipline*

Whether one is new to the industry or a seasoned veteran, the ability to manage the present apart from the future is predicated on understanding this evolution and reframing thinking beyond the boundaries of the current reality. To rise above the turbulence of the industry forces and to identify and achieve opportunities for creating the future beyond the present day-to-day dilemmas, it is imperative to understand the interdependencies at play between the industry and their translation to operations (see Table 4.1).

The evolution of health care organizations continues to accelerate at a breathtaking pace. The current tension is for fundamental changes that will demonstrate significant and more rapid results in terms of the *whats*, such as the following:

- Reductions in the cost of care
- Reductions in the cost of illness
- Improvements in health care access
- Improvements in overall health status

These changes are being driven by several facets, the *whys*.

- Government-mandated health care reform
- Health care industry activity and maturation
- Global economics among purchasers
- Increasing consumerism (expectations and accountability)

The industry is responding to the drivers with these transitional initiatives, the *hows*.

- Financial shift from fee-for-service to capitation
- Mergers, acquisitions, and affiliations between physician groups, hospitals, and managed care organizations in a race to integrate and consolidate in order to demonstrate better value
- Public disclosure with competition based on quality and cost of health care, with increased focus on outcomes measurement related to health and satisfaction
- Technology acquisition assessments increasingly based on cost/benefit trade-offs, with shift away from competition based on high-tech niche

Table 4.1. The evolution of focus in the health care industry.

Period	Industry focus	Management implications
1960s–1970s	• Bricks and mortar	• Build it, they will come • Mechanics and task management
1970s–1980s	• Technology and innovation	• Physician relations and decisions to support doctor-centered treatment and medical intervention: magic bullet theory • Provide infrastructure to treat illness and disease • Decisions made with hospitals, physicians, and other medical providers as revenue centers
1980s–1990s	• Managed care and cost containment	• Competition for market share • Strategy development to diversify business beyond the acute care hospital • Development of core competencies • Financial strategy and bottom-line management—how to do more with less • Decisions made with hospitals, physicians, and other medical providers as cost centers • Quality improvement and cost reduction initiatives • Development structures and processes • Responsibility for a person each time that he/she presents him/herself as a patient
1990s–2000s	• Outcomes and value	• Collaboration and alliance building • Alignment of incentives and consolidation of care components—seamless • Patient-centered and family-centered choices from a continuum of care • Health status of community, with increased focus on prevention and health management • Development of systems, people, and intellectual property • Functional outcome and well-being • Responsibility for a defined population over a period of time, whether or not the individual ever becomes a patient

- Cultural shift toward health promotion
- Responsibility for the health of a community, across the continuum of care
- Systems integration of people, products/services, and profits
- Alignment of incentives, in particular between physicians and institutional providers, as well as with consumers

These changes, drivers, and responses have led the evolution of the hospital to the integrated delivery system (IDS). The IDS is structurally a series of strategic alliances among physicians, institutions, and health plans for meeting the health needs of a population. Functionally it must bear risk for the health expenditures of the population that it serves and ultimately improve the population's health status.

With the IDS, health care has moved beyond the walls of the hospital and fragmented care components and is being reframed in terms of seamless webs of care designed to meet the community's health needs. Current reality for many emerging IDS is a focus on structure and strategy. However, the future success of the IDS will be the ability of today's leaders to transform the structural elements into a value-added system of coordinated care that improves health, manages risk, and demonstrates efficiency and value. By the twenty-first century, a new pattern of service delivery, financing, and incentives will prevail—and we are in the process of transforming the current reality to this transformed model.

Conventional thinking often centers on the IDS as an improved hospital–physician system for treating illness, with a greater emphasis on prevention and early detection. This is a significant improvement and has value, but is only an interim destination. Beyond conventional thinking is the progressive understanding and visionary leadership that centers on the ultimate realization of the IDS as an information- and knowledge-based living entity that has the opportunity to improve the health of the community. The greater opportunity for the IDS is to unearth its intellectual property, regarding care management and health promotion, and marry it with existing medical technology and innovative information-age technology that allows for a proactive partnership of health with the community.

It is not by accident that the wealthiest individual and company in the United States today is Bill Gates and his company Microsoft. The source of this wealth is not based on natural resources (such as gold or oil) or industrial economies (manufacturing or processing). The success is based on intellectual property. The key to the future in health care is our ability to harness intellectual property and use it to create greater value for communities. The new interdependencies and system dynamics are already moving into place.

The Leader's Toolbox

> *The best way to predict the future is to create it.*
>
> —Russell Ackoff, *Creating the Corporate Future*

> *Success is a lousy teacher; it seduces smart people into thinking they can't lose. And it is an unreliable guide to the future.*
>
> —Bill Gates, *The Road Ahead*

Today's health care executive is being challenged to manage and improve the *current* system while concurrently rebuilding and redesigning the *future* system. This challenge has been likened to flying a 747 airliner, while trying to rebuild it in midflight, and travel to a destination that has never been reached before. And by the way, there isn't a well-defined map to guide the journey. Difficult, but not impossible with the proper tools.

The key questions for today's managers and leaders are no longer issues of task and structure, but questions of purpose, values, change mastery, and systems thinking. This takes the ability to learn, adjust, and implement at a faster pace than ever experienced in health care. These are new tasks for the health care executive, which require a new set of tools. The key concepts outlined here, from Peter Senge's *The Fifth Discipline*, are a prerequisite for all health care executives trying to lead and navigate through this multidimensional period.[1]

Systems Thinking

- The concept that business is a web of interrelated, visible, and invisible parts and actions.

- To create change in business is to first understand the interconnectivity of the parts and actions—the patterns versus the snapshot.

- The goal is to be able to optimize the whole over the parts and to understand the implications that will result.

    —Practical first step: Look at the IDS as whole and move inward, rather than trying to improve individual components within the organization. Identify the value chain within the organization. What may be positive for the IDS may not be optimal for an operating unit.

Personal Mastery

- The concept that one must be disciplined to continually clarify and broaden one's personal vision, and to challenge and monitor one's own learning and performance.

- The goal is to stay grounded in personal values and to monitor the translation of values into professional reality.

    —Practical first step: Clarify personal values and set up aims on how these values may get realized and developed in the professional arena. Take ownership of one's role, responsibility, and actions. Then challenge the executive team members to do the same on an individual basis. Follow up with group discussion on the process, implications, and insights.

Mental Models

- The concept that we all operate from deeply ingrained beliefs and a frame of reference based upon our historical experience.

- These mental models affect the way we view situations and our decision-making patterns.

    —Practical first step: Turn inward. Examine and clarify one's own mental models and make them vulnerable to challenge and new influences. Then challenge the executive team members to do the same. Follow up with group discussion on the process, implications, and insights.

Shared Vision

- The concept that a truly defined picture of the IDS is painted and understood in the minds and hearts of those throughout the organization.

- The benefits of the IDS must be powerfully shared and conveyed among those who will be building, working in, and/or using the IDS if we are to realize the full power and intent of its concept.

    —Practical first step: Begin with the executive team in exploring and co-creating "pictures of the future" in a manner that creates ownership and empowerment, rather than just creating shared understanding. Then challenge the executive team members to do the same with their teams. The goal is to create good leaders, not just good followers, throughout the IDS.

Team Learning

- The concept that learning is more than memorizing facts or transferring information. It is about creating understanding and new knowledge about who we are, what we make, and how we make it.

- The goal is to deliberately examine events and concepts, identify leverage points and barriers, and recognize consequences and impact of actions and decisions; to share points of view, explore other perspectives, and consider their possibility.

  —Practical first step: Create an environment that encourages the free flow of thoughts and ideas. Establish ground rules and expectations for discussion that explore questions and alternate viewpoints in a "safe container." Designate discussion time on meeting agendas, and use a trained meeting facilitator as a dialogue coach.

From the beginning, the health care industry has been a fragmented consortium of elements operating somewhat disjointedly. We now have the opportunity to reshape the pieces of the puzzle and glue them together in a manner that will create a new system. There aren't any cookbook methodologies. The reality is that we don't have a clear path to follow in health care today, as we are pioneering into new territories. However, consistent application of this ensemble of tools, on both an individual and team basis, can help to further the journey and galvanize creativity.

Executive Competencies

> *Today, loving change, tumult, even chaos is a prerequisite for survival.*
>
> —Tom Peters, *Thriving on Chaos*

> *You can't count on conventional wisdom. That only makes sense in conventional markets.*
>
> —Bill Gates, *The Road Ahead*

Just as the industry is evolving, so is the leader's role. Leaders who are transformational to the industry evolution are those who are able to stay in tune with the needs of the industry, the community, and the organization, and to respond appropriately to these needs.

It's as if the global industry is undergoing 10 major medical interventions at once, and it's the health care executives' role to stabilize, revitalize, and strengthen their respective local enterprises. In this analogy, a practitioner would need the proper tools and technology; skills and competencies would be equally important.

Previously in this chapter, the tools for leaders in an emerging IDS were identified; the tools and competencies are complementary, and their effectiveness is interdependent. Here are the competencies, which go hand-in-hand with the tools and should serve as key focus areas for the role of the health care executive.

Steward and Guide

- Promulgate a sense of ownership and accountability.
- Galvanize values and philosophies that capture the heart of the organization's higher purpose and most inner truth. This is a shift from traditional strategic intent to corporate purpose.

- Operate in a new context, away from competition with a primary focus on profitability to a primary focus on ideals that are pursued in a profitable manner.

- Liberate people to unleash their creativity and innovation.

- Accept responsibility for the overall well-being of the organization—from the personal level to the organizational level to the community level.

- Recognize that people do not get out of bed every morning to increase productivity and market share; people get out of bed because someone has flipped a switch in them that matters.

- Values cannot be instilled through a crash course. They are the existing strengths of the organization that must be revered and practiced. Employees must be able to identify with them and to see how these play out in the day-to-day activities and decisions.

  —We have an annual internal campaign we call "Family Appeal." Through the foundation, we collect and distribute funds employees can access in times of need. At the beginning of each campaign year, a videotape is viewed by everyone throughout the organization. The video highlights fund recipients and pictorializes the role our IDS plays within the employee community. The video includes action footage of various employees throughout the organization going about their daily lives. The program, and the video itself, offer powerful testimonials that galvanize the purpose and value of our coming together each day. Examples and opportunities for us to "walk the walk," such as this program, go far beyond the effect of the proverbial vision statement. Both have a purpose, but it takes both.

Sense Maker

- Create an organization with the ability to think globally and act locally.

- It is vital that a health care organization's role and actions make sense for the community. Once plans are developed and implemented, will the results and actions be valuable to the community?

- Define reality and make sense of the organization and its environment. These are chaotic times, but constancy of purpose and clarity of direction can give a method to the madness that will anchor the organization.

- Create shared vision and a genuine sense of purpose. As a leader you bring your ability to see, read, hear, and feel the company's greater destiny; serve as the catalyst for the organization to participate in this.

- Pursue higher aims and ideals first—not focusing on profits—but pursue them profitability. Put profits in their proper context.

  —The profitability pendulum for health care organizations can vary greatly. In writing this chapter, we authors compared our organizations: One is operating in a strong financial arena, and the other has a history of financial turbulence. What we realized in comparing notes is that there is danger in both of these zones. Without the proper context, profits (whether ample or strained) can alter the way in which an organization defines and pursues its aims. The former runs the risk of being lulled into a false sense of stability because of the insulation that profits can have on the tension for change. The latter runs the risk of foregoing visionary change for the sake of frenzied operational improvements as an attempt to alleviate financial pressures. However, our organizations have avoided these pitfalls by staying grounded in our guiding principles. At both of our organizations we've spent a lot of time talking about the three Ps—people, products, and profits. Our role as leaders has been to guide our boards and our senior management team in keeping these in perspective and in the right order. In health care, people have to come first. The products (whether you define them as care delivery or health promotion) or profits should not be the primary reason for decisions.

Facilitator and Coach

- When it is all said and done, it is people, not strategies, that make the difference.

- The leader's job is to get everyone involved and to see the reality (apparent or not). When people understand the situation and the challenges, the need for change takes over and they actively seek to create and innovate. You don't change people and culture; you coach their growth and development.

- Encourage critical thinking. Create a safe environment that promotes free thinking and vulnerability.

- Allow differences and work through them.

- Establish up front that no one person has all the answers and that as a team, solutions must be sought and discovered.

- Be the orchestra conductor, not an emperor or referee.

- In essence, become a servant to those in your organization to help them become more effective as individuals and as teams.

  —We have a system management council meeting once a month. Three tiers of management are present at this meeting. A portion of the meeting is devoted to strategic direction, where as a team we discuss our vision, environmental developments, and operational implications. A second objective in the meeting is to talk about operational progress and link it to our strategic direction—discussion of actions being taken and developed. The remainder of the meeting is devoted to addressing the needs of the operational managers. The key questions are asked by senior managers; we probe the next two layers of managers to find out what resources or support they need from us to accomplish their goals and objectives. In this forum, the primary goal of the senior executives is to ask questions and identify leverage points for supporting management. It is a meeting where senior executives coach and facilitate; we are there to support the managers and to hear them.

Integrator

- Create a seamless web of care, with aligned stakeholders (physicians, providers, purchaser, patients, prepatients/at-risk population).

- Move structural elements into a high-performing system with interdependencies that are leveraged to maximize the value chain.

- Identify the stakeholders and provide incentives to form interdependent relationships that work toward the same goal. If these incentives are aligned properly, then real change efforts will be self-promulgating.

Collaborator and Alliance Builder

- Deals are driven by products, business plans, and financial statements. Alliances are driven by chemistry and ideals that, if successfully developed, will prove to also be financially sound.
- Seek to create win–win scenarios that focus on the greater good.
- Coalesce parties to work toward accomplishing something of a higher order, versus trying to work the best position for their turf.
    - —This spans both within and beyond the inner virtual walls of the IDS. We recently completed an alliance for a medical clinic comprised of more than 70 physicians to relocate to our campuses and align their practice with our IDS. We began this process by exploring our values, the needs of the community, and our vision for meeting these needs; we spent hours and months talking about these ideals. This intellectual and emotional bond solidified and carried us through the structure and negotiation stages. When the difficult decisions were put on the table, rather than competitive and adversarial forces taking over, a sense of "we cannot *not* do this" would emerge. Obstacles became rallying points for us to overcome collaboratively. Our strategic intent wasn't focused on the dollars or market share, but on the value of what we were creating for the community. It took more time on the front end, and tremendous patience with the process, but the rewards are in the value of what was created. We accomplished the unrealistic.

Educator

- Create within the organization an environment embedded with a routine of deliberate learning.
- Involve the board of directors early in the process.
- Build a web of new knowledge and thinking centered around a consistent image of the IDS you are developing. View the pieces in the interrelated dimensions that exist within the organization and that span to the community.
- Build the IDS by not just constructing new departments and a new organizational chart. Create a system of interdependencies that work in tandem to produce health. This will require managers and physicians to learn and apply the principles of systems thinking and other tools new to the trade.
- Couple the tools training with continuous education about the state of the industry, both nationally and locally. People can change when educated about where we are, what got us here, and that inevitably we are headed somewhere else. It is vital for the leader to assume this responsibility and to fulfill it proficiently.

Communicator

- Job one is to first understand and unearth the existing information and knowledge. The most important communication attribute for the health care executive is the ability to listen.
- Job two is to keep everybody on the same page with noncensored communication.
- It is the leaders' responsibility to make sure that "real" information is being shared both up and down the organization—not just messages "from on high," but real truth, from all levels and in all directions.

- The sharing of real information encourages people to take responsibility and ownership.

  —We went through a time when our profitability and viability were hemorrhaging. We set up regular "town meetings" with employees throughout the company and weekly management meetings that dipped down into the middle layer. There was no sugar coating—the problems were laid out, and the need for change was made clear. What we did not dictate was the solutions—we sought those together. Operational readings were given from the top down, as well as from the bottom up. In a nine-month period, we implemented changes that resulted in $6 million of improved profitability. The key was communication—both sharing the facts and listening to other viewpoints.

Risk Taker

- Leaders have to lead, even if they aren't fully sure of the next steps. This crucial responsibility is central to the leaders' role and cannot be delegated.

- The development of the IDS is a risk in and of itself. At this juncture there isn't a set of tried and tested blueprints.

- Expose to others that you don't have all of the answers—and furthermore, there might not even be one perfect answer, but together we can seek answers.

- Identifying the risk elements and your personal vulnerability is essential because it enables others to expose their needs as well. It is awesome to see how creative mutually vulnerable individuals can be in dealing with a challenge.

- Failing to be honest and failing to take risks only leads to greater risk, as progress and development will be seriously impeded.

- Risk taking by leaders is a personal responsibility rather than a corporate responsibility, as leadership by its very nature is personal not corporate. Corporations don't lead; people lead. And it is people who make choices and bear the risk.

- As a leader pioneering through health care during today's tumult, recognize that risk goes with the territory.

Change Agent and Time Keeper

- Create change.

- Manage change.

- Monitor the rate of change. Timing is important. If the development or implementation moves too rapidly or too slowly, effectiveness is lost.

- Evaluate change. Differentiate between one-shot episodic improvements and dramatic, sustainable redesign.

  —An IDS is a web of interconnections; much like a mobile. I often find that as change is created within one segment, the effects ripple to other segments. A perfect example of this lies within the interconnectedness between our provider-owned health plan and our acute care hospital. To respond to increased managed care pressures from the market and to improve the performance of our health plan, we reduced the physician panel fees. The health plan improved financially as well as in its performance measures. But our IDS didn't fare so well overall initially. We proactively attempted to prevent, as well as mitigate and address, the inevitable—physician backlash aimed at the hospital side of the business (for example, through decreased patronage). We moved through this by managing the implementation to correspond with real market pressures and with an organized communication plan from the IDS. We explained the market dynamics, the changes and pain that we were experiencing, and the context of the physician changes. Making this kind of change isn't mechanistic or delegatable, and it often offers unexpected challenges. The fundamental key of the leaders' role is to manage the dynamics across the boundaries of the IDS. Change doesn't happen in isolated vacuums.

Champion of the Customer

- The key questions that must first be answered by today's health care executive are

  —Who do we serve?

  —What do we provide them?

  —How do we deliver it?

  —How do we improve?

- The realization that there are internal and hidden customers, as well as external customers, is new thinking for many in the industry. We've always respected the community, medical staff, patients, and employees. What must be clarified is their specific roles, expectations, and needs as customers of the IDS.

- In building the IDS, don't repeat the cycle of the past by building from the providers'/institutions' perspective. Begin with the ultimate customers—the community—and work backward.

- Don't assume that we know what customers want. Find out what they want from them directly.

- Keep the perspective alive that meeting and exceeding the health needs of the community, in a prudent manner, is the reason for the IDS. Without the community (which includes those for whose health the IDS is responsible), there is no cash for the chief financial officer to flow, no business for the chief operating officer to operate, and nothing for the chief financial officer to execute. The IDS is about the community, not about institutional survival.

- Weave the IDS into the very fabric of the community.

  —The cornerstone of our IDS is a tertiary, academic medical center located in an inner-city area. We created a community development organization that focuses on revitalizing and improving the socioeconomic conditions of this geographic area. Realizing that this community is our customer and that our charge is to make it a healthier community, abandoning this once-decaying area was not an option. Instead we formed an action-oriented cooperative and embraced the community. In return, it embraced us. It has been a learning endeavor for all of us in rebuilding the infrastructure of the environment in which we all live. The health of the community and the health of our organization has prospered as a result. This is a priceless demonstration of core values centered on meeting and exceeding customer needs—and marrying our organization with the community. When an organization focuses on creating community benefit and value for its customers, it ensures its own prosperity.

Discussion Questions for a One-Hour Executive Committee Meeting

1. What are my personal values?

2. How do these translate into my professional values and goals?

3. How can I break through to the next level of potentiality and superior performance?

4. What new knowledge and learning do I need to seek?

5. How can I use the tools and develop the competencies identified?

6. What actions do I need to take to ensure that I am fulfilling my role?

7. How can I approach the responsibility of changing a complex system?

8. How will I measure my progress and effectiveness?

9. What is my plan for identifying and making improvements in my performance?

10. Who are my customers?

11. What do my customers need from me?

12. How can I help other health care executives grow and develop?

Note

1. Peter M. Senge, *The Fifth Discipline: The Art and Practice of the Learning Organization* (New York: Doubleday, 1990).

Kimberly E. Sangari is a vice president with Pitts Management Associates, Inc. PMA is a consulting and strategic advisory firm specializing in strategy development, mergers, and consolidations in the health care industry. Her health care experience includes strategic and financial planning, operations development, and partnering and alliance development.

Before joining PMA, she worked for five years as a senior-level director with General Health System in Baton Rouge, Louisiana, a $450 million provider-insurer, organized as a regional integrated delivery system, with an HMO, care delivery components comprising the full continuum of care, and strategic alliances with physicians.

Prior to working with General Health, Sangari was a senior consultant with Price Waterhouse in Houston, Texas. She specialized in management consulting related to financial and operational issues. She performed financial and business analysis and due diligence associated with money center bank financings, bond offerings, corporate strategy development, corporate recovery, business development ventures, and litigation matters.

Sangari holds a master's degree in health care administration from the University of Houston-Clear Lake and a bachelor's degree in business administration from the University of Texas at Austin.

Chapter 5

Strategic Deployment in an Integrated Delivery System

Sherry Bright

Strategy is both the *what* and the *how* of how organizations choose to make their way in their environment. Strategy is the aggregation of the choices made, built one on top of the other. It begins with the skillful plan, but most important is the focused implementation that accomplishes the objective. Too often organizations focus on the plan—the what—and neglect the implementation—the how. Without implementation, strategy is a dead artifact of the organization and has little meaning.

Considering the turmoil in which the health care industry finds itself, it seems impossible to make plans, much less commit to them, with horizons stretching years into the future. Instead, it is more realistic to play the balls—or hand grenades—as they are tossed. Keeping the ball in focus takes energy and an absorption with the present. This reactive mode is intense and leaves little time for thinking about such ideas as strategic planning. Indeed, market dynamics make it seem nonsensical or presumptuous to seriously consider planning for a future so clearly unknown.

Counterintuitive though it may be, the process of strategic planning, decision making, and commitment is most valuable when the environment is changing rapidly and organizations are facing great challenges. A misstep, when the margin for error is smaller than ever, can be costly. And, whether consciously acknowledged or not, organizations make decisions of strategic import every day: new services to initiate, mature services to abandon, markets to enter, and partnerships and affiliations to make. The interrelationship and dynamics of these separate decisions combine to define the strategy of the organization, for good or ill.

Organizations choose one of two mental models with which to face turbulent times: reactive, responding to the environment and competitive changes; or proactive, consciously making choices that define a desired future and proceeding toward it with deliberate speed. Both organizations will have pursued a strategy. One will have done so with a sense of momentum and manifest destiny, while the other is likely to feel tossed about by external forces. In this chapter, I will argue for the use of consciously developed and deployed strategy as the driver for organizational change, especially in times when the future is anything but clear.

Making skillful choices is only the first step in mastering strategic deployment. Skillful execution of the operational implications of those choices is the key. When the future cannot be predicted with any certainty, there may well be several diverse routes to success. The degree to which this implementation is successful determines both the power of the initial decision and how the organization's strategic plan will be evaluated in the future. It is the organization's actual operations—not what is found in a binder in the boardroom—that are the DNA of strategy.

This begs the question of how it is possible for large and complex organizations—metamorphosing and combining under the forces of the market—to reach high-leverage strategic business decisions that are then effectively implemented. It is said that fish don't notice the water in which they swim. Organizations, management teams, medical staffs, and employees don't notice their own culture or its effect on them. It is like the very air they breathe. And understanding the organization's internal environment and culture and their leverage for obstructing or fueling change is critical to the success of the effort. Even though intangible and therefore hard to command and control, it has to come before the attention needed for successful deployment will be committed. Making these issues explicit and overt will allow creation of internal congruence around the choices made, the rationale for those choices, and the energy necessary to implement them. This congruence is based on understanding the mental models at work in the organization—crafting a means to elicit ideas, innovation, and creativity while creating coherence around values and outcomes. The processes are convergent and divergent at the same time. It is establishing consistent thinking while avoiding groupthink. The building blocks are ideas and mental models; the mortar is process management. The resulting infrastructure is the skeleton of the organization, critical for strength and endurance.

This realm of mental constructs is complicated, but there are other emotional as well as more tangible obstacles to success. One is that this work is not glamorous, high tech, or flashy. Yet it is the real work of leadership. Linking the mundane, everyday tasks of care delivery to the power of a vision that is transforming requires reflection on the characteristics of the organization and the people and groups that comprise it. In an almost anthropological way, leaders must observe, surface, and confirm the mental models and values at work in the organization. Leaders must be honest and recognize the difference between the values that are espoused and those that are acted on every day.

An espoused value included in many organizations' lists of cultural characteristics may be employee empowerment. The question leaders must ask of themselves is whether or not the behaviors of their managers and staff demonstrate a sense of empowerment. Do they even know what an empowered organization would look like? This is tough work—looking in the mirror and acknowledging what is seen. If the image does not reflect the characteristic, then leaders must ask themselves what they are doing or reinforcing that contributes to the real world of the workplace. If their own behaviors are inconsistent with the stated desired value, either the statement or the behaviors must change.

One group of senior leaders at an urban hospital was widely quoted for its commitment to total quality management. When challenged with the need to rapidly remove cost, the team chose to act in a fashion consistent with its stated values and work through an accelerated program of process improvement to achieve its goals.

This attention to details that are not financial—not data driven in the traditional sense—may be a stretch for many leadership teams. Examining their own actions and the role modeling they represent may be difficult, intellectually as well as emotionally. There is likely to be no clear path that identifies the right set of questions to ask to fully understand the inner workings of the organization. Finding the way and beginning this journey, a requisite component of effective deployment and execution of the change strategies needed by health care organizations today, requires trust and communication. This work of leadership is nondelegable and difficult.

This chapter is organized around the central theme of effectively delegating challenging change-oriented strategies in an integrated delivery system. It will cover theories of transformation through sharing a vision and creating tension for change. Importantly, it will discuss the management of the transition period, a time of driving nitroglycerin-loaded trucks over rough and rocky roads. It will cover the importance of clear processes for decision making, accountability, and ownership. Fundamental to all is the ability and willingness of those at the top to think clearly, accept ownership and accountability, and act with internal coherence.

The concepts of strategy management as daily work life, and the criticality of not separating what an organization actually does from either its short- or long-term strategic intent, are then addressed. Making the vision real to everyone in the organization and demonstrating with them its substantive impact on their lives is the only way to truly engage the mental, emotional, and physical resources of the people involved. We'll examine a learning experiment as an example of how this deployment and engagement process might work. The example itself is irrelevant; the learning comes from the process of identifying leverage points and developing impactful actions to make use of them.

The chapter then considers the challenge faced by today's health care organizations as they seek to become integrated delivery systems: How might energy for change be created within the organizations themselves? The necessity for formulating pull strategies that motivate and incentives forward momentum, as well as possible tactics for doing so, will be surfaced. In this instance, it is important to articulate assumptions made about the common characteristics integrated delivery systems face, on which these approaches are based. Those assumptions will not hold true in all environments, but it is hoped that an understanding of the techniques of deployment (in the context of those assumptions) will have value for organizations faced with different market forces.

Based on the set of strategies developed from the assumptions, the chapter follows those strategies into action through the use of planning cycles and action-oriented monitoring systems that support learning, course correction, and improvement. Some ideas will be shared on how the market may be monitored and thought about to keep the plan evergreen.

Case studies of strategy deployment in two different integrated delivery systems are offered. The first looks at the implementation of a business planning process driven by the system's strategy and the accountability system designed to manage its progress. The second looks at the process of restructuring an evolving system to bring it into alignment with its business strategy. Both are still in process. The final chapters of those organizations' stories are far from written, but the approach they are using may be instructive.

The last narrative component of the chapter is a look back at the lessons learned from the experiences discussed. Salient points are considered that may be helpful in the steps of creating strategy, deploying it, managing its implementation, and improving it.

Finally, sample agendas and discussion questions that could be used for senior executive meetings, board meetings, and process owner meetings are given. Cautions and suggestions for use accompany these samples.

The Strategic Challenge of Transformation

The first question organizations must answer in this process is "Transforming to what?" The need for articulating and owning a common idea of the desired end state is fundamental to any change effort or the thorough implementation of any strategic initiative. In most health care organizations the board of directors is largely composed of interested and committed community leaders—not health care delivery, administrative, or business professionals. It is, therefore, critical that the management team provide a vivid context for the visioning process, actively leading or facilitating its development. At the same time, a vision that is not owned at the governance level is a risky proposition. It may not have the strength of conviction when important trade-offs must be made. The vision must be a picture of how the organization desires and expects to interact with its future environment, adequately compelling to drive tough decisions. Working toward something deeply desired provides the rationale for sacrifice in a way nothing else can.

It is said that strategy is crafted, that a good vision is a work of art. In the sense that its vitality evokes an emotional response of commitment and willingness to work to achieve it, strategy is an art form. The raw materials necessary to bring such a vision into being are the interest and energy of the governing body, the knowledge and insights of management, the concerns and desires of the organization's customers, and the enthusiasm and shared ownership of the organization's employees. The process of bringing these energies together to create a vision sufficiently worthy of those disparate energies is not something that happens by default—and should not be delegated to any outside agent. The successful deployment of strategy for an integrated delivery system starts here, as does its ownership and accountability.

The governing board is clearly interested in the organization's current and future success, or the hours of dedicated (and usually volunteer) service would not be given. Often, the board's interest may be in protecting the organization's history. Failure to replace this backward-looking perspective with one more fitting for tomorrow's challenge can sink the enterprise from the start. Leaders must help the board focus on its mission as the driving force and consider various scenarios for achieving it. Providing information on market trends, reinforced with human interest anecdotes, can create the tension for change so necessary to fuel creation of and commitment to a new approach to mission achievement.

Similarly, management and medical staff may be resistant to the degree of change needed. Market-based data, paired with predictions of potential—even alternative—futures may get their attention. It is relatively easy to demonstrate the need for improvement in cost structures. Government programs alone highlight that fact. There is evidence from other markets, even other countries, of both significantly lower and different utilization with no negative impact on clinical outcome. After such a presentation, probing these knowledgeable leaders on why and how such results could be achieved with significantly lower resource consumption is a start to shaking assumptions and beliefs and both the status quo and the future.

The organization's customers, patients or purchasers, can also be relied on to provide a wake-up call. Focus groups of community residents candidly offering their opinions on the health care system as they encounter it today, as well as their fears of the future, can be used to motivate redesign. Experiencing the incredulity of a group around the issue of the cottage industry of fragmented health care providers working together to optimize patient benefit can cause health care professionals to question their past improvement efforts. The public is calling for fundamental change—a new type of delivery system—and hearing their request can stimulate proactively. Employees both act in the creation of this vision and are acted on. They, too, know at a visceral level the opportunities for improvement. They experience firsthand the frustration, fear, and needs of their patients. Harnessing this understanding to create an end-state picture and to mobilize around efforts to make better outcomes is a powerful rallying cry.

Establish a team sensitive to the political realities of each organization's environment and select a visioning process that fits the organization's culture. Tools and techniques are readily available; it is not the technique that is used but the energy and involvement with which the tool is wielded that will make the difference. Identify the core constituencies that must be involved: those who can both empower and energize the process as well as those who can negate its implementation. The concept of concentric circles may work well for this analysis. In the innermost circle will be the organization's leaders, who are pulling the process by the saliency of their awareness of need for it. Immediately beyond them are those who are authorized to shape it on behalf of the larger community. Beyond this ring are woven rings of medical staff, management, and employees. All need to hear the same core message, feel the need for change, and recognize why participating in a successful change is important for them. This set of concentric circles, then, is really rings divided by semipermeable membranes through which communication and understanding must pass. Figure 5.1 captures this concept.

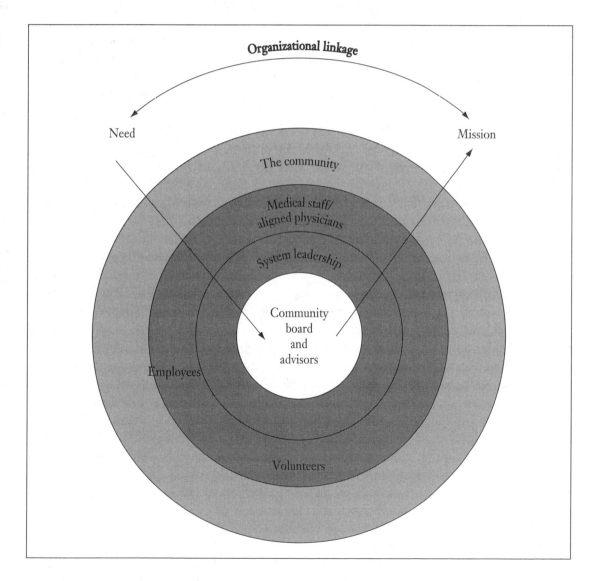

Figure 5.1. The rings through which communication and understanding must pass.

Visioning the future without a commitment to tangible change is no more than fantasizing to pass the time. A goal without resources applied to achieve it is a daydream: no more. Members of organizations are rightly skeptical of the "new" vision and direction when they see the same activities budgeted in the same way and their managers and leaders acting as they always have. Taking the first of many steps from the tried and true in a direction that is new and toward an end point that is clear but distant requires a real leap of faith. The tendency will be to creep along the familiar, testing the future tentatively and with hope of feeling some certainty. In today's health care environment, certainty is not to be had. Even the most progressive markets do not provide operational recipes for what steps to take. It is apparent that the dynamics of tomorrow's health care delivery system will be quite different from those of today. Still, it is fairly clear the direction those dynamics will take: cost reduction, demonstration of quality and outcome. This must be enough to begin. Staying too long in the past, relatively comfortable environment may, in fact, so compromise an organization's strength that it will be unable to successfully navigate the rapids when it encounters them.

A visual image commonly used for this is that of a burning platform, on the theory that a person afraid of heights who feels the heat and smells the smoke of the fire in the room behind will leap even into an unknown. The vision statement, if emotionally compelling, will help the jumpers feel that they are leaping toward a known end that they value rather than falling off a cliff. For this to be the result, there must be tangible motivation for the action itself.

This is where many change efforts fall short—and successful deployment of a new business strategy is a change effort. They may articulate, publish, and disseminate a vision that is fingerprinted by the organization. They may have created such a sense of the raging fire that people—physicians, managers, and frontline care givers—feel singed. But they cannot stop there, move their focus to a different critical issue, and expect the change process to continue. Establishing a self-perpetuating set of reinforcers for the entire organization (in whatever language and medium is most effective) to continually see the vision and feel the heat is mandated. This early transition period, when the new strategic paradigm is being tested, accepted, and deployed, is the most critical period in the fragile new strategy's life.

Think of the vision and its related activities as mechanisms that pull one forward; the burning platform is a pusher—maybe even a shove. Motivation on the scale needed to move all the components of today's delivery system in concert will require judicious use of both. Opportunities to highlight the vision and make elements of it real to various parts of the organization should be sought and leveraged. Setting up field tests or learning laboratories where decisions, choices, and policy characteristics can be played with and felt can go a long way toward helping people see that the change they are engaged in has a purpose and an end point they value. An example of this could be creating a game or mock-up of a particular process (patient transfer, for example) and letting staff engage in the acts of transfer as they were envisioned. This learning lab is also a great way to involve the staff in fingerprinting the vision as it is deployed; create feedback loops from such an experience that inform the process and policy design of implementation. Bringing in speakers who have real-life trench-time with other organizations seeking to accomplish a similar result can help staff members realize that they are not in the struggle alone and that other people have experienced some of the same feelings. Let these explorers mingle with the various groups without constantly being shepherded by senior management. It adds to the speaker's credibility and to management's ability to relinquish control. Send staff on road trips to bring back stories of how other organizations and individuals have surmounted some of the same challenges.

In the early 1990s, when one health care organization was in the design and development stage of a new facility's vision, several of these techniques were employed. The annual board retreat centered around the words and lessons learned by a chief executive officer of a system in a more advanced market to pique the interest of the board and leadership in attempting something new for the market. The design team visited facilities driven by similar end-state values and objectives in states from Florida to California. A mock-up of a patient room, designed to include amenities surfaced through community focus groups, was constructed. Hundreds of employees and community members wandered through, leaving comments behind.

As for the burning platform: It seems easier, or at least more natural, for management to excel at creating a sense of gloom and doom rather than one of excitement and anticipation. Creation of a sense of tension for change is good, but leverage the information leading to depression to motivate action that challenges the feared results. When detailing the negative impacts being felt by the organization—Medicare cuts, managed care contracts pushing revenue down, competition from the organization across town—include some specific action individuals can take to improve their own and the organization's chance of success. The instinct to take action—whether it is flight or fight—is deeply ingrained in the human animal. Management's responsibility is to clearly define the enemy and the road to victory, arm the combatants with knowledge and tools, support their efforts, and identify a specific target at which to shoot.

Strategy Is What You Do, Not What You Say You Do

Strategy is defined as "overall planning and conduct of large-scale operations," "a plan of action," and "the art or skill of using stratagems."[1] In all of these definitions the word carries two connotations. The first is the more passive one: the design or creation of a plan of action. Too often this is where organizations stop in their strategic planning efforts. They create a plan—in some cases in great detail—that is put into a three-ring binder, translated into overheads, presented to the board and selected other constituents, and then placed in a prominent place on a shelf. The manager intends to use it as a guideline and even as a monitor or milestone check for progress toward agreed-upon goals. In some cases some incentive may even be tied to it. But somehow "it" doesn't happen. Somehow, real life happens instead while the manager is intending to implement the strategic plan. In time, the commitments outlined in the plan erode in the face of the discontinuity of not being able to take the action determined. It is uncomfortable to have to carry the knowledge of a plan committed to, but not implemented. To resolve this feeling, managers must either lower their performance expectations or change their reaction to the fires encountered on a daily basis. The tendency to lower one's goals is so common it has been described as a system archetype called "drifting goals."[2] It is an even more common result when strategy—and the strategic plan—is viewed only with this first definition.

The second definition conveys a sense of action: the conduct of operations using stratagems. Warren Bennis, well-known as an advocate of leadership, wrote that "the single defining quality of leaders is the capacity to *create and realize a vision*" (emphasis added).[3] How an organization actually conducts itself—what tactics, schemes, programs, and activities it employs to recruit physicians, contract with purchasers, generate customer loyalty, improve operations, and manage its resources—is the true embodiment of its strategy. This can be a scary thought that underscores the importance of walking the talk. If future success as described in the vision requires an environment of trust among and between administration and the medical staff, and if the strategic plan contains an objective for increasing medical staff representation in leadership forums, but the organization's operations are characterized by an us-versus-them mental model, *that* is the organization's real values in action and its strategy. If the principles of total quality are espoused in the vision and addressed in the strategic plan, but management continues to make decisions without data and without an understanding of work as a process, the strategic plan will never come to be. To better ensure successful deployment of a new strategic direction, an organization should critically appraise its current operations—its strategies and values in practice—for how well they mesh with those that will be necessary for and congruent with the vision.

Peter Senge has said, "It's not what a vision is . . . it is what a vision does."[4] It is this responsibility for true, visible, and tangible change in the way an organization works, when fueled by a powerful vision, guided by well-defined strategies and committed actions matched to the written word, that is leadership's role as organizational midwife.

As mentioned, the aggregation of daily work life and daily work decisions of the thousands of individuals of the organization brings a vision to life. The marketing discipline has long known that in order to complete a purchase, customers must both believe—and act on the belief—that the purchase directly benefits them. This principle, known as WIIFM (or "what's in it for me") is at the root of all effective marketing campaigns. They appeal to the specific needs customers feel and the promise that the product's features will address them. This is why both Suburbans and Corvettes are made and profitably sold: The need is only simplistically for transportation. Both the cars themselves and the manner in which they are positioned and sold respond to an emotional or mental need customers have. In the end, to create loyal customers who will buy again, customers must feel they got a good bargain and received value.

General management can take a page out of marketing's book to be successful in this complicated area of strategy deployment. Gaining understanding and support for a vision and set of strategies substantive enough to change behaviors is an outcome worthy of the best marketing approach leadership can develop. In a service business as complex as health care, it is important that organizational change be orchestrated so that the patient's needs, entwined in the process of care delivery, are consistently met in a smoothly functioning way. Using a mechanistic metaphor, to achieve this outcome, each cog of the sophisticated delivery system must contribute to the end result. Under the theory of push/pull incentives discussed previously, managing the deployment and implementation of strategy should include identifying specific tactics to link groups and individuals with the push or pull that has the most meaning for them. For some, the threat of competitive action forcing downsizing may be the most powerful motivation. For others it may be the opportunity to take on a new challenge and learn a new way of doing things. Successful strategic deployment requires an understanding of the drivers of different individuals and groups and how the successful implementation of the strategy will impact their motivation.

Following this train of thought, senior management must clearly assign accountability and responsibility for successful deployment. The CEO and the board chair are the ultimate owners of this and all else, and their willingness to acknowledge that may well go a long way in helping the organization understand the importance of deployment. An analogy that may be helpful is that of building a brick house. Each brick must be well made for strength, endurance, and beauty. The architect must design a house that is functional and pleasing. Contractors must make sure that the electrical wiring and pipes go to the right places. The order to begin construction and its sequencing must be given. The process of strategy deployment is like the mortar that holds the bricks in place, provides protection for the system infrastructure of pipes and wires, and allows the edifice to be created as designed. Builders are as careful about the mix they use for mortar as they are of any element of the design. Managers tend to think that this element of cohesion will happen by itself.

This makes it all the more important to be clear about ownership and responsibility. Failure to specifically highlight it in the plan or leadership dialogue sends a message that it is not important and/or that it will happen by default. A cliché is true: What belongs to everyone belongs to no one.

The tactics put into place to manage this critical area must be interconnected, linked, and synergistic. This cannot happen from aggregating strategic and operational objectives and teams that never convene to talk about how their new work is going. Assign an individual and authorize the creation of a team whose primary function is managing deployment.

- Understand the way the organization has changed in the past
- Communicate and generate commitment to the vision
- Accept and own the vision
- Monitor the heat of the fire being felt
- Mix the push and pull mechanisms designed specifically to move the organization forward along the strategic track

These are the navigators watching the organization's dashboard for early warning signs of the need for special efforts.

Once assigned and with accountability accepted, senior management must ask about performance. People do what they are reinforced to do. In management parlance, that tends to boil down to doing what one is asked about. In the same way that no one will pick up the strategic plan who doesn't have to report on its progress, no one will serve as organizational conscience and change mentor if these actions are not encouraged and reinforced.

Specific time should be set aside on the board and senior management agendas to ask how the deployment process is working. Specific and measurable process outcomes or milestones should be solicited and then monitored. Managers' ongoing role as leaders and communicators should be leveraged as an implementation tactic. When resistance to change is encountered and is too strong for the personnel assigned, it may be necessary to enlist the direct support of management in finding the right mix of push and pull to overcome it.

In the same way that business strategies of creating a vehicle for physician/hospital collaboration, for example, are monitored and reviewed, so should be the movement of the organization in understanding, accepting, embracing, and enacting new strategy. Agreed-upon indicators of the strategy's success should be stated: cycle time of policy implementation, efficiency of process redesign, and degree of awareness of new information may all be examples of such indicators. Other chapters in this book relate to a variety of methods or techniques that might be used as monitoring tools. Again, the tool is much less important than that senior managers *use* the tool to measure the rate at which strategic deployment of key initiatives is taking place. It is their use of the tool and their asking of the questions, routinely and consistently, that sends the message that this deployment process is important.

The Challenge Before Us

Health care organizations have an abundance of talented managers—intelligent and intuitive leaders who care deeply about providing quality health care to the people of the United States. The literature is full of the necessary criterion for success under the new industrial paradigm. The overall direction has been charted, though each organization comes from its own unique position and must find its own unique course. Across the nation, organizations large and small are

- Successfully improving alignment with other components of the delivery system
- Focusing on cost reduction

- Documenting quality of care outcomes
- Strengthening their ability to contract successfully with managed care

Yet it is obvious that not all organizations can win, and some won't even survive the next few years.

If there is no real secret about knowing what to do, and we agree that we care enough to do it, we must ask why more change has not happened within the industry—that is, led by the industry as opposed to being forced from outside. Possibly the real issue is overcoming inertia and the fear of change inherent in moving forward into the unknown. Yes, the industry may need to retrench—but not hunker down where it has been over the last decades. It must move to a new, more defensible, and stronger position from which it can more successfully launch its efforts.

As discussed, there are beliefs and mental models that underlie a decision to deal with these issues head-on or to avoid them. Those models make up the milieu of an organization's culture and spirit. Without recognizing the need for adaptation in these deeply embedded beliefs and values the organization breathes, any change initiative will be short-lived. With that recognition, then, comes the challenge of making the specific strategies to be employed and the actions taken tangible.

Skills in making the imperatives for and the barriers to change visible will be necessary in this time of transition. This assumes the underlying skill set of identifying and leveraging the motivators and drivers of action. The future is both unknown and unknowable. With the accelerated pace of change and development we encounter, the probability of predicting a future with any degree of confidence is minimal. Yet the future cannot be denied, and we must prepare ourselves and our organizations. The future will be painted by the dynamic forces present today and as they evolve over time. These forces are subliminal, and their systemic interaction even less apparent.

Systems thinking tools such as causal loops and the archetypes documented in *The Systems Thinker*[5] are examples of the types of tools that can be used by a skillful practitioner to help make the invisible visible. Through a process of surfacing underlying assumptions and relationships, validating them explicitly, and discussing their relative weight and impact, it is possible to engage larger groups of people in understanding the underlying structure of the change. Beginning to talk in the language of systemic interaction and recognizing the delays inherent in action/reaction can begin to raise the consciousness of the organization. When people are able to converse intelligently about their market and environment, even when they don't have all the answers, their confidence in their ability to drive their own path increases.

This may seem a daunting task, but it need not be so. Start with a generally accepted cause-and-effect relationship fundamental to a strategic effort. Working with your peer group, ask what that relationship is and how it works. For example, there is an assumed relationship between physician commitment and the ability to improve quality. If this is so, does improving quality strengthen physician commitment? Or does improved physician commitment drive the ability to improve quality? Is there consensus within the group on which is the driver characteristic? What assumptions lie behind this belief? Does talking about this relationship suggest actions that could be taken to increase the positive results through working on different leverage points than those traditionally chosen?

The old adage "better the devil you know than the one you don't" rings true in this instance. Through naming and defining forces acting in the market and pushing on old traditions, the force is no longer a faceless specter but a dynamic that can be recognized and measured. Health care professionals are, by and large, scientists in nature. Give them the opportunity to analyze a problem—measure it, weigh it, give it a litmus test for reaction—and they can deal with not only large and complex issues, but also those where the prognosis is not positive. It is the unknown that causes fear and resistance.

Articulating the forces and surfacing properties consistent with other, more familiar dynamics can free people up to take action. An example of this is the current absorption in managed care and the tumult that the pressure to handle it successfully creates in each market where it emerges. A look at what about managed care invokes fear is worthwhile. Most people in an integrated delivery system are related to care giving. On their own, caregivers aren't certain what the implications of managed care are for them. Who defines the care? Who manages it? How do we know? How will we find out? All of these questions swirl in the mind of a nurse manager who is told by her CEO to "get ready" for managed care.

Aside from the fact that the first hurdle is being included in a contract so that the nurse manager can deliver care, there is really very little that will be different for the frontline caregivers. Health care organizations have been working on improving the value of their service and demonstrating outcomes for many years now. To this point, by far the focus has been on acute care and managing the efficiency of a given diagnosis. Managed care will expand the boundaries and the scope at which improvement may be aimed, but the guiding principles (the right care for the right patient at the right time delivered in the right way) are unchanged. With current relationship dynamics, this aim is difficult to achieve. Incentives will be changed through the use of risk pools, but the *aim* remains the same. In fact, well-designed risk pools motivate commitment to that aim and reinforce actions to achieve it. A simple dialogue to help caregivers see that their imperatives for quality and demonstrated value have not changed could go a long way toward easing their fears. Once the energy diverted to worrying is released, they will allow themselves to focus on those parts of the delivery continuum and the strategy being deployed over which they have control. It is the necessary act of calming a fear or naming the unknown that must happen before most individuals free their minds up adequately to work on appropriate new challenges. There is a nearly tangible sigh of relief when an organization's caregivers are authorized to do what they do best—with an imperative for improvement.

Key performance outputs of an integrated delivery system will of necessity include financial profitability, clinical outcomes, process innovation/performance improvement, and satisfaction. One means of building staff understanding of the strategy would be to work through how these (or other) measures relate to the staff's work; further, to show how balanced successful performance across all indicators describes a viable operation, which translates to continued job security. This is *what's in it for them* and will help them grasp market dynamics, the importance of organizational reaction, and their role in its success. This empowers them and motivates them. Beyond this, their understanding that such a balanced scorecard is needed to monitor the organization's current performance as well as to have leading indicators of longer-term success will stand the organization in very good stead.

Common Characteristics of Current Reality

The health care "system" has never been a true system. Rather, it is a set of programs, services, financing vehicles, and care providers linked—often against their will—by their need for each other to treat and cure patients. Patients and payors/purchasers have most frequently been viewed as outside the "system," which, if defined at all, was simplistically viewed as physicians and their workshops, hospitals. Physicians and hospitals formed an uncomfortable alliance where hospitals depended on physicians to bring them patients and so courted those physicians who came most frequently and with the most lucrative demands. The reimbursement system—also not operating in a systemic way—encouraged episodic utilization and treatment models. Over the last 10 years, changes in payment mechanisms have largely driven changes in the way care is organized and delivered. In many markets today the hodgepodge of payment mechanisms—from fee-for-service to global capitation—has created a perverse set of incentives that divide the continuum of providers and reinforce their competition instead of their collaboration.

A *system* is defined as a group of interacting elements forming a complex whole.[6] Many traditional health care organizations have tacked the word *system* onto their names with few, if any, substantive changes in the way they define their work, work processes, or outcomes.

The theory behind the development of integrated delivery systems designed to successfully accept and manage risk are a strategic response to the insanity of these misaligned incentives that not only increase the cost of care, but also have the potential to negatively impact quality. The challenge is that the mental models necessary to conceive, design, and implement systemic integration is in many ways counter to those that have led to success in the traditional health care industry. This is the imperative for today's system managers: to provide incentives, reinforcement, logic, and mandate for the competitive components of care delivery to recognize the mutual benefit of collaboration. These benefits must be defined in terms of the immediate constituents—the pieces and parts of the soon-to-be system—and the larger constituency of the community. Effective deployment for strategy implementation requires effective deployment of a shared understanding of these benefits. Concurrently, it will be critical to change the measurements of success by which individual organizations or components are governed. Application of collaborative values and systems theory in tandem with tangible rewards for performance will be effective in moving the industry's leadership to a new perspective.

The indicators of successful performance today—profitability, satisfaction, and clinical outcome—will continue to be the indicators of success for tomorrow's systems. The difference will be in their breadth of application. Instead of measuring profit purely on the basis of unit revenue minus unit cost, it will be determined by the delivery system's ability to provide a health outcome for an individual at a price set by the market. Satisfaction will address a member's assessment of the entire experience, including transitions from one site to another. The loyalty factor—how committed the patient/member is to remaining in the system—will matter more than simple satisfaction. Outcome will move beyond mortality, infection, or episode-specific results to functional health status.

If it is true that people and systems produce what they are reinforced to produce, the question for leadership is how to transition organizational targets from one set of performance standards to the other, aligning the organization in this new and expanded direction. Making certain that this new scorecard is consistent with the espoused values of the organization and drives strategies that achieve its vision is one critical element of leaders' new work.

The Dynamics of Systemic Change

At root, it is necessary to understand the dynamics of the system. Only by understanding the action/reaction of different components of the system can its real structure be understood. Through that approach, it is possible to understand the motivators and reinforcers that have kept the current system in its historical state of equilibrium. From that, it is a natural progression to recognize what factors have changed, thereby destroying the balance within the industry and its markets, and a new picture can be drawn that provides necessary perspective for understanding leverage points for today and tomorrow. This understanding is a prerequisite for successfully deployed and executed strategies.

Figure 5.2 offers a generic model reflecting, at a high level, the changes in the system. The loops to the left reflect an understanding of the current dynamics of purchaser pressure for downward prices, limiting unit revenues. The right loop depicts a theory of how provider ability to capitate—and

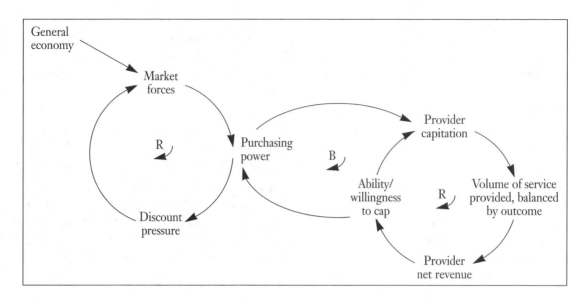

Figure 5.2. Theory of change.

pull business into capitated contracts—can change this dynamic, increase the purchaser's perception of value, and release pressure on unit price decreases.

For each organization developing its own strategy and deployment plan, it would be important for that leadership team to understand and articulate its own theories leading to identification of leverage points. Figure 5.2 is an example of how a deeper understanding is built on the broader assessment and theory of change. This process positions leaders for two important acts. First, it helps them think through their own beliefs and assumptions about their market and organization and identify if there are significant assumption discrepancies within the leadership team. Second, it provides a framework for dialogue within the organization at multiple levels. This conversation is often neglected because it does not lead directly to a specific decision or action. That belief is fatally flawed. It is through conversation that shares a fundamental understanding of the market conditions in which the organization exists that a recognition of the need for change and the willingness to step outside traditional boundaries and begin redesign comes. The success of the organization in its transition is directly correlated to the degree to which the workers—care deliverers, support staff, and administrators—all commit to the effort. Commitment cannot be mandated.

Leverage points are those vital few elements of the system that have a disproportionately large influence on the system's performance and direction. When one needs to change the direction of a large boat, the rudder position is altered. As the water flows over the rudder it pushes the bow with opposite force, and the directional change is accomplished with greater efficiency than by trying to push on the bow directly. The rudder provides leverage for the boat. The larger the boat, the heavier the rudder, and the harder it is to push it against the water's flow. In some cases a smaller trim rudder is attached to the main rudder. It operates in exactly the same fashion; shifting its direction changes the flow of water, and the water pushes the rudder around and results in the bow's movement. The trim rudder is a far more efficient way to accomplish the directional goal.

Efficient strategy deployment should use the same concept and seek the leverage points that will have a trim rudder effect on the organization. Often, these factors are overlooked because they may not be mainstream. They may have to do with environmental factors that are subtle. The results of working on the leverage points may not be dramatic, but are robust in sustaining the change process.

Building Strategy Based on Leverage

Using the example given, a priority goal may be to reduce waste throughout a defined service continuum in order to be successful under a changed reimbursement system rewarding lower costs. This new question—how to accomplish this goal—can be considered from a systemic structure perspective and from one of interpersonal commitment. The first dialogue will help the team identify the critical point in the structure or care delivery process where a small change can have larger impact. The second dialogue will surface the issues and frames of the people involved, allowing a strategic initiative to address both concurrently. Figure 5.3 is an example of how such a set of dynamics may be drawn out to generate thoughtful discussion. It translates a system archetype known as "limits to growth" to the health care environment, given one theory of how constraints on governmental ability to raise taxes and cut Medicare benefits will impact the growth in Medicare risk products.

Strategy and Action

Translating Strategy to Action

Once the key points for action are identified, it is a simple matter to bring together those limited players with knowledge about the action or change needed and the element or factor being acted upon. If the higher level stories have been communicated, the team members will understand the organizational imperative for their success and the implications upstream and downstream of action taken. Having this context, their appreciation for the need to take action will drive their initiative. Tools learned through process/quality improvement teams come in handy in this new change effort.

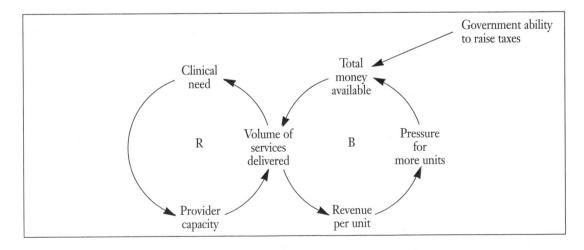

Figure 5.3. Change model for growth in Medicare risk products.

Neither the health care industry nor specific markets and organizations remain in a period of simple, continuous change. Instead, they are characterized by complex, discontinuous change. Trend lines and projections of impact are useful from a directional standpoint, but the market's dynamics are so intense that organizations must be able to mobilize resources quickly to address new opportunities and threats as they arise. This requires an orientation toward building in excess management capacity in an era heralding "lean and mean" as an operating style. Again, the power of an entire organization conversant with the market and its undulations is clearly one important way to manage this apparently conflicting need. An organization focused on achieving a shared vision, with a commonly held understanding of the importance and value of change and the knowledge to understand the rationale behind a particular strategic initiative, will be better able to fill in the gaps, operationally, when parts of the organization are pulled off line to fight other fires.

This is not an argument for curtailing routine organizational efforts in continuous strategic and business planning. While it is true that specific crises or opportunities may not be predictable, a thorough understanding of the market's dynamics can predict trends and tendencies and facilitate an ever-ready preparedness. Successful ambushes will be less frequent. A good leadership team will build organizational competencies in response to likely demands resulting from those trends, and should be doing so routinely.

The business planning cycle and a marketplace tracking system should be concurrently developed and operating, providing critical information for iterative, double-loop learning. The understanding of the marketplace as a whole should lead to identification of specific actions the organization should take in response and/or to new competencies it should be building for the long haul. The impact those initiatives have on the market should be captured within the tracking system, and course corrections made. To use a sailing analogy; the vision of the organization is the compass course the boat charts. The specific point of sail used at any particular time is a function of the wind, the seas, the hullspeed, and the design capacity of the boat. It will tack back and forth across its course to achieve its ends. It is the same with the use of a strategic business plan with a multiyear directional end point. Each time the business plan cycles through, that end point is revalidated and the course is reset along with the planned series of tacks needed in the foreseeable future. Throughout that series, gusts of wind, the presence or absence of other boats, or other factors may necessitate a shift in the sequence, but the end point and directional effort remain constant.

By its very nature, the degree of progress toward that end point is not always apparent. Depending on wind direction, for example, there are times when it actually seems the boat is moving away from its goal. This can be very confusing to the crew members, who are struggling mightily to keep on course and maintain speed. A technique for helping them understand and continue their efforts is the set of linked scorecards. These scorecards should be correlated to the defined business strategy and actions and should be deployed in a fashion consistent with the implementation effort needed down through the organization. The scorecard should reflect the intersection of the organization's beliefs and values about what is important for long-term success and the decisions on critical action variables.[7]

For many organizations, the operational budget is the only scoring system deployed vertically and horizontally throughout the organization. That budget, increasingly focused on unit cost management, is often the most current and pervasive indicator of how the budget unit is performing. Unfortunately, budgets may be prepared and disseminated without explicitly linking them to business initiatives or understanding their implications for related results. Often budgets are built on history, a sure way to reinforce that doing the same things in basically the same ways is the road to success. This is inconsistent with encouraging fundamentally different performance and thinking. The sole indicator being used, then, is not connected to the organization's goals and is sometimes perceived to be arbitrary. The budget can be a very effective component of a scorecard that tells a story to each unit of what the organization expects from that unit and how that expectation is linked to the expectations and needs the organization has of itself as a whole.

Capital allocation is another key indicator of the organization's strategic intent that is seldom explicitly tied to stated strategy. Particularly in this era when organizations need to change their mental models, it is interesting to consider how many organizations continue to allocate capital to traditional needs. Review of the journals demonstrates the dichotomy. On facing pages to articles dealing with the need to resize delivery systems are reports on dollars committed to bricks-and-mortar initiatives. Garnering headlines are stories of multimillion-dollar commitments to build information systems and other infrastructure issues. If the industry is over-bedded and over-resourced and it is known that new and more timely ways to acquire and manipulate information will be an increasingly critical success factor, why do the trade journals treat one decision as though it is natural and the other as particular enough to deserve special mention? By explicitly tying capital allocation—for equipment, technology, and other hard assets—to strategy, this gap will demand attention and may be better addressed. Similarly, decisions to commit capital to hard assets instead of to development of people and their competencies may also come under review.

Strategy for a Moving Target

Referenced previously was the need for a tracking system for organizations and their markets. Historically, the best organizations were quite conversant with their performance and the drivers of that performance. Over the last few years they have become interested in their competitors' performance and have developed tools and data repositories to allow analysis of aggregate provider performance in most markets. A need to understand the market, its preferences, and pressures is a relatively recently phenomenon for many health care organizations. It comes from a product mentality: This is a clinical service we can deliver (and/or expand). If we build it, they will come. If the indications of the future are correct, this mind-set will lead to an increasing number of unneeded programs all requiring support from organizations with limited discretionary resources. What is needed, then, is skill in recognizing the forces of change and preference in the market and the ability to translate those to needs that will be realized. A corollary skill will be the ability to communicate those needs to the providing organization in a sufficiently compelling manner that it chooses to respond to those needs rather than to its own preferences.

Given the importance of monitoring the environment and customers, the available data are often contradictory and unclear. One response in that situation is simply to rely on what is known—which by definition means reviewing history and using it to project forward. This is like driving down a highway at night by looking only in the rearview mirror. Even if the headlights do not provide a bright view of the road far ahead, looking in that direction will surely bode better for the organization.

A technique developed about 20 years ago by Royal Dutch Shell, when attempting to plan for the dynamic oil industry, is scenario planning. In essence, this is a process of painting several alternative futures in some detail. Each needs to be reasonable, given the dynamics at play. One approach is to develop one picture driven by dynamics that fall in a relatively positive way, one where everything that could go wrong does, and one with a mix of good and bad events. Spending time among the leadership building the scenarios goes a long way in further cementing the relationships at the root of the ability to implement decisions made. Surfacing the various strategic initiatives and imperatives that the organization should take to deal with each scenario develops a breadth of choices. Typically, a very limited number of options will surface consistently among all three scenarios. These may well be the context for the leverage points that can have the greatest impact on the organization's success.

Other techniques are available to assist the organization in selecting strategies for its future. The critical issue is that leadership accept the responsibility for driving the organization to its future, rather than managing its current performance. Time spent understanding this imperative will be time well spent. It will set the expectation throughout the organization that development and change are important. It focuses governance and leadership on modifying practice, habits, and policies inconsistent with future needs. This translates rapidly to middle management and frontline employees and, when followed by consistent and clear guidance on priorities and pace, brings the organization into alignment.

The process of deploying specific initiatives, along with discerning the role of various departments and units, can be delegated. This is the intersection of organizational development, strategic deployment, operational implementation, and scorecards. How it is communicated, the focus and priority, the daily work trade-off and actions, and the process for evaluation all must be explicitly integrated. This integration need not be orchestrated by the leaders, the need for it must be mandated by them. Accountability for success of the integration is owned at the CEO level, making it apparent to all that the organization's future success is contingent on organizational commitment to a set of interactive strategic initiatives.

Case Studies

ABC Health Care System, an organization composed of acute care, primary care, long-term care, behavioral health care, and a financing/insurance component, was challenged with making all the pieces work together to create an integrated health care delivery system capable of accepting and managing financial and clinical risk for its contracted population. Over the years it had learned that, left alone, the manifest destiny approach of each of its business units would lead to conflict and internal competition—expenditure of resources against each other rather than against market forces. The system's senior leadership engaged in a planning process, built on an assessment of the external market and its requirements as a customer of the system. The result left the group far from complacent. Radical improvement in productivity of the system in accomplishing wholly new outcomes would be needed to be successful. The role of system leadership in setting the parameters of success, providing forums in which managers could address their issues and resolve differences, and providing resources (information, time, and process) to work through the issues was accepted and action taken.

In an effort to ensure deployment, the organization's leaders surfaced their beliefs relative to the core businesses and business practices or disciplines of the system. Care delivery, care management, covered life acquisition, and business system support were the four core processes identified. The purpose and role of each of these was clearly articulated as each pertained to the system's vision of itself. Additionally, the inherent conflicts and potential synergies of the core processes with each other were surfaced. Leaders of the areas were identified, not necessarily operational leaders over the functions incorporated in the core processes.

Management was brought together to understand the system's perception of the roles, responsibilities, and deliverables of each area, and teams were chartered at the system level and for each core process. Just as the work of each core process was subordinate to that of the system, the planning cycle was also designed in a cascaded format. As the strategic plan identified system work, deliverables, and measurable results, it set the expectation for the work of each of the core processes. The planning activity within each area identified priority areas for work, which were considered for systemic implications. When these were understood, clarity in direction and pace could be stated for each core process's work, and deliverables and measures would be developed. In the same way, the entities and/or functional areas composing the core processes would be provided direction and then allowed to develop their own approach within higher level parameters.

This process accomplished several objectives. First, it ensured linkage in focus, resource allocation, and implementation throughout the system's organizational initiatives. Second, it improved the knowledge base of all those in the system as to why certain commitments were being made. Third, it allowed maximum autonomy at increasingly lower levels of the organization as to how work would be done, tied together by outcome and scorecards rather than by micromanagement and control.

XYZ Health System, in a different market, was faced with transitioning an organization acknowledged as highly successful in its current environment to a similarly successful position in a vastly different and evolving market. The senior team, again, forced itself to spend the necessary time together to come to a common understanding of what the expected changes were in the market and its dynamics. On the basis of that shared common group, the question of how the organization could best respond —functionally—was asked. In this organization, the preeminence of clinical care was unquestioned. The central capability, then, was clearly in improving the care delivery process across the continuum. It became apparent that administrative involvement would be inadequate to appropriately design or to engage the commitment of clinicians. Rather, they needed to feel independently and legitimately involved in work critical to the organization's success.

Leveraging the organization's traditional team-oriented and egalitarian management approach, it was determined that clinical operations would be divided into institutional and physician components and that hospital-based services delivered by employed physicians would be led through the physician component, not the institutional. Conversely, the traditional medical staff support functions would remain within the purview of the institutional component, because the medical staff has no reason for existence outside the hospital. Other leadership functions were placed on par with that critical one. A council incorporating the traditional leadership was established to provide direction to the organization. Another council, designed for consistent, clear communication and rapid-fire response/execution was named to incorporate the heads of all the various operating entities and key support functions. It was further determined that a strategic operations team was needed to translate the direction from the strategy council into the increasingly hard trade-off decisions demanded by the changing health care environment.

Over the ensuing months, the team rearticulated and committed to the strategic imperative for development and execution that would further change its management systems and potential structure. The dialogue was held in the open and under conditions of absolute integrity and honesty. Though a difficult process, and one that demands tact and a strong humanistic orientation, delicate subjects were raised and addressed.

On the basis of this clarity at the senior level, it is now possible for the organization to commit itself—from the leadership level all the way to frontline employees and medical staff—to new methods of behavior to accomplish the aim established by the board years previously. Most importantly, the team determined not to attempt substantive decision making that lasts over time without the active engagement of the management team.

With this central core of commitment, deployment of the strategic intent through the organization can be carried out by any member of the management team, with confidence that the message being sent is consistent. Even more important, by thrashing out the basis for decisions and their probable trade-off in terms of resource allocation, the senior team has committed itself, in unison, to stand behind the actions to be taken.

Lessons Learned
Creating/Developing Strategy

• This is a new day, and the formation of strategy is organic, evolving as the dialogue continues. This is in contrast to the old days when projections of future growth and revenues was more formulaic and hospital strategic planning largely meant selecting between various bricks-and-mortar options. Today's strategy requires building, but building of new relationships and alliances to build synergistic organizations.

• Leadership teams need diversity in terms of knowledge base, mental models, and starting positions. That means there will also be diversity in the ability or speed of all team members to grasp certain new concepts. The need to explain, diagram, and be explicit should be thought of as a benefit, forcing the resulting strategies to pass high hurdles for logic and power.

• At the same time, most leadership teams have been at the same work for a number of years, reinforced into a similar mental model of the market's dynamics. With these dynamics radically changing, it should be expected that there will be resistance among the team members to surfacing and dealing with the new questions just because they are outside the framework of their experience. It must be noted: Leaders did not get to be leaders by failing—their beliefs about how the world works have been effective for them and their organizations for many years.

• There must be a compelling reason to change to lift the leadership team members to a new altitude from which they can consider their environment. Because of the diversity of the team members, that reason must be translatable into several different implications. Some should be forward looking, pulling the team to a positive new horizon. Some must be threatening, like thundering clouds at their back.

Deploying Strategy

• Today's strategies are founded on the interactions of people and organizations much more than on hard assets. As one management team learned, "When I'm in the room it is planning, and when I'm not it is plotting." This need to be involved, to understand, and to fingerprint the resulting decision is important. While clearly not everyone can be in the room where the highest leverage decisions are made, the days are past when effective deployment merely means giving marching orders. Organizations today must engage the minds and wills of their people, in addition to their hands. This requires a new commitment to communication and building understanding throughout the organization.

• One means of accomplishing this is to use the concept of cascading communication and strategic implications. The higher level cannot design an implementation process as effectively as those involved in the implementation who do the work. This theory of deployment requires trust—the needed outcomes are expressed and a dialogue held with staff where they are given an opportunity to understand and test the strategy, and then are asked to develop their plans consistent with that of the higher level and are explicitly trusted to do so. In turn, they will need to explain to their subordinates and team members their intent, engage their commitment, and then trust the next level.

- All of this is supported by a similarly deployed accountability system, but one where people are expected to play a strong self-policing role. The role of senior leaders, then, is to role model the new behaviors, asking new sets of questions and overtly carving out those activities that reinforced the old way of doing business. If the strategic inept is clearly tied to both measures of outcome and to reinforcement systems deployed throughout the organization, alignment will follow. The stronger the measures and reinforcement systems, the more rapid and tight the alignment.

Managing Strategic Implementation

- The command-and-control mentality requires a "dot every *i*/cross every *t*" orientation. If that was ever effective, it won't be today. The market is moving too quickly, and the relationships on which successful achievement of most strategic aims depend are too dynamic. Again, trust plays a role. The direction must be set. Unacceptable behaviors, choices, and detours must be articulated in a broad policy way—not in a list of do nots. Staff members can be held accountable for judgment within these parameters. This gives them more flexibility and more empowerment and will lead to better results.

- Accountability is deployed, however, along with flexibility. Through this process, organizational control will be gained on the basis of self-control.

- The last 10 years have seen a significant number of management methods applied to improve results. Build on these tools, don't attempt to replace them. Total quality management, operations improvement, reengineering, and work redesign are all full of tactical tools that can be used to enhance the process of implementation. Use those that the organization has already invested in developing.

Course Corrections and Improvement

- View deviations from the set course as opportunities for learning, not as errors to be expunged. Why did it appear necessary to alter the plan's implementation? If the deviation was accidental, what could make the process more robust and less apt to be subject to whims and external pressures?

- Build a storehouse of knowledge about how well the process works to create alignment, as well as how accurately the predictions and assumptions on which the plan was built play out. Consciously review this learning, at least at the point in time when the cycle begins again, if not more frequently.

- When a course correction is appropriate, demand an explicit statement explaining it. Were the assumptions on which the course was set in error? Did new events occur that changed the dynamics? Were capabilities or capacity misunderstood? It is through examination of these and similar questions that the new course can be set more effectively.

Conclusion

Two critical success facts seem to be absolutely central to effective deployment of strategy in an integrated delivery system. Both are within the complete control of the senior leadership of the organization. The first is the creation of a line-of-sight goal or vision that all members of the organization can see as clearly as can leadership. Buttressing this is a line of communication, stretching from the board through frontline workers. This communication line may use different words and methods, but must contain a message that never falters from the line-of-sight goal. Supporting these is a line of measures, linked to each other and consistently deployed throughout.

The second is a unified management team committed to the core to the same outcome. The time that must be spent to make sure that the team is in true agreement and truly supports the vision, and acknowledges the trade-off inherent in reaching it, is the most powerful weapon the organization has. That team may need to be reconfigured, as physicians need to be much more intimately involved in the macrodecisions a health system makes. Regardless of its make-up, it must present a united front in order to mobilize the organization effectively and efficiently.

Discussion Questions for a One-Hour Senior Executive Meeting

1. What are the strongest forces, external to the organization, driving change? How do those forces interact?

2. What are the strongest forces, internal to the organization, holding us in status quo or resisting change?

3. How do the external and internal forces act on each other today? What could make that interaction change? Would that change likely increase our organization's strength and flexibility, or weaken it?

4. How might we impact that leverage point?

5. What can we, as the senior management team, do to accomplish that?

Discussion Questions for a One-Hour Governing Board Meeting

Present the board with an overview of the environment and its dynamics.

1. Brainstorm and then use a nominal group process to surface answers to the question, "What must the organization do to remain successful in this new environment?"

2. Use a paired comparison process (hoshin planning's interrelationship digraph is an effective tool) to identify drivers and results. On the basis of this, dialogue about prioritization of effort.

3. Focus on differences between causes and effects and what management tools are appropriate.

4. Discuss the board's support for those management tools/skills needed to impact the high-leverage drivers.

Discussion Questions for a One-Hour Process Owners Meeting

Present them with the pictures developed by the board and senior management. Spend time explaining the theory at work behind the pictures.

1. What will the end result of these dynamics look like if change is not successful?

2. How might each of you take this direction and make change happen—using the leverage points identified—in your areas?

3. What result would you expect?

4. How will you know if you achieved that result?

5. What barriers or impediments do you see to taking this action?

6. What incentives or reinforcements exist to support this action?

Notes

1. *American Heritage Concise Dictionary*, 3rd ed. Microsoft ENCARTA '95, 1992-94 Microsoft Corporation.

2. Dan Kim, *Systems Thinking Tools: A User's Reference Guide* (Cambridge, Mass.: Pegasus Communications, 1995), 20.

3. Marshall Loeb, "Where Leaders Come From," *Fortune*, September 1994, 241–242,

4. Peter Senge, Core Competency course, MIT/Organizational Learning Center, September 1994.

5. Dan Kim, *The Systems Thinker* (Cambridge, Mass.: Pegasus Communications).

6. *American Heritage Concise Dictionary*.

7. Chip Caldwell, *Mentoring Strategic Change in Health Care* (Milwaukee: ASQC Quality Press, 1995), 97–132.

Chapter 6

Managing Quality in PROs

Vicki S. Davis

This chapter is designed to share an example of the strategy, implementation, and results of peer review organizations (PROs) in their quest to perform as change agents within health care. By receiving this information as presented from the perspective of a quality improvement coach inside the PRO community, readers have the opportunity to experience this information from within the actual working system.

Total quality management (TQM) is an exciting concept. It usually takes little exposure to create a genuine desire to practice its theory. While compiling these data, I continued to discover that people are interested in doing their jobs well, teamwork really does produce a greater output, and variation is seriously under attack.

The purpose of this chapter is to provide a practical handbook for implementing quality improvement within a PRO and to create a stronger curiosity in each of us about how to direct our efforts toward creating a more streamlined system that will increase appropriate and timely care for the Medicare population. This chapter provides a short history of PROs, including why they exist, and the vision of the Health Care Finance Administration (HCFA) to be carried out by PROs. Also covered is HCFA's definition of quality, how it is measured, what we mean by "partnering" with providers, the training and development of teams, and how all of this relates to the daily work of the PRO. Information management plays a major role in the continued success of process improvement by documenting the approach, progress, and results of improvement efforts for future replication. This chapter looks at the most recent communication system offered to PROs. Finally, a few lessons learned along the way will be shared, with the hope that the efforts of others will result in even better outcomes.

Peer review organizations (PROs) were born in 1982 as a method to provide oversight to the DRG system of financing health care.[1] The goals of the PRO program were to determine if health care services funded by Medicare were reasonable and medically necessary, furnished at the appropriate level of care, and receiving proper billing.[2] Over time, the role of the PRO program evolved into one of mandating quality through a series of contracts with the HCFA. These contracts are referred to as "scopes of work" and generally last three years each.[3] The first three scopes of work focused on issues ranging from detecting inappropriate admissions to identifying problems concerning quality of care. Any apparently inappropriate findings were reviewed by PROs, with hospital physician involvement, and the quality concerns were resolved.

The fourth scope of work shifted its objective to increasing the health status of the Medicare beneficiary by developing and sharing information on patterns of care and outcomes. This information was presented to providers as benchmarks. Both hospitals and physicians alike were more willing to cooperate and even to partner (participate with equal willingness, interest, and effort toward a common goal) with PROs in this benchmarking effort.

The Health Care Quality Improvement Program (HCQIP), created in the Fourth Scope of Work, focuses on the effectiveness and efficiency of services to Medicare beneficiaries. The Fifth Scope of Work, which began staggered implementation across states in April 1996, describes five program goals as the method of accomplishing this mission.[4] They are:

1. Monitoring and improving quality of care

2. Strengthening the community of those committed to improving care

3. Communicating with beneficiaries, providers, practitioners, and plans in order to promote informed health choices

4. Protecting beneficiaries from poor care

5. Strengthening infrastructure

It is through the efforts of HCQIP that HCFA sees the method for attaining its vision: "to guarantee equal access to the best health care."[5] Currently, 53 PROs across the country serve as contractors to HCFA and provide the connection between having a vision and transforming it into reality.[6]

HCFA's strategic plan defines continuous quality improvement (CQI) as "the ongoing state of making better the services provided to customers."[7] HCQIP strives to improve the efficiency and effectiveness of health care to its customers and, as such, CQI is the logical vehicle to satisfy HCFA's definition of quality. To get there, HCFA has carefully outlined its expectations of PROs concerning the implementation of quality.[8]

1. All leadership, management, and staff of contractors must be trained in TQM and CQI concepts, tools, and techniques.

2. Contractors will have a deep understanding of TQM basic philosophy, principles, methods, and terminology.

3. Contractors will be active participants in organizing a system under the TQM philosophy to mobilize the organization toward a single focus.

4. Utilize a TQM and CQI approach in daily operation and demonstrate continued commitment to this approach.

5. Support the development of innovation approaches and implementation strategies to improve the quality of the HCQIP and the way in which it is administered by working with HCFA and other contractors.

6. Define and implement methods and approaches to improve the efficiency and productivity of the processes defined in the contract.

7. Employ CQI techniques, such as statistical quality control, in the development of these improvements and employ these techniques to discover and document special and common causes of process variations that need correction.

8. Participate in exchanges with peers designed to share best methods, forward suggestions for improvement to HCFA on a regular basis, and participate in multidisciplinary quality improvement teams.

These customer requirements are targeted by PROs when identifying measures of success in meeting HCFA's goals of continuously improving the quality of health care for the Medicare population.

Developed as the application of CQI theory to meet HCFA's overall goals, HCQIP is a program of quality improvement activities deemphasizing case review and promoting collaborative efforts. This approach enhances the quality of care for Medicare beneficiaries by supplying providers with information that focuses on patterns of care and identifies current best practices. Another incentive for the hospital to participate in this program is its ability to support Joint Commission on Accreditation of Healthcare Organizations (JCAHO) accreditation standards. Satisfying multiple requirements while increasing the quality of health care to a growing population is an attractive opportunity for the provider community. While each PRO serves the same mission, the details of the processes may be different. The flowchart in Figure 6.1 identifies the steps of an HCQIP cooperative project as defined by HCFA. Each PRO then develops a more detailed process for efficiently implementing the generic plan.

Chapter appendix A is an example of how the Oklahoma Foundation for Medical Quality, which has the PRO contract for the state of Oklahoma, implements projects for HCQIP.[9] This plan is particularly meaningful because of its detail. The design allows a date to be entered as teams move from step to step. This provides an opportunity to understand the impact of variation on total process turnaround time. The summary of tasks to be completed in the HCQIP process at Health Care Excel, the recipient of the PRO contract for Kentucky and Indiana, is illustrated in Figure 6.2. This road map of activity provides steps to be completed, the duration of the task, and the team members responsible for each step in the process.

Another illustration of work to be completed within the HCQIP project process is in chapter appendix B, "Integration Matrix—CIP Timeline and Center Work Phases," as developed by the CIP Engineering Core Work Team at the Michigan Peer Review Organization.[10] The matrix guides team members through the project process by identifying specific boundaries and tasks within each step of the HCQIP process.

Knowing what opportunities to target for improvement is an important detail for PROs selecting new projects. HCFA has assisted PROs in selecting priority projects by providing minimum performance standards in the fifth scope of work. These standards are based on the needs of the Medicare population. The Michigan PRO has developed idea evaluation criteria to help select projects that satisfy HCFA's performance standards (see Figure 6.3).

HCQIP projects originate from a variety of sources ranging from HCFA-directed national efforts to local replications. The most common is probably the analysis of Medicare data. The analysis compares a set of indicators regarding a particular outcome from an individual hospital to a related peer group and to national outcomes. The comparison provides hospitals with a view of clinical outcomes in relation to both groups. Hospitals can use these data in their improvement efforts without fear of disclosure under the Social Security Act (Section 1160) governing peer review organization information, as well as federal confidentiality regulations found in Title 42, Code of Federal Regulations, Part 476, subpart B.[11]

Local projects may be formed as replications of projects done in other PROs. Feedback from the health care community is another important example of an effective way to identify meaningful

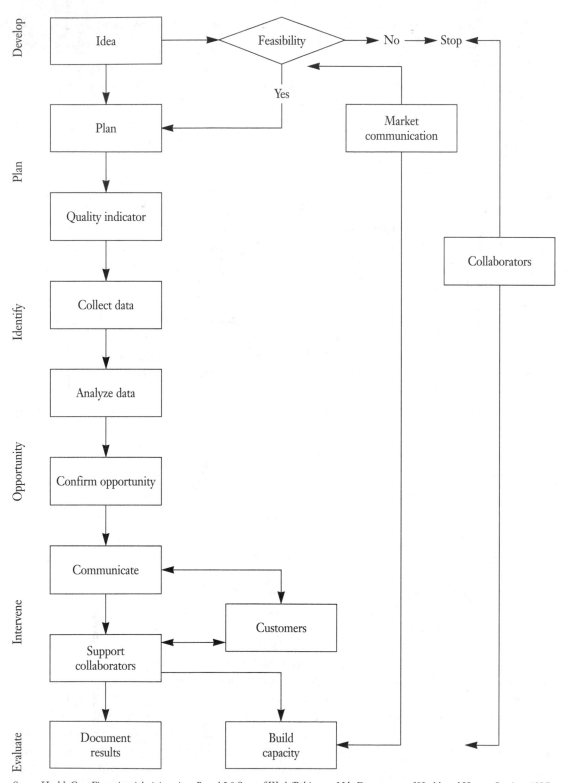

Source: Health Care Financing Administration, *Round 5.0 Scope of Work* (Baltimore, Md.: Department of Health and Human Services, 1995).

Figure 6.1. The steps of an HCQIP cooperative project.

Summary tasks

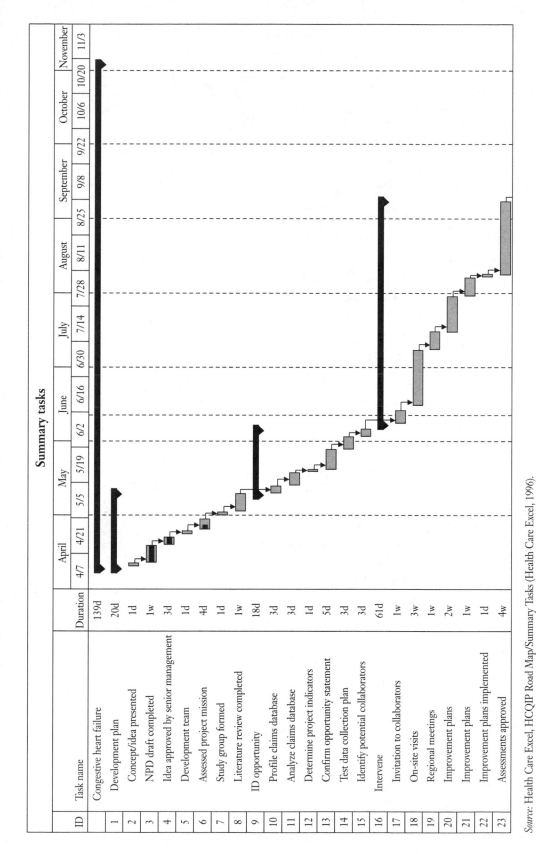

ID	Task name	Duration
	Congestive heart failure	139d
1	Development plan	20d
2	Concept/idea presented	1d
3	NPD draft completed	1w
4	Idea approved by senior management	3d
5	Development team	1d
6	Assessed project mission	4d
7	Study group formed	1d
8	Literature review completed	1w
9	ID opportunity	18d
10	Profile claims database	3d
11	Analyze claims database	3d
12	Determine project indicators	1d
13	Confirm opportunity statement	5d
14	Test data collection plan	3d
15	Identify potential collaborators	3d
16	Intervene	61d
17	Invitation to collaborators	1w
18	On-site visits	3w
19	Regional meetings	1w
20	Improvement plans	2w
21	Improvement plans	1w
22	Improvement plans implemented	1d
23	Assessments approved	4w

Source: Health Care Excel, HCQIP Road Map/Summary Tasks (Health Care Excel, 1996).

Figure 6.2. Summary of tasks to be completed in the HCQIP process.

129

Criteria question	Response
1. What is the goal of the project?	
2. Summarize the support for the medical literature. Identify clinical trials, academic research, or recognized guideline(s) that have been published.	
3. What processes of care does the CIP address? What outcomes will be affected by the process improvement?	
4. How many beneficiaries are affected? (Provide estimates from medical literature applied to Michigan population or from MedPRO.) What will be the impact on beneficiaries? a. Clinical health status? b. Quality of life? c. Specific targeted group (for example, minorities, caregivers)?	
5. Which providers will be targeted for collaboration? What are the barriers to their making improvement?	
6. Is it an issue that Michigan providers will be interested in? How can you substantiate this?	
7. Which specialty societies are interested in this issue? (List, with contact person.) Has each given its support?	
8. Which customer(s) will accrue benefit (beneficiaries, ambulatory setting, hospital inpatient, HCFA)?	
9. Would beneficiaries be interested in this information? In what way?	
10. Is there a beneficiary feedback loop? Would elder services networks support this? How can you substantiate this? Have they been queried?	
11. What barriers exist to the timely completion as a CIP?	
12. How will the cost effectiveness of the CIP be measured for each of the groups listed in item 9?	
13. Anticipated need for PDC—number of records?	

Source: Michigan Peer Review Organization, Idea Evaluation Criteria (Michigan Peer Review Organization, 1996).

Figure 6.3. Idea evaluation criteria.

projects. The examples here show how California Medical Review (see Figure 6.4), the Louisiana Health Care Review (see Figure 6.5), and The Peer Review Organization of New Jersey (see Figure 6.6) request suggestions from the health care community on projects of interest. Simply identifying appropriate projects, however, is not enough. Even the most efficient work can be rendered meaningless if its effects cannot be measured. In fact, measurement has often been described as the most difficult part of the quality improvement process. We think we know when something is better but, in reality, a measurable indicator is the only thing that differentiates an improvement from mere change. Measurement in the fourth scope of work focused on building capacity for quality improvement and thus valued the number of projects completed. The fifth scope of work requires measurement relating

Partners in Quality Improvement

Based in part on suggestions from California hospitals, CMRI is initiating the nine Health Care Quality Improvement Program (HCQIP) projects listed below. We welcome the interest and participation of California's hospital representatives, physicians, and other health care professionals in all our HCQIP projects. We continue to receive recommendations from the health care community for future projects. If you have comments or ideas for us, please take a few minutes to complete the form below and return it, via fax or mail.

FACILITY_____

NAME_____ TITLE_____

DEPARTMENT _____ TELEPHONE NUMBER _____

FAX NUMBER _____

ADDRESS _____

                street   city   state   zip code

PROJECTS

Yes–I'm interested in collaborating with CMRI on this project— please call me.	*I'm not interested in collaborating at this time, but please send me more information about this project.*	Return by Fax: **(415) 882-5991**	Return by Mail: CMRI 60 Spear Street, Suite 500, San Francisco, CA 94105 Attn: Health Services Evaluation and Research

❑	❑	Osteoporosis: Diagnosis and Treatment in Patients with Femoral Head/Neck Fractures
❑	❑	Use of ACE Inhibitors in Congestive Heart Failure
❑	❑	Unstable Angina and LV Ejection Fraction Evaluation
❑	❑	Use of Aspirin in Peripheral Arterial Atherosclerosis
❑	❑	Necessity of Combined Right/Left Heart Catheterization
❑	❑	Use of Endoscopy in UGI Bleeding
❑	❑	Use of ACE Inhibitors in Diabetic Nephropathy
❑	❑	Antibiotic Prophylaxis in Selected Surgeries: Aneurysm Repair and Bowel Resections
❑	❑	Potentially Inappropriate Medication Usage

Are you currently studying any of these projects? If so, please indicate which ones, along with their status.

_____

_____

_____

_____

Are there other projects you'd like to recommend?_____

_____

_____

Is there other information you'd like to read about in this publication? Let us know!_____

_____

For more information, contact your CMRI Region Office: Ann C. Hayman, D.P.A., Regional Director, CMRI Southern Region, Equitable Plaza, 3435 Wilshire Blvd., Suite 200, Los Angeles, CA 90010, (213) 738-5400; or Terry Ramirez, Regional Director, CMRI Northern Region, 60 Spear Street, Suite 550, San Francisco, CA 94105, (415) 882-0934.

Source: California Medical Review, *Health Care Quality Improvement Report* (San Francisco: California Medical Review, 1995).

Figure 6.4. California Medical Review's suggestion form.

Collaborative Projects: New Topic Ideas

Louisiana physicians and providers are encouraged to identify new topics that could provide the basis for a collaborative project effort with LHCR. Current LHCR project ideas are spawned in a variety of ways including independent research, ideas proposed by our research advisory council as well as current health care issues. However, LHCR is also interested in providers' successes in their own CQI project efforts. Thus, we welcome ideas that the Louisiana health care community is currently working on or has a concerted interest in developing. For their part, collaborating hospitals will be able to utilize LHCR's broad database of claims data for provider-specific and comparative reporting, software packages for data collection, and personnel resources in these projects.

Hospitals should also note that participation with LHCR on a cooperative project may be used to meet Joint Commission on Accreditation standards as documented in the last issue of *PRO Report*.

Submitted by: _____   Title: _____

Facility: _____   Phone: _____

Address: _____

Statement of Project/Idea:

Source: Louisiana Health Care Review, *PRO Report: Health Care Quality Improvement Program Newsletter* (March 1994).

Figure 6.5. Louisiana Health Care Review's suggestion form.

to the mission of HCQIP, which is "to promote the quality, effectiveness, and efficiency of services to Medicare beneficiaries." The success of a PRO's process improvement efforts is measured by its achievement of increased timeliness, accuracy, efficiency, and effectiveness in the following areas.[12]

- Cooperative projects
- Mandatory case review
- Beneficiary information on Medicare rights
- Continuous quality improvement
- Data reporting requirements
- Financial management

These areas represent customer expectations; specifically, HCFA's expectations as the primary customer. To improve the measured outcome, it is first necessary to identify the process or processes that impact the measurement of the areas. One process owned by the PRO that produces measurable care improvements is the HCQIP project process. HCFA suggests using a numerator/denominator–type indicator such as the percentage of total projects resulting in measurable improvements (that is, 93 percent of 44 cooperative projects showed improvement).

Chapter appendix C shows current indicators of process performance for the Michigan Peer Review Organization.[13] Measurement of actual processes themselves is discussed as follows.

"No man is an island," nor is any health care organization. CQI has proven the importance of teamwork over and over again. In today's health care environment, the surest way to produce genuine

We'd like to hear from you . . .

Name: _____

Title:_____

Facility:_____

Address: _____

Telephone Number: _____ Fax: _____

Cooperative Projects: New Topics

Physicians and facilities are encouraged to identify new topics that could form the basis of a possible cooperative project. This form is designed as a means of conveying ideas for new topics to The PRO.

Statement of the idea:

What brought this issue to your attention or makes you think it's important?

Do you have any data on this yet?

Have you read any articles that support the idea as an important one?

What is the question to be answered (i.e., what is the hypothesis)?

What could be measured to demonstrate that the intervention is having an effect?

How do you think this project should be pursued?

The Quality Improvement Report

Is the content of this newsletter beneficial?

What other information would you like to read about in this newsletter?

Source: The Peer Review Organization of New Jersey, *The PROs Quality Improvement Report* (April 1995).

Figure 6.6. The Peer Review Organization of New Jersey's suggestion form.

improvement is through the combined efforts of knowledgeable parties from the point of initiation to completion. Likewise, all players must come to the table when attempting to understand the possibilities for improvement.

The Connecticut Peer Review Organization (CPRO) explains its understanding of this concept and the role played by the PRO in a semiannual report, which reads as follows:

> *The fundamental premise of CPRO's efforts to improve the quality of care delivered to Connecticut patients is continuous quality improvement through collaboration. Because of the health care system's complexity, effecting change can be an enormous challenge. That is why HCFA and the PRO community have actively engaged as many different players as possible in the new Health Care Quality Improvement Program (HCQIP). Buy-in is critical to all of our efforts. CPRO is in a unique position to bring these players to a neutral table at which innovations can be developed and exchanged, all for the improvement of health care quality.*[14]

Figure 6.7 identifies some of the collaborators participating in Connecticut's effort to improve health care quality for Medicare beneficiaries. Including collaborators provides the opportunity to view the projects from a more systematic perspective. Individual collaborators can detail parts of the system to get closer to waste, rework, and needless complexities that, when eliminated, can create greater customer satisfaction.

The major expectation of collaborators is that they participate in the measurement of improvement. PROs operationalize this by requesting that hospitals that collaborate in projects respond to the data with improvement plans: documents that outline the hospital's intent to use the data to create measurable improvement in the process under study. For reasons supporting administrative and timeliness issues, PROs ask the hospitals to return this information to them within 30 days of receiving data.

As HCFA identified in the fifth scope of work, the expectation of PROs is to train employees at all levels in the concepts, tools, and techniques of CQI. Not only is this a requirement, but it is a necessity for effective implementation of quality methodology. To manage with quality, a transformation must take place within the organization. To make the transformation effective, all players need a common understanding of how business will be conducted and what language will be spoken. Tools and techniques create a new approach to making things better, but trying to learn to use them effectively can create a great deal of anxiety for the person who feels untrained.

Many PROs rely on outside conferences and workshops to educate and develop management and supervisory staff in TQM philosophy, principles, methods, and terminology. At one such session in February 1995 called "Partnership for Improvement," Donald Berwick of the Institute for Healthcare Improvement and others introduced members of PRO senior management to an overview of CQI. Since that time, PROs have continued to attend outside events to learn more about all areas of this methodology.

Detailed introduction of CQI concepts to individual PROs has usually been presented by an outside consultant who begins teaching senior leaders the philosophy, followed by an introduction to the actual tools and techniques. Variation seems to occur after this point. Some PROs continue to work with consultants in a variety of ways, such as additional training, facilitating teams, or mentoring the PRO's efforts. Regardless of the method taken, the important thing to note is that training and development must be continuous.

Collaborator	Project(s)
Health care providers • Physicians • Nurses • Hospitals • Ancillary personnel	All
Insurers • United Health Care Insurance Co.	Mammography outreach
Government entities • Commission on Aging • Department of Health Services • Health Care Financing Administration • Veterans Affairs	Mammography outreach, myocardial infarction project–II, all MQIS projects
Managed care organizations	HIV readmissions, mammography outreach
Academic medical centers • Yale University • University of Connecticut Health Center • University of Virginia • University of Pittsburgh • Cleveland Clinic	Cooperative cardiovascular project, myocardial infarction project–II, community-acquired pneumonia, all Medicare quality indicator system (MQIS) projects, unstable angina, mammography outreach, HIV readmissions
Private organizations • American Cancer Society • Elderly Health Screening Services	Mammography outreach
Health services researchers • Thomas Jefferson Health Policy Institute • Agency for Health Care Policy and Research • Patient outcomes research teams	Community-acquired pneumonia, all MQIS projects, blood transfusion, carotid endarterectomy
Other PROs • Alabama, Colorado, Florida, Georgia, Idaho, Iowa, Oklahoma, Utah, Virginia	All MQIS projects, blood transfusion
Consumers • AARP	All
Professional organizations • Connecticut Hospital Association • Connecticut Health Information Management Association • Connecticut State Medical Society • Medical specialty societies • American Medical Association • American Heart Association	Cooperative cardiovascular project, community-acquired pneumonia, all MQIS projects, mammography outreach

Source: Connecticut Peer Review Organization, *Commitment to Quality Semi-Annual Report* (October 1993–March 1994).

Figure 6.7. Some of CPRO's collaborators.

Process improvement teams have played a big role in developing the skills learned in training sessions. Just-in-time training or experiential learning allows staff to make the connection between the tool or technique and how it actually helps to improve the process being addressed.

Team teaching is another method found to be successful in at least one PRO. At Georgia Medical Care Foundation (GMCF), the staff of the PRO department recognized the need for more than introductory training. The department, which is structured in independent work teams, agreed that a refresher course on tools and techniques would increase confidence in using the process improvement methodology in daily work. The approach would not be classroom lecture, and everyone was to be involved. Remaining consistent with the team approach, one person was selected from each work team to participate on a teaching team to research a tool and teach it to the remainder of the department. The criteria used for the teaching teams was that the content of the session had to be accurate and thorough and there had to be some way of knowing the audience both understood and could use the tool or technique. Above all, it should be fun. The CQI coach participated in a support role to all the teams.

In this way, teams covered each tool and technique used within the department. Training took place over a period of four weeks, and the results were memorable. Team members not only benefitted by learning tools, they also had the opportunity to work with different people within the department, creating a common bond and strengthening a culture supportive of CQI. In addition, each person within the work teams had the opportunity to teach at least two tools, thereby ensuring a team resource for every tool used.

Storyboards are also a useful teaching tool. By displaying the work of process improvement teams, staff has the opportunity to see how tools were used throughout the improvement process. Storyboards keep everyone informed by documenting team progress as it occurs. By hanging storyboards in high-traffic areas within an organization, teams celebrate their efforts through peer recognition of their work. Figure 6.8 illustrates the storyboard created by the staff of GMCF'S PRO department while learning to use the storyboard as a tool to educate, communicate, and celebrate team activity.

Maintaining consistency in the education process throughout the organization can be a challenge. KePRO, who holds the PRO contract for Pennsylvania, uses a checklist to ensure the proper training and development of staff at all levels (see Figure 6.9).

Checklists have also proven to be the answer for KePRO to keep teams on track as they go through the improvement process (see chapter appendix D).[15] By relying on written next steps, the team's focus can remain on creating a successful outcome and documenting results to support replication of the project in the future.

Once the initial educational process has been completed, it is natural to feel a great sense of accomplishment. A lot of information has been consumed, the normal work schedule has been interrupted, and it feels like it is time for things to return to normal. Sometimes people comment about being glad to get back to their "real" jobs. The truth is, the work has only just begun. Celebrating the successful completion of the first steps is important and deserves recognition, but knowing how to use a cause-and-effect diagram or be able to recite the definition of a process is still a long way from the desired end results of TQM.

So how do we transform the theory of TQM into the reality of daily work? HCFA's definition that CQI is "the ongoing state of making better the services provided to customers" is a good starting point, since it is a reminder that the process will go on and on. There is no returning to "real" work, because this *is* the real work. All work will now be done based on how it can be done better. No longer

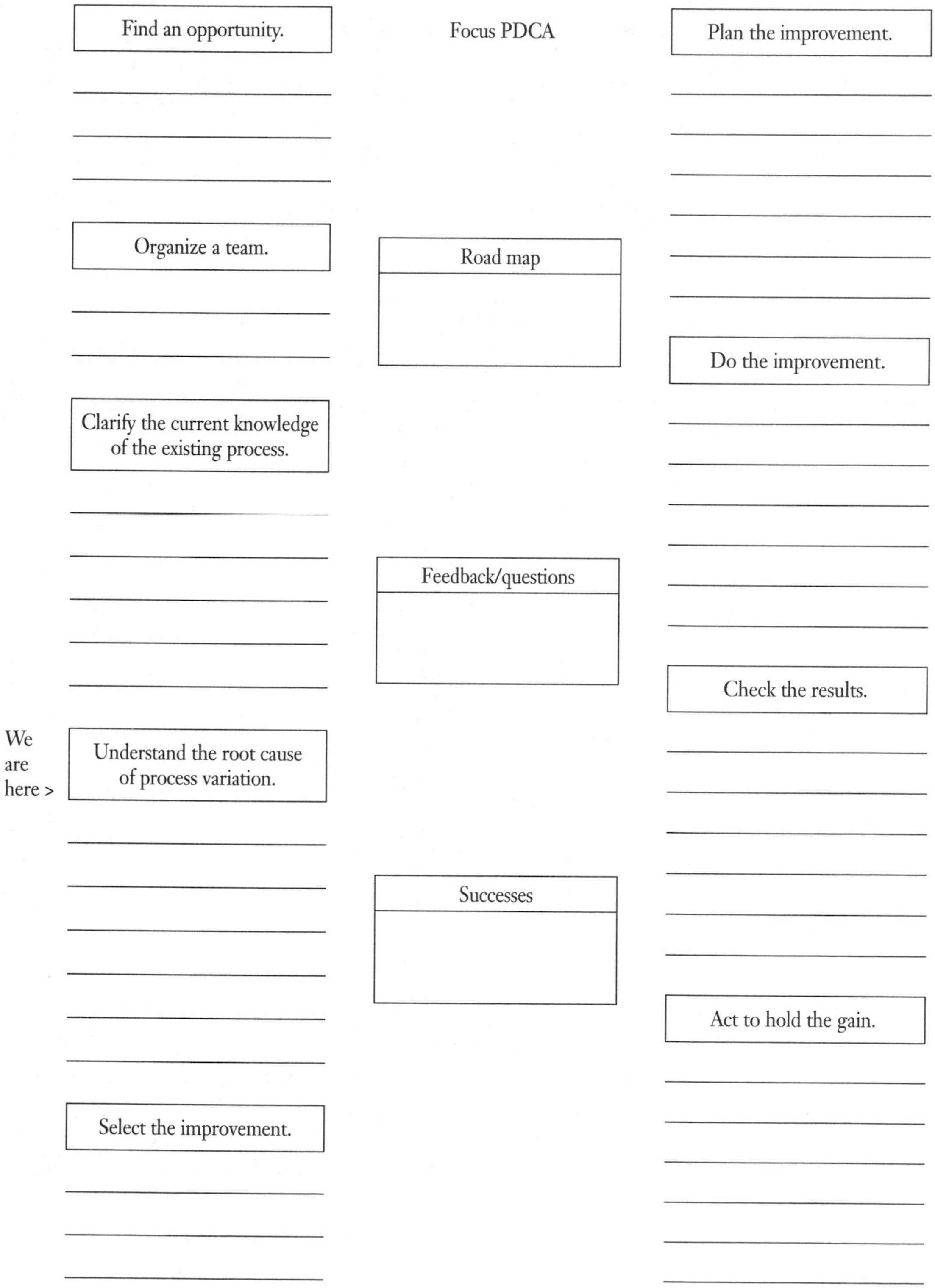

Find an opportunity.

Focus PDCA

Plan the improvement.

Organize a team.

Road map

Do the improvement.

Clarify the current knowledge
of the existing process.

Feedback/questions

Check the results.

We
are
here >

Understand the root cause
of process variation.

Successes

Act to hold the gain.

Select the improvement.

Source: Georgia Medical Care Foundation, 1996.

Figure 6.8. GMCF's PRO department storyboard.

Continuous improvement training/education			
Who	What	When	By whom
Policy and planning committee	TQM/CQI overview; strategies, quality gurus; TQM tools/techniques overview; team-building skills	Initial: August/ September 93 plus ongoing inservices	TQM consultant
Management/supervisory staff	TQM/CQI overview; leadership skills; team-building skills; TQM tools and techniques; problem-solving skills and techniques; empowerment	Initiated: February 94 Monthly 1.5 hours	P&P committee CI/SD staff Outside consultants
Facilitators	TQM/CQI overview; quality gurus; team-building skills; in-depth TQM/CQI tools and techniques	Prior to team/committee assignment and ongoing inservices	TQM consultant P&P sponsor
Committee/team leaders	TQM/CQI overview; leadership skills; team-building skills	Participation on team/ committee	Facilitator
Committees	TQM/CQI overview; tools/ techniques; problem-solving skills; team-building skills	JIT (just in time)	Facilitators, P&P members, outside seminars
Quality improvement teams	TQM/CQI overview; tools/techniques; problem-solving skills; team-building skills	JIT (just in time)	Facilitators
General staff	TQM/CQI philosophies and overview; team-building skills; communication skills	Introductory sessions: May 94 and ongoing	Communications and Awareness Committee and P&P committee
Project data collection team	Data collection training, disease philology/process	Prior to designing the PDC instrument	Project leader
Project data collection abstractors	Data collection training, disease philology/process	Prior to collection of PDC	Staff epidemiologist and other expert staff as project dictates

Source: KePRO, 1996.

Figure 6.9. KePRO's training and development checklist.

will the target be the completion of a task, but rather the understanding and improvement of each process required to produce a successful outcome compared to customer expectations. This includes the identification of waste, rework, and variation.

There is a key word in HCFA's definition of quality: *customers*. The reason we exist is to satisfy or exceed customer expectations, and this is the first step in the CQI transformation. The following questions regarding organizing the production of health care as a system should be asked of all senior PRO staff.[16]

- Who are the primary customers of the PRO?

- What are the needs and expectations of our customers?

- What does the PRO provide to meet those needs and expectations?

- What indicators are used by the PRO to measure the success of meeting customer needs and expectations?

- What plan is used by the PRO to improve the process or processes performed routinely to satisfy customer needs and expectations?

- What measurement is used to show improvement in processes?

The following illustrates how Georgia Medical Care Foundation answered those questions and used the answers to tie theory to reality.

1. Who are the primary customers of the PRO?
   —Health care facilities
   —Doctors
   —HCFA
   —Medicare beneficiaries
   —Managed care companies
   —Coworkers
   —Board of directors
   —Federal and state agencies

2. What are the needs and expectations of customers?
   —Data
   —Support
   —Health care security means appropriate, effective, and efficient care and billing
   —Meaningful work
   —Dissemination of credible information on which to base improvements
   —Staff at all levels educated in continuous improvement
   —A strategy that provides evidence of achieving a vision
   —Measured improvements in all areas supporting the strategy
   —Widespread replication of improvement and innovation
   —Fiscal appropriateness

3. What does the PRO provide to meet those needs and expectations?
   —Data analysis
   —HCQIP cooperative projects
   —Interagency coordination
   —Information
   —Education/consultation
   —Improved clinical management
   —Capacity for improvement
   —Plan for improvement (strategy)
   —Communication/marketing
   —Product evaluation/measurement

4. What indicators are used by the PRO to measure the success of meeting needs and expectations?
   —Percentage of projects resulting in a measured improvement
   —Number of provider process improvement teams generated as a result of an HCQIP project
   —Number of agencies represented on each PRO-initiated coalition
   —Number of provider feedback sessions

—Number of Medicare program informational sessions
—Number of projects entered into QIP
—Percentage of reviews done on time out of total number of reviews
—Percentage of projects addressing multiple objectives
—Percentage of duplicated projects out of total number of projects
—Turnaround time for HCQIP project from point of idea generation to first hospital feedback

5. What plan is used by the PRO to improve the process or processes performed routinely to satisfy customer needs and expectations?
   —A project selection matrix is used as a method to select initial process improvement teams based on customer expectations (see Figure 6.10).
   —Organizing the production of health care as a system[17] (establishes the strategy and tactics for achieving the PRO's vision based on customers' needs, expectations, and definition of quality).

6. What measurement is used to show improvement in processes?
   —A key quality characteristic (indicator) is selected for each process.
   —A baseline measurement and a follow-up measurement are taken to prove improvement versus change.

Georgia Medical Care Foundation answered these questions after the completion of the exercise referenced in question five, organizing the production of health care as a system, as explained by Batalden and Stoltz.[18] This exercise allowed the PRO to connect daily work with the improvement of that work and related both the work and its improvement to the vision of the PRO. Figure 6.11 illustrates the process map developed as a result of this exercise to identify the core processes, support processes, and where customers enter and exit the system. The map was used as a vehicle for the staff to understand how customers experience the work of the department and served to help employees identify their own part in making the customers' experience better. The snapshot of the department's work as a whole connected every individual to some part of the customers' experience and brought new value to the work being done.

The culture of an organization plays a large role in its ability to implement TQM. Culture is playing a big part in the successful transformation to CQI at GMCF, where the embracing of teamwork and risk taking is supported even by the structure of the organization. Each team has a leader that serves in a capacity unlike a traditional manager or supervisor. Team leaders have the specific responsibility of supporting a cooperative environment, promoting a high level of interaction among members, and facilitating team performance through effectively coordinating team skills and encouraging leadership skills in all team members. Because team leaders serve as facilitators for other teams, they possess a higher knowledge of tools and practice facilitation techniques. The result is a better understanding of customer/supplier relationships between teams. Figure 6.12 illustrates the structure of GMCF's PRO department.

Note that team leaders are members of the work teams who provide a technical skill set necessary to successfully complete the work of the team. Individuals are not selected to be team leaders on the basis of technical skills, but rather leadership skills, and the willingness to take on additional responsibilities that include supporting the established culture. As illustrated in Figure 6.12, the department is divided into work teams and support roles. Let's take a closer look at the specifics of the teams.

Expectations	Impact	Customers	Process	Process	Process	Indicators
Cooperative projects Timely Accurate Efficient Effective						
Mandatory case review Timely Accurate Efficient Effective						
Benefit information on Medicare rights Timely Accurate Efficient Effective						
CQI Timely Accurate Efficient Effective						
Data reporting requirements Timely Accurate Efficient Effective						
Financial management Timely Accurate Efficient Effective						

Heavy impact   Moderate impact   Slight impact   No impact

Source: Georgia Medical Care Foundation, 1996.

Figure 6.10. Project selection matrix.

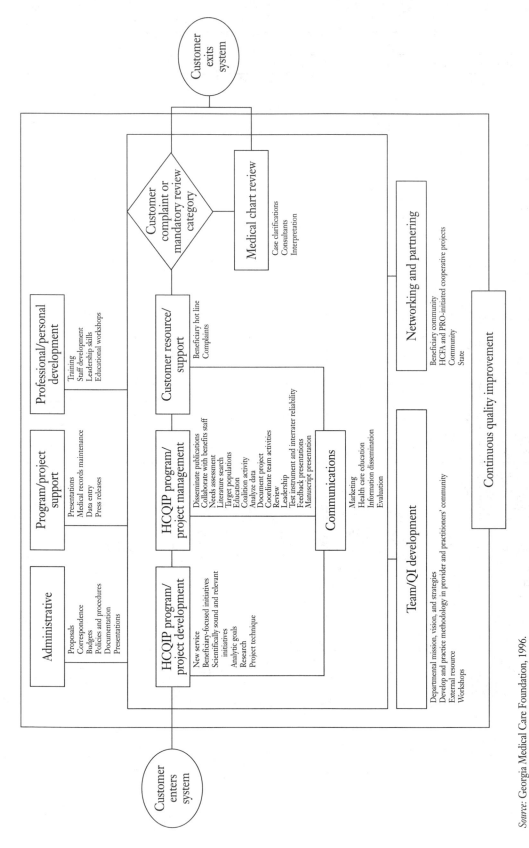

Source: Georgia Medical Care Foundation, 1996.

Figure 6.11. Process map that identifies core and support processes.

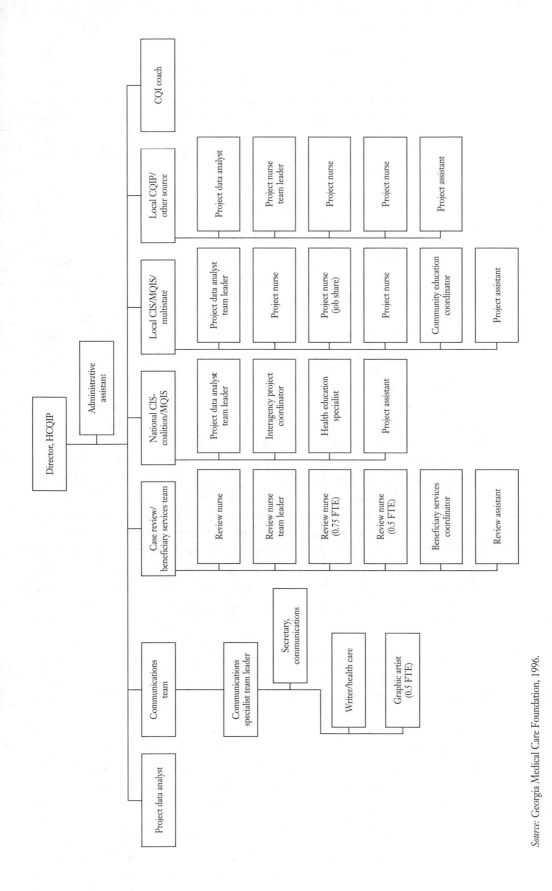

Source: Georgia Medical Care Foundation, 1996.

Figure 6.12. The structure of GMCF's PRO department.

The communications team assumes responsibility for supporting the HCQIP in areas of information dissemination and staff development to better communicate findings to customers. This team also develops and directs the consumer information strategies (CIS) campaigns in partnership with the national CIS-coalition/MQIS team and produces information for beneficiaries by developing brochures and newsletters. The communications team supports the administration of the foundation by producing the annual report and the memorandums of understanding contracts to providers.

The case review/beneficiary services team performs any mandatory fee-for-service reviews or any reviews performed as the result of a beneficiary complaint. This team also supports beneficiaries by presenting informational programs and exhibits, participating in congressional meetings, and supporting the beneficiary hot line.

The national CIS-coalition/MQIS team facilitates and directs the activities of Georgia coalitions related to national initiatives by networking with public and private agencies with interest in the focus area. It also processes and analyzes all HCFA-directed national data sets, including the cooperative cardiovascular project and all MQIS projects, and conducts statewide feedback on these efforts.

Finally, the local CIS/MQIS/multistate team develops local projects from MQIS CIS campaigns and participates in multistate projects. The local collaborative quality improvement partnership (CQIP)/other source team also develops local projects replicated from other PROs or generated from national surveillance data or CQIP.

There are three positions on the chart outside the team structure. These positions—project data analyst, administrative assistant, and CQI coach—support the work of the entire department. This project data analyst supports the multidisciplinary work teams and works with colleagues to develop, implement, and complete national and local quality improvement projects by performing quantitative and qualitative analysis of HCFA claims/surveillance/MQIS data, PRO-originated project data, and other data sources to identify patterns of improvable care and patterns of interest. The administrative assistant supports the entire department in administrative responsibilities to meet HCQIP fifth scope of work expectations and participates on process improvement teams to produce better outcomes in this area. Last, the CQI coach facilitates the development and practice of the quality improvement methodology within the HCQIP department. This person coaches positive change by planning, developing, documenting, and measuring the implementation and growth of the process improvement strategy and activities of the department. The CQI coach works closely with the HCQIP director to provide a department road map based on continuous assessment of current status compared to short-term goals and the long-term vision of the department. Figure 6.13 addresses activities to be completed in order to develop the desired environment. This tree diagram provided the sequence of events for the department's road map. The CQI coach also supports providers throughout the state by providing optional assistance in the development of quality improvement plans for HCQIP projects or any other related needs.

There are specific characteristics required of the individuals hired to fill all department positions in order to support the culture of continuous improvement. Adapted from attributes identified in *Workplace 2000*, some of the characteristics include the ability to demonstrate daily commitment to the mission, vision, and values of GMCF, the HCQIP department, and the HCQIP work team; the ability to demonstrate measurable improvement in meeting and exceeding customer expectations by studying, learning, and practicing process improvement techniques in daily work; and demonstrating a commitment to continuous learning by first understanding the conditions under which learning occurs best. With the start of the fifth scope of work, GMCF put the new structure of the PRO department in place. Since evidence of the required attributes was present, it became important to

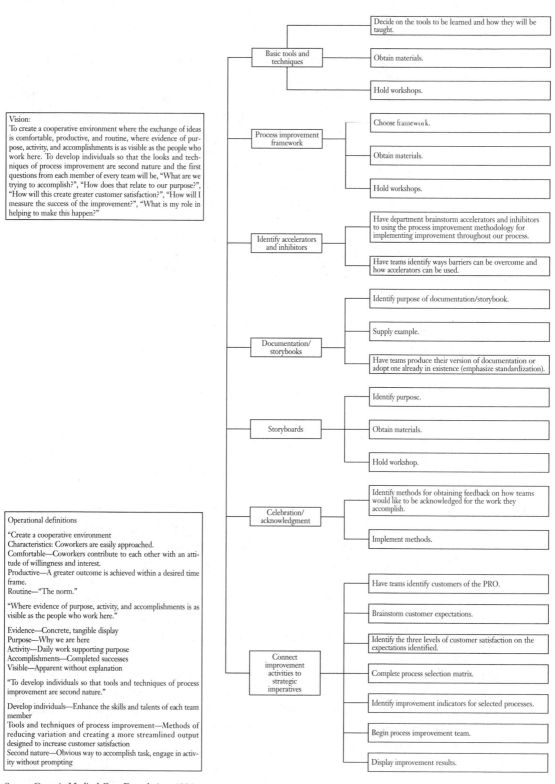

Vision:
To create a cooperative environment where the exchange of ideas is comfortable, productive, and routine, where evidence of purpose, activity, and accomplishments is as visible as the people who work here. To develop individuals so that the looks and techniques of process improvement are second nature and the first questions from each member of every team will be, "What are we trying to accomplish?", "How does that relate to our purpose?", "How will this create greater customer satisfaction?", "How will I measure the success of the improvement?", "What is my role in helping to make this happen?"

Operational definitions

"Create a cooperative environment
Characteristics: Coworkers are easily approached.
Comfortable—Coworkers contribute to each other with an attitude of willingness and interest.
Productive—A greater outcome is achieved within a desired time frame.
Routine—"The norm."

"Where evidence of purpose, activity, and accomplishments is as visible as the people who work here."

Evidence—Concrete, tangible display
Purpose—Why we are here
Activity—Daily work supporting purpose
Accomplishments—Completed successes
Visible—Apparent without explanation

"To develop individuals so that tools and techniques of process improvement are second nature."

Develop individuals—Enhance the skills and talents of each team member
Tools and techniques of process improvement—Methods of reducing variation and creating a more streamlined output designed to increase customer satisfaction
Second nature—Obvious way to accomplish task, engage in activity without prompting

Basic tools and techniques
- Decide on the tools to be learned and how they will be taught.
- Obtain materials.
- Hold workshops.

Process improvement framework
- Choose framework.
- Obtain materials.
- Hold workshops.

Identify accelerators and inhibitors
- Have department brainstorm accelerators and inhibitors to using the process improvement methodology for implementing improvement throughout our process.
- Have teams identify ways barriers can be overcome and how accelerators can be used.

Documentation/ storybooks
- Identify purpose of documentation/storybook.
- Supply example.
- Have teams produce their version of documentation or adopt one already in existence (emphasize standardization).

Storyboards
- Identify purpose.
- Obtain materials.
- Hold workshop.

Celebration/ acknowledgment
- Identify methods for obtaining feedback on how teams would like to be acknowledged for the work they accomplish.
- Implement methods.

Connect improvement activities to strategic imperatives
- Have teams identify customers of the PRO.
- Brainstorm customer expectations.
- Identify the three levels of customer satisfaction on the expectations identified.
- Complete process selection matrix.
- Identify improvement indicators for selected processes.
- Begin process improvement team.
- Display improvement results.

Source: Georgia Medical Care Foundation, 1996.

Figure 6.13. Activities in developing the desired environment.

145

have a structure of mechanical processes that would allow staff to support each other in achieving the desired result of operating as a system.

Each work team began to examine its work as a system, which allowed a common focus for improving daily work. Indicators were developed based on core processes of the work teams that would align with the overall department indicators selected to measure success in satisfying customer expectations. As this did not happen overnight, the initial concern was to practice the skills developed during the departmental training sessions on tools and techniques before they got cold and it became difficult to make them a natural part of daily work.

The process selection matrix as shown in Figure 6.10 was used to help each work team identify a process for improvement where not only an output could be improved, but the improvement would also result in increasing satisfaction in an area known to be important to customers. By identifying the degree of impact each team had on the expectations listed, they could systematically identify the specific work processes that affected the outcome. Teams agreed on a measurement to be used with the selected process in order to confirm improvement. This method allowed teams to practice their skills on work that was meaningful to their customers.

One such process improvement example was a team called "action seekers." The team originated at the GMCF with an opportunity to impact the timeliness and effectiveness of four out of six expectations listed on the process selection matrix. The team recognized an opportunity to streamline the process of requesting and accepting quality improvement plans from collaborating hospitals committing to improving the processes related to the outcomes identified in the HCQIP project study groups. The team's intent was to increase the number of improvement plans received within 30 days of project feedback and to increase the number of appropriate improvement plans received on the first submission. These two indicators would measure the reduction of delays and rework within the PRO process for disseminating data to hospitals. As mentioned earlier, the improvement plans represent hospital efforts to eliminate waste and inefficiency in processes.

One change in the project process was to develop a standardized collaborative project report to streamline feedback of data to hospitals. The report included project findings, hospital-specific information, suggested opportunities to target for improvement, and specific information to be included by hospitals in their improvement plan. The team also developed a suggested format for hospitals to use to reduce variation among plans and to assist hospitals in the actual construction of the plan. Creation of the report improvement was aided by the Mid-South Foundation for Medical Care in Tennessee through information shared as a result of similar opportunities. Chapter appendix E illustrates the suggested format for hospital quality improvement plans developed by the team.[19]

As in this example, PROs often use each other as resources to create widespread improvement. Individual networking serves the purpose of sharing ideas and methods to some degree. The American Peer Review Association (AMPRA), the PROs' trade association, supports these services and others on a national scale. AMPRA's mission is to be "a charitable, educational, not-for-profit national membership association dedicated to health care quality through community-based, independent quality evaluation and improvement programs."[20] AMPRA offers certified medical education activities and conferences where member PROs can network and learn together. These include annual technical conferences as well as the National Quality Symposium. In addition, AMPRA publishes the *Quality Advocate* newsletter, among others, which shares information on quality-related topics.

As improvement efforts continue, the process of documenting and sharing the progress made demands improvement itself. At the time this chapter was being written, a new software module was being introduced to PROs. The software is called *PROvantage* and the module for quality improvement documentation is called *QIP*. Representatives from the PRO community, regional offices, and the central office of HCFA worked together as a team to define data fields, validate values, standardize definitions, and produce the narrative project document through a two-year consensus development effort.

QIP is designed to collect high-level descriptive data on HCQIP projects. The system meets the needs of PROs by helping to more efficiently manage projects and by creating an easier way to share lessons learned. QIP also facilitates widespread project replication between PROs. Variation in the documentation process is reduced by utilizing standard software, thus less time is required to locate information in the familiar format. The data structure emphasizes the HCQIP project plan, measurement of project impact, and collaborations or partnerships developed.

HCFA envisions equal access to the best health care for Medicare beneficiaries. This vision can be attained through HCQIP by supporting the continuous improvement of the processes performed within the health care community. By focusing on this vision, the individual improvement efforts of each PRO will decrease the time it takes to make the vision a reality. To date, we have experienced some important successes and, just as importantly, some serious challenges.

Identifying accelerators and inhibitors to the process is almost as important as the process of implementation itself. The ability to identify the factors of success and failure creates a more thorough understanding of implementing CQI, which in turn produces positive outcomes ranging from decreased time for implementation to greater measured results. Some of the accelerating and inhibiting factors noted so far are listed as follows:

Accelerators

- Storyboards (visual documentation of progress)
- Measurement (understanding how success will be determined)
- Meaningful work (what I do to contribute to the big picture)
- Networking (AMPRA's CQI network for learning and sharing)
- Road maps (estimated timeline and opportunity to access progress)
- Documentation (specifics of how improvements were achieved)

Inhibitors

- High variation between the 53 PROs concerning structure and implementation
- Impact on PROs when changes in requirements are made by HCFA
- Finding time for implementing CQI

Even with the high degree of change required to make the transition to CQI and the uneasiness that results from change, we have come to a point where we all agree on the mission. The following quote from Donald Berwick summarizes the true aim of managing quality in PROs.

> *Until we learn to work together, we will not achieve the level of health and the quality of health care that this country deserves, at a cost it can afford. Working together has to cross institutional boundaries. It has to cross professional boundaries. It has to cross historical boundaries. It will take courage. It will take the willingness of people accustomed to working within a system of separate pieces to stand up and say, "We can accomplish much more together than we can separately."*[21]

PROs across the country have embraced a serious paradigm shift by the Health Care Financing Administration. Focusing on the improvement of processes of care is replacing inspection to correct errors. Benchmarks replace standards, and partnerships are forming where adversarial relationships once existed. These are evidences of the changes taking place due to a commitment to continuously improve the way the work of PROs is carried out in order to exceed the expectations of customers.

To help apply the concepts in this chapter to your work, the following questions can be used as discussion guides for meetings for senior executives, the governing body, and process owners.

Questions for a One-Hour Senior Executive Meeting

1. Knowing the shared vision of this PRO, what things are in place to support the achievement of the vision?

2. What barriers prevent the achievement of the vision?

3. How can senior leaders lessen or remove the identified barriers?

4. What measurements should be tracked to identify the success of the vision?

Questions for a One-Hour Process Owners Meeting

1. Where does my daily work support the achievement of the shared vision?

2. What factors exist that make this work successful in accomplishing the vision?

3. Where do I need help in removing obstacles to achieving a better outcome?

4. How will I measure the success of these processes?

Questions for a One-Hour Governing Body Meeting

1. What is the shared vision of this PRO?

2. What role does this governing body play in facilitating the success of the PRO?

Notes

1. American Peer Review Association, *By-laws*, 1996.

2. M. L. Millman, The Health Care Quality Improvement Program, unpublished presentation, 1995.

3. J. B. Grant, R. P. Hayes, R. D. Pates, K. S. Edward, and D. J. Ballard, "HCFA's Health Care Quality Improvement Program: The Medical Information Challenge," *The Journal of the American Medical Informatics Association*, 3, no. 1 (1996): 15–16.

4. Health Care Financing Administration, *Round 5.0 Scope of Work*, Version May 1, 1995, Section H (Contract no. 500-96-P704) (Baltimore, Md.: Department of Health and Human Services, 1995).

5. Ibid.

6. American Peer Review Association, *Quality Improvement in Health Care*, 1994.

7. HCFA, *Round 5.0 Scope of Work*.

8. Ibid.

9. Oklahoma Foundation for Peer Review, Cooperative Project Flow Diagram, 1996.

10. Michigan Peer Review Organization, Integration Matrix: CIP Timeline and Center Work Phases, 1996.

11. Louisiana Health Care Review, *PRO Report: Health Care Quality Improvement Program Newsletter* (March 1994).

12. HCFA, *Round 5.0 Scope of Work.*

13. Michigan Peer Review Organization, Current Indicators of Process Performance, 1996.

14. Connecticut Peer Review Organization, *Commitment to Quality Semi-Annual Report* (October 1993–March 1994).

15. KePRO, Team Checklists, 1996.

16. P. B. Batalden and P. K. Stoltz, "A Framework for the Continual Improvement of Health: Building and Applying Professional and Improvement Knowledge to Test Changes in Daily Work." *The Joint Commission Journal on Quality Improvement* 19, no. 10 (1993): 440.

17. Ibid.

18. Ibid.

19. Georgia Medical Care Foundation, Hospital Quality Improvement Plan, 1996.

20. American Peer Review Association, *By-Laws.*

21. L. A. Headrick, M. Knapp, D. Neuhauser, S. Gelmon, L. Norman, D. Quinn, and R. Baker. "Working from Upstream to Improve Health Care: The IHI Interdisciplinary Professional Eduction Collaborative," *The Joint Commission Journal on Quality Improvement* 22, no. 3 (1996): 152.

Appendix A: The Oklahoma Foundation for Medical Quality Cooperative Project Flow Diagram

Project name: _____

Team leader: _____

Date of initiation: _____

Developmental

Code: _____

Literature search
- TL working with the PCC requests articles and/or medline search
- PC/TM obtains articles
- TL/PCC reviews articles for selection in study
- PC/TM completes journal directory of articles
- PC/TM prepares a reference list

Develop quality indicators
- TL working with PM and PCC develops the proposed quality indicators for the study
- Project team reviews the proposed quality indicators prior to the study group

Develop concept
- TL working with PM and PCC develops a written concept for review at the study group
- Collaboration criteria are established (for example, DRGs, ICD-9-CM codes, sampling time frame, inclusions, and exclusions)
- Project team reviews the proposed concept prior to the study group

Develop PDC tool
- PC working with the TL, PM, and PCC develops the tool
- Statistician evaluates tool to ensure all elements required for analysis are included and the tool addresses the quality indicators
- Tool is tested using charts from the file room, if possible
- If appropriate, tool is sent to ACC for comments
- TL meets with programmer to begin the initial programming
- Project team reviews the proposed PDC tool prior to study group

ACC recruitment
- PCC working with the team will decide whether to use an ACC on the project
- PCC will recruit an ACC agreed on by the team

 __/__/__/

 __/__/__/

HCQIP team
PCC: Principal clinical coordinator
ACC: Associate clinical coordinator
PM: Project manager
TL: Team leader
PC: Project coordinator
TM: Team member
Biostatistican

Project name:_____

Identify partners
- Statistician working with TL/PM/PCC analyzes the claims or other database to determine number of cases for time frame and number of cases per provider
- Taking into consideration the project concept, the team will select partners
- If possible, benchmarks and focus providers will be selected
- Selection of partners may include
  —Set number of providers selected
  —Population-based random sample (number of providers determined by beneficiary sample)
  —Other

Credential study group members
Depending on project design, the selection of study group members may include
- Physicians and/or HCPOTPs selected from each/or a portion of the partners
- Opinion leaders in the field under study
The PCC works with the team researchers to determine which staff members would best serve on the study group

Notification to study group members and/or partners
- Operations secretary sends letters to each of the study group members and/or the partners (who will select study group members) with an attendance form attached to return to OFMQ
- Operations secretary will finalize attendance and make arrangements prior to the meeting

Identify and select medical records
Depending on the study design, PDC may be performed on-site at the provider or the medical records may be mailed in
- PM determines review methodology and schedules on-site or mail-in reviews
- TL working with the statistician identifies IQC sample that must be mailed in for second reviewer review
- PM provides PDC sample to operations secretary for request and notification of PDC review
- Medical record request/scheduling letters are sent by operations secretary

Administrative support documentation
- Operations secretary begins and continues to maintain correspondence and information files on all projects
- Administrative support personnel initiate and help to maintain chart lists, logs, and the correspondence/information files
- PROVIDER.LST
- FINALIQC.LST
- 1STLEVEL.IQC
- FINAL.IQC
- COLLABOR.LOG

Project name:_____

Finalize study group meeting preparations
- TL working with the team will finalize the slide show presentation
- TL working with the team will finalize the study group booklets
- TL working with the team will decide on appropriate questions that need to be addressed by the study group

Study group meeting
- PCC will lead study group meeting with the assistance of the team

The study group should address and finalize
- Project design (for example, sampling, inclusions, exclusions)
- Project concept
- PDC tool
- Journal directory

Finalize project
- TL and PC will modify the elements of the study to reflect the consensus of the study group
  —Project design (for example, sampling, inclusions, exclusions)
  —Project concept
  —PDC tool
  —Journal directory
- Programmer working with the TL will finalize the PDC entry screen using the finalized PDC tool
- Statistician will produce a STATA program to analyze the abstracted data

Solicit collaborators
- Following the study group meeting, collaborator letters will be sent to all providers selected to participate in the project. The letter will explain the collaboration process and will request their collaboration. The letter will also include a project booklet that will include the following information:
  —Project design (for example, sampling, inclusions, exclusions)
  —Project concept
  —PDC tool
  —Journal directory
- TL will maintain the collaborator log for the project. This log will keep a record of which providers agreed to collaborate and following feedback that providers submitted improvement efforts.

Implementation

Code: _____

Project name:_____

Develop initial budget
- TL will initiate a worksheet for project budget
Calculation for completion by the COO

Initiate PIR and PAMS
- TL is responsible for the initiation and monthly maintenance of PIR and PAMS

Preparations prior to abstractor training
- PCC will complete review of "gold standard" cases for use during the training
- PC will complete initial IQC charts
- TL and PC work with programmer to ensure the entry screen/database are complete and all possible edits are in place
- TL and PC prepare a PDC instruction booklet, which provides information regarding all elements of the study
- TL and PC finalize the PDC instructions
- TL consults with PCC regarding requirements for training

Abstractor training
- TM will be assigned to projects by the PM
- The time frame and length of the training period will be dependent on the complexity of the project and PDC tool
- TL is responsible for training with the assistance of the PC
- All elements of the study will be discussed (for example, concept, objectives, quality indicators, PDC tool, and journal directory)
- PCC may assist with training as necessary
- "Gold standard" cases will be completed by abstractors and checked by TL
- After "gold standard" review is satisfactorily completed, the abstractors will complete initial IQC review (according to IQC process flow diagram)
- Abstractors will be allowed to abstract cases only after IQC process has been followed and completed

Abstraction
- PC will complete review of final IQC charts while abstraction is taking place
- Abstractors will perform abstraction of cases as scheduled
- The 10 percent gold standard review will be included in the review and an error rate assessed
- Problems encountered during abstraction should be immediately reported to the TL
- TL and PC will be available for questions during the abstraction process
- Final IQC will be accomplished during the abstraction process as available
- Final IQC error rate will be reported at the conclusion of the abstraction process

Project name:_____

Merge abstractor's databases
- At the conclusion of the review and IQC process, the TL will notify the programmer, who will then merge the abstractors' databases
- Programmer will produce the initial database reports to be used by the statistician

---

Analysis
- Statistician will work with TL/PC to ensure the integrity of the database
- Statistician will analyze the data using the STATA analytic program
- Statistician will work with the team and any ACCs during this process
- Team leader meetings (statistician, PM, PCC, and TLs) will be held during all stages of the HCQIP project process in order for the TLs to have an as-needed forum for questions regarding their projects

---

Feedback methodology development
- At the conclusion of analysis, the team will agree on a feedback methodology that may include
  —Feedback meetings scheduled at all providers participating in the project
  —Feedback meetings scheduled at a portion of the providers participating (for example, population-based random sample)
  —Regional feedback meetings (for example, population-based random sample)
- The team will define a target audience at the providers and the operations secretary will schedule the meetings at the providers

---

Feedback presentation development
- TL is responsible for the design and execution of the feedback slide show presentation and booklet
- TL working with the PCC is responsible for the design and execution of the feedback slide presentation
- Team will finalize feedback slide show presentation
- Each hospital will be provided 10 presentation booklets, which will include
  —Hard copy of the slide show
  —Color result graphs and tables
  —Potential root causes for variations
  —Sample improvement effort plan
  —PDC tool and instructions
  —Journal directory
- Each person attending the meeting will be asked to sign the attendance sheet
- Handouts will be provided to others attending (>10 people) the meeting, which will include
  —Hard copy of the slide show (four slides per page)
  —Result tables
  —Other information, depending on the project presentation
- Evaluation forms will be provided to each person attending the meeting
- HCQIP questionnaire will be provided to each person attending the meeting to solicit ideas for future HCQIP projects
- "Join the HCQIP team" forms will be provided to each person attending the meeting to solicit OFMQ member (physicians) and nonphysician HCQIP team members

Project name:_____

Travel to the provider's location
- PCC and TL will attend each meeting and other staff may attend as appropriate

---

Provide project feedback to collaborators
Each provider selected to participate in a project will receive feedback of project results
- For on-site feedback the PCC/ACC will present the feedback information to the target audience (physicians and HCPOTPs)
  —Project booklets and all aforementioned handouts will be distributed at the meeting
- For those projects where a large number of hospitals participated (for example, population-based random sample), all participating providers may not receive on-site feedback. The PCC will, however, mail a feedback letter including their results and other project information
- For regional feedback, the PCC/ACC will present the feedback information to the target audience (physicians and HCPOTPs)
- All aforementioned handouts will be distributed at the meeting

---

Solicit improvement letter
- Improvement effort solicitation letter will be delivered to each provider selected to participate in the study. This will either be hand-delivered at the meeting or mailed with the project information letter sent by the PCC. A handout describing potential improvement efforts will be included with the request letter.
- TL will maintain the collaborator log by updating the log with any improvement efforts received
- An assigned TM will receive copies of all improvement efforts and will apply the provider level of participation improvement project to each document or verbal commitment submitted by the provider
- An HCQIP improvement effort grid will be maintained by the TM in order to track provider level of participation

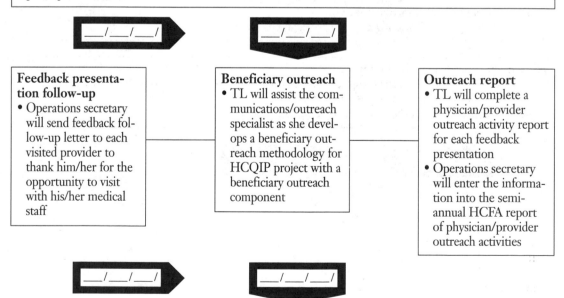

Feedback presentation follow-up
- Operations secretary will send feedback follow-up letter to each visited provider to thank him/her for the opportunity to visit with his/her medical staff

Beneficiary outreach
- TL will assist the communications/outreach specialist as she develops a beneficiary outreach methodology for HCQIP project with a beneficiary outreach component

Outreach report
- TL will complete a physician/provider outreach activity report for each feedback presentation
- Operations secretary will enter the information into the semi-annual HCFA report of physician/provider outreach activities

Assessment

Code: _____

Project name: _____

Dissemination of HCQIP projects
- The PCC working with the team will develop a project report for each project, which will provide
  —Abstract
  —Introduction
  —Methods
  —Results (including tables and graphs)
  —Discussion
  —Conclusion
  —References
- A variety of dissemination methodologies may be employed but, at a minimum, copies of the report will be mailed to every provider in the state
- Additional copies may be distributed
  —At regional meetings
  —At other project feedback meetings
  —To other interested agencies (that is, physician associations, state health department, Cancer Society, and so on)
- Information on HCQIP projects will also be accomplished through
  —Publication of project information in the *HCQIP News*
  —Notification of HCQIP project information during regional meetings
  —Notification of HCQIP project information during other project feedback meetings
  —Notification of HCQIP project information at other meetings where OFMQ staff are invited to participate

---

Collaborators perform improvement efforts
- TL will maintain collaborator log after the project is completed

---

Assessment sampling methodology
- Six to nine months following the completion of feedback, the statistician will do preliminary analysis of claims or other data to determine possible sample sizes
- The team will agree on an appropriate sample size for project assessment

---

Project name:_____

<table>
<tr>
<td>

Identify and request assessment sample
- Due to decreased sample size, these reviews will probably be done as mail-ins
- Operations secretary will send reassessment chart request letter to all providers participating in the study

</td>
<td>

Administrative support documentation
- Administrative support personnel initiate and help maintain chart lists, logs, and the correspondence/information files
  —PROVIDER.LST
  —FINALIQC.LST
  —1STLEVEL.IQC
  —FINAL.IQC

</td>
</tr>
</table>

Abstractor training
- PM will assign one abstractor to perform the assessment review
- TL will work with the abstractor to retrain her on the review she initially performed
- Abstractor will complete initial IQC review (according to IQC process flow diagram)

Assessment PDC review
- PC will complete review of final IQC charts while abstraction is taking place
- Abstractor will perform abstraction of cases as scheduled
- Problems encountered during abstraction should be immediately reported to the TL
- TL and PC will be available for questions during the abstraction process
- Final IQC will be accomplished during the abstraction process as available
- Final IQC error rate will be reported at the conclusion of the abstraction process

Assessment analysis
- Statistician will work with TL/PC to ensure the integrity of the database
- Statistician will analyze the data using the STATA analytic program
- Statistician will work with the team and any ACCs during this process

Project name:_____

Assessment of improvement
• The team will meet to discuss improvement achieved by the participating providers

---

Dissemination of assessment review
• The team will determine an appropriate feedback methodology to disseminate the assessment review, which may include
   —Mailing the results of the review to each of the participating providers
   —Scheduling an on-site visit if indicated
• Information on assessment of HCQIP projects will also be accomplished through
   —Publication of project information in the *HCQIP News*
   —Notification of HCQIP project information during regional meetings
   —Notification of HCQIP project information during other project feedback meetings
   —Notification of HCQIP project information at other meetings where OFMQ staff are invited to participate

Appendix B: Integration Matrix—CIP Timeline* and Center Work Phases[†]

CIP timeline SOW-5	Center work phases	From	To	Includes
Project development a. Idea development	Phase one: Idea generation	Project idea conceived	Idea has been "selected" by CIP staff at periodic meeting and project team assigned	Informal idea generation development Initial bib/lit search Entering ideas into archive CIP staff review Project team assigned Start IMS
Project development (continued) b. Feasibility	Phase two: Project development	Idea selected and team assigned	CIP staff agree to take forward to steering committee as a project	Additional lit search Bib development Medpro data analysis (Macro) Small number of records requested Initial contact with speciality societies and AHP reps Project database created Members of expert panel determined Add info to IMS Steering committee materials prepared
Project development (continued) c. Project plan	Phase three: Project setup	CIP staff agreement to take to steering committee	Collaboration with partners established	Steering committee Project shared with • Provider community • Other groups • Other PROs Collaborators (partners) identified Submit IMS
Identification of opportunities to improve care a. Measurable quality indicators				Identification of measurable quality indicators Develop/test tool Test for reliability of tool PDC on preliminary data Analysis of preliminary PDC Hold study group Data collection tool finalized PDC to create "gold standard" records for validity testing Abstractors trained

*As referenced in HCQIP scope of work—round 5, and shown in italics.
[†]As drafted by the center's CIP engineering team.

CIP timeline SOW–5	Center work phases	From	To	Includes
Identification of opportunities to improve care (continued) b. Collect data	Phase four: Baseline measurement	Request for medical records for PDC	Data feedback reports completed	Medical records requested for collaborators Execution of PDC Validity conducted during PDC
Identification of opportunities to improve care (continued) c. Analyze data d. Confirm the opportunity for improvement				Collected data analyzed Baseline data reports created Update IMS
Comprehensive intervention a. Communication with health care providers and/or beneficiaries	Phase five: Preparing the collaborators	Site visits with collaborators	Collaborators ready to initiate project	Site visits with baseline data Improvement plans requested from collaborators Facilitate intervention design Assist in improvement plan design Provide optional CQI assistance Improvement plans received and endorsed
Comprehensive intervention (continued) b. Support of quality improvement activities	Phase six: Implementation by collaborators	Improvement plans endorsed	Completion of improvement plans	Collaborators commence improvement plans Collaborators send monitoring data Support CQI efforts Collaborators complete improvement plans
Measuring impact and project evaluation	Phase seven: Project evaluation	Improvement plans completed	Postintervention measurement and assessment by collaborators	Follow-up PDC to measure change Commence long-term, routine monitoring of project effectiveness Ongoing communication and assistance as needed Project assessment, summary, and communication Provider satisfaction assessment Complete IMS

Appendix C: Current Indicators of Process Performance

CIP Topic _____

Date submitted _____

Related to the key quality characteristics of . . .	Indicator	Measurement	Target	Current indicator measure-ment	Responsible person
Timeliness	On-time performance of project start and finish target dates in a given month (separate indicators related to start and finish target dates)	Number of start or finish target dates missed ——————— Total number of start or finish target dates occurring in a given month	Smaller percentage is better; zero or NA (not applicable, that is, none missed) is best [P]		IQC
Timeliness	Adherence to overall work plan timelines	Number of untimely projects ——————— Number of projects	Smaller percentage is better; zero or NA (not applicable, that is, none missed) is best [P]		IQC
Timeliness	Cumulative lag time in start and finish target dates at close of month (separate indicators related to start and finish dates)	Number of net delay days for start or finish target dates at close of month for all active projects combined ——————— Number of active projects	Smaller percentage is better; zero or NA (not applicable, that is, no days) is best [XmR]		IQC
Timeliness	Delay analysis documentation success percentage per month	Number of times project delay documentation not initiated ——————— Number of actual delays	Smaller percentage is better; zero or NA (not applicable, that is, no delays) is best [P]		IQC
Data accuracy and integrity	Data rerun rate per month	Number of rerun requests for data ——————— Total number of data requests	Smaller percentage is better; zero is best [P]		Data
Data accuracy and integrity	Successful team meeting #5 Percentage per quarter	Number of team meeting 5s where available data do not fit analysis and project goals ——————— Number of team meeting 5s	Smaller percentage is better; zero or NA (not applicable, that is, no delays) is best [P]		Data and project team
Effectiveness and efficiency	Improvement plan completion rate per CIP	Number of collaborators not completing improvement plans ——————— Number of providers at end of phase 3	Smaller percentage is better; zero or NA (not applicable, that is, no collaborators without complete plan) is best [P]		Project trackers

Related to the key quality characteristics of . . .	Indicator	Measurement	Target	Current indicator measure-ment	Responsible person
Effectiveness and efficiency	Study group participation rate per month	Number of Michigan hospitals that have indicated interest by participating in a study group meeting (by month)	Larger is better		Project trackers
Effectiveness and efficiency	Site visit rate per month	Number of hospitals that have indicated an interest in collaborating in projects by participating in a site visit	Larger is better		Project trackers
Effectiveness and efficiency	Hospital collaboration rate per quarter	Number of Michigan hospitals that haven't completed at least one CIP ———————— Number of Michigan hospitals	Smaller percentage is better; zero or NA (not applicable, that is, no providers without agreement) is best [P]		Project trackers
Effectiveness and efficiency	Formal agreement rate per CIP	Number of providers not completing formal agreement ———————— Number of providers initially targeted	Smaller percentage is better; zero or NA (not applicable, that is, no providers without agreement) is best [P]		Project trackers
Impact on beneficiaries	Change rate per completed CIP	Number of providers without "significant" indicator change ———————— Total number of providers in CIP	Smaller percentage is better; zero or NA (not applicable, that is, no providers without change) is best [P]		CC/EF
Collaborator satisfaction	Percentage of collaborator ratings at or below satisfied (ratings on multiple indicators assumed)	Number of ratings at or below satisfied ———————— Number of ratings	Smaller percentage is better; zero or NA (not applicable, that is, none rating this way) is best [P]		Project trackers
Effectiveness and efficiency	Total process time	Number of total days to complete a CIP			IQC
Effectiveness and efficiency	Compliance with monthly schedule of idea evaluation meetings	Scheduled monthly meeting occurs and projects are evaluated	100 percent compliance		CG
Effectiveness and efficiency	Number of new CIPs approved for steering committee compared to target number	Number of new CIPs approved at monthly evaluation meeting ———————— Target number	Larger number is better. 100 percent is best.		CG

Appendix D: Team Checklist

Tasks—getting started	Completed	Date
Train new team members.		
Distribute team handbook to members and leaders.		
Finalize charter and set ground rules.		
Send a copy of finalized charter to Pat Eley (Florida operations).		
Determine sunset.		
Assign member(s) for maintaining team binder.		
Assign member(s) for updated storyboard.		
Review team assessment tool.		
Review guidelines for reporting to P&P and functional area(s).		

Tasks throughout process—have we . . .	Completed	Date
Kept team binder updated?		
Kept storyboard updated?		
Kept sponsor informed?		
Documented our lessons learned as we went along?		
Obtained external/input customer input?		
Collected data and made decisions based on data?		
Operationalized improvements?		
Kept two-way communication with functional area and had their buy-in?		
Quantified our improvements?		
Measured the system/process/perceptions prior to initiating changes/improvements?		
Determined our post-measurement of improvement (that is, how will we know improvements were successful)?		
Set up a system to collect and evaluate ongoing trending information (that is, set up key indicators and thresholds)?		
Evaluated whether our changes will potentially impact an external customer?		
Eliminated manual processes wherever possible?		
Identified the root cause(s) of the problems identified?		
Standardized processes where possible?		
Used the applicable CI tools and techniques?		

Tasks—wrapping up	Completed	Date
Complete team assessment tool.		
Schedule lessons learned (facilitator/sponsor).		
Hold lessons learned session.		
Update relevant individuals/groups.		
Transfer responsibility to appropriate functional areas/person.		
Celebrate!		

Distribution: Facilitators, chairpersons, team leaders, team members (team member handbook update)

Appendix E: Hospital Quality Improvement Plan (Suggested Format)

1. Describe the strengths and weaknesses of the data and quality indicators presented by GMCF.

_____
_____
_____
_____
_____
_____
_____

2. Please provide the name and telephone number of the contact person with whom GMCF can discuss the improvement plan. _____
_____

3. List the name and position of each member of the multidisciplinary team who will develop and implement the quality improvement plan.

    Name   Position

_____
_____
_____
_____
_____
_____
_____

4. List the quality indicators selected to be addressed by the team.

_____
_____
_____

5. Complete a timeline for planning and implementing the improvement plan (sample attached).

6. What process(es) were selected for improvement?

_____
_____
_____
_____

7. Attach a description of the specific actions to be taken to resolve the underlying cause of variation within the process(es) selected. Complete the following information concerning measurement of the described action.

*Indicator(s) of the selected process to be measured for improvement.

_____

_____

_____

*The baseline measurement of the process indicator(s). _____

_____

_____

_____

8. Attach or send updates on progress. This may be minutes or other forms of documentation used by the hospital. Include lessons learned by the process team (pitfalls and positives) that might be beneficial to others working on this process.

9. Upon completion of project:
Provide the follow-up measurement of the process indicator(s) after the improvement has been implemented (measurement could be after 30, 60, or 90 days).

Improvement plan timeline

Task	Time projected																Assigned
Return QI plan to GMCF																	
Week	1	2	3	4	5	6	7	8	9	10	11	12	13	14	15	16	

Year: _____

_____   ██████████
Incomplete   Complete

Vicki S. Davis coaches the implementation of continuous quality improvement at Georgia Medical Care Foundation in Atlanta, Georgia. GMCF is the Health Care Quality Improvement Organization for the state of Georgia (formerly known as Peer Review Organizations). HCQIOs contract with the Health Care Finance Administration to improve the efficiency and effectiveness of health care services to Medicare beneficiaries. Davis served as director of quality resources at West Paces Medical Center in Atlanta from 1988 until 1993 and as corporate director of quality for National Linen Service before joining GMCF in late 1995.

Chapter 7

Quality Management in Military Medicine

Charles B. Mount

This chapter is dedicated to all the men and women of the U.S. armed forces who, even under the most arduous circumstances, have been able to use the tools and principles of quality management (QM) to achieve success. In the Army, Navy, Air Force, Marine Corps, and countless other agencies of the U.S. Department of Defense (DoD), it is the individual employees—active duty and reserve, officer and enlisted, military and civilian—who have made the difference. They are the unsung heros of the successes of QM. Military medicine is highlighted in this chapter as a clear example of how resistance can be overcome and change instituted through the use of QM.

The power of QM in military medicine is its ability to transcend many layers of bureaucracy and the many years of tradition such as those often found in military hospitals and teaching centers. This is often the case when introducing a new management philosophy into the military: One must overcome years of well-entrenched tradition. The "old way" of doing business can often become the *only* way. The personal need for command and control, if not watched carefully, can stifle creativity. Military employees often wish that QM could become a permanent part of the military culture. Others would claim that QM can, at best, only partially succeed in a military setting because of the need for control. This author believes that military medicine needs all of the facets of QM and, with them, can be very successful. Observations of men and women at work in military health care over the past six to seven years have amply demonstrated this.

What is the major difference between military and civilian medicine? *Command and control* and *readiness for war* are two frequent themes of military medicine. The success of the military is in its ability to effectively blend those themes during a crisis. It is a hard-won success. Each of these themes competes for a limited supply of money, people, and equipment. The era of large military and health care budgets is over. The excesses of the 1980s have been given over almost totally to downsizing, cost containment, and managed care.

However, the *power* of military medicine—despite these challenges—is in its unique capacity to focus its efforts on selected areas, appoint key leaders to lead the way, and mobilize the efforts of hundreds—if not thousands—of men and women. And this aptly describes the military way of life. It is a lifestyle built around creating a command-and-control environment in which someone is always in charge. And therein lies the predominant strength of the military for more than 200 years: No matter what project or task is being developed, someone is told to be in charge and is accountable to senior leadership. This is true for all aspects of the military, whether it be training new staff, driving tanks, refueling ships at sea, launching new aircraft, or treating patients. Someone is put in charge to make it happen. As W. Edwards Deming and Joseph M. Juran have correctly noted, leadership begins at the top. QM has the same requirement: Leadership starts with the senior staff and then cascades down to managers, supervisors, and line employees.

Quality management can be defined in part as the scientific application of statistical tools and data analysis to improve processes, steps of procedures, or activities within an organization. It is a management philosophy—a way of describing the organization's business practices. *Continuous quality improvement* (CQI), *total quality management* (TQM), and *total quality leadership* (TQL) are often used interchangeably by military and civilian staff as synonymous with *quality management*. They are similar to each other, with only minor differences in how the tools and principles are actually used in a specific organization.

A quick look at the strengths and weaknesses of the military demonstrates where QM might work in military health care and where it struggles to compete with other activities.

Strengths of the Military

The strengths of the military include the following:

- Ready to fight wars on near and distant shores
- Pride in serving the United States
- Reacts quickly to crises
- Works from the top down
- Mission is clearly defined
- Established channels of communication
- Clear lines of authority
- High degree of esprit de corps within units or departments
- Prepared to respond on short notice

When one visits military medical and dental treatment facilities (medical centers, hospitals, clinics, ships, field units, and sick bays) throughout the world, one fact stands out loud and clear: The men and women in military medicine are fanatically committed to their patients. They are not paid any more or less depending on how many patients they treat each day. Often they must provide health care in old buildings with minimal equipment. The word they would often use in describing these buildings is *austere*. When the call comes, the active duty or reserve personnel go anywhere in the world to provide care. Separation from families and friends is the norm, often for long periods. If they must work long hours into the night or on weekends or holidays to get the job done, they will. They may complain, but they'll never let the patient down. Patients are never left to fend for themselves.

With these strengths in mind, there are several areas left over from the military of the 1970s and 1980s that could stand some improvement. Leaders at all levels of the military are well acquainted with these.

Opportunities to Improve

The military's opportunities to improve include the following:

- Facts are often heavily outweighed by government politics in making decisions.
- Fire fighting or applying band-aids makes planning for the future difficult.
- Small incidents quickly become crises without notice.
- Leaders often look for the guilty party (hunt for the "bad apple").
- Instructions are written in an attempt to cover all aspects of military life; therefore, they lose their effectiveness.
- Creativity is not well tolerated, nor is thinking outside of the box.
- There is a low tolerance for ambiguity.
- The mission becomes the end unto itself.
- The old way of doing things often becomes the only way.
- The lowest-ranking people (who are closest to the actual processes) are often not consulted.

Old Way vs. New Way

Opportunities to improve in any organization should be taken for what they are: opportunities. In previous years, this was a very hard sell in the military. Today, the phrase *opportunities to improve* is no longer a joke but is gaining a strong, firm foothold throughout all agencies of the DoD. One of the great lessons of QM is that nearly all processes can be improved, especially those that existed as part of the old way of health care—military and civilian—for many years. While establishing the National Demonstration Project and the Quality Management Network, Don Berwick compared health care's pre- and post-QM days as the old way (see Table 7.1). His lessons of health care moving from the old way to the new way are directly applicable to today's military health care system.

Overcoming the Old Way. Beginning in the mid-1980s, it became clear to the DoD that the industrial use of TQM could have a major impact on the DoD and each of the branches of the military services. The old way of doing business was simply too costly. Then, as well as today, the United States spent a great deal of taxpayers' money on maintaining a national defense. The price of freedom for America comes at the cost of continually procuring new weapons systems, equipping and training troops, treating soldiers and sailors and their families 24 hours a day, and maintaining the infrastructure of military bases throughout the world.

Table 7.1. The old way vs. the new way.

Old way	New way
Quality is just fine.	Quality can and must be improved.
Poor quality comes from people.	Poor quality comes from processes.
Checking and reporting creates quality.	Analysis and understanding of processes leads to quality.

In the past, the perception of the military was that money was often spent buying and maintaining duplicate equipment. Beginning in the early 1980s, many military and DoD experts saw the enormous potential of eliminating this duplication through the use of QM. The old way of "quality is just fine" had become a bad joke. Employees frequently used the phrase "if it's good enough for the government, it's good enough for anyone else." Clearly DoD and military leaders were eager to change this attitude. To do so would require reducing redundancy, reducing the cost of poor quality, and eliminating non–value-added steps. The attitude of "good enough" could no longer be the government's standard.

Thanks to the talents of many men and women in the federal government, much of the "good enough" attitude has been overridden. The costly overruns and duplicate equipment purchases had in fact wreaked havoc on morale and performance. QM overcame that with the use of scientific tools for data gathering and decision making, combined with employee-based action teams. Without the use of QM, cost overruns might have continued for several more years.

Equally destructive is the old-way philosophy that poor quality comes from people. This has been an especially dangerous practice as found in military and civilian organizations. Too often, it is far easier to find the guilty parties and punish them. Taking the time and energy to examine the processes is seen as wasted time by many managers and supervisors. Profit and not-for-profit organizations both use this tactic. Organizations want quick action. "Find who is at fault" is the cry of management. Punishment is seen as a sign that someone is really doing something. It implies that someone—the leader, manager, or supervisor—has taken quick, effective action and therefore is demonstrating great leadership. Unfortunately, with this approach the process never gets the attention or focus on permanent improvement that it deserves. Fear and punishment—quick fixes, especially as driven from the top—can squelch even the very best of QM efforts.

Paralleling the industry-based old-way/new-way changes in the late 1980s were changes in our nation's civilian and military health care system. Changes in one frequently affect the other. With hundreds of military medical and dental treatment facilities scattered throughout the world, military medicine impacts almost all aspects of the system: direct patient care, research and development, and education and training. As an example, beginning in late 1988, the Joint Commission on Accreditation of Healthcare Organizations (JCAHO) embarked upon its "Agenda for Change," in which the principles of TQM/CQI would be infused throughout its survey process for accrediting hospitals and other health care organizations. With a careful, watchful eye on approximately 5400 civilian and military hospitals that undergo accreditation every three years, JCAHO clearly expected that improvements would be visibly demonstrated in each institution, using scientific tools rather than random, isolated quick fixes. The JCAHO survey process was intended to highlight improvements in health care processes that serve the needs of the community and the hospitals' customers. While never mandating the use of a specific QM method (such as CQI or TQM) or a preference for a specific model (such as that of Juran, Deming, Philip Crosby, or others), JCAHO did expect then (and very definitely does today) the use of QM-based tools such as

- Process flowcharting

- Cause-and-effect diagrams

- Data gathering: histograms, scatter diagrams, trend analysis

- Priority setting, brainstorming, multivoting

- Data analysis: run charts, control charts

This meant that the old way of checking and reporting, endless inspections, and quick fixes had to give way to the new way of analysis and understanding of processes. This meant using the tools of QM such as those listed to demonstrate visible improvements in processes.

Inspections simply do not improve processes—people do. This author's experience for 30 years in military health care is that countless inspections, reporting and checking, double checking, and using quick fixes only creates massive fear and mistrust, not improvement. As a result, problems are driven underground where they may remain hidden for years. Valuable time is lost while focusing on the visible, superficial, quick remedy, which leaves no time or incentive to solve the real problems, where the greatest impact would be felt.

Since the tour of duty at a given location for most military active duty health care staff (which includes an enormous array of physicians, nurses, administrators, dentists, medics, hospital corpsmen, and support personnel) is for only two to three years, the problem of staff turnover becomes acute. Problems can easily be covered up, overcome by other pressing military priorities, or completely pushed aside in favor of crises after crises. This pattern can continue until the new person takes command; then the problems resurface. The new way of analysis and understanding of processes is at least a partial answer for overcoming this. The new way allows all personnel involved in the process (regardless of whether they have been in the organization for two weeks or more than 20 years) to design long-term processes and solutions to cope with rapid changes in staff and senior leadership.

Health care, military or civilian, is by almost every known measure a complicated and exhausting business. The pace is hectic, the hours are long and unpredictable, patients are often angry at the system, and the rewards often seem few and far between. The increased use of same-day surgery centers, high-volume ambulatory care settings, and overcrowded emergency rooms or trauma centers place added stress on health care workers. Heavy patient care workloads during the late night hours, weekends, and holidays, plus the endless requirements for documentation, take their toll. Taking a break during the middle of the day or night shift to focus on improving a process doesn't come easily for hospital employees. Administrators often complain that they don't have time for quality (see Table 7.2). Physicians, nurses, and support staff say that they have even less time.

No one, be they physicians, dentists, nurses, physician assistants, hospital corpsmen, medics, licensed vocational nurses, or nurses aides, has it any easier than the others. For all employees in the health care industry, there are simply more patients to treat than staff available. Cost containment, one of the cornerstones of today's managed care practices, forestalls any immediate hiring of more staff to alleviate the workload imbalance. Directors of military medical and dental centers are frequently pressed to maintain productivity levels, find time for readiness training, and face ever-declining budgets and staff downsizing. To them, quality measures carry a big cost; they just don't have the time or money.

One of the recent solutions to the military's dilemma of patient care demands vice readiness training is the DoD's TRICARE system, which combines military hospitals with civilian physicians and

Table 7.2. More old way vs. new way: the cost of quality.

Old way	New way
Quality costs money.	Quality *saves* money.
We don't have time for quality.	We don't have time not to improve quality.

networks to provide medical and dental care to military personnel and families stationed in the United States and overseas. The TRICARE system provides patient care in community and military hospitals and provides resources for readiness training without sacrificing the quality of either. TRICARE offers excellent opportunities to see the tools of QM in action, combining the best health care practices to improve access to care, reduce waiting times, and improve customer service using scarce resources. TRICARE is a superb example of demonstrating that piecemeal quick fixes or crisis management do not solve health care problems—quality management does.

As a resource, time is in short supply. The key concern facing most military hospitals and clinics is the dual mission required of wartime medicine: (1) the peace time care of military families and retirees, and (2) wartime training requirements to maintain proficiency for the battlefield. Unfortunately, time can be split only so many ways. The dual demands of military medicine require more than 24 hours a day. The old-way adages that we don't have time for quality and that quality costs money are particularly meaningful to military medicine.

The good news is that today there are some leaders in military medicine who believe that the use of QM will save money and time, even if it is in the long term. These are the courageous leaders. They are the astute ones, the leaders of tomorrow. For others, this long-term view of improvement is not an easy sell. Their focus is on the short-term, immediate, day-to-day needs of their patients. Time constraints, productivity pressures, and readiness for war all create a sense of immediacy that can effectively block out long-term thinking of even six to 12 months down the road. Frequently, the military requires its leaders to focus their planning efforts in terms of hours and days, not months.

To the commanding officer of a hospital, the three to four months that a process action team may need to complete an important project sounds like an eternity. Occasionally, a team will need even more time. This can scare senior leaders. All health care professionals wish it could be true, but most health care systems are not likely candidates for quick fixes. If one could hover over a process action team in progress and look down at the problem from the 5000-foot level, the need for a team to take four to six months to resolve a tough problem may seem quite appropriate. However, at ground zero in a busy hospital or clinic, this can seem like forever.

Readiness for War. Just mentioning the words *readiness* or *operational readiness* can invoke feelings of acute anxiety or apprehension with any member of the armed forces. Readiness for war goes by many names, such as the following:

- Operational readiness
- Operational tempo
- Battlefield medicine
- Battlefield deployment

At its core is the fundamental fact that active duty and many reserve officers and enlisted personnel can be sent anywhere in the world. This includes medical and dental staff. With minimal notice, they can be on their way to Bosnia, the Persian Gulf, Vietnam, Korea, or Guantanamo Bay, Cuba. Anywhere the President of the United States orders infantry or battlefield troops or ships, military medicine goes as well. If the troops pull out tonight for distant shores, the response is immediate, and their medical staff goes out side-by-side with them. Medical staff of the Army, Navy, Air Force, and Marine Corps all have the same responsibility. Wherever their troops go, the "doc" goes as well. Perhaps just the knowledge that you could be sent tomorrow to care for the wounded near the battleline creates such anxiety and fear—tomorrow! Who will take care of the parents or children tonight? What about the house or lawn? Are the wills and insurance policies up to date? Who will take care of the bills?

Even more striking is the training environment for wartime medicine. Some wartime training can be conducted in the larger hospital and medical centers near large cities or communities. Often, however, field medical training must be conducted in remote areas, far from families, friends, and the community. Infantry troops, air squadrons, or ships train in remote locations for reasons of security and safety. The psychological and physical pressure of wartime training far from families can take its toll.

Fortunately, there are some solutions. For one, many military hospitals have an excellent cadre of civilian employees. It is their day-to-day steadfast work in the military's hospital and dental clinics that helps ensure that the patients and their families are well cared for. After the active duty or Reserve staff have departed to their next wartime training assignment, the civilian employees are still hard at work treating the patients, welcoming new batches of officers and enlisted staff, and carrying on the normal, day-to-day administrative functions of a busy hospital or clinic.

More good news is that a large number of the civilian employees are well trained in the tools and practices of quality management. Moreover, they are only too happy to show the "newbees" the results of their process improvements. In fact, when officers and enlisted personnel report in, they would do well to ask their civilian employees to show off their improvements. Everyone likes to show off their success stories.

No one ever said that being in the military is easy. It is not; it takes its toll on the officers and enlisted personnel and on their families. Among their greatest challenges is that of being on call 24 hours a day and ready to respond in times of crisis. And yet, it is exactly in this environment that quality management can, must, and does flourish. No one ever said that using QM would be easy. Work processes must be done right the first time, with the least down time and the fewest number of redundant steps. The quality of work must be improved daily.

This author's experience has been that people need frequent reminders that using QM tools should be a natural part of the day, not an extension. It is a mistake to view QM as an add-on activity. Military personnel are especially prone to thinking that QM comes at the end of the work day, after the patients have been treated and cared for. If QM is relegated to after the "real" work is done, the defects or problems are quickly forgotten in the haste of getting more work done. Sadly, when they are forgotten, they tend to reappear at the least likely time and cost twice as much to fix. Given the stresses of the health care industry, especially in giving care to severely ill patients, a great many hospital employees see QM as a huge added burden. They prefer the faster, easier route and focus on short-term fixes.

One of the most powerful ways to visibly see the stresses and the resulting impact of QM is in contrasting the old-way/new-way patterns of communications and patient flow. In the old-way style of communication, control is maintained by using one-way dialogue from the top down to employees (see Figure 7.1). In civilian or military health care, the need for control is much the same. The old-way communication is used to keep only certain people informed, basically on a need-to-know basis. Who is *excluded* from the communication is often as important as who is included. Consequently, any system or process problems that might be voiced by the junior-ranked staff can be squelched in the pursuit of control. In fact, QM may well be a major threat to the old way's basic need for maximum control. Organizations that thrive on maintaining tight control view QM as a real enemy of time and resources.

Old Way

- Mission statement: Who knows?
- Communication: One way
- Leaders in the executive area
- Community efforts = diffuse

Ambition: To survive

Figure 7.1. The old-way style of communication.

In the old way, not only was the organization's mission statement rarely known, but few leaders were in touch with the actual work flow. Senior leaders often did not know how the majority of work was actually performed. Under the new way, communication goes two ways and is highly visible throughout the entire organization (see Figure 7.2). Leaders are out and about, looking at the health care processes and their impact on the customers/patients, practicing MBWA: managing by wandering about. Leaders who hide in their offices quickly lose touch with the real work. They lose contact with the employees and their customers. When asked during TQM training sessions "How many of you have ever been evaluated by someone who doesn't have the foggiest idea what you do?" the response from most employees is overwhelmingly strong; hundreds of hands are immediately raised.

What yields the loudest responses from employees in TQM-oriented training classes is their personal experiences as a patient. Some people are excited and have had very positive experiences. Most, unfortunately, describe their time as a patient as one of great frustration: long waiting times in the emergency room or the pharmacy, clinic appointments that are double-booked or canceled, rudeness from the hospital staff, being shuffled from one area to the next, herded like cattle into patient waiting rooms only to discover the waiting time is in hours, not minutes. The list is long and distinguished!

New Way

- Mission statement stresses quality
- Communication visible up and down
- Leaders in touch with the work
- Leaders practice MBWA

Ambition: Be the best

Figure 7.2. The new-way style of communication.

Rarely do TQM/TQL instructors encounter from their students such emotionally gut-wrenching experiences as these. Everyone has had experience with poor treatment or service. The problems encountered as a patient are remembered vividly for many years. For these students, the health care industry desperately needs improvement—the sooner the better.

As Figure 7.3 illustrates, hospitals are often arranged like many organizations: hierarchically and according to departmental function (laboratory, pharmacy, X-ray, admissions office, and so on). Military hospitals add even more structure and control to the departmental organization chart. Yet it is well-known that patient care cuts across multiple departments, starting with the time patients enter the hospital until they leave. Patients believe quite honestly that everyone in the medical and dental care environment who comes in contact with them should know who they are, know what type of care is safest and most effective for them, and be able to answer their specific questions accurately and with utmost privacy. These are just a few of the basic, fundamental beliefs of most patients. What is surprising is that, in military and civilian health care, the end result is often the same pattern: Employees believe that they are doing their best. Each thinks that his or her portion of the process is just fine. To them, quality improvement means getting other people to do their job right! Perhaps if each person's part of the process was in fact fine, there would be less problems in health care.

Rarely does one person know and understand the whole of any major process. Each sees only his or her part. QM takes a different track than many other styles of management. It forces health care professionals to view the hospital or clinic through the patients' eyes and to do this nondefensively. Under QM, it has to be okay for the patient to say, "Your system (hospital, clinic) just doesn't work well." Military hospital commanders (and civilian CEOs) must hear those words not as another attack on them and their hospital, but as a genuine opportunity to improve. Patients care about their hospital or clinic; employees care about their hospital. Those in senior leadership positions must do so as

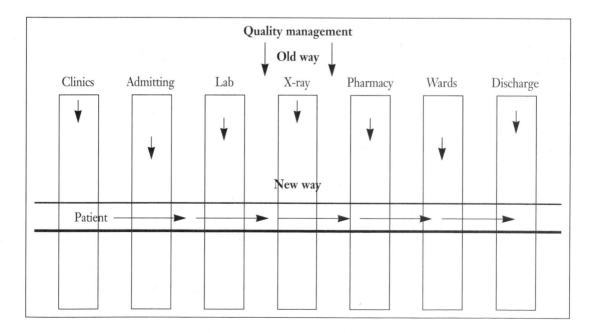

Figure 7.3. Vertical vs. horizontal view of how hospitals are organized.

well. The kind of honesty where patients can complain, be heard, and have their ideas considered important is often missing, but is sorely needed in all areas of the health care industry.

Given the hundreds of processes that go on 24 hours a day in most busy hospitals—drawing blood, administering medications, starting intravenous solutions, obtaining a history and physical, taking X-rays, giving preoperative teaching, preparing patients for discharge, transferring patients from one unit to another, giving nutritional and dietetic counseling, and so on—the stage is set for a variation on Murphy's Law: "If it can go wrong, it will."

As a case example, a 24-year-old male patient is admitted to a large, urban hospital with intense abdominal pain and some signs of acute appendicitis. In the civilian setting, the patient may have been driven to the emergency room by a family member or relative, or the patient may be referred to the ER by the family physician. In any event, acute appendicitis is considered an emergency, requiring immediate response from the health care team.

This patient will probably do well in the hospital and go on to live a normal, productive life if

1. The ER is not overly crowded with other patients, and the staff is attuned to triaging ill patients.

2. The right blood work is drawn and labeled correctly, and the blood tubes are not broken in transit to the laboratory or set aside on a countertop waiting to be tested.

3. The patient's signs and symptoms are accurately diagnosed and differentiated from other illnesses.

4. The operating room is readily available or, if multiple surgical cases are booked, there is a short turnover time between other cases.

5. The instruments for the surgery are properly prepared, sterilized, and immediately available for emergency surgeries such as this.

6. The anesthesia staff and operating room staff are fresh and have not been working all day and well into the night.

Note that the first and last problems—overcrowding of emergency rooms and hospital staff working long hours at night and on weekends—are very common in military medicine.

It is possible that if these situations can be avoided or minimized, this patient will recover quickly and leave the hospital minus his appendix. The good news about this patient is that he is young, only 24 years old. With most illnesses and minor goofs in the hospital, young patients recover quickly. This is not true for patients in their 50s, 60s, and older.

Having worked in hospitals for more than 30 years, this author wonders what happens when the treatment processes are suboptimized. What if the blood tubes are lost, mislabeled, or dropped, or if the quantity drawn is insufficient for testing, requiring a redraw of the blood? What if the ER is very crowded on a busy Saturday night, with minimal staffing? What if the wrong patient is operated on? To outsiders, these seem like improbable events. They are true stories about the health care industry. The industry has a history of long delays, numerous handoffs, multiple decision points, and just plain sloppiness. Any process in the health care environment can easily become suboptimized. Hospitals and clinics often have numerous handoffs (see Figure 7.4), multiple bureaucracies, tight staffing, and declining budgets. It is hard to know who is in charge of the patient, who is supposed to coordinate the handoffs, and who is to balance the patient's needs with the budget. Without coordination or left unchecked, handoffs can multiply beyond belief. Treatments can be delayed; problems can occur in

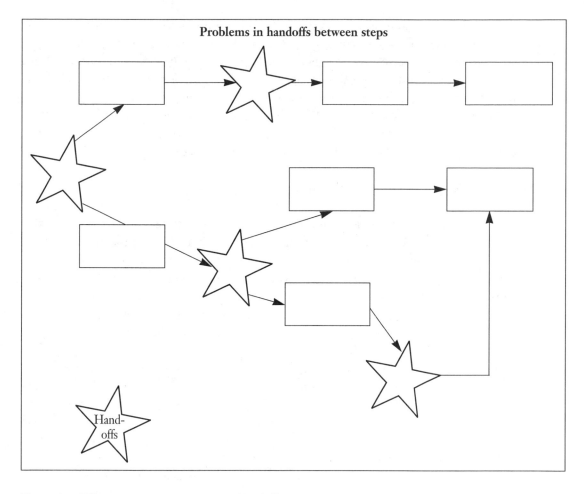

Figure 7.4. What can go wrong in a process: Handoffs.

any area of the hospital or clinic. Bureaucratic processes can slow down the recovery of any patient. A quick glance at a hospital, clinic, field aid station, or shipboard sick bay reveals a host of well-known problems, including the following:

- Minimal staffing or inexperienced staff
- Crowded, busy schedules late in the evenings or on weekends
- Long waiting lines
- Broken or misplaced specimen containers
- Lost laboratory or radiology reports
- Misplaced health records
- Poorly displayed signs or, worse yet, no signs
- Tired, irritated staff with minimal customer focus
- Outdated or broken equipment

These problems are by no means the exception. It is not hard to imagine the impact when cost reduction (that is, saving dollars and reducing staff) becomes the overarching goal. In the end, the patient suffers. Now, add to this scenario the military environment of preparing for wartime medicine. The situation becomes even more complicated. Quick fixes, instant decisions, and short-term thinking can steamroll any well-intentioned process improvement. Changing to a longer-range mode of thinking, as found in the practice of QM, is not easy. Most military organizations tend to resist change. They prefer keeping things on an even keel and preserving the status quo. Change, even with the best of intentions, creates instability. After all, it is far easier to provide control when the target (the organization) is not moving. Quality management very definitely means change; control means slowing down the change. Resistance helps stop the change. In many ways, the practice of QM can collide head-on with the need for control.

Although much has been written about quality management, it is important to recognize what it is and is not (see Figure 7.5). QM is a cultural change and is the responsibility of top management. It is not fighting fires or a management tool to be used only by specialists. Unless the senior leadership of the organization is exceptionally well trained and committed to quality management, it will become a short-term, slogan-ridden program—and preserving the status quo will win every time. Personal experiences by this author have been that when there is a conflict between the needs of the individual and the needs of the organization—military or civilian—the individual usually loses. Preserving the status quo can become a means unto itself.

In the example, the 24-year-old patient could be a member of the armed forces, deployed out in the field with a tank or infantry battalion, aboard a surface ship or submarine, stationed overseas in a remote location, or flying in a jet aircraft. Care for this type of patient is first provided by a Navy hospital corpsman, Army/Air Force medic, independent duty hospital corpsmen (IDC), physician assistant (PA), a young flight surgeon, or a general medical officer (GMO), depending on the requirements of their service or field units. Training for a military caregiver varies from 10 to 14 weeks of basic hospital and field medical training for the hospital corpsman or medic to more extensive training for the IDC or PA to full-fledged medical school training for the flight surgeon or GMO. The levels of wartime medical training varies widely. Some caregivers have had years of extensive field or emergency training; others have had little.

Once the diagnosis of our young military patient has been made, the next challenge is where this patient will get the necessary care. The patient may be lucky and be near a well-staffed medical center

Is	Is not
Cultural change	Overnight cure
Responsibility of top management	Delegated to subordinates
Systematic	New program
Structure	"Fighting fires"
Long term	Short term
Conveyed by action	Slogans
Action by everyone	Only specialists

Figure 7.5. What QM is and is not.

with superb operating room capabilities. Or the patient may have to be treated at a small field battalion aid station, a quickly erected field hospital, a hospital ship, or at a small clinic in the middle of the desert. Such is the variation among the military's treatment facilities. Fortunately, the military devotes a considerable amount of time training its personnel to function in these facilities. The successes of battlefield medicine as seen in World War II, Korea, Vietnam, the Persian Gulf, and Bosnia have been due to this training.

Spanning approximately 50 years, the basic processes of military emergency or wartime medicine have remained basically the same: triage, immediate diagnosis, stabilize, treat, and recuperate or evacuate. Today, medicine faces the same difficulties as in World War II: Getting the ill and injured to definitive medical care as fast as possible. Here is an excellent opportunity for the practice of quality management to shine. Properly applied, QM tools can save time, reduce rework, and redistribute scarce resources. Every minute of treatment or evacuation time that can be saved is time that can be used elsewhere. Reducing rework, eliminating redundant procedures, reducing handoffs, providing quicker response times—all of these mean safer and more effective recovery for the patient (and ultimately less cost to the health care system).

Delays in treatment, diagnosis, or evacuation can impair the mission of the military unit. Military medicine's goal has always been to treat the ill or wounded and return them to duty as fast as possible or medically evacuate them to definitive care. Anything less creates risk, prolongs treatment, and increases the number of casualties. If the ill and wounded can be immediately returned to their units, so much the better. Then the unit's mission is only slightly impacted. Rapid diagnosis and triage are critical processes; they must be done right the first time. Without them, the rest of the treatment process is compromised.

What happens if the patient in the military environment is treated on the spot and needs only some rest and brief recuperation? Getting this needed rest may be a big problem. Unlike civilian patients, military patients cannot simply be sent home to recover. Home can be a ship at sea, an air squadron in some remote location, a submarine underwater, or a field unit in the desert. Military patients are far from the comforts of their real homes. What if the patient needs definitive care and cannot be sent anywhere? Then, in keeping with the unit's mission, the patients are treated as best they can be where they lay. Hospitals in the civilian community do not often face these problems. The military health care system is designed to work as a system: (1) triage, (2) immediate diagnosis, (3) stabilize, (4) treat, and (5) recuperate or (6) evacuate. Any delays or unplanned changes in this system can suboptimize the entire spectrum of care. Military planners spend days, weeks, or months perfecting this system.

No matter who the health care provider is—hospital corpsmen, medic, registered nurse, IDC, PA, flight surgeon, or GMO—the motto is "You go with what you have." It is up to the commander of the squadron, battalion, or vessel to help arrange for the medical evacuation. That is one of the critical jobs of senior military leadership: ensuring that the sick and injured are properly cared for and then arranging for medical evacuation. This often means balancing the mission of the unit against the severity of the illness or injury. Getting the patient to definitive care is a big issue. Safety is a big issue. Medical evacuations by airplane or helicopter can be dangerous. They require precision planning and flawless execution.

One exciting alternative to cope with injuries in the field and limited availability of medical evacuation is the use of "telemedicine," in which the field medic or physician is connected to a base hospital. As an example, digital X-rays from the field or ship can be coupled with voice or electronic communication and transmitted to more experienced physicians and nurses at a major medical or dental treatment facility. Staff at the major facility can read the X-rays and respond to the field with appropriate treatments. Military units can receive superb field treatment by telemedicine. In many instances, patients can be treated there without further evacuation. The patient can then be returned to the field for duty or at least can be stabilized in the field and await less emergent care after the unit has returned to its home base. This is an exciting process to watch that holds great promise for the future. Note that prior to telemedicine, patients were routinely medically evacuated at great cost and risk. Whenever anyone is medically evacuated, there are no "temporaries" than can be immediately brought in to backfill critical skills of those evacuated. Staffing levels of units or ships are already tight; there are never enough personnel to go around.

Over the past several years this author has learned a great deal from military and civilian experts about using quality management to improve military medicine. The lessons have been learned first-hand in Navy hospitals and clinics. Additionally, hundreds of lessons were learned by collaborating with health care professionals in Army and Air Force clinics and hospitals throughout the world. Each lesson learned has been an opportunity to teach others as they begin their QM journey.

An example of lessons learned is at the Naval Medical Center San Diego (NMCSD), located in San Diego, California. This author acknowledges that similar lessons can be found every day in the Army and Air Force hospitals. The staff of Army and Air Force hospitals have every right to be just as proud of their QM accomplishments as does San Diego. What matters is that lessons are learned and shared freely among all three branches of the services and the civilian sector.

The Navy successes and lessons learned at NMCSD span a period of six years from October 1989 to September 1995, with this author intimately involved in planning, coordinating, and facilitating NMCSD's QM journey. NMCSD is similar in size and scope to other large teaching medical centers in the Army and Air Force. The commanding officer or commander of NMCSD is a senior Naval officer, usually a one-star or two-star admiral. As a large and complex military medical center, it has to work harder than many smaller hospitals to maintain the delicate balance between the military's wartime need for operational readiness and the peacetime health care needs of the active duty military personnel reserves, military retirees, and their families. With a staff of approximately 4500, the medical center and seven outlying medical clinics log more than a million outpatient visits a year. Southern California has one of the largest active duty and military retiree populations in the United States. Consequently, NMCSD must provide care and support for hundreds of thousands of patients each year.

NMCSD was introduced in 1989 to quality management TQM/TQL by two great visionaries of military medicine: the then Navy Surgeon General, Vice Admiral James Zimble, MC, USN, and the hospital commander at that time, Rear Admiral Robert Halder, MC, USN. "Balboa" as NMCSD is affectionately known, is one of the world's largest military medical and teaching centers. It is considered a multiservice treatment center, serving men and women from all services—Army, Navy, Air Force, Marine Corps, and Coast Guard—retirees, and their families. Patients come from as far away as Japan and the Pacific Rim. Balboa is a key component in the DoD TRICARE system.

As Balboa's commanding officer in 1989, Halder had just returned from a conference on improving health care quality, coordinated by Zimble at Navy medicine's headquarters in Washington, D.C. The course was taught by Donald Berwick and his staff from the National Demonstration Project located near Boston. Zimble had heard of Berwick's work in quality management and had been eager for quite some time to use QM principles in Navy hospitals and clinics to resolve recurring problems such as access to care, long waiting times in ambulatory clinics, delays in procedures, and long waiting times for prescription refills.

In the late 1980s, health care was changing rapidly for all of the military hospitals, clinics, and field units. Population demographics and treatment protocols were changing, and change was coming rapidly. As the Navy Surgeon General, Zimble wanted to successfully lead Navy medicine through these upcoming changes. He wanted to avoid crisis management as a method to solve problems. He viewed quality management as a powerful tool to overcome crisis management, improve the delivery of health care, and get all military medical and dental employees involved.

In September 1989, Zimble invited almost 150 of his senior-most health care leaders to the conference. Probably one of the biggest lessons shared by Berwick during the conference was that any organization seriously interested in using QM practices must start at the top. If the organization's top leadership does not buy in, neither will anyone else. Without it, any big change such as QM is doomed. It will die a quick death. Quality management requires radical changes from the status quo; it requires commitment, respect, and trust, especially from the leaders in the organization who control the resources. Implementing QM requires committing resources up front: labor, equipment, and dollars. Only the organization's leaders can determine the priority for allocating these resources.

What Halder saw as a vision during the 1989 conference is still alive today. He saw the power of quality management. He saw a unique opportunity for thousands of junior and senior hospital employees to make a difference in the lives of their patients, families, and community. His was a vision of a large military hospital that could one day serve its customers without endless bureaucracy, long waiting lines, hundreds of complicated forms, and staff worn-out from daily frustrations. He shared this vision in great detail with his senior staff at Balboa as soon as the conference was over.

In 1989, the health care industry's use of quality management was certainly in its infancy, both for military and civilian institutions. During this time, the military was using the term *TQM* to describe its use of quality management tools and methodologies. Soon afterward the Navy changed the name to TQL—total quality leadership—to emphasize the leadership aspects of QM. Even today, TQM and TQL are used interchangeably by military audiences in describing quality management. By 1995 and 1996, the definition of QM was expanded to include some of the tools and principles of business process reengineering.

On his return to San Diego from the conference with Zimble, Halder announced to the senior directors and managers that he was going to implement TQL at Balboa and that he would personally lead the transformation. This proved later to be an extremely valuable lesson for any health care organization undertaking quality management. *It takes a transformation to enact a profound change such as quality management.* Without transforming the organization, the changes are only temporary and are seen by the employees as just another program to which they give lip service. Had Halder not taken the time and energy to create a transformation, quality management would have quickly died at Balboa. Sadly, other large military facilities had started QM initiatives using crisis management techniques and had failed.

Among Halder's first actions was to appoint a quality management (TQL) coordinator (this fortunate author) and form an executive steering committee (ESC) to help lead the way at Balboa. He then sought the commitment and active participation of the senior physicians, nurses, administrators, and senior enlisted staff to be members of the ESC. He got their commitment. Halder made participation on the ESC voluntary. He made it clear in the beginning that there would be no hard feelings toward those who chose not to join the ESC. He only requested that they not block his efforts at creating an ESC and implementing quality management. It would have been very easy for Halder to simply order everyone at Balboa to use QM. That would have been the classic military model. Had he ordered the use of QM, predictably, he would have been met with massive resistance and malicious compliance.

Wisely, Halder chose a smoother and more practical method to begin implementing QM. He gained slowly, over a period of time, the cautious trust and commitment of the ESC members, all of whom volunteered for the assignment. For many senior leaders in military medicine, trust and commitment do not come easy. Years of government bureaucracy, last-minute crises, and half-started schemes have taught them to be very cautious. With numerous flavor-of-the-month management programs having been forced on them, it is very easy to understand the skepticism, especially from the physicians.

Civilian doctors are wary of any administrative scheme, such as a committee or task group, that takes them away from their patients. No matter how rational the meeting or project, time away from patients is money lost. Military physicians are just as skeptical. They have even less confidence in bureaucracies that take time away from their patients. Over the years, they have witnessed a variety of military management schemes fade away after a few weeks or months. This is especially true for physicians who are midlevel managers and supervisors. With pressures coming up from their subordinates and down from their seniors, they are caught in the middle. They are very reluctant to try any new management idea until it has been thoroughly tested. They don't have time to waste on untested or novel schemes. This leads to another lesson learned at Balboa and elsewhere: *Don't expect new styles of management to be adopted by managers at any level of the organization without a lot of soul-searching, agonizing, and much consternation.* The pressure is on all managers, middle and upper, to get the work done *now*. New ideas such as QM sound like long-winded schemes to them, not solutions to their problems.

After he had established the ESC, Halder's next step was to articulate his vision—the same one he saw at the conference. This is not any easy task in the military. In a culture where today's military mission often clashes with tomorrow's vision of the future, it is imperative that the vision created in the military environment is clear, honest, and compelling. Perhaps that was one of Halder's greatest gifts to his staff at Balboa: He clearly saw a day when quality management would become a way of life. When asked some specifics about his vision, he said he envisioned that whenever a patient or family member or guest walked around the hospital and clinics, looking lost, the staff would automatically reach out to that person and ask, "How can we help you?" Halder, a physician as well as a senior military commander, easily understood how patients can become lost in a hospital or clinic as they are shuffled from one place to the next. He also envisioned that just as the patients were getting ready to leave the physician's office, the clinic, or the ward, the staff would automatically ask, "How could we have made your stay more comfortable?" Halder's vision was that QM would become so well established that these two questions would become a natural part of the work day. Additionally, the staff would listen with open ears to the answers and respond in a caring, helpful manner.

With a quality management (TQL) coordinator appointed, an ESC established, and a vision given to his staff, Halder spent the next several months ensuring that training in QM tools and methodologies was provided to the hospital staff at all levels. Senior managers received extensive training; so did middle managers and junior employees. Some of the training was obtained from Berwick's National Demonstration Project and newly formed Quality Management Network. Some of the training came from local community and military resources. The rest came from within the hospital.

During this time another powerful and enduring lesson was learned at Balboa: "The local community offers superb training opportunities." So great was the input from the nearby community hospitals that Halder and a civilian hospital director, Michael Stringer, from the University of California at San Diego Medical Center, formed the Southern California Coalition for Improving Healthcare

Quality. Its purpose was to create a support network for new health care quality management coordinators and to build communitywide training opportunities in QM tools and methodologies. So great was the impact of this coalition that it was felt for many years after it had started.

The membership of the coalition included 28 military and civilian hospital/health care organizations. The hospitals included some as far away as 40 to 60 miles in Orange and Imperial Counties. Members often drove an hour each way for the meetings. The meetings were held at the coalition members' hospitals on a rotating basis. The meeting agenda included discussions on strategies for implementing QM, use of statistical tools, lessons learned, and how to overcome resistance to change. Visitors came to the meetings from Los Angeles, Nevada, and Arizona. QM-related training conferences were sponsored by the coalition once or twice every three to four months.

Another rich source for the staff at Balboa to receive QM training was from the Navy ships home ported in San Diego and the Marine Corps field units stationed at Camp Pendleton, California. The Marine Corps was always eager to assist its Navy colleagues at Balboa. The ship staffs were equally eager to teach what they had learned as they implemented QM practices. They willingly volunteered their time, talent, and resources. Wherever the training resources could be found, local and far away, they were used without hesitation.

Newly established in Bethesda, Maryland, the Naval Medical Quality Institute (NMQI) quickly became another source of excellent training courses and guidelines. Halder sent many nurses, physicians, administrators, and technicians to the NMQI courses. Later, other training resources were used, such as those from Air Force and Army units and at Veterans Affairs hospitals in California and most of the United States. In each instance, the reaction from these organizations was the same when Halder requested their assistance: "What can we do to help?"

In addition to the QM coordinators, facilitators for Balboa's process action teams (PATs) were also trained in the local community. The San Diego Deming User Group and the San Diego–based Institute for Quality and Productivity provided state-of-the-art training in statistical tools, principles, and QM methodologies. Both of these groups quickly became the mainstay for learning new ideas, advanced training in statistical tools, and building PATs. Eventually, hundreds of other organizations in San Diego and Southern California were also tapped for facilitator and team training. For Balboa, it was "The dawn of a new era." Balboa had, in fact, arrived at the doorstep of the quality movement. There was a sense of teamwork at Balboa and in the community—a sense of being together at the start of something bigger than all the organizations put together.

When Balboa staffers asked for help, they received it sevenfold. Collaboration, teams, and networking became the norm rather than the exception. Reports from many other Navy hospitals and those of the Air Force and Army indicated much the same thing: When help was requested, it came in bucketfuls! For example, it was during a site visit to Chip Caldwell and his employees at West Paces Ferry Hospital in Atlanta, Georgia, that Halder saw the power and success of quality management. He knew then that he had made the right choice for Balboa. Here was a hospital, astutely guided by Caldwell, that had successfully instituted Quality Management. QM practices were found throughout the entire hospital—not just in a textbook, but in offices, clinics, departments, and services of a renowned hospital. It wasn't a fluke; it was real.

At West Paces Ferry, Halder and his quality management coordinator also discovered the power of the FOCUS-PDCA cycle (see Figure 7.6). The actual creator of the model was HCA: Hospital Corporation of American. Seeing the FOCUS-PDCA model in action was exciting. Storyboards had been created at West Paces Ferry using this model. Each team's progress was clearly displayed. Because

Find a process to improve.

Organize to improve the process; select a team or individual who understands the process.

Clarify the current knowledge of the process.

Uncover the sources of process variation or poor quality.

Start the plan-do-check-act cycle.

Plan a pilot process improvement.

Do the improvement; collect and analyze the data.

Check the results and lessons learned.

Act to hold the gain by adopting, adjusting, or abandoning the change.

Figure 7.6. FOCUS-PDCA model.

the FOCUS-PDCA model requires a disciplined approach to problem solving, it gives structure and guidance to new and old teams. Structure is critical to success in the military; as is discipline of using sound, well-established management tools. As a result of seeing the storyboards in action, NMCSD adopted the FOCUS-PDCA model.

Once Halder had established a variety of QM training programs at Balboa, he created several pilot PATs to gain real-time practice in using QM tools. The first PATs included the following:

- Linen handling
- Surgical scrubs
- Admissions procedures
- Patient consult procedures
- Needle disposal
- Management information: hospitalwide databases
- Maternal–child: admission and discharge
- Pharmacy: dispensing of medications
- Visitor and staff parking
- Nursing staffing procedures

Over the next several years, scores of other PATs were created that dramatically changed the culture of Balboa. Problems that required the use of PATs were drawn from customer complaints, feedback from patients and their families, and discussions with the hospital staff. Some PATs were created by single departments or services such as laboratory, pharmacy, and nursing services. Others were more cross functional in nature and needed to be chartered by the ESC. To manage the growing number of teams, midlevel quality management boards (QMBs) were subsequently created to provide hands-on, direct support and administrative guidance to the PATs. The QMBs were especially helpful to new teams that were just starting their journey. Each QMB was required to provide supervision, technical guidance, just-in-time training, and moral support to its PATs. The QMBs also coached and prepared the PATs as they presented their FOCUS-PDCA storyboards to the ESC.

The time from 1989 to the early 1990s was a period of rapid growth in quality management at Balboa. Today, QM has evolved into a mature, relatively stable system at Balboa and elsewhere in military medicine. Some military hospitals and clinics have gone on to use business process reengineering practices or other management methodologies. Others have quietly incorporated the PATs and QMBs into their everyday business life without much fanfare. Sadly, some have let their teams and processes wither away, only to be used in preparation for their next JCAHO accreditation visit. But back in 1989 and the early 1990s, quality management was big stuff. There was much discussion about QM: You were either for it or wished it would go away. Rarely was anyone neutral about QM. PATs were constantly being started, reviewed, and completed.

In those days, so many processes in health care needed improvement (the need is still great in today's environment) that it was hard for hospitals to prioritize them. Although the ESC chose to charter many formal PATs at Balboa, some of the clinics and departments chose to create informal PATs or work groups to address more specific needs. In the end, these informal groups provided Balboa with some of its greatest QM successes. The informal PATs included those listed in Table 7.3.

As other hospitals have also found, teams are able to dramatically improve processes. Some processes require only minimal tweaking and do not require teams. Some teams are started with good intentions by management, but are later shelved due to higher priorities. The constant rotation of hospital staff creates membership problems for many teams at many hospitals. Yet most teams succeed because they persevere. Their challenge is to improve processes, eliminate outdated procedures, and overcome organizational barriers and hurdles while, at the same time, handling the other day-to-day health care crises. The teams listed in Table 7.3 faced these challenges head-on, dealt with the everyday crises, and achieved much success.

From these informal teams came another important lesson: *Young hospital employees, closest to the process, are often the best sources of vitality and energy to improve processes.* Not only was every team not a total success; not every team member was skilled at using quality management. Many team members

Table 7.3. Some of the informal PATs at Balboa.

Department/unit	Process or work flow
Optometry unit	New tracking system to ensure rapid patient follow-up.
Medical nursing	Safety risk factors for patients on medications such as Halcyon.
	Needle sticks: Implementing the needleless system.
Respiratory therapy	Adult resuscitation bags: Switching to disposable units.
Surgical nursing	Tube feedings: Switching from multiple feeding control devices to a single brand enteral feeding pump.
Post-anesthesia care unit (PACU)	Patient visits: Encouraging family members to visit patients in the PACU. Family is notified soon after the patient is admitted.
Dental department	Patient flow: differentiating between routine and emergency care; reducing waiting time for appointments.
Orthopedic department	Consult backlogs: using PAs in the hand and knee clinic to greatly reduce backlog of consults.
Physical therapy/occupational therapy	Fleet (shipboard) support: established physical therapy services aboard the aircraft carrier *USS Kitty Hawk*.

required much training, guidance, and support in learning the tools of QM. Yet after working on their teams, often for up to six to nine months, these team members (especially the younger ones) still displayed great enthusiasm and energy. Just when a team was ready to quit, these employees would urge the other team members to keep on going. That often made the difference between a team's success or failure. This is not to say anything against the more seasoned or older hospital staff. We expect them to ride out the ups and downs of any team activity. But when the going gets tough, youthful energy and persistence can sometimes make a world of difference.

A quick look at one of Balboa's PATs—linen handling—demonstrates this point very well. At Balboa, informal PATs could be chartered by the department heads, supervisors, and managers if the process was solely within their own area. They did not need the blessing of the ESC. If the processes crossed into several departments, then they became formal teams, requiring approval by the ESC. The linen PAT was chartered by the ESC because of the increasing cost of linen supplies. A hospital the size of Balboa uses a lot of linen each day. Hospitals use their linen supplies 24 hours a day, seven days a week; it is never-ending. A medical center can easily be compared to a major hotel in terms of its linen supplies. Linen is a high-cost item. The cost of purchasing, laundering, repairing, and replacing bed sheets, pillow cases, bath towels, and surgical scrubs was approximately $300,000–$400,000 per year at Balboa.

When Halder was first approached about the problem, he asked, "What does the $300,000–$400,000 get me?" The answer was "Until next year," which meant that each year he would have to spend the same amount of money purchasing new linen supplies, with no real net gain. The cost would be the same or higher each succeeding year. Intuitively Halder knew that there had to be a better way.

Once Halder and the ESC had chartered the linen PAT, the team members used the QM tools of process flowcharting and cause-and-effect tools to look at the problem from multiple views. The process flowchart showed numerous problems in the handling of patient care linen.

- Most of the linen to be cleaned was contracted out to private businesses.

- Dirty linen had to be presorted into several categories (routine, contaminated, and so on) and labeled as such before it was sent to the contractor.

- The process of sorting was a dirty job that no one wanted to do.

- Sharp objects were occasionally found in the sorted linen.

- The linen appeared to be wearing out prematurely.

- There was never enough linen for the evening shifts or weekends.

Military hospitals are notorious for running out of linen at night and on weekends. Every military nurse, medic, or hospital corpsmen who has worked the inpatient wards during these hours knows this situation by heart, especially over the three-day holiday weekends. By noon on Saturday, the linen supply is already running low, and some items run out.

The linen at Balboa was wearing out much faster than would be normally expected. The problem was getting worse. Linen was returned from the contractor with holes and tears. Multiple patches were needed on the sheets. If the linen was too badly worn, it had to be replaced. The sheets and pillowcases were often lasting for only four or five washes. As the team used the FOCUS-PDCA cycle, the cause-and-effect diagram shed some light on some of the suspected causes for the linen problem.

- The contractor was purposely ripping the linen.

- The contractor's equipment was obsolete.

- Linen was purchased from low-bid sources.

- Linen was being taken home by a variety of sources.

- Harsh detergents were wearing out the linen.

- The amount of dirty linen sent to the contractor did not match the amount returned.

- Areas that had no linen were "borrowing" from other areas.

In all, nearly 40 suspected causes were highlighted in the team's FOCUS-PDCA cycle. After several weeks of analysis and discussion, the team finally uncovered two of the most important causes of the linen problem: (1) low-bid linen was in fact wearing out prematurely; and (2) very ingenious hospital corpsmen on the night and weekend shifts were secretly hoarding the linen to prevent running out. Hoarding has been a time-honored tradition for thousands of hospital corpsmen and medics. They pride themselves on coming up with the linen when none was to be had.

The linen team's solution to the low-bid linen problem was to work with the federal regulations and supply ordering personnel to purchase new linen from a higher-quality source. The solution to hoarding was to prevent having to hoard in the first place. One of the young hospital corpsmen on the linen PAT showed the team members how hoarding worked. The hospital corpsmen from the patient care areas, who are in charge of the linen, did not trust the delivery timeliness or the amount of linen received from the linen room. They knew they would be short-changed, and hence run out at night and on weekends. They had experienced this for years. Despite spending more and more money, the problem remain unchanged. And that led to another lesson in quality management: *Throwing money at a problem usually only makes it worse.* If money were the ultimate solution, the hospital would have gone broke years ago. Fixing the problem up front—eliminating the need for hoarding—became the focus of the linen PAT's efforts.

The story behind this problem is that before the use of the FOCUS-PDCA cycle and QM tools, there were hundreds of informal, anecdotal suggestions from the hospital staff to fix the problem, including the following:

- Change contractors.

- Bill the contractor for the torn linen.

- Load the wards and clinics with more linen on Fridays.

- Budget more money each year for linen; take the money from other departments.

- Hire a new security force to patrol the parking lots looking for theft.

None of these solutions was based on any scientific analysis. If Halder had chosen any of these solutions, they would have only made the problem worse—much worse. Thankfully, QM tools showed the PAT members a clearer and more accurate view of the problem. The results of the team's work was a dramatic reduction—$200,000—in linen costs per year. Balboa could easily have taken the easy way out and blamed the contractor, employees, and patients. Instead, the staff chose a more pragmatic and long-term solution to the linen problem. The story of the linen PATs suspected causes can be repeated for many other teams at Balboa. Once the process is thoroughly examined, the initial suspected causes for many problems rarely turn out to be the real causes. All PATs can use the scientific tools to overcome wild guesses, myths, perceptions, and distortions. All PATs, informal or formal, can therefore make a big impact upon the customers, patients, staff, and community. All PATs can use the FOCUS-PDCA cycle proven to keep their teams on track, document their results, and make the best use of their team members' talents and expertise.

Balboa serves as a good example of how quality management, properly applied and nurtured, can achieve cost savings, reduce waiting times, eliminate needless duplication, and better serve its customers. After Halder retired from Balboa, Rear Admiral Ridenour, MC, USN, and later Rear Admiral Nelson, MC, USN, took command. They put their distinctive touches on the QM processes at Balboa. They saw new opportunities for the thousands of military and civilian health care staff to work together to make a difference for the patients at Balboa.

Halder's QM vision was subsequently shaped, molded, and refined by both the patients and the staff at Balboa. The patients benefited from the efforts of the PATs to improve customer service; the community benefited as well. In turn, Navy medicine learned a lot about quality management from the staff at Balboa. In addition to Balboa, all military hospitals, clinics, and field units have learned valuable lessons in QM and have freely shared them.

Zimble retired from the Navy as Surgeon General knowing that he had successfully instituted a major change in military medicine through QM. He was followed by other Surgeon Generals of the Navy: Vice Admiral Donald Hagan, MC, USN, and currently Vice Admiral Harold Koenig, MC, USN. Each of these Surgeon Generals chose the difficult road of continuing the journey toward quality management. Choosing quality management as a way of doing business in the military carries big risks. QM takes time, energy, commitment, and perseverance; however, this author is convinced that the results of QM definitely outweigh the risks and initial costs.

Overcoming Barriers and Learning New Lessons

In addition to the lessons learned outlined in this chapter, new lessons have been learned and barriers have been overcome. These come from informal teams and small groups at Balboa and discussions with other QM professionals in other military and community hospitals. Overcoming barriers and learning new lessons is never easy, but can lead to remarkable successes.

Barriers. There are many barriers to implementing quality management.

- The norm is crisis management
- Productivity at the expense of quality
- Multiple and conflicting customers
- The fix-it-later syndrome
- Inspections, inspections, and more inspections
- Don't have time to plan, do, check, and act
- "Fire, ready, aim"

One of the biggest barriers to overcome is crisis management. Crisis management is often used to demonstrate action or that "something is getting done." Watching crisis management in action gives a false sense of security. It looks like the organization is proactive and getting results. When crisis management becomes the only method, processes often break down. People take shortcuts to save time. Improvements are put off until there is more time. Quick productivity takes precedence over quality. *Counting* something is viewed as far better than improving it. The fix-it-later syndrome is seductive. It implies that "good enough" is just fine. In other words, why waste time fixing things that aren't really broken? Inspections, like crisis management, are viewed as necessary evils that get the job done now and eventually lead to improvement. Both allow the organization to find a guilty party—the person who is slowing down the process and not getting the work done fast enough. Blame can then be fixed on someone. PATs aren't good targets for blaming; individuals are, especially during inspections.

Additional Barriers. The list continues.

- One-way communication
- Front-office, ivory-tower approach
- Lowest bidder
- Unconscious waste of resources
- Priorities based on politics versus facts (or no priorities at all)

One-way communication is a great deterrent to creativity. If a leader doesn't care for improvements or feels threatened by them, limiting communications is a superb killer for any quality management initiative. The front office staff members can become far removed from the real work. They can use the ivory-tower approach and assume that their policies and procedures are correct and are the only ones to be followed. This gives an impression that management knows what is best for the employees. The low-bidder syndrome can masquerade as saving money. Often the organization winds up with inferior products, which can be dangerous to staff and patients. Basing priorities on politics instead of facts is very common. Unfortunately, employees know it and become very suspicious of management. Politics often sacrifice the hard work of employees so that someone else can get what he or she wants. Each of these barriers can undermine the best of efforts.

Difficult Barriers. Two barriers are particularly difficult to overcome. They are slowly being driven out of the military culture.

- The fear of saying no
- Evaluations based on quantity versus quality

The fear or inability to say "no" in an organization is enormously destructive to any QM initiative. It immediately creates distrust and stifles productive feedback. Employees are fearful of being fired. Exposing any weaknesses or faults labels the employee as a troublemaker. Employees are then very distrustful of any management scheme that talks of empowerment. If they don't see empowerment or trust in action, they will correctly decide that it doesn't really exist. If their evaluations are based on the quantity of work performed, process improvement will be seen as a waste of time. Their view is, "Why spend the time required to fix processes?" For them, management's over-focus on short-term tasks or projects gives visible (but false) evidence that real work is being done.

Sinking the QM Ship. Using the analogy of sinking a ship, there are many ways to "sink" the quality management ship.

- Myopia: The pressure for short-term results
- The B-movie syndrome: Ineffective cast and stars
- TQM band-aid: Cultural change is not by accident
- Failure by numbers
- Minimize/downsize: Education gets cut
- Solve world crises

A quick killer to any QM activity is the pressure for short-term, quick-gain results. This myopia forces an individual or team to take a superficial look at the process, select a cause, and then jump into action rather than holding the gains made for the long haul. The B-movie syndrome is equally destructive. Like many of the B-movies made in Hollywood in the 1950s and 1960s, it assumes that any work group or team can be put together to solve a problem. In other words, any team will do; they'll eventually figure out what to do. If the leader, facilitator, and members are not properly selected, trained, and supported, the results are predictable: not a showcase event.

Cultures do not change by accident. TQM is not a band-aid. Cultures are changed by creating ownership within the workplace and creating open and effective communications. Downsizing and getting rid of departments such as education or human resources is not an accidental event. It is a deliberate and fast way to save money for the short run. A perfect target for downsizing appears to be education and training departments. The belief is that it can always be made up later. Downsizing the workforce without reducing the workload is not an efficient management strategy: *You cannot downsize to greatness.* Solving world crises is a quick and painful way to sink the efforts of any team effort. It assumes that tackling a bigger problem is far better than tackling smaller ones. After all, there is only so much time available to solve problems; we might as well work on the big ones. Sad to say, this tactic has ruined many teams and work groups. They simply take on too big of a project at one time, then frustration settles in. Morale plummets, productivity comes to a standstill, and team members get bogged down in the complexity of an overwhelming project.

New Lessons Learned at the Executive Level. There are many lessons to be learned at the executive level of an organization. These two are clear standouts.

- Senior leadership must demonstrate commitment.
- Senior leadership must constantly seek ways to improve the organization's systems and processes.

The commitment from senior leaders cannot be lukewarm. Everyone in the organization looks to leadership for priorities, expectation, and the rules to work by. Any speech, policy, or action that is seen as half-hearted will be quickly viewed as not important. Employees are well accustomed to lip service; quality management, TQM, and TQL can easily become "total quality lip service." If the commitment is not there at the executive level, don't expect the employees to be enthusiastic. Senior leaders must be relentless in seeking new ways to improve the organization and its processes. Every organization—military or civilian—must analyze, upgrade, restructure, or dramatically improve its processes to remain competitive and to stay in business. Executive leaders are responsible for helping maintain that competitive edge. Lukewarm enthusiasm rarely succeeds; half-hearted improvements don't work either.

New Lessons Learned at the PAT Level. PATs are great sources for learning new lessons. Among the new lessons, two are clear standouts.

- QM/TQL is not effective for crisis management or instant solutions.
- Changes to processes must be confirmed on a trial basis.

Quality management activities are not designed for quick fixes, instant solutions, or any activity where data and analysis are short-changed. Successful process improvement requires allowing PATs the time to collect accurate data and conduct an analysis. Crisis management should not become the norm in a QM-oriented organization. It is waste of the team's time to expect constant quick fixes. Once changes are determined by the team, they must be confirmed by a trial PDCA cycle. Changes should be tested on a pilot basis to confirm that the right processes are being improved with the correct tools, based upon accurate data. Large-scale changes without a pilot test are an invitation to disaster.

Suggested Actions for Leaders. From the lessons learned come some actions that leaders of all organizations can use, including the following:

- Senior leaders should lead by example.
- Practice daily doing it right the first time.
- Drive out fear: Be open to different ideas.
- Make decisions on what's best for the organization.
- Practice two-way communications at all levels.
- Prioritize.

If quality management is to be successful, it deserves the example of senior leadership: Do what you say and say what you do. Everyone watches to see what the real priorities of the leaders are. Employees have a built-in radar for lip service; they can spot it a mile away. They also know when things are being done right. They expect senior leaders to help them do things right the first time and to serve as role models. Quality management should be an opportunity for senior leaders to showcase their leadership in action. What kills quality management the fastest? Fear—it can destroy people in minutes. The cure for this problem is to drive out fear. Employees want the leaders to be open to new or different ideas. Fear squelches creativity and innovation. Equally bad is making decisions based on what's best for an individual. The "I win, you lose" philosophy is still alive in many organizations. The focus should be on what's best for the entire organization or department. A word of caution: In organizations with multiple departments, optimizing one department may well suboptimize the others. Unless the process is fully analyzed by a trained, cross-departmental or cross-functional team, suboptimization can result.

More Suggested Actions at All Levels. These suggested actions can be used at all levels of the organization.

- Long-term planning includes customers.
- Identify the customer's needs—listen.
- Make decisions based on data.

All levels of the organization should automatically involve the customer(s) in any level of planning. Quality management means understanding and meeting or exceeding the customer's expectations. The focus is on the customer. If the only intent is to serve the organization's parochial interests, without involving the customer, customers will eventually figure it out and go somewhere else. Once the customers have been identified, listening is the greatest skill that management can acquire. Listen for the true needs of customers. Listen nondefensively. It has to be okay for customers to tell managers what they really think and believe. Listening with closed ears is the same as tuning out the data. Customer-oriented decisions based on data lead to success. Decisions based on poor data, hunches, or wild guesses drain the organization's resources.

And, when in doubt, just do it! It is far better to be proactive and begin using quality management than to delay starting it. Delays breed more delays. QM can be highly successful at all levels of an organization, whether practiced by individuals, small work groups, or the entire organization. QM can be used to make decisions and improve planning in the community, home, church, or for leisure-time activities. Waiting to be told to start QM is like waiting for your ship to "come in." It may be at sea for a long time. The time to start is now!

Summary

Quality management, as highlighted by the example of Balboa and the lessons learned, can be a very powerful tool in military medicine. It can achieve successes often found in the civilian sector. In the culture of the military, QM competes with the military's need for command and control. It further competes with military medicine's dual mission of peacetime health care and readiness for war. And yet, QM has the ability to override the multiple layers of government bureaucracy, eliminate redundancy, reduce rework, and streamline outdated or obsolete procedures. Health care—military and civilian—owes much to the unsung heros of QM: the employees of hospitals, clinics, and other organizations. While the military often calls it *total quality management* and the Navy changed it to *total quality leadership*, quality management is clearly a positive and successful move from the old way to the new way. QM goes a long way toward overcoming the belief that poor processes only come from people, or that checking and endless reporting or endless inspections are good practices. Quite the opposite: QM is about giving health care employees an opportunity to improve processes—to improve the care they want to give to patients.

The work of Zimble and Halder lives on today. Naval Medical Center San Diego is one example of a military medical center that successfully started the journey. It is still on that journey. All hospitals, clinics, field units, squadrons, and ships of the Army, Navy, Marine Corps, and Air Force can claim their own QM successes. Other agencies of the DoD can do so as well. With numerous barriers to quality management, many new and continuing lessons have been learned. Senior leadership must be committed to leading the way. TQM is not a band-aid. Short-term fixes usually lead to more problems. It is likely that many more lessons will be learned in the coming years. With the lessons learned has come much success—success in overcoming bureaucracy and years of status quo. When asked whether someone should begin using TQL, Halder said, "Just do it!"

Discussion Questions for a One-Hour Senior Executive Meeting

1. What is the role of executive leadership in implementing quality management?
2. What does resistance sound like at the executive and middle management levels?
3. Is benchmarking with other successful organizations an executive-level responsibility? If not, who has the responsibility?
4. What lessons can be learned from executive leaders in private industry?
5. How can the organization's overall resistance to QM be overcome?
6. How can the conflicts between downsizing and quality management be resolved?
7. What happens when politics routinely outweigh the facts?
8. If QM training opportunities are cut, what is the responsibility of senior leadership?
9. What are the hallmarks of successful quality management outcomes for leaders?
10. How can executive leaders overcome the "crisis management" mentality?
11. What if the first few QM initiatives aren't fully successful—what is the role of senior leadership?

Discussion Questions for a One-Hour Governing Body Meeting

1. How does this hospital/organization fit in with the community's needs?

2. What do internal and external customers say about health care at this institution?

3. What is the board's vision for this hospital five to eight years from now?

4. Who is doing what we do better, and how can we learn from them?

5. What new trends in our society must we start addressing now?

6. How does new technology help or hinder our institution?

7. Are we just giving lip service to quality management?

8. Reengineering appears to be very popular in our community—are we strong enough in QM to begin using it?

9. Downsizing is very popular—how can we prevent losing our brightest and best employees?

10. What is this hospital's/organization's role in preventive care?

Discussion Questions for a One-Hour Process Owners Meeting

1. What are the best ways for employees in our organization to identify processes that need improvement?

2. What successes have we already achieved in QM? What can we learn from them?

3. What is the best way to ensure attendance at team meetings?

4. What should teams do when they get stuck or frustrated?

5. Are we identifying special cause as well as common cause variation?

6. Many employees are frustrated with the organization's slow progress—what words of encouragement can we give them?

7. Employees read about the "death" or "failure" of QM—what's the real story?

8. JCAHO surveyors are coming in nine months—what successes do we want to showcase?

9. We seem to be always working on only administrative processes—what about clinical processes?

10. Some of the doctors are working with us; others aren't—how can we get more of them involved?

Suggested Reading

Berwick, Donald. *Curing Health Care.* San Francisco: Jossey-Bass, 1990.

Berwick, Donald, et. al. *Striving Towards Improvement: Six Hospitals in Search of Quality.* Oakbrook Terrace, Ill.: JCAHO Press, 1992.

Collins, James C., and Jerry I. Porras. *Built to Last: Successful Habits.* New York: HarperCollins Publishers, 1994.

Deming, W. Edwards. *Out of the Crisis.* Cambridge, Mass.: Massachusetts Institute of Technology, 1986.

Deming, W. Edwards. *The New Economics.* Cambridge, Mass.: Massachusetts Institute of Technology, 1993.

Dienemann, J. *Continuous Quality Improvement in Nursing.* Washington, D.C.: American Nurses Publishing, 1992.

Executive Learning. *Continuous Improvement Handbook.* Brentwood, Tenn.: Executive Learning, 1993.

Gaucher, Ellen, and Richard Coffey. *Total Quality in Healthcare.* San Francisco: Jossey-Bass, 1993.

Goonan, Kathleen J. *The Juran Prescription.* Wilton, Conn.: Juran Institute, 1995.

Champy, James. *Reengineering Management: The Mandate for New Leadership.* New York: HarperCollins Publishers, 1995.

Harrington, H. James. *Total Improvement Management: The Next Generation in Performance Improvement.* New York: McGraw-Hill, 1995.

Juran, J. M. *Juran on Leadership for Quality.* New York: Free Press, 1989.

Sloan, M. Daniel. *How to Lower Health Care Costs by Improving Health Care Quality.* Milwaukee: ASQC Quality Press, 1994.

Waitley, Denis. *Empires of the Mind: Lessons to Lead and Succeed in a Knowledge-Based World.* New York: William Morrow and Company, 1995.

Capt. Charles B. Mount, NC, USN is the director of education and training standards at the Navy Bureau of Medicine and Surgery in Washington, D.C. In 1989 he became the quality management/total quality leadership (TQL) coordinator for the Naval Medical Center in San Diego, California. He served in that capacity until 1995, after which he was the TQL coordinator for the TRICARE health care system co-located at Naval Medical Center San Diego. For six years, Mount served as a coach, facilitator, trainer, and advisor to hundreds of military and civilian health care professionals throughout Southern California. He was promoted to Navy Captain in July 1996.

Mount was president of the Southern California Coalition for Improving Healthcare Quality for six years. He served as education coordinator, vice president, and then president of the San Diego Deming User Group. For his expertise in quality management and outreach to the community, he was awarded numerous honors and cited in *Who's Who in Business.*

Mount resides with his wife in Reston, Virginia, and continues his active teaching and facilitation in quality management.

Chapter 8

Quality Management in Veterans Health Administration

Galen L. Barbour

Background of the VA Health Care System

America's proud tradition of honoring and caring for those who have fought its wars and worn its uniform began on this continent nearly 150 years before the founding of the country itself. Building on the English custom in which monetary benefits were paid to anyone injured in the service of the Crown, the early settlers in Plymouth Colony adopted a law in 1636 that provided benefits to those wounded in military actions on the behalf of the colony. The United States, as a new government, continued that tradition by assigning to itself a responsibility to provide for the veterans of the Revolutionary War. Several key acts by the U.S. Congress continued the recognized responsibility and enlarged the scope and depth of the benefits. Specific structures were built for the provision of medical care: the Naval Asylum (1811) in Philadelphia that later became the first prepaid closed panel group health plan in the country,[1] and the U.S. Soldier's and Airmen's Home (1851) that also provided domiciliary care.

In the aftermath of the Civil War, Congress recognized the unmet need of wounded soldiers and created the system of hospitals known as the National Home for Disabled Volunteer Soldiers. Most of these institutions provided domiciliary care for the most part, but also provided medical care, both ambulatory and hospital-based. A federally funded system of hospitals, run under the aegis of the Public Health Service to care explicitly for veterans, began in 1920. Congress had authorized the use of funds to construct and purchase facilities to care for the veterans returning to the country after the Great War in Europe.

It was during that same time, the early part of the twentieth century, that American business leaders recognized the "plain horse sense" of providing health insurance to their workers in industry, manufacturing, and other climes such as mining.[2] A direct extension of this reasoning culminated in the passage of the War Risk Insurance Act of 1914. Although the Act was primarily aimed at providing disability benefits, it was carried on a tide of recognition that the federal government was a major employer and that certain of its employees—the soldiers and sailors involved in armed conflict—were involved in an occupation that was at least as risky as that of civilians who were covered by employer-provided health insurance. There was also some recognition that the federal government's responsibilities to provide for the military conscript do not end with the cessation of hostilities. So, in 1921, the

Congress created an independent bureau—the Veterans Bureau—to oversee the military veteran hospital system that until then was the responsibility of the Public Health Service.

In 1930, Congress created the Veterans Administration (VA) by combining three other federal agencies: the National Homes for Disabled Volunteer Soldiers, the Veterans Bureau, and the Bureau of Pensions. That new system was primarily based in its 47 hospitals and its 22,700 beds, most of which came from folding the structures of the National Homes into the new system. The Public Health Service continued to operate its facilities separately to care for some active duty personnel and their dependents.

At the close of World War II, only 15 years after its creation, the Veterans Administration faced the enormous challenge of caring for the expected large influx of veterans returning from Europe and Asia with a hospital system that was largely underfunded and understaffed. Two major and long-reaching changes to the bureaucratic structure of the system were made at that time, largely on the basis of recommendations of VA Administrator, Omar Bradley, and his chief medical advisor, Paul Magnusson. These two individuals engineered a change in the Civil Service Act to allow the creation of a separate personnel system for the hiring of physicians and constructed a partnership between the VA and America's medical schools. The separate personnel system allowed the VA to hire trained and skillful professionals to meet specific needs that were not contained in the Civil Service ranks and to recompense them accordingly. The partnership with medical schools was a clear win–win for both; the schools had little access to patient care settings in which to teach their students, and the VA hospital had far too few physician workers. This marriage between the practical realm of delivering medical care and the world of academe has brought untold benefits to both systems over the past 50 years. The affiliation has allowed VA to recruit highly qualified and talented physician staff; the presence of medical students and other trainees has created an environment of inquiry and questioning that has built consistent expectations for improvement and a drive for the highest-possible quality in care delivery and outcomes. Part of this drive has resulted in the development of research programs in VA that have made many significant contributions to the understanding of disease and its cure in American medicine. Two VA researchers have won Nobel prizes for their pioneering work.[3,4] Others have developed the CAT scanner[5] and the cardiac pacemaker;[6] proper treatments for hypertension,[7] tuberculosis,[8] and schizophrenia;[9] or the role of surgery in coronary artery disease;[10] laser treatment for prostatic cancer;[11] timing of drug protocols for AIDS;[12] and the protective effect of aspirin in heart disease.[13] VA researchers have also developed a variety of prosthetic devices and diagnostic equipment for use by the profession.

The impact of the marriage of American medical education with the VA was also quite positive. At present, more than half of the practicing physicians in America have had a significant portion of their medical training within the VA. Currently, all 55 of the nation's dental schools and 105 of the 126 medical schools are actively affiliated with the VA; in the 1970s, Congress passed the Manpower Grant program that allowed the creation of five new medical schools, and each of them has a VA facility as the parent teaching institution. Approximately 12 percent of the nation's residency training positions in the fields of psychiatry, surgery, and internal medicine are funded by the VA. Each year more than 30,000 medical residents and 22,000 medical students spend substantive training time in VA facilities rotating through those positions in traditional mainstream educational programs. The VA has also been instrumental in developing new, nontraditional training programs. For more than a decade, the VA's academic policy has included using some portion of its medical educational budget to establish superior training opportunities in nonaccredited fields; its leadership in the training of geriatric specialists provided impetus to the designation of geriatric medicine as a recognized specialty by the

Accreditation Council for Graduate Medical Education in 1988. Similar status accrued to geriatric psychiatry in 1994. As these programs joined the mainstream, the VA has shifted that support to other nonaccredited programs with special meaning for veterans: spinal-cord injury care, treatment of substance abuse, understanding the biologic basis for mental illness, traumatic brain injury, ambulatory medical care, clinical pharmacology, health care delivery methods, and even medical informatics.

For nearly 20 years, the number of VA hospitals (called *medical centers* because each of them has capacity and activity in outpatient care, acute hospital care, and extended care such as hospice or nursing home) has remained about constant at 172 with at least one in every state in the union. Recently, 18 of those facilities merged their administrative structures to create some dual division medical centers; the number of individual facilities officially dropped after that exercise to 159, but the health care delivery sites did not close. However organized, for the past decade VA medical centers have accounted for 900,000–1,000,000 discharges from acute care and 24–25 million outpatient visits each year. To accomplish this huge task, the VA employs about 240,000 people—roughly one in every thousand Americans works for the VA and contributes to the benefits delivered to our veteran patients.

The Veterans Administration (1930–1989) was comprised of three separate divisions. each with its own set of responsibilities. The Department of Medicine & Surgery (DM&S) provided the health care and medical education and training. Most VA employees worked for DM&S (about 190,000–200,000). The Department of Veterans Benefits (DVB) was responsible for administrating the veterans benefits programs for education, disability, home loans, and so on. DVB handles and disburses most of the money appropriated to the VA by Congress. The third division was the Department of Memorial Affairs (DMA), which was responsible for the upkeep and maintenance of cemeteries and providing for burial of veterans. In 1989, Congress raised the VA to cabinet level by creating the Department of Veterans Affairs (still to be known as *VA*, but without the *the*). This new VA also had three newly named divisions, doing the same work as before: DM&S became Veterans Health Service and Research Administration (VHS&RA), DVB became Veterans Benefits Administration (VBA), and DMA became the National Cemetery Service (NCS). In 1991, VSH&RA was retitled the Veterans Health Administration, or VHA.

There have been questions recently about the role VA should play in the delivery of health care in the United States. Some have considered that the department is no longer necessary since the number of veterans in the population is steadily declining. Although this is true, the absolute number of veterans seeking care from VA is remaining about constant, a steadily rising percentage of the overall veteran population. Although veterans, as a part of society, have a higher level of education and income than the national average, the group of patients seen by VA is largely composed of individuals without health insurance from any other source and with quite low income. VA's health care programs are clearly providing a safety net for many of these patients; without the system their care would be either shifted to other parts of the health care system (probably uncompensated) or would be left undone.

History of Quality Assurance Activities in VHA Prior to 1990

Like much of the rest of the medical care systems in America, VHA's involvement with quality assurance (QA) activities had begun in the 1960s and 1970s as an outgrowth of quality control. The usual QA activities amounted to measuring the number of times (or the rate) that bad things occurred (for example, death following a procedure). Any such focus on bad things tends to color the reason for collecting the information as well as the people that perform the collection. It didn't take long for the QA staff in almost every hospital to be seen as the "quality police;" their reports often identified individual practitioners as outliers in the grand scheme of things and then the hospital administration treated that individual as an outlaw and used one or another punitive method to try and get them to change.

The net result of such activity should have been predictable: Physicians were distrustful of the process; things didn't really change; and the administrative "solution" often was to hire more "police," collect more data, and search ever more diligently for bad things. Physicians didn't trust the system for a variety of reasons. They usually were not consulted about the measures beforehand (and often found reasons not to be involved, anyway) and considered them inappropriate when they were finally published. They rigorously questioned the data elements; much of the information was collected by employees who were not part of the direct care system and had little knowledge about the need for accuracy or how the data could or would be used. Often the interpretation of the data was also considered flawed by the physicians; in many instances, since the primary data of interest was not available, administrators had selected surrogate measures that were not reasonable in the physicians' eyes. And, importantly, the physicians knew two important facts that seemed to be largely ignored by everyone else. First, they knew that the care of a given patient was not totally influenced by their actions; the process of care generally took place outside of their control or direct influence (with the obvious exception of the operating room). They knew that some, but not all, of the bad things that happen were attributable to them; they felt unfairly persecuted when things went wrong and they were singled out for criticism and punishment when the error was nothing they could affect. Second, they knew what the errors were in the process of care, and they saw no real attempt to improve these parts of the system. They knew that these problems continued to exist in spite of much QA staff effort at collecting data, and they felt—often rightly so—that all the QA activity did was churn and churn: Real problems didn't get fixed, but one of them was going to get blamed if anything went awry.

From the administrators' standpoint, QA activities were also a problem. The data that got collected sometimes indicated that their facility was performing less well, sometimes significantly less well, than their counterparts. That information might be perceived by headquarters staff as evidence that they were not doing a good job; a real fear of measurement, data, and information began to grow in the organization. Very few wanted real measurement of anything because such information was often used in a punitive manner, and the ones held responsible did not feel it was in their power to fix whatever was wrong. That didn't stop them from trying, however, often by collecting ever more information in an attempt to find out who was responsible for the poor performance. In the decade leading up to 1991, several public occurrences of data disclosure tainted VA's reputation. In virtually all of these instances there was a real adverse event, but the unscientific approach of investigators blew the circumstances out of proportion, ignored the number of good things that happened, and took some form of pride in "exposing" the problems of "poor care" at one or more VA medical centers. Almost invariably, the centers that were most criticized were active affiliates of the local medical school. The staff physicians at the VA held faculty teaching positions at the medical school, and the local press and population were very proud of the care delivered at that medical school—and failed to see the connection. On one occasion, Congressional subcommittee staff developed their own "methodology" to determine the quality of care at VA hospitals. Their process was to count the number of certain bad things that occurred over a year; surprisingly, the hospitals that scored the worst were the largest hospitals, the ones giving the most care—often the most complex care as well—and they were academic affiliates of medical schools rated by a national magazine as among the top hospitals in the country. The absence of risk adjustment or comparisons of rates rather than raw numbers was challenged scientifically, but the damage to VA's reputation had already been done by then.

In late 1990, VHA underwent a major turnover of top-level management in its central office. A new chief medical director, James Holsinger Jr., was named; he brought with him several individuals new to that level of the department. Among the actions he took was to reorganize several of the administrative functions, including that of quality assurance. Before that time, the Office of Quality Assurance in VHA was placed several layers below that of the chief medical director (CMD). From this point in the organization, the staff of the QA office found that they were not able to make much headway in the department for needed change. Holsinger's reorganization moved the office nearly to the top, renamed it the Office of Quality Management, and gave it significant support for changes to be made throughout the system. It was from this new vantage point that some significant changes in VHA's measurement strategy for quality began to move through the system.

With the understanding and backing of the new chief medical director, we set a goal for VHA to be recognized as a leader in quality health care by 1995. In order to attain that goal, each of the problems already identified would have to be addressed and resolved. That process turned out to take the full five years and involved four phases of change.

First Steps of Change: Development of a Creed and a Definition of Quality

Late in 1990, the new Office of Quality Management (OQM) completed a series of consultative visits with quality managers in some of the medical centers, senior leaders of the new central office management team, and clinical leaders throughout the system and reviewed recent investigations and criticisms of VHA's QA activities. For VHA to reach its goal of being recognized as a leader in quality health care, we determined that three specific objectives would have to be attained. First, and perhaps most critical, was the development of a reputation for credibility in all that we did—including recognizing, acknowledging, and repairing any significant problems in the system. The credibility had to exist with Congress, the media, and especially with our partners in academic medicine. A second objective was to establish VHA as a clear leader in some key and important areas of health care. The third objective, never completely separable from the first two, was to bring a solid foundation of science to the measurement of quality within VHA, a foundation so firm and convincing that we could build our credibility and our leadership upon it.

As a beginning point, the new OQM set forth an operating creed to guide the day-to-day decisions needed to move toward the objectives. That creed simply stated the beliefs of the staff in OQM and did so publicly to allow others in the system to understand the reasoning behind certain actions. The creed said,

> *We believe that, in a health care system:*
>
> *1. Quality is assured at the point of patient contact*
>
> *2. Quality is improved at the point of patient contact*
>
> *3. Quality improvement is data driven, therefore*
>
> *4. All data must go to the point of patient contact.*

Using this creed, we began to determine the flow of data in the organization and to direct it outward toward the periphery, where patient care was occurring. We emphasized the responsibility of every person in the data collection and reporting cycle to see that the information was put into the hands of the only people in VA who could actually improve health care processes—the people in direct contact with patients. Not unimportantly, we also used the creed to establish an expectation for improvements and to use data and measurement both to make decisions as well as to document any changes.

Credibility. As noted, VHA had been the subject of several investigations of its QA processes and some instances of bad outcomes in the preceding decade. The absence of general information about quality of care for VHA to use in rebuttal or by way of explanation led the responsible administrators to take a defensive posture and to try and minimize the damage to the system from bad publicity. Two specific issues were important in this regard: VHA's grid scores on surveys done by the Joint Commission for Accreditation of Healthcare Organizations (JCAHO) were consistently lower than those of the rest of the nation, and VHA's internal peer review organization was based in individual districts around the country and was unable to provide a national data set about quality of care in any discrete area. At the national level, these two situations were addressed vigorously by developing a model program of employee education about JCAHO standards and by creating a national peer review system based on community standards and criteria that used non-VA physicians to review the care.

Many inside VHA believed that the primary reason for the low JCAHO scores was the institution of a new multihospital survey process in which JCAHO dedicated a team of surveyors to reviewing only VA medical centers in a geographic region over a several month period. These surveyors certainly became familiar with the VHA system and were better able to determine whether we were meeting the standards than they had been previously when their experience with a VA hospital was infrequent. Because the VHA scores averaged nearly 10 points below the rest of the nation, VHA began in 1989 to put significant resources into helping the hospitals meet the standards; most of the time this assistance came through hiring consultants to visit individual hospitals and perform critical mock surveys. In 1990, we began a program of educating VHA staff about the purpose and intent of the JCAHO standards rather than focusing all attention to the symptom of low scores. In association with VHA's Office of Academic Affairs, OQM developed and piloted a five-day educational program at JCAHO headquarters in Oakbrook Terrace, Illinois. The course instructors were JCAHO surveyors, and the material they covered emphasized the background and reasoning for the various standards. The first four classes of 25 individuals were composed of physicians from hospitals scheduled for surveys in the next year. A fifth class that first year was composed of quality managers. The classes were considered so successful by the attendees that their number grew to about 10 classes each year through 1996. Beginning in 1994, the classes were aimed at teams of individuals from the same medical center—usually three individuals—to enhance the concept of teamwork in addressing any improvement needs. By 1991, VHA's grid scores consistently averaged five to 10 points above those of the rest of the nation and gave some important credibility to claims that the quality of care in VA is high.

In addressing the problem of the peer review, we determined that the main issue was the credibility of performing peer review within the system—a concern outside the system that the "foxes were guarding the henhouse." Accordingly, we dissolved the internal peer review program (called MEDIPRO for Medical District Initiated Peer Review Organization) and contracted with an outside peer review organization to review a sample of cases in every hospital across the country. The contract called for the reviewer, West Virginia Medical Institute, to establish criteria using practicing physicians who were not associated with VA and to use those criteria to review a random sample of 5 percent to 6 percent of high-volume and high-risk cases across the system. Using these putative community standards and a random sample of cases, we have been able to show that VHA's care for these patients meets or exceeds the community standard more than 98 percent of the time. The steady accrual of this kind of information—generally lacking in other hospital systems—has provided VA administrators leverage and balance in discussions with outside parties about the care delivered in any particular medical center or in the system as a whole.

While these two activities were addressing the credibility of the system to outside critics, we felt a need to make improvements in internal credibility as well. We began to provide internal reports to the individual medical centers of data they had been sending to the central office for several years (two specific reports dealt with the rate of new pressure sores in patients in extended care facilities and the average length of stay in the hospital preoperatively for patients undergoing elective procedures). Staff in these hospitals were initially suspicious of the reports, questioning the data elements and what was expected of them in reply. Over time, however, they came to understand that only they could take this data and use it for substantive improvements in care and outcomes; the lack of attention to the reports or their findings by any central office helped to confirm our assertion that these data belonged to them, the ones at the point of patient contact. Another action taken over several months and in different venues involved direct attempts to reduce mandated workload, reduce the confusion in centralized policies and procedures, and develop mechanisms for the staff to get access to local data for quality management activities. Overall, throughout the five-year period from 1990 to 1995, these actions brought steady improvement in credibility for the system and for the central office with the various staff members in the local medical centers.

Leadership. Internal leadership required providing VHA physicians with a reason for their personal involvement in developing and using quality management programs. We felt that any new programs should be driven by the ultimate users, and the role of leadership was to not only motivate these users and practitioners to become involved but also to find and direct the resources to the development of the best quality management tools we could. A conscious effort was made to contact physician leaders throughout the system for their constructive input and then to ask for their continued involvement in improving the tools we had available or in development. Over the five-year period, more than 100 different physicians spent time actively engaged in the process of constructing new tools or making major changes and improvements in existing measurement tools. These individuals were not only valuable to the effort in these very direct ways, but also as ambassadors of change and specifically the local use of the tools they were familiar with. The use of scientific collection methods and analysis also attracted physician support for the new tools, and we tried to build around that key point in teaching about the new tools during any pilot phase or when they were released for use throughout the system.

Externally, leadership was best exhibited by the types of tools and measures we determined to be of value. One specific instance involved the development of an automated checklist for quality indicators over a few months after the VA secretary declared the need for such an instrument. The mechanism developed, the Quality Improvement Checklist (QUIC), enabled the VA hospital system to accomplish what the JCAHO was attempting to do with its Indicator Measurement System—to use automated databases to determine how well the hospital is operating within specified guidelines. In another instance the development and finding of a mechanism to collect risk-adjusted data of patients preoperatively and use that data to assess quality of care postoperatively provided an opportunity for VHA to establish itself as a national leader in setting and measuring surgical standards of care.

Science. Incorporation of the best scientific methods was necessary for us to accomplish both the recruitment of VA physicians to the quality improvement model and to develop useful tools to measure quality that would bear the scrutiny of outside critics. As noted, we put considerable effort into listening to the needs and desires of the physician staff in our medical centers—we considered them an important customer group. Several of the initiatives and modifications undertaken by OQM in the early 1990s were directly attributable to comments, suggestions, or complaints raised by the physician staff.

The respect of the academic world, however, took more than a listening ear. We used the expertise of VHA's health services research community to bring to bear the cutting-edge concepts in clinical assessment for new measurements of quality. These concepts included case-mix analysis of patient populations, risk adjustment of specific patient cohorts, the use of patient (customer) information to design and remake programs and services, and ensuring adequate connection between intervention and outcome (even when that meant extended follow-up).

Second Steps: Determining Where We Were and What Is Needed to Improve

Several key issues demanded recognition and correction. For many of the reasons noted, quality management was essentially invisible in the organization; it lacked leadership, cohesion, and philosophy. Continuous improvement was not a goal, and efforts to manage or measure quality were considered micromanagement. The fear of data and measurement was pervasive and dominated the system. The QA staff being regarded as quality police made their job much more difficult, and this was compounded by a lack of any structured quality improvement education program. Access to existing data was poor, even though VA has one of the best integrated data systems in health care; the impediments at the local level to use that data were significant and prevented engaging the clinical staff. National aggregation of data was done annually and not used for any significant review of activities. There was little use of the department's scientific resources in developing and measuring quality; the patient satisfaction instrument had little face validity and had not changed substantively in the preceding 20 years. In sum, the quality management function in VHA and generated by the central office had virtually no credibility in the clinics and medical centers across the system.

At about this time, certain of the medical center staff began to question us about the information we were sending them, inquiring what we expected them to do with it. As we discussed with them the possible local interpretations and uses, other more significant questions arose. Why were we sending this particular data and information to them? Why didn't we send them something that would be more useful? The truth was, we were just sending the information we had; we began asking a different question: "What is the right data and information to provide to clinicians in the medical centers?" The answer seemed to be that we should focus on returning *encounter* data, which comes from the encounter of the patient with the health care system and is collected during the history, physical examination, or testing procedures for diagnostic or therapeutic purposes. There should also be data reported on the *outcome* of any treatments applied, to allow the connection between what was done and what happened as a result. Even with this clear restriction on the type of data to be provided to practitioners, there was an enormous body of data to be considered; the next difficult task was to settle on the most important of those data elements

Definition of Quality Health Care. To address the question of which pieces of information to collect and provide to the medical centers, OQM undertook to develop a definition of quality health care.[14] We settled on the following seven attributes. "Quality health care is care that is *needed* and delivered in a manner that is *competent, caring, cost-effective, timely,* and that *minimizes risk* and *achieves achievable benefits.*"

Needed implies that the health care provided is what that patient needed and was appropriate for that patient at that time. It means "doing the right thing." There is also an intent to reflect the access to care for individual patients or patient populations.

Competent means that the health care processes were carried out in ways that are consonant to the best knowledge or accepted guidelines of care. It means "doing the thing right."

Caring is intended to reflect that the patient's judgment about the care processes or services will be taken into account. The quality of mercy will be considered.

Cost-effective means that the cost of care was considered along the process and that resources were not squandered.

Timely implies that the care was delivered at the appropriate moment to produce the most favorable outcome (for example, leucovorin rescue during chemotherapy, thrombolytic therapy in myocardial infarction) or to meet patient expectations (short waiting time for clinic appointment or prompt delivery of requested pain medication).

Minimizes risk means that the health care system takes conscious steps to prevent patients from being harmed by its processes; it also means there is intent to prevent harm or injury to caregivers and the community as well.

Achieves achievable benefits may be the most difficult aspect to attain. It means that the process of care leads to the best possible outcome. To accomplish this attribute, practitioners must have substantial knowledge about the disease and its natural history. Patient participation in the treatment process is necessary. As knowledge expands and patients become increasingly involved in their own care, this particular attribute may well become the single most important measure of quality health care.

We used this definition to create a matrix for the display of quality measures; the attributes of quality were placed on a vertical axis, and the horizontal axis was composed of the various types of services provided by VHA (for example, outpatient medical care, acute inpatient care, outpatient surgery, inpatient surgery, outpatient psychiatry, inpatient psychiatry, and extended care). This 7 × 7 matrix allowed us to place the many pieces of data and measurements routinely collected in the name of quality into individual cells that corresponded to the type of service measured and the aspect of quality it represented (for example, mortality rate after acute myocardial infarction was placed in the cell where *competency* intersects with *acute inpatient care*; the length of stay following cholecystectomy was placed in the intersection of *cost-effectiveness* with *inpatient surgery*). After placing all the current measures used in VHA in this matrix, we recognized two distinct patterns. Several of the cells contained many different measurements (for example, the cell intersection of *competency* and *acute inpatient care* contained 114), while some others contained none (for example, the intersection of *cost-effectiveness* and *outpatient psychiatry*). The recognition of these patterns led us to focus attention over the next few years on winnowing the cells with too many measures and developing tools for determining quality in the cells that were empty. The planned development of tools to measure specific aspects of quality intended to fill the cells of the matrix became the third phase of change in OQM.

Third Steps: Development and Testing of New Tools

The VA health care system has three unique advantages as a development and testing ground for quality tools. First is its national status; the presence of a VA facility in every state and the large number of veteran patients seen each year provide an ample database that is relatively free of geographic bias. Second, the high degree of affiliation with academic medicine assures VHA that its actions to measure quality will be closely and carefully scrutinized and that we will have scholarly input to any new programs. Third, the entire VHA system is united around a common, computerized database with identical structure and capabilities. This computer system—called the Decentralized Hospital-based Computer Program (DHCP)—connects all the pertinent functions in each hospital (for example, administrative, clinical, laboratory, fiscal, and imaging capabilities are linked). This large database enhances the value of the large hospital system and patient population by providing developers and researchers with a (potential) national database that stretches back into the early 1980s and provides a national networking system for the thousands of health care professionals in VA.[15]

In early 1991, after assessment of the needs for quality measurement and the recognition that new tools and support to the medical center staff would be required, OQM began a series of undertakings that provided activity in both of these areas simultaneously and continuously over the next five years. We began to develop new measurement instruments by congregating some of the best clinicians, informatics experts, and administrators in the system and using their expertise about practical capabilities to try pilot ventures and improve them to working stages rather quickly. The areas chosen for this type of development had been identified through the analysis of the matrix display of current measures that identified key areas in which we were not adequately monitoring our activity. The second type of undertaking was to provide more immediate (and ongoing) educational support to the hospital personnel expected to contribute most of the effort toward actual measurement of quality—the quality managers and their staff in the individual medical centers.

Support for Local Quality Managers. The creed of OQM states that "quality is assured at the point of patient contact," recognizing that all health care, like politics, is local. In order to enhance the likelihood that local care would be improved by the use of new tools and the feedback of data, we felt that effort should be made to provide the local quality managers and their staff with specific information and training. One of the first identified needs for this group dealt with the lack of a single document regarding the wide variety of QA mandates and activities in the system. VHA's activities in QA began more than 25 years before and were constantly being added to or changed; rarely did any of the changes make reference to the remainder of the expectations for the staff. Several senior quality managers made mention to their need for some form of short "cheat sheet" to understand the full breadth of the local QA programs.

In early 1991, a group of quality managers, some with many years of experience and others relatively junior in the system, spent an intensive week reviewing all VHA publications that dealt with quality assurance or quality management programs. They compiled a standard set of data elements about each program: the history of the program, data elements required for collection (including suggestions about where that data might be found in the system), the frequency of mandated collection, and the particulars about reporting the information (to whom and in what format). They also appended a list of the pertinent VA publications and the Joint Commission's Accreditation Manual for future reference. The information about each of the listed programs was displayed on one or two pages, a glossary and some explanatory narrative was written, and the material was published and circulated throughout the system as a 74-page booklet. Over the next few years the booklet became an important teaching aid for quality managers to use within their facility to increase awareness of their activities on the part of clinical and administrative staff as well as to use it in the orientation of new QA staff.

Also in 1991, VHA created a freestanding entity for the purpose of focusing educational efforts in the area of quality management—the Quality Management Institute (QMI). The Institute was conceived and funded to provide direct support to the quality management staff at the individual hospitals in at least three spheres: education, research, and informatics. The education support ultimately came in the form of regular national and regional meetings, course offerings at the institute, and distance learning opportunities coordinated by the Institute staff and also involving academic faculty from a variety of affiliated universities. The research support included the encouragement and active support (with consultation, data analysis, and occasional personnel) of local endeavors to develop or test new concepts about quality management that could be used throughout the system. Informatics support focused on the data access, acquisition collation, and analysis capabilities of the local quality management offices; over the next few years the Institute provided automated data-handling capability in the form of hardware (486 workstation, modem, printer, disk drives, and so on) and software, including both off-the-shelf items and material written by Institute staff solely for the use of VA personnel. One of the programs written by Institute staff, the Clinical Indicator Workbook, is an electronic document containing programmed learning examples on how to choose and develop clinical indicators for use in any environment. It includes tools to help with flowcharting, run chart construction, and so on, and contains examples of indicators that can be modified for local use. The workbook was widely circulated throughout VA, and the Department of Commerce now offers it to purchasers through its National Technical Information Service at a nominal cost. In 1994 the Institute published a comprehensive data management directory that compiled all available educational programs, hardware, software, or other audiovisual or hardcopy publications dealing with any aspect of data management, from collection to analysis. QMI staff have directly contributed to improving the data handling and analysis capability for quality management purposes within VHA, and the enhanced ability of quality management staff to use automated systems can also be traced to the diligence and dedication of the highly professional Institute staff.

It is a well-known phenomenon that bad news travels quickly while good news does not. While most of the VHA system might be aware of a problem at one of the hospitals, we were usually unaware of individual medical center successes and achievements and this, too, seemed a fertile place to assist the local staff. In 1994 OQM compiled and published a booklet of 80 innovative techniques and approaches to common problems within the system. The stories were solicited from the medical centers and reviewed by a series of appropriate clinicians for impact, practicality, and exportability. Each story was confined to two pages in the booklet and followed a stylized presentation that included the problem addressed, the people who resolved the issue, the tools they used, and the outcome obtained. Telephone numbers were given so that direct contact could be made for additional information. Shortly after the booklets were distributed to VHA, the Health Care Financing Administration requested an additional quantity so that it would have copies to distribute to each state's peer review organization to demonstrate how quality management activities can make improvements in the health care system.

Consistently, OQM believed that the local quality managers were our primary customer. They represented the doorway for our educational efforts and the feedback reports into the individual medical centers. We centered a significant amount of time and other resources to providing this critical cadre with active support information, and enhanced capability. The vast majority of the improvements in actual patient care came at these local sites and was supported and encouraged by the local quality staff.

Development of Specific Tools. Since the assessment of need driven by the matrix analysis in 1991, VHA has constructed a number of instruments to collect and report information in targeted areas. Each instrument was developed with input and consultation from clinical and administrative leaders in the VA system, including many end users (clinicians at the point of patient contact). Just as the direct involvement of users in the development of a new process or tool was considered important, we also focused on the manner in which the information obtained would be disseminated and its usefulness at the local level. We coupled planned educational programs to assist medical center staff and practitioners to use the data for the improvement of processes and outcomes.

The use of data from national tools for reflecting quality of care has at least two, sometimes seemingly disparate, functions. One important use is to provide a thoughtful evaluation of the national experience in some of the key areas of clinical and administrative activity within VHA. To get this picture requires a sampling of the activity at each medical center, but that sample may be too small to acquire statistical importance at the medical center level. The second function of the national tools, then, is not to make statistically valid interpretations of clinical quality at every medical center, but rather to call attention at that local level to performance that may be out of line with expectations. Those local areas of interest will require additional data to determine if a real problem exists. In most instances the national tool contains the capability for the local staff to obtain the necessary information from their own data and use their data for analysis and to measure progress if changes are needed.

Quality Improvement Checklist. In 1991, VHA developed a method to use the DHCP data files to feed an automated instrument that calculates incidence rates and occurrences for about 40 different indicators.[16] The secretary of veterans affairs decided that the system needed a means of determining whether individual hospitals were "operating up to standard," and this new tool—the Quality Improvement Checklist (QUIC)—was specifically constructed to measure and reflect VHA's activity and quality of care in a few critical areas. The DHCP data and some manually collected information is entered into an electronic report form that can be reviewed and approved by the facility, electronically signed, and then transmitted to a national center for aggregation. From there, a national report is produced in hard copy, with comparisons of the answers to each indicator from each of the medical centers. The national data collection is performed at six-month intervals and provides every hospital the ability to track its own progress in each area.

The QUIC was developed by a task force of VHA employees with clinical, administrative, research, and academic backgrounds. As the task force members considered the development of the checklist, they were aware of the system's need for better means of measuring *competency* of care as well as *timeliness,* and they chose to use a format grounded on literature-based clinical guidelines and clinical indicators that could reflect these key attributes. Their goals for the checklist were for it to emphasize the clinical activities of VHA, provide information in critical areas that can be used for improvement, and stimulate the use of data and measurement for decisions. They also wanted a tool that was relatively short and that could be interpreted as a whole, not by focusing on specific questions. The decision by the task force to base the QUIC in clinical indicators was grounded in the belief that clinical guidelines can improve compliance with treatment recommendations and possibly even clinical outcomes.

The task force constructed a series of some 53 questions in a standardized format containing a clear statement of the question to be answered, definitions of terms, a short rationale with literature references about the importance of the topic, and an explanation of the data sources and calculations to be used (there were no black boxes in the checklist). Two-thirds of the questions were answerable with either a simple yes or no (total of 15) or by data automatically extracted from the DHCP (total of 21); only 17 questions required data collection by the facility staff, but were considered important enough to justify this effort. One such question asked for the rate of nosocornial pneumonia in patients that were ventilator dependent; this information is not routinely collected and stored in DHCP but is an important reflection of quality of care.

Since its inception, the QUIC has been modified a number of times. Questions have been dropped from the tool and new ones constructed with DHCP support for most of the every-six-months collection periods. With each set of changes, the QUIC emphasized more clinical activity and reduced the number of questions focused on administrative matters. The changes also included some additions that had been requested by the primary users, the quality managers in the system. A capability to construct, plot, and print graphic displays of statistical trends for each of the data-related questions was developed within spreadsheet application. Some of the JCAHO monitors from the Indicator Measurement System were also added to provide assistance to the local facilities in preparing for their surveys. Adjustments to the DHCP routines were also made to allow the local staff to choose the time frames and the diagnoses to be searched; such changes opened the QUIC to use far beyond that of simply reporting the information on national issues once every six months. Overall, these changes steadily increased the positive feedback and the use of the QUIC data in quality improvement activities at the local level. A national survey regarding the usefulness of the QUIC was performed in 1995 and found 81 percent of respondents (103 of 172 hospitals) rated the usefulness as above average for a quality management tool and similarly positive for its impact on patient care outcomes. Although the respondents gave high marks to the validity and reliability of most questions, more than half reported that they only made the required measurements and never used the QUIC capability for local inquiries.

The existence of an automated, data-driven system with regular reporting cycles has many important uses to a national health care system like VHA. The obvious uses include the consistent monitoring of a critical few high-risk, high-volume clinical areas to assure VA administrators that individual hospitals are performing well on usual and customary standards of care. QUIC also provides a quick and flexible way to obtain valid and comparable answers to high-priority questions and issues. Issues such as how well VA hospitals are meeting recently set customer service standards could only be answered by a measurement system like QUIC. There may be both a push and a pull for quality improvement from the implementation of QUIC. The requirement to make a report at six-month intervals pushes every facility to look at a number of nationally important issues and become cognizant of their own performance; it is a rare hospital that does not respond to such demands by trying to ensure that its data are accurate and thorough. Later, when the comparative data are reported to the facility, there is a clear pull to make improvements in those areas where the facility did not perform as well as expected. Both forces have created significant changes in quality in individual hospitals in the VHA since 1991.[17,18] From both ends of the interest spectrum—the headquarters and the local facilities—there is agreement that the instrument has many strengths and can be further adapted to enhance local use.

External Peer Review Program. As noted, VHA was aware that its internal peer review program in 1990–1991 did not provide a national picture of practice patterns and results. The internal nature of the review system—using VHA physicians from one facility to review the care provided at another facility in reference to locally determined care standards—did not seem to be sufficiently disinterested to satisfy outside critics. Further, that system of review, like virtually all others in the country at the time, was largely based on the use of implicit criteria drawn from the experience of a single, qualified expert. As VHA set out to construct a new national peer review system, the intent was to address each of these drawbacks, then develop a program that would remedy the weakness and that would complement a national agenda while addressing the identified needs of new measurement capabilities in the area of needed care and the competency and timeliness of that care. VHA decided to pattern its new peer review program after the one the Department of Defense (DoD) had been operating, using clinical guidelines to provide a yardstick for measuring the quality of care in DoD facilities. After setting expectations in a national request for proposals and working with possible contractors, VHA was finally ready in late 1992 to proceed with implementing a systemwide peer review program that would evaluate the quality of care provided in VHA, assist in stimulating improvement in care processes, and provide a national database to allow comparison of VHA care to the private community.

The new peer review program—the external peer review program (EPRP)—was designed to address the shortcomings mentioned involving implicit criteria and single reviewer bias by using non-VA physicians to endorse clinical guidelines and algorithms for use in measuring care process quality.[19] Clinical topics for review were chosen by OQM staff from the most common and most difficult types of cases seen in VA hospitals; initial review areas included medical diagnoses such as cancer of the lung, colon, or prostate; diabetes; acute myocardial infarction; pneumonia and gastrointestinal bleeding; and surgical care such as cholecystectomy, prostate resection, coronary bypass, carotid endarterectomy, and abdominal aneurysm repair. The contractor in charge of developing the EPRP was the West Virginia Medical Institute (WVMI), which also runs the peer review program for the state of West Virginia. The physicians chosen by WVMI to serve on peer review panels were required to be in active practice in a JCAHO accredited hospital, have no connection with VA, and be board certified in the area of their expertise for the EPRP. These physicians reviewed existing clinical guidelines in the areas of interest and made practical changes in the recommendations that were agreed upon by the members of the appropriate panel. Key steps were then extracted from the guidelines and written into a diagnosis and treatment algorithm and programmed into a laptop computer. Record review technicians used these algorithms to evaluate care in a random sample of cases at virtually every VA hospital every month; a total of nearly 60,000 cases are reviewed each year.

Cases for review represented a 5 percent sample of the cases (or 30 cases, whichever is greater) in each hospital in each clinical topic. A random selection of cases was fulfilled from a cohort of patients discharged one month previously; a list of cases was prepared and the medical records obtained. The records were then compared to the algorithm by the medical record technicians; those cases which met all steps in the algorithm "passed." Cases that did not pass the initial review were abstracted and sent to the physician panel for further review where the experts would judge the circumstances of care as a panel and make a decision. As noted, the review using these "community" standards by outside physicians found that VA care met or exceeded the standards more than 97 percent of the time; these findings were satisfying for both VA physicians and administrators, as they provided an unbiased basis for judging VA care as at least equivalent to that provided in non-VA hospitals across the country.

The EPRP provided VHA with several additional advantages, as well. One of those benefits revolved around the need for VHA to perform internal peer review on cases that qualified as meeting certain occurrence screens that were set to detect circumstances where care may not have met appropriate standards. These screens involved issues such as readmissions within a few days of discharge, returns to the operating room, death, cardiac arrest, and so on. VHA physicians have been reviewing such cases regularly since 1989 with an eye toward identifying system or practitioner errors that may need correction. Over several years, these reviews have consumed a good deal of time and yet have not uncovered major problems in either the systems of care or the practitioner patterns of care; most of the time less than 4 percent of cases referred were judged to represent examples of poor quality of care. The EPRP review mechanism provided VHA an unusual opportunity to test the accuracy of its internal peer review program and to determine whether we could accomplish this same activity without requiring VHA physicians to spend time away from providing care while reviewing cases that usually did not identify significant issues for the hospital staff.

The results of review of the occurrence screening program by EPRP physicians disclosed striking consistency; overall, 87 percent of the cases reviewed by the outside reviewers were judged the same by the non-VA physicians as they were by those physicians within the system. In 7 percent of the cases the outside reviewers felt that VA physicians had been too strict in their judgment about the quality of care, while the remaining 6 percent felt the VA review had been too lenient. This high proportion of agreement was generally felt to represent validation of VHA's own internal peer review (which had been considered too likely to be forgiving of errors to have credence). In addition, the level of agreement between the two systems of review indicated that VHA could easily move the peer review function of the occurrence screen program to the EPRP without creating internal difficulties with the review findings.

Given that VHA needed to have a peer review mechanism of some type in operation, an additional benefit that accrued from switching to the EPRP instead of staying with the internal review program was a significant cost reduction. Contrary to conventional wisdom, the internal peer review program in VHA was significantly more costly than EPRP. For several years in the late 1980s, VHA's internal peer review program employed coordinators in its 27 medical districts and arranged for reviewers from various hospitals to travel to other facilities for meetings and reviews. The salary costs and the travel expenses across the nation accounted for slightly more than a $7 million cost for the program; as previously noted, the program did not provide uniform reviews across the system and did not create a national database. The EPRP, on the other hand, was crafted to use national standards and to create just such a database, and did so in reviewing a scientifically selected sample of the nationwide experience. The 50,000 reviews each year were accomplished at a cost of $100 each, an annual cost of only $5 million for a more useful product.

As the program matured, several other review functions were added to the EPRP list of responsibilities in 1995: resident supervision and tort claim reviews. Resident supervision oversight can be accomplished through adequate medical record documentation and outside review of that documentation at regular intervals; like some of the occurrence screen reviews, this type of oversight may be more readily accepted from outsiders than from internal staff. Similarly, when a tort claim is filed against VA and the adjudication results in the system being found at fault, a prompt review of the practitioner's role in the error must be made in order to make appropriate reports to the National Practitioner Data Bank. Such reviews can be quickly made by the EPRP system and physician reviewers without creating the necessity for internal reviews by physicians in the same facility or requiring that other VA reviewers travel to accomplish the task.

The EPRP program began in 1992 with a clear focus on the acute care, inpatient programs of medical care and surgery. Over the next two years, two facts became increasingly evident: (1) the clinical care under review by the program had little need of improvement, and (2) the VHA care programs were shifting steadily away from the inpatient setting toward more ambulatory care and extended care (for example, nursing home, psychiatric, and extended care). Accordingly, the oversight body for the EPRP, the Field Advisory Council, began to direct the selection of new clinical topics for the contractor to develop criteria sets for review. As certain original topics were eliminated (decubitus ulcer, pneumonia, gastrointestinal bleeding, intestinal obstruction), other areas were developed for inclusion in the list of review topics. New review areas included hip fracture, major depressive disorder, alcohol abuse, bipolar disorder, urinary incontinence in nursing home patients, and the outpatient care of insulin-dependent diabetes mellitus. As well as developing these new review algorithms, the EPRP program turned attention to generating VA guidelines for the treatment of specific populations of patients of interest to the system: patients with stroke, amputation, or ischemic heart disease.

In spite of the general success of the EPRP at the national level (documenting the high quality of care in VA) and the common perception of its credibility at the local level, the program has not been uniformly well received or totally successful. Across the hospital system there is striking variation in the penetration of the program expectations and results into the clinical ranks. The causes of this poor penetration may be either disinterested clinicians or a malfunctioning internal communication system, but the result is the same: Valuable results are not being reviewed and used by those at the point of patient contact. Two problems with the program itself are being addressed and will comprise major improvements in the next generation of studies. The first of these is an improved reporting mechanism that incorporates feedback from the primary users into making the written report to the facility more user-friendly. The second improvement relates to moving the program away from being entirely based on case-by-case review and more of an analysis of trends in the processes of care. Overall, however, the EPRP is seen as credible by outside critics because of its reliance on scientific criteria, non-VA reviewers, and the use of putative community standards. Inside the system, the program has credibility at the local level due to its scientific basis and at the national level by its demonstration of the high quality of care regularly delivered in VA hospitals across the country.

Surgical Quality Improvement Program. Since 1972, VHA's cardiac surgery consultants committee has met twice a year to review the results of cardiac surgery programs in the system. Over the years they have used raw, unadjusted mortality rates to decide whether a program should have a site visit or stop doing cardiac surgery because of poor outcomes. The committee members recognized that many of the programs they visited because of high mortality rates were actually operating on very sick patients and doing a superb job both technically and clinically; the majority of their cases survived, but the few that did not were making their rates unacceptably high. The committee wrestled with the issue of developing a risk adjustment for cardiac patients and finally, in 1987, began to prospectively collect risk factors on all patients undergoing cardiac surgery in VHA facilities. The information they collected was used in conjunction with outcomes to construct risk profiles and to assist them in determining the expected mortality or morbidity that would be seen in a cohort of patients with a particular set of risk characteristics. By using these measurements and comparing the actual or observed (O) outcomes in a cohort of patients to the expected (E) outcomes that cohort should exhibit, the committee was able to determine the ratio of these outcomes (O/E) to better determine which programs were not operating up to standard. Programs with O/E ratios less than 1.0 were producing better outcomes in their patients than the risk characteristics would suggest; conversely, those programs with O/E ratios greater than 1.0 had worse outcomes than would be expected on the basis of patient characteristics alone. These programs were then subject to site visit reviews to determine whether they should be allowed to remain active. Over the first five years of following the O/E ratio for cardiac surgical cases, the VHA overall mortality rate for this type of surgery fell by nearly 24 percent; the systemwide mortality rate had been unchanged for more than five years prior to the institution of this form of risk-adjusted monitoring and oversight.[20,21]

In 1991, recognizing that VHA needed a mechanism to determine whether the care processes were achieving achievable benefits, we determined to export the cardiac surgery consultants risk adjustment concepts to the field of general surgery. In conjunction with The Office of Health Services Research and Development, the Office of Quality Management and the Office of Clinical Programs developed a mechanism to collect preoperative risk factor information on virtually all patients undergoing any type of surgical procedure in VHA. The program was operated as a clinical research project under the title National VA Surgical Risk Study (NVASRS). As part of the study, a panel of reviewers and advisors was created with experts from the fields of surgery, health policy, research, epidemiology, and biostatistics. These experts regularly reviewed the accumulating data and advised VHA on the implementation of the overall program. Their involvement helped add credibility to the endeavor to VA and non-VA physicians and scientists, but also provided a ready mechanism for the dissemination of the study results when it was completed.

There were some key decisions and activities made in support of this developing program that ensured its success. One was the identification of designated personnel at each of the original 44 hospitals in the program to collect all necessary data pre- and postoperatively; the cardiac surgery database had often been slighted in terms of input because there were not designated data collection personnel in that system. The original 44 sites for the NVASRS were the same sites where VHA had cardiac surgery programs. This selection was made for two important reasons: these programs already had some experience with this type of data collection, and it was recognized that the NVASRS data collector could also obtain the needed data for the cardiac program and increase the data capture and information relevance. The presence of an identified data collector—commonly a nurse—may have been the single most important decision made in the information of the program. With a dedicated person seeing to the record completion at each site, virtually every program accomplished more than 95 percent data capture in time for reporting.

A second important decision was to support the local data capture specialists with a nurse coordinator and two traveling nurse consultants to assist them in solving local problems with data accrual. Without these key individuals, the local data nurses may well have wandered off course several times. Another key decision was to handle the data intake and analysis for the first 80,000 to 100,000 cases as a research project; this compelled us to collect the information without providing feedback to the individual hospitals about their O/E ratios until we had collected sufficient data to ensure that the prediction models were statistically valid.

The methodology of the NVASRS has been described elsewhere.[22] Briefly, data were collected on most patients scheduled for major surgical procedures to be performed under general, spinal, or epidural anesthesia. Certain high-volume, low-risk procedures, such as transurethral resection of the prostate, were not all selected for inclusion; a random selection of patients undergoing these procedures was included each week from those sites performing those types of surgery. There were 63 preoperative risk variables, 16 intraoperative variables, and 23 postoperative or outcome measurements collected for every case. Each surgical procedure was given a complexity score by panels of surgeons in each specialty; this score helped to account for variation in the difficulty of the operation between hospitals and among the different specialties. Patients were followed postoperatively to the 30th day whether or not they had been discharged from the hospital, to ensure that the follow-up information was the same in all cases. The locally collected information was entered into the DHCP and automatically transmitted to the study data center at the Hines VA hospital in Chicago, Illinois. At the center, data validation and analysis were performed using forward stepwise logistic regression to identify most important variables in the preoperative risk factors.

After 26 months of data accrual from the 44 hospitals, we had collected more than 87,000 individual surgical cases in the database. At that point we terminated the initial phase of the program—the research phase—and began providing feedback of study results to the participating hospitals. It was clear to all involved, from the staff in the central offices to the surgical staff at the individual hospitals, that the database was unique and the input of additional data should not be interrupted. We decided to expand the operation of the NVASRS to all VHA facilities with surgical programs, a total of 132 facilities, and to change the name of the program to the National Surgical Quality Improvement Program (NSQIP). The research aspect of data collection ended December 31, 1993; between April and October 1994 the program was extended throughout the VHA system and all surgical programs began adding their operative data to the database. By September 30, 1995, more than 183,000 major surgical cases had been entered into the database.

The range in the volume of surgical cases entered into the database by the individual facilities varied widely from 25 cases per month to more than 270 cases per month. As might be expected in a VA hospital, the most common procedures came from the specialties of general surgery, orthopedics, urology, peripheral vascular surgery, thoracic surgery, neurosurgery, otolaryngology, and plastic surgery. The most common procedures were transurethral resections of the prostate, total hip or total knee replacement, partial colectomy, carotid endarterectomy, and pulmonary resections. Unadjusted mortality and morbidity rates at 30 days postoperatively for the common procedures were comparable to those reported in the peer review literature over the past 10 years. Certain risk factors were identified as important in almost every setting: preoperative serum albumin, the patient's functional score on the American Society of Anesthesiology rating system (ASA class), the patient's overall function (for example, independent or partially/fully disabled), the patient's age, and the blood urea nitrogen level. Data reports are available to the local surgeons as outputs from the DHCP. This information is often used by the physician staff to address questions of research, quality assurance, or personal interest. Semiannual reports from the data center provide the local surgeons with information about their mortality and morbidity rates compared to other VA hospitals and to help them identify patient risk profiles, intraoperative processes, or outcomes that are in need of improvement. These reports are presented with comparisons to the other VA hospitals' performance as well as providing information about the local experience trended over time. Because of the emphasis on performance improvement, the major focus of the information is to highlight those facilities with the lower O/E ratios and better-than-expected outcomes. Individual programs and surgeons interested in finding out more about the practices that allow such high performance to occur are encouraged to make direct contact with the high-performing hospital.

The existence of the database has allowed several additional studies of practice patterns and outcomes by VA investigators. Topics studied include the development and implementation of new surgical techniques in the system, such as laparoscopic surgery for gallbladder disease or other circumstances. Some investigators are concentrating attention to the outcomes of specific surgical procedures like pulmonary resection, partial colectomy, or radical prostatectomy. Still others are focusing their interest on the connection between risk profiles and outcomes in selected veteran patient cohorts such as women or the elderly. This rich and growing database of surgical experience has already been recognized as a national resource by non-VA constituencies such as the American College of Surgeons. Certainly the emphasis on measuring quality health care requires a methodology that can provide credible, scientifically based risk adjustment while not punishing those institutions that cater to patients that are truly older and sicker than the average; the National VA Surgical Quality Improvement Program contributes just such capability to the profession. Further, as recognition rises that the best reflection of quality care may well be whether it achieves achievable benefits, instruments that can compare what happened with what should have happened will be more in demand and VHA's experience with both the NVASQIP and the cardiac surgery data will provide meaningful direction for the country.

The Patient Feedback Program. Although VHA had been measuring patient satisfaction since 1972, the instrument employed was not useful for understanding or identifying areas for improvement. The instrument, about 40 questions each requiring an answer on a five-point Likert scale, was generally given to patients during a clinic visit or just before they were discharged from an inpatient stay. The questions had changed little in the 20-year usage of the survey instrument, and the source of the questions ranged from administrative interest to Congressional mandate and addressed mostly issues of hotel services such as food service, cleanliness, and friendliness. On the five-point scale, VHA facilities averaged a score of 4.2 for most of the preceding 20 years with little variation. Although this generally high score was of some comfort to VA administrators, and seemed quite comparable to satisfaction scores in the private sector,[23] we identified a lack of useful measurement of the caring component of quality health care and determined to make improvements in our instrument.

Recent literature has contained persuasive information in two regards to suggest that we should change the focus of the patient satisfaction instrument. First, there is increasing data that the most reliable systems for reflecting patient concerns and satisfaction have distinct features in common: they place the customer's wishes as the primary driver for the measurement mechanism, and they recognize that patients may be better *reporters* of what happened during their care than *raters* of how good that care was. Second, management literature was emphasizing that successful enterprises also put their customer's wishes as the primary driver in their internal assessment of how well they were doing and in choosing what areas needed improvement. In both of these areas, VHA's patient satisfaction instrument fell short.

Clearly, the first step needed in the development of a new patient satisfaction measurement tool was to obtain direct input from our customers—the veteran patients seen in our hospital and clinics across the country. We held focus group meetings with patients, eight to 12 in a group, at a variety of VA hospitals and clinics around the system: we chose to go to each of the four geographic regions of the system to minimize any regional biases in expectations. The groups, which included patients recently discharged from inpatient care and those being actively treated in outpatient clinics, were asked to describe what they thought a high-quality health care experience would look like. Follow-up questions pressed for more detail and tried to tie the expectations to specific measurable behaviors on the part of VA employees. Videotapes and audiotapes of those sessions were reviewed by multiple individuals interested in the development of patient-based standards of care. Their understanding of the major themes and patients' concerns in these focus groups was utilized to create VHA's national customer standards and to draw from there a series of new questions for the patient satisfaction survey instrument. The new instrument was developed over a period of several months in cooperation with the University Hospital Consortium and with Picker Institute; the Institute's primary interests are in the development of valid measures of patient feedback about medical care.

The key issues from the veteran patients' perspective were adhering to their personal preferences, providing emotional support, seeing to their physical comfort, providing coordinated care with proper transition between care sites, continuity of care, timeliness and access to care, overall staff courtesy, providing them information (education) about their disease, and involving their family in their care.[24] Some of these concerns related only to the outpatient phase of care (access and continuity). In each area, highly specific questions were developed and tested for clarity and understanding by veteran patients before placing them in the final instrument. In general, the questions were worded to reflect the patients' perception of how often VA employees' behavior was consistent with high-quality care.

In late 1994, the new National Customer Feedback Center (NCFC)—created and staffed for the purpose of providing VHA with the capability and expertise to carry out national satisfaction surveys that would have some usefulness at the local level—sent out the first survey in the new format to recently discharged inpatients. A total of more than 69,000 randomly selected patients—some from every acute care VA hospital who had been discharged in June, July, or August—received a 49-item questionnaire in the mail with a return envelope. A few of the questions inquired about the general health and capability of the patient and allowed for some internal risk adjustment of responses. Using targeted reminders for slow responders, an overall return rate of 68 percent was obtained after 10 weeks—a response judged to be very good by academic survey research standards. Results of the inpatient survey were released to the individual VA hospitals early in 1995, and plans for follow-up include repeating the national mailing on an annual basis.

In fall of 1995, the NCFC mailed the first new feedback instrument aimed at the patients receiving outpatient care in a VHA clinic. Another random sample of patients, some from every clinic site, was selected, and surveys were mailed to nearly 41,000 individuals who had visited a VHA clinic sometime between mid-May and mid-July 1995. Reminders were again used, and this time a national response rate of 76 percent was obtained. In both surveys the NCFC was able to use demographic information about the selected patients to determine that response rates and types of answers (positive or negative) were not affected by the age, gender, race, or service-connected status of the veteran patient.

Both reports were returned to the individual hospital in a format intended to help them interpret the results, identify which areas needed improvement, and identify what could be addressed to bring about that improvement. The report includes an executive summary that points out the national results and contrasts the individual hospital's or clinic's results. Analysis of the national data permitted the NCFC to determine which questions were most closely related to the overall rating given to the hospital or clinic by specific patients. This analysis led to identifying those areas considered by patients to be critically important, very important, or important in their judgment of the overall value and quality of the health care they had received. Each clinic or hospital performance in each of the customer standards was compared to that of the other VHA facilities and rated as either high, meaning that the individual score was better than the 95 percent confidence limits for the nation in that area, average by being within the confidence limits, or low, meaning a score worse than the confidence limits. Each facility's results were categorized by importance (nationally) and performance (locally) in a table in the executive summary. The report also included a listing of the VHA facilities with scores in the high range for any of the customer standards; this identification of best performers is intended to stimulate interest in the means by which that score was accomplished. Several facilities are noted for appearing in more than one of the lists.

The report goes on to provide explicit feedback on the performance of the individual facility in each of the areas and on each of the questions, including a comparison to known benchmarks. Initially, the only comparisons available for inclusion in the report were the VHA averages and national experience. In time we hope to add the results of surveys done by the University Hospital Consortium in their member hospitals and those of the Picker instrument reflecting the performance of private hospitals. At the end of the report is a tabular display of the demographic and background characteristics of the respondents to the survey; the national distribution can be compared to those of the individual facility to help local officials determine whether there is any significant difference between their patients and the national sample.

VHA's results from these two new survey tools is quite different from that seen with the use of the previous instrument. Specifically, by using the focus of the patient perspective there is new appreciation of the measurement itself, and the breadth of the questions in the new instrument allows for better understanding of the areas where poor performance is reported. In addition, tying the patient/customer response to explicit behaviors of the employees enables local managers and staff to focus their improvement efforts directly on the areas which patients are reporting as unsatisfactory. For example, in the previous survey the food might have been rated as unsatisfactory, but we didn't know if that was due to taste, temperature, timeliness, or what. In the new survey, a specific question about courtesy asks, "Did your provider look you in the eye when you talked, rather than at your chart or elsewhere?" Problem scores in this area are easily understood and addressed with counseling and education to the staff about expectations.

Specifically, VHA has been told by its customers that we need to improve at a national level in paying attention to patients' preferences and in providing emotional support, patient education, and coordinating care. Each of these areas has become a focal point for local and national attention in the first year after the results of the survey were published. Specifically, VHA has undertaken a national campaign based on the admonition of Secretary of Veterans Affairs Jesse Brown to "put veterans first." We have published customer service standards in every facility, based those standards on the focus group findings, and modified them to be more demanding in those localities where the local patient expectation was even higher than that of the national standard. (For example, the national standard calls for a scheduled patient to be seen within 30 minutes of the scheduled time; certain areas indicate that the community standard is 20 minutes, and those facilities are setting their local standards accordingly.) A similar national push for identifying a primary care provider for every veteran patient is intended to address the coordination of care and its continuity. Before the end of 1996, every VA hospital and clinic is expected to have organized its health care delivery system into an emphasis on primary care and to have virtually every patient's health care assigned to a single provider or group of providers. The primary intent of this expectation is to address the customer/patient desire to have a single provider, but there is a concomitant belief that such a primary care program will also reduce the costs of care generally associated with using a delivery system composed mostly of disconnected subspecialty clinics. Whether any degree of cost savings will be realized is unknown at present and may not actually occur.[25]

VHA's new patient feedback system, with national and local reports of performance judged against customer-driven standards, has provided the system with a measurable capability to determine the degree to which it is meeting the caring component of its definition of quality health care.

Fourth Steps: Refinement and Developing a Set of Measures

The development of a series of new measurement tools had enhanced VHA's capability to determine its performance at both the local and the national level in virtually all of the defined aspects of quality in each of the areas in which VHA provides care. The various cells of the quality matrix now have several measures in them, and the measures reflect valid and useful determinations that can be used for improvement of identified deficiencies. There still seemed to be a structure lacking to interpret and use this information at any level other than simply to react to identified shortcomings. Further, from long experience we knew that reactive change often ignores the impact that it may have on other, closely allied parts of the system. This type of reactive change may qualify for what W. Edwards Deming called "tampering." What seemed needed at this time was both a philosophic construct in which improvement/change would take its effect on related aspects of care into consideration and a coordinated management methodology to address the prioritization of changes. The first of these needs led to the development of a concept of using a balanced set or family of measures; the second concern caused VHA to adopt the principles of the Malcolm Baldrige National Quality Award (MBNQA) criteria to guide its management decisions.

*A **Balanced Set of Measures.*** As noted, there is always the risk that attention to cost reduction may compromise the quality of the final product; certainly this is the concern of many in and outside of the medical profession when health care reform is discussed. There is an implicit understanding that "health care reform" actually means "health care financing reform," and that means "cost cutting." There should be some perception of the impact that cost reductions have on the measurable aspects of quality care; VHA's new set of measurement tools permits the connection between these two spheres. Recognizing that the real search in health care today is for value, we should also understand that value is the quality of product for the cost paid. Thus, quality-of-care measures can be logically linked to the cost of the care as a means of determining the value of the care to the treated population. The quality component may be taken to be composed of the seven attributes mentioned in the definition of quality health care; cost-effectiveness is included as a property of quality and should perhaps be moved from the quality side of measurement to the cost side. In addition, one of the other attributes of quality, patient satisfaction measured by the aspect of caring, seems worthy of importance apart from the rest of the components. With these concepts in mind, OQM proposed that VHA consider using a family of measures in each of the areas under scrutiny. The family of measures should represent a balance between the outcomes of care as defined by the organization, the cost of producing those outcomes, and the customer/patient satisfaction with the product (see Figure 8.1).

This triad of measures would include both global and specific measures at national, systemwide, and local levels for the important determinants of quality outcome as defined by the practitioners (for example, mortality rates, functional state of the patient, and so on), patient satisfaction as determined by the customer standards, and cost as determined by the fiscal parts of the system (cost per visit, per day of care, per patient per year, and so on). VHA endorses the use of clinical guidelines, whether

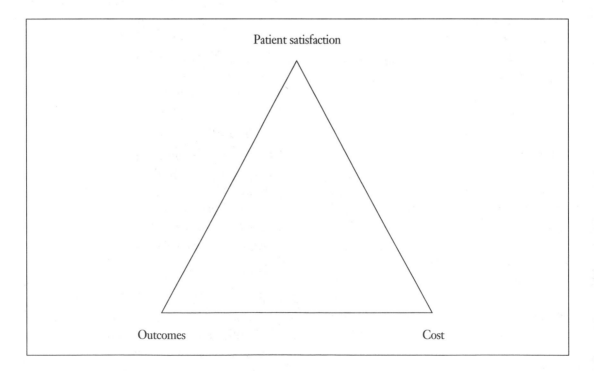

Figure 8.1. The triad of measures.

adopted directly from national organizations or societies or adapted to local specifics, as the principal means of determining whether care is needed and whether it is being delivered in a competent manner. Even with this emphasis on using scientifically derived standards for measurement, the current state of the art judges care to be of high quality if the care processes do not create adverse outcomes. Another needed emphasis in the near future is to show the benefit of care by measuring the improvement in function of patients receiving care.

Any specific triad of measures would have to be applied to a consistent cohort of patients for rational interpretation (there is no point to determining the patient satisfaction with outpatient dermatology, the cost of coronary artery surgery, and the mortality rate of pneumonia). The initial attempt to find appropriate cohorts of patients and make the requisite measurements involved identifying the high-volume diagnoses within the VHA system.

We were able to select eight cohorts of patients with sufficient size and that are reasonably consistent by using very specific diagnosis-related groupings (DRGs) and some adjacent DRGs (ADRGs). The eight cohorts and the number of patients (N) are: (1) chronic obstructive pulmonary disease (COPD) ($N = 59,276$), (2) pneumonia and pleurisy ($N = 69,245$), (3) congestive heart failure ($N = 63,204$), (4) angina pectoris/chest pain ($N = 102,596$), (5) diabetes mellitus ($N = 46,607$), (6) chronic renal failure ($N = 26,898$), (7) major depressive disorder (MDD) ($N = 38,500$), and (8) bipolar disorder ($N = 28,061$). These conditions and diagnoses account for about 20 percent of the discharges from VHA's inpatient case load each year and were intentionally chosen because they are mostly chronic conditions. Using the DHCP, patients were added to these cohorts at an early point in their disease and followed for the next four or five years to determine outcome (mortality) and resource utilization as a surrogate for direct measurement of cost (admissions, days of care, visits to the clinic, and so on). The cohorts were dynamic, with patients leaving through death and new patients being added continually, so calculations were based on "patient years at risk." Just as occurs in the private sector, this apportionment process identifies and includes enrollees that do not consume any resources in a given year, in spite of the fact that they have chronic illnesses. No patient was included in more than one cohort, and each remained in the cohort to which he or she was initially assigned.

Initial evaluation of the data from this type of cohort analysis indicates that, across the breadth of the country and the variety of VHA facilities, there is remarkably little variation in the risk-adjusted mortality rate for patients in any cohort. There is, however, a fair degree of variation in the use of resources to accomplish that outcome, in some instances there is as much as a threefold use of resources between facilities or networks of facilities without any discernable impact on outcome as reflected by the mortality rate. The VHA system is beginning to focus on these combined measures as a means for improvement. Attention to adding the patient satisfaction dimension to this set of measures is a high-priority item, as is beginning to better understand the reasons for the variation in resource consumption.

Malcolm Baldrige National Quality Award Criteria. A careful determination of the need for a systematic way of approaching planning and the distribution of increasingly scarce resources led VHA to decide that the structure and interrelatedness of the MBNQA criteria would provide the system with a means of coordinating its planning and performance improvement activities. The MBNQA criteria are categorized into seven key areas: leadership, information management, process management, human resource management, strategic planning, customer satisfaction, and organizational performance and results. Each area relates to several others and is comprised of a set of steps to be taken and questions to be answered to ensure that the organization is moving in the right direction and using all of its attributes most effectively. VHA has determined that the best use of the MBNQA criteria initially is for self-assessment purposes at the local level; as areas needing improvement are identified and resources dedicated to making the improvements, the reapplication of the criteria will provide evidence of the degree of improvement.

In support of its decision to base management actions in a coordinating environment, VHA has developed a training series of modules for dissemination across the system. More than two dozen master trainers and educators have been identified to use the modules at VHA sites that request training in the basic concepts of the MBNQA criteria. Beginning in the middle of 1996, these trainers are fanning across the system and helping the individual facilities understand the concepts and use of the MBNQA criteria in their own self-assessment. The findings from that assessment should provide the direction, along with the systemwide goals, for each hospital or clinic to set priorities for improvement activities in the next one to three years.

Melding the concept of a balanced set of measures with the structure provided by the MBNQA criteria allows VHA to pursue the development of performance measures that begin at the top of the organization and cascade downward. Each succeeding lower level will have increasingly more specific measures, and those measures will stress areas in which the control of the activity rests at that same level of the organization. This cascading of measures will help everyone in the organization understand their role in supporting the overall mission of VHA and will also help focus resource use and activity on the high-priority items in the system. An example of such a cascade is as follows:

Organizational level	Measurement
Headquarters	Overall patient satisfaction
Network	Emphasis on primary care
Hospital	Shift to outpatient care
Department	Reduce inappropriate admissions
Section	Reduce lengths of stay and bed days of care
Unit	Adoption of clinical pathways

Summary and Conclusions

Between 1990 and 1995, VHA developed a number of concepts and tools in quality management that enabled the organization to address its concerns about the quality of care in VA hospitals. A major concept was a working definition for quality health care that allowed a common terminology throughout the system during the development of new tools. The definition was used to drive an assessment of the capacity of the organization to measure its quality and to recognize the shortcomings of the measurement capability with the tools and instruments of 1990. This important needs assessment became a catalyst for targeted development of new devices for the evaluation and analysis of quality in health care; as opportunities arose over the next five years, resources were directed to the planning and implementation of measurement concepts and capabilities for the department.

Results of the application of these new tools to the health care processes of VHA generally show that VA care is good care. Perhaps more important, however, the use of the tools also shows where this federal health care system needs to make improvements and indicates our willingness to address those issues and make necessary changes.

Most of the philosophic concepts used to drive the changes in capability and attitude in VHA are adaptable to other settings; there is no need for a federal environment for the use of these ideas. In addition, the specific tools for measuring quality—the quality improvement checklist, the external peer review program, the surgical quality improvement program, and the patient feedback program—have direct applicability and usefulness in any type of health care setting. The measurement of quality health care is just beginning, and the more widely used every instrument is, the sooner the profession will be able to discern which are the most useful and concentrate efforts on the use of those tools that are best able to move us in the direction of continuous improvement.

Notes

1. J.A. Gronvall, "The VA's Affiliation with Academic Medicine: An Emergency Post-War Strategy Becomes a Permanent Partnership," *Academic Medicine* 64:61–66 (1989).

2. R. Stevens, "Can the Government Govern? Lessons from the Formation of the Veterans Administration," *Journal of Health Politics, Policy and Law* 16:281–305 (1991).

3. A. V. Schally, C. Y. Bowers, T. W. Redding, and J. F. Barrett, "Isolation of Thyrotropin Releasing Factor (TRF) from Porcine Hypothalamus," *Biochemical and Biophysical Research Communications* 25:165–169 (1966).

4. R. S. Yalow and S. A. Berson, "Size Heterogeneity of Immunoreactive Human ACTH in Plasma and in Extracts of Pituitary Glands and ACTH-Producing Thymoma," *Biochemical and Biophysial Research Communications* 44:439–445 (1971).

5. W. H. Oldendorf, "Isolated Flying-Spot Detection of Radiodensity Discontinuities: Displaying the Internal Structural Pattern of a Complex Object," *IRE Transactions on Biomedical Electronics* 8:68–72 (1961).

6. W. M. Chardack, A. A. Gage, and W. Greatbatch, "A Transistorized Self-Oriented Implantable Pacemaker for the Long-Term Correction of Complete Heart Block," *Surgery* 48:643–654 (1960).

7. B. J. Materson, D. J. Rea, W. C. Cushman, B. M. Massie, E. D. Freis, M. S. Kochar, R. J. Hamburger, C. Frye, R. Lakshman, J. Gottdiener and Associates, "Single-Drug Therapy for Hypertension in Men: A Comparison of Six Anti-Hypertensive Agents with Placebo," *New England Journal of Medicine* 38:959–961 (1993).

8. W. B. Tucker, "The Evolution of the Cooperative Studies in the Chemotherapy of Tuberculosis of the Veterans Administration and Armed Forces of the USA," *Advanced Tuberculosis Research* 10:1–68 (1960).

9. J. F. Casey, C. J. Lindley, L. Hollister, M. H. Gordon, and N. N. Springer, "Drug Therapy in Schizophrenia: A Controlled Study of the Relative Effectiveness of Chlorpromazine, Promazine, Phenobarbital and Placebo," *Archives of General Psychiatry* 4:381–389 (1961).

10. P. Peduzzi and H. Hultgren, "Effect of Medical vs. Surgical Treatment on Symptoms in Stable Angina Pectoris: The Veterans Administration Cooperative Study of Surgery for Coronary Arterial Occlusive Disease," *Circulation* 60:888–900 (1979).

11. J. N. Kabalin, H. S. Gill, "Urolase Laser Prostatectomy in Patients on Warfain Anticoagulation: A Safe Treatment Alternative for Bladder Outlet Obstruction," *Urology* 42:738–740 (1993).

12. J. D. Hamilton, P. M. Hartigan, M. S. Simberkoff, P. L. Day, G. R. Diamond, G. M. Dickinson, G. L. Drusano, M. J. Egorin, W. L. George, F. M. Gordon, and Associates, "A Controlled Trial of Early Versus Late Treatment with Zidovudine in Symptomatic Human Immunodeficiency Virus Infection," *New England Journal of Medicine* 326:437–443 (1992).

13. H. D. Lewis Jr., J. W. Davis, D. G. Archibald, W. E. Steinke, T. C. Smitherman, J. E. Doherty III, H. W. Schapner, and Associates, "Protective Effects of Aspirin Against Acute Myocardial Infarction and Death in Men with Unstable Angina," *New England Journal of Medicine* 309:396–403 (1983).

14. G. L. Barbour, "Assuring Quality in the Department of Veterans Affairs: What Can the Private Sector Learn?" *Journal of Clinical Outcomes Management* 2:67–76 (1995).

15. R. E. Dayhoff and D. L. Maloney, "Exchange of Veterans Affairs Medical Data Using National and Local Networks," *Annals of the New York Academy of Science* 670:50–66 (1992).

16. G. L. Barbour, "Development of a Quality Checklist for the Department of Veterans Affairs," *Joint Commission Journal of Quality Improvement* 20:127–139 (1994).

17. G. L. Barbour, "Assuring Quality . . ."

18. G. L. Barbour, "Development of a Quality Checklist . . ."

19. D. Walder, G. L. Barbour, H. Weeks et al., "VA's External Peer Review Program: Measuring Quality of Care," *Federal Practitioner* 12:31–38 (1995).

20. F. L. Grover, K. E. Hammermeister, C. Burchfield, and the Cardiac Surgeons of the Department of Veterans Affairs, "Initial Report of the Veterans Health Administration Preoperative Risk Assessment Study for Cardiac Surgery," *Annals of Thoracic Surgery* 50:12–28 (1990).

21. F. L. Grover, R. R. Johnson, A. L. Shroyer, et al., "The VA Continuous Improvement in Cardiac Surgery Study: From an Oversight Committee to a Continuous Improvement Model," *Annals of Thoracic Surgery* 58:1845–1851 (1994).

22. S. F. Khuri, J. Daley, W. Henderson et al., "The National Veterans Administration Surgical Risk Study: Risk Adjustment for the Comparative Assessment of the Quality of Surgical Care," *Journal of the American College of Surgeons* 180:519–531 (1995).

23. R. J. Rollins, "Patient Satisfaction in VA Medical Centers and Private Sector Hospitals: A Comparison," *Health Care Supervisor* 12:44–50 (1994).

24. N. J. Wilson, P. D. Cleary, and G. L. Barbour, "Correlates of Patient Reported Quality of Care in Veterans Affairs Hospitals" (paper presented at the Association for Health Services Research Annual Conference, San Diego, Calif., 1994).

25. M. Weinbeger, E. Z. Oddone, and W. G. Henderson, "The Veterans Affairs Cooperative Study Group on Primary Care and Hospital Readmission, *New England Journal of Medicine* 334:1441–1447 (1996).

Galen L. Barbour, M.D., currently serves as the director of strategic planning, employee and academic education programs and the performance improvement activities of one of the Veterans Affairs major tertiary care hospitals located in Washington, D.C. Barbour is a career VA employee with more than 30 years' experience in the system. Between 1990 and 1995 he held the position of associate chief medical director for quality management for the entire 172 hospitals of the VA system; in that role he directed the quality assessment, risk management, and utilization management programs of the nation's largest health care system—including the system's relationship with the Joint Commission for Accreditation of Healthcare Organizations—managing a nationwide peer review program and developing new tools for the measurement and improvement of health care quality.

Barbour earned his medical degree from the University of Arkansas in 1965. He is board certified in both internal medicine and nephrology.

Dr. Barbour is a Fellow of the American College of Physicians and a member of AOA, Sigma Xi, and other learned societies in medicine and research. He became a certified health executive (CHE) in the College of Healthcare Executives in 1993. As an active researcher and teacher, Barbour has published widely on the topics of medicine, nephrology, and medical care quality, including two books about the quality of care in the VA system. He is currently a reviewer for several medical journals.

Section II
Strategic Measures

Chapter 9

Measuring Clinical Outcomes at the Front Line

Eugene C. Nelson, Mark E. Splaine, Paul B. Batalden, and Stephen K. Plume

The aim of this chapter is to provide practical advice about measuring the outcomes of clinical care. The intended audiences for this chapter are frontline clinical teams who provide care to patients and clinical improvement teams aiming to create high-quality and high-value clinical management systems for frontline use.

The chapter is *not* intended to provide a comprehensive approach to outcomes measurement for clinical researchers, health services researchers, program evaluators, or policy analysts. Much has already been written for this purpose.[1]

Framework for Measuring and Improving Clinical Outcomes
The Context of Patient Care.

To understand outcomes, we first must set a context for delivering patient care. To illustrate some of the main points about the context of medical care and outcomes, refer to Figure 9.1 for a view of the basic framework.[2]

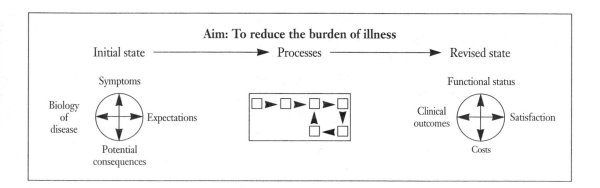

Figure 9.1. A framework for thinking about aims, activities, participants, and results in health care.

The framework involves an episode of care that begins with an individual experiencing a health need and ends with a determination that the health need has been met. The framework blends the measurement of outcomes with the delivery process associated with these outcomes and the patient mix characteristics that influence both the nature of the delivery process (what is done for what reason) as well as the outcomes experienced by the individual (that is, clinical outcomes, functional status, satisfaction against need, and total cost results).[3]

The episode of care begins with a patient, or a panel of patients, presenting with a health need such as the need for treatment of a minor acute problem (for example, cystitis, upper respiratory infection (URI)), a medical emergency (for example, acute myocardial infarction (MI), fractured hip), chronic disease care (for example, hypertension, diabetes), or primary prevention and early detection of treatable problems (for example, mammography or cervical cancer screening). The patient, or panel of patients, can be described at the beginning of the care episode based on their demographic and health characteristics at the point of time at which they enter the health care system. These patient characteristics (that is, case mix variables) are often used to describe the case, or the mix of cases in the panel, at the beginning of a treatment episode.

The episode of care continues in stepwise fashion (often with feedback loops), as the care-giving/care-receiving process unfolds. The patient (1) accesses the system of care; (2) is assessed by the clinical team based on history, physical, and diagnostic tests; (3) receives a diagnosis; (4) negotiates a treatment plan with the clinician; and (5) cooperates, more or less, with the regimen and is followed by the clinician for reassessment, diagnosis, and ongoing treatment planning.

The episode of care usually ends in a ragged manner, unless the patient expires. The ragged ending of an episode exists because of the arbitrary nature of determining end points for care outcomes. For example, the respective end points for cystitis, URI, acute MI care, hypertension control, diabetes treatment, and health maintenance do not occur at one precise moment in time. Rather, the patient, or cohort of patients, are followed for a reasonable period of time—based on clinical knowledge about the course of disease and recovery—to determine their outcomes at a specified, somewhat arbitrary, point in time.

If we take a longer-term view of a patient—for example, over a period of five years—it becomes clear that each person experiences a sequence of illnesses that are strung together over time. Consider the patient described next.

> ***Mary Holland—Part 1.*** *Mary Holland is a 64-year-old woman who considers herself to be in "fairly good health . . . all things considered." She is under treatment for essential hypertension, which is well controlled with medications and dietary restrictions. Mrs. Holland is a member of Good Neighbor HMO and has a personal physician Dr. Drake, a general internist, whom she has seen three to five times per year for the past seven years.*
>
> *During the past 12 months, Mrs. Holland visited Dr. Drake in August for a routine health maintenance visit, saw him again in October about recurrent cystitis, and visited his office three more times—in November, February, and May—to check her blood pressure and cardiovascular health.*
>
> *Her only serious health problem took place three years ago when she was admitted to the hospital for severe chest pain. She had suffered an acute MI and proceeded to have cardiac catheritization and to undergo a coronary artery bypass grafting (CABG) procedure. Her recovery progress post-discharge was uneventful; within six months she felt fully recovered from both the acute MI and the CABG operation.*

The Mary Holland case could be viewed as a series of longitudinal care episodes. At the beginning of each episode, she could be described in terms of her clinical status, functional status, her expectations for care to be received, and her past medical care costs (that is, the total medical care resources consumed to date). At the end of each episode, Mary Holland could once again be described in terms of her clinical status, functional status, satisfaction, and incremental costs (that is, the new costs associated with the care that she received). For example, Figure 9.2 shows a framework for understanding Mary Holland's episode of cystitis.

Some general principles arise from this case.

- *Longitudinal care.* Health needs of the patient, as managed by the clinician, may be thought of as longitudinal episodes of care that may either be distinct and separated or overlapping one another.

- *Transitions.* Most outcomes are better thought of as transitions in health status over time (for example, changes in urinary symptoms from cystitis, hip pain, blood sugar, physical function, mental health, and so on).

- *Specific outcomes.* Some outcomes are specific to the particular health need experienced at the beginning of the episode (for example, cystitis-specific results related to symptoms, hip fracture results related to pain and mobility, diabetes control level as measured by serum glycosolated hemoglobin and degree of end organ damage, and so on).

- *Generic outcomes.* Some outcomes are generic to all individuals (for example, physical function, mental health, health-related role limitations, bodily pain, overall satisfaction with the clinician or clinical team, outpatient costs, and so on).

- *Multiple outcomes.* There are multiple, important outcomes that relate to different aspects of the quality of care (clinical, functional, satisfaction, and so on) and to the costs associated with illness and receiving health care.

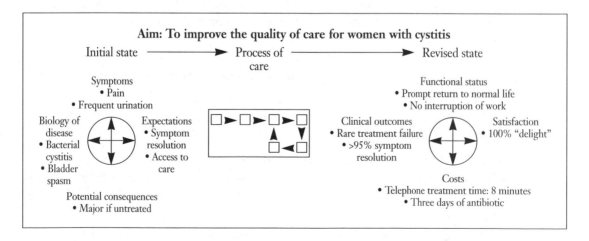

Figure 9.2. A framework for thinking about the relevant issues for a patient with cystitis. These issues are presented for her initial state prior to treatment and for her revised state following therapy with antibiotics.

- *Value: quality and costs.* The overall value of care is a function of both the quality of the outcomes as well as their costs (that is, amount of resources used to achieve the outcomes). This relationship can be stated as follows:

$$\text{Value} = \frac{\text{Quality of outcomes}}{\text{Cost}}$$

Outcomes of Care

The outcomes of health care may be thought of as a set of results, or consequences of care, that are associated with the delivery of health care services. These health care outcomes may be desirable or undesirable, expected or unexpected. In the past, the outcomes of care were, for the most part, viewed simply as a matter of toting up the four *D*s.

- Death

- Disease

- Disability

- Dollars

It always will be important to assess outcomes with respect to mortality, morbidity, and costs. Death, disease, and disability are useful indicators of clinical results; they reflect underlying biological processes and often link directly to the therapeutic interventions performed by physicians. Society must then account for the resources consumed, using dollars as the gauge.

As the saying goes, however, "For every complex problem, there is a simple answer that is usually wrong."

During the past several decades, the concept of medical outcomes has been expanded to include many additional elements (going beyond mortality and morbidity) such as functional status, perceived well-being, health risk status, satisfaction with care, perceived benefit of treatment, and costs of care.[4] This new view of outcomes is more sophisticated than the earlier view and has huge potential, but could be overwhelming.[5] Thus, for the purpose of making the measurement and improvement of care both well-rounded and practical, it is helpful to focus on the four cardinal domains of outcomes that are illustrated in Figure 9.3.

There are many types of outcomes related to many different types of people with myriad health problems and needs. In general, however, the consequences of treatment for a patient fall into four very broad categories.

1. *Clinical outcomes.* The biological status of the individual, often expressed in terms of organ system function or pathophysiological values.

2. *Functional status and well-being.* The physical, mental, social/role function of individuals, which reflects their ability to perform in their normal environment, and the individuals' level of well-being as reflected in their personal assessment of their health status and their level of health risk.

3. *Expectations and satisfaction against need.* The evaluation of the individual about the goodness of the health care delivery process and the extent to which their health needs were met.

4. *Total costs.* The direct costs associated with resources consumed in delivering care, and the indirect social costs associated with receiving care and being unable to carry out normal role activities (for example, working, taking care of family, going to school, and so on).

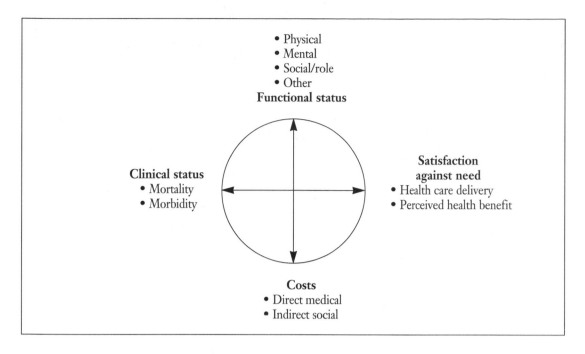

Figure 9.3. The clinical value compass.

The clinical value compass, illustrated in Figure 9.3, provides an easy-to-remember and easy-to-apply method for conceptualizing critical types of health outcomes. It suggests that there are four major quadrants of the health outcomes territory that exist and that may be (1) explored, (2) understood, (3) defined, (4) measured, (5) managed, and (6) improved over time.

The clinical value compass approach can be used to describe a patient at a point in time or a population of patients that share a health problem. It has been used for many different purposes including the measurement of value of acute MI care in three hospitals,[6] the management of a clinical product line—CABG patients—in a tertiary care center,[7] the clinical management of panels of elderly patients being cared for in primary care medical practices,[8] and to launch rapid-change-cycle clinical improvements by frontline teams of practitioners.[9] An example of a value compass for CABG surgery is presented in Figure 9.4.

Improving Patient Care

There is no reason to measure outcomes except to improve the outcomes of care for individuals or populations. Improvement in outcomes may actually occur, but cannot be known to have been achieved without measurement. Improvement has many faces:

- *Regimen planning.* Matching the treatment plan to the patient's need based on standardized, patient-based assessments of the individual's overall health need (for example, feeding forward important information on the patient's health status to be used by the primary physician to design a treatment plan for a frail elderly patient)

- *Clinical monitoring.* Observing that critical clinical results are going out of control and taking fast action to return them to normal or safe levels (for example, blood sugar monitoring of

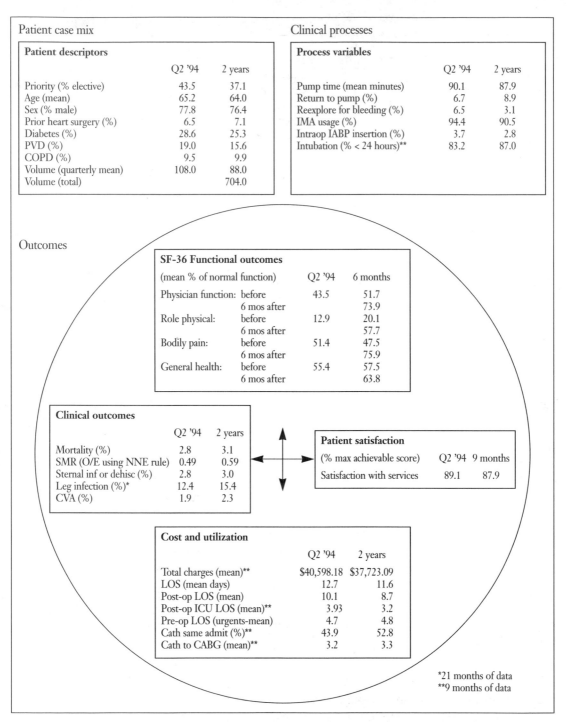

Patient case mix

Patient descriptors

	Q2 '94	2 years
Priority (% elective)	43.5	37.1
Age (mean)	65.2	64.0
Sex (% male)	77.8	76.4
Prior heart surgery (%)	6.5	7.1
Diabetes (%)	28.6	25.3
PVD (%)	19.0	15.6
COPD (%)	9.5	9.9
Volume (quarterly mean)	108.0	88.0
Volume (total)		704.0

Clinical processes

Process variables

	Q2 '94	2 years
Pump time (mean minutes)	90.1	87.9
Return to pump (%)	6.7	8.9
Reexplore for bleeding (%)	6.5	3.1
IMA usage (%)	94.4	90.5
Intraop IABP insertion (%)	3.7	2.8
Intubation (% < 24 hours)**	83.2	87.0

Outcomes

SF-36 Functional outcomes

(mean % of normal function)		Q2 '94	6 months
Physician function:	before	43.5	51.7
	6 mos after		73.9
Role physical:	before	12.9	20.1
	6 mos after		57.7
Bodily pain:	before	51.4	47.5
	6 mos after		75.9
General health:	before	55.4	57.5
	6 mos after		63.8

Clinical outcomes

	Q2 '94	2 years
Mortality (%)	2.8	3.1
SMR (O/E using NNE rule)	0.49	0.59
Sternal inf or dehisc (%)	2.8	3.0
Leg infection (%)*	12.4	15.4
CVA (%)	1.9	2.3

Patient satisfaction

(% max achievable score)	Q2 '94	9 months
Satisfaction with services	89.1	87.9

Cost and utilization

	Q2 '94	2 years
Total charges (mean)**	$40,598.18	$37,723.09
LOS (mean days)	12.7	11.6
Post-op LOS (mean)	10.1	8.7
Post-op ICU LOS (mean)**	3.93	3.2
Pre-op LOS (urgents-mean)	4.7	4.8
Cath same admit (%)**	43.9	52.8
Cath to CABG (mean)**	3.2	3.3

*21 months of data
**9 months of data

This shows the instrument panel used to summarize the CABG process at one hospital. Note that, in the functional outcomes data, the six-month follow-up data for Q2 '94 are pending. PVD = peripheral vascular disease; COPD = chronic obstructive pulmonary disease; IMA = internal mammary artery; IABP = intra-aortic balloon pump; SMR = standardized mortality ratio; O/E = observed/expected; NNE = Northern New England Cardiovascular Disease Study Group; CVA = cerebrovascular accident; LOS = length of stay.

Figure 9.4. A clinical value compass for a CABG patient.

diabetics, body weight monitoring of congestive heart failure patients, blood-clotting times of patients on coumadin, post-surgical wound infection rates, and so on)

- *Clinical benchmarking.* Reviewing the health outcomes for a cohort of patients that have recently received care in a particular location and observing that some critical outcomes are below the levels achieved by other practitioners caring for similar patients (for example, benchmarking of one group's results against best known results for similar patients)

- *Care innovation.* Designing new clinical management systems and evaluating the success of the new system (versus the old system) based on the differences in quality-related and cost-related results (for example, reengineering the care delivery process in an intensive care unit by cross-training and use of lower-skilled workers in teams with more advanced clinicians)

All of these potential improvements in clinical care depend on measurement of outcomes to know if a change is having the desired results and is free from major unwanted outcomes. The clinical improvement worksheet, described in the next section, can be used to provide a flexible path forward for improving clinical care. The next section aims to provide guidance about outcomes measurement using case examples.

Measuring Clinical Value: What to Measure, How to Measure It, and How to Make It Useful

Basic Approach

Our approach is to build the measurement of health outcomes into a process of continual improvement at the front line of care delivery. To make this work easy and flexible, we use the clinical improvement worksheet shown in Figures 9.5a and 9.5b. The worksheet's purpose is to accelerate clinical improvement by linking outcomes measurement and process knowledge with pilot tests of changes with the potential of improving care.

Side A of the worksheet frames the work by specifying the clinical target population, the outcomes of interest, the delivery process, and potential changes that could be made that may produce superior results. Side B of the worksheet hones in on a specific pilot test or change cycle. It guides the test of change by clarifying the specific aim, the measures that will be used to determine success, and a description of the planned test of change. It then proceeds with the detailed plan and execution of the change cycle using the familiar plan-do-check-act (PDCA) approach—planning the pilot, doing the test of change, checking/studying the impact of the test, and acting to hold the gains or abandoning the pilot if it fails to achieve the hypothesized results.

In the next section, we use this approach and apply it to three case examples to illustrate the use of measurement at different levels in the delivery of health care: a hospital, a clinical practice, and a patient. We will focus specifically on the measurement of outcomes.

Specific Examples

Case 1—Acute MI: Internal Benchmarking and Clinical Instrument Panel to Identify Improvement Opportunities for a Hospital. This case is based on work done in three community hospitals in the southeastern United States that were part of an investor-owned health care company.[10] A synopsis of the case follows, using the worksheet's format to summarize the information.

- *Aim.* To develop a method for measuring the outcomes and processes of acute MI care for the purpose of improving outcomes and reducing costs. The first step will be to gather baseline data on

232

Clinical Improvement Worksheet

Aim: Accelerate clinical improvement by linking outcomes measurements and process knowledge with the design and conduct of pilot tests of change.

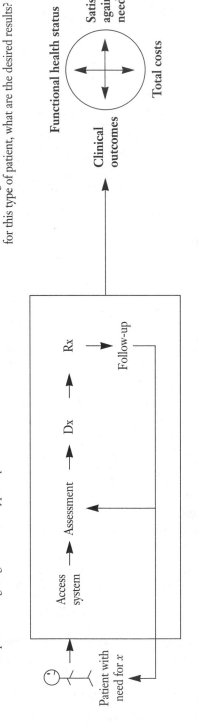

② Process ⟶ **Analyze the process.**

What's the process for giving care to this type of patient?

Access system ⟶ Assessment ⟶ Dx ⟶ Rx ⟶ Follow-up

Patient with need for *x*

③ Changes ⟶ **Generate change ideas.**

What ideas do we have for changing what's done (process) to get better results?

• • • •

Figure 9.5a. Clinical improvement worksheet: Side A.

Measurement

outcome
outcome

process
process
PDCA

Process

① Outcomes ⟶ **Select a population.**

What's the general aim? Given our wish to limit/reduce the illness burden for this type of patient, what are the desired results?

Functional health status

Satisfaction against needs

Clinical outcomes

Total costs

④ Pilot ⟶ **Select the first/next change for pilot testing.**

How can we pilot test an improvement idea using the plan-do-check-act method?

Making Improvements: Clinical Improvement Worksheet

Team members ⟶ Who should work on this improvement?

1. *Leader*   5. _____
2. *Facilitator*   6. _____
3. _____   7. _____
4. _____   8. _____

Coach _____   Admin Support _____

A. Aim ⟶ What are we trying to accomplish? (more specific aim)

B. Measures ⟶ How will we know that a change is an improvement?

C. Selected change ⟶ How would you describe the change that you have selected for testing?

D. Plan ⟶ How shall we *plan* the pilot?
- Who? Does what? When? With what tools and training?
- Baseline data to be collected?

E. Do ⟶ What are we learning as we *do* the pilot?

F. Check ⟶ As we *check* and *study* what happened, what have we learned?
- Did the original outcomes improve?

G. Act ⟶ As we *act* to hold the gains or abandon our pilot efforts, what needs to be done?

Figure 9.5b. Clinical improvement worksheet: Side B.

case mix, processes, outcomes, and costs of care for internal benchmarking and for constructing hospital-specific instrument panels to show case mix, processes, and outcomes/costs.

- *Measures*. A partial listing of measures is displayed in Table 9.1.

- *Plan*. A consecutive series of confirmed acute MI patients admitted directly to each of three hospitals will be studied to obtain baseline results. Inpatient medical records will be reviewed to collect information on patient mix, clinical process, and some outcomes (for example, mortality, readmissions), and hospital billing information will be used to obtain data on costs. Patients will be interviewed at eight weeks post-discharge to obtain data on satisfaction with care, functioning, and some clinical measures (for example, angina).

- *Check*. Figure 9.6 shows the internal benchmarking results after statistical adjustment for patient mix differences across hospitals. Hospital A had the lowest cost, while Hospital C was highest ($24,580 vs. $31,525). On the other hand, Hospital C had the best level of physical functioning at eight weeks (75 percent of maximum score for Hospital C vs. 63 percent for Hospital A and 49 percent for Hospital B). Differences in mortality and overall hospital satisfaction were not significant, although if the trend were to hold, the mortality differential would have become statistically significant with the addition of more cases.

The instrument panel for Hospital C is shown in Figure 9.7; this presents the unadjusted (actual) results. This can be used to gain a panoramic view of patient mix, process, outcomes, and the patient's ratings of selected aspects of care. The instrument panel shows that on average it took three hours for patients to get to the emergency department after experiencing the onset of chest pain. Nine percent of patients had high severity of symptoms and 69 percent low. Only 14 percent received thrombolytic

Table 9.1. A list of some of the categories of measurement and associated specific measures for a hospital trying to improve the care of patients with acute MI.

Category	Specific measure
Patient mix	Demographics Comorbidity Illness severity
Clinical processes	Diagnostic tests Therapeutic interventions
Elapsed times	Onset of chest pain to arrival in ED Arrival in ED to reading of ECG Arrival in ED to thrombolytic therapy
Clinical status at eight weeks	Mortality Angina severity
Functional status at eight weeks	Overall health Physical function Time to resuming normal work/life
Satisfaction	Overall satisfaction with hospital Patient ratings of specific information needs being met
Costs	Hospital charges Length of stay Readmission within eight weeks

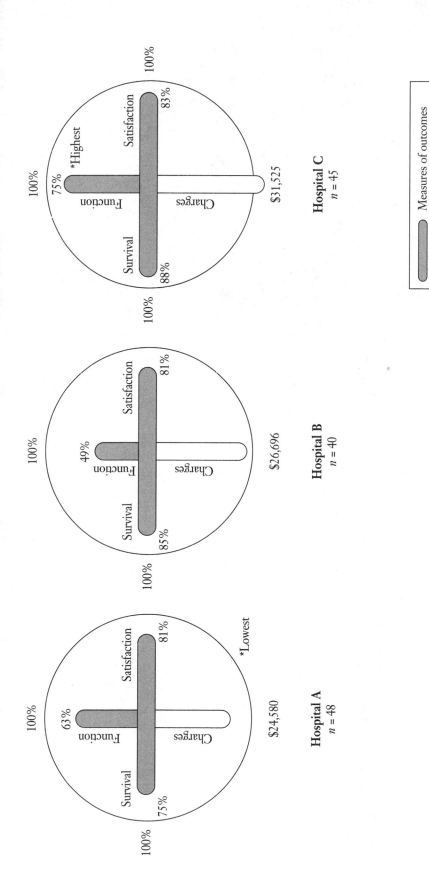

Figure 9.6. Outcomes and costs of care for acute MI patients seen in three hospitals: Adjusted results.

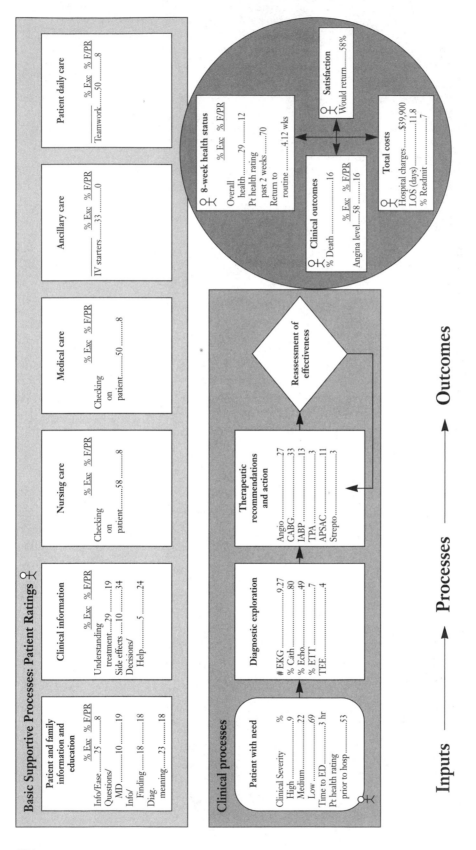

Basic Supportive Processes: Patient Ratings ⚥

Patient and family information and education

	% Exc	% F/PR
Info/Ease	25	8
Questions/ MD	10	19
Info/ Finding	18	18
Diag. meaning	23	18

Clinical information

	% Exc	% F/PR
Understanding treatment	29	19
Side effects	10	34
Decisions/ Help	5	24

Nursing care

	% Exc	% F/PR
Checking on patient	58	8

Medical care

	% Exc	% F/PR
Checking on patient	50	8

Ancillary care

	% Exc	% F/PR
IV starters	33	0

Patient daily care

	% Exc	% F/PR
Teamwork	50	8

Clinical processes

Patient with need

Clinical Severity	%
High	9
Medium	22
Low	69
Time to ED	3 hr
Pt health rating prior to hosp.	53

⚥

Diagnostic exploration

# EKG	9.27
% Cath.	80
% Echo.	49
% ETT	7
TEE	4

Therapeutic recommendations and action

Angio	27
CABG	33
IABP	13
TPA	3
APSAC	11
Strepto.	3

Reassessment of effectiveness

8-week health status ⚥

	% Exc	% F/PR
Overall health	29	12
Pt health rating past 2 weeks		70
Return to routine		4.12 wks

Satisfaction ⚥

Would return......58%

Clinical outcomes ⚥

	% Exc	% F/PR
% Death		16
Angina level	58	16

Total costs ⚥

Hospital charges	$39,900
LOS (days)	11.8
% Readmit	7

Inputs ⟶ Processes ⟶ Outcomes

Figure 9.7. Instrument panel for acute MI patients seen in one hospital: Unadjusted results (based on consecutive series of 45 nontransfer acute MI patients).

therapy whereas 33 percent went on to have a CABG and 27 percent an angioplasty. The mortality rate at eight weeks was 16 percent, and 16 percent of survivors had substantial angina. On average it took 4.12 weeks for patients to return to work or normal routine, and their level of functioning now averaged 70 percent vs. 53 percent prior to admission. The length of stay averaged 11.8 days and hospital charges averaged $39,900. Patients' ratings of care for specific features showed both areas of strength and weaknesses (for example, 34 percent rated their understanding of potential side effects fair or poor).

• *Act.* The comparative results prompted several actions. Hospital C reviewed its costs and treatment patterns—for example, the levels of CABG and angioplasty were scrutinized. Hospital A wished to study its trend in mortality to determine if its rate was atypical for the series of patients under study. Hospital B became interested in finding ways to speed the recovery of patients' physical function. The instrument panel results prompted improvement work in several areas including public education on recognition of chest pain, medical staff education on indications for thrombolytic therapy, redesign of the patient education process, and redesign of the initial management of chest pain in the emergency department to accelerate rapid diagnosis and early intervention.

This case includes several important measurement issues. A few of these are detailed as follows.

• *Case mix adjustment.* The three-hospital outcome results were adjusted to provide fair comparisons across hospitals. Adjustment was done by using multivariate analysis to control for the effects of patient mix differences (for example, age, gender, disease severity, and comorbidity). This was done to allow a more accurate understanding of the level of differences in survival, function, satisfaction, and charges after removing variation associated with case mix differences. The hospital-specific instrument panel results were not adjusted because the intent was to analyze the actual results for this series of patients.

• *Patient ratings of the process of care.* The patients were asked a set of specific questions related to meeting needs associated with discrete facets of the treatment process. The list of questions was developed after conducting a focus group of recent acute MI patients and family members. These condition-specific patient evaluations of process quality were beneficial in targeting improvements in patient education linked to distinct parts of the delivery process.

• *Measurement of costs.* There is a real distinction between actual costs (amount of resources consumed) and charges (amount billed to payors). It is often difficult to obtain data on actual costs, and it is therefore useful to use measures of resource intensity that are proxies for costs. In this case, LOS (length of stay) is a good example of a proxy variable for costs. Charges to the payor represent the billed amount and may reflect actual level of payment (cost to the payor) or could have been discounted and therefore not be a good indication of the payment actually rendered.

• *Use of multiple data sources.* Three sources of data were used: the medical record, the billing and administrative databases, and patient self-report. It is often possible to obtain reasonably accurate information on some variables from routine sources (records, bills, and so on); however, one frequently must use prospective data collection from patients or providers to measure needed variables. Collection of prospective data—from patients or providers—should be kept to the minimum needed to answer critical questions.

Case 2—Health Assessment and Health Maintenance to Match Treatment Regimen to Patient Health Need in a Clinical Practice. This case is based on the COOP Clinical Improvement System that has been designed to improve care for elderly patients, adults, and adolescents. Once again we provide a case synopsis followed by a discussion of relevant measurement issues.

• *Aim.* To make the best match between patient need and the treatment plan by feeding forward patient-based information into the complete health maintenance visit. The information can be used to forge a partnership between the patient and the physician, to activate the patient to better manage his or her own health care, to provide standard data on the patient's health transitions over time, and to provide the clinician with uniform feedback on the health outcomes of the panel of patients.

• *Measures.* Some of the patient-based measures are listed in Table 9.2.

• *Plan.* Patients age 70 and older complete a comprehensive, self-administered questionnaire before seeing their personal physician for their annual health assessment. The information (which covers clinical symptoms, functioning, health risks, satisfaction with care received, and so on), is entered instantly into a computer (using bar coding, optical scans, or a touch-screen device). The computer automatically produces (1) a flowsheet for the doctor that summarizes the patient's health profile (enabling the doctor to quickly focus on problem areas and to note any important transitions from the prior year), and (2) a personal recommendation/advice letter for the patient that points out areas of concern and suggests actions to take. The clinician completes the health assessment by taking the history, doing a physical examination, and ordering diagnostic tests. The treatment plan is discussed with the patient, and the patient is given a medical encyclopedia to take home and is given specific reading assignments related to areas of health concern. The data are then used to (1) produce a summary of the clinician's panel of patients compared to other peer practices, (2) identify practice improvement opportunities, and (3) monitor changes in the clinician's panel of patients from year to year.

Table 9.2. A list of some of the categories of measurement and associated specific measures for a clinical practice trying to improve the care for all of its patients.

Category	Specific measure
Patient mix	Demographics Comorbidity
Risk status	Immunizations Personal habits (exercise, smoking, alcohol use) Environmental (household hazards, for example) Advanced directives
Clinical status	Common problems Symptoms and side effects
Functional status	Overall daily activities Physical function Mental function Social activities Pain

Satisfaction	Patient ratings of
	   Physician's treatment of problems
	   Explanation given about treatment
	   Health benefit from treatment

Costs	Hospital stays in the past six months Medications

• *Check.* Selected results for one physician's first 75 patients who used the new system are illustrated in Figure 9.8. The findings highlight the percentage defective, which means the proportion of patients that have a problem in each particular area listed. Traveling around the value compass shows that 22 percent of the panel have hearing problems and from 13 percent to 11 percent have problems sleeping, thinking, or with their feet. Substantial limitations in physical functioning are common (37 percent), while 16 percent and 13 percent respectively suffer from pain or limitations in social activities. With respect to health risks, immunizations are often not up to date (76 percent to 25 percent are not current on tetanus, pneumovax, and influenza), more than half do not have advanced directives in place, and 28 percent report consuming three or more drinks per day. With respect to satisfaction with their doctor's care for specific problems, 14 percent did not understand their physician's explanations of physical functioning problems and 33 percent indicated that they had not benefited from their treatment. Finally, on the cost side, 44 percent of patients report spending $60 or more per month on prescribed drugs and 18 percent have been hospitalized in the past six months.

• *Act.* The initial results on this physician's panel reveal many opportunities for improvement. It would be easy to be overwhelmed by the number of areas. To avoid this, the clinician would be wise to work with the clinical team to select important problem areas that are relatively easy to improve rapidly and which can be targeted for sequential tests of change. For example, three cycles of change

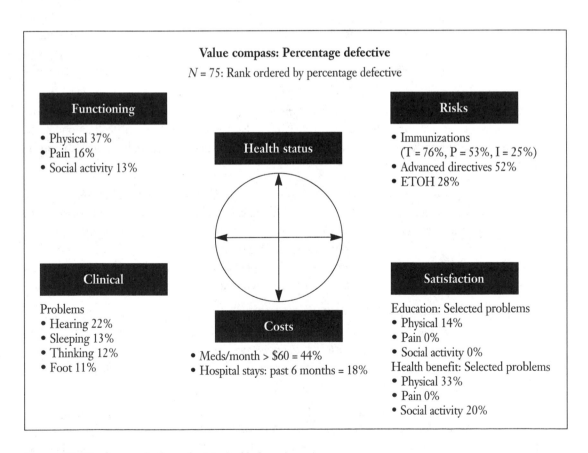

Figure 9.8. Baseline results for a physician's elderly patients.

could be planned: (1) start with immunizations by building them into routine chronic care follow-up visits, (2) tackle advanced directives by including this in the annual assessment process and training a member of the office staff to handle this important issue, and (3) address medication costs by reviewing them at the annual assessment, trimming unnecessary medicines, and substituting lower-cost drugs for higher-cost medications when possible.

A few of the measurement issues embedded in this case are highlighted next.

• *Techniques for measuring health status and satisfaction.* There are some validated methods for measuring health status and satisfaction that can be used in busy clinical settings. Some of the best known and most widely used brief measures of general health status are the MOS SF-36,[11] the MOS SF-12, and the Dartmouth COOP charts.[12,13] There are also some widely used patient satisfaction questionnaires that can be used or adapted for use in a variety of settings including medical offices,[14] inpatient settings,[15] and health plans.[16]

• *Link health outcomes with satisfaction.* In the past, it was common to study clinical or functional outcomes and not to connect these health results to satisfaction. This is often a mistake, because the perceived health benefit derived from care is a critical aspect of satisfaction.[17] Figure 9.9 illustrates how this was accomplished in the case study. Patients rate their functional status on a COOP chart and, if they score poorly, they proceed to answer questions on satisfaction with treatment effects and communication.

• *Build outcomes measurement into daily work.* For many purposes, the best time to gather data on the health status of the patient is at the time that care is rendered. It has the benefits of measuring status at time of treatment, can be used as part of the patient assessment, and can be done efficiently without building a separate (added cost) system for gathering outcomes data.

• *Use information systems to improve care and the cost-effectiveness of data collection.* It is now possible to use a variety of techniques to automate data entry, data analysis, and report production and to use the information instantly—in real time—as care is being provided. These technologies should be exploited.

Case 3—Assessing and Improving the Management of a Common Clinical Problem for a Patient. Earlier in the chapter, we used the Mary Holland case to illustrate the concepts of episodes of illness and multiple outcomes. In this section we provide an example to illustrate the measurement of outcomes relevant to some of Mary Holland's health needs during her episode of recurrent cystitis.

This case is based on work done in nine medical practices in New Hampshire and Massachusetts that are part of a multispecialty group practice. A patient scenario and a synopsis of the case follows.

> ***Mary Holland—Part 2.*** *Mary Holland develops symptoms of frequent urination with associated pain and burning. She does not have a fever, chills, back pain, nausea, or vomiting. These symptoms, she recalls, are the same ones she had 10 years ago when she was treated for a UTI. Aside from her hypertension, she has been in excellent health since her acute MI and CABG surgery three years ago.*

• *Aim.* To improve the care of a woman with a UTI, starting from the time she contacts the office with symptoms until the resolution of her symptoms. The first step in this work is to design a clinical protocol based on knowledge of the medical literature. The protocol can then be used to guide management of patients with UTIs, serve as a data collection instrument, and provide the basis for clinical research.

Using the chart below, circle the number beside the category that best describes you.

FEELINGS

During the past four weeks . . .

How much have you been bothered by emotional problems such as feeling anxious, depressed, irritable, sad, or downhearted and blue?

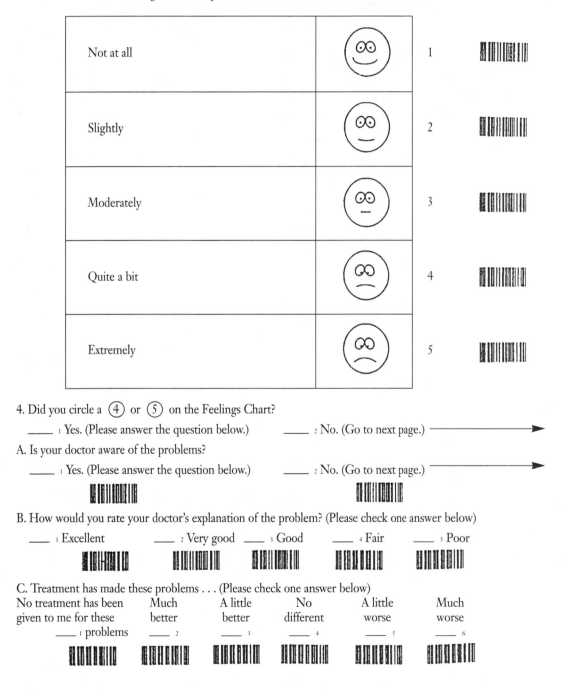

4. Did you circle a ④ or ⑤ on the Feelings Chart?

_____ ₁ Yes. (Please answer the question below.)   _____ ₂ No. (Go to next page.) ⟶

A. Is your doctor aware of the problems?

_____ ₁ Yes. (Please answer the question below.)   _____ ₂ No. (Go to next page.) ⟶

B. How would you rate your doctor's explanation of the problem? (Please check one answer below)

_____ ₁ Excellent   _____ ₂ Very good _____ ₃ Good   _____ ₄ Fair   _____ ₅ Poor

C. Treatment has made these problems . . . (Please check one answer below)

| No treatment has been given to me for these _____ ₁ problems | Much better _____ ₂ | A little better _____ ₃ | No different _____ ₄ | A little worse _____ ₅ | Much worse _____ ₆ |

Figure 9.9. Sample page from the COOP Clinical Improvement System survey for elderly patients.

- *Measures.* Table 9.3 presents some of the measures to evaluate a patient with a UTI.

- *Plan.* A protocol for triaging and managing UTIs is established in the clinic where Mary Holland receives her care. When Mary calls the office, she speaks to a nurse who obtains baseline information on Mary's age, medical history, previous UTIs, and current symptoms. Since Mary has no risk factors for a complicated infection, the nurse suggests that Mary come to the clinic at her earliest convenience to test her urine for infection. At the clinic, Mary provides a sample of her urine, which tests positive. She is treated by the nurse with three days of antibiotics and is given education about signs and symptoms to look for if the UTI is not improving. Finally, Mary is called by a nurse seven days after her treatment started to make sure her symptoms have resolved and to assess her satisfaction with care. Mary's entire episode of care occurs without a visit to her physician and is recorded on a single data sheet that also becomes part of her medical record.

- *Check.* The actual results of the use of the UTI clinical protocol for patients like Mary Holland with uncomplicated UTIs are displayed for a single practice in Figure 9.10. Although Mary was not at high risk for a complicated infection, 37 percent of patients were at high risk and treated with antibiotics for seven rather than three days. Side effects from antibiotics occurred in 9 percent of patients. Failure of antibiotic therapy occurred 12 percent of the time. Satisfaction with care was high; 100 percent of patients were delighted with the convenience of not having to schedule and wait for an appointment with a physician and with receiving a follow-up phone call from a nurse. Costs are also decreased by eliminating a physician office visit and standardizing urine testing; the total reduction in charges for a single practice is $52,000. The effect of the clinical protocol on the use of urine cultures (a more expensive and unnecessary test for patients with a simple UTI) in the practice as a whole is shown in Figure 9.11.

- *Act.* The use of a protocol for managing UTIs has generated several additional developments. One clinical practice decided to study Mary Holland's insight that her symptoms were the same as her previous infection. This group compared the accuracy of a patient's self-diagnosis with the accuracy of

Table 9.3. A list of some of the categories of measurement and associated specific measures for a patient with a UTI.

Category	Specific measure
Patient mix	Demographics Comorbidity
Clinical status	Symptoms (urinary frequency, pain) Risk of complicated infection Medication side effects Failure rate of antibiotic therapy
Functional status	Ability to perform daily activities
Satisfaction	Patient ratings of overall satisfaction with care Prompt resolution of symptoms
Costs	Time away from work or daily role Diagnostic testing Antibiotics

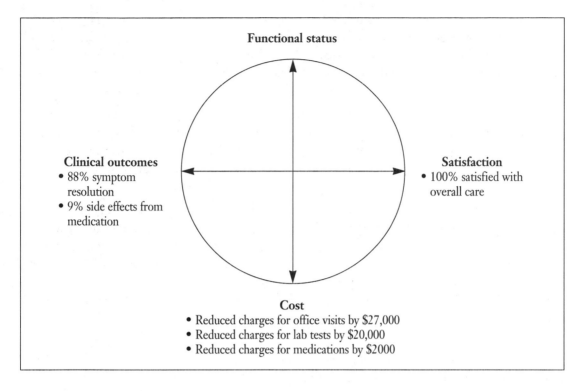

Figure 9.10. Results for women age 18 to 65 with uncomplicated cystitis from the use of protocol for managing UTIs at one clinical practice.

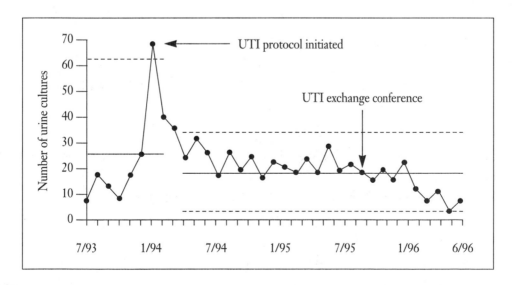

Figure 9.11. The number of urine cultures ordered monthly in a participating clinic for women age 18 to 65 with a simple UTI. The use of a clinical protocol began in January 1994 in this practice. The practice participated in a conference on the use of UTI protocols in September 1995.

a urine dipstick test, using a urine culture as the gold standard. They found that the women were able to predict just as well as the dipstick whether an infection was truly present. In addition, the low antibiotic failure rate, high patient satisfaction with care, and demonstration of wise use of testing over time has convinced other practices to begin using a UTI protocol.

Some of the measurement issues highlighted by this case are described as follows.

• *Use a self-coding data sheet.* The careful design of a data collection sheet is critical to the success of measurement over time. The sheet should be easy to use and limited to one page. Self-coding is a standardization of the possible data entries (that is, response choices) for any particular variable or step in a protocol. Use of this technique minimizes confusion over what each data point represents and facilitates data entry.

• *Measure and display data over time.* This method is a powerful tool for understanding the results of any change in a process. A control chart (shown in Figure 9.11) is one method for displaying data over time. First described by Shewhart,[18] the control chart allows one to observe the central tendency and the inherent variation of any process. The addition of computed control limits helps inform the observer about when the process is out of statistical control (for example, a point outside the control limit that is more than three standard deviations from the mean) and when action on the process is required vs. when not to take action (that is, because the process is acting within its normal inherent variation).

• *Use clinical protocols to study specific aspects of care.* One clear advantage of the use of clinical protocols is the definition of the process of care. Clarifying the process can be used to focus measurement on key steps. When the measurement is in place, one then has the ability to change the process of care and study the results of the change. This method of designing measurement into the daily work of practitioners makes clinical research more accessible for anyone interested in studying specific aspects of a care process.

Final Comments: Lessons Learned and Challenges for the Future

Lessons Learned

Experience in measuring outcomes has taught us some lessons. A few of these are listed next, using a question-and-answer format.

How can we make measurement useful?

1. Start with the concept of continual improvement, running rapid and repeated tests of change.[19]

2. Use a framework such as the COOP Clinical Improvement Worksheet.[20]

3. Ask the users of the information how they will use the data and what could be done to make the data most useful.[21]

4. Construct instrument panels to display results.[22]

5. Label each instrument panel with critical information regarding the user, the uses, the sources of data, the sample size, and the time period of data collection.

What should we measure?

6. Measure case mix, key processes, and a balanced set of outcomes and costs. The same process that produces the health care outcomes also produces the health care costs.

How can we measure outcomes?

7. Use condition-specific and generic measures of outcomes.

8. Be sure to specify each outcome variable by writing both conceptual and operational definitions to enable valid information to be gathered in a reliable manner.[23]

How can we make measurement fit into clinical practice?

9. Design data collection into the patient flow and the clinical delivery process.

10. Start small, with bite-size chunks of data that are needed to answer critical questions.

11. Use available data when possible.

12. For data that must be collected prospectively, design self-coding data sheets to be used by patients, clinicians, and support staff as work is performed.

Challenges and Final Comment

This chapter has introduced an approach for measuring and improving health outcomes and value. The methods can be used for inpatient and outpatient care. We hope that more and more clinicians who are practicing medicine in busy delivery settings will begin making the measurement and improvement of outcomes and costs an active participant sport that they themselves engage in and enjoy.

The challenge is clear! Better outcomes. Lower costs. No excuses. Be part of the solution.

Acknowledgments

The authors wish to express their gratitude for the clinical case examples that were made possible by the following people: John H. Wasson, assessment of the elderly; Harold Sox and Marjorie Godfrey, treatment of cystitis; and William Nugent, William Schults, and their colleagues' monitoring of cardiac care. We also wish to thank Denise Nelson for her work in preparing the manuscript and the figures used to illustrate the text.

This chapter is based on an oral presentation delivered at the Institute for Healthcare Improvement's National Forum in Orlando, Florida, in December 1995.

Notes

1. N. Goldfield, M. Pine, and J. Pine, *Measuring and Managing Health Care Quality: Procedures, Techniques, and Protocols* (Gaithersburg, Md.: Aspen Publishers, 1996).

2. E. C. Nelson and J. H. Wasson, "Using Patient-Based Information to Rapidly Redesign Care," *Healthcare Forum Journal* 37:25–29 (1994).

3. P. B. Batalden, E. C. Nelson, and J. S. Roberts, "Linking Outcomes Measurement to Continual Improvement: The Serial 'V' Way of Thinking About Improving Clinical Care," *Jt Comm J Qual Improv* 20:167–80 (1994).

4. S. Greenfield and E. C. Nelson, "Recent Developments and Future Issues in the Use of Health Status Assessment Measures in Clinical Settings," *Med Care* 30:MS23–41 (1992).

5. P. M. Ellwood, "Outcomes Management: A Technology of Patient Experience," *N Engl J. Med* 1549–1556 (1988).

6. E. C. Nelson, S. Greenfield, R. D. Hays, C. Larson, B. Leopold, and P. B. Batalden, "Comparing Outcomes and Charges for Patients with Acute Myocardial Infarction in Three Community Hospitals: An Approach for Assessing 'Value,'" *Int J Qual Health Care* 7:95–108 (1995).

7. W. C. Nugent, W. C. Schults, S. K. Plume, P. B. Batalden, and E. C. Nelson, "Designing an Instrument Panel to Monitor and Improve Coronary Artery Bypass Grafting," *JCOM* 1:57–64 (1994).

8. Nelson and Wasson, "Using Patient Based Information . . ."

9. E. C. Nelson, I. L. Mohr, P. B. Batalden, and S. K. Plume, "Improving Health Care, Part 1: The Clinical Value Compass," *Jt Comm J Qual Improv* 22:243–258 (1996).

10. Nelson, Greenfield, Hays, Larson, Leopold, and Batalden, "Comparing Outcomes and Charges . . ."

11. J. E. Ware and C. D. Sherbourne, "The MOS 36-Item Short-Form Health Survey (SF-36): I. Conceptual Framework and Item Selection," *Medical Care* 30:473–483 (1992).

12. J. E. Ware, M. Kosinski, and S. D. Keller, "A 12-Item Short-Form Health Survey: Construction and Scales and Preliminary Tests of Reliability and Validity," *Medical Care* 34:220–233 (1996).

13. E. C. Nelson, J. M. Landgraf, R. D. Hayes, J. H. Wasson, and J. W. Kird, "The Functional Status of Patients: How Can It Be Measured in Physicians' Offices? *Med Care* 28:1111–1126 (1990).

14. J. E. Ware and R. D. Hayes, "Methods for Measuring Patient Satisfaction with Specific Medical Encounters," *Medical Care* 26:393 (1988).

15. M. Meterko, E. C. Nelson, and H. R. Rubin, *Patient Judgments of Hospital Quality: Report of a Pilot Study* (Philadelphia, Pa.: J. B. Lippincott Company, 1990).

16. A. R. Davies, and J. E. Ware, *GHAA's Consumer Satisfaction Survey and User's Manual* (Washington, D.C.: Group Health Association of America, 1991).

17. A. Donabedian, *Explorations in Quality Assessment and Monitoring, Vol. I: The Definition of Quality and Approaches to Its Assessment* (Ann Arbor, Mich.: Health Administration Press, 1980).

18. D. J. Wheeler, *Advanced Topics in Statistical Process Control: The Power of Shewhart's Charts* (Knoxville, Tenn.: SPC Press, 1995).

19. P. B. Batalden and P. K. Stoltz, "A Framework for the Continual Improvement of Health Care: Building and Applying Professional and Improvement Knowledge to Test Changes in Daily Work," *Jt Comm J Qual Improv* 19:424–47; discussion 19:448–452 (1993).

20. E. C. Nelson, P. B. Batalden, S. K. Plume, and J. J. Mohr, "Improving Health Care, Part 2: A Clinical Improvement Worksheet and Users' Manual," *Jt Comm J Qual Improv* 22:531–548 (1996).

21. E. C. Nelson, P. B. Batalden, "Patient-Based Quality Measurement Systems," *Quality Management in Health Care* 2:18–30 (1993).

22. E. C. Nelson, P. B. Batalden, S. K. Plume, N. T. Mihevc, and W. G. Swartz, "Report Cards or Instrument Panels: Who Needs What?" *Jt Comm J Qual Improv* 21:155–166 (1995).

23. Nelson, Mohr, Batalden, and Plume, "Improving Health Care, Part I."

Eugene C. Nelson, D.Sc., MPH, is the director of quality education, measurement, and research at Lahey Hitchcock Clinic, Lebanon, New Hampshire, and a professor in the department of community and family medicine at Dartmouth Medical School in Hanover, New Hampshire.

Mark E. Splaine, M.D., M.S., is the senior scientist for measurement and statistics of Lahey Hitchcock Clinic in Lebanon, New Hampshire, and an instructor in the department of medicine at Dartmouth Medical School, Hanover, New Hampshire.

Paul B. Batalden, M.D., is a professor in the department of pediatrics and the department of community and family medicine at Dartmouth Medical School and the director of health care improvement leadership development at Dartmouth Medical School in Hanover, New Hampshire; the director of clinical process improvement and leadership development at Dartmouth-Hitchcock Medical Center in Lebanon, New Hampshire; and vice president and breech chair in the department of health care, quality improvement, education, and research at the Henry Ford Health System in Detroit, Michigan.

Stephen K. Plume, M.D., is the president at Lahey Hitchcock Clinic in Lebanon, New Hampshire, and a professor in the department of surgery at Dartmouth Medical School in Hanover, New Hampshire.

Chapter 10

Measuring Health Care System Quality and Performance

Eugene C. Nelson, Nancy Mihevc, Mary Gentry, Deborah Kehne,
April Levine, Paul B. Batalden, and Stephen K. Plume

Medical leaders are struggling to create integrated delivery systems and secure their position in an increasingly competitive environment. They must (1) reduce the costs of providing services to meet purchaser price demands, (2) increase the measured quality of care to show value to consumers, (3) increase the number of primary care outlets to enhance patient choice and access to services, and (4) skillfully manage the clinical care of patients, particularly those with serious medical problems, to provide needed services in the right way at the right place at the right time. These are some of the strategic imperatives faced by health care system leaders.[1] Amidst this turmoil, there is a clear accountability mandate—measure the quality and costs of care, quantify your delivery system's performance, and ensure best achievable outcomes.[2] The demand to measure organizational performance and to quantify results comes from many directions.[3] Purchasers often lead the way by calling for report cards on the quality and costs of care rendered to their members.[4] Accrediting organizations now require measures of clinical results, preventive care, customer satisfaction, and organizational performance.[5,6] Some states are promoting uniform measures of quality while medical professional organizations—such as the Northern New England Cardiovascular Study Group—are forming outcome measurement networks for physician-directed improvement.[7,8]

The need for health care organizations to change, grow, and be accountable is clear.[9] Yet measures of system performance, such as case-mix severity, clinical processes, utilization, health outcomes, satisfaction, costs, and operating margins, in and of themselves, will not necessarily help senior leaders or frontline physicians deliver the high-quality, low-cost care that purchasers demand and patients desire. System performance measures must be balanced, accurate, timely, interpreted correctly, and used intelligently if they are to have a positive impact on performance.[10] For this reason, it is helpful to think of measures contributing to an "instrument panel" that can be used to monitor performance, take wise action, and improve results.

The aim of this chapter is to show how a delivery system can design and use measurement to manage and improve performance. This report will (1) describe an approach to developing measures of performance, (2) provide highlights of results associated with particular uses, (3) summarize lessons learned, and (4) suggest features that performance measurement systems should have to be useful.

Methods

In this section we summarize methods used to develop helpful data displays (that is, instrument panels) for measuring system performance.

Background and Setting

Work to construct measures of system performance (MSP) began in 1993 when senior leaders decided to develop a way to measure their organizations' success. The delivery system was composed of three interdependent, nonprofit organizations that served New Hampshire and Vermont.

- *The Hitchcock Clinic:* A 450-physician, multispecialty group practice with approximately 30 delivery sites serving New Hampshire and eastern Vermont

- *Mary Hitchcock Memorial Hospital:* A 400-bed academic tertiary care hospital with 18,000 discharges per year

- *Matthew Thornton Health Plan:* A New Hampshire health maintenance organization with 130,000 members

Selection of Performance Measures

To select a manageable number of performance indicators, the leadership teams followed a process that helped them view their organization as a system.[11] This involved clarifying organizational aims, core processes, strategic priorities, and summarizing this work in a graphical format. After studying related work done by other health care and non–health care organizations,[12,13] leadership agreed on these principles to guide selection of measures.

- *Balance.* Select a well-rounded set of critical performance metrics (for example, clinical, financial, strategic, and so on).

- *Parsimony.* Select a small, manageable set of measures that reflect overall performance (for example, 10 to 15 indicators were considered adequate for getting started).

- *High level.* Begin with aggregated, high-level measures that reflect overall performance, realizing that, over time, it will likely be necessary to disaggregate the measures.

- *Real time.* Begin to track performance over time, and report results frequently and close to the time of occurrence.

- *Instrument panels.* Use instrument panel thinking to track multiple aspects of performance simultaneously.

- *Gradual ramp up.* Assume that the development of accurate and useful performance metrics will take time to design, implement, revise, and make fit for use.

This process led to the selection of an initial set of 17 performance measures that fit into six categories.

Patient Satisfaction

1. Patient satisfaction*
2. Patient access*

Customer Satisfaction

3. Employee satisfaction*

4. Employer (purchaser) satisfaction*

5. Referring physician satisfaction*

6. Community image (resident satisfaction)*

Health–Clinical

7. General functional health status*

8. Selected clinical indicators

Utilization

9. Outpatient visits

10. Inpatient discharges and length of stay

11. Number of HMO members

12. Productivity: physicians, inpatient

Financial

13. Operating margins: outpatient, inpatient, HMO

14. Costs: inpatient costs per adjusted discharge, HMO per member per month

Other

15. Employee view of management process*

16. Research (ratings about research and productivity)*

17. Employee view of information system*

The measures marked with an asterisk are aggregate measures composed of multiple items and are based on interviews with random samples of individuals within specific groups. For example, outpatient satisfaction was a composite score that was calculated by combining several different items that are related to the general concept of patient satisfaction.

Databases and Data Collection Methods

The data cover the time period extending from July 1993 to January 1996. To simplify the presentation, we focus on a particular region within the delivery system (that is, the "northern region" based at the Dartmouth Hitchcock Medical Center located in Lebanon, New Hampshire). Two databases were used: (1) the general MSP database covering the six categories of measures listed, and (2) a clinical database on bowel surgery (DRG 148-149, elective admissions). The MSP database used to produce Figures 10.1 to 10.4 covers a 25-month period (July 1993 to July 1995), whereas the bowel surgery database used for Figure 10.5 covers 16 months (October 1994 to January 1996).

All satisfaction measures were collected using telephone interviews. Thirty-two individuals per month (eight per week) from each respective respondent group (that is, outpatients, inpatients, community residents, referring physicians, employers/purchasers, and employees) were sampled at random to ensure representativeness. Eight patients (or other types of respondents) per week were selected because this would provide a large enough sample of patients to (1) reflect month-to-month variation using statistical process control chart methods (n = 32 per month) and (2) produce reasonably accurate estimates of satisfaction on an annual basis (n = 416 per year).

Selected individuals were telephoned by a professional interviewer employed by an independent survey research firm. A confidential, structured interview was conducted; the interviews ranged from 10 to 20 minutes in duration and included both fixed-response and open-ended questions to determine the individuals' evaluations of quality of care and to obtain reports on the health care system. To achieve high response rates, individuals were called up to six times at different times of the day and on different days of the week. Appointments for interviews were arranged as needed for respondent convenience. Average monthly response rates range from just over 50 percent for community residents to more than 70 percent for employees.

The other performance indicators (that is, measures that are not based on the evaluations of patients or other groups) were retrieved from internal administrative, financial, medical, or other databases and were reprocessed to produce performance indicators. For example, data on utilization came from routine inpatient and outpatient management reporting systems, data on financial performance came from standard accounting systems, data on clinical indicators were accessed from internal clinical monitoring systems, and information on research productivity was extracted from online library reference databases.

Uses of Measures and Analysis Methods

MSP reports were used by senior leaders for five purposes: (1) monitor key trends, (2) evaluate success of strategic actions, (3) identify variables that explain variation in satisfaction, (4) identify negative interactions within the system (push-down/pop-up effects), and (5) evaluate the impact of planned changes.

Conventional analytic methods were used, and the results were communicated in MSP reports that used graphical data display techniques. Quantitative data were analyzed using run charts, statistical process control charts, histograms, bar charts, and multiple regression. Statistical process control charts (for example *XmR* charts) were produced using standard methods to show monthly variations and longitudinal trends.[14,15] Histograms were generated to provide information on the distribution of individual variables. Composite scores of patient-based and customer-based measures (for example, satisfaction, access, community image) were used for summarizing overall trends and to limit the number of measures to small and manageable size. However, these composite measures may hide important information, therefore, individual items (or more specific indicators) were used whenever there was a need to focus on specific issues or trends.

Stepwise multiple regression was used to determine which independent variables have the greatest independent influence on explaining variation in patients' overall level of visit satisfaction. Strictly speaking, it is not possible to establish cause-and-effect relationships without observing independent and dependent variables in time-ordered sequence under controlled conditions; the randomized controlled trial is the classical method for establishing causality. However, without the opportunity to run prospective, controlled trials, investigators can generate explanatory hypotheses using multivariate analysis. Therefore, we used a form of multivariate analysis (stepwise multiple regression) to identify the factors most responsible for explaining variation in patient satisfaction ratings for ambulatory care patients seen by medical specialists (that is, non–primary care physicians) who practice medicine at the tertiary medical center in the northern region.

Results

Use A: Monitor Key Trends

Figure 10.1 offers a high-level view of performance trends in the northern region. This instrument panel has 12 control charts and is the first page in a monthly MSP report. The results show that (1) outpatient visits and inpatient discharges have increased modestly over time while average length of stay has decreased by one day; (2) costs per adjusted discharge have increased then decreased, whereas financial margins from operations (NOI) have been small consistently; (3) customer satisfaction has ranged from 50 percent of maximum achievable score (community image) to more than 80 percent (patient satisfaction); and (4) employees' ratings of management process issues, after being exceedingly stable, increased sharply in the final month of observation. Patient satisfaction and functional health status after receiving care vary within a performance zone of 70 percent to 80 percent of maximum achievable. Community image and referring physician satisfaction are running in lower performance zones, tending to vary around 60 percent of maximum.

Figure 10.1 has some special cause signals (that is, scores on measures that are outside of statistically determined upper and lower natural process limits), which leaders need to be aware of. For example, patients' ratings of access to services decreased in July 1995 (that is, fell below the lower natural process control limit), whereas employee satisfaction and employees' ratings of management process both improved.

Use B: Evaluate Success of Strategic Actions

A tertiary medical center depends on the goodwill of community-based physicians who refer patients in need of highly specialized or technical services that cannot be provided locally. For this reason, senior leadership selected referring physician services as one of five strategic themes for improvement. The board of governors appointed a clinical leader and committee to lead the improvement of referring physician services. The referring physician team began working on changes in three areas: (1) awareness of referring physicians about available services, (2) access of referred patients to services, and (3) communications with referring physicians.

Figure 10.2 provides sobering information on the quality of referring physician services as evaluated by recent referrers. After 15 months of work, the control chart reveals that there has been no overall improvement in the composite measure of referring physician satisfaction. While the overall referral process was rated favorably (the modal rating was 7 on a 1 to 10 scale), more than 30 percent of referring physicians reported that they had complained about the service while fewer than 10 percent had bragged. Moving to specific subareas, the process of communicating showed the greatest level of dissatisfaction—almost 30 percent of referring physicians rated it fair or poor—whereas there was no dissatisfaction with awareness of physicians to whom you refer (approximately 40 percent rated this excellent), and about 10 percent rated appointment access fair or poor while almost 50 percent rated it excellent.

Use C: Identify Variables That Explain Variation in Satisfaction

Figure 10.3 shows the results from a multiple regression analysis on factors explaining variation in overall visit satisfaction. The results on $N = 246$ randomly selected patients seen between July 1994 and May 1995 show that 72 percent of the variation in overall visit satisfaction was explained by just two factors—the patients' ratings of the competence of the physician that they saw, and the patients' level of satisfaction with office wait time. The other seven variables that were potential predictors of

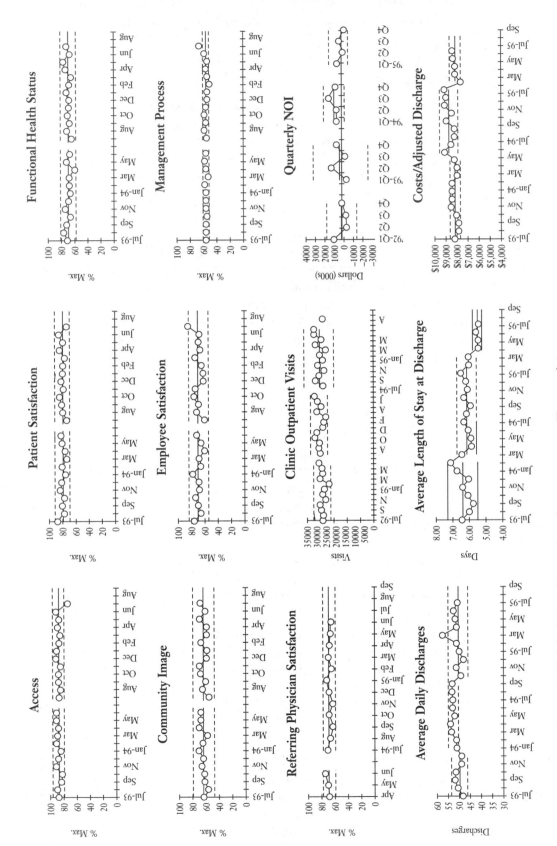

Figure 10.1. Monitor key trends. High-level view of important performance measures: Time trends.

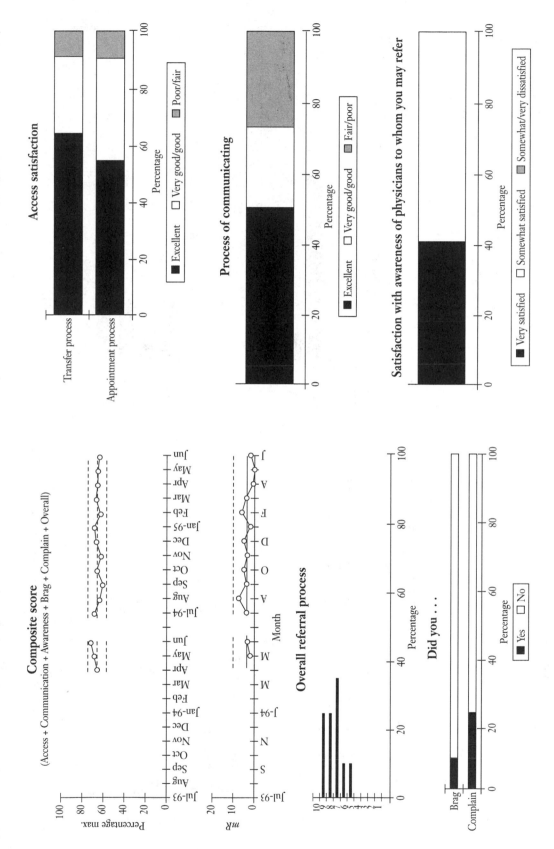

Figure 10.2. Strategic actions. Referring physician satisfaction: Time trends and specific indicators.

255

256

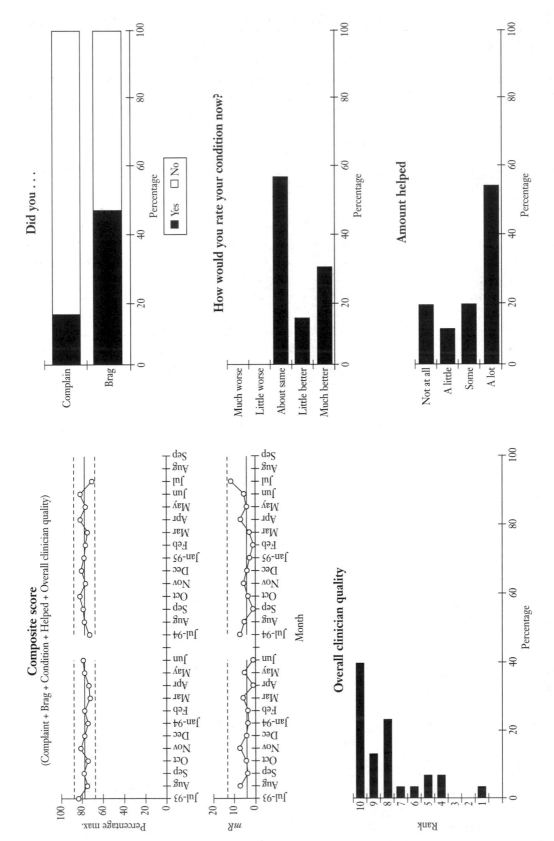

Figure 10.3. Explaining satisfaction. Variables that explain variation in overall patient satisfaction.

satisfaction were all significantly and positively correlated with overall visit satisfaction (that is, the zero-order correlations ranged from 0.27 for physical and emotional health now to 0.88 for provider choice), but they failed to add any substantial gain to explaining variation in overall visit satisfaction. These results suggest that improvement could be highly targeted in just two areas.

Use D: Identify Negative Interactions Within System

Most delivery systems are struggling to reduce costs without sacrificing quality of care and satisfaction. Reducing staff is a common cost-reduction tactic. Figure 10.4 sounds an alarm. One measure used to track employee satisfaction is a question that asks, "Is this organization a better or worse place to work compared to 12 months ago?" This question was first asked of hospital employees in March 1994 and has been monitored on a monthly basis since then. Figure 10.4 shows that there was a crossover; the percentage of employees rating the hospital better exceeded the percentage rating it worse until May 1995, at which time the proportion rating it worse exceeded the proportion rating it better. This negative crossover persisted for the next four months. Further analysis as to the reasons for the negative response (that is, reporting it to be worse) were, in rank order, management attitudes and cutbacks in staffing. This may be a faint alarm, but it has been registered and is a cause for concern since the mission calls for the organization to be a superior place both for patients to receive care and for physicians, nurses, and other staff to work.

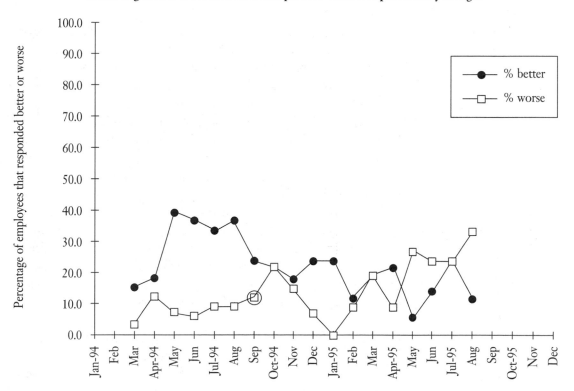

Figure 10.4. Negative interactions. Crossover in employees rating the organization a better or worse place to work.

Use E: Evaluate the Impact of Planned Changes

A challenge facing most medical systems is to find ways to reduce costs in specific clinical services while maintaining or improving quality. Our delivery system has attempted to accelerate clinical improvement in certain high-volume, high-cost, high-opportunity areas. Bowel surgery (DRG 148/149) was the first area selected.

Figure 10.5 shows cost and quality-related results for consecutive nonurgent bowel surgery patients (DRG 148/149, elective admissions) over a 20-month period. The LOS has fallen from 11.5 days (Oct. 94–Jan. 95) to 6.5 days (Oct. 95–Jan. 96) over the period of observation. More detailed results show that post-anesthesia care unit (PACU) and operating room (OR) hours both decreased (from 6.8 and 4.8 hours to 4.8 and 3.5 hours respectively) and chemical laboratory tests fell from an average of 45 per patient to 17. While direct costs of care were being lowered, the surgical procedure continued to be safe (the mortality rate remained at zero) and complications declined (the percentage of patients readmitted within 30 days dropped from 22 percent to 8 percent).

The reasons for these positive changes included (1) making changes in the use of same day services; (2) standardizing preop bowel preparation; and (3) developing a clinical pathway, standing orders, and an enhanced patient education process. These changes (that is, interventions) took place in the period between February 1995 to September 1995; the four-month time period before February 1995 was considered the preintervention phase, whereas the four-month period after September 1995 was considered the postintervention phase.

Discussion

Some Results and Their Implications

Patient satisfaction is one critical component of quality. The results show that it is possible to track variation in overall satisfaction over time, to decompose satisfaction into distinct dimensions, to assess performance monthly, to break out and analyze patient satisfaction results for particular market segments (for example, patients of specialists in a region), and to isolate a small number of variables that explain satisfaction. The implication is that the measurement infrastructure required for tracking, decomposing, and teasing out potential satisfaction drivers is greater than that which exists in most delivery systems today. Furthermore, this "peeling the onion" work can be done only in areas where there is rich experience to draw on. More is known about the causal system behind patient satisfaction than about the independent variables that contribute most to explaining the health outcomes for asthma, congestive heart failure, or depression.

The referring physician satisfaction findings remind us that it is far easier to point to a problem and say "fix it" than to make substantial improvements in large and complicated processes involving thousands of people. These results also show that the referral process works well for some physicians and poorly for others, particularly vis-á-vis communicating important information in a timely manner. This variation is itself the product of differences in individual physician performance, individual department performance, local culture, and organizational performance of basic services such as dictation and transcription.

The rise in employee dissatisfaction that coincided with the reduction of a relatively small number of positions (about 15 positions in a medical center with more than 3000 employees) suggests how tightly intertwined different aspects of the organization are. Small "doses" of management actions may trigger large "toxic" effects that would be easy to miss without accurate and balanced measurements.

Trends Across Time

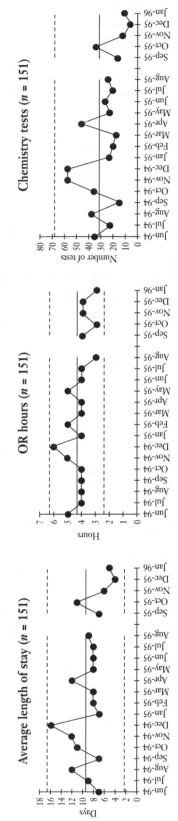

Snapshots in Time

	Implementation		
	Oct. 94–Jan. 95 (*n* = 33)	Oct. 95–Jan. 96 (*n* = 31)	Difference
Clinical outcomes			
• Mortality %	0	0	0
• 30-day readmit %	22	8	–14
Cost measures			
• LOS days	11.5	6.5	5
• PACU hours	6.8	4.8	2
• OR hours	4.8	3.5	1.3
• Chemical tests	45	17	28
Demographics			
• Age	66	62	
• Female %	59	52	

Figure 10.5. Evaluate impact. Clinical and cost outcomes for consecutive series of bowel surgery patients, DRG 148/149 (elective admissions only).

259

Better Measurement, More Utility

In the spring of 1995, our measurement team interviewed more than 30 people (a mix of senior leaders, clinicians, and managers) that currently use—or could use—the performance measures. The aim of the interviews was to improve the utility of the measurement system. When asked what could be done to provide measures with high utility, their responses suggested that the performance measurement system should possess these key features.

- *Actionable.* Measures should be disaggregated or stratified in a manner that allows identification of where to act and what to do.

- *Accurate.* Metrics should be representative, reliable, and valid.

- *Timely.* Indicators should be reported with minimum lag time between event occurrence and feedback of data.

- *Standard.* Some measures should be standardized across all sites within the delivery system.

- *Flexible.* Some metrics should be tailored to reflect local priorities and conditions.

- *Easy to understand.* The meaning of the signal given off by the display of the measures should be clear and easy to interpret.

- *Trending over time.* Some indicators must be tracked longitudinally to provide understanding of common cause (endogenous) variation versus special cause (exogenous) variation.

- *Graphical displays.* Graphical data displays are easier to understand and have more impact than written text or numeric tables.

These factors are being used by the measurement team to (1) redesign the feedback reports (for example, routinely include radar plots, control charts, Pareto charts, and explanatory analyses) and (2) develop a series of educational programs to assist users in understanding how to interpret the reports and take wise action.

A second way in which the measurement system needs to be improved is to begin to routinely gather data on clinical/functional/satisfaction and cost outcomes for selected high-volume, high-cost, high-opportunity clinical services. Current strategy calls for involving both frontline clinical teams and senior leadership in taking actions to accelerate clinical improvement of quality and value for 15 different patient populations. Rapid reduction in actual costs and real improvements in quality-related outcomes require measurement of patient case mix, clinical process changes, and associated results (clinical, functional, satisfaction, and costs). Consequently, there is a fundamental need to refine the measurement system for the management and improvement of clinical care. Much of this improved clinical measurement should, we believe, be built into the routine delivery process at the front line of care and be incorporated into the daily work of receptionists, nurses, physicians, and others directly involved in patient care. This "design-measurement-in" approach contrasts with the "add-measurement-on" methods used for research or periodic monitoring of overall performance.

Limitations and Lessons Learned

Although some real progress has been made in developing a useful performance measurement system, we have learned that the gap between what's needed and what's being done is enormous. There are many problems and limitations. A few of the major ones are listed next. First, we tend to give lip service to the need for measurement rather than to design and use it in our daily work. Moving to a work culture that uses measurement for daily management and improvement will take time and knowledge.

Second, all measurements are imperfect due to sources of bias and error associated with reliability, validity, sampling, response rates, and other factors. Third, it is easier to measure results than to measure the system that produces the results. Improvement of results requires knowledge of the process—the upstream causal system—which is often tangled, complicated, and resistant to easy quantification. Fourth, many measures are displayed in ways that have embodied within them far too much noise and far too little signal. One important antidote to this common problem is careful stratification of observations into meaningful, homogeneous subgroups (for example, group elderly patients with severe diabetes and other comorbidities separately from middle age diabetics without other complications). Fifth, measurement takes time and resources, which can draw needed energy away from other important areas such as delivering needed care in the correct manner.

Conclusion

It is imperative that physicians, health care leaders, and other health professionals find ways to accelerate improvements in the quality and value of care. Measurement of performance is one essential ingredient needed to accomplish this. Taking an aggressive, evolutionary, and balanced approach to the creation of instrument panels for use at the front line and in the front office may be better than a crash program of outcomes measurement or satisfaction assessment or cost accounting of strategic gains. Over the long run, measurement must become embedded in the total fabric of the organization (top to bottom, side to side, front to back), should involve everyone, and should be used wisely for learning, taking prompt corrective action, monitoring performance, making improvements, devising innovations, and evaluating the success of planned changes.

Acknowledgments

The authors would like to thank the team of people who produce the Measures of System Performance, which includes Jennifer Eames, Joel Finnell, Kathleen Iannacchino, David Krause, Kathy Mook, Terri Rodee, and Judi Simoneau. We also wish to recognize the members of the Accelerating Clinical Improvement Bowel Surgery Team at Dartmouth-Hitchcock Medical Center who performed the clinical work reported in the paper: John Birkmeyer, Thomas A. Colacchio, Judith Dixon, Stuart R. Gordon, Christina C. Mahoney, Wendy Manganiello, William Mroz, Cathy Pallatroni, John E. Sutton, Jr., Gayle Thomson, and Charles L. Townsend. Finally we wish to thank Denise Nelson for preparing and editing the manuscript.

Notes

1. D. Blumenthal and S. O. Thier, "Managed Care and Medical Education: The New Fundamentals, *JAMA* 276:725–727 (1996).

2. R. H. Brooks, E. A. McGlynn, and P. D. Cleary, "Quality of Health Care, Part 2: Measuring Quality of Care," *N Engl J Med* 335:996–970 (1996).

3. H. B. Noble, "Quality Is Focus for Health Plans," *New York Times* A1 (1995).

4. M. Chase, "Health Journal: Doctor Report Cards Don't Tell Consumers Whole Story on Care, *Wall Street Journal* B1 (1996).

5. J. M. Loeb and D. S. O'Leary, "A Call for Collaboration in Performance Measurement," *JAMA* 273:1405 (1995).

6. Committee on Performance Measurement, *Hedis 3.0 Health Plan Employer Data & Information Set* (Washington, D.C.: National Committee for Quality Assurance, 1996).

7. G. T. O'Connor, S. K. Plume, E. M. Olmstead et al. "A Regional Intervention to Improve the Hospital Mortality Associated with Coronary Artery Bypass Graft Surgery: The Northern New England Cardiovascular Disease Study Group" *JAMA* 275:841–846 (1996).

8. E. L. Hannan, H. J. Kilburn, M. Racz, E. Shields, and M. R. Chassin, "Improving the Outcomes of Coronary Artery Bypass Surgery in New York State," *JAMA* 271:761–766 (1996).

9. A. R. Tarlov, J. E. Ware, S. Greenfield, E. C. Nelson, E. Perrin, and M. Zubkoff, "The Medical Outcomes Study: An Application of Methods for Monitoring the Results for Medical Care," *JAMA* 262:925–930 (1989).

10. R. S. Kaplan and D. P. Norton, *The Balanced Scorecard: Translating Strategy into Action* (Boston: Harvard Business School Press, 1996).

11. W. E. Deming, *The New Economics for Industry, Government Education* (Cambridge, Mass.: MIT Center for Advanced Engineering Study, 1993).

12. R. S. Kaplan and D. P. Norton, "The Balanced Scorecard—Measures That Drive Performance," *Harvard Business Review* (1992).

13. R. S. Kaplan and D. P. Norton, "Putting the Balanced Scorecard to Work," *Harvard Business Review* (1993).

14. D. J. Wheeler, *Understanding Variation: The Key to Managing Chaos* (Knoxville, Tenn.: SPC Press, 1993).

15. D. J. Wheeler, *Advanced Topics in Statistical Process Control: The Power of Shewhart's Charts* (Knoxville, Tenn.: SPC Press, 1995).

Eugene C. Nelson, D.Sc., MPH, is the director of quality education, measurement, and research at Lahey Hitchcock Clinic in Lebanon, New Hampshire, and is a professor in the department of community and family medicine at Dartmouth Medical School, Hanover, New Hampshire.

Nancy Mihevc, Ph.D., is the director of measures of system performance at Lahey Hitchcock Clinic in Lebanon, New Hampshire.

Mary Gentry, MHSA, is a quality resource analyst at Mary Hitchcock Memorial Hospital in Lebanon, New Hampshire.

Deborah Kehne, B.A., is a quality research analyst at Lahey Hitchcock Clinic in Lebanon, New Hampshire.

April Levine, M.S., is a Ph.D. student at the Center for Clinical and Evaluative Sciences at Dartmouth Medical School.

Paul B. Batalden, M.D., is a professor in the departments of pediatrics, community and family medicine at Dartmouth Medical School and is the director of health care improvement leadership development at Dartmouth Medical School in Hanover, New Hampshire. He is also the vice president and breech chair in the department of health care, quality improvement, education, and research at Henry Ford Health System in Detroit, Michigan.

Stephen K. Plume, M.D., is the president of Lahey Hitchcock Clinic, Lebanon, New Hampshire, and a professor in the department of surgery at Dartmouth Medical School in Hanover, New Hampshire.

Section III
Key Strategies

Chapter 11

Costs of Poor Quality: An Opportunity in Health Care

Harvey Dershin and Julie A. Magrath

There is no escaping the fact that cost is a key driver in health care today. As much as we would like to think otherwise, it is the overarching concern for cost that has motivated government and private purchasers of services to become involved and push for change in this sector of the economy. The forces of the market have finally appeared on the health care scene.

This is an uncomfortable and unfamiliar environment for many providers. Not that the subject of cost control has not been raised before; cost containment has been in the air since the 1970s, but then it was "voluntary" and the powerful health care lobbies had little trouble burying the notion. Real cost control probably started in the early 1980s, with Medicare DRGs. Initially generous, DRG reimbursement tightened as national rates took effect, forcing providers to cost-shift in order to make budgeted bottom lines. Eventually, the price distortions resulting from cost-shifting became visible and serious to private payors, who were dealing with their own cost control issues. As a result, during the late 1980s and early 1990s, the health care "market" came to life with a vengeance.

The signs are now familiar: contraction of inpatient census, hospital closures and consolidations, shrinking bottom lines, managed care, brokered care, preferred contracting, utilization management, hospital/physician associations of various sorts, and, in many locales, fierce competition. And the end is not yet in sight. As long as the supply of providers exceeds the demand for service, the industry will continue to face a buyer's market. Costs—and prices—will have to be managed and controlled.

But squeezing cost out of an organization can be a tough challenge, particularly for people who spent decades maximizing reimbursement. At first it seemed easy. As managers put together their annual budgets, they felt a slight pinch in revenue and responded by trimming a bit here and there, denying requests for additional staff and holding back on raises. As time moved on and the squeeze continued, this type of action was not sufficient and managers were forced to take more drastic action. The industry had its first encounter with such things as salary and hiring freezes, across-the-board cuts, and elimination or sharp reduction of such items as travel and education expenses. But in some settings even these actions were not enough. When it became clear that the problem was not a transient one, deeper cuts were made through downsizing, restructuring, and elimination of programs. In some highly competitive environments, even these actions did not do the job, and the slash-and-burn specialists had to be brought in to save organizations or arrange to sell or close them.

At times it appears that the industry has given itself over to the financial managers and that cost cutting is being carried out with little regard for its effect on the quality of care provided. On the other hand, who can deny that the actions are appropriate? How else can a health care organization survive in today's competitive environment? It seems obvious to think that, because availability of funds is the problem, those who know about money must have the solutions.

But perhaps there is another way. Is there perhaps some benefit to thinking like a clinician instead of an accountant? Maybe the industry has been locked into a one-dimensional view with respect to this issue. It is akin to thinking that every medical problem has a surgical solution.

Searching for costs of poor quality (COPQ) offers another view. If excessive costs are the disease, is poor quality one of the root causes? If this is so, then excising or otherwise curing the disease at its source can have the dual benefit of reducing cost and improving quality. And that is the theme of this chapter: reducing cost while improving quality.

Definitions

One can think of health care, or any other costs for that matter, in two categories.

- *Production or value-added costs:* Costs associated with essential activities required to get the work done. Examples include performing a diagnosis, filling a prescription, bathing a patient, or removing a gallbladder. Billing insurance companies, paying vendors, or mopping floors are also production costs.

- *Costs of poor quality:* Costs associated with providing and ensuring a high-quality product or service. These costs would disappear if every task was performed perfectly.

Quality costs can be described in the following four categories:

- *Appraisal or inspection:* Inspections designed to ensure that work measures up to standards; costs incurred to prevent errors or defects before customers are affected. Utilization review, checking drug orders for contraindications, daily checks of crash carts, inspection of new equipment, and preoperative checklists are all types of appraisal.

- *Internal failures:* These include costs that arise to correct internal errors and deficiencies before the customer notices. Internal failure costs are also incurred to repair, replace, or discard defective work. Here is where we find rework, waste, reprocessing, and scrap. Internal failure costs include those associated with replacing lost linen, repeating blood tests because specimens have been spoiled, running STAT labs (because results are late), repeating X-ray exams because of poor quality or improper patient preparation, and forcing nurses to pick up drugs because deliveries are late. They are distinguished from external failures only in that the external customer does not observe them directly.

- *External failures:* These are the costs incurred when a failure happens and the customer knows about it. This is the hip surgery done for no charge because someone's grandmother fell out of bed (not to mention the malpractice settlement); these are the penalties levied by insurance payors because bills are late; these are the hospital-acquired infections. The effects of external failures are doubly damaging because they increase costs directly, to correct mistakes, but also have the potential to adversely affect future revenues because they erode customer confidence and increase customer dissatisfaction.

- *Non–value-added:* In studying work processes one also finds process segments that seem to serve no useful purpose. They may not be the result of, or create, failures of any sort but their purpose defies reason. They may include rarely used financial systems, excessive filing and retrieving of records, reports never looked at, or irrelevant procedures.

Appraisal costs hurt when they become excessive. They cannot be eliminated altogether because some health care processes are so critical as to permit no errors, for example, type and cross match of blood, or perfusion (that is, flawless functioning of a heart/lung machine). But internal and external failures and non–value-added costs are nothing short of disasters for any business. They represent money spent on work that is of no value to the customer or the business. No one benefits from these expenses. And their order of magnitude can be shocking. One should not be surprised to find 10 percent to 30 percent of a department's budget tied up in this type of work.

Methodology

There are many ways to find costs of poor quality. The common theme described in this chapter is to search for activities that provide no value and may even do harm to patients or other customers. Three approaches will be described.

- The defects-driven method
- The gold standard method
- The process flow method

Each method offers its own benefits, and each has certain shortcomings. All three should be considered when undertaking a COPQ analysis.

Defects-Driven Method

This approach begins with the identification of the various defects that occur in the delivery of service. Of particular interest are those that are dangerous to patients, have a high frequency of occurrence, and have the potential for being expensive to correct. Examples include things like falls, infections, late discharges, inappropriate admissions, returns to surgery, missing or incorrect patient billing addresses, or readmissions to a care setting. Each of these incidents creates costs of poor quality. The effort then is to simply calculate the dollar content of each type of failure and sum it over the entire organization. A few examples follow.

Unit Cost Approach. This approach requires two pieces of data.

- The number of times a particular deficiency occurs
- The average cost for correcting and recovering from that deficiency

Examples might include calling a doctor because an order is not clear, retaking an X-ray because the film quality was poor, or administrative recovery from a patient complaint.

To illustrate, suppose a hospital has a chronic problem of late delivery of medications. Data show that nurses on a typical unit spend 1000 hours per year going to the pharmacy for medications. If there are 10 units in the hospital, and nursing salaries average $20/hour (averaged for different types of nurses) then the total cost of poor quality for this activity is as follows:

$$1000 \times 10 \times \$20 = \$200,000 \text{ per year}$$

A not unusual amount for a typical hospital.

Total Resource Approach. This approach also requires two pieces of data.

- Total resources consumed
- Percentage of those resources consumed for activities associated with cost of poor quality

Examples might include the percentage of time patient accounts clerks spend chasing after improperly registered patients, the percent of time spent by operating room staff waiting for cases to begin, or the percentage of time nurses spend looking for missing supplies. The following example illustrates the method.

The medical records department at Couldn't Be Better Hospital employs five registered technicians and five clerks. Their primary job is to see to it that the history of each patient's care is recorded and archived in accordance with the highest professional standards. Over the years, their work has grown to accommodate the requirements of third-party payors, utilization reviewers, and various government agencies. As a result, the department has become a sort of intermediary between various hospital professionals (that is, doctors, nurses, administrators) and the outside world.

What used to be a fairly straightforward job of collecting, coding, filing, and retrieving information has expanded to include satisfying the requirements of dozens of external customers. This means that each record is filed and retrieved at least 10 times before it is completed. Most of the filing and retrieving is done by the clerks. In fact, this occupies 50 percent of their time. But medical records technicians are also involved in this work. At least 20 percent of their time is spent filing and retrieving.

The department director believes that all this filing and retrieving is a waste of effort and has urged the administration to install computer software to simplify the work. The administration is reluctant to spend the $50,000 required for the software. The director feels they are spending the money anyway, as a result of this inefficient process.

Medical records clerks are paid $8 per hour, and technicians are paid $12. The following worksheet demonstrates the cost of poor quality for the process.

Resource	Annual salary cost	Benefits (at 30%)	Total annual cost	Number of positions	Percent non–value-added	COPQ
Clerks	$16,640	$4992	$21,632	5	50%	$54,080
Technicians	$24,960	$7488	$32,449	5	20%	$32,450
Total COPQ						$86,530

Clearly, the COPQ outweighs the cost of the software.

Gold Standard Method

This method begins with the identification of high-cost services or service elements that can be compared to a quality benchmark, either internal or external. The entire sphere of costs associated with the direct provision of care can fall into this category. Benchmarks can be external (to comparable institutions) or internal (with respect to best practices). A DRG-based example follows.

Figure 11.1 shows total patient cost for DRG XXX versus excess length of stay (that is, length of stay beyond the expected standard). Each dot refers to the average cost and excess length of stay for a particular physician. The number next to each dot refers to the number of cases associated with each practitioner. Figure 11.2 profiles the highest-, median-, and lowest-cost physicians. Also shown is the best demonstrated practice—that is, a theoretical cost profile constructed by assembling the lowest costs for each service (blood, respiratory therapy, and so on) from the entire group. One could think of costs of poor quality in three different ways. If costs could be brought to a level no higher than the

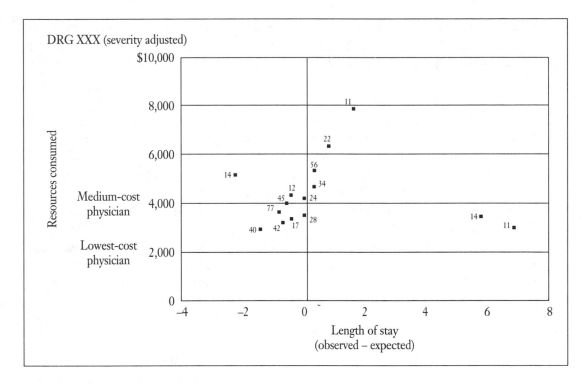

Figure 11.1. Total patient cost versus length of stay.

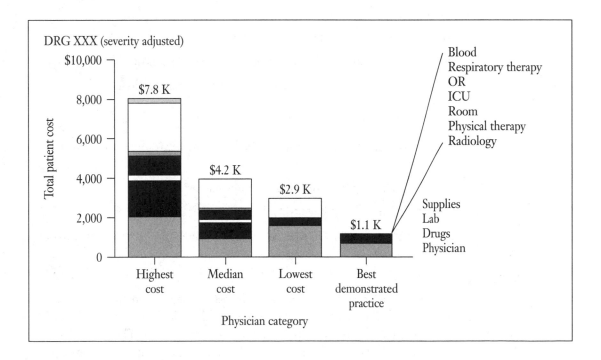

Figure 11.2. Total patient cost best demonstrated practice analysis.

mean, savings would be about $180,000. If each physician could be brought to the level of the lowest-cost physician, savings would be about $460,000. If all physicians could work at the level of the theoretical best practice, savings would be about $1.3 million.

Process Flow Method

When it comes to developing insight and understanding about how a particular type of work is carried out, there is nothing quite so informative as drawing the actual process flow diagram. The exercise is so enlightening, and often so much fun, that it is sometimes hard to get quality teams to move on to other tasks. People love the act of discovery that is at the heart of the flowcharting effort. Rarely do team members complete this task without learning something surprising about a process they thought they knew well. The process flow diagrams are often full of "black holes," inexplicable rework loops, and tasks that seem to have little purpose.

The process flow method builds on this by providing methodology for calculating costs. Teams can determine the cost of an entire process and, at the same time, extract the cost components that relate to costs of poor quality. The result is a clear, quantitative statement about the potentially recoverable costs associated with a process.

The work itself can be facilitated through a series of spreadsheet templates. These are shown in chapter appendix A and cover the following calculations.

- Table 11.1 itemizes the tasks associated with a process and calculates the labor hour content of each task. This document is also used to sort the tasks into production and COPQ activities.

- Table 11.2 captures the COPQ-related labor hours, converts them into costs, and adds nonlabor costs.

- Table 11.3 captures nonlabor costs such as costs of money, discounts, and penalties.

- Table 11.4 calculates the cost of the entire process.

- Table 11.5 summarizes all cost information and calculates the percent cost of poor quality.

An example illustrating the use of the spreadsheets is included as chapter appendix B.

Conclusions

Some quotes and anecdotes from health care employees give life to the frustrations caused by costs of poor quality.

- "I spend 20 percent of my time just correcting billing [problems] . . ."

- "Finding a coding error at the billing stage adds at least another 10 days to the process."

- "We have to inspect 100 percent of the medical records because 99.9 percent of them have mistakes."

From department managers,

- A director of a cardiac cath lab revealed that a recent downsizing had caused him to lay off a full-time person. However, since nothing had been done about the scheduling system (first come, first serve), he had to rely on overtime to provide the necessary service. The net result: *extra* costs of more than $100,000 per year. This is a classic result of cutting staff without eliminating unnecessary work.

- A director of radiology told us that 50 percent of all orders had to be followed up with phone calls because the orders were incomplete.

- An occupational health clinic manager told us that more than 50 percent of invoices were returned from the payor because of incomplete or incorrect information.

- A physician's office manager revealed that 70 percent of invoices were returned for reprocessing.

- A nursing director found that nurses were spending 10,000 hours per year on trips to the pharmacy because drug delivery was so slow.

The stories go on and on. What's interesting, though, is that the people trapped in these ineffective processes do not change them. Why? Because they are so caught up in the day-to-day business of just taking care of their departments that they have no time. Also, in most cases, while they are conscious of the pain, they don't know what's causing it. That's one reason why the COPQ analysis can be helpful. People quickly come to understand the causes of their pain and see ways to correct things.

An organization can identify costs of quality by any of the three methods described. All are useful and complement each other. Taken together, they can be powerful drivers for quality. One must look hard and dig for cost-saving opportunities. They will not turn up by themselves. But once found, the numbers can help prioritize improvement opportunities, motivate managers, and provide a framework for measuring the success of a quality effort.

We all know that one of the biggest challenges in health care today is to reduce costs without sacrificing quality. But how can we do this? The answers may be right under our noses but, like so many things, they are not obvious. How many quality directors despair because project nominations are meager in number or scope? The truth is that important, high-yielding projects (in terms of cost) will not jump out and bite you. You have to find them. They have to be dug out from the interstices of an organization. People do not nominate them because they do not know they exist!

That's what COPQ analysis is all about. It helps people identify the high-yielding, costly work that can be eliminated from an organization without sacrificing quality. It won't solve problems, but it will tell you where to look. It will create targets for quality projects and quantify the potential savings from each. Also, because the analysis can easily involve frontline managers and supervisors, it provides a way to deploy quality skills throughout an entire organization. Because costs are identified by managers themselves, buy-in is easy. It is not a matter of persuading people to take some sort of pledge for quality.

Perhaps most important is that management follow through and help make the changes identified; commission quality teams if need be, provide resources to redesign local processes, or correct the obvious deficiencies immediately.

Appendix A: Process Flow Worksheets

Table 11.1. COPQ worksheet 1: Analysis of COPQ labor hours.

Case study: Billing for occupational health services clinic

(1) Step number	(2) Activity	(3) Responsible position(s)	(4) Process volume items/week/ individual	(5) Hours/ week/ individual	(6) Number of individuals	(7) Total labor hours/week (5) × (6)	(8) COPQ activity? (yes or no)	(9) COPQ labor hours/week (yes only)
	Total this page					0		

Table 11.2. COPQ worksheet 2: COPQ salary and related costs (only).

1 Step number	2 Activity	3 Responsible position(s)	4 COPQ labor hours/week/ activity	5 COPQ labor hours/year/ activity (3) × 52	6 Salary and related cost/hour	7 Salary and related cost/ activity/year (5) × (6)	8 Fringe benefit multiplier (1.3)	9 Total salary and fringe (7) × (8)	10 Related supplies/ materials dollars/year	11 Other costs dollars/year (see Table 11.3)	12 Total COPQ cost/activity (9) + (10) + (11)
Total											

Table 11.3. COPQ worksheet 3: Other costs.

1 Step number	2 Activity	3 Contracted services	4 Cost of money	5 Penalties and missed discounts	6 Premium prices difference	7 Other	8 Total	Notes
Total								

Table 11.4. COPQ worksheet 4: Cost of the total process.

1 Step number	2 Activity	3 Responsible position(s)	4 Total labor hours/week/ activity	5 Total labor hours/year/ activity $(3) \times 52$	6 Salary and related cost/hour	7 Salary and related cost/ activity/year $(5) \times (6)$	8 Fringe benefit multiplier (1.3)	9 Total salary and fringe $(7) \times (8)$	10 Related supplies/ materials dollars/year	11 Other costs dollars/year (see Table 11.3)	12 Total cost/ activity $(9) + (10) + (11)$	
Total this page												

Table 11.5. COPQ worksheet 5: Summary.

Total COPQ	
Cost of the total process (see Table 11.4, column 12)	
Percent cost of poor quality	

The completed worksheets follow (see Tables 11.6–11.10). The COPQ in this case is 56 percent of total process cost.

Table 11.6. COPQ answer sheet 1: Analysis of COPQ labor hours.

Case study: Billing for occupational health services clinic

(1) Step number	(2) Activity	(3) Responsible position(s)	(4) Process volume items/week/individual	(5) Hours/week/individual	(6) Number of individuals	(7) Total labor hours/week (5) × (6)	(8) COPQ activity? (yes or no)	(9) COPQ labor hours/week (7) × (18)
1	Treat patient	OT	40	20	2	40	No	0
2	Fill out medical record	OT	40	6.7	2	13.4	No	0
3	File medical record	OT	40	1.3	2	2.6	No	0
4	Fill out charge slip	OT	40	3.3	2	6.6	No	0
5	Mail charge slips to business office	OT	1	0	1	0	No	0
6	Receive and sort charge slips	Clerk	5	1.25	2	2.5	No	0
7	Bundle charge slips and forward to information systems department	Clerk	5	0.4	2	0.8	No	0
8	Receive and sort bundles	IS clerk	5	0.8	2	1.6	No	0
9	Data entry	IS clerk	40	6.7	2	13.4	No	0
10	Run invoice	Technician	1	1	2	2	No	0
11	Separate invoice and forward to depts.	Clerk	1	5	2	10	Yes	10
12	Receive invoice report and retrieve medical record	Clerk	80	2.7	1	2.7	Yes	2.7
13	Enter treatment info, return to business office, and refile medical record	OT	40	6.7	2	13.4	Yes	13.4
14	Receive invoice and file till end of month	Clerk	1	1	1	1	Yes	1
15	Retrieve filed invoice and forward to mailroom	Clerk	1	1	1	1	Yes	1
16	Receive invoice and file	Mail clerk	1	1	1	1	No	0
17	Package invoice and mail	Mail clerk	1	1	1	1	No	0
18	Receive invoice and process	Ins. clerk						
19	Decision okay/not okay	Ins. analyst						
20	Okay—process check	Ins. clerk						
21	Not okay—return to provider	Ins. clerk						
22	Receive letter, forward to business office	Clerk	1	0.25	1	0.25	Yes	0.25
23	Post check	Clerk	1	0.25	1	0.25	No	
24	Determine reason for failure	Clerk	40	3.3	1	3.3	Yes	3.3
25	Return to clinic	Clerk	40	0.5	1	0.5	Yes	0.5
26	Receive invoice and analyze	OT	20	1	2	2	Yes	2
27	Pull medical record	OT	20	1	2	2	Yes	2
28	Correct invoice	OT	20	1	2	2	Yes	2
29	Return to business office	OT	1	0.25	1	0.25	Yes	0.25
30	Repeat steps 6–10 and so on	Clerk	40	10.1	1	10.1	Yes	10.1
31	Repeat steps 14–17	Clerk	40	2	1	2	Yes	2
	Total					135.7		50.4

Table 11.7. COPQ answer sheet 2: COPQ salary and related costs (only).

1 Step number	2 Activity	3 Responsible position(s)	4 COQ labor hours/week/activity	5 COQ labor hours/year/activity (3) × 52	6 Salary and related cost/hour	7 Salary and related cost/activity/year (5) × (6)	8 Fringe benefit multiplier (1.3)	9 Total salary and fringe (7) × (8)	10 Related supplies/materials dollars/year	11 Other costs dollars/year (see Table 11.8)	12 Total quality cost/activity (9) + (10) + (11)
11	Separate and forward to depts.	Clerk	10	520	$9	$4680	1.3	$6084	$1,040		$7124
12	Receive invoice and retrieve medical record	Clerk	2.7	140.4	$9	$1264	1.3	$1643			$18,117
13	Enter treatment information, return to business office, and refile medical record	OT	13.4	696.8	$20	$13,936	1.3	$18,117			$18,117
14	Receive invoice and file till end of month	Clerk	1	52	$9	$468	1.3	$608			$608
15	Retrieve filed invoice and forward to mailroom	Clerk	1	52	$9	$468	1.3	$608			$608
21	Not okay, return to provider	Ins. clerk								$10,000	$10,000
22	Receive letter, forward to business office	Clerk	0.25	13	$9	$117	1.3	$152			$2008
24	Determine reason for failure	Clerk	3.3	171.6	$9	$1544	1.3	$2008			$2008
25	Return to clinic	Clerk	0.5	26	$9	$234	1.3	$304			$304
26	Receive invoice and analyze	OT	2	104	$20	$2080	1.3	$2704			$2704
27	Pull medical record	OT	2	104	$20	$2080	1.3	$2704			$2704
28	Correct invoice	OT	2	104	$20	$2080	1.3	$2704			$2704
29	Return to business office	OT	0.25	13	$20	$26	1.3	$338			$338
30	Repeat steps 6–10	Clerk	10.1	525.2	$9	$4727	1.3	$6145		$1000	$7145
31	Repeat steps 14–17	Clerk	2	104	$9	$936	1.3	$1217			$1217
	Total COPQ salary-related costs					$34,874		$45,336	$1,040	$11,000	$57,376

Table 11.8. COPQ answer sheet 3: Other costs.

1 Step number	2 Activity	3 Contracted services	4 Cost of money	5 Penalties and missed discounts	6 Premium prices difference	7 Other	8 Total	Notes
11	Separate invoice and forward to depts.							
12	Receive invoice and retrieve medical record							
13	Enter treatment information and return to business office							
14	Receive invoice and file till end of month			$10,000			$10,000	
15	Retrieve filed invoice and forward to mailroom							
22	Receive letter, forward to business office							
24	Determine reason for failure							
25	Return to clinic							
26	Receive invoice and analyze							
27	Pull medical record							
28	Correct invoice							
29	Return to business office							
30	Repeat steps 6–10		$1000				$1000	
31	Repeat steps 14–17							
Total other costs		$0	$1,000	$10,000	$0	$0	$11,000	

279

Table 11.9. COPQ answer sheet 4: Cost of the total process.

1 Step number	2 Activity	3 Responsible position(s)	4 Total labor hours/week/activity	5 Total labor hours/year/activity (3)×52	6 Salary and related cost/hour	7 Salary and related cost/year/activity (5)×(6)	8 Fringe benefit multiplier (1.3)	9 Total salary and fringe (7)×(8)	10 Related supplies/materials dollars/year	11 Other costs dollars/year (see Table 11.8)	12 Total cost/activity (9)+(10)+(11)
1	Treat patient	OT	40	2080	$20	N/A	1.3				
2	Fill out medical record	OT	13.4	696.8	$20	$13,936	1.3	$18,117			$18,117
3	File medical record	OT	2.6	135.2	$20	$2,704	1.3	$3,515			$3,515
4	Fill out charge slip	OT	6.6	343.2	$20	$6,864	1.3	$8,923			$8,923
5	Mail charge slips to business office	OT	0	0	$20	$0	1.3	$0			$0
6	Receive and sort charge slips	Clerk	2.5	130	$9	$1,170	1.3	$1,521			$1,521
7	Bundle charge slips and forward to information systems	Clerk	0.8	41.6	$9	$374	1.3	$487			$487
8	Receive and sort bundles	IS clerk	1.6	83.2	$9	$749	1.3	$973			$973
9	Data entry	IS clerk	13.4	696.8	$9	$6,271	1.3	$8,153			$8,153
10	Run invoice	Technician	2	104	$15	$1,560	1.3	$2,028			$2,028
11	Separate and forward to depts.	Clerk	10	520	$9	$4,680	1.3	$6,084	$1,040		$7,124
12	Receive invoice and retrieve medical record	Clerk	2.7	140.4	$9	$1,264	1.3	$1,643			$1,643
13	Enter treatment information, return to business office and refile medical record	OT	13.4	696.8	$20	$13,936	1.3	$18,117			$18,117
14	Receive invoice and file till end of month	Clerk	1	52	$9	$468	1.3	$608			$608
15	Retrieve filed invoice and forward to mailroom	Clerk	1	52	$9	$468	1.3	$608			$608
16	Receive invoice and file	Mail clerk	1	52	$9	$468	1.3	$608			$608
17	Package invoice and mail	Mail clerk	1	52	$9	$468	1.3	$608			$608
18	Receive invoice and process	Ins. clerk									
19	Decision okay/not okay	Ins. analyst									
20	Okay, process check	Ins. clerk									
21	Not okay, return to provider	Ins. clerk								$10,000	$10,000
22	Receive letter, forward to business office	Clerk	0.25	13	$9	$117	1.3	$152			$152
23	Post check	Clerk	0.25	13	$9	$117	1.3	$152			$152
24	Determine reason for failure	Clerk	3.3	171.6	$9	$1,544	1.3	$2,008			$2,008
25	Return to clinic	Clerk	0.5	26	$9	$234	1.3	$304			$304
26	Receive invoice and analyze	OT	2	104	$20	$2,080	1.3	$2,704			$2,704
27	Pull medical record	OT	2	104	$20	$2,080	1.3	$2,704			$2,704
28	Correct invoice	OT	2	104	$20	$2,080	1.3	$2,704			$2,704
29	Return to business office	OT	0.25	13	$20	$260	1.3	$338			$338
30	Repeat steps 6–10 and so on	Clerk	10.1	525.2	$9	$4,727	1.3	$6,145		$1,000	$7,145
31	Repeat steps 14–17	Clerk	2	104	$9	$936	1.3	$1,217			$1,217
Total			135.7	7053.8		$69,555		$90,422		$11,000	$102,462

Table 11.10. COPQ answer sheet 5: Summary.

Total COPQ	$57,376
Cost of the total process	
Percent cost of poor quality	56.00%

Appendix B: Process Flow Example

Following is a description of a process within a real hospital (the names are altered to protect the innocent).

Colossal Health Care System consists of operating hospitals, nursing homes, medical clinics, and other outpatient facilities in five states. Colossal recently purchased a string of outpatient facilities offering acute and rehabilitative treatment for injured workers. The strategy is to associate each of these occupational health clinics with one of the hospitals, to serve as feeders of patients. The purchase was made with Colossal's usual lightning speed, and services were immediately integrated with those of the hospitals.

After six months of operation, people were beginning to talk about serious deficiencies with the integration. In particular, it seemed that occupational therapists at the occupational health clinic were seeing fewer patients, unit costs of these services appeared to be on the increase, and cash flow was a bit short. A COPQ team was assembled to study the process and see if this was really a problem.

At the team meeting, team members were told by the clinic's occupational therapist that the new billing procedure, now integrated with that of the hospital, was cumbersome, time-consuming, and a prime contributor to the problem. The team decided to construct a process flow diagram to understand how the system worked.

Representative staff from occupational therapy, business office, information systems, and the mailroom were assembled to describe the process.

Occupational Therapy. "After I treat a patient, I have to fill out the medical record, fill out a charge slip, file the record, and mail the charge slip to the business office. I usually hold the slips until the end of the day and send them over in one package. If I have time, I'll file the medical records right away. If I'm busy, they pile up, and I try to file them before I go home.

"Of course, that's not the end of it. Every few days, I get a package back from the business office with insurance forms that need clinical information. Then I have to pull the records again, go through them to figure out what I did for the patient, and enter treatment codes on the forms. When I send a package over to the business office, I include these forms.

"But it's still not over: Every other day, it seems, I get back forms that have gone to the insurance company but have been denied. About half of the forms come back. Then I have to repeat the process all over again: Pull the charts, figure out what I did, decide what was wrong, and send them back to accounting one more time. No wonder I have no time to see patients."

Business Office. "Well, we get charge slips from all over the place all day long. We have to sort them by department, bundle them up, and send them to data entry. They produce the billing reports, but then we have to take the reports apart and send them back to the departments to be coded with clinical information. When we get them back from the departments, we hold them until the start of the billing cycle, that is, until the end of the month. Then we send them to the insurance companies.

"Of course, that's not the end of it. A lot of the bills are wrong. It's not our fault. But when they're wrong, we have to figure out what the problem is. Then we send them back to the departments to be corrected, because that's usually where the trouble starts. When we get the bills back from the departments, we have to go through the whole process with data entry again. At least we don't have to wait till the end of the month to send them out. They usually go out right away.

"It's no wonder I'm so busy. I never get to go home until after 6:00 P.M."

Information Systems. "We just run the computer. I don't count how many times I have to run everyone's report. It's enough that we have to take them apart and bundle them by department for the business office people. I think that should be *their* job. We're specialists, not clerks."

Mailroom. "I just package stuff up and ship it out. I send out whatever people give me. As long as the address is correct and I have a code to charge for shipping, the stuff goes. If stuff comes back it's not my fault, unless the address is wrong. The postage is always right."

A representative from an insurance company could not be present for the meeting, but the team was told that the bill is either right or wrong. If it's right, Colossal gets paid. If it's wrong, the bill is returned. The insurance person did say, however, that the company reduces payments by 10 percent if bills are delayed more than 60 days. Over the course of a year, this results in payment reductions of about $10,000 for the Occupational Health Clinic.

Figure 11.3 is a flowchart depicting the process.

Harvey Dershin is vice president of Juran Institute in Wilton, Connecticut, specializing in quality management in health care. He provides services in the United States and Canada as well as overseas.

Before joining Juran Institute he spent 13 years as a senior executive of Grant Hospital in Chicago, seven years as senior vice president for professional services, and six years as executive vice president/chief operating officer. Before joining Grant, Dershin was active in public health, serving as Director of a Model Cities Neighborhood Health Center Project, a lecturer at Tulane's School of Public Health and Tropical Medicine, a consultant to the World Health Organization, and director of the statewide family planning program in Illinois.

He earned an M.S. degree from UCLA and a bachelor of mechanical engineering degree from the City University of New York. He is a member of the American College of Health Care Executives and American Society for Quality.

Julie A. Magrath is an independent consultant. She is the former vice president of organization and management effectiveness at Juran Institute in Wilton, Connecticut. Prior to joining Juran Institute, Magrath specialized in organization and leadership effectiveness with senior-level executives for the Delta Consulting Group in New York. There, she consulted with clients in the areas of organizational assessment and change, quality management, and strategic planning and implementation. As vice president and principal at Executive Development Associates in Westport, Connecticut, she designed and developed executive education and development programs customized to help clients achieve their key business strategies. Other experience of note includes management training and development positions with AMF, Inland Steel Company, Marine Midland Bank, and G.D. Searle.

Magrath is a graduate of Ripon College, with a B.A. degree in psychology and education. She earned an M.S. degree from Loyola University in industrial relations and personnel management. She is a member of the Conference Board, American Management Association, Human Resource Planning Society, American Society for Planning and Development, and the Business Resource Group.

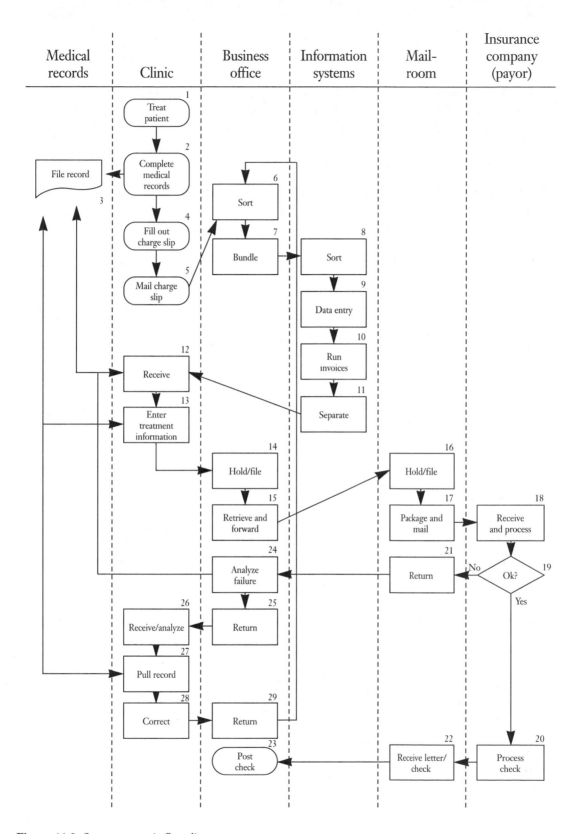

Figure 11.3. Summary matrix flow diagram.

Chapter 12

Cost-of-Poor-Quality Analysis: The Prescription for Profitable Change Management

Anthony J. Romagnole

A significant amount of cost savings and customer value creation has been realized by leading health care providers who have systematically identified and quantified opportunities for improvement within their businesses. Organizations such as Mayo Clinic,[1] in Rochester, Minnesota, Suburban Hospital in Bethesda, Maryland,[2] and General Health System in Baton Rouge, Louisiana,[3] are using data to prioritize projects, to gain consensus for organizational change, and to allocate resources and efforts toward those activities that will yield the highest returns on investments. As a result, millions of dollars have been saved, quality of care has improved, and competitive positions have been enhanced.

This chapter will explain the different forms of cost of poor quality (COPQ) and provide some examples of how they can be quantified. Internal cost of poor quality—deficiencies that occur before and during service delivery—and external cost of poor quality—deficiencies occurring after the service is delivered—will be explored. The lives of two CEOs will provide examples of unsuccessful and successful change management and how COPQ can make a difference. A lessons learned section outlines key success factors in implementing a COPQ program.

There are a number of terms and methodologies being used today to capture similar results. Some of these names include *operational reviews, continuous improvement opportunity analysis*, and *reengineering assessments*. All have some element that includes systematic discovery and quantification of ideas for improvement. The techniques mentioned in this chapter can replace or supplement any form of these activities.

COPQ Definition

Cost of poor quality is the total cost that results from problems occurring before and after a product or service is delivered. These costs arise from both internal and external sources. Internal poor-quality costs increase a company's costs of operation (for example, rework, billing errors, and other avoidable process losses). External poor-quality costs result in lost incremental revenue (for example, readmittances, lawsuits, and lost business).

A COPQ *analysis* identifies the sources of poor quality and develops estimates of their economic value. This information then allows organizations to prioritize their improvement efforts and focus resources on the opportunities with the greatest leverage. It also provides tangible targets to assist improvement teams in achieving significant cost savings, quality breakthroughs, and customer loyalty.

The line between internal and external cost of poor quality is not clear-cut. Many suboptimal processes and functions can contribute to both increased costs *and* customer disloyalty. However, it is useful to separate the two for analysis, because internal COPQ studies can generally be conducted with little customer input, whereas external COPQ studies require intense customer feedback methodologies. These distinct techniques will be discussed separately.

Internal Cost of Poor Quality

Internal cost of poor quality is the total amount of operating cost associated with non–value-added activities. Common categories of these costs are as follows:

• *Rework* represents the cost incurred by failing to provide the service correctly the first time. An example would be having a phlebotomist revisit and restick a patient due to hemolization caused by poor turnaround time in the lab or improper technique.

• *Work around* refers to existing processes that have become so cumbersome that various participants have developed their own, informal way of coping with the problems—sometimes bypassing the process altogether. This can lead to uncoordinated and haphazard bursts of activity downstream with a chaotic effect on hospital operations. An example would be holding medical records after discharge due to excess paperwork or inefficient delivery systems, which in turn causes lost records, billing inaccuracies, and delayed billing and collection.

• *Excess inspection* is the situation that arises from having a process so measured and controlled that the costs associated with checking the intermediate or final outputs become greater than the benefit of doing so. In service businesses such as health care, this often manifests itself in the form of excessive sign-offs. Another example would be 100 percent inspection of diagnosis code capturing when errors rarely occur and sampling techniques could do the job adequately.

• *Inadequate facility or staff utilization* occurs when processes, department staff, or sets of equipment are underutilized relative to the amount of services they can deliver in a given period. It is not possible to run at capacity all the time, but numerous studies have shown that a typical health care facility's utilization averages are much lower than other service industries (50 percent to 60 percent range versus 70 percent to 90 percent)—some so low that the facility would be out of business in any other environment. An example is shown in Figure 12.1, where expensive radiology equipment is used only 60 percent of the time throughout the year.

• *Scrap or waste* refers to materials and equipment discarded without being used for an organization or customer benefit. An example is inventory spoilage of vascular graphs due to expiration (which may be caused by having too many vendors).

• *Suboptimal process* is a catch-all term to describe a process that at least works well generally but could be taken to a new level of effectiveness and efficiency. An example is a scheduled admission process that requires a lot of manual entry or coping when a computerized process would result in higher levels of accuracy and productivity.

• *Excess process variation* is a form of suboptimal process that seems to work well sometimes or in some situations, but results in excess costs or lower quality in others. An example would be a routine hip replacement on a relatively homogeneous set of patients (severity-adjusted population) that yields

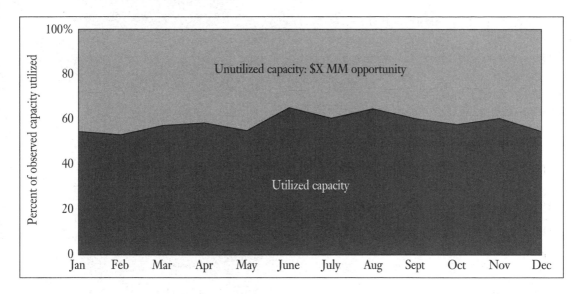

Figure 12.1. Average radiology utilization (normal hours).

wildly different costs—double or triple—throughout the year. Substantial opportunities arise when health care organizations find the cause of the variation and reduce it.

Figure 12.2 shows a simplified example of the results of analyzing a hospital emergency room. It is useful to map the processes in some way in order to understand where handoff problems can occur and to pinpoint where opportunities occur. Figure 12.2 also shows the dollar amount of each category's opportunities to make an impression about what efforts in the emergency room will yield the highest returns. After all target areas around the organization are analyzed, an overall list of opportunities can be formed and ranked by financial benefit.

A distinction needs to be made between processes that occur within a department or functional area and processes that wind their way through departments and functions. Concerning the latter, a reengineering assessment is typically employed to analyze the effectiveness of a multifunctional process. However, large-scale reengineering efforts of select processes may not address other inefficiencies occurring *within* each functional silo. Certainly you do not want to optimize the function and create a bottleneck that suboptimizes the larger process (patient throughput, for example). But a reengineered mainstream process may ignore, say, low-capacity utilization of medical equipment. Therefore, both the process and the functions must be analyzed.

Internal COPQ analysis can be separated into clinical issues, such as radiological processes, and administrative issues that support and facilitate the clinical services, such as the admissions process. Other examples of clinical and administrative issues are shown in Figure 12.3.

Benefits of Internal COPQ Analysis

Understanding and focusing on internal poor-quality costs can result in substantial cost savings and improved quality and organizational profitability. Study after study in both manufacturing and service organizations—and particularly in health care—shows that costs associated with wasted effort and rework are between 20 percent and 40 percent of total operating expenses. In addition, the impact of

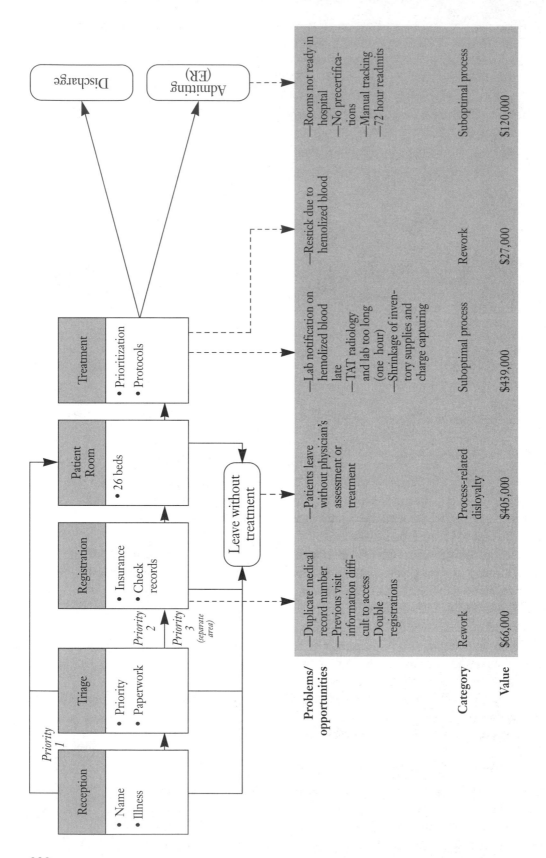

Figure 12.2. Emergency room patient flow.

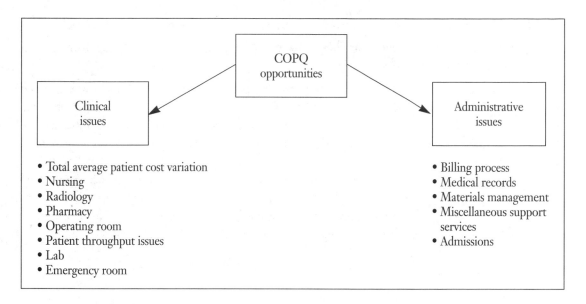

Figure 12.3. Internal COPQ focus areas.

customer defections can reduce profits by half. It is not unusual for organizations to begin realizing millions of dollars in savings as a result of projects identified through systematic internal COPQ studies.

Internal COPQ assessments are particularly useful for addressing the following:

- Decreasing profitability

- Increasing price competition

- Frequent patient readmittance or high legal expenses

- Lack of internal management buy-in to the need for change

- Few, or confusing, internal efficiency measures

- Unclear benefit of investing in quality improvement projects

- Many projects underway without overriding prioritization or consensus

Action Steps for Internal COPQ Assessments

Typically, a team is commissioned by executive management to conduct a data-based analysis of the organization's processes to identify sources of poor quality and to develop estimates of their economic value. All techniques utilized are based on extensive interviews, hard data, and rigorous analysis. Some of the tools used include the following:

- *Internal best demonstrated practice* compares the performance of like processes within an organization to identify the best demonstrated practice and quantify the gaps.

- *External comparisons* measure the performance of select processes with the performance of the same processes in other organizations.

- *Failure unit-cost analysis* identifies and quantifies the frequency and cost of failures in processes, products, and services.

- *Variation analysis* measures the variation of processes and quantifies the cost of excess variation.

- *Proportionate resource allocation* identifies proportions of specific resources expended on non–value-added activities.

The name of the tool is not as important as simply applying investigative thought to the area of study. As an example, Figure 12.4 shows the operating room utilization of a hospital with 11 operating suites. This graphic was based on using the log data at the scheduling station for daytime hours of operation (when the majority of the operations occurred). At an average utilization of 44 percent, it was clear that some suites' work could be combined—at a potential savings of more than $600,000 in reduced services and support. However, blocked-time requirements for certain physicians and practices prohibited major change. Figure 12.5 shows that while blocked-time was required, it was not utilized to its fullest. Blocked-time utilization was not known to the various physicians that used the space. These data allowed the hospital to measure the degree of efficiency, to quantify the impact, and to gain consensus for changes.

A typical project includes the following steps.

1. Identify the activities resulting in poor quality.

2. Decide on specific methodologies to estimate the costs for each activity.

3. Collect the data, estimate the costs, and build a database for comparisons.

4. Analyze the results and represent the opportunities graphically.

5. Present improvement projects, with associated profit impacts.

6. Assign improvement responsibilities with specific accountabilities.

7. Incorporate measurements, investments, and savings into the budget, the financial plans, and the strategic plan.

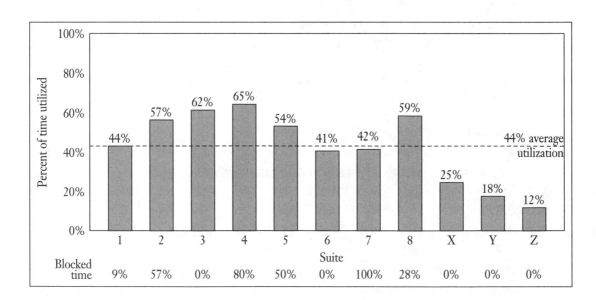

Figure 12.4. OR utilization during core hours.

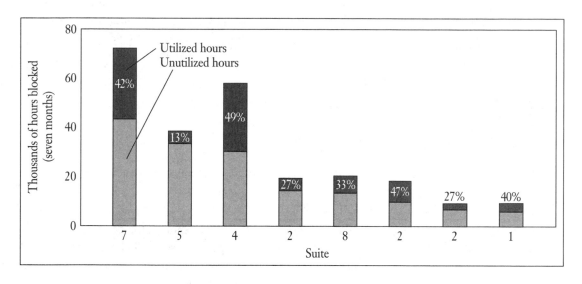

Figure 12.5. OR block utilization.

Diagnosis-Related Group Variation Analysis: A Special Measure of Internal COPQ

Diagnosis-related group (DRG) variation analysis is a rigorous, data-based examination of resources used by physicians performing procedures within a hospital. The analysis quantifies the financial benefit of developing pathways and reengineering processes for each DRG or group of DRGs.

Different physicians practicing within the same environment will consume widely varying amounts of hospital resources, even within a severity-adjusted DRG. Studies have shown that this practice variation raises costs associated with similar procedures by as much as 200 percent on average. Studies have also shown that the extra costs involved do not necessarily result in increased quality of care and often result in *decreased* care quality.

Quantifying and examining practice variation can be used as a foundation for organizational and process change. Studies based on this technique will uncover the following:

- Potential savings of reducing practice variation within each severity-adjusted DRG
- Ranking of DRG opportunities by potential savings and by other variation measures
- Identification of internal best-practicing physicians as benchmarks
- Relationship between physician experience and average cost per patient

This information allows organizations to prioritize their quality improvement efforts and focus resources on the opportunities with the greatest leverage. It also provides tangible targets to assist quality improvement teams in achieving cost savings and quality breakthroughs.

Benefits of DRG Variation Analysis

Understanding and focusing on DRG variation can result in substantial cost savings while improving quality and profitability. Studies conducted by the Juran Institute show that costs associated with practice variation are between 10 percent and 25 percent of total operating expenses, with a significant portion of these costs realizable within a one- to two-year time frame. Mayo Clinic saved $4 million annually by improving processes and developing procedures for key medical interventions.[4]

DRG assessments are particularly useful for addressing the following:

- An increasingly capitated case mix

- A lack of management and physician buy-in to improvement projects

- Cost rationalization and price decreases by competitors

- Unclear benefit of investing in quality improvement projects

- Many projects underway without overriding prioritization or consensus

The Significance of DRG Variation Analysis

Figure 12.6 shows a typical graph of a severity-adjusted DRG. Each point on the graph represents the practicing physician in charge of the procedure (usually the surgeon for surgical DRGs, or the attending physician for medical DRGs). The y axis represents the average resources consumed per patient per physician during a given year. The x axis shows the corresponding average length of stay per patient per year.

As expected, the trend generally shows a higher cost with increasing length of stay. However, there are some questions that need to be answered. First, why is there such a wide range of costs for a given length of stay? For instance, for five days the costs range from approximately $5000 to $10,000—a 100 percent difference. Second, for that matter, if the severity-adjusted DRG represents a fairly homogeneous group of patients, why should the average costs for these patients range from $5000 to more than $30,000—a sixfold difference?

The answers to these questions can be determined only by doing an in-depth analysis of the activities associated with the cases during the year. From that analysis, a group of recommendations could

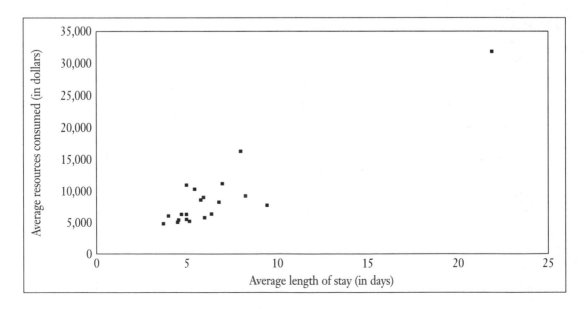

Figure 12.6. Average charge versus average length of stay for DRG XXX.

be formulated, discussed, and implemented. However, there are nearly 500 DRGs to inspect. How would a hospital decide which DRGs represent the best targets in terms of potential improvement?

I have looked at numerous, readily available variables to correlate with costs in order to get a reliable predictor of average cost per patient. What I have discovered is that one of the primary drivers of costs is physician (or case team) experience. Figure 12.7 shows the same data with the number of cases per physician per year next to each physician's point on the graph. Notice that, generally, the most experienced physicians tend to have lower costs. Figure 12.8 shows that by plotting these same costs against the number of patients per year to which a physician supplies services in the DRG, you observe a downward-sloping physician experience curve—similar to experience curves that have been observed in all types of industries over the years. This suggests that physician experience is a factor in costs. It also suggests, for this and many other DRGs plotted for numerous environments, that there is a point at which costs level off. In this example, the physicians that conducted a minimum of 10 cases per year generally stayed in the $5000 to $6000 range.

You might conclude that some of the less-experienced physicians were unlucky—that they were in charge of one or two tough cases, whereas those types of patients were lost in the averages of the more-experienced physicians. If that were the case (ignoring the fact that the data were severity-adjusted), you would expect the average of all of the less-experienced physicians to be closer to the averages represented by the more experienced physicians. Figure 12.8 shows that the physicians with 10 or more cases averaged $5908 per case, whereas those with fewer than 10 cases per year averaged $9037 per case—50 percent higher costs.

A significant feature of this comparison is that all physicians in a given hospital operate in the same environment. Benchmarks comparing various regional or national hospitals are often viewed with great skepticism, as each hospital is considered to have unique operating requirements. Thus, an internal benchmark may be more acceptable to the various practices, and it can be used to establish a first target for improvement.

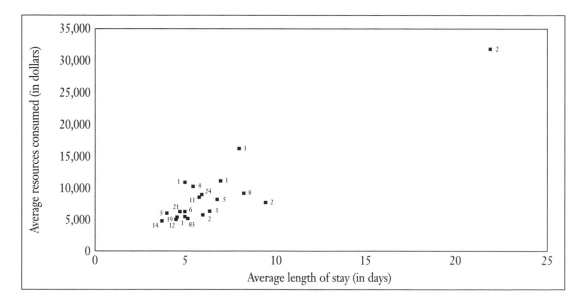

Figure 12.7. Average charge versus average length of stay for DRG XXX.

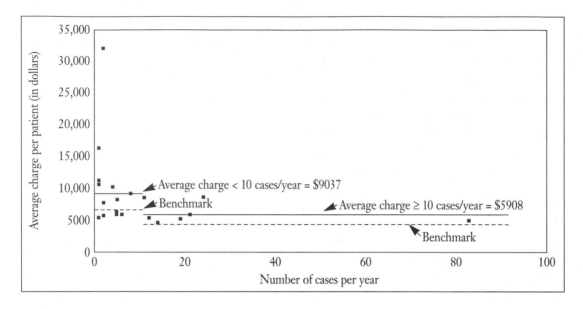

Figure 12.8. Physician experience curve analysis for DRG XXX.

Given that physician experience is a predictor of resource consumption, it is interesting to see the practice concentration profile of a typical hospital. Figure 12.9 shows such a profile. This example reveals that only 2 percent of the physicians in this hospital perform 10 or more procedures within a DRG each year. In fact, the bar chart on the right side of the figure shows that more than 80 percent of the procedures are being performed by physicians with fewer than 10 cases per year in a particular DRG. One-third of the cases are performed by physicians with one patient in a given DRG!

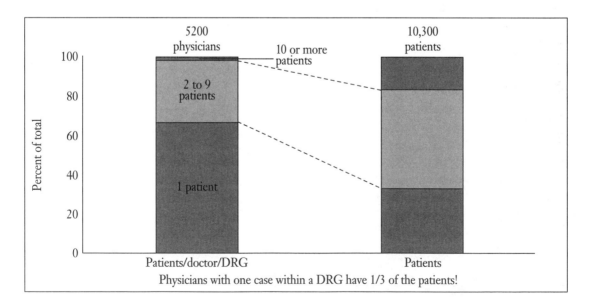

Figure 12.9. Practice concentrations.

Quantifying the impact of excessive practice variation is a powerful tool in identifying those DRGs with high potential for financial and quality gains through process improvement and pathway development.

Action Steps for DRG Variation Analysis

A team is commissioned by executive management to conduct an analysis of the organization's database to identify sources of practice variation and to develop estimates of their economic value. Some of the tools used include the following:

• *Internal best demonstrated practice* compares the performance of physicians within an organization to identify the best practices and quantify the gaps. The gaps are quantified by comparing the average cost per patient with the best experienced physician (BEP)—that physician who performed the most cases in a year—within a DRG. The difference represents improvement potential.

• *Variation analysis* measures the resource use variation among practices and quantifies the cost of excess variation. In this alternative technique, the standard deviation of average costs per physician for each DRG—a measure of the spread of costs—is multiplied by the number of procedures performed in the DRG. This measurement is used to rank the DRGs by cost variation within a DRG rather than by cost differences between physicians.

The benefit of using these techniques is that the organization can quickly hone in on those DRGs that will yield the highest results. Figure 12.10 illustrates an example of a hospital where 20 percent of the DRGs with more than 10 total cases per year represented 70 percent of the potential savings.

A typical project includes the following activities.

1. Identify the accuracy and scope of available data.

2. Develop proxies for data that may not be directly available.

3. Collect, format, and process the data.

4. Analyze the results and identify patterns within the data.

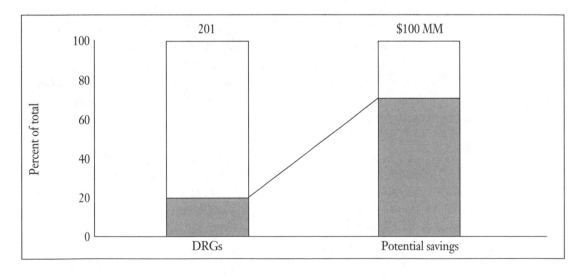

Figure 12.10. DRG variability analysis.

5. Graphically represent the opportunities.

6. Present improvement projects and the associated profit impacts.

7. Assign improvement responsibilities, with specific accountabilities.

8. Incorporate measurements, investments, and savings into financial and strategic plans.

External COPQ: Customer Loyalty

Customer loyalty is a bond between a targeted customer and a supplier characterized by the customer consistently spending most or all of its budget on the supplier's goods or services. Loyal customers add value to an organization's bottom line by

- Providing a consistent cash flow over time
- Generating new sales by referring other customers
- Paying a price premium
- Buying a broader mix of goods and services
- Co-developing leading-edge products that can be sold to other customers
- Reducing the company's selling and servicing costs

Enhancing loyalty in target customers can lead to sustainable and profitable sales growth.

Customer loyalty analysis provides a framework for enhancing revenues by building customer loyalty. Generally, these studies are conducted for organizations that wish to increase customer retention, market share, and overall customer focus. The recommendations that result from these studies can be implemented immediately—with benefits, based on experience, of up to 50 percent of current net income. A typical customer loyalty analysis includes the design and implementation of an unfiltered customer feedback system that prioritizes opportunities based on bottom-line impact. This system provides essential inputs into clients' strategic plans and a powerful mechanism to lead and motivate change.

The Difference Between Customer Loyalty and Customer Satisfaction

While many organizations track and manage customer satisfaction, most of them see no connection between the satisfaction scores and the bottom line. What we have discovered is that even if a customer is satisfied, the customer may still shift some or all of its business to a competing supplier. This is because satisfaction measures customer *preferences,* which are often unrelated to their behavior. For example, while price is frequently cited as a leading cause for dissatisfaction, it is almost never the most significant reason why a customer leaves. Customer loyalty, on the other hand, is based on customer buying behavior, and its measurement is directly linked to profits.

Benefits of Customer Loyalty Analysis

Studies have found that companies employing customer loyalty management have been able to improve their net income by as much as 50 percent.[5] Many leading health maintenance organizations are beginning to focus on customer loyalty because disenrollments significantly impact financial performance.

A customer loyalty analysis is particularly useful for addressing:

- Declining market share, sales, or profitability
- High levels of customer churn (and the resulting need to replace lost business)

- Unclear benefit of investing in quality improvement projects
- Many projects underway without overriding prioritization or consensus

Customer churn—replacing lost customers with new customers—is particularly detrimental to an organization's potential for growth. Figure 12.11 shows two scenarios for growth of an insurance company's membership: high churn and low churn. By reducing the amount of controllable loss of business, the company can significantly increase its growth rate.

The aim of customer loyalty research is to determine why customers become loyal or disloyal. An organization must be able to identify disloyal and loyal customers, measure the level of disloyalty, and draw a connection between loyalty rate and profitability. Then, specific actions need to be identified to increase loyalty and guide the organization through improvement efforts.

A customer loyalty study results in the identification of specific actions linked to and prioritized by impact on the bottom line. This allows organizations to align their product and service offerings with factors driving customer spending behavior. The study also provides key market information such as competitor strengths and weaknesses, segmentation based on behavior, and market perceptions.

Action Steps for a Customer Loyalty Analysis

Customer loyalty analysis is a highly customized activity that should be designed and executed specifically for the target organization and its competitive environment.

A typical project includes the following steps.

1. Determine the appropriate methodology for measuring customer loyalty.

2. Identify target product/customer segments.

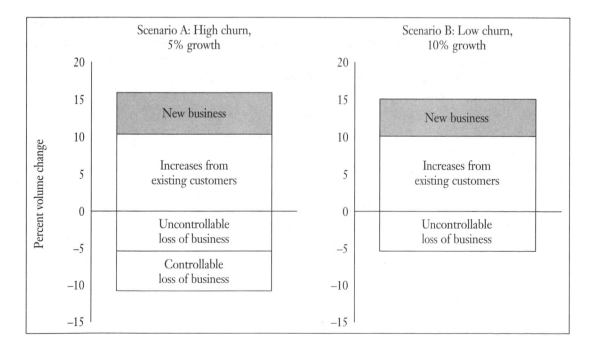

Figure 12.11. Two scenarios for growth.

3. Conduct customer interviews.

4. Develop a customer loyalty database; formulate algorithms for data analysis.

5. Develop a prioritized list of improvement opportunities.

6. Present project results, with profit impacts.

7. Assign customer-focused improvement responsibilities, with specific accountabilities.

8. Refine the understanding of customer profitability and market segmentation.

9. Incorporate measurements, investments, and savings into financial and strategic plans.

Case Studies: The Success and Failure of TWO CEOs

Problems: One CEO's Experience

Changing Environment but Resistance to Internal Change. Due to increasing revenue capitation, a large regional hospital is placed in an unfamiliar position of having to reduce costs to maintain profitability. The CEO and executive committee decide that a 10 percent reduction in the hospital budget is needed. All department heads are called in to determine how much they can sacrifice without disrupting operations. The meetings reveal that most departments claim they are at capacity and that any reduction in costs will affect patient care.

Physicians practicing at the hospital have the greatest influence on how the resources are spent. They are solicited to help reduce lengths of stay and to use standardized procedures. Some of the physicians disagree with the effort as it may decrease care and increase liability. Others show interest but are perplexed as to how to go about gaining consensus and making improvements—much less, measuring improvements. All parties arrive at a stalemate.

Unfocused Efforts Leading to Lower Costs, But Lower Quality and Competitiveness. The executive committee decides to take matters into its own hands. It starts looking at the largest expenditure items in the hospital. Staff, particularly nursing, will have to be cut. Orders are sent out to all departments to reduce staff by 10 percent across the board, phased out over the fiscal year. Hospital morale declines.

During the year, some departments seem to get by despite previous hardship claims. However, in other departments, the remaining personnel are taking on more and more work. Morale declines even further as reality sets in. Turnover increases. Recruitment costs rise. Productivity gains, produced by fewer staff, level off and start to decline while new staff members learn the hospital's procedures. Above all, patient care declines—just as the department heads had warned.

A new problem springs up: a declining number of patients—and the impact is far greater than the cost reductions sought. Physician groups start to refer patients to alternative health care facilities. Competitors start to specialize in certain procedures and seem to be doing a better job at a lower cost. Word gets around the community, and market share declines. Soon after, a hospital group calls to discuss the possibility of buying the facility.

Solution: Another CEO's Experience

Formulating a Plan for Managing Change. On the other side of town, the primary competitive hospital is faced with the same increasing revenue capitation and the same unfamiliar position of having to reduce costs to maintain profitability. This CEO understands that the organization has a capacity to absorb change and that there would be plenty of resistance to it. There was no one to blame. The situation had developed due to a change in the environment, before which the hospital ran quite competitively.

On the cost side, the CEO and executive management team all know that, due to a previous focus on growth and increasing complexity, inefficiencies have developed in the system over time and have become institutionalized. Complaints are coming in from all areas of the hospital and the community: employees, physicians, patients, friends, and neighbors. Even as customers themselves, everyone knows that there is a better way to operate.

The executive team members realize that unless the policies and procedures change, eliminating jobs and services would only result in chaos. But where do they start? It seems there are plenty of ideas, but which ones should they go after? After all, there are limited resources and a limited time in which to create change. And more important, how will they get the organization to accept change without using a stick?

Bringing Data into the Decisions: A Snapshot in Time of All Opportunities. What is apparent is that the organization is missing objective data to be used to gain consensus and to drive change. Of course, the executive team knows that it has to take into account political and cultural factors in steering a new course for the hospital. However, it needs facts in hand to counteract unsubstantiated and emotional arguments.

The executives commission a team to systematically uncover all cost reduction (and quality-enhancing) opportunities in the hospital and to estimate the impact each idea has on costs. The hospital ranks those opportunities by economic value, estimates the time frames for implementation, and thereby provides a road map for change—both short term and long term. It is this snapshot in time that provides the basis for all decisions regarding where the organization can best leverage its resources and time.

Interestingly enough, the amount of waste and inefficiency identified far exceeds the 10 percent target set for cost reduction. By distinguishing between the high-impact and low-impact projects, the hospital can focus its efforts in the right directions and maximize gains while increasing quality.

Communicating Findings and Constructing a Clear Implementation Plan with Accountabilities. In the spirit of improvement and in light of competitive realities, the results of the study are communicated throughout the organization. Objections, endorsements, and concerns are anticipated and handled in subgroups—especially those involving the issue of potential layoffs.

Ultimately, consensus is reached, and project leaders are assigned to achieve measurable results. "Quick hits" are executed for immediate results and to demonstrate the efficacy of the program. A small portion of the financial benefits gained are used to fund more ambitious strategic and infrastructural changes.

Executing a Plan to Decrease Customer Defections and to Increase Revenues. Within a few months, the hospital is on the road to recovery by improving productivity and quality. However, cost cutting only aligns capacity with demand. A significant part of the hospital is underutilized, and it is clear that adding revenues is immensely more valuable than cutting costs. After all, the fixed costs are in place, and any increase in revenues would only be reduced by the variable costs incurred. Thus, each additional incremental dollar in revenue results in a higher-than-average percentage flowing to the bottom line.

From defecting (or disloyal) customers, the team members learn what factors drove the customers to use competing facilities—based on both perceptions and reality. Likewise, from loyal customers they learn their competitive strengths. As with the internal cost study, these external customer issues are quantified and prioritized by bottom-line impact.

During the year, efforts are focused on the most leveraged activities to eliminate inefficiencies and to increase customer loyalty. Most staff reductions are achieved through attrition. As positions are eliminated, the non–value-added activities associated with them are eliminated. The remaining personnel are working the same amount, but are doing more things that are valuable to patients and to themselves—no more unnecessary tasks! Morale and pride increases. Word starts to spread around the community, and the hospital becomes the health care facility of choice.

Lessons Learned: Success and Failure Factors for COPQ

The CEO dilemma examples give a sense of what can go right and what can go wrong. The following items are some of the key factors in successfully executing a COPQ analysis.

• *Get top management endorsement.* All of the decisions that result in the completion of a study and, eventually, implementing recommendations need top management support and oversight. If endorsement cannot be achieved, the chances of success become remote.

• *Do not get obsessed with the need for perfect data.* Remember that while this analysis is conducted to supply realistic data to decisions, it is only an estimate. Do not get sidetracked (or let anyone derail your efforts) by engaging in overanalysis or "analysis paralysis." No perfect data exist to give estimates to the penny. Being within an order of magnitude is usually sufficient to make informed decisions and can be achieved within a short time frame.

• *Provide the necessary resources to get the analysis completed within a desired time frame.* Obviously, no one is sitting idly waiting for another full-time assignment to be dropped in his or her lap. If the study is to be done by internal staff, clearing them of other (lower value-added) responsibilities will ensure that they have time to focus on the project and to complete it. Many efforts have been started but were not finished—or worse, they were completed very slowly. It is very dangerous to embark on an improvement effort based on inadequate analysis. If no one (or no expertise) is available internally, then it may be worthwhile to engage external help for facilitation, speed, and learning.

• *Try to convey analyses, ideas, and results in graphical form.* It is said that "a picture speaks a thousand words." Graphics also have a lot more impact than lengthy prose or pages of tables of numbers. Collecting the data is easier than assimilating them into intelligence and simplifying the conclusions in a powerful graphic. But the latter must be done if the analysis is going to be used to influence people in the organization. Do not skimp on packaging the message, even if it requires a little extra time. If your organization lacks the skills or resources initially, get help and learn how to do it.

• *Be careful about the tone of the results.* To be accepted by the majority of the managers and employees of the organization, the output of the study must be presented in a tone that is appropriate to the culture and circumstances. It is useful to be positive, pointing toward the possibilities, rather than pointing fingers and assigning blame.

• *Distinguish between the amount of change and rate of change.* Once the path to prosperity is known, it is common for management to want to do everything by tomorrow. Unfortunately, that is neither possible nor prudent. Decisions must be guided by the rate of change possible given the culture of the organization, its present capabilities, and its past experiences. It is important to be realistic about an implementation time frame and to allow for contingencies. The pace can be quickened only by increasing investments—both monetarily and physically—in the short term. These investments can take the form of training, added staff, or outside help.

• *Provide a clear implementation plan, with accountabilities and resources.* Many great analyses fall short of transforming into reality because implementation rarely just happens—it frequently requires tenacity and hard work. There are a host of techniques available to make things happen, but minimally someone should be appointed, with time and resources, to be accountable to get the action items accomplished. The person should be rewarded handsomely when the results materialize, both monetarily and through public recognition.

• *Prioritize actions, get moving, and make progress.* Movement toward improvement should start the day the results are known. Do not let the intelligence sit. Start something, somewhere. The few projects worth doing will be apparent.

Conclusion

Many quality improvement efforts are being implemented with only a vague indication of financial benefits. There is little, if any, knowledge of what the investments in time and resources will yield in terms of profit improvement and customer value. Cost reduction decisions are often made with detrimental medium- and long-term consequences for employees, customers, and shareholders. Customers—patients, physicians, insurance companies, HMOs, and employers—switch their business to competing facilities, and the primary reasons for those defections are not corrected until a crisis develops. The financial consequences of internal inefficiencies and external customer defections is usually unquantified, yet largely debated based on emotional grounds.

Combining market, operational, and financial data is very powerful in making tactical and strategic decisions. Until recently, this was not necessary because of the cost-plus structure of the health care industry. Now, with increasing cost and competitive pressures and with the proliferation of technology, the market is changing more rapidly than ever before. This has made the need for some version of cost-of-poor-quality analysis essential for survival. You can bet that at least one of your competitors is doing it to gain an edge.

The purpose of the COPQ assessment is to understand what the total opportunity is and where, specifically, the organization can gain financially by improving customer service. This allows the following:

• Prioritization of targets

• Practical implementation plans

• Organizational concurrence and acceptance of change

• Measurement and documentation of improvements

The last point suggests that in order for the analysis to be most effective, a new COPQ study should be conducted periodically (typically annually) to measure efficacy of implementation processes.

By understanding all of your organization's options to reduce administrative and clinical costs, to increase customer loyalty and to measure progress toward improvement, an aggressive plan could be executed confidently knowing that all efforts will assure increasing customer and stakeholder value. Ultimately, the focus of change management will be toward managing for growth rather than managing for survival.

Questions for a One-Hour Executive Council Meeting

Internal Cost of Poor Quality

1. What are the significant non-value-added activities in the organization?

2. How much is each opportunity worth?

3. How do we get agreement internally that the analysis is correct?

4. How do we implement the improvements in a timely fashion?

5. Who should lead this effort?

Customer Loyalty

1. What are our competitive strengths and weaknesses from the customers' standpoint?

2. What is the rank, in importance, of each competitive strength and weakness?

3. How much is each competitive strength and weakness worth on the bottom line?

4. How can we get agreement from each function in the organization, at all levels of management, that the answers to questions 1 through 3 are correct?

5. How do we turn this competitive market intelligence into action and, ultimately, customer and shareholder value?

Notes

1. Carleton T. Rider, "Aligning Your Improvement Strategy for the Biggest Payback," *IMPRO®95 Conference Proceedings* (Wilton, Conn.: Juran Institute (1995), 7E1-1; R. R. Waller, M.D., "The Best of Both Worlds: Better Care and Lower Costs," *IMPRO®96 Conference Proceedings* (Wilton, Conn.: Juran Institute (1996), 1-1.

2. M. D. Minogue, F. William, and Elizabeth H. Dougherty, "Re-engineering the Surgical Process: Landmarks & Landmines," *IMPRO®95 Conference Proceedings* (Wilton, Conn.: Juran Institute (1995), 6E-1.

3. James L. Brexler, and B. Eugene Beyt, M.D., "Quality Basics and Basic Quality: A Healthcare Example," *IMPRO®93 Conference Proceedings* (Wilton, Conn.: Juran Institute (1993), 5-1.

4. Rider, "Aligning Your Improvement Strategy . . .;" Waller, "The Best of Both Words."

5. Robert McPherson, "Customer Loyalty Management at CSI," *IMPRO®93 Conference Proceedings* (Wilton, Conn.: Juran Institute (1993), 8A2-1.

Anthony J. Romagnole, vice president of Juran Institute, Inc., is a member of the Customer and Process Analysis Group that develops and implements quality-based strategies and initiatives for clients at the business unit and corporate levels. The Customer and Process Analysis Group is focused at the crossroad of traditional management concerns (such as the balance sheet and income statement) and management for quality. Emphasis is placed on measurable improvement to net income and shareholder value.

Prior to joining Juran Institute, Romagnole was vice president in charge of regional sales, marketing, and operations at Guardsmark, Inc., a leading national building security firm. Prior to that, he was with International Business Machines.

Romagnole earned a B.S. degree, summa cum laude, in civil and urban engineering from the University of Pennsylvania, and an M.B.A. degree from the Harvard Business School.

Chapter 13

Process and Organization Structure for JCAHO Accreditation

Howard B. Nussman

Most health care organizations today participate voluntarily in one or more accreditation processes as a means of demonstrating and providing evidence of the quality of care they deliver. This chapter will identify several key processes and structures which, when put in place, strengthen the health care organization's compliance with accreditation standards set forth by the Joint Commission on Accreditation of Healthcare Organizations (JCAHO). Many of the key principles set forth by JCAHO have been influenced by or have influenced other sets of criteria for organizational performance, such as the Malcolm Baldrige National Quality Award criteria or the National Committee for Quality Assurance criteria. Thus the processes and structures discussed here will often apply to an organization's efforts to achieve compliance with the standards and criteria published by other similar agencies.

Several common traits are observable in health care organizations that receive high scores in JCAHO accreditation surveys, particularly in those that receive accreditation with commendation, the JCAHO's highest level of recognition. These traits include the following:

- *Strategic alignment*—A clear understanding among those in the organization of its purpose and strategic direction, accompanied by actions that are consistent with the purpose and direction

- *Integration of services*—Teamwork and collaboration in daily work activities among staff from various departments, hospital staff and medical staff, and staff from within the organization and others external to the organization but important in provision of services

- *Data-based decision making*—The proper use of data and information in the decision-making process, including most notably data regarding the needs and expectations of the organization's important customers and external data comparisons that add value to the organization's assessment of its own performance

- *Current competence*—The ability to confirm that those who work within the organization possess the knowledge and skills to fulfill the expectations and requirements of the jobs they perform, especially those who provide patient care

- *Continuous improvement*—Evidence that the organization has embraced and applied the principles of continuous quality improvement, including observable results

Each organization faces unique challenges in developing these traits, which are highly dependent on the management style and culture within the organization. In the remaining sections of this chapter, we will highlight six key issues or activities organizations must address to comply with JCAHO standards. These include

1. Executive leadership

2. Focus on processes

3. Performance improvement

4. Patient care

5. Information management

6. Environment

As each of these key issues or activities is presented the discussion will be organized to address the traits described previously. Refer to Figure 13.1.

In recent years, the JCAHO standards have evolved to set forth a broad framework for organizational effectiveness as opposed to a prior emphasis on department- or service-specific requirements. As

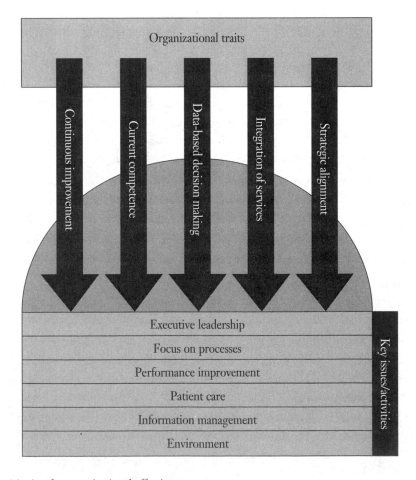

Figure 13.1. Positioning for organizational effectiveness.

a result, the standards are far less prescriptive or limiting with respect to implementation. As health care organizations vary in culture, size, and scope of services, resources, and so on, their approaches to achieving compliance also vary. The strategies discussed in this chapter are fairly universal and can be applied to almost any organization. They should be viewed as strategies for enhancing the effectiveness of the organization. A successful accreditation survey is merely a beneficial by-product.

Key Issues and Activities

Executive Leadership

The first step in moving the organization toward and even exceeding compliance with the JCAHO standards and sustaining that level of compliance over time is to address senior leadership roles, reporting relationships, and the manner in which the senior leaders support and build a culture that exhibits the traits of an effective organization.

JCAHO has defined a set of important functions or key processes of health care organizations, and through the accreditation survey process attempts to assess how effectively organizations perform these functions. Many organizations trip over poorly defined leadership responsibilities and traditional organization structures as they try to carry out these important functions. While certainly not an all-inclusive list, the following checkpoints are key to positioning your organization for compliance with JCAHO standards.

Strategic Alignment. The beginning point—regardless of the size, scope of services, or organization chart of the organization—is for the senior leaders to understand and fulfill their role in establishing the strategic direction for the organization. Board and executive management must clearly articulate the organization's mission, vision, values, and strategic goals and objectives.

Most health care organizations have defined or recently revised their mission, vision, and values either as part of their strategic planning process or as part of their implementation of total quality management. An all-too-common observation is that these are not compelling documents that guide and inspire. They tend to become decorations for the hallways—soon forgotten and most certainly overlooked in daily work and decision making.

To avoid such a fate, the mission, vision, and values must have meaning to executive management and to the rest of the organization. Meaning is often lost in vague wording and jargon not commonly used throughout the organization. Meaning is also lost for the organization as a whole when the senior leadership team fails to employ mission, vision, and values as a compass to provide direction in the decision-making process.

Mission, vision, values, and strategies are defined as follows:

- *Mission:* The mission should clearly and concisely define the purpose of the organization's existence. It should address the role of the organization in its community, answering the question, "Why are we here?"

- *Vision:* State the vision for the future in terms that are measurable and observable. Probably the most misunderstood of the planning documents, the vision statement should describe to the best of your knowledge how the organization will look, and what those who are associated with that organization will be doing, at some future point in time. As you evaluate your own vision statement, ask the question "Does the vision statement tell what you likely will be doing tomorrow that is different from today?"

- *Values:* Describe the behaviors that are expected of those working in the organization and the desired culture. Again, state them in clear terms, using observable examples to ensure consistency in interpretation across the organization. When establishing the organization's values, don't stop at the point of having articulated what you desire as a culture for the organization. Take the next step and measure the gap between the present state and the desired future state.

- *Strategic goals:* Strategic goals and objectives define the specific actions, usually with assigned accountability, that have top priority and will move the organization toward its vision. Develop the organization's strategic plan (goals, objectives, tactics) with the organization's key customers and key processes in mind. A process that incorporates the development of organizationwide or team goals and objectives, supported by department- or service-specific goals, is helpful in achieving strategic alignment.

Once meaningful mission, vision, values, and strategic objectives have been established, executive and middle management must devise a plan for communicating the strategic direction across the organization. The communication plan should include a variety of methods. Some that have proven effective are as follows:

- CEO meetings with employees

- Incorporating mission, vision, values, and key strategies in new employee orientation and reorientation for existing staff

- Department leaders facilitating discussions with staff around the application of the mission, vision, values, and key strategies in their departments

- Department leaders and staff articulating mission, vision, values, and key strategies for their departments or services based on the organizationwide documents

- Creation of a vision alignment matrix that identifies the organization's current key strategies and illustrates the relationship between performance improvement or other major team initiatives and those key strategies

- Direct feedback to staff during the performance evaluation regarding contribution to mission, vision, key strategies, or specific behaviors supporting the organization's values

- Daily role modeling and reinforcement by the leadership team

Various methods of posting these documents—for example, framed posters, displaying them on the back of employee name tags, coffee cups, and so on—can be valuable in creating reminders or points of reference for staff. However, these displays alone are not effective tools for building a common understanding within the ranks as to the purpose, strategic direction, or desired culture of the organization.

The vision, values, and strategic goals and objectives are often referred to as a road map that the organization follows. Effectively communicating that road map is essential to achieving strategic alignment. Once leaders below the level of executive management understand the strategic direction, they must operationalize them—using the mission, vision, values, and strategies as a test in the decision-making process—including resource allocation, new service development or changes to existing scope of services, measurement systems, performance improvement efforts, and staff development.

Integration of Services. Effective integration of the numerous departments and services within today's health care organization is not a trivial task. To be successful, integration must be an expectation at all levels of the organization. The values espoused by the organization should in some manner address integration as an expectation.

Both executive and middle managers have a responsibility to model the integrated behavior they expect to see demonstrated across the organization. It is unusual to find high levels of collaboration and teamwork sustained over time among the ranks when they are not practiced and part of the culture of the leaders at the top of the organization.

A crucial component of the integrated organization structure is the inclusion of the medical staff. The integration of the medical staff must be evident at all levels, including the following:

- Representation on the board and in board-level committees and functions

- Partnership between traditional administration and the leadership of the medical staff

- As the leader of and/or a participant on the patient care team

The integration of the medical staff includes

- Ownership in the mission, vision, values, and strategic direction of the organization

- Regular involvement and participation in the decision-making process

- Communication of performance measures related to progress toward the vision and strategies and the performance of the organization in general

The JCAHO standards clearly define the responsibilities of executive and medical staff leaders. It is common to see those responsibilities incorporated in the bylaws of a health care organization. However, when the integration of the medical staff falls short, the lack of integration is often a symptom of a lack of understanding and implementation of those responsibilities, both on the part of the executive managers and the appointed leaders of the medical staff.

Further down in the organization, integration is greatly impacted by the organizational relationships that have been imposed through the organization chart. Evaluate your organization's reporting relationships. Do they support integration of departments and services? Many health care organizations are leaving the traditional nursing/ancillary/support department structure for more integrated models based on service and product lines or clustering of clinical versus nonclinical areas.

Data-Based Decision Making. Executive leaders, including medical staff, should exercise restraint and make wise choices when selecting the data and information they will routinely review and assess regarding progress toward the vision and performance of the organization. The quality of the information and its relationship to the overall success of the organization should be elements of the selection process.

An important activity for any senior leadership team is identifying the critical success factors for the organization and establishing a process for generating a periodic scorecard of the organization's effectiveness. Indicators on the scorecard may include

- Measures based on the vision and/or strategic goals

- Organizationwide indicators of the performance of the important processes/functions of the organization

- Financial indicators
- Indicators of the satisfaction of the organization's most important customer groups

Build the process around an executive information system (manual or automated) that places current data for the critical success factors in the appropriate hands in a timely fashion. Establish the appropriate leadership forum(s) for evaluating and discussing the measures as a leadership team and for making informed decisions based on the data.

Leaders at all levels must be disciplined to demand (of themselves and others in the organization) the use of appropriate data in the decision-making process—again, modeling the behavior desired within the organization.

Current Competence. Two separate processes must be in place to ensure that the people who provide patient care (as well as nonclinical staff within the organization) possess appropriate qualifications and are competent in the work they perform. For the medical staff (including some nonphysician practitioners), there must be a sound credentialing and privileging process that verifies the credentials of physicians applying for appointment or reappointment to the medical staff and confirms that the individual's background and experience reflect competence relative to the privileges sought. For all others, there must be a job description–based performance evaluation and competency assessment. The organization's board and executive leaders are responsible for ensuring that these processes are in place and are carried out in a consistent fashion across the organization.

JCAHO requires that the following basic criteria be addressed.

- Current licensure
- Relevant training or experience
- Current competence
- Ability to perform the privileges requested

Key elements of the job description–based performance appraisal include the following:

- Adequate definition within the job description of the qualifications and scope of the work expected by job title (including ages of patients served for clinical positions)
- Identification of critical competencies for the position (unique to the position/department) addressing critical skills, knowledge, and critical thinking/decision making
- Periodic assessment of the individual's performance of the defined job responsibilities and verification of the critical competencies
- Thorough orientation of new employees to their assigned function/department
- Performance improvement/quality assessment data incorporated with the employee appraisal process

As these processes for assessing the performance of individuals providing care and services within the organization are implemented, leadership should review and consider aggregate data relative to performance and competency and prioritize staff development investments, in-service, and continuing education accordingly.

Continuous improvement. A major component of the JCAHO accreditation survey has always been the assessment and improvement of the quality of patient care. Though somewhat different in perspective, performance improvement is still a critical piece. Relative to executive leadership roles, the board and executive management team must create a linkage between quality management or performance improvement activities and the vision and key strategies of the organization.

Failure to establish congruence between strategy and performance improvement spells future apathy, if not disaster, for the quality management function. Similarly, the organization becomes frustrated in its attempt to achieve the future vision and key strategies when important systems and processes fail to perform at desired levels of quality and customer satisfaction.

Strategic planning by the executive team should set the agenda for managing for quality through the identification of a set of quality goals or priorities for performance improvement. These articulate to the entire organization where performance improvement energy will focus. This important step is often overlooked by health care executives.

To determine whether your organization has adequately established a relationship between the strategic plan and the performance improvement function, create a matrix of key strategies and performance improvement efforts similar to the one in Figure 13.2. There should be a strong relationship between each of the high-profile, interdisciplinary improvement efforts and at least one of the key strategies of the organization.

Quality planning and improvement projects	Key strategies				Important functions									
	Develop an integrated delivery system	Improve E.D. image in community	Decrease cost of poor quality	Develop cardiac center of excellence	Patients rights and ethics	Assessment of patients	Care of patients	Education of patients and families	Continuum of care	Improving organizational performance leadership	Mgt. of environment of care	Mgt. of human resources	Mgt. of information	Surveillance, prevention, and control of infections
Reduce E.D. waits		●				●								
Reduce E.D. admit time		●							●					
Hip replacement path	)		●			●	)	)						
C-section path	)		●			●	●	●						
Design physician office info system	●												●	
Improve TPA admin time			●			●	●							
CABG path	)		●				●	)						

● = High impact   ) = Moderate impact

Figure 13.2. Performance improvement priorities matrix.

Focus on Processes

Recognizing that the important work accomplished in an organization takes place between departments and functions in major processes as opposed to within a single department, JCAHO set out to identify and build standards around the key processes or important functions of the health care organization. JCAHO's list of important functions includes the following related to the care of the patient.

Patient-focused

- Patients' rights and organization ethics
- Assessment of patients
- Care of patients
- Education
- Continuum of care

JCAHO has also defined a set of important functions that otherwise support the provision of patient care.

Organization

- Improving organization performance leadership
- Management of environment of care
- Management of human resources
- Management of information
- Surveillance, prevention, and control of infections

It is a significant accomplishment when the organization is able to recognize the value of focusing attention on its key processes and the management of processes versus departments.

Strategic Alignment. It has already been mentioned that the senior leadership team's role is to establish priorities for improving performance. As the organization makes the transition away from emphasizing departmental operations to managing the key processes that cross departmental lines, those decisions regarding where to initiate design and improvement efforts for the key processes or important functions should be based on the future vision and strategic goals and objectives. You can't do everything at once; prioritize based on vision and strategy.

Does the organization's vision for the future point toward managing care outside the walls of the hospital? If so, leaders and those involved in managing the important functions should begin to evaluate the impact on design and improvement of the important functions when the continuum of care extends beyond traditional boundaries. For example, an element of providing for and protecting the rights of patients is the communication and fulfillment of a patient's advance directives. When the hospital expands its horizons into the home care and hospice components of the health care delivery system, a reasonable expectation is that accurate information regarding the patient's advance directives flows with the patient regardless of the setting and that patient care providers are properly informed. Thus, design and improvement efforts would likely include participants from the hospital, home care provider, and hospice working together to design a process that provides accurate and timely communication and documentation of a patient's wishes regardless of the setting of care.

Integration of Services. Integration of services lies at the heart of any organization's initiative to focus on processes. A cultural change must occur for those with ownership in the traditional department management structure to begin to support the emphasis on managing processes. Beyond modeling collaborative behavior at the senior management level, education and communication that focus attention on a clear vision for the organization's future and recognition of customer requirements are key. Building incentives around collaboration and team goals can also yield positive results.

As the organization begins to recognize and emphasize its key processes, it will begin to uncover variation in the performance of those processes across the organization. JCAHO expects and requires by standard the "uniform performance of patient care." The same concept can be applied to nonclinical functions; that is, a nonclinical process such as providing for and documenting orientation of new employees should be implemented consistently across the organization. A new electrician in the engineering department has no less need for orientation to patients' rights issues, safety hazards, normal operating procedures within the department, and so on than a staff nurse on a patient care unit. The content of the orientation will vary by functional area and job responsibilities. The process for developing the content, providing the orientation, creating supplemental materials for the employee, and documenting the results of orientation should be consistent.

The practice in the past was to have department-specific policies and procedures. The requirement for uniform performance and emphasis on the important functions or key processes leads an organization to fewer department-specific policies and procedures and more global, organizationwide policies. Examples include the use of conscious sedation, providing for patients' rights, maintaining confidentiality of patient and organization-sensitive data, assessment prior to an invasive procedure, and so on.

Leadership must carefully plan the transition toward focus on and management of processes organizationwide. One approach has been to appoint process teams responsible for guiding the organization through the transition relative to a specific important function or key process. Tasks include the following:

- Establish a clear definition of each important function that the organization will understand and identify with.

- Inventory the policies and procedures across the organization (existing within various departments) related to the important function, looking for opportunities to replace department policies and procedures with organizationwide policies and procedures.

- Identify the variations in practice/performance of the function, targeting those that must be brought to consistency.

- Inventory the various measurements (typically department quality indicators) of the important function and identify which, if any, would serve as a key organizationwide indicator of the performance of the function.

- Identify what improvement efforts are currently underway, recently completed, or planned for the important function.

The overall goals should be to provide for uniform performance of the function across the organization, establish a measure(s) to provide ongoing assessment of the performance of the function, and provide support to any performance improvement efforts underway.

Data-Based Decision Making. If the organization is truly committed to taking action and basing decisions on data, the focus on important functions and key processes should include sound data collection and assessment of the performance of these functions. It is usually revealing to take an inventory of data collected across the organization to identify and categorize the existing measurements in place related to the important functions. The data gathered might include process measures, assessing the steps in the process and verifying that the process performs as intended (for example, how long customers wait for service, how long it takes to complete a certain step, and so on) and outcome measures, addressing the end results (such as costs, revenue generated, customer satisfaction, and mortality).

If there are no measures, develop them with input from individuals whose job it is to make the process work. Some of the important functions or key processes are less likely to be measured in existing measurement systems. An overabundance of data are collected relative to utilization of clinical resources, unexpected outcomes, and other indicators and screens that have been established under traditional quality assurance programs. Measurement of indicators of process performance related to patients' rights, leadership, or improving organizational performance are less prevalent.

Current Competence. Traditional performance evaluation and competency assessment for hospital staff center around the department or service in which the employee resides. A challenge for complex organizations attempting to achieve uniform performance of key processes across the organization is to establish consistency in assessing staff competency relative to the performance of cross-functional processes when staff reside in multiple departments. For example, the nursing department will often implement comprehensive competency testing related to medications, addressing the process to follow for medication administration, dosing for emergency medications, monitoring for adverse effects, and so on. Nurses and other clinical professionals in nonnursing departments are responsible for being competent in medication administration, but may not be held to the same standards because the testing is focused on the department rather than important functions.

As the organization begins to increase its focus on processes and managing the effectiveness of its important functions, the critical competency issues for each process should be identified and implemented for staff working in those processes, regardless of the department considered home base.

Continuous Improvement. Those who are charged with oversight and leadership for the organization's important functions should strive for ongoing continuous improvement. Target an important function for dramatic improvement or intensive redesign efforts when called for by the organization's vision and strategic plan. Look for opportunities to replicate improvements in an important function that might have been identified and implemented in one part of the organization but was overlooked in other areas where the process is also performed.

Performance Improvement

JCAHO uses the term *improving organizational performance* for the important function that might be defined as managing for quality or implementing the principles of total quality management (TQM) on an ongoing basis. Within the scope of this function lies planning for and designing new processes and services, problem solving and continuously improving existing processes and services, and quality control activities associated with the measurement and analysis of data reflecting the performance of processes.

The management and improvement of quality has always been a major focus of accreditation surveys by JCAHO and therefore warrants both close attention and participation by the leadership of the organization.

Strategic Alignment. It is absolutely essential to have a direct linkage between the organization's quality management or performance improvement function and the organization's strategic plan and vision of the future. As noted previously, the executive management team is where this generally occurs.

It is not uncommon to see the quality council of a health care organization deploying teams to work on process improvements and tracking the progress of improvement efforts that offer little correlation to the strategic imperatives that drive all of their other actions and decisions. These organizations fail the test of strategic alignment.

Does the performance improvement function within your organization fail the test of strategic alignment? Symptoms to watch for include the following:

- Poor attendance of the organization's leaders at meetings whose agendas include improvement team reports or planning for new performance improvement teams (poor attendance can be masked by mandatory quality council meetings)

- Performance improvement teams that never end

- Failure to show any measurement of the impact of the improvements implemented

- Declining enthusiasm for performance improvement across the organization

- Leaders of the organization have difficulty answering the question, "What have been our most significant improvements during the past year?"

JCAHO requires delineation of a set of priorities for performance improvement. It is through this exercise that leaders often begin to appreciate the importance of the linkage between strategy and performance improvement and the potential impact the performance improvement function can have for the organization. Figure 13.3 provides an example of criteria a leadership team might use to prioritize improvement projects and develop its list of priorities for improvement. Regardless of the methodology used, the end result must be performance improvement activities that specifically address the organization's strategic goals and objectives.

Integration of Services. In a health care organization, performance improvement must be a collaborative effort between the hospital departments and services (as well as other providers, such as home care or long-term care) and the medical staff. In the beginning stages of TQM implementation, many hospitals choose to postpone involvement of the medical staff until the organization has demonstrated a successful implementation. The result has been duplication of effort as the TQM function has grown and more traditional medical staff monitoring and evaluation activities have also remained intact.

Bringing the two together can be a challenge. There is fear that additional work is being added to the time physicians already spend in committees and performance improvement activities. Turf battles create resistance to the merger of the two entities that have been mutually exclusive for a period of several years. Some fear letting go of activities long promoted as "required by JCAHO."

The first step toward leaving these obstacles behind and implementing a fully integrated performance improvement function is to ensure that there is a senior leadership coordinating group or

Criteria	Explanation
Relationship to vision/strategies	Extent to which project will enable the organization to achieve some component of the future vision or current strategic objectives.
Chronic problem	Are there data to substantiate that the problem is a chronic one that has not been resolved in prior attempts?
Potential cost impact	Expected significance of results relative to cost
Potential clinical quality impact	Expected significance of results relative to the quality of patient care
Potential customer service impact	Expected significance of results relative to customer service measures
Key customer issue	Extent to which the project addresses needs of key customer group(s)—internal or external
Key process impact	Extent to which the project improves performance of one of the organization's key processes
Probability of success	Likelihood of success, including the ability to overcome resistance to change and political barriers

Figure 13.3. Criteria for prioritizing performance improvement projects.

council that is itself fully integrated. All departments or functions, including the medical staff, should be represented. This doesn't mean there should be a representative from every department of the organization, but rather someone at an administrative level providing representation.

In beginning stages, most organizations established a quality council to oversee the implementation of TQM and the quality management activities of the organization. The long-term goal should be to have performance improvement/quality management activities so well integrated with the ongoing management of the organization that a separate quality council and quality council meetings are not needed.

Performance improvement and managing for quality occur on at least two distinct planes within a health care organization.

- *Organizationwide*—Highly collaborative and cross-functional design, measurement, assessment, and improvement efforts relative to the organization's important processes or functions.

- *Departmental*—Each leader/manager monitors and continuously improves the quality of the services provided within his/her own area of responsibility.

Other levels begin to emerge as organizations become experienced and more sophisticated in their approach to quality management, reflecting the complexity and various subdivisions of the organizational structure. These additional levels of measurement and improvement might include multidepartment divisions, business units, or service lines.

The greatest impact will usually be with the organizationwide performance improvement activities, assuming that they are strategically aligned. The senior leadership should focus attention on these organizationwide activities, while ensuring that mechanisms are in place to facilitate, encourage, and support the other less-strategic activity.

Integration and collaboration are implemented at the grassroots level through the use of teams that are chartered or deployed to investigate improvement opportunities and recommend process changes. Teams can include not only traditional continuous quality improvement (CQI) teams, but also planning teams designing new processes or service lines for the organization, clinical pathway teams, or reengineering teams.

Successful integration of the medical staff often calls for a reevaluation of committee structure. Committees put in place to satisfy JCAHO standards in years past (such as the surgical case review committee) may no longer add value, especially if the monitoring, evaluation, and improvement activities once assigned to these committees are taking place within other interdisciplinary teams (for example, clinical process improvement teams or clinical pathway teams). Evaluating and streamlining the committee structure helps to overcome some of the integration obstacles.

Data-Based Decision Making. A primary objective of the organization's performance improvement initiative should be to establish a precedent within the organization for measuring and basing decisions on sound data and information. In fact, improving the management of information is a worthy improvement priority for most organizations.

Measurement should be systematic. Most health care organizations are inundated with measurement that originated in the early days of JCAHO standards for quality assurance. Most admit that it is of little value. To be truly systematic in your approach to measurement, you must begin to take on the task of inventorying existing measurement activity, evaluating each indicator's contribution to the assessment of the performance of the important functions, and revising the measurement to eliminate wasted effort and ensure comprehensive assessment of performance across the organization.

Figure 13.4 shows a format for inventorying the performance measures of the important functions organizationwide. This approach makes it easy to verify that there are indicators for each of the important functions and the relationship of the specific measures back to the organization's strategic objectives.

As noted, quality management occurs on at least two levels in the organization. Measurement is similarly structured. There should be indicators that are reviewed routinely by the senior leaders of the organization as they monitor the performance of the organization as a whole and progress toward the future vision. There should also be indicators tracked by individual department or function leaders as they monitor the performance of their areas of responsibility.

A common practice in many health care organizations, which is a holdover from early quality assurance initiatives, is to have a senior-level meeting to review department-level performance data. That activity has yielded very little benefit in the past. The department- and service-specific performance data should be reviewed and discussed as part of the ongoing review of operations between a department leader and his or her immediate supervisor. Should the department-level monitoring activity identify significant improvement opportunities that cross department boundaries, those issues can and should be brought to a higher level for prioritization and determination of a course of action.

In addition to the ongoing measurement and assessment activities of the organization, performance improvement teams should have structured processes to follow that guide them through appropriate data collection, assessment, and analysis to support accurately identifying the root causes of poor performance and making sound recommendations for process improvement. Juran Institute's QI Process, for example, guides quality improvement teams through a sequence of steps—analysis of symptoms, testing theories, proving effectiveness of solutions, and so on—with emphasis on using data to ensure that the team is in fact moving toward achieving its objective. The group coordinating the organization's performance improvement efforts and responsible for deploying performance improvement teams should be firm in its expectation that teams be rigorous in their measurement and assessment efforts.

Performance improvement data inventory				Important function measured										
Indicator	Where measured	Frequency	Where reported	Patients' rights	Assessment	Care of patient	Education	Continuum of care	Improving performance	Leadership	Mgt. of environment	Mgt. of human resources	Mgt. of information	Infection control

Figure 13.4. Matrix of performance improvement indicators.

A key step in implementing an effective performance improvement function is the development of internal resources for basic statistical analysis of data. Data-based decision making relies on sound data that are analyzed with proper statistical tools. Health care organizations have typically been weak in this area. You can strengthen your organization's capability for assessing data by

- Acquiring the tools and training resources to support the proper analysis of data
- Training leaders and others who routinely collect and assess data in basic statistical methods so that they are able to use the tools
- Training all leaders and staff who work with data to interpret the output of the analytical tools

Leaders of the organization should challenge themselves to model the desired behavior, using the statistical tools and expecting others to use them as well.

Along with the systematic measurement of performance and the use of appropriate statistical tools to transform the data into useful information, an effective performance improvement function depends on valid external comparisons of the organization's performance data. Assessing performance by simply comparing one's own data over time yields opportunities for improvement—up to a point. More dramatic opportunities for improvement have been uncovered by making external comparisons.

Current Competence. Assessment of the performance and competence of medical staff and health care employees should incorporate data generated through the organization's performance improvement activities. Those responsible for gathering and providing data within the organization must exercise caution, however, to ensure that data reflecting the performance of an individual are presented and discussed in the proper setting.

Teams and other multidisciplinary groups should focus attention on aggregate data reflecting how a process works. Data related to the performance of an individual should follow a flow designed by the organization that channels physician-specific data through the organization's peer review and reappointment process and channels hospital employee data into the hands of the appropriate manager. Trends related to performance across the organization—that is, more than one employee/physician— should also trigger organizationwide staff development and education activities.

Continuous Improvement. Improvement means results. Results should be seen on at least two levels in the organization. Most critically, there should be evidence of improvement in the important organizationwide functions. These results should address the organization's priorities for improvement, linked to the vision and key strategies. Additionally, there should be evidence all around the organization of the results of the empowerment of departments and staff to implement improvements within their areas of responsibility as opportunities are identified.

Leadership should periodically assess the effectiveness of the quality management function and revise the process as needed. As with the other key processes or important functions of the organization, the function of improving and managing quality can also be assessed and improved.

The assessment of the performance improvement function should address each of the major elements defined in the JCAHO standards, namely,

- *Plan:* How well has the overall infrastructure and plan worked? What further changes will be implemented to continue the transition to a single, coordinated performance improvement function?

- *Design:* To what extent have the major new service implementations been driven by customer expectations? Have the tools and methods of quality improvement been applied in new service design? Have the design efforts been collaborative, with representation from the appropriate disciplines?

- *Measure:* How effective have the current scorecards been? Are the organizationwide measures truly reflecting the performance of the important functions? Are there other aspects of the important functions that should be monitored in addition to or instead of those that have been monitored? Are all departments/services appropriately monitoring their individual performance?

- *Assess:* Are those responsible for the assessment of performance improvement data, both organizationwide and departmental, using appropriate statistical methods? Have more intensive reviews been initiated when assessment shows a significant variation or opportunity to improve? Are the sentinel events and variations listed in the JCAHO standards (adverse drug reactions and so on) assessed as required?

- *Improve:* Where has there been impact? Are teams establishing measurement activities that will enable the leadership to determine the amount of improvement resulting from process changes? Have actual improvements been documented for each of the improvement priorities and to the extent desired? How many of the important functions have been improved? Is there evidence throughout the organization of the philosophy of continuous improvement put into action by an empowered workforce?

The assessment of performance improvement function effectiveness should not simply be a written report providing evidence that the exercise was performed, but, more importantly, should result in changes implemented to the process that will provide measurable and observable increases in function effectiveness from that point forward.

Patient Care

JCAHO has identified the following patient-focused functions related to the clinical care of the patient and the involvement of the family.

- Patients' rights and organization ethics
- Assessment of patients
- Care of patients
- Education
- Continuum of care

Rather than address these individually, this section explores the interaction between the organizational traits that are so critical to a successful survey and all of these patient-focused functions as a whole.

Strategic Alignment. The organization's strategic plan should address all of the important functions or key processes, including those related to the care of the patient. Important patient groups or customers of the organization should be identified in the planning process. The plan should then provide guidance regarding future initiatives in the design and improvement of patient care processes in order to meet the needs of the important customers.

Another consideration for the organization as it strives to demonstrate strategic alignment in the provision of patient care is the application of the organization's values in the performance of the patient care processes. How will the staff operationalize the desired values of the organization as they carry out these patient care processes? If the values of the organization include respect and compassion in care delivery, or teamwork and collaboration with other health care professionals, how are staff coached and provided direction regarding how these behaviors should be demonstrated?

One approach is to have team leaders and middle managers facilitate dialogue with staff emphasizing the organization's values and allowing the staff to articulate specific examples of each value put into practice in daily work. Recognizing and celebrating shining examples of staff living the desired values helps illustrate how to operationalize the values and reinforces their importance. Leaders should also provide direct feedback and coaching when opportunities to demonstrate the desired values are missed.

Integration of Services. Collaboration in the provision of patient care is expected. Very few patients come into a health care organization and receive care from a single discipline. Whether formally or informally, patient care is usually provided by a team of health care professionals. Effective teams establish goals and plans for the care of the patient that are commonly shared. Clinical pathways are an excellent tool for establishing, documenting, and communicating interdisciplinary goals and plans for patient care. When these tools have not yet been implemented, other interdisciplinary patient care planning sessions and interdisciplinary charting formats are excellent avenues for supporting collaboration among disciplines.

As the organization promotes collaboration among patient care providers, the uniform performance of patient care processes can also be addressed. As previously noted, this is of particular interest to JCAHO survey teams. The health care organization must establish requirements for qualifications and specific care standards for the key patient care processes performed in various locations by various kinds of staff. Once these care standards are defined, the expectation is that they will be implemented consistently regardless of the locale.

Ensure that consistency is achieved through the following:

- Organizationwide policies and procedures instead of individual department policies and procedures for the patient care processes performed in multiple sites

- Adequate orientation, training, and—where justified—competency testing to ensure that staff participating in the process are skilled and knowledgeable

- Measurement of critical steps or outcomes related to the process, sampling from each location where the process is performed

- Feedback to caregivers regarding performance against the organization's standards

Data-Based Decision Making. Within the patient-focused functions, data-based decision making can be viewed from two perspectives. First are the patient-specific decisions made by the care team—implementing a plan of care based on diagnostic data and observations of a specific patient. There are various checkpoints and controls in place to verify that procedures and therapies implemented are appropriate based on clinical findings. Traditional quality assurance and peer review systems have been established to identify patterns of care that vary from generally accepted norms.

The second area of data-based decision making relates to the design and implementation of patient care *processes* rather than the care of an individual patient. As noted, one method of ensuring consistency in the performance of a patient care process across the organization is to have a measurement system that monitors critical steps in the process and/or process outcomes from each of the various sites where the process occurs. In health care there has been much more of a focus in the past on having sufficient patient-specific data and on gathering data on a case-by-case basis for peer review purposes than on establishing sound controls to measure the performance of a process organization-wide. This is where there is work to be done.

The systematic measurement of the performance of key processes described in the "Performance Improvement" section should be implemented for the important patient care functions. Accurately measure the level of performance of each patient-focused process. Rather than duplicating or increasing the volume of measurements, incorporate whenever possible the existing measurements from sources such as clinical pathway teams, risk management, utilization review, medical record review, or department-based monitoring activity. Assess both process performance and outcomes. Empower caregivers to continuously improve by routinely providing feedback regarding their performance. Leaders of these processes should also look for improvement opportunities by benchmarking and comparing data externally.

Current Competence. There is no other area where having mechanisms in place to ensure current competency is more important than in the patient-focused functions. It is also an area that has confounded many hospitals.

JCAHO's publication *Perspectives* listed competence assessment as number two in the top 10 problematic standards for hospitals.[1] This finding is based on survey results for the first half of 1995.

A starting point for organizations that have not been able to make progress in establishing a mechanism for assessing competency includes the following suggestions.

- Identify patient care processes that, for the organization or for certain categories of employees, occur infrequently and present high risk to patients or staff.

- Recognize age-related issues in the performance of patient care processes, where skills and knowledge required vary with the age of the patient.

- Provide for consistency across the organization in competency expectations and measurement.

Continuous Improvement. As the organization implements performance improvement, focusing on the important functions and the strategically selected priorities for improvement, there will most certainly be activity within the patient-focused functions. One caution: Don't confuse process changes with improvement. Challenge and expect the teams redesigning and improving patient care processes (clinical pathway teams, CQI teams, reengineering teams, and so on) to measure the amount of improvement and impact on patient care and outcomes.

Identify at the beginning of the improvement effort the desired amount of improvement in the process or patient outcome. Establish measurements that will allow the organization to determine whether those targets have been achieved.

Information Management

The impact of the organizational trait of data-based decision making is seen throughout the key activities and elements of the health care organization. While JCAHO has always given attention to the documentation of patient care in the medical record, just since the initiation of the Agenda for Change has it begun to recognize the importance of sound practices and well-planned processes for managing information, both clinical and nonclinical, across the organization.

Strategic Alignment. The leadership of the health care organization must assess the capabilities of its information systems, including both automated and manual components, compared to the future vision and strategic goals and objectives it seeks to achieve. Medical staff participation in the assessment, as primary customers and suppliers within the management of information function, is key. While conducting the assessment of current capabilities, consider the extent to which the present capabilities provide the data and information needed to track progress toward the organization's future vision and key strategies.

The output of the planning process should be an established set of priorities for closing the gap between current capabilities and desired capabilities. These priorities and plans for developing the information management function should be integrated with the overall strategic goals and objectives of the organization and its corresponding priorities for performance improvement. This connection must be made to achieve strategic alignment.

Integration of Services. Data and information systems must be integrated. Performance of patient care processes often depends on the transfer and integration of clinical data residing in the information systems in various departments. Clinical data originating and/or maintained in one department can impact the patient care provided by another. Examples include drug orders that create dietary restrictions to avoid drug-food interaction or results from laboratory tests that provide guidance in accurately dosing medications.

There are also integration issues to address between health care professionals as they collaborate on the care of specific patients. This information integration takes place within the medical record. Approaches frequently seen include multidisciplinary progress notes, patient education documentation, and assessment forms.

Data-Based Decision Making. The most basic first step toward implementation of this trait relative to the management of information is to provide decision makers with good data. The JCAHO standards specify the critical factors to address, including uniformity in data definitions and reliable data collection methods. Well-established standardized coding schemes and data definitions are used for uniform reporting of specific data elements for health care organizations, and yet it is not uncommon to see conflicting data within a hospital regarding, for example, the number of admissions during a specified period of time or the number of outpatient visits or births because of unique definitions within different departments or services or varying data-gathering methods. Several methods for overcoming this problem include the following:

- Internally publish a dictionary of data definitions for the vital few or most frequently measured and reported statistics.

- Include in the dictionary of data definitions and the formulas for correctly performing some of the frequently used calculations such as length of stay, adjusted patient day, or full-time equivalent employee.

- Eliminate unnecessary or duplicative measurement activity.

External benchmarking has already been identified as an important component of data-based decision making. Again, sound decision making should encompass a comparison of performance to others external to the organization, rather than solely a comparison of the organization to itself over time.

Establish through policy and process a means for ensuring confidentiality when sharing data outside the organization. Enhance the value of comparisons through careful understanding of the data element definitions and accurately mapping your data to the database.

Current Competence. Identify places within the organization where information management processes constitute core competencies for staff. Ensure that the leaders who must make decisions based on data, and the staff who gather data analyze it, and make decisions, are competent in measurement and statistical tools. A well-rounded training program to develop competencies around information management might include the following:

- Review and discussion of the organization's data definitions and standard coding schemes for commonly used data elements and internal sources for data and information

- Data collection methodologies, including design of data collection tools, sampling, and data stratification

- Basic statistical analysis, including how to use and interpret analytical tools such as control charts, Pareto analysis, histograms, and so on

- Instruction in software applications that support the analytical tools

Continuous Improvement. As with the other key processes of the organization, strive for continuous improvement in all aspects of information management. Focus resources through cross-functional teams as called for in the organization's priorities for improvement. As with other important functions, measure the amount of improvement, identifying where possible the improved outcomes as the information management processes improve.

Environment

Managing the environment within the health care organization is a function that has received significant attention from JCAHO because of the potentially significant impact to patients, visitors, and staff when defects exist related to the environment or when staff are ill-prepared to deal with emergency situations related to the environment, such as fire, chemical spills, and so on.

Strategic Alignment. JCAHO requires that the organization establish specific plans, policies, and procedures that provide for the proper management of the care environment. These should reflect the mission and vision of the organization. For example, if the future vision addresses the development of patient care services provided within the home that make use of staff and equipment from the health care organization, the plan for managing medical equipment should encompass the proper orientation and training of staff working in the home care environment regarding safe use of the equipment and guidelines for ensuring that equipment placed in a patient's home is safe and functioning properly.

JCAHO's definition of the environment of care includes the following seven components.

- Safety
- Security
- Control of hazardous materials and waste
- Emergency preparedness
- Life safety
- Medical equipment
- Utility systems

The strategic planning process carried out by the organization's leadership should take into consideration a current assessment of the environment of care. All of the components listed should be assessed. Priorities for improvement should be established as needed.

Integration of Services. Implementing the plans, policies, and procedures that provide for a safe care environment is a task requiring participation and cooperation from all departments and services. Thus, deficiencies in integration and collaboration between departments are often readily apparent through carefully observing the environment and the results of monitoring response to emergency drills or actual emergency situations.

Assuming a culture exists that promotes integration and collaboration, the key to achieving collaboration in the management of the care environment is the clear definition of roles and responsibilities, with feedback regarding performance. These roles and responsibilities are spelled out in the care environment plans, policies, and procedures. When roles and responsibilities are unique to a department or service, such as security issues related to abduction prevention in the nursery and pediatrics ward, department-specific plans and/or policies are required to spell out those unique elements.

Data-Based Decision Making. Information and data requirements relative to management of the care environment should be considered in the assessment of the organization's information management function. A comprehensive data collection and assessment process, measuring the performance of the organization implementing the care environment plans, is required. JCAHO has specified several categories of performance standards that should be monitored. Some of these are staff knowledge and skills, staff participation, monitoring and inspection activities related to the specific components of the environment of care, and emergency and incident reporting.

Most of the monitoring elements listed in the accreditation manual are currently measured in health care organizations. An inventory of indicators and measurement activity similar to the one described in the "Performance Improvement" section will identify gaps and will be helpful in implementing a systematic process for data collection. Look for opportunities to

- Combine and streamline data collection.
- Make use of existing data sources.
- Employ random sampling techniques to ensure that data collection is cost-effective.

Current Competence. Staff knowledge regarding management of the care environment is critical to the successful implementation of the care environment plans. The term *staff* includes students, volunteers, and members of the medical staff. Staff should be well-informed regarding response to emergency situations, the risks inherent in their daily work environment (to themselves, as well as to patients and visitors), and their roles and responsibilities in the implementation of procedures to ensure a safe environment.

Continuous Improvement. JCAHO expects an annual evaluation of the effectiveness of care environment plan implementation using the performance standards mentioned. Each of the seven components should be specifically and thoroughly assessed. Where opportunities for improvement are identified, some plan of action should be formulated for follow-up. Where improvements are cited, data must be provided measuring the amount of improvement.

Note

1. *Joint Commission Perspectives*, January/February 1996.

Howard B. Nussman, vice president and principal at Premier, is responsible for training and consulting services for Premier owner organizations in the areas of organizational effectiveness, accreditation, and quality management. He works closely with executives and middle managers to build effective leadership teams, implement approaches for total quality management, and foster collaboration in process design.

In 1991, Nussman assumed the role of director of quality services to lead the development of an array of programs and services for alliance partners to support their TQM implementation. These programs and services included a partnership agreement for quality training and support through Juran Institute, regional roundtable/educational meetings for quality professionals, 60 quality improvement demonstration projects to explore the applicability of quality methods in solving chronic process failures, development of a set of criteria based on the Malcolm Baldrige National Quality Award criteria for health care providers to use in assessing organizational effectiveness, and quality workshops and forums for showcasing partner hospitals' lessons learned.

For more than 10 years he has provided consultation and training to health care organizations as they prepare for accreditation surveys from the Joint Commission. As the leader of Premier's presurvey team, he helps organizations assess their current level of compliance with accreditation standards and develop strategies for overcoming areas of weakness.

Nussman joined Premier, formerly SunHealth, in 1978 to provide systems improvement consultation to members of the health care alliance. He earned a bachelor's degree from the Georgia Institute of Technology and a master of science in health systems degree, also from Georgia Tech.

Chapter 14

Using the Malcolm Baldrige National Quality Award Process to Stimulate Organizational Excellence

Ellen J. Gaucher

As organizations in all industries struggle to deal with rapid environmental change, the importance of a continuous improvement philosophy becomes apparent. To compete in ever-changing markets, organizations must produce high-quality products and services at a reasonable price. Outstanding product quality and service translates into enhanced customer satisfaction, customer loyalty, and increased market share. Data also exist indicating that quality improvement can enhance profitability. Figure 14.1 shows how both conformance to quality—meeting customer needs—and perceived quality—exceeding customer needs—can improve organizational profitability.

In today's environment, executives place greater scrutiny on new and existing products, services, and programs. Accordingly, they may also examine their quality programs to assess their effectiveness and return on investment. Key questions in such an assessment include the following:

- Is there a way to evaluate your improvement process?

- Are you exceeding customer requirements?

- How do your customer approaches compare with those of world-class companies?

- Can you determine how embedded your quality initiative is in the corporate culture?

- Is there a way to determine existing areas for improvement that, when addressed, will greatly strengthen your progress?

- Are quality efforts providing a positive return on investment?

Clearly, other questions will emerge as well. Fortunately there is a sound, well-tested quality assessment approach embraced across the spectrum of industries. Since 1987, the Malcolm Baldrige National Quality Award criteria have been recognized as the preeminent approach for quality assessment in industry. This chapter examines the evolution of U.S. quality approaches and assessment in industry and health care. It then explores the Baldrige Award framework and how the criteria can be used to evaluate and improve organizations. Next, it suggests key steps to follow when embarking on a self-assessment or preparing a Baldrige Award–based application. Finally, it offers questions for executives, the Board of Directors, and process owners to consider in preparing for an assessment process.

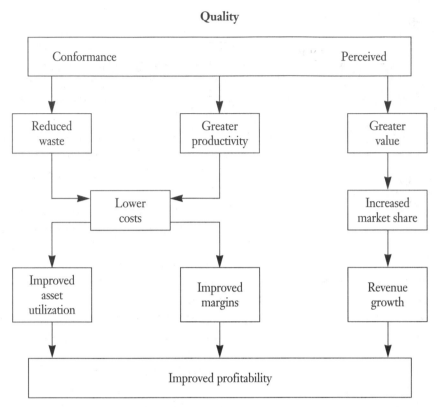

Quality

Source: S. George and A. Weimerskirch, *Total Quality Management: Strategies and Techniques Proven at Today's Most Successful Companies* (New York: John Wiley & Sons, 1994), 8.

Figure 14.1. The relationship between quality and profitability: Quality improvement increases profitability.

Quality Progress in the United States

After World War II, two American quality leaders began assisting the Japanese with rebuilding their industrial base. W. Edwards Deming and Joseph M. Juran brought the principles of quality management to Japan. For many years American industry ignored the teachings of Deming and Juran. Then, in 1951, Juran wrote *The Quality Control Handbook.* He proposed that quality ought not to be seen solely as an expense, but as an investment in profitability. He argued that avoidable quality losses were, in fact, a business unto themselves; care in reducing them had the potential, by his calculations, of saving as much as $1000 per worker per year.[1] Other experts, such as Armand Feigenbaum and Philip B. Crosby, joined Deming and Juran in the call for a more formal approach to quality management. While their approaches varied, each of these experts encouraged attention to quality improvement and cost reduction.

In the 1980s, the United States slipped into a deep recession. The emerging global marketplace weakened the dominance of American products. Better-quality products at lower prices were becoming available worldwide in a variety of industries. The significant market penetration of Japanese products has been well-documented. It was obvious to almost everyone that new, more effective approaches were necessary to help American products compete more effectively.

In 1987 Ronald Reagan signed the Malcolm Baldrige Quality Improvement Act into law, and a new era in American industry began. The purpose of the award, named after a former Secretary of Commerce, was to stimulate and promote total quality management as an approach to improve the competitiveness of American industry. The responsibility for the award process was entrusted to what is now the National Institute of Standards and Technology (NIST). NIST, collaborating with industry and academic experts, defined the criteria and the process. American Soceity for Quality assists NIST in administering the award process. The Baldrige Award board of examiners evaluates applications, prepares feedback reports, completes site visits, and makes recommendations on winning companies to the Secretary of Commerce and ultimately to the U.S. President. There are 270 examiners, 50 senior examiners, and nine judges on the board. These individuals, selected through a competitive process, come from industry, academia, and consulting.

The Baldrige Award will be 10 years old in 1997, and there have been many changes to the award process. What started out as an incremental approach of statistical analysis, quality training, and a team approach to improvement has become a sophisticated means for monitoring and achieving organizational excellence. Juran, one of the leading quality experts and consultants for more than 50 years, related in a recent interview that "Right now the most complete list of actions to achieve world class quality are contained in the Malcolm Baldrige National Quality Award."[2] Mark Graham Brown, a Baldrige Award examiner and consultant, notes that "The Baldrige has done more to improve the quality of U.S. products and services than anything that has come before it. Quality is now something that almost every company in America is working on."[3]

The Baldrige Award is the most imitated quality award in the world. Baldrige Award–based awards have been established in more than 40 states and communities in the United States. Many countries, including Argentina, Brazil, Canada, and India, have established similar awards, and the Baldrige Award criteria also serve as the basis for the European Quality Award. In addition, many organizations have internal Baldrige Award–based processes. Companies such as Baxter Healthcare, Johnson & Johnson, IBM, Whirlpool, and Kodak regularly use the criteria for self-assessment and improvement.

History of the Baldrige Award in Health Care

Many health care organizations have used the Baldrige Award criteria to complete an organizational assessment. The Baldrige Award criteria are a validated set of measures that allow you to measure the effectiveness and efficiency of institutional processes. Assessment isn't a new strategy for the health care industry. Health care organizations have used quality assessments since the Joint Commission on Accreditation of Healthcare Organizations (JCAHO) was formed in 1915. However, the JCAHO assessments tended to be focused on standards and basic requirements rather than on the drive to be best in class and achieve stretch goals, as required by the Baldrige Award criteria. Since 1994, the JCAHO standards have incorporated principles and techniques to foster continuous improvement. Also in 1994, JCAHO changed its standards and review process to focus on functions or processes within an organization, rather than the departmental approach previously used. In the past, nursing, pharmacy, and other departments were evaluated separately. Now functions like the medication process, management information, and continuity of care are the focus, and people throughout the health care organization are asked how they contribute to these processes.

Since JCAHO accreditation is essential for health care organizations, many executives are interested in how the Baldrige Award criteria relate to the JCAHO standards. Francis Jackson, an experienced

Baldrige Award examiner and consultant with the Institute for Healthcare Improvement, recently published a book titled *Crosswalk Assessment*. This publication illustrates how the JCAHO survey and the Baldrige Award criteria are linked. Jackson's work is useful in helping organizations identify how to focus their resources on meeting JCAHO requirements while creating a structure for continuous improvement.[4]

Despite the growth and maturity of the quality management field in health care, most health care organizations are not eligible to apply for the Baldrige Award because of two restrictions. Not-for-profit organizations cannot apply, and units within a for-profit company (such as one hospital from a multihospital chain) cannot independently apply.[5]

Over the past decade, many health care executives pressed for a Baldrige Award for health care. After several years of study, NIST recommended to Congress that a pilot project be funded to assess the readiness of health care and education for a formal award process. The pilot was seen as a prerequisite to the introduction of a Baldrige Award for health care.[6] In 1995, Baldrige Award pilot evaluations were conducted for education and health care. While specific criteria were tailored to the particulars of each industry, the categories, framework, and scoring remained the same. The pilots were supported by federal funds. Volunteer examiners and judges completed the assessment process for 46 health care organizations and 19 educational organizations. Among the health care organizations, two were selected for site visits. All of the participating organizations received formal feedback to facilitate continued progress and enhance their strategic planning. Currently there is a movement to create a foundation that supports a formal award process for health care. In the meantime, most state award processes include health care organizations; there have been several health care winners, including the following:

1994	Nevada	Mercy Medical Services, Las Vegas
1994	Nevada	Valley Hospital and Medical Center, Las Vegas
1994	Nevada	Hightech Health Care Services, Las Vegas
1994	Florida	Florida Hospital, Orlando
1994	Florida	Sacred Heart Hospital, Pensacola
1994	Michigan	University of Michigan Hospitals, Ann Arbor
1994	Missouri	St. Luke's Hospital, Kansas City
1995	Mississippi	Baptist Memorial Hospital, Desoto
1995	Mississippi	Methodist, Hattiesburg
1995	Mississippi	Forest General Hospital, Hattiesburg
1995	Mississippi	St. Dominic's Memorial, Jackson
1995	North Carolina	St. Joseph's, Asheville
1995	New Hampshire	St. Joseph's, Nashua
1995	Louisiana	Rapides Regional Medical Center, Alexandria

Understanding the Baldrige Award Framework

"The best way to understand the Baldrige Award criteria is as a audit framework, an encompassing set of categories that tells companies where, and in what ways, they must demonstrate proficiency—but not how to proceed."[7] In other words, the criteria are not prescriptive.

The 1997 Baldrige Award criteria focus on a balance of business results and customer satisfaction. The criteria are divided into seven categories, with 20 examination items (each focusing on a major requirement) and 30 areas to address. The format is illustrated in Table 14.1.

Table 14.1. Format of Baldrige Award elements.

Category	Number of items	Number of areas to address	Points	Percentage of points
1. Leadership	2	3	110	11
2. Strategic planning	2	5	80	8
3. Customer and market focus	2	3	80	8
4. Information and analysis	3	4	80	8
5. Human resource development and management	3	6	100	10
6. Process management	3	4	100	10
7. Business results	5	5	450	45
Totals	**20**	**30**	**1000**	**100**

Source: National Institute of Standards and Technology, *Malcolm Baldrige National Quality Award 1997 Criteria for Performance Excellence* (Gaithersburg, Md.: NIST, 1997).

Figure 14.2 illustrates how the categories, items, and areas to address are related. The example is from Category 1, Leadership. Leadership is defined as the driver of the Baldrige Award system. Figure 14.3 illustrates the Baldrige Award criteria framework. This framework provides the structure for the sets of criteria to assess different aspects of quality.

The Baldrige Award Scoring System

The scoring system is based on three dimensions: approach, deployment, and results. *Approach* refers to the methods, tools, and techniques that are applied to all requirements of the item. Overall, approaches should be systematic, integrated, and consistently applied. An approach should be prevention-based to avoid errors or defects in products or services, and therefore avoid the cost of poor quality. The approach should demonstrate cycles of improvement as well. Questions to think about relative to approach are: How have practices and processes been evaluated and improved over time? Are the processes targeted for improvement key to customer satisfaction or business performance? Is there a record of evaluation and improvement? Do we have positive improvement trends? Do the methods accomplish our stated objectives? Do the approaches appear to be systematic and consistently applied?

Deployment refers to the extent to which approaches are applied throughout the organization. Are the same tools and techniques utilized throughout the organization, with all operations and processes? Are the same strategies utilized for all products and services? Are the methods used by all work units? Do any gaps exist? Are there plans to close the gaps? Are methods systematically evaluated for effectiveness? When we make changes in our methods and how do we communicate them? Are the improvements replicated elsewhere in the organization?

Results refer to whether the approach and deployment processes generate results in key business processes. What are our current performance levels? How satisfied are our customers? Is there measurable improvement in quality levels of all products and services? How do we compare to our peers? Do we have competitive comparisons? Can we demonstrate sustained improvement?

The scoring range for each item is 0 percent and 100 percent based on sound systematic approaches that are fully deployed leading to industry and benchmark leadership.

1.1 Leadership System (80 pts.)

Describe how senior leaders guide the company in setting directions and in developing and sustaining an effective leadership system.

In your response, address the following Area:

a. *Leadership System*

How the company's senior leaders provide effective leadership, taking into account the needs and expectations of all key stakeholders. Include:

(1) how senior leaders set company directions and seek future opportunities for the company;

(2) a description of the company's leadership system and how it incorporates clear values, company directions, high performance expectations, a strong customer focus, and continuous learning;

(3) how senior leaders communicate and reinforce values, directions, expectations, customer focus, and their commitment to learning throughout the work force; and

(4) how senior leaders review the company's overall performance, and use the review process to reinforce company directions and improve the leadership system.

1.2 Company Responsibility and Citizenship (30 pts.)

Describe how the company addresses its responsibilities to the public and how the company practices good citizenship.

In your response, address the following Areas:

a. *Societal Responsibilities*

How the company addresses the current and potential impacts on society of its products, services, facilities, and operations. Include:

(1) key practices, measures, and targets for regulatory, legal, and ethical requirements and for risks associated with managing company operations; and

(2) how the company anticipates public concerns, assesses potential impacts on society, and addresses these issues in a proactive manner.

b. *Community Involvement*

How the company and its employees support and strengthen their key communities.

Source: National Institute of Standards and Technology, *Malcolm Baldrige National Quality Award 1997 Criteria for Performance Excellence* (Gaithersburg, Md.: NIST, 1997), 5.

Figure 14.2. An example of a category, items, and areas to address.

Approaches to Assessment

There are several types of Baldrige Award–based assessments to consider. The appropriate approach for your organization will vary depending on the support of leadership and the readiness of the organization. Many organizations choose to begin with a department or division assessment before attempting an organizationwide process. If your scores are in the range of 600 to 1000 points, you are probably ready for the application process. If you score lower than 600, identify the gaps in your processes and set up teams to close the gaps. Plan to resurvey in a year.

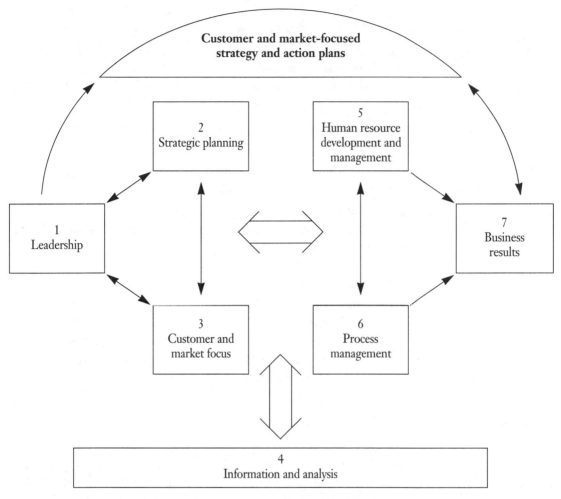

Source: National Institute of Standards and Technology, *Malcolm Baldrige National Quality Award 1997 Criteria for Performance Excellence* (Gaithersburg, Md.: NIST, 1997), 42.

Figure 14.3. The Baldrige Award criteria framework: A systems perspective.

Self-Assessment

As the term suggests, self-assessment is an internally focused process to determine the level of quality progress. There are two main types of self-assessment.

Discussion-Based. The management team may use the Baldrige Award criteria or a simple form of assessment to determine progress. Many organizations have developed tools suited to their own business, with simple summary statements and simple scoring devices. A sample assessment tool developed by the University of Michigan Hospitals is included in the chapter appendix. This assessment process can be completed by a department, by a division, or organizationwide, and results shared with all employees. Many employees can participate in this process because the questions are organizationally and industry specific, and minimal training is needed. This type of assessment can be accomplished for a low cost.

Data-Based. In the data-based approach, the complete Baldrige Award process is utilized and a thorough data-gathering approach is used. With a data-based approach, there are several choices.

- *Do it on your own.* Use internal staff to collect data, write the report, score the application, and provide feedback on strengths and areas for improvement. Many organizations use this process to create an internal chairman's or president's award to recognize and stimulate the quality progress of internal teams, departments, or divisions.

- *Collaborate.* Internal staff collect data and write the report, but scoring and feedback—and perhaps strategic planning assistance—are provided by external experts.

- *Use outside experts.* Outside experts assist with data collection, writing, scoring, and feedback functions. This method provides the most objective process.

Each of these approaches requires a different level of resources including staff time and consulting fees. A careful analysis should be undertaken to choose the approach that best fits organizational needs, the resources available, and the maturity of the quality initiative.

Application for State or National Award

Preparation of an application for a state or national award is a rigorous process. It requires an extensive planning and orientation process. Therefore, there is a higher cost associated with this type of assessment. If you choose this approach, a complete application is developed and submitted following the process detailed in Figures 14.4 and 14.5. Because of the level of expert review, this model provides the greatest level of objectivity and detailed feedback that can be used to continue the improvement process.

Step 1: Project Planning

- *Making the commitment.* The executive leadership team should make the decision whether to complete an application process for a state or national quality award. To determine organizational readiness, review the core values of the award process with the executive leadership team and discuss how your organization is doing relative to these values. A series of questions can be used as a first-step assessment. A sample of questions is included in the "Questions for a One-Hour Executive Session" section. Any "how" questions should be discussed by the team to achieve consensus. Remember that methods should be deployed throughout the organization, not just in one department or division. For the other questions, a simple ranking of yes, weak, strong, or no will help you determine if you are ready to go on to a more sophisticated level of assessment. If the executive team needs additional information to assess progress, there are several things you can suggest.

1. Arrange a benchmarking visit to a company that has won a quality award at the state or national level.

2. Invite the quality director of a company that has won quality awards to visit with your executive leadership team.

3. Bring in a consultant to train the executive team.

4. Arrange an in-house training session to further educate the executive team.

If the executive team scores the organization well, it may be time for a higher level of assessment. The team should review the seven categories and briefly discuss which categories are strengths and which are areas for improvement. The next step would be a mock Baldrige Award application, with

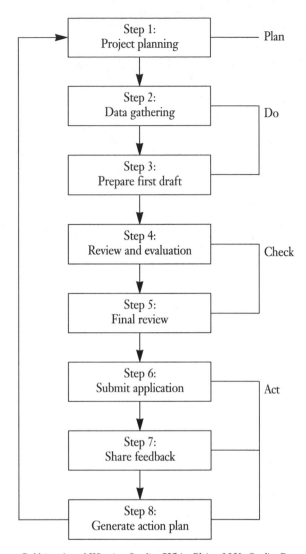

Source: Adapted from M. G. Brown, *Baldrige Award Winning Quality* (White Plains, N.Y.: Quality Resources, 1995), 47.

Figure 14.4. Application flowchart for state/national quality award.

review and scoring by Baldrige Award examiners. If no one internal to the organization holds these credentials, call NIST for a list of examiners in your state or contact your state quality award office.

• *Assigning leadership.* The best person to lead the overall application process is someone who has been through formal Baldrige Award training and has served as an examiner for the state- or national-level awards. This individual should also have a broad knowledge of the organization. In most organizations this would be the vice president of quality. The Baldrige Award language and requirements are complex. Having internal expertise means less time will be spent understanding the process. Institutional learning can be enhanced by having an executive leader serve as a champion and leader for each category. As leaders become more sophisticated with the tool, and more expert in quality assessment in general, they tend to share this knowledge and encourage additional quality efforts.

	Key tasks	Subtasks	Lead	Time frame
Step 1: Project planning	1. Making the commitment	Review Baldrige Award values	Executive team	Week 1
	2. Assigning leadership	Assess strengths and weaknesses by category		
	3. Creating the steering committee	Select leader for application process	CEO	Week 1
		Develop business overview	CEO	Week 1
	4. Building the application team, categories 1–7	Benchmark application process	VP of quality	Week 1
		Develop work plan	Team	Week 2
		Organize by category	CEO/VP of quality	Week 2
	5. Creating the training team	Assign executive champion as lead	CEO	Week 2
		Ensure team alignment	VP of quality	Week 2
	6. Creating the communication team	Develop curriculum	Training team	Week 2
		Develop timetable for education	Training team	Week 2
		Implement training	Training team	Week 3
		Develop plan to inform all employees	Communication team	Week 3
		Use flowchart and planning checklist	Communication team	Ongoing
		Develop timetable	Communication team	Ongoing
		Implement		Ongoing
Step 2: Data gathering	1. Develop interview tool	Announce requirements	CEO	Week 2
		Arrange interviews	Application team	Week 2
	2. Develop and maintain log	Log progress	Category team members	Week 2
	3. Focus on trended data	Review need for minimum three years of data	VP of quality	Week 2
	4. Prepare good graphics		Application team	Throughput process
Step 3: Prepare first draft	1. Remember the page limit	Assign page count by importance weight	Steering committee	Week 2
	2. Assign main editors	Take responsibility for smoothing style	VP of quality	Week 2
	3. Be concise, factual, and quantitative	Keep explanations simple	Application team	Throughput process
		Don't duplicate graphics in text	Application team	Throughput process
	4. Address all linkages	Check across teams frequently; check again after first draft	All teams	Throughput process

Source: Adapted from M. G. Brown, *Baldrige Award Winning Quality* (White Plains, N.Y.: Quality Resources, 1995), 47.

Figure 14.5. Application planning checklist.

	Key tasks	Subtasks	Lead	Time frame
Step 4: Review and evaluate	1. Encourage process owner to review application	Ensure accuracy of examples	VP of quality	Ongoing
	2. Use business overview to review application	Check for integration of all critical elements	VP of quality	Ongoing
	3. Use expert scoring	Train examiners Hire external examiners	VP of quality	Week 6
	4. Capture areas for improvement	Steering committee should review and make any team assignments required	Steering committee	Week 6
Step 5: Final review	1. Check each category and item	Review each category, item, and area to address against the criteria	Main editor and category leaders	Week 9
	2. Revise and check again	CEO check and assign readers not serving on application team	CEO/VP of quality	Week 9
	3. Decide how to customize application	Gather pictures, graphics for use	Main editor and steering committee	Week 10
Step 6: Submit application	1. Plan site visit	Plan control center	Steering committee	Week 11
	2. Make and distribute copies of the application	Establish escort teams	Steering committee	Week 12
	3. Send the application and celebrate		Steering committee and application team	Week 12
Step 7: Share feedback	1. Develop a process for sharing feedback	Each category leader presents (+) and (–) aspects by category	Steering committee	Week 12
	2. Clarify all strengths and areas for improvement	Review with executive team Review with all employees	Category leader Category leader and area manager	When feedback is received
	3. Develop a Pareto analysis for each category	Separate critical few from trivial many	Category leader	When feedback is received

Source: Adapted from M. G. Brown, *Baldrige Award Winning Quality* (White Plains, N.Y.: Quality Resources, 1995), 47.

Figure 14.5. *Continued.*

	Key tasks	Subtasks	Lead	Time frame
Step 8: Generate action plan	1. Set up teams to close identified gaps	Assign teams Develop individual action plans for each team	Executive committee	Within two weeks of feedback report
	2. Adjust the strategic plan	Set new stretch goals	Executive committee	Annual strategic planning
	3. Prepare to survey again in one year	Evaluate the process Prepare plan for resurvey	Executive committee	Retreat

Source: Adapted from M. G. Brown, *Baldrige Award Winning Quality* (White Plains, N.Y.: Quality Resources, 1995), 47.

Figure 14.5. *Continued.*

• *Creating the steering committee.* A steering committee should be assigned to lead and monitor the application process. A proposed membership group is suggested in Figure 14.6. The first task of the steering committee is to develop the business overview. This overview serves as a guide for data collection and application writing. Key business issues mentioned in the overview must be addressed in the body of the application. It is also a critical document for the examiners and judges who will be evaluating your application. The overview has five sections.

1. A basic description of the company

2. Customer requirements

3. Supplier relationships

4. Competitive factors

5. Other factors important to the applicant

Another important task of the committee is to benchmark the application process with state or national award winners. Even if the organizations are unwilling to share their actual application, the quality director may be willing to share valuable lessons learned during the process.

• *Building the application team.* Each category also requires a team that will be responsible for data collection, collation of the material, and documentation of the category. The people chosen for each category team should be knowledgeable about the organization and be excellent interviewers and writers. During the data gathering, process teams should create a notebook for each category to maintain a data audit trail.

As each category leader develops a work plan, the meetings schedule should be addressed. Due to many linkages required across categories, sets of teams should meet together weekly. These sets include teams for categories 1 and 2 and teams for 4, 6, and 7 (see Figure 14.7). At least every other week the entire application team should meet to share progress and align efforts. Also, it is important to have one individual serve as process lead and editor to tie the application together, emphasize the linkages, and create a consistent whole.

• *Creating the training team.* Many employees will participate in the application process. An effective training plan takes into consideration the multiple roles people will play, and develops a

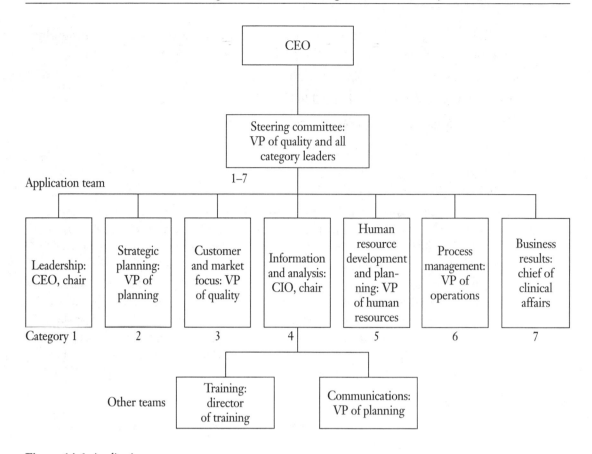

Figure 14.6. Application teams.

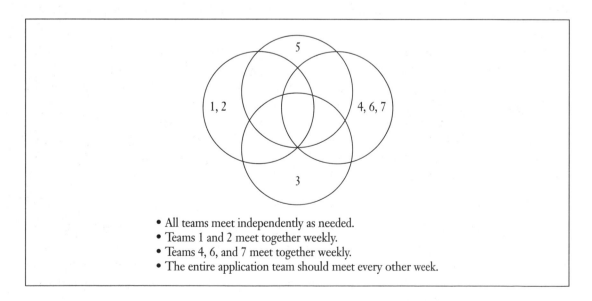

Figure 14.7. Relationships of team meetings.

strategic plan that includes time frames. The training should reinforce the key principles of the quality process for your organization. Key elements of the curriculum should include the following:

—Orientation to the award criteria, framework, scoring, and application process

—The actual process the organization will follow to submit the application

—Roles and responsibilities of various groups during the process

—Key institutional quality principles

There are several groups to consider, including executives, members of the board of directors, physicians, managers, process owners, and employees.

• *Creating the communication team.* This team should develop a communication plan to inform people of the various steps in the process. The typical questions of *who, what, where, when, why, how,* and *what's in it for me* should be covered in the plan. The development of a process flowchart and planning checklist such as shown in Figures 14.4 and 14.5 can be broadly shared and can help set expectations. Stories in the organization's newsletters can be utilized to ask for additional examples of process improvement. All staff need to know items such as: What types of data need to be collected? When will the teams be seeking information? Who should be called with examples that can be shared?

The process can be shared both through cascade meetings and in all print materials. This is also an ideal time to focus on sharing once again the mission, vision, key indicators and measures, and other key principles to enhance understanding and deployment of these concepts.

Step 2: Data Gathering

• *Develop interview tool.* The use of a standard interview tool will help when it is time to write up the examples. Figure 14.8 contains a sample interview tool.

• *Develop and maintain a log for future reference.* The log should contain data such as who was interviewed, when the interview occurred, what data were collected, and who the contact people are for follow-up.

• *Focus on trended data.* An announcement of the type of information you are looking for should be made as soon as the decision is made to apply for the award. In many cases you will have to make several phone calls to track down process improvement information with factual results. Make sure the examples you choose to highlight are clear, with appropriate trended data. Keep in mind that a trend is three or more years of data. Anecdotal stories are not effective. Remember also that each category has elements in which approach, deployment, and results are asked for. Responses must reflect appropriate requirements. Appropriate benchmark information can demonstrate your market leadership. Competitive comparisons are a critical element of the application.

Step 3: Prepare the First Draft

• *Remember the page limit.* There is a 50-page limit for the application, so much of the planning should be around the best way to display critical information. Note that the point values for categories are weighted according to importance; for example, category 7 is worth 45 percent, while strategic planning is worth 8 percent. When preparing an application, many organizations allocate category pages based on their performance weight.

• *Assign a main editor.* This will ensure a smooth style throughout the application and reduce the potential for jarring changes in style and disconnects between categories. It is easy to identify those applicants prepared by committee without a main editor.

Interview Tool

Describe the process that was improved.

Who are the customers of the process?

What were the key results?

Was customer satisfaction evaluated?

How were the results measured?

What were the cause-and-effect relationships between actions and the results?

Is there an evaluation and improvement cycle built into the approach?

Do the results bring the organization closer to its long-term objectives?

Are there actions that would build on this success?

Date:

Person interviewed:

Department interviewer:

Figure 14.8. Data gathering.

• *Be concise, factual, and quantitative.* Keep explanations simple. Don't try to substitute creative writing for data. The examiners are well trained and can discriminate fact from fiction. When you see words such as *trends, results,* or *data,* use graphs to respond. Don't duplicate information presented in graphics in the text. Don't use too many abbreviations, because it makes the application hard to read.

• *Be sure to address all of the linkages required.* The collaborative teams' assignments are to check linkages at each meeting. The criteria are part of an integrated system; therefore, the application should be checked frequently for content, completeness, consistency, redundancy, and alignment. The 1997 award criteria[8] contain notes to provide information on where linkages and consistency should be checked. When the application is complete, have several people review it again to look for these linkages.

Step 4: Review and Evaluation

• *Encourage process owner review.* Encourage process owners to review and check all examples for accuracy. When data are collected and condensed, there is always the possibility that the example is compromised.

• *Use the business overview to ascertain whether all key customer, supplier, employee, and operations issues are addressed.* Integration of the key factors across the categories and the entire application is essential.

• *Use expert scoring.* If you are fortunate enough to have employees who are experienced examiners, have them review and score the final product. This will give you a rough idea of your numerical score. You can also train internal examiners to perform this function. With internal examiners, objectivity is always an issue. Some will score the organization low because they know all the problems; some will score too high because they are less objective.

• *Capture areas for improvement.* Develop a list of any areas for improvement found during the data-gathering process. This process will highlight areas for improvement that you can begin to address immediately.

Step 5: Revision and Final Review

• *Check each category and item.* There are requirements for appropriate approach, deployment, and results responses. Make certain the response is appropriate to the question.

• *Revise and check again.* After revisions are made, check the application again.

• *Decide how to customize the application.* Many teams choose to make the application unique. This can be accomplished by adding pictures on the category header pages or on the cover. Such small touches will help to distinguish your application from others.

Step 6: Submit Application

• *Check to be sure all elements are included.* Elements of an application must include the application form, site listing and description form, application report, the 50-page document, and a five-page business overview.

• *Plan site visit.* Develop a site visit plan to avoid a last-minute scramble. Discuss where the control center could be located, what documents and people need to be on hand, and where supporting notebooks will be stored. It is also important to identify who will serve on the site visit escort teams. You could consider running a mock survey.

• *Distribute copies of the final application.* Share copies of the application with employees. This will enhance communication about the process and give people a sense of assignments if a site visit occurs. It will also help to celebrate completion of the project.

• *Send the application and celebrate.* The entire organization should mark this time with a celebration. It is an important milestone for improvement efforts.

Step 7: Share Feedback

• *Develop a process for sharing feedback with the organization.* In this way you maximize the efforts of the process and complete the plan-do-check-act cycle.

• *Clarify all strengths and areas for improvement.* Do you understand each comment? Do you agree with the comments? Did the scoring framework for the Baldrige Award provide a system to help you analyze strengths and areas for improvement? Each category team leader should work with his or her team to develop a formal process to review strengths and areas for improvement within the category. Share the results first with the executive team and then in a cascade fashion with all employees.

• *Develop a Pareto analysis to identify the most important issues.* There will be many areas where improvement is needed. Organizations can be overwhelmed by the data. A Pareto analysis allows you to set priorities and focus on key areas first. Any areas for improvement that are visible to customers should also be prioritized quickly.

Step 8: Generate Action Plan

• *Set up teams to close identified gaps.* When critical gaps have been identified, set up teams to close the gaps. Set time frames for completion of the improvement process.

• *Adjust the strategic plan.* When the key areas for improvement have been identified, the strategic plan should reflect these issues and the assignments to remove gaps.

The Review Process

Once the application is received, there is a four-stage review process at both the state and national levels.

1. Independent review and scoring of the application by at least five examiners. The panel of judges meets to determine which applications proceed to stage 2.

2. Consensus review. The examiners review the application a second time and arrange a meeting, by phone or in person, to reach consensus on the application scoring. The judges meet to determine which applications will go on to stage 3.

3. A site visit is made to the high-scoring organizations to verify and clarify the information in the application. The examiners have an extensive plan to validate information. The scoring for this part of the process is simple. The numerical scores of the application are not adjusted; the site visit team simply recommends raising or lowering the score by a large or small amount, or keeping the score the same.

4. The judges meet to determine which organizations will be recommended as winning companies. There may be up to two Baldrige Award winners in each category: small business, service, and manufacturing. Some state awards have different categories.

All applicants receive feedback reports detailing strengths and areas for improvement.

Lessons Learned at the University of Michigan Hospitals

In 1987, we began our quality journey at the University of Michigan Hospitals. Inspired by our participation in the National Demonstration Project, which was cosponsored by the Harvard Community Health Plan and the Hartford Foundation, we began our first improvement process. The results of this first process improvement, to reduce waiting time in our admitting department, were impressive. We reduced wait times from 140 minutes on average to less than 10 minutes. In subsequent efforts, times were reduced even further. Because the changes occurred in a department that was very visible, others wanted to use the techniques that led to the process improvement.

The executive team committed to a full quality improvement process. Key steps included the creation of a quality council, adoption of a quality curriculum (we utilized Qualtec Quality Services to begin our employee education process), a comprehensive human resources strategic plan, and a focused approach on improving operating and financial performance and enhancing customer satisfaction.

In 1990, after winning the Health Care Forum Commitment to Quality Award, the executive team developed a tool for an annual assessment that was simple and specific to our organization and our industry. A sample of this tool is included in chapter appendix A. The vice presidents used the tool with their subordinates to determine a progress ranking by department and division. The vice presidents reported divisional scores at the annual planning retreat, and the executive team then reached a scoring consensus on an organizationwide basis. There was a great deal of heated discussion and tremendous variation in scoring. Some departments and divisions had made substantive gains and others had yet to begin.

The executive team then identified key gaps in the quality process and developed a new strategic plan. Improvement teams were assigned to close the gaps. The same format was followed for two consecutive years. As the executive team became more sophisticated, the scoring became more critical.

In 1993, we used the Baldrige Award criteria to assess our organizational progress. The scores were very low, but the benefit was in highlighting critical gaps with a well-established and validated tool. In 1994 our repeat scores were much higher and the executive team decided we were ready for external evaluation and feedback.

The State of Michigan Quality Leadership Award, based on the Baldrige Award, was developed in 1993; the executive team made the commitment to complete an application. The goal was to have a rigorous external review. The application team worked hard to accomplish the task of completing the application. There was a tremendous amount of learning at all levels in the organization. We were extremely pleased to be notified that we had been chosen for a site visit.

Key Lessons

The following lists include the key lessons learned during our application for the State of Michigan Quality Leadership Award in 1994. First, the positive.

• *Applying for the award was motivating.* Many process owners called to tell us about results that were previously unknown. The process owners got a chance to tell their stories and receive positive feedback.

• *Many people were excited about the application and the site visit.* The process was highlighted in the local and state press and gave a sense of pride to employees.

- *We established a site visit escort team.* We assigned two application team members to escort the examiners. Sometimes it was necessary for the escorts to act as translators for the questions of the examiners, who were from manufacturing industries and occasionally used different terminology. The examiners and the staff felt that this was beneficial.

- *We held a critique at the end of each day of the site visit process.* This helped us compare notes and prepare for the next day. We discussed missing information and had a chance to locate data that would help answer questions. We also could identify problems to be rectified or at least note them for future reference.

Other lessons indicated room for improvement.

- *Ask questions about benchmarking during the data collection process.* Many of our teams reported benchmarking experiences; however, when the examiners asked them to document changes they had made in their processes as a result of benchmarking, we could not document these changes.

- *Have process owners review the application for accuracy.* We called a process owner to meet with an examiner during the site visit, and the process owner told us the example was wrong. It was a stressful experience for everyone involved.

- *Prepare for the site visit during the application process.* Then if you are notified that you will be site visited, you will be prepared. Preparing for the site visit requires significant time and effort. If you do not proceed to the site visit stage, you have a plan to review the next time you apply. We did not expect a site visit with our first application; we only had two week's notice, and we scrambled to get ready.

- *Establish a realistic schedule.* At the site visit, many more people than we had time for wanted to tell their story. They were disappointed when they could not.

The entire process—from the decision to apply, to the mailing day of the application, to the phone call informing us we had won, to the excitement of the celebration black-tie dinner—was an incredible experience. The whole organization felt rewarded for work well done. We also recognized, however, that there was much more work to accomplish.

Summary

The process of self-assessment or applying for a Baldrige Award–based quality award can yield many benefits for an organization. The benefits range from simply raising organizational awareness of the current quality progress to stimulating employees to set even higher goals for process improvement and customer satisfaction. Quality is a moving target. As Hart and Bogan indicate, "When quality is done right, it becomes a kind of obsession, one that begins in the hearts and minds of top management and is transmitted from there down through every nook and cranny of even the largest multinational corporation."[9] Extensive planning, doing, checking, and acting are required to improve processes and exceed customer requirements. As Mark Graham Brown indicated, "Having an impressive total quality management program is not what the Baldrige criteria are about. Baldrige now focuses on the evidence of fundamental changes in the way the organization does its day-to-day business."[10]

Questions for a One-Hour Executive Session

One way to set the stage for an assessment process is to determine how the executive team feels about quality progress. The following questions can be used for a one-hour executive session. They are formulated around the 11 Baldrige Award values and include the following:

1. *Customer-driven quality.* Have we identified important customer groups? Do we measure customer satisfaction? Do we have improvement strategies for all groups of customers? Are the satisfaction trends positive? Do we compare favorably to our peers? Do we make it easy for customers to complain? How quickly do we respond to complaints? Do leaders talk to customers to determine requirements? What roles do customers play in strategic planning?

2. *Leadership.* Do we provide leadership to improve performance and capabilities across the organization? Do we evaluate our organizational progress? Do we evaluate and improve the progress of the leadership team? How do we personally communicate values, vision, expectations, and directions? Are the mission, vision, values, key processes, and key measurements understood by all staff? How do we validate this knowledge? Are we visible quality advocates? Do we have empowering leadership styles? Do we encourage decision making at the customer level?

3. *Continuous improvement and learning.* Do we measure improvement at the worker and unit level? Do we know the required competencies for all types of our workers? Are our educational programs tied to building these competencies and capabilities? How do we personally make evident the need for continuous learning? Do we participate in teaching others throughout the organization?

4. *Employee participation and development.* Are all employees empowered to act to meet customer needs? Do we have an effective reward and recognition program? How do we seek to improve the skills and motivation of the staff? How do we demonstrate investment in the workforce? Is our human resource strategic plan integrated with the business plan? Are our employees satisfied? How do our employee satisfaction measures compare with those of our peers?

5. *Fast response.* Have we improved cycle time for the development of new programs or services? Can we make rapid changes when customers express concern about processes? Are customers pleased with wait times for admission, appointments, visits, tests, treatments, phone calls, and so on? Do we have an organizationwide strategy to reduce cycle time?

6. *Design quality and prevention.* Are we focused on problem prevention? Do we address quality while building or delivering a service rather than retrospectively, when a customer complains? Do we take the voice of the customer into consideration when we are planning new products or services? Do we involve suppliers in the planning process?

7. *Long-range view of the future.* Do we have a strong future orientation? What is the range for short-term and long-term planning? Do we understand who our customers and competitors will be in five or 10 years? Do we involve customers, suppliers, and employees in planning processes?

8. *Management by fact.* Is our business system built on a framework of measurement, information, data, and analysis? Have we identified all key processes? Do we measure key processes and trend improvements? Have we benchmarked key processes and used the results to facilitate

further improvement? Do we have trend analysis on customers by market segment? Do the measures we collect relate clearly to our strategic plan and goals? Do process measures correlate to customer satisfaction or financial performance? Do we have effective information systems?

9. *Partnership development.* Do we build internal and external partnerships? How can we demonstrate partnership with employees? What examples do we have of partnership with suppliers? Have we partnered with the community? What examples of alliances do we have to share?

10. *Corporate responsibility and leadership.* How dedicated are we to the needs of our community? How do we monitor ethical behavior? How do we protect the health and safety of our employees and customers? What role do employees play in planning health and safety programs? What unique environmental issues do we face? Do we have effective plans to reduce environmental impact? How do we address resource conservation and waste? Do we share quality knowledge with our community?

11. *Results orientation.* Has our organization shown steady improvement in the quality of products and services? How do our results compare with peer organizations? Do our financial and operational trends compare favorably with benchmarks? Can we demonstrate positive trends in our support services departments? Can we demonstrate suppliers' contributions to our quality results?

Questions for a One-Hour Board Session

Prior to submitting an application at the state or national level, at least a one-hour meeting should be set with the board. It is critical to set the right expectations with the board. Developing a Baldrige Award–type application can be a great learning experience. However, even Baldrige Award winners report that they have 50 or more items for improvement from their feedback reports. The commitment must be one of continued process improvement, not just a one-time event. Few organizations have won a state or national quality award on the first try. It is critical to emphasize that the best reason for applying is to receive the benefit of expert review and feedback, not just to win.

The agenda should allow time to review the core values of the Baldrige Award, cover the benefits and risks in applying, review the framework and process for the award, and review examples chosen from the application to demonstrate organizational progress.

Sample Benefits

- Responding to the criteria helps develop a common language within the organization.

- An organizationwide focus can stimulate quality progress by highlighting successes and existing gaps.

- Managers can learn more effective means of evaluating customer and supplier relationships by using both internal and external best practices learned during the process.

- Involving a large number of employees can lead to integration and alignment of improvement activities.

- The process provides an opportunity to share success stories and create positive momentum.

Sample Risks

- The feedback may indicate a score much lower than the organization expected, and it can serve as a demotivator.

- Without a comprehensive plan, the cost can be very high with a poor return on investment.

Questions for a One-Hour Process Owners Meeting

The process owners meeting should kick off the data collection process. An introduction to set the tone for the award process should include a review of the completed business overview.

The key questions for discussion include the following:

- Have we identified all key processes?

- Have we flowcharted all processes?

- How do the processes relate to key customer and business requirements?

- What do the key process indicators tell us?

- How do our measures compare with our peers?

- What are the trends, and how are trends shared with all employees?

- What success stories do we have to tell?

- What areas for improvement do we have?

Appendix: Self-Assessment Tool for Health Care Organizations Based on the Baldrige Award Criteria

The Leadership category (110 points, 11 percent) represents the executives' personal leadership, involvement, and communication of quality goals and values throughout the organization; how the executives create and sustain a customer focus and meet community health care goals is key.

Rank

10 Quality is the number-one priority of the leadership team of the organization and department. The leadership team establishes the strategic direction for the organization and the targets that will lead to achievement.

9 The organization and department have assessed community health care needs, developed an action plan to meet those needs, and communicated their goals.

8 Leaders and department heads establish personal improvement plans to evaluate and enhance quality leadership and involvement in the quality process. The organizational leaders model quality behaviors and lead the quality effort.

7 Quality values are integrated with the daily management behaviors of leaders, as indicated by employee surveys.

6 Quality issues are part of every agenda. The quality process drives all meetings.

5 Rewards and recognition reinforce the quality improvement process. The executives and department heads participate in reward and recognition efforts formally and informally.

4 Leaders and department heads meet with customers and suppliers to determine requirements and assess satisfaction.

3 Leadership is concerned about breaking down interdepartmental barriers to the quality process. Leadership is accessible and keeps employees informed on quality progress.

2 Executives/department heads are visible advocates for quality. They lead or serve on teams and teach quality courses. They exhibit quality behaviors, such as reinforcing a customer focus and planning and reviewing progress toward quality.

1 Organizational and departmental mission, values, and vision are developed and shared broadly with all employees.

Source: E. Gaucher and R. J. Coffey, *Total Quality in Healthcare* (San Francisco: Jossey-Bass, 1993).

Notes

1. J. M. Juran, ed., *The Quality Control Handbook* (New York: McGraw-Hill, 1951), 37.

2. J. M. Juran, "The Upcoming Century of Quality," *Quality Progress* 27, no. 8 (August 1994): 34.

3. M. G. Brown, *Baldrige Award Winning Quality: How To Interpret the Malcolm Baldrige Award Criteria* (White Plains, N.Y.: Quality Resources, 1995), xi.

4. Francis Jackson, *Crosswalk Assessment* (Kingsport, Tenn.: Bishop Associates, 1995).

5. E. Kratochwill and Ellen Gaucher, "Using the Baldrige Criteria as a Self-Assessment Tool: A Case Study from the University of Michigan Medical Center," *The Journal of Healthcare Information and Management Systems Society* 8, no. 4 (1994): 25.

6. H. S. Hertz, C. W. Riemann, and M. C. Bostwick, "The Malcolm Baldrige National Quality Award Concept: Could It Help Stimulate or Accelerate Healthcare Improvement?" *Quality Management in Healthcare* 2, no. 4 (1994): 71.

7. D. Garvin, "How the Baldrige Award Really Works," *Harvard Business Review* 69, no. 6 (November-December 1991): 82.

8. National Institute of Standards and Technology, *Malcolm Baldrige National Quality Award 1997 Criteria for Performance Excellence* (Gaithersburg, Md.: NIST, 1997).

9. Hart, C. W. L., and C. E. Bogan. *The Baldrige: What Is It, How It's Won, How to Improve Quality in Your Company* (New York: McGraw-Hill, 1992).

10. M. G. Brown, "Measuring Up Against the 1995 Baldrige Criteria," *Journal for Quality and Participation* 17, no. 7, (December 1994): 66.

Ellen J. Gaucher, MSN, MSPH, is the vice president for quality and customer satisfaction at Wellmark Inc. Blue Cross and Blue Shield of Iowa and South Dakota. She previously served as the senior associate hospital director of the University of Michigan Health System in Ann Arbor, Michigan. She currently holds faculty appointments in the School of Nursing and the School of Public Health at the University of Michigan. She holds master of science degrees in public health and nursing. She has more than 20 years of experience in senior management positions in health care organizations.

Gaucher coauthored a book entitled *Transforming Healthcare Organizations: How to Achieve and Sustain Organizational Excellence*, which won the 1992 James A. Hamilton Book award given by the American College of Healthcare Executives. A second book, entitled *Total Quality in Healthcare: From Therapy to Practice*, was published in May 1993 and won the American Nurses Association Book of the Year in 1994. Gaucher has published numerous articles and book chapters, including "Teams in Total Quality Management: The Healthcare Pioneers 1992," and lectures internationally in the field of hospital management, systems development, and quality improvement.

She is a board member of the Institute for Healthcare Improvement, The Quality Letter Editorial Board, the Editorial Advisory Board of QI/TQM (Quality Improvement through Total Quality Management), and the Editorial Board for Healthcare Competition Week, and is an associate editor of *Quality Management in Health Care Journal*. She is a fellow in the American Academy of Nursing.

Gaucher also served on the panel of judges for the Malcolm Baldrige National Quality Award from 1992 to 1995 and currently serves as a judge for the State of Michigan Quality Award.

Chapter 15

Public Disclosure of Quality and Performance Information in Managed Care

Cary Sennett and Margaret O'Kane

The past decades have been years of extraordinary change in the health care system. Medical science has created new strategies and developed new technologies to radically alter the approach to therapy for literally millions of patients. The emergence of new diseases—like AIDS—has created challenges that were completely unpredictable even 20 years ago.

But perhaps no change in the health care system is as profound as the movement of managed care into the mainstream. Twenty years ago, health maintenance organizations (HMOs) were a brave social experiment: isolated efforts to try to improve the quality of life for insured Americans by maintaining health through strategies that focused on disease prevention and health promotion. Today managed care is very much the norm, with more than 50,000,000 privately insured enrollees in HMOs, and scores of millions more enrolled in other managed care offerings: preferred provider organizations (PPOs), point-of-service (POSs) products, "managed indemnity" plans, and other products that are appearing at an ever-increasing rate. More than that, managed care has significantly penetrated the public sector: In 1996, more than 10,000,000 publicly insured (Medicare and Medicaid) beneficiaries were enrolled in HMOs, and rates of growth among these populations exceed those in the private sector.

This rapid expansion of managed care into the mainstream of the U.S. health care system has created some concern, and with it a substantial demand for quality assurance. The concern comes from some of the realities of managed care: The limitations on provider choice that are an essential element of virtually all managed care networks and the incentives and systems that exist in most managed care systems to limit the delivery of care. Both of these have the potential to greatly enhance quality. Limiting the network to only those providers that meet high standards promises to create a *higher*—not lower—quality system. Incentives to motivate the delivery of relatively lower-cost health-promoting and disease-preventing services and to limit the delivery of unnecessary, typically high-cost, and often morbid acute and restorative care has the potential not only to reduce cost but to improve member health and functionality. It is also clear that both have the potential to significantly and profoundly compromise quality as well. Limiting choice may compromise access to high quality providers if the provider network is poorly designed, and incentives and systems to limit the delivery of inappropriate care may restrict access to needed care if the incentives and systems are poorly designed or excessive.

In this context, the public and private organizations that purchase health benefits—and the consumers of health care themselves—have increasingly demanded that adequate quality assurance mechanisms operate on (or in) managed care to provide protection against the risks inherent in managed care systems. While these quality assurance mechanisms are quite diverse, they are largely of two types: (1) those depending on regulatory initiatives to superimpose a quality assurance mechanism onto managed care operations, and (2) those attempting to use market forces to create appropriate incentives that motivate managed care firms to deliver high-quality care.

Clearly, an effective quality assurance mechanism should take advantage of both regulation and market forces. A detailed discussion of regulatory approaches is beyond the scope of this chapter. Here we would like to summarize some of the issues suggesting to us that regulatory solutions alone will not achieve the efficiency we believe is possible, and then discuss in more detail information-driven strategies for creating a market for managed care services in which high-quality care becomes probable because economic incentives exist for managed care firms to deliver high-quality care.

The Limits to Regulation

Experience with regulation suggests that it has an important, but limited, role in assuring quality in health care in general and managed care in particular. This is so because of the following:

1. *Regulation may limit creativity and innovation.* While regulations have the potential to institutionalize best practices, the process of developing, modifying, and implementing regulations can be slow and filled with inertia. To the extent that that is so, regulations may fail to permit creativity and may be slow to recognize innovation when it has occurred.

2. *Regulatory processes are essentially political; they may drive to the status quo.* That regulatory processes are political seems indisputable; as political processes, they are subject to influence from those who wield political influence. It is usually the case that the politically influential have reason to resist change—the influence that they have in the current world may be threatened by that change. As a result, political processes have a tendency to enshrine the status quo; regulators may be slow to embrace strategies that threaten to rock the boat.

3. *States and governments have the power to shut down organizations; this has focused regulation on ensuring that "bad apples" are identified, rather than on driving continuous improvement.* While state and federal governments are clearly interested in improvement in the marketplace, they have a special obligation to protect the public, and therefore to detect the truly substandard providers. This drives regulatory activity toward the identification and elimination of "bad apples" (a strategy antithetical to the continuous improvement we believe competition can foster) and, further, may create some reluctance for intervention at the margin. (Where the state's authority rests in its ability to terminate a license and literally put an individual or an organization out of business, the level of evidence required for action may be so high that action is taken only in the most egregious cases.) Again, these limit the potential of governmental actors to ensure—and certainly to improve—the quality of managed care firm operations and products.

The Role of Competition

As a result, we believe that competitive pressure can and should be a powerful force to drive quality improvement in the market for managed care, as it has been in the markets for other goods and services in the United States and internationally. However, there is little doubt that the market for health care services is different. Health care is not a commodity like gasoline or airline travel, and many aspects of health care purchasing are unique, to which conventional economic theory does not apply. It is appropriate, therefore, to begin our discussion of market mechanisms for quality assurance in managed care in general—and the role of public information in assuring discipline in that market in particular—by considering the two assumptions on which that discipline depends: namely, that (1) given economic incentives to improve quality, managed care organizations (MCOs) will behave rationally and levels of quality will rise; and (2) given adequate information about the quality and performance of managed care firms, those who drive the market (purchasers and consumers) will elect to purchase and consume care from those organizations that provide the highest quality.

It does not seem unreasonable to accept the first assumption as axiomatic. Certainly, there is no reason to doubt that managed care firms behave in some manner that is consistent with basic economic theory—and much evidence (some anecdotal, some not) that managed care firms are capable of generating sometimes very large profits. There seems little reason to doubt that MCOs respond to economic incentives in much the same way as other firms; to the extent that that is so, quality is ensured if purchasers and consumers are willing to reward higher-quality firms with their business (assuming that purchasers and consumers have the ability to recognize the MCOs that are providing higher quality).

Is it true that purchasers and consumers will vote for higher-quality managed care firms with their pocketbooks? This seems less clear. On the one hand, an increasing number of corporations are, for example, mandating that managed care firms interested in their business distinguish themselves through achieving accreditation by an objective evaluator such as the National Committee for Quality Assurance (NCQA). On the other hand, there seems no question but that price was the dominant market force in 1996. Anecdotally, the major determinants of plan choice appear to be price, price, and price.

What does this mean? Clearly, it means that competition *is* possible in the market for managed care services. While some have argued that that market is imperfect (and we've no doubt but that it is), it is not noncompetitive. Rather, it is aggressively price competitive. But this does not establish that competition based on quality is impossible. First of all, in the absence of information about quality, it is hard to understand how anyone might expect to see anything *but* price competition. More than that, it is difficult to predict what will be the basis for competition when truly competitive (that is, marginal cost) prices have been achieved and managed care becomes something of a commodity. It seems more than likely that—at some point probably quite soon—only small differences in price will distinguish one managed care firm from another. When that is so, it seems highly likely that quality will be the feature distinguishing one MCO from another in the marketplace.

It also seems likely that growing consumer interest will spark quality-based competition in the near future to a greater extent than in the past. As managed care becomes a reality for more consumers, a critical mass will become interested in quality and it will move from the perimeter toward the center of MCO radar screens. In fact, consumer interest in quality—sparked by the growth of HMOs (especially growth among the influential elderly, for whom health care quality is an issue of paramount importance) and fueled by the greater availability of information about quality—may prove to be the force that drives the quality-competitive marketplace.

Providing Information to Purchasers and Consumers

If we postulate that there is group purchaser and individual consumer demand for quality, then what is needed to create an environment in which MCOs are motivated to provide higher levels of quality is the ability to distinguish managed care firms that provide higher quality. This, of course, is the essential role of publicly disclosed quality and performance information: to make available to the health care purchasing and consuming public the information they need in order to make it possible for them to express preferences in an informed manner. It is critical, therefore, to begin our discussion with some consideration of what we know about the information needs of consumers and purchasers.

NCQA has conducted a number of focus groups with consumers—both privately insured and those enrolled in the Medicare and Medicaid programs—as part of its ongoing research on consumer information needs. The focus groups included individual interviews, followed by group discussions, and testing of model report card components. The focus groups revealed a number of key points about report cards and consumers' evaluation of health plans.

- *Consumers are interested in health plan report cards, and such report cards do expand the way they think about health plans.* They generally think they lack sufficient knowledge and understanding about plan choices and describe the selection process as challenging and frustrating. However, they are very interested in detailed, systematic, and informative data from sources they consider trustworthy.

- *Consumers are able to critically evaluate data when they are presented in an easy-to-use form.*

- *Different consumers have different information needs.* However, when they were shown model report cards, there was less difference among different types of consumers than between individuals. This indicates that a basic format might be appropriate for all consumers, with some variations in supplementary material to provide more detailed, personalized information for individuals.

- *Consumers' differing information needs appear to be related to demographics, individual knowledge about health care issues and plan types, and individual plan type preferences.*

- *In all three focus group studies, virtually every type of consumer positively mentioned* Consumer Reports *and its typical data presentation format.* Consumers perceive the magazine as independent, neutral, objective, conscientious, thorough, and without any conflict of interest—therefore trustworthy—and they consider its format very useful.

- *Quality and performance measures such as the Health Plan Employer Data and Information Set (HEDIS; NCQA's core set of performance measures) are generally new to consumers, and they are most interested in measures they see as personally relevant.* Also, consumers do not always understand how individual performance measures reflect on health plans and need this explained to them.

- *Consumers have mixed reactions to patient satisfaction measures.* They believe these results can be skewed or misrepresented by plans to make them look better to potential members. Consumers are also inclined to discount patients' quality evaluations because they don't believe patients are knowledgeable enough to judge health plan quality. However, consumers are very interested in patient evaluations of access to care.

- *Consumers sometimes do not realize that they don't understand the differences among plan types or how they work. This affects their evaluation of health plans and must be considered when information sources present their data to consumers.* For example, not only does the degree to which consumers understand the HMO concept affect their choice of a plan, it also affects levels of satisfaction and disenrollment. Research shows that a major reason for disenrollment is a lack of understanding of how the HMO works. Conversely, those HMO members who best understand HMOs tend to be most satisfied.

- *Consumers are suspicious of any single source of information. Impartiality is the most important criterion to them.*

- *Consumers currently rely most on family members, friends, and workplace colleagues for recommendations on health plans and to find out how they have fared under a particular plan.* These opinions carry more weight than information from any other source.

- *If faced with conflicting information, consumers rely on the experiences reported by friends over information supplied by the plans.*

- *Employer-provided materials and information appear to rank second in importance, particularly if a health committee or union group is involved.* However, consumers know that many people are self-employed or retired, so employer information may not apply to all potential plan members.

- *Information from health plans and governments (state and federal) ranked third and fourth, respectively.* Some consumers are skeptical about health plans' honesty in representing their advantages over competing plans. Governments ranked lower than either employers or nonprofit groups in credibility because governments are perceived as too bogged down in red tape and moving too slowly. Medicaid beneficiaries were the most distrustful of government information, more so than Medicare beneficiaries.

- *Information from physician groups or associations is viewed with skepticism.* Consumers felt this way because physicians may supply evaluations that are too technical or because the physicians have a vested interest in consumers' plan choices.

- *Nevertheless, some consumers mentioned discussing their health plan choices with their family physicians.* In fact, some study participants made their plan selections according to whether or not their physicians were included in a given plan's network.

- *Despite their enthusiasm for* Consumer Reports, *study participants gave consumer groups mixed reviews as an information source regarding health plan quality.* Some consumers thought these groups lacked sufficient expertise to evaluate health plans and needed more plan information than the groups would have as laypersons. Consumers were even skeptical about information provided by organizations for or representing the elderly.

- *To consumers, the best solution would be to have a combination of different groups, agencies, and information sources collaborate to provide the public with health plan information.*

The focus groups also revealed that participants were confused by many of the terms used to describe and discuss health insurance choices, such as *HMO, preferred provider option, accreditation,* and *board certification.* The terms in question had to be explained on several occasions to the focus group participants. In addition, virtually every focus group mentioned the magazine *Consumer Reports,* leading us to conclude that using a format similar to the one used by *Consumer Reports* might be useful for presenting report care data.

Consumers' opinions of what they want to know about health plans are related to their views on quality. How do consumers define quality? Consumers appear to agree that the quality of health care involves a reasonable balance of cost, coverage, choice of physician, accessibility, "value for money," and other important factors. In other words, consumers' quality judgments start with physicians, but go well beyond that.

To consumers, the concept of quality of care includes the idea that one's own particular health issues and conditions will be covered—that is, not only basic, routine urgent, and emergency care, but also preventive care, annual physicals and screenings, and prescription drug, dental, and eye care. In other words, basic care really means comprehensive care, not bare-bones catastrophic coverage. People who have chronic conditions are also concerned about and interested in coverage for catastrophic illnesses and extended care. Quality of care also means that patients are treated immediately and appropriately; plan members should be able to receive care at the nearest location.

A high-quality health plan, in the eyes of consumers, also has a number of other distinguishing characteristics. First, it is reasonable in cost and allows access to any necessary medical facility (the key here may be in how consumers define "any necessary" facility; their definition may be quite different from the plan's definition of which facility is necessary). Second, it runs smoothly, with easy referrals, good follow-up care, efficient appointment making, short office waits, and good communications, particularly over the phone. It has enough practitioners to handle the membership and isn't overloaded with patients. Third, the plan covers essential services free or with minimal out-of-pocket cost to the member. Fourth, it is a hassle-free system that gives patients access to their own medical records and informs them of their rights and the grievance or appeals procedures. Fifth, it knows how to help patients help themselves by offering preventive care and patient education; competent, cutting-edge medical care from providers who listen to and trust what patients tell them; and rehabilitation when patients need it through creative home-based strategies.

Older consumers and those with chronic conditions also want plans and practitioners to be able to make excellent referrals in times of crisis; the elderly also stress being listened to, comforted, and not rushed. Lower-income consumers want a plan that will correctly diagnose and effectively treat them the first time, because they cannot afford to take time off work to get second opinions or go from specialist to specialist; they also want doctors to listen to family histories, accept responsibility for mistakes, and trust them and be trustworthy in return.

The Overarching Need for Standardization

While this discussion makes it clear that the information needs of purchasers and consumers are complex and varied, it is clear to us that there is at least one requirement any information set must fulfill. If information is to be useful to assist in making choices, then information must be standardized so that comparisons are possible. While it may be unrealistic to expect a single standard set of performance measures for each discrete segment of the health care system, the need to make comparisons drives toward at least a standardized core of measurements that all or most players in a given segment are required to produce and report the same way.

Without a standardized core set of measures, it is difficult to envision how competition based on quality can occur. If health plans or provider organizations are forced to report on multiple sets of measures, it limits the ability of any one set to provide a comprehensive picture of quality. Since there is no theoretical limit to the number of measures that can be developed, and since one can imagine many individual organizations and stakeholder groups wanting to know about the performance that they believe is most important, the result would quickly become so burdensome that the organizations being evaluated could be expected to refuse to cooperate. Even in the event that the organizations sought to cooperate with multiple powerful constituencies, the presence of competing measurement sets would limit the ability of all to move forward coherently unless some basis for cooperation could be established.

In an alternate scenario, plans could be expected to pick and choose among a variety of measures and measurement sets. In this case, organizations almost certainly would report on the measures that most favorably reflect their organization's performance. If there were a large number of measures and the average organization in a particular class only reported on a small subset, there would be little overlap between the measures; the ability to make comparisons across organizations would not exist. In the health plan world, this would take us back to the situation in the late 1980s, when each corporate purchaser asked (often only slightly) different questions about a health plan's performance and there was little useful information that could be gleaned from the resultant data.

Current Sources for Health Plan Information

Clearly, less information is available to purchasers and consumers than is required to create an informed (and therefore disciplined), quality-driven market; however, there is good reason to believe that this state of affairs will not continue for much longer. We would like to discuss two efforts underway at NCQA—NCQA accreditation and HEDIS performance measurement—to provide information to users that can assist them with health plan selection. As this information becomes more readily available—and as more potential users realize that it is—we believe that competition based on quality will be more and more evident.

NCQA's accreditation program is a strategy for evaluating whether a health plan can document that it operates in a manner expected to result in care and service that meet the needs of its membership. NCQA accreditation is organized around standards that represent statements of excellent managed care business practice—developed and maintained by industry experts in managed care and quality improvement—in six functional domains.

1. *Quality management and improvement.* Can the health plan demonstrate that it is working to improve quality? Can it document that it has necessary structures and processes in place, that they are adequately resourced, and that they are operating as they were designed to operate? Can the health plan document that it has achieved improvements and that these improvements are sustained?

2. *Utilization management.* Can the health plan document that it has the structures and processes in place to ensure that utilization of care will be appropriate? Is there adequate protection against underservice in a health plan that creates financial incentives to providers to limit the delivery of care? Are decisions about medical appropriateness informed by clinical science? Are decisions made by individuals with sufficient expertise to make them? Are decision-making processes systematic and consistent? Are they timely? Does the health plan have well-defined and fair processes for resolving disputes about the appropriateness of care?

3. *Credentialing.* Does the health plan have a rigorous process for establishing that providers have the credentials they represent they have, or that are necessary to the delivery of the care they provide? Can the health plan document that its credentialing activities conform to that process; that is, is there evidence that credentials have been verified, and verification noted by accountable health plan management? Does the health plan incorporate information from ongoing performance reviews of providers with recredrentialing decisions?

4. *Preventive health.* Can the health plan document that it is effectively using preventive care to maintain the health of its enrolled population? Is there evidence that guidelines for preventive care are developed and are communicated to providers and patients as appropriate? Is there evidence of monitoring of the success of preventive care? Is there evidence of improvement where monitoring suggests an opportunity?

5. *Members' rights and responsibilities.* How does the health plan document that it recognizes and respects the rights of its membership? Is there a statement of rights and responsibilities that has been communicated to the member? Is there evidence that the plan has diligently tried to educate its members about important policies and procedures? Are there effective complaint and grievance processes? Do they motivate action? Is there closure?

6. *Medical records.* Is the medical record documentation adequate? Is essential information in the chart? Is it organized? Is it legible? Is there evidence that patient information (laboratory results, consultant notes) is reviewed by the primary care physician? Is there evidence of continuity of care and of follow-up? Is there evidence that care is appropriate—both that necessary care is given and that unnecessary care is not?

The accreditation process involves a site review, undertaken by a team of physician and nonphysician quality experts; typically three to five reviewers work for three or more days. Data from the on-site review are summarized in a report, which is reviewed by a committee (the review oversight committee) of senior physicians and executives from the industry, who make the accreditation determination. A health plan may receive full (three-year) or one-year accreditation, or may receive a provisional accreditation that is valid for one year. Only about one-half of plans receive full accreditation. Some 10 percent fail accreditation outright. The standards are high—deliberately so. Accreditation is a rigorous process, and a health plan truly must be capable of operating at a high level across all critical functions in order to achieve full accreditation.

Accreditation produces summary information about health plan capability and control: an explicit evaluation of whether a health plan is capable of doing the things it must in order to deliver high-quality care and service, and whether it can document that it is in fact doing those things successfully. Performance measurement provides information complementary to that; it is NCQA's work to assess the actual results that health plans achieve. Our long-term vision for performance measurement is one in which the full range of information about health plan performance is available to let purchasers and consumers make comparisons and to support health plan efforts to improve. To achieve that vision, we have focused our efforts in five areas.

1. Developing a precisely specified information set (HEDIS) that can serve as an industry standard, responsive to the needs of purchasers and consumers.

2. Developing an audit process to ensure that production of HEDIS data conforms with the precise specifications laid out by NCQA and that HEDIS data are credible to purchasers and consumers. As HEDIS data become more and more available, it will be critical to ensure that results do not misrepresent performance and thus lead users to incorrect conclusions.

3. Bringing data together to make them more accessible to users and to permit benchmarking and analysis.

4. Investigating the information needs of consumers to ensure that future generations of HEDIS will be more responsive to those.

5. Exploring ways to make HEDIS data more meaningful and accessible to users.

HEDIS 2.0, NCQA's first product released in November 1993, included some 60 statistics that focused on a broad array of issues ranging from clinical process to financial performance. HEDIS 2.0 (or a technical update, version 2.5) is being produced by more than 87 percent of HMOs and is the basis for virtually all health plan report cards. We have recently introduced a significantly enhanced version of HEDIS—HEDIS 3.0—that far more comprehensively covers the range of issues that matter not only to private purchasers, but also to those who manage the Medicare and Medicaid programs, and to the beneficiaries who receive care whether privately insured or publicly insured. HEDIS 3.0 is far more outcome oriented than was the earlier version; the set of measures is organized into eight domains that are the areas in which purchasers and consumers have told us the measures needed to focus.

1. Effectiveness of care: Is care achieving the gains in health expected?

2. Accessibility and availability of care: Is care available to those who need it, without inappropriate barriers and delay?

3. Satisfaction with the experience of care: Is the experience of care satisfying, as well as clinically effective?

4. Cost of care: Is care "high value?"

5. Stability of the health plan: Is the health plan stable—or will I experience the sort of change that could disrupt my care?

6. Informed health care choices: Is the health plan successful at helping members to be active and informed partners in health care decisions?

7. Use of services: How are resources used? Is there evidence of too much—or too little—care?

8. Plan descriptive information: How is the plan organized? What type of doctors participate, and how many?

About 75 measures in HEDIS 3.0 are intended to serve as national reporting requirements for managed care firms. These measures are precisely specified so that rules for calculation are unambiguous. In addition to these, an additional 30 or so measures are included as a testing set of measures. Measures in this testing set are for evaluation; these measures were felt to be important and promising, but significant concern existed about their usefulness for health plan comparison in 1996. The objective of the testing set is to create a mechanism to generate evidence about the characteristics of these measures—so as to better evaluate their potential usefulness for future generations of HEDIS—and to refine those that evidence suggests have great utility. It is also intended to signal where HEDIS is headed—to provide managed care firms with more lead time to prepare care management and information systems addressing areas that are not addressed by the 3.0 reporting set.

Formats and Distribution Methods

In order to be useful to the purchasers and consumers of health care, information not only has to be responsive to the issues that matter to them—and not only has to be standardized as we have suggested—but it has to be presented to them in a way that is comprehensible and needs to be available when they need it. While theoretically less challenging, our work suggests that these operational issues are no less problematic and no less important to consider.

Certain themes have emerged from the work that we and others have done to understand how to display and deliver information to the public. To summarize,

• Information must be in a user-friendly format.

• The quality information presented and the discussion of the information's meaning must be easily comprehensible to the intended users.

- The information must be easy to access and available when and where users need it.

- The existence of multiple users (with different needs and levels of sophistication) means that multiple formats—printed material, 24-hour help lines, consumer-accessible computerized databases, videotapes, even multimedia presentations—will generally be more successful than any one format alone.

There is also general agreement that the more distribution mechanisms used and the greater the variety of mechanisms the better, for several reasons. Different users may have access to some sources but not others; also, this can vary over time for the same user. One day, a written report might suffice; at another time, a database may be more convenient. Access to and effectiveness of distribution improves with redundancy of information outlets. Also, as with other kinds of information, customer use and understanding of the data improve with repetition.

A number of organizations have been successful in making quality and performance information available to the public. Xerox—a large Fortune 100 company that has been a leader in the quality movement—provides highly customized reports to Xerox employees. Xerox's reports go so far as to provide employees with information on the health plans that operate within the ZIP codes in which they live. This saves workers from having to wade through a nationwide or regional list of plans, benefit packages, and performance data. Xerox employees, a high percentage of whom are computer literate, have also requested electronic access to the information. Xerox is currently setting up a World Wide Web site with online NCQA accreditation information and some information about HEDIS measures; the company hopes to have the full set of HEDIS measures online next year. Xerox also hopes to have a referral link with Joint Commission on Accreditation of Healthcare Organizations hospital accreditation summaries, as well as online connections to its participating HealthLink HMOs.

HealthLink is a seven-year-old benefit program that assembles all participating HMOs into seven oversized networks with each managed by an appointed systems manager, itself an HMO company that has undergone a bidding and evaluation process. Systems managers are responsible for collecting, analyzing, and applying performance and other data from the HMOs assigned to them, with the intention of helping plans learn to do better. The performance reports issued to employees are part of the HealthLink program.

NCQA's work has revealed differences among socioeconomic groups regarding the preferred method for distributing information about health plan performance. Medicare beneficiaries generally prefer written materials and personal counseling over videotapes and computerized information. Not surprisingly, videotapes and computers get better ratings from younger people questioned.

HealthPartners, a Minneapolis, Minnesota–based HMO company with a variety of plan member types, is in the process of providing members with benefit and provider information electronically. Consumer Choice, an interactive computer system designed for consumer use, was introduced to members in November 1995. The system uses laptop computers and touch-screen microcomputers to provide plan members with information on more than 4500 physicians and about 300 clinic sites and medical centers affiliated with the company's traditional and open-ended HMOs and PPO. The data include detailed accounts of each practitioner's training, areas of expertise, and personal care philosophy, including a biography written and submitted by the individual physicians. In addition, the system provides a generous amount of patient satisfaction information (obtained by an independent surveying firm) and performance rankings for physicians and clinics in four categories: childhood immunization rates, prenatal care, mammography, and cholesterol screening. Consumers can even conduct a brief health risk analysis for themselves and see a list of member education classes available on various medical conditions.

The technology used by the HMO firm has existed for years in the credit card and banking industries, but this is its first application in managed care. HealthPartners began thinking about the system's design a few years ago. It wanted a system that could be transferred at some point to a web page, a CD-ROM, or even an employer's own computer system. The HMO company plans to exchange laptops for microcomputers and microcomputers for mobile workstations or kiosks (in larger locations). This will be followed by applications for network users, local networks of employers, and CD-ROMs. More categories of performance and quality measures will be added in the future.

Consumers aren't the only ones who find point-of-service information useful. Dean Medical Center, in Madison, Wisconsin, uses computerized analysis of patient-supplied clinical, health status, and functional status information. The information is solicited before patients' appointments, filled out before they go to their appointment, and scanned into the system so that data are immediately available for use during the office visit. The data are being collected for three areas: asthma treatment, internal medicine, and psychiatry. The value of the psychiatry data is still being assessed, but physicians and nurses alike report that physician-patient communication has improved for asthma patients and in internal medicine encounters. Whether patients perceive improved communication is not yet known; some physicians, though, have changed their treatment because of the information reported by patients via the survey.

Performance information has been released as HEDIS report cards, by organizations spawned by purchasing coalitions, and by the lay press. We have watched with interest and excitement as coalitions of purchasers and health plans—like the California Cooperative HEDIS Reporting Initiative (CCHRI) and the New England HEDIS Coalition—have produced HEDIS report cards, and as large and influential employers like Xerox and CalPERS (the California Public Employees and Retirees System) make data on plans available to employees at the time of enrollment choice. HEDIS and NCQA accreditation results have been published in specialized publications (such as *Health Pages*, a journal on health information for consumers) and in the lay press (such as in *Barrons* and *Newsweek*). And accreditation data are available from NCQA, where requests (for written reports or "hits" to our Internet home page) suggest that more than 8000 organizations and individuals seek that information monthly.

Efforts to make information more available are underway. In August 1996, NCQA began to offer *Quality Compass* reports. These reports—which flow from a national database of health plan quality information that NCQA has developed—enable users to get both NCQA accreditation and HEDIS results on multiple health plans, in formats that will permit easy comparison of one plan to another or to national or regional benchmarks. Reports on CD-ROM will permit users to sort and aggregate data; over the next two to three years, we expect to offer users online access to the HEDIS database and a toolkit that will permit even more flexible analyses. This first version of *Quality Compass* is intended to increase the accessibility of data as well as make it more comprehensible; over time, NCQA hopes to give users online access to the database through a set of tools that will permit users to query it directly and interactively.

Finally, a small number of states have indicated to us that they intend to release (or are working with us to prepare to release) performance information for public use. Similar efforts have occurred for other types of data—for example, a number of states (including New York, Pennsylvania, and California) have been releasing hospital- and sometimes surgeon-specific data on selected outcomes (for example, mortality rate for patients undergoing coronary artery bypass graft surgery), and the Minnesota Health Data Institute has recently published satisfaction survey data on all health plans in the state. Clearly, the state can be a powerful force for moving information to the public, and some states have already begun to provide leadership in this regard.

While efforts clearly are underway to produce information to support decision making, it is clear that such efforts are not fully mature. Why, one is forced to ask, is there so little information about the quality and performance of health care plans? And what should be done to further close the gaps that still exist?

Why Isn't More Information Available?

We believe there are several reasons that national capacity for measurement is limited. Some of these are technical; some are more cultural. Among the most important are the following:

1. *The data required for performance measurement are often unavailable or, if available, are only available at a high cost.* The performance measurement process requires transforming data that describe the process and outcomes of care into performance information. Data about the process of care may be available from electronic transaction data sets (claims, encounters, laboratory or pharmacy records, and so on); such data, however, typically lack the clinical detail necessary to understand the context in which care was delivered and rarely provide a window on the clinical and functional outcomes (or even the physiologic results) achieved as a consequence of the service. While valid measures of clinical process are possible from such data, there are limits to the knowledge that can be gleaned without additional detail. This detail is typically available only by extracting data from another—typically far more costly—source: from the medical record via abstraction, or from the patient via survey. Although theoretically capable, measurement that depends on these data sources rapidly becomes problematic—given the large sample sizes needed to generate the statistical power to discriminate between health plans, measures based on medical record abstraction or patient survey have, of necessity, been used sparingly. We anticipate that improvements in information systems will make necessary clinical and functional status data more readily available in the future, and that the rate at which information flows to the public will accelerate qualitatively as this occurs.

2. *Substantial technical problems are associated with health plan performance measurement, above and beyond the problem of obtaining necessary data.* We have already mentioned the large sample sizes needed; this is problematic not only because of the cost, but because many health plans are quite small (the median size of an HMO in the United States in 1996 was approximately 40,000 enrollees). As a result, the size of a population of interest may be too small to permit discrimination between plans. For example, given an estimated incidence of breast cancer of 60 cases per 100,000 population, the median health plan would be expected to have only 24 incident cases annually. Estimates of, for example, five-year mortality rate (one proposed, and certainly face valid, measure of outcome relevant to evaluating health plan quality) in such a small population will be subject to large swings based on chance. Furthermore, given the range of values that is likely to represent the spectrum of current performance, it seems extremely unlikely that such small samples would permit the best plans to be distinguished even from the worst plans (never mind the average plan) with any confidence that we are looking at anything other than chance variation.

The problem is even worse than that, though. We have already intimated that there may be a need for clinical detail to understand the context in which care is delivered. When one is considering an outcome measure (rather than a process measure), that need is even greater. Here the need is to understand what confounders there may be; that is, what other factors may account for an observed outcome, other than the factor of interest (health plan performance). This is the problem of risk adjustment, which is a big problem for health plan performance measurement. Where another factor (such as a characteristic of the patient: if we are looking at breast cancer mortality rate, it might be the stage at which that cancer was diagnosed, or it might be the presence or absence of comorbid illness) can affect the probability of some outcome (such as death), there is a need to adjust for that factor in order to develop a performance measure that validly and reliably estimates health plan quality. Techniques for such risk adjustment are both data intensive and typically quite far from perfect; the usefulness of many conceptually valid measures of outcome for assessing plan quality has been limited by the difficulties of adequately risk-adjusting the measures.

There are yet other technical reasons why performance information has been slow to materialize. Among those, one that bears special mention is what we call the problem of controllability. A health plan should be held accountable only for what it can control (or at least significantly influence); where an outcome is beyond the control of a health plan, it makes little sense to measure it (no matter how important it may be). To some extent, this is the problem of risk adjustment restated—if the probability that a woman will die from breast cancer is high because she has significant comorbid disease, then we obviously do not want to view that death as an indicator of poor plan performance. But another aspect of controllability is worth pointing out that relates to the long timelines over which many outcomes proceed. What plan is accountable for a potentially avertable death from breast cancer if a woman changes plans two years after her diagnosis? What plan is accountable for the development of heart disease in a patient whose high cholesterol is undetected in any of the six plans in which he enrolled during the 25-year period when his heart disease developed? The long time frames over which outcomes proceed, and the propensity that individuals have to change health plans with some frequency, individually and collectively make performance measurement (especially outcomes measurement) particularly difficult. It is far easier in a randomized, controlled, clinical trial.

3. *Standardization of measurement has been absent; without standardization, measurement provides no information for comparison.* Until recently, there had been no success at achieving standardization of measurement; that is, of creating rules that were universally applied to all managed care firms reporting information. The reasons for this are likely as much cultural as technical. Although differences in the amount and nature of available data probably account for some of the variation, it is also probably true that most measurement efforts were fairly local in scope (so the need for national standardization was not apparent).

The need for national standardization is, however, profound. On the one hand, there is a clear desire among those who purchase benefits at sites across the nation (Health Care Financing Agency, multisite employers such as Xerox and GTE) to be able to compare the performance of health plans not only locally but nationally. Also, clear value is associated with the development and elaboration of benchmarks—benchmarks that permit others to set realistic targets (that are neither too high nor too low), and benchmarks that permit best-in-class organizations to be identified and their underlying best processes studied and disseminated. Benchmarking can proceed only when measurement is standardized.

Another important issue bears on standardization. For purposes of efficiency, it is desirable that measurement strategies be developed centrally. The cost of supporting the development of HEDIS 3.0 was in excess of $1 million over the year during which it was built; we estimate that it may require another $3 million to $5 million to test and refine some of the component measures and to develop measures to address key gaps. Building and maintaining multiple structures to achieve the same end seems an inefficient use of the very limited resources available to support this work. While centralization is not the same as standardization, the latter will surely follow the former. It is, of course, possible to have standardization with redundant management processes. We have already suggested that that is inefficient; we will further suggest that it is potentially dangerous.

Is Competition in the Market for Public Information a Good Thing?

NCQA accreditation clearly represents the gold standard in health plan evaluation, and HEDIS is unquestionably the reference set for health plan performance assessment. Yet competitors are emerging, both to NCQA accreditation and to HEDIS. Is this a good thing?

As an organization firmly committed to the notion that competition in the market for managed care services will drive health plan performance to higher levels, it might seem incongruous for us to argue against competition here. And yet we will, for we feel that competition represents a real threat—not to NCQA, but to the work to which we are committed.

Competition—meaningful competition—is desirable and appropriate when consumers can distinguish sufficiently well among the range of products offered to make informed choices among them that truly reflect their preferences. We have argued that meaningful competition in the market for managed care services is possible, but will require that consumers have a better ability to distinguish among the range of health plans offered to make informed choices among them that truly reflect their preferences for some combination of price, clinical effectiveness, service effectiveness, access, and so on. Obviously we believe that the key to enabling consumers to distinguish among health plans is to equip them with information about the quality of the organization and operation of the plan (derived from expert judgment through NCQA's accreditation program) and with information about the results plans achieve in these several domains (through objective results from the application of HEDIS measurement standards). We see competition as possible, and standardized information about the quality of offerings as the key to making it happen.

Similarly, we believe that competition in the market for health plan evaluation is (theoretically) possible; to realize it, consumers must be able to distinguish between the quality of the offerings of NCQA and potential competitors. And that, we think, is practically impossible. The processes used to evaluate health plans are sufficiently arcane and technically complex as to make it unrealistic to think that consumers will be able to judge which source for information is the more reliable and valid. Without the ability to make that judgment, though, there is no possibility for competition.

What *is* possible is confusion. If competing evaluative systems exist, of variable quality, then conflicting results are likely. Without the ability to distinguish which system is of higher quality, the consumer is certain to become confused. The product of that confusion could go beyond rejection of a specific finding (that is, the specific point on which there is disagreement). We fear that consumers may be very intolerant when those who claim expertise themselves cannot agree. The risk is that that intolerance will lead to rejection—not of a specific finding, but of the process of (and prospect of) performance evaluation. We worry that disagreement among the evaluators could lead consumers to wish "a plague on all our houses" and an entire body of work to be rejected.

The solution to this could be, of course, to have an evaluator of the evaluators—an objective third party to evaluate the quality of the evaluations that NCQA and its competitors provide. Of course, there could be competition at this level (why not?), so another layer of evaluator will be required to help the public understand which objective third-party evaluator of health plan evaluators to believe. And so on, until the system topples under its own weight and we return to the void that has marked the past and that we so desperately hope is not the future.

It seems far better to suggest—given the recognition that competition must end at some point—that we admit that competition in the market for evaluation is not the means by which to achieve the public good we seek. Rather, we would argue in favor of a singular process, in which quality is ensured through openness rather than competition. In particular, we believe that the process of developing standards for health plan evaluation—be they accreditation standards that speak to health plan structure and operations, or measurement standards that address health plan results—should be singular but open, and driven by the stakeholders to the work. Openness ensures both that input from the best sources will be possible and that accountability can be achieved. Both provide quality assurance; both can occur in a not-for-profit public service environment. Stakeholder control ensures not only relevance, but is the closest thing possible to informed consumerism. Providing stakeholders to the work the opportunity to guide it creates a mechanism for a small group that represents the driving market forces to gain and use the information they need to ensure that evaluative mechanisms are built well and operate effectively. We think that this model of quality assurance—a model ensuring that quality is built in through oversight of design and implementation—is more appropriate to the need that exists and will lead, effectively and efficiently, to the standards that are needed to respond to the public's need for information about the quality and performance of health plans.

The Consequences of Public Disclosure of Health Plan Performance Information

What has been—and what will be—the impact of the release of more and more information to the public? We offer the following short list.

1. *Health plans will feel increasing pressure to demonstrate excellence and to improve the quality of the care and service they provide.* Increasing this pressure—and driving this improvement—is, of course, the primary objective of producing and releasing quality information. We see this already, and expect to see it grow over time as more information is available and as more of those for whom it is intended recognize that it is and become familiar with its use.

2. *Other health care organizations will feel the same pressure that health plans do.* To some extent, this is (and will be) a consequence of parallel efforts to measure and report on the performance of hospitals, physicians, and other components of the health care system. Some of these efforts are underway, but have not moved as quickly as have those we have described. But to some extent, pressure will rise elsewhere within the system because managed care firms—which are being held accountable for results—recognize that they need information about the quality of care and service delivered to their members by those with whom they contract if they are going to manage quality the way they are now expected to. This transmitted pressure is a positive force that will help both to improve quality at the provider level and help to coordinate quality improvement efforts at different levels of the system. It will create increasing discomfort, though, as organizations and individuals begin to feel the pressure for accountability that managed care firms have felt intensely for nearly a decade.

3. *Organizational strategic planning will focus on improving performance in those areas where information is released to the public.* There is both an upside and downside to this: The visibility of results will lead to the allocation (or reallocation) of resources to areas where improvement is evidently most needed. This is good—health plans (and others) will invest in improving clinical and service performance and (at least to some extent) in proportion to the need. The risk here is that investment will be limited to areas where there are performance measures—that *only* what gets measured will get done.

As it is impossible (at least impossibly costly) to require the public release of information for all issues that might be important, there is some risk that important issues will not get the attention they should because no public reporting is required.

Strategies exist for dealing with this. One, of course, is to ensure that expert evaluation of organizations continues to be a component of the overall evaluation system. To the extent that experts are involved in detailed inspection of a health care organization, there is an opportunity to gain assurance that the organization's efforts to manage quality are not too narrowly focused and an opportunity for the health care organization to be rewarded for investing resources in areas where there is a need for it to do so, whether or not that investment is apparent through a public reporting process. Even so, those who develop strategies for public reporting are well advised to consider the responsibility that activity implies: Laying out the public reporting agenda is tantamount to setting strategic priorities for health care organizations, and the potential to do harm by misdirecting resources is real and must be considered.

4. *In the long run, the consumer will become a smarter purchaser; this will move quality assurance deep into the system.* While we expect the availability of comparative information to assist consumers to make choices more in line with their preferences—and expect to see a positive impact on the marketplace as a result—we think the longer-term impact of the public release of information will be bigger than that. We believe—and our work with consumers suggests it is more than an article of faith—that performance information can have a powerful effect to stimulate consumers to become more aware of the issues important to them; reports cards are a tool both for communicating information *and for stimulating consumers to learn about the issues the information addresses.* Knowing about the mammography rates of two plans tells consumers something (we think, something important) about the priorities those health plans have and about their success in successfully achieving results in line with their priorities. But information about mammography rates also raises awareness of the importance of mammography (and of the importance of other related information—such as whether mammograms are read accurately and whether abnormal results are followed up in a timely manner) and of the health plan's role in ensuring that women receive preventive care. This awareness will help consumers better understand what else they need to know and to ask the questions of their provider and their plan that matter to them. Educated consumers will raise levels of accountability to unprecedented heights; the public release of information is both a part of, and a powerful stimulus to, that consumer education.

Cary Sennett, M.D., Ph.D., is executive vice president at the National Committee for Quality Assurance (NCQA). He is responsible for overseeing all functions—from strategic planning and marketing to policy and product development—that support NCQA's efforts to develop products responsive to the marketplace's need for information to enable value-based purchasing and selection of managed care plans.

Sennett is a board-certified internist with considerable training and experience both in the science and application of clinical measurement for quality improvement in managed care. Prior to joining NCQA, Sennett had quality leadership roles at Group Health Cooperative of Puget Sound, at US Healthcare's US Quality Algorithms subsidiary, and at Aetna Health Plans. He received an M.D. degree from Yale and did his residency in internal medicine at Harvard's Brigham and Women's Hospital. After his clinical training, Sennett completed a Kaiser Foundation Fellowship in Health Policy and Management at the Massachusetts Institute of Technology, from which he received a Ph.D. degree.

Sennett is a frequent speaker and author on issues of quality measurement and quality improvement in health care, and is a member of the editorial boards of *The Joint Commission Journal on Quality Improvement* and *Quality Management in Health Care.*

Margaret O'Kane is the president of the National Committee for Quality Assurance (NCQA), an independent, nonprofit organization that reviews and assesses the quality of managed care plans. Under O'Kane's leadership, NCQA has become the nation's leading accrediting organization for health plans, and the organization-developed performance measures have become the industry standard. NCQA is headquartered in Washington, D.C.

O'Kane, who has worked in the quality field since 1986, has many years of experience in developing health care policy and in research. She has served as director of quality management for the Group Health Association, a large staff model HMO, and was staff director for the Medical Directors Division of Group Health Association of America. In addition, she was a special assistant to the director of the National Center for Health Services Research, was a Public Health Services Fellow, and has worked for various other research and government entities.

O'Kane earned a master's degree from the Johns Hopkins School of Hygiene and Public Health.

Chapter 16

The Joint Commission's Agenda for Change and Beyond

Paul M. Schyve and Dennis S. O'Leary

Today's Health Care Environment

In recent years, U.S. health care organizations have faced escalating challenges. Cries have come from all sides that health care costs are out of control. Employers, especially, have expressed concern that their competitiveness—especially in a global economy—is being hurt by the magnitude and escalation of health care costs. Relatedly, employees complain that they are asked to pay more out-of-pocket costs for their health care. And advocates for the underinsured and uninsured are fearful that rising costs restrict access to needed prevention and timely detection and treatment services.

This focus on costs has led to a rising demand for the health care system's accountability to the health care consumer—the public—and the purchasers of health care. This demand has focused on the answers to three sets of questions.

- Which treatments are efficacious and effective? Why is there a paucity of scientific studies to support widely accepted interventions? Why is there professional disagreement over specific preventive tactics, such as screening mammography, and medical interventions, such as coronary artery bypass graft surgery?

- Which treatment is appropriate for a given individual? Why are there variations from geographic area to area in the rates that certain treatments are used, even where patient populations are similar and no differences in outcomes have been demonstrated? Why are patients sometimes admitted to hospitals, while similar patients are managed on an ambulatory basis? Why are patients sometimes discharged when follow-up care is not available?

- Why does health care cost so much? Why has its cost risen faster than inflation? Why does an aspirin tablet cost $5.00 in the hospital?

These are all clear and understandable questions. They can best be summed up in one question: How do consumers and purchasers know that they are getting their money's worth in health care—that they are getting *value* for their dollars? And since the value provided is likely to differ among health care organizations, can information be provided that permits them to select the *best* value?

In this environment there has been a fundamental shift in the relationship between health care professionals and providers and the rest of society. For decades, health care professionals said, "We know best; trust us." Now society demands accountability to a shared "community of interests"—a community composed not only of health care providers and professionals, but also of consumers, payors and employers, regulators, and policy makers.

The Health Care System's Response

The health care system has reacted to this shifting relationship by recognizing the need to focus on efficiency and quality and by integrating health care delivery and health care financing to improve both efficiency and service. Traditional quality assurance had assumed that classic quality expectations (that is, efficacy, effectiveness, appropriateness, and safety) were being met, and that the goal was to prevent their erosion—usually by investing more, rather than fewer, resources into care. But the lessons learned from other industries suggested that the focus should be on continuous improvement, not just on detecting and correcting errors.[1] And with this new focus came a commitment to improve efficiency as well as quality; that is, to reduce resource use for the same or even improved outcomes. The key to this new focus is the evaluation of outcomes—the results of health care—whether measured by clinical or functional outcomes, by the satisfaction of those receiving care, or by the costs of the care. Measuring these results, as well as the processes used to achieve them, is becoming the core of a data-driven approach to managing health care organizations and continuously improving health outcomes.

Which outcomes are most important to improve? Again, learning from other industries, providers are shifting from determining desired outcomes almost exclusively from their own perspectives to recognizing the importance of understanding and responding to the needs and expectations of the other stakeholders in the community of interests. These especially include purchasers, enrollees in health plans, and patients receiving care.[2]

Next, once the outcomes at interest are identified, how can better outcomes be achieved? Here, health care has responded by developing clinical practice guidelines, clinical protocols, and critical pathways. All are mechanisms that translate scientifically based (data-driven) process design into tools that can guide practitioners and organizations in practice, while accommodating the consumer's preferences.[3] These tools, in guiding process redesign and implementation, can also be helpful in enhancing efficiency while simultaneously improving quality. Combining an understanding of consumer needs and expectations with the use of scientific knowledge to design improved processes has created opportunities to address health outcomes, satisfaction, and costs at the same time.

While these shifts in the health care system's approach to quality and efficiency were primarily imported from outside health care, the other major response to the changed environment has been generated within the health care system itself: the movement toward integration.[4] Organizations that once offered one type of service (for example, acute inpatient care) have progressively become providers of a spectrum of services (for example, acute care, long-term care, home care, and ambulatory care). And from what were once aggregates of discreet services, some organizations have begun to provide a truly integrated continuum of services for the individuals they serve.

With this integration has come the ability to manage *health*, not just illness. As organizations have learned, solid investments in health promotion, disease prevention, and early detection of disease can reduce the downstream costs of treatment, and patients can be shifted to home care and ambulatory care from inpatient care with advanced, coordinated planning. More recently, the integration of health services has led to linkages with health care financing. This most commonly involves the management of health benefits for a defined group of healthy and sick individuals, that is, a population whose health status is one of the outcomes of the health care system.[5]

But the integration of health delivery and health financing in the form of managed care has created new challenges. The public fears that an emphasis on efficiency will result in underutilization or even underavailability of needed services and that management of care will reduce responsiveness to their preferences—or choices—with regard to practitioners, provider organizations, or treatment options. In a related fashion, physicians and other practitioners fear that their clinical autonomy to make decisions in the interests of their patients may be limited. There are also concerns—commonly expressed in the media—that economic incentives may tempt provider organizations and individual practitioners to act in their own interests rather than in the interest of patients, thus eroding the public's confidence in the beneficence of the health care system. And all stakeholders worry that improvements in both quality and efficiency, while possible in theory, may not be linked in practice. Thus, the drive for efficiency may in fact compromise quality and undermine the value in the health care system.

The Role of Accreditation

Within the context of this challenging environment, how can an accrediting body contribute value? First, it provides tangible support to the full range of mainstream health care organizations in effectively improving *both* their quality and efficiency (that is, their performance) and in helping them understand the needs and expectations of the larger community of interests. Second, the accrediting body conducts credible and comprehensive evaluations of health care organizations and makes useful performance information publicly available to help health care consumers and purchasers choose those providers that offer the best value. In addition, the accrediting body can provide direct assistance in the interpretation and use of performance data for all stakeholders in the community of interests.

Third, the accrediting body facilitates the development of consensus within the larger community of interests about expectations for health care quality and efficiency. It does so by involving consumers, practitioners, provider organizations, regulators, and payors and purchasers in forums for designing, evaluating, and setting priorities for the tools and measures used to evaluate health care organization performance (for example, standards, performance measures) and for integrating these tools and measures into a comprehensive evaluation process.

The Joint Commission's Agenda for Change

Consistent with these accreditation-related roles, the mission of the Joint Commission is to improve the quality of care provided to the public through the provision of health care accreditation and related services that support performance improvement in health care organizations. In 1986 the Joint Commission set a new direction to create services that would better serve users of the health care delivery system, accredited health care organizations, and the larger community of interests.[6] By so doing, the Joint Commission itself would contribute value to the U.S. health care system. This new direction was called the Agenda for Change.

The Agenda for Change would, in effect, entail a complete reengineering of the accreditation process. The new process was to focus on what a health care organization *does*—and *should do*—that is most relevant to patient care outcomes. This meant, first, focusing the standards and survey process on important systems and processes in the organization (called *important functions* by the Joint Commission), rather than on the structures of the organization, such as individual departments, services, or committees. Second, it meant shifting the focus of the accreditation evaluation from the *capability* of the organization to provide good care—as reflected by the existence of important structures, systems, and processes—to the actual *performance* of these important systems and processes—as reflected in their effectiveness and efficiency in achieving desired health care outcomes. Third, it meant fostering *continuous improvement* in performance, rather than only maintaining the current level of performance, which had been the traditional role of quality assurance. Finally, this emphasis on performance explicitly acknowledged that the accreditation process must in some fashion incorporate the actual results being achieved, that is, health outcomes.

With this emphasis on continuous improvement in performance came the intent to support the rapid innovation—and even restructuring—required of health care organizations to meet public demands for more effective, efficient, and integrated care. This meant creating an accreditation process that was adaptable and could not only accommodate but also actually guide the evolution of new organizations capable of meeting the public's objectives.

Finally, the added value of the Joint Commission's new direction was to be manifest both in its service to accredited organizations in their efforts to improve and in its service to the public by making useful information available about the performance of accredited organizations. The value added by the Joint Commission would be enhanced by improving the efficiency of the accreditation process itself.

Over the past decade, this Agenda for Change has guided the Joint Commission's developmental priorities. As the structure and nature of the health care system have evolved, the Agenda for Change has been tailored to meet the needs emerging from this evolution. The goals of the Agenda for Change that were envisioned a decade ago have indeed stood the test of time, and the new accreditation process is now in place. How does the new accreditation process meet contemporary needs and add value to the health care system?

Refocusing the Standards

Historically, the basis for evaluating (and accrediting) a health care organization has been to assess its compliance with standards. Whether these standards set expectations for structures or for systems and processes, the standards themselves have been established through a process that relies on scientific knowledge, expert consensus, and real-world relevance. That is, the current state of knowledge has been reviewed for information that contributes to understanding the role of the structure or system or process in achieving good outcomes—or, often, avoiding bad outcomes. Current knowledge has been evaluated by various content experts to arrive at consensus on translating knowledge into standards. Sometimes the scientific knowledge base is insufficient, and experts have needed to extrapolate from the limited information base and their personal experience to create proposed standards.

While standards should reflect *desirable* goals, they also need to be *achievable* goals. Even if they are stretch goals, they need to be within the reach of most health care organizations with regard to both technology and resources. If they are not achievable, they are not appropriate as standards. To determine that a proposed standard is achievable requires input from more than just the experts. It requires a review process that involves clinicians and administrators in health care organizations, consumers (the patients) who ultimately benefit from the standards, and others who rely on the accreditation process. As will be discussed, even with the incorporation of performance measures (including patient outcomes) into the accreditation process, standards-based evaluation will continue to drive the accreditation process in the future. Continued attention will therefore need to be directed to the effectiveness of the standards development process.

How was this process used to refocus the standards as part of the Agenda for Change? The goal was to generate a set of standards that address the performance of important functions—that is, those systems, processes, and activities that have the greatest direct and indirect impacts on patient outcomes. The first step in reaching this goal was to review the many existing standards; there were, for example, more than 2500 standards for hospitals. Joint Commission staff, with the advice of committees composed of practicing clinicians and administrators, eliminated standards that did not clearly relate to patient outcomes or were thought to be but one of multiple ways to achieve the same desirable outcome.

The resulting substantially reduced numbers of standards now had to be recast in a *performance-based* framework. But performance from whose point of view? The ultimate beneficiary of the health care system is the public, including enrollees in health plans, patients, and their families. This same public, it was reasoned, should also be the ultimate beneficiary of accreditation. Therefore, what could be more appropriate than to view an organization's performance on the basis of how well it meets the needs of the patient—that is, to make the standards *patient-centered*?

With the assistance of health services researchers at Northwestern University and both ad hoc and standing advisory committees, the Joint Commission generated a new framework for organizing its standards that was both performance-based and patient-centered. The framework begins by focusing on those systems and processes whose direct customer is the patient, and then moves behind the scenes to address those systems and processes that must be performed well if the patient-centered processes are to be effective. The former set of systems and processes (or, in Joint Commission parlance, functions) are called patient-focused functions, and the second set are called organization functions.

The patient-focused functions, as they were subsequently refined, are as follows:

- Patient rights (including the organization's ethical code of business practice)
- Patient assessment (including imaging and laboratory testing)
- Patient care (including anesthesia and conscious sedation, medication use, operative and other invasive procedures, rehabilitation, and use of restraint and seclusion)
- Patient education (including health promotion, disease prevention, and family education)
- Continuum of care (including admission, discharge planning, and transfer among practitioners and providers)

The organization functions, as they were subsequently refined, are as follows:

- Leadership (including governance, management, and clinical leadership)
- Human resources management (including determination of staff competence and staff education)
- Information management (including health care records, aggregate performance data, comparative data, and knowledge-based literature)
- Environmental management (including security, safety, equipment management, and the physical and psychosocial environments)
- Infection surveillance, prevention, and control
- Improving organization performance (including the design of systems and processes, measurement, assessment, priority setting, and continuous improvement)

Because these important functions were identified in a patient-centered, performance-based framework, it rapidly became obvious that these same functions are relevant to all types of organizations that directly deliver care. These include organizations providing ambulatory care,[7] behavioral health care (including services for chemical dependency and mental retardation/developmental disabilities),[8] home care (including hospice services),[9] inpatient care (including psychiatric, rehabilitation, and other specialty services),[10] and long-term care (including dementia, subacute, and pharmacy services).[11]

Organizations that do not deliver care directly almost always have similar organization functions, but do not perform patient-focused functions. Thus, the accreditation standards for laboratories are organized around the organization functions, with additional chapters on the technical functions of quality control and CLIA-waived testing.[12] Likewise, integrated organizations that provide a spectrum of services—for example, health maintenance organizations and provider-sponsored networks—are themselves evaluated against standards for relevant organization functions, while actual care delivery sites are evaluated against standards for patient-focused and organization functions that are appropriate to the care setting.[13]

But a narrowed list of standards that are patient-centered and organized around important functions are not necessarily performance-focused. The standards themselves needed to be restated as *performance objectives*; that is, there was a need to be clear about the goals—the desired results—of the functions. For example, having good systems and processes in place to support patient rights or to educate patients would not be sufficient. The important questions for consumers, health care organizations, and an accrediting body were, and are: Are patients' rights actually being respected? Are patients being educated effectively?

So the patient-focused, functionally aligned standards were recast as objectives that described intended *results*. These would not be the ultimate results reflected by patient health outcomes, whose measurement and interpretation are technically challenging (for example, because of the need for risk adjustment) but they would be the intermediate results of the important functions. For example, the standards would expect timely patient assessments that contain sufficient data for treatment planning and the undertaking of interventions that are appropriate to the individual patient. These intermediate results provide assurance that an organization has the needed systems and processes—both patient-focused and organization functions—in place; that these systems and processes are well designed, reflect current knowledge, and are stable; that the systems and processes are measured and monitored to identify any changes in their stability; and that, in response to any changes in stability or new knowledge, the systems and processes are redesigned to improve their effectiveness and efficiency. The achievement of good intermediate results, in turn, increases the probability that good ultimate results—patient health outcomes—will also be achieved, and that the risk of undesirable ultimate results will be reduced.

In sum, the patient-centered, performance-based standards focus on the effective implementation of important systems and processes, rather than only on their existence. And effective implementation is judged by results, not simply by acceptable design. The development of performance objectives as the central theme of the new standards framework also permitted the elimination of much prescriptive detail from the then-existing standards and encouraged the preparation of multiple examples of acceptable performance and implementation for inclusion in the standards manuals. While standards state what *must* be done to be accredited, the examples are just that—examples of *acceptable* methods of meeting the performance objectives articulated in the new standards. Other equally or more effective methods are also acceptable, and innovation in the spirit of continuous improvement is not only permitted, but encouraged. The intent statement for a standard, which is also found in the scoring guidelines, helps to explain what the organization would normally be *expected* to do to comply with the standard, but the surveyor(s) may still use his or her judgment if the organization can show how its alternative approach complies with the standard. This approach to standards and scoring guidelines allows the flexibility the organization needs to be able to improve its efficiency as well as its quality (that is, to improve its overall performance).

Notwithstanding the new standards framework, an approach that enables continuous improvement in performance does not necessarily set an expectation for continuous improvement. To set an expectation for continuous improvement, certain specific concepts also needed to be included in the standards. Today, most of the concepts that underlie continuous quality improvement (CQI) and total quality management (TQM) underlie the approach found in Joint Commission standards. These concepts include the following:

- The importance of identifying the organization's customers and of understanding their needs and expectations, their levels of satisfaction with how well their needs and expectations are being met, and their priorities for improvement.

- The important role of the organization's leaders—governance, managerial, and clinical—in establishing and making widely known the organization's mission, vision, and priorities for improvement throughout the organization.

- The role of human resources management in matching individuals' skills and knowledge to the processes in which they will work, in providing new process knowledge needed for improvement, and in supporting the positive attitude and application of the knowledge and skills (that is, profound knowledge and improvement tools) needed to drive improvement in the organization.

- An emphasis on understanding and changing the design of systems and processes, rather than focusing on isolated individual performance, as the principal source of improvement opportunities.

- The realization that important systems and processes usually directly or indirectly involve multiple departments, services, and individuals within the organization, and, therefore, that their effectiveness and improvement require cooperation and collaboration across the organization's structures and boundaries.

- The importance of good design and testing of new processes, instead of relying on inspection and correction of errors and defects after the fact.

- The role of measurement of outcomes—including clinical results, health status, satisfaction, and costs—and of the processes that yield those outcomes, and appropriate assessment of the data.

- The use of properly assessed data (that is, good information) to understand the cause-effect relationships between processes and outcomes, to set priorities for improvement, to establish a basis for evaluating process redesigns, and to monitor the stability of existing or revised processes.

- Attention to all relevant dimensions of performance, including efficiency, as the proper subjects of improvement activities. These dimensions include efficacy, appropriateness, availability, timeliness, effectiveness, continuity, safety, and respect and caring, as well as efficiency.

- An emphasis on continuous improvement in performance, rather than only on quality assurance that maintains current levels of quality and corrects defects.

In addition to these CQI/TQM concepts, the Joint Commission approach to performance improvement also incorporates the use of external, comparative databases (that is, reference databases). These databases can provide comparisons that are useful to the organization for assessing its performance on a relative basis, for setting improvement priorities, and for benchmarking processes and outcomes.[14] In addition, Joint Commission standards emphasize the use of up-to-date sources of scientifically based process knowledge, such as clinical practice guidelines, in designing, assessing, and redesigning the organization's processes.

These concepts, including the use of reference databases and clinical practice guidelines, underlie four chapters in each accreditation manual: Leadership, Management of Human Resources, Management of Information, and Improving Organization (or Network) Performance. The Improving Organization Performance chapter not only includes these concepts, but in its design-measure-assess-improve cycle, it also recapitulates the steps of the plan-do-check (or study)-act cycle of Shewhart and Deming.[15]

And as a final footnote to the standards transition, the number of standards for hospitals was reduced from 2500 to 500, creating the foundation for an accreditation process that is both more focused and more demanding than its predecessor.

A Survey Process to Match

The realignment of the standards to be patient-centered, functionally oriented, and performance-based, and the incorporation of continuous improvement concepts into this standards framework, were intended both to stimulate and to guide health care organizations in their efforts to improve. The new standards were intended as well, however, to provide yardsticks against which organizations are measured in order to reach accreditation decisions.

If the yardsticks had been radically altered—as they had—the methods for applying these measurement instruments would also require radical redesign, not simply from a technical standpoint but also in a fashion consistent with the principles underlying the standards. To this end, the survey process has been redesigned to evaluate cross-organizational systems and processes, rather than the activities of individual departments, services, or disciplines. To conduct this cross-organizational assessment and to model cross-organizational collaboration and teamwork, the surveyors function as a multidisciplinary team—viewing different parts of the organization from the same overall perspective and integrating their observations into findings related to the performance of patient-focused and organization functions throughout the organization.

The surveyor's focus is on performance—is the job done well?—rather than on the presence of policies, procedures, structures, or equipment. Assessing actual performance is clearly more challenging than reading policy and procedure manuals, meeting minutes, and patient records. It takes interviews with patients, with staff, and with the organization's leaders and clinicians. And it takes visits to patient care units to observe care and to discuss patient records with the actual caregivers from multiple disciplines. This increased interaction with staff at all levels has the ancillary benefit of providing a more consultative survey process, and daily briefings with the organization's leadership provide immediate educational feedback about the organization's strengths and opportunities for improvement.

To maximize the utility of the survey process to the organization, feedback from the surveyors should be reliable and timely. Reliability is dependent on the clarity of the standards, consistency in surveyor judgments, effective integration of related data and information from across the organization, and accurate judgments about the impact of surveyor conclusions on the organization's accreditation decision. The latter include identification of significant areas of performance that need improvement, which are referred to as Type I recommendations.

The revision of the standards and the reengineering of the survey process were designed with the forgoing outcomes in mind. Not only have the standards been simplified and reduced in number, as described, they have been rewritten by writers from outside the Joint Commission who were not steeped in Joint Commission jargon. This was done because the standards had to be understandable to their primary users, the health care organizations, while still reflecting the professional intents behind the standards. This translation of standards into "plain English" has not only improved communications between surveyor and organization staff, but also between surveyor and surveyor and between surveyor and Joint Commission central office staff, thereby increasing the consistency of standards interpretation. Further, the sharing of information among members of the survey team, and the new requirement that they reach consensus on scoring of each standard, virtually eliminates any idiosyncratic standards interpretations at an individual surveyor level. This sharing of data and development of consensus on findings also means that the surveyor findings are informed by multiple observations from throughout the organization, rather than only by observations of the portions of the organization one individual surveyed.

The survey team's conclusions are used to reach decisions about the organization's accreditation status and to determine Type I recommendations, if any, that will require follow-up either through an on-site visit or review of a written progress report from the organization. The organization must resolve all Type I recommendations within specific time frames in order to retain its accreditation. For the typical accreditation survey, the translation of findings related to hundreds of standards into consistent accreditation decisions is a significant challenge. To meet this challenge, computerized algorithms using so-called aggregation and decision rules have been developed. These rules consistently group related survey findings together, weight the relative importance of survey findings, and produce numerical ratings for each of a series of identified performance areas.

These rules have long been publicly available, but their application in the field without computer support stretched human capabilities. Thus, in the past, the surveyors had great difficulty in accurately predicting the likelihood of Type I recommendations at the conclusion of a survey. This problem, together with other identified needs, led to the decision to provide laptop computer support for surveyors in the field.

Today, the findings from multiple surveyors can be entered into a single software program, differences in surveyor judgments flagged for discussion, and consensus scores finalized. The findings can then be shared with the organization's leaders at the end of the survey, providing an opportunity to discuss and validate the findings with the leaders. The laptop computers also permit application of the aggregation and decision rules to the findings and the production of a preliminary accreditation report that is left with the organization's leaders. Because this report is generated using the same computer algorithms applied to the validated findings in the Central Office, there has been a dramatic reduction in the number of differences between the survey team's preliminary conclusions and the final written report. The preliminary report that the surveyors now leave on-site is therefore providing immediate useful feedback to the organization. Finally, the reduced processing requirements for the accreditation report in the central office is permitting more rapid transmission of the final report to the organization. This has most recently averaged 45 days from the end of the survey.

If accreditation is to add value to the health care system, the accreditation process itself must be continuously improved. To this end, the Joint Commission launched the Orion Project in 1995. This project is an initiative to create a "mobile laboratory" to test innovative concepts that have significant potential to improve the quality and value of accreditation services. The intent is then to transition successfully tested methods, products, and services into the mainstream accreditation process. The overall goals of the Orion Project have been to

- Create a continuous accreditation process at the local level that supports health care organizations' efforts to improve their performance.
- Use regionally dedicated surveyors who are sensitive to local issues and needs.
- Tailor performance measurement activities to the scope of services and data-gathering capability of individual organizations.
- Work with local and state external review agencies to reduce duplication of activities.
- Foster ongoing communication with the Joint Commission.
- Provide dedicated, continuing support to accredited organizations.
- Expand educational opportunities for health care organizations.

The idea of an experimental project for testing new accreditation approaches was proposed by the Joint Commission's Work Group on Accreditation Issues for Small and Rural Hospitals, a group of users—and critics—of the Joint Commission accreditation services. The Orion initiative allows for the unfettered testing of new accreditation concepts before any broad-scale national implementation proceeds.

Orion Project testing is being conducted in selected geographic areas to provide for controlled, yet flexible, experimentation. A region in central Pennsylvania was identified as the first test site beginning in April 1995. Sixty-eight hospitals and freestanding ambulatory care, home care, long-term care, and behavioral health care organizations are currently participating in this site where testing is addressing the following four concepts.

1. Implementation of a regional representative program. A Joint Commission staff person serves as the regional representative. This person works in the region to facilitate ongoing communication between health care organizations and the Joint Commission, and also provides performance improvement support to these organizations.
2. Assignment of a dedicated survey team to the region, which knows the local environment and is sensitive to issues that area organizations face.
3. Adaptation of relevant performance measures. The regional representative assists organizations in identifying and using performance measures appropriate to the care they provide.
4. Reduction of duplicative external review activities. The Joint Commission is actively working with other health care review organizations—state, local, and voluntary—to reduce redundant surveys and other review activities.

Arizona was selected as the second project site and began site testing in September 1995. Enrollment includes more than 147 health care organizations. The Orion Project is testing the following concepts in Arizona.

- Designation of a coordinating surveyor. This surveyor organizes survey activities and participates in surveys when appropriate. The coordinating surveyor also helps to decentralize scheduling and management of survey activities, to the extent possible, and serves as a liaison between surveyors and the central office service team.

- Establishment of a regional service team at the Joint Commission's central office. This team provides the services of a regional representative, but does so electronically from the Joint Commission's central office.

The third project, Orion-Tennessee, has been designed as a value-added accreditation support program. The program, a refinement of the original ideas tested in Orion-Pennsylvania, constitutes the first embodiment of the continuous accreditation process envisioned when the Orion Project was launched. This program is a self-funded experiment being conducted in cooperation with the Tennessee Hospital Association. The Orion-Tennessee model incorporates three key components.

1. A train-the-trainer program for hospital staff having leadership responsibilities for quality improvement.

2. A series of 12 structured on-site consultations by the regional representative, based on scheduled self-assessments against defined groups of the standards.

3. Customized packages of print materials that address common standards compliance and quality improvement issues.

The primary objective of the Orion Project is to continuously improve the value of accreditation for the accredited organization. The concepts being tested are steadily laying the groundwork for the introduction of performance measures into the accreditation process—a transition that will eventually define accreditation as a continuous process.

The Role of Performance Measures in Accreditation

Performance measures are quantitative evaluation tools that can be used to identify and guide improvement opportunities in health care. They are commonly measures of health outcomes, including clinical results, functional status, satisfaction of the patient and patient's family, and the costs incurred in achieving these outcomes. Performance measures also include measures of processes and resulting intermediate outcomes (for example, the degree to which a clinical practice guideline is followed in treating breast cancer, the mammography rate) that are causally linked to the outcomes of interest (in this example, survival and quality of life for patients with breast cancer).[16]

Good outcomes are the ultimate goal of health care. At the outset of the Agenda for Change, the Joint Commission recognized that the day was approaching in which the evaluation of a health care organization would not be credible if it did not take into account the actual outcomes the organization produced. That is, a standards-based evaluation alone would not be sufficient. Only by examining health outcomes as part of the accreditation process could organization evaluations yield the type of useful information about the organization's performance sought by providers, consumers, and purchasers. For the provider, its own outcomes—especially in comparison to others—help it to identify opportunities and priorities for improving its performance. For the consumer, comparative performance information—especially that information relevant to his or her personal situation—may help in choosing among providers. Likewise, for purchasers, comparative outcomes provide one basis for contracting with providers to offer employee or beneficiary services.

At the advent of the Agenda for Change, the development of performance measures—especially outcome measures—was seen as opening the door to a future accreditation process that would no longer require the use of standards and an on-site survey process (except, perhaps, to audit data). Is it possible for accreditation to be entirely driven by performance measures? A decade's experience in the development and use of performance measures, combined with the insights provided by the statistical quality control principles that underlie CQI and TQM approaches, suggest not. While the ultimate goal of health care is good outcomes, these outcomes are always the product of *past* processes. That is, today's outcomes result from yesterday's work. But most decisions that consumers and purchasers make in health care are based on expectations surrounding *future* performance: "Where should I go for care?" "With whom should we contract?" To predicate tomorrow's outcomes on today's outcomes, the answers to the following three questions must be answerable in the affirmative.

1. Are the processes that yielded today's outcomes designed well; that is, are they designed in accordance with contemporary knowledge and likely to be stable over time?

2. Does the organization measure these processes to monitor their stability, and does it take action to return them to stability when unexpected variation occurs?

3. Since current knowledge in health care is steadily advancing, does the organization systematically and continuously improve its processes—and thereby its outcomes—in light of new knowledge?

The answers to these questions are not evident from the outcomes themselves. However, these questions are precisely the foundation of the modern accreditation process that seeks to minimize risks, optimize outcomes, and foster continuous improvement. Over time, good outcomes are not random events. They occur because organizations do the right things (processes) and do them well (intermediate outcomes). The codification of these expectations occurs in the form of standards. Good outcomes should generally validate effective standards compliance, while less satisfactory outcomes establish the baseline for and provide guidance toward improved future performance. Thus, the credible, comprehensive accreditation process of the future needs to combine the effective application of standards and performance measures. The two complementary views of an organization provided through these evaluation tools will be progressively refined as their relationships are empirically tested through incremental refinements in the future accreditation process.

A decade ago, when the Joint Commission first determined that outcomes measures needed to be incorporated into the accreditation process, it was assumed that this would be a relatively easy and inexpensive process. But it soon became clear that measures that were adequate for this purpose had not already been developed. Consequently, the Joint Commission itself embarked on an arduous and relatively expensive process of developing and testing performance measures. This culminated in the introduction of the Indicator Measurement System (IMSystem) in 1994.[17]

In keeping with the original vision, the intent was to progressively require all accredited organizations (beginning with hospitals) to participate in the IMSystem as part of the accreditation process. This system would then provide the Joint Commission with relevant, reliable, valid, and risk-adjusted data on each accredited organization's performance that could be incorporated into the accreditation process. The benefits were, the Joint Commission thought, self-evident: good, nationally comparable data that would assist accredited organizations in their quality improvement efforts, improve the usefulness of the accreditation decisions, and, someday, provide health care organizations with a source of data that could be used to meet the increasing demands from consumers and purchasers for outcomes data.

But by late 1994, the quality evaluation environment had changed. First, in contrast to a decade earlier, there were now hundreds of performance measures and numerous performance measurement systems available. This change had occurred both because of the growing interest in health care outcomes which had been inspired in part by the work of Wennberg and others on small area variation,[18,19] and because of the increasing technical capacity to store and manipulate data. In addition, by 1994, some accredited organizations were already participating in one of these other measurement systems, either voluntarily or because participation was mandated (for example, by state law). And finally, some providers correctly concluded that the IMSystem did not have the short-term capability to meet their specific data needs.

In light of these factors, the Joint Commission reassessed its plans in early 1995 and concluded that the needs of the future accreditation process for performance data might be better satisfied by a combination of measurement systems, including the IMSystem. Consequently, the Joint Commission announced a plan to include a variety of measurement systems in its accreditation process, thus affirming the prerogative of choice for accredited organizations.[20] An organization would be allowed to select, from a group of systems judged to be acceptable, the system that best met its needs. It would also be able to choose those performance measures that were most applicable to the patient care services it provides. In the future, organizations seeking accreditation would be expected to participate in one of these approved measurement systems.

To implement this plan, the Joint Commission issued a Request for Measurement Systems in 1995, inviting a large number of measurement systems to become involved in the future accreditation process.[21] Approximately 150 systems responded, and subsequently more than 70 submitted specifications for review by a special Council on Performance Measurement. This Council on Performance Measurement, comprising nationally known experts in outcomes measurement, established a framework to support the review and evaluation of performance measurement systems.[22] The framework incorporates six broad characteristics or "attributes of conformance" and identifies specific criteria relating to each attribute. The attributes include the following:

1. The performance measures that comprise the system

2. Database capability

3. Data quality

4. Risk adjustment and stratification

5. Provision of data feedback to participating organizations

6. Relevance to the Joint Commission's accreditation process

As of this writing, the council is using the attributes and the related criteria to evaluate the initial group of applicant systems, and in late 1996 recommended to the Joint Commission's board of commissioners those systems that have met the screening criteria. With its anticipated approval of the initial list in early 1997, the board will concurrently set a timetable for expected accredited organization participation in an approved system as part of the accreditation process. This timetable will likely require selection of an approved system by each accredited hospital and long-term care facility by January 1998, and submission of actual performance data to the Joint Commission by January 1999. The new accreditation requirements for other types of health care organizations would proceed on a similar timetable that would begin in January 1998. Meanwhile, the review and approval of measurement systems will be an ongoing process, as new systems qualify for the list.

The Joint Commission's IMSystem is an applicant system undergoing review by the Council on Performance Measurement. The IMSystem currently contains 42 performance measures applicable to hospital-level obstetrical, perioperative, cardiovascular, oncology, and trauma care. In addition, performance measures for infection control and medication use have been fully tested and are being integrated into the system. Each of the measures in the IMSystem was developed by expert panels of academicians and practitioners, and was initially tested in the field for face validity, adequacy of uniform data element definitions, and feasibility of data collection. This initial testing eliminated some measures and led to the modification of others. The revised measures were then tested for two years in 100 to 200 sites for reliability, validity, and discrimination capability, during which time the Joint Commission developed models for data analysis and feedback.[23]

As of mid-1996, nearly 200 hospitals were enrolled in the IMSystem, and the database contained data from approximately 500,000 cases. Each enrolled organization continuously collects data for the measures it has selected, in accordance with data element definitions and collection procedures detailed by the Joint Commission. Each enrolled organization can either develop itself, or work with a vendor to develop, appropriate data collection and transmission software that meets the specifications issued by the Joint Commission. PC-based software is also available for purchase. The software must contain, at a minimum, certain specified edits for data quality (for example, allowable values for specific data elements) and algorithms for calculating indicator rates, as well as the capability of generating reports for the organization.

Patient-level data (without patient or practitioner identifiers) from each participating organization are transmitted quarterly to the Joint Commission database vendor, Computer Sciences Corporation (San Diego, California), where the data are further checked for completeness and errors, and either returned to the sender for completion or clean-up or entered into the database. The data are risk adjusted using a method based on logistic regression, and each organization is then compared to the others in the database. On a quarterly basis, each participant receives feedback reports that contain, for each measure, run charts of the organization's performance, risk-adjusted comparisons to the other organizations in the database, and selected tables of further analysis (for example, C-section rates by maternal age group). This feedback is designed to assist the participating organization in its efforts to improve its performance.

Because good performance measures are now available from other sources, the Joint Commission has discontinued its own new indicator development activities. In place of these efforts, the Joint Commission now issues periodic Requests for Indicators (RFIs) to identify performance measures that might be candidates for inclusion in the IMSystem and eventually in other measurement systems that are participating in the accreditation process.[24] The first RFI—for health care networks and health plans—was issued early in 1995, and RFIs for ambulatory care, behavioral health care, home care, and long-term care services were issued in the spring of 1996.

The response to the RFIs has been excellent. More than 900 measures were submitted in response to the network and health plan RFI, and thousands for the subsequent RFIs. To evaluate the submitted measures, national panels of content experts (for example, experts in managed care for the network indicators) review the submissions for face validity. That is, the panel judges whether the measure is relevant and important and assesses its potential for identifying opportunities to improve care. The expert panel for the network and health plan indicators eventually determined that 230 of the 907 submitted measures were nonduplicative and had face validity.

As the Joint Commission initiated the RFI process, it became clear that there was an opportunity not only to enrich existing measurement systems, but also to create a resource for health care organizations and others interested in quality measurement. In effect, the Joint Commission was compiling a systematic national database of known performance measures having face validity. The decision was made, therefore, to make this information widely available in a *National Library of Healthcare Indicators*™ (*NLHI*).[25] NLHI is intended to serve as a comprehensive catalog of performance measures judged by content experts to have face validity for application to various types of health care organizations. The first *NLHI* publication will focus on network and health plan indicators and is expected to be issued early in 1997.

The performance indicators in *NLHI* will be classified into four broad categories.

1. Priority clinical conditions arrayed against domains of performance (for example, effectiveness of care, appropriateness of care)

2. Priority clinical conditions arrayed against domains of functional status (for example, ability to work, psychological function)

3. Satisfaction from the perspectives of patients/enrollees, practitioners, and purchasers

4. Administrative and financial aspects of organizational performance

Each performance measure in *NLHI* will have its own profile that defines the measure; describes its focus and rationale; specifies its numerator and denominator where applicable; details its characteristics, including risk adjustment and stratification, if any; portrays its applicability to various health care delivery settings; delineates the degree to which the indicator has been formally tested; and identifies its developer and source.

Ultimately, *NLHI* will serve as a continuous source of promising indicators for the IMSystem and other performance measurement systems that the Council on Performance Measurement may approve. Meanwhile, it will be an immediate resource for health care organizations that are interested in further developing their performance measurement and quality improvement capabilities, as well as a resource for purchasers, consumers, researchers, and others. Periodic RFIs will continue to be issued to ensure that contemporary indicators applicable to the full range of health care delivery organizations are included in *NLHI*. By late 1997, *NLHI* is expected to be available in electronic form.

The Joint Commission's pioneering efforts in the development and testing of indicators, creation of the IMSystem, initiation of the RFMS and RFI processes, and now establishment of *NLHI* all stem from the initial decision to incorporate performance measures into the accreditation process. While the precise timetable for implementation is pending, the sequence of incorporation will be the same for most types of accredited organizations.

- Enrollment by the accredited organization in an approved measurement system

- Use of specific measures in the system by the organization that are relevant to a specified portion of its patient population, with stepwise expansion in the scope and application of the measures over time

- Quarterly transmission of the data gathered for the specified measures to the Joint Commission, preferably by the measurement system in which the organization participates

- Use by the organization of the resulting data, including comparisons of its performance to the cohort in its measurement system, for its own performance improvement activities

- Use of the data by the Joint Commission to monitor organization performance and, where appropriate, to initiate interventions between triennial on-site surveys, for example through telephone inquiries, requests for additional information, and even on-site follow-up visits if indicated by the circumstances

- Use of the data by the Joint Commission to design the agenda for the organization's triennial survey and to select specific surveyors for the survey in order to focus both evaluation and consultation on areas having the greatest potential for benefiting from such attention

Fostering and Evaluating Integration of Health Care

From its inception, the Agenda for Change contemplated a more adaptable accreditation process that would provide relevant performance-based standards, outcomes measures, and a constructive survey process. The resulting work products include a common set of functionally oriented standards that can be applied across all types of health care organizations, a smaller proportion of similar standards that are applicable only in selected settings, and a growing spectrum of performance measures that at least touches on major areas of interest in health care. These work products can readily be shaped into evaluation modules and have now given the Joint Commission the capability to adapt its accreditation process to virtually any type of organization configuration in health care. This capability has proven to be not simply an asset, but rather a necessity, in today's rapidly evolving delivery system.

The health care system is clearly experiencing a shift toward organizations that provide an integrated continuum of services and are responsible for managing the financing of these services. At the same time, this shift is far from universal. Organizations providing single services, clinically integrated organizations that do not manage financial risk, and everything in between continue to populate the health care landscape. This is seemingly inevitable in a pluralistic, market-driven health care system. It is also therefore inevitable that the quality oversight approaches undertaken by health care accrediting bodies must accommodate a spectrum of organizations, from the simplest home health agency or physician organization to the most complex integrated delivery network. Today's Joint Commission is especially well positioned to assume these responsibilities.

To blend together its new capabilities, the Joint Commission inaugurated an accreditation program for health care networks and health plans in late 1994. The standards and survey process for this program were designed to apply to any entity that provides (or provides for) integrated health care services to a defined population. Entities are eligible whether the services they provide are comprehensive across the spectrum of health care needs or are focused on a specialty area (for example, behavioral health care). The entity must have a central structure of some sort that integrates the care provided through its delivery sites, which include component organizations (like hospitals or outpatient surgery centers) and practitioners' offices. While the entity must be able to define the population it serves, this population need not be an enrolled population, as in a managed care organization. It should be noted that the flexibility of this approach contrasts with that of the Joint Commission's late 1980s managed care accreditation program—and with that of other present day managed care accrediting bodies—in that the current approach can be applied both to entities that manage health benefits and financial risk and to integrated delivery systems that do not. A module of standards related to the management of health benefits and financial risk are applied only when these functions are within the entity's responsibility, that is, where it functions as a managed care organization.

The types of entities addressed by this new accreditation program include health plans, integrated delivery systems, physician-hospital organizations, preferred provider organizations, provider-sponsored networks, specialty service systems (for example, managed behavioral health care), and similar types of emerging organizations. But regardless of its type, a network is viewed as having two major functions—managing and integrating its care system, and providing direct patient care. A health plan or other managed care organization has the additional function of benefits and financial risk management. To be meaningful from the consumer and purchaser points of view, the evaluation of these complex entities needs to be comprehensive, encompassing not only the network's central functions, but also the systems and processes in the actual care delivery sites (that is, from hospitals to practitioner offices).

For this reason, the Joint Commission network accreditation process applies a set of organization function standards (described earlier) to the network's central function and requires that each component organization in the network meet one of the following criteria.

- Accredited by the Joint Commission.

- Accredited by another accrediting body with whom the Joint Commission has a cooperative agreement (for example, Community Health Accreditation Program for home care, College of American Pathologists, and Commission on Office Laboratory Accreditation for laboratories).

- If a hospital, Medicare certified based on a survey within the preceding three years.

- Be subject, on a sampling basis, to a survey using a subset of component-specific accreditation standards that are published in appendices in the accreditation manual for networks. The sample selection is based on the level of care provided by the type of component and the number of such components in the network.

In addition, a sample of practitioners' offices are surveyed on-site to determine whether the offices are effectively implementing relevant network policies (for example, with respect to patient rights and record keeping) and whether the network's central function is providing adequate support to the practitioner.

Thus, when a network applies for accreditation, the selection of standards and the survey process are customized to the organization as a function of (1) the scope and types of services it provides, (2) whether it manages benefits and financial risk, (3) the types and numbers of component delivery sites in the network, (4) the existing accreditation status of the component sites, and (5) the number and types of practitioners' offices in the network. This customization process permits the network accreditation program to be applicable to the full spectrum of entities that provide integrated health services to defined populations. Where significant numbers of similar, reasonably well-defined entities already exist, the Joint Commission is currently developing standardized modular-based accreditation products that can be further customized for each applicant organization. Thus, separate accreditation manuals will soon exist for networks and health plans, for preferred provider organizations, and for managed behavioral health care entities.

In developing the network standards, special attention was paid to public and provider concerns about the ethical risks that are associated with managed care. These risks include potential limitations on a patient's right to participate in decision making about his or her care; patient access to information about alternative treatments; the potential influence of financial incentives on physician clinical decisions; and the patient's ability to choose from a practitioner panel constituted on the basis of ability to provide good care, notwithstanding considerations about practitioner financial performance. To address these issues, the standards applied to all networks include provisions that:

- Each member be given clear, concise explanations as to his or her condition and proposed treatments or procedures; the potential benefits and drawbacks of the proposed treatments; the likelihood of success; any significant alternative treatments or procedures; which services are covered by the benefit package and which are not; and how to obtain services not covered by the benefit package (in sum, no gag clauses).

- The network's code of ethical business behavior protects the integrity of clinical decision making. That is, decisions are made in the patient's best interest, regardless of how the network compensates or shares financial risk with its leaders, staff, and practitioners.

- Decisions on appointments or reappointments to practitioner panels take into consideration the impact of these decisions on the quality of care provided through the network.

Along with efforts to customize the evaluation process to the full spectrum of entities that provide integrated care to defined populations, the network accreditation program has also been designed to reduce duplicative evaluation activities for the surveyed organization. First, component delivery sites that are already accredited, and hospitals that achieved Medicare certification within the preceding three years, do not need to be evaluated again during the network accreditation process. Second, unaccredited organizations that as part of the survey of one network have undergone an evaluation using a subset of component-specific accreditation standards within the preceding year do not need to be reevaluated if they are selected as part of the component sample for another network. Third, the Joint Commission is actively negotiating collaborative agreements with a number of additional accrediting bodies that will make it possible for other evaluations to satisfy the accreditation requirements for components in the network. Fourth, the Joint Commission is working with state regulatory bodies, including through the Orion Project, to reduce duplicative evaluations by utilizing the findings from other reviews, in whole or in part, in the accreditation process. Finally, the Joint Commission has been able to demonstrate the alignment of Joint Commission standards to the Malcolm Baldrige National Quality Award criteria so that an organization using the Baldrige Award criteria for self-assessment can conduct a standards-based assessment simultaneously.[26,27] Thus, the customization process is also being designed to reduce unnecessary evaluation expense for organizations and to optimize the efficiency of the accreditation process.

Providing More Helpful Information to the Public

The public's call for accountability in health care is reflected by the demand for greater disclosure of information about health care organization performance. To help accredited health care organizations meet this demand, and to meet the demand directly, the Joint Commission has begun to release performance reports on organizations accredited by the Joint Commission.[28] These reports are distilled from the somewhat technical official accreditation reports prepared for each organization and are designed to provide useful and understandable information for public consumption. The Joint Commission began releasing these organization-specific performance reports in December 1994 for all health care organizations undergoing a full survey after January 1, 1994. Performance reports for entities accredited under the Joint Commission's newer programs for laboratories and networks are expected to become available in late 1996 and in 1997, respectively.

After an accreditation decision is reached, the surveyed organization receives its own draft performance report and is offered the opportunity to submit a commentary of up to two pages long that will accompany publicly released reports for these organizations. Each report includes the following:

- A brief overview of the accreditation process
- The accreditation decision and date
- The organization's overall performance level
- The organization's performance level for each performance area evaluated
- Those performance areas having recommendations for improvement (that is, Type I recommendations)
- National comparative data for the overall performance level and each performance area level

Included with the report is an explanatory document that describes the Joint Commission's accreditation process, the several accreditation categories, what is addressed in each performance area, and how each area is evaluated. The reports are available to anyone who requests them.

Based on focus groups and interviews with providers, consumers, and purchasers, the reports have been redesigned for organizations surveyed in 1996. In addition to a series of user-friendly refinements, the performance areas and scoring system in the publicly released report will now be aligned with the performance areas and scoring system used in the organization's official accreditation report. Further, the performance report will display both the original and updated scores for performance areas where improvements have been achieved, as well as the original and updated overall score (capped at 94 out of 100) when improvements in individual performance areas are sufficient to be reflected in the organization's overall performance.

The current performance reports are based on the results of current standards-based evaluations. It is anticipated that after performance measures, including outcomes, are incorporated into the accreditation process, data and information based on interpreted risk-adjusted comparative outcomes will also begin to be included in the performance reports.

A Challenge for the Future

The Agenda for Change has created an accreditation process that focuses on those systems and processes believed to be most relevant to actual results, that facilitates and sets expectations for innovation and continuous improvement in organization performance, and that can be customized to comprehensively evaluate the broad spectrum of individual health care organizations and integrated delivery systems that provide services in the evolving health care system. This new accreditation process is producing performance information that is both critical to health care organization efforts to improve and useful in helping health care organizations meet the increased public demand for accountability—that is, the demand that health care organizations demonstrate what they are achieving and its value.

But the effective use of performance information for either improvement or accountability purposes depends on an understanding of the relationship between what a health care organization *does* and the *results* that are achieved. It is this relationship, after all, that underlies both the ability of an organization to improve its results by changing its systems and processes, and the degree to which an organization can be accountable for its results. An organization can be accountable only for those results over which it can exercise substantial control—those results that would be expected to change if the organization changed its systems and processes. Herein lies the real opportunity to manage outcomes in the future.

Today, however, as the public becomes more restive, the need for a better understanding of the relationship between what a health care organization does and the results that are achieved has become compelling. This is especially true in relation to growing awareness of serious, undesirable occurrences in health care organizations—occurrences that may involve the loss of patient life, limb, or function. These "sentinel events," as they are called, gain added significance in an atmosphere where there has been a shift in public attitude from trust in the beneficence of its health care system to one in which practitioners' and providers' motives and the scientific basis of medical care are increasingly being questioned. And sentinel events are also raising serious concerns among health care practitioners and provider organizations themselves, as evidence is presented suggesting that their frequency is much higher than previously believed.[29] Against this backdrop, it is more than fair to ask how the health care organization, the accrediting body, and the public should respond to a sentinel event.

First, how should a health care organization respond to a sentinel event? An organization should focus its efforts on seeking to identify the underlying, or root, cause(s) of the event. It should begin by asking itself, "Is this event the result of a common cause(s) or a special cause(s)?" Any adverse occurrence, including a sentinel event, may be the result of either a common cause(s) or a special cause(s) or both, or, in the alternative, of uncontrollable human error or other factors. In undertaking a root-cause analysis, the organization bears the burden of reaching credible conclusions that either lead to appropriate actions or clearly demonstrate it had already taken all reasonable, correct steps to avoid the event.

There is always a strong immediate temptation to attribute the sentinel event to the special cause of human error—and stop there. But whether any cause is common or special depends on the frame of reference. That is, the concepts of "common" and "special" are not *attributes* of a cause, but rather express the *relationship* of a specific cause to a specific process. For example, a death may result from the loss of electrical power during a surgical procedure. This undesirable variation in function is the result of a special cause in the operating room, but may also be the result of a common cause in the organization's system for preparing for a utility failure. In fact, in most cases, a special cause of variation in one process will be found to relate to a common cause of variation in the larger system (that is, the larger set of processes) of which the immediate process is a part.

This analysis leads to the conclusion that the identification of a special cause for a sentinel event is only the first step in a full evaluation of the event. The second step is to identify the larger system in which there may be one or more common causes. This larger system then becomes the focus for potential improvement, because only it can be redesigned to eliminate the common cause of the adverse event. The component process cannot easily correct a special cause within itself.

What meaning does this have in a clinical context? It acknowledges that all clinical processes in the organization are part of larger systems in the organization. Thus, special cause sentinel events that occur in the care of patients are frequently the result of common causes in organization systems.

For example, when individual physicians are admonished to avoid prescribing medications that lead to adverse drug-drug interactions, they may try very hard to do so. But the number of possible drug-drug interactions and the constantly growing knowledge base in this area make it impossible for physicians to remember all of the possible interactions. Errors in memory *will* occur. The individual physician prescribing process is likely to be improved only when it is seen as part of the larger medication use system that involves the pharmacy, nursing, and information management. One solution some organizations are using is a computer-based ordering system that is linked to a real-time expert system that provides feedback to the physician about potential adverse drug-drug interactions, thus enabling better-informed clinical judgment. Here, the solution to the problem has been found by addressing the common cause in the design of an organization's information management system, not by focusing on the special cause in the clinical process, that is, the physician's memory.

To summarize, for the health care organization, identification of a special cause for a clinical sentinel event should automatically lead to a search for the common cause(s) in the system(s) of which the process is a part. It is the larger system (and its managers), not the process (or process owners), that is accountable for the redesigns that will reduce the likelihood of future sentinel events. Thus, errors by individual physicians, nurses, pharmacists, or others should generate evaluations of the organizational systems in which they work and that support their work. These systems include the credentialing and privileging processes for physicians and other licensed independent practitioners, and the hiring and competency review processes for others; the continuing education of staff; the management of information, including facilitation of communication, access to knowledge-based information, and linkage of information sources; and the measurement of performance with respect to both processes and outcomes. It is the responsibility of the organization's management and clinical leaders to focus attention on systems that can be redesigned for improvement, rather than on people who cannot control the causes that affect their performance. The systems cited, and others, are in fact just the functions now addressed in Joint Commission standards. However, where knowledge about organization function is still growing, future changes in these standards—including potential new standards—are likely over time.

How should an accrediting body respond to a sentinel event? When a sentinel event occurs in an accredited organization, the goals of the accrediting body are twofold.

1. To focus the attention of the organization that has experienced the event on understanding the causes that underlie that event and on making changes in the organization's systems and processes to reduce the probability of such an event in the future

2. To inform the public about the *possibility* of a safety-related issue in the organization and provide assurances that the issue is being effectively addressed

To achieve these goals, the Joint Commission has adopted a policy that, when it is notified of a possible sentinel event, it will confirm the event's occurrence and determine whether there is a potential opportunity for future improvement in the organization. If these things are so, the Joint Commission places the organization on Accreditation Watch. This designation—borrowed from corresponding terminology in the financial community—is intended to be nonjudgmental. It means that no conclusions have yet been reached about the specific underlying cause(s) of the event or about what the organization might do to prevent similar events in the future.

An organization so designated is expected to undertake a root-cause analysis of the event, as described. The Joint Commission then reviews the organization's root-cause analysis for its adequacy, including its thoroughness and credibility. If it is inadequate, further analysis—supported by Joint Commission consultative assistance, if necessary—is to be undertaken. Once the root-cause analysis is satisfactory, the Accreditation Watch designation is removed, and the organization receives any Type I recommendation(s) related to standards compliance issues that have not yet been corrected. A follow-up on-site survey is conducted within six months to evaluate the organization's implementation of the system and process improvements identified through its root-cause analysis. Based on this follow-up survey, the organization's accreditation status is either maintained or changed.

Finally, how should the public respond to a sentinel event in a health care organization? How can the public's expectations and health care organizations' reasonable accountabilities be aligned? This is a challenge for health care organizations and the Joint Commission collectively. The answer cannot be that every sentinel event is simply "human error" and does not reflect on the organization. As discussed, the organization has within its control systems and processes that can help reduce the risk of human error. On the other hand, the knowledge that an organization *can* change its systems and processes to help reduce risk in the future does not necessarily mean that it *should* have made those changes already. Failure to install systems and processes that are expected to be in place in health care organizations today (for example, systems and processes described in Joint Commission standards) is quite different from not having already designed new systems and processes that will reduce future risk. It is important to help the public understand this distinction.

While only one step toward this end, the Joint Commission's policy on responding to sentinel events in accredited organizations is designed to convey this distinction. It tells the public that the health care organization and the Joint Commission can be trusted to recognize that a serious event has occurred, to evaluate it thoroughly, to reach conclusions about whether the organization is meeting existing expectations, and regardless of existing expectations, to try to prevent similar events in the future. This message needs to be accompanied by the corollary reality message that serious undesirable events do occur and cannot be completely eliminated. What should be of greatest importance to the public is the health care organization's response: Did the organization try to improve its systems and processes, and do the results demonstrate its success in this effort?

This combination of the organization's response, the accrediting body's action, and the public's understanding should synergistically contribute to future continuous improvement in the quality and safety of health care.

Conclusion

In the rapidly changing health care system, the need to focus on the quality and efficiency of health care organizations is more important than ever. This focus should be aligned with and guided by the entire community of interests. The evaluation of performance must use the most contemporary methods and tools—including patient-centered, performance-based standards and relevant, reliable, and valid performance measures. Information from the evaluation process must be useful to and used by health care organizations to improve their performance, and also be available to meet public—consumer and purchaser—demands for accountability. The Joint Commission will continue to play central roles in convening the community of interests; developing, using, and continuously improving contemporary approaches to evaluating performance; and providing public access to the evaluation results in a constructive fashion that serves the interests of health care organizations and the public.

Notes

1. D. Berwick, "Continuous Improvement as an Ideal in Health Care," *New England Journal of Medicine* (1989): 53–56.

2. M. Gerteis, et al., *Through the Patient's Eyes* (San Francisco: Jossey-Bass Publishers, 1993).

3. M. J. Field and K. N. Lohr, eds., *Guidelines for Clinical Practice: From Development to Use* (Washington, D.C.: National Academy Press, 1992).

4. S. M. Shortell, et al., "The New World of Managed Care: Creating Organized Delivery Systems," *Health Affairs* 13, no. 5 (1994): 46–64.

5. B. M. Zajac, et al., "Health Status of Populations as a Measure of Health System Performance," *Managed Care Quarterly* 3, no. 1 (1995): 29–38.

6. D. S. O'Leary, "Agenda for Change Objectives Stay the Course," *Joint Commission Perspectives* 14, no. 1 (1994): 2–3.

7. Joint Commission on Accreditation of Healthcare Organizations, *1996 Comprehensive Accreditation Manual for Ambulatory Care* (Oakbrook Terrace, Ill.: Joint Commission on Accreditation of Healthcare Organizations, 1995).

8. Joint Commission on Accreditation of Healthcare Organizations, *1997–98 Comprehensive Accreditation Manual for Behavioral Health Care* (Oakbrook Terrace, Ill.: Joint Commission on Accreditation of Healthcare Organizations, 1996).

9. Joint Commission on Accreditation of Healthcare Organizations, *1997–98 Comprehensive Accreditation Manual for Home Care* (Oakbrook Terrace, Ill.: Joint Commission on Accreditation of Healthcare Organizations, 1996).

10. Joint Commission on Accreditation of Healthcare Organizations, *Comprehensive Accreditation Manual for Hospitals: The Official Handbook* (Oakbrook Terrace, Ill.: Joint Commission on Accreditation of Healthcare Organizations, 1996).

11. Joint Commission on Accreditation of Healthcare Organizations, *1996 Comprehensive Accreditation Manual for Long Term Care* (Oakbrook Terrace, Ill.: Joint Commission on Accreditation of Healthcare Organizations, 1996).

12. Joint Commission on Accreditation of Healthcare Organizations, *1996 Comprehensive Accreditation Manual for Pathology and Clinical Laboratory Services* (Oakbrook Terrace, Ill.: Joint Commission on Accreditation of Healthcare Organizations, 1996).

13. Joint Commission on Accreditation of Healthcare Organizations, *1996 Comprehensive Accreditation Manual for Health Care Networks* (Oakbrook Terrace, Ill.: Joint Commission on Accreditation of Healthcare Organizations, 1996).

14. Joint Commission on Accreditation of Healthcare Organizations, *The Measurement Mandate: On the Road to Performance Improvement in Health Care* (Oakbrook Terrace, Ill.: Joint Commission on Accreditation of Healthcare Organizations, 1993).

15. W. A. Shewhart, *Economic Control of Quality of Manufactured Product* (New York: Van Nostrand, 1931).

16. Paul M. Schyve, "Outcomes as Performance Measures," in *Using Clinical Practice Guidelines to Evaluate Quality of Care, Volume I: Issues* (Washington, D.C.: Agency for Health Care Policy and Research, 1995), 27–34.

17. D. M. Nadzam, et al., "Data-Driven Performance Improvement in Health Care: The Joint Commission's Indicator Measurement System (IMSystem)," *The Joint Commission Journal on Quality Improvement* 19, no. 11 (1993): 492–500.

18. J. E. Wennberg and A. Gittelsohn, "Small Area Variations in Health Care Delivery," *Science* 182, no. 117 (1973): 1102–1108.

19. Dartmouth Medical School Center for Evaluative Clinical Sciences, *The Dartmouth Atlas of Health Care* (Chicago: American Hospital Publishing, 1996).

20. Joint Commission on Accreditation of Healthcare Organizations, "Performance Measurement Strategy Evolves, Offers Flexibility," *Joint Commission Perspectives* 15, no. 2 (1995): 1, 5.

21. J. M. Loeb and D. S. O'Leary, "A Call for Collaboration in Performance Measurement (from the Joint Commission on Accreditation of Healthcare Organizations)," *JAMA* 273, no. 18 (1995): 1405.

22. J. M. Loeb, and A. S. Buck, "Framework for Selection of Performance Measurement Systems: Attributes of Conformance (from the Joint Commission on Accreditation of Healthcare Organizations)," *JAMA* 275, no. 7 (1996): 508.

23. M. R. O'Leary, *Clinical Performance Data: A Guide to Interpretation* (Oakbrook Terrace, Ill.: Joint Commission on Accreditation of Healthcare Organizations, 1996).

24. J. Seidenfield, et al., "A New Tool—Request for Indicators (from the Joint Commission on Accreditation of Healthcare Organizations)," *JAMA* 273 no. 9 (1995): 691.

25. Joint Commission on Accreditation of Healthcare Organizations, "Joint Commission to Create National Library of Healthcare Indicators," *Joint Commission Perspectives* 16, no. 2 (1996): 1, 4.

26. D. Cesarone, *Assess for Success: Achieving Excellence with Joint Commission Standards and Baldrige Criteria* (Oakbrook Terrace, Ill.: Joint Commission on Accreditation of Healthcare Organizations, 1997).

27. M. P. Carr and F. W. Jackson, *The Crosswalk: Joint Commission Standards and Baldrige Criteria* (Oakbrook Terrace, Ill.: Joint Commission on Accreditation of Healthcare Organizations, 1997).

28. Joint Commission on Accreditation of Healthcare Organizations, "Joint Commission to Release Organization-Specific Performance Information," *Joint Commission Perspectives* 15, no. 5 (1994): 1, 6–7.

29. L. L. Leape, "Error in Medicine," *JAMA* 272, no. 23 (1994): 1851–1857.

Paul M. Schyve, M.D., is the senior vice president for the Joint Commission on Accreditation of Healthcare Organizations. In this role, he is responsible for facilitating quality improvement throughout the Joint Commission; for working with key professional, patient, consumer, purchaser, and government organizations in furthering improvements in the quality of care provided to the public; and he oversees Joint Commission education and publication efforts.

Prior to joining the Joint Commission, Schyve was clinical director of the State of Illinois' Department of Mental Health and Developmental Disabilities, an integrated network of 22 hospitals and community-based outpatient and residential programs. He also has served as the director of the Illinois State Psychiatric Institute, a research and teaching hospital in Chicago.

In addition to his clinical and administrative experience, Schyve was a clinical associate professor of psychiatry at the Pritzker School of Medicine, University of Chicago, and an instructor and United States Public Health Service Fellow in psychiatry at the University of Rochester School of Medicine and Dentistry, Rochester, New York.

Schyve is a fellow of the American Psychiatric Association and a member of the Illinois Psychiatric Society, the Chicago Medical Society, and the American Medical Association. In addition, he is the author of numerous published articles and book chapters in the areas of psychiatric treatment and research, quality assurance, and continuous quality improvement.

Schyve received a bachelor's degree from the University of Rochester, Rochester, New York, where he was elected to Phi Beta Kappa. He completed his medical education and residency in psychiatry at the University of Rochester School of Medicine and Dentistry. Schyve is certified in psychiatry by the American Board of Psychiatry and Neurology.

Dennis S. O'Leary, M.D., is president of the Joint Commission on Accreditation of Healthcare Organizations. Under his leadership, the Joint Commission has successfully transformed its accreditation process to emphasize evaluation of actual organization performance. The transformation has se the stage for the progressive introduction of outcomes measures into the accreditation process.

O'Leary has also spearheaded the launch of the Joint Commission's newest accreditation program for health plans, integrated delivery systems, and other types of health care networks. This initiative, coupled with his successful efforts to make organization-specific performance reports available to the public, has permitted the Joint Commission to make giant strides toward meeting its public accountabilities for improving the quality of care provided by health care organizations.

Prior to joining the Joint Commission, O'Leary served as dean for clinical affairs at the George Washington University Medical Center and vice president of the George Washington University Health Plan, an academic HMO. Additionally, he was president and chairman of the board of the District of Columbia Medical Society and a founding member of the National Capital Area Health Care Coalition.

O'Leary earned a bachelor of arts degree from Harvard College and a doctor of medicine degree from Cornell University. After two years of internal medicine training at the University of Minnesota Hospital, he completed his residency at Strong Memorial Hospital in Rochester, New York. He is board certified in internal medicine and hematology.

Section IV

Change Concepts

Chapter 17

Reengineering the Surgical Process

Elizabeth H. Dougherty, William F. Minogue, and Jay B. Mathur

In 1995, Suburban Hospital—a community-based, not-for-profit, acute care hospital located in Bethesda, Maryland—undertook a project to redesign its surgical process. The surgical process was defined as beginning when a patient made the decision to undergo a procedure and ending with a post-surgical assessment six to 12 months later. As of the summer of 1996, the hospital was implementing a number of the recommendations that grew out of this initiative. Suburban's experience to date is highlighted in this chapter, serving as a case study for those interested in one hospital's operational insight into deploying and managing a major reengineering initiative. The chapter attempts to share both the good news and the bad news about the initiative; raise questions for readers to consider; and serve as an educational piece for management, boards, caregivers, and those directly involved in process management. The body of the chapter is set up to reflect the phases of the hospital's reengineering initiative: preparation, assessment, design, and implementation. Following these sections are lessons learned, a summary, and questions to stimulate discussion (for executives, process owners, and team members).

Preparation: Overview

In late 1994, the executive staff (the president and the senior vice presidents) of Suburban Hospital concluded that although a continuous quality improvement (CQI) initiative was underway at the hospital, the incremental improvements gained through such efforts would not be sufficient enough to align Suburban with the competitive position desired. Making the decision to undertake fundamental process redesign—reengineering—the executive staff interviewed a variety of consulting firms to assist in this initiative. Important to their selection of a consultant was the fact that the hospital was in a good financial position, embarking on reengineering as a proactive strategy rather than a reactive response. Because of this, slash-and-burn and quick-fix philosophies were rejected by the executive staff members who were interested in enhancing (and accelerating) progress made through the hospital's cultural shift to a management philosophy of CQI. The Juran Institute—a world-class leader in process management consulting—was selected to help the hospital initiate and manage a reengineering project.

Preparation: Project Selection and Structure

At a retreat in early 1995, the executive staff developed the overall focus and supporting structure for Suburban's reengineering project. The details of the project are listed as follows:

- *Focus:* The surgical process, which encompasses the diagnosis, treatment, and recovery of the patient, not simply the surgical event itself. This represented 20 percent of the hospital's expense budget.

- *Executive sponsor:* The chief operating officer.

- *Core team:* Nine department managers who devote approximately 50 percent of their time to reengineering. The following departments were represented: operative services, inpatient services, radiology, pharmacy, laboratory, management information services, admitting and patient accounting, nursing clinical education, and quality. A consultant from the Juran Institute also served as part of the core team during the assessment and design phases of the project.

- *Time frame:* A 12- to 18-month process.

The management structure of the project required the core team to drive the progress of the reengineering initiative with input and exchange from the executive staff. However, the structure, as seen in Figure 17.1, was designed to also involve other managers and staff members at appropriate points throughout the project.

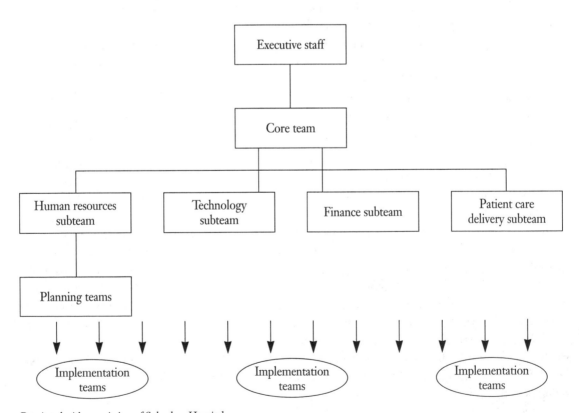

Reprinted with permission of Suburban Hospital.

Figure 17.1. Surgical reengineering project structure.

For communication purposes, the project was segmented into the following phases.

Phase	Answers the question(s) . . .
Assessment	What do we do today? How well do we do it?
Design	What do we want to do? How would we like to do it?
Implementation	How are we going to reconcile what we do and what we'd like to do? What are we actually going to implement, and how?
Maintenance	What do we need to do to ensure that the process is working, over time, as expected?

Although the timeline for these phases was laid out sequentially for the purposes of presentation to stakeholders outside of the core team, the reality is that the process of reengineering is more fluid and less linear. With that stated, the general time frame for the phases was identified as follows:

Phase	Timeline
Assessment	February 1995–June 1995
Design	July 1995–December 1995
Implementation	January 1996–April 1996
Maintenance	Ongoing after April 1996

Since the project's initiation, the timeline has been modified. The majority of the implementation phase activities were timed to coincide with the hospital's fiscal year that began July 1, 1996.

Assessment: Conceptual Understanding of the Process

Answering the questions "What do we do today?" and "How well do we do it?" requires progression through an iterative process of learning. The progress through the assessment phase can be likened to looking out an airplane window while in flight. At 30,000 feet, the passengers know where they left from and where they are going, but when they look out the window, they can't see much of what is below. As the plane descends to lower and lower altitudes, passengers can begin to distinguish more and more of the landscape with increasing detail. This is the journey that the core team must travel. To understand how the process actually works today, the team must progress toward a deeper and more thorough comprehension of the current system's complexity.

The core team's first task was to define the overall boundaries (similar to the origin and destination of the airplane passengers) of the surgical process. For the purpose of this initiative, the team identified the starting point as the step at which the patient concurs that surgery is the required treatment. Depending on the patient type (for example, emergency versus nonemergency), the location of the starting point was different. The ending point was somewhat less concrete—the point at which a postoperative assessment of the patient is conducted, usually six to 12 months after the procedure. The logic of Suburban's boundary setting was to ensure that the entire continuum of care was captured.

Once defined, the core team organized the overall surgical experience into 10 subprocesses, which are listed as follows:

1. Decision

2. Pretesting for outpatients

3. Preoperative for inpatients

4. Preoperative for emergency patients

5. Preoperative for outpatients and patients admitted in the morning of their day of surgery

6. Intraoperative

7. Postoperative for inpatients

8. Postoperative for outpatients

9. Discharge

10. Follow-up

To gain a clearer understanding of each of these subprocesses, a flowchart was developed. Figure 17.2 is an example of such a chart.

Assessment: Assessing an Activity's Value

Although the activity level flowcharts were useful in visually tracking the process, more detailed information was needed about how the subprocesses actually were completed to move beyond a conceptual level. To optimize the efficiency, effectiveness, and data integrity, and to begin to build awareness of the initiative, the core team opted to collect data about each subprocess from a sampling of employees who actually do the work. For each step of each subprocess, a list of activities necessary to complete the step was developed by position. For example, if a step in the subprocess was "preauthorize patient for procedure," the activity list might read "call patient for insurance information; contact insurance company for authorization; and complete appropriate hospital authorization form." Approximately 800 activities were ultimately identified and served as the basis for the data collection effort.

More than 150 employees from 50 distinct positions were asked to provide data about how someone in their job would complete the activities outlined for each step of each subprocess. Figure 17.3

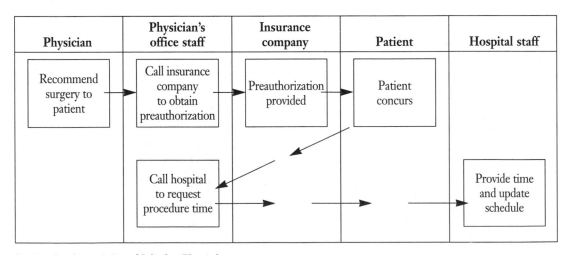

Reprinted with permission of Suburban Hospital.

Figure 17.2. Sample flowchart.

Employee Data Collection Form

Department _____   Process number _____

Job code _____   Subprocess number _____

Activity number _____

Activity description _____

How often is the activity done? [day, week, month, quarter, year]   _____

How long does it take each time? [in minutes]   _____

How many times is it done?   _____

Under the best circumstances, how long should it take?   _____

Is this a critical activity?   _____

Is this activity a normal and regular part of the job?   _____

Date _____   Page _____

Reprinted with permission of Suburban Hospital.

Figure 17.3. Sample data collection form.

illustrates, with a sample data collection form, the types of information elements solicited. The four major elements that were derived from the data collection form were: (1) frequency (how often the activity is completed); (2) processing time (how long the activity takes to complete, assuming that employees have what they need, such as information, supplies, a specimen, or the patient); (3) cycle time (the processing time plus any time the employee spends waiting for needed resources); and (4) cost (how much human resource is expended in completing the activity).

To illustrate processing and cycle time, consider an activity of a hospital admissions employee: obtaining patient preauthorization from an insurance company. The admissions employee, armed with all of the necessary patient information, calls the insurance company. If he or she is able to immediately interact with an insurance representative and obtain the preauthorization, the processing time and the cycle time are the same. If, however, the admissions employee is put on hold or must call back multiple times before the preauthorization can be acquired, the cycle time would be far greater than the processing time since cycle time includes the time spent waiting to receive the necessary preauthorization. Thus, in an ideal scenario, the cycle time equals the processing time, and wait time is nonexistent.

Understanding how (and how well) work currently gets done not only requires information about how often activities occur, how long activities take to complete, and how much each costs, but also the value—the benefit—that each activity contributes to the overall process. Value assessment requires that each activity be evaluated and placed in one of the following categories.

- *Customer value added (CVA):* The activity helps meet customer requirements (for example, evaluating a patient or educating the family on a patient's care needs).

- *Business value added (BVA):* The activity does not help meet customer requirements, but contributes to meeting business requirements (for example, producing a financial report or keeping records to comply with state regulatory agencies).

- *Non–value-added (NVA):* The activity does *not* contribute to meeting customer or business requirements (for example, asking the patient for the same demographic information multiple times during a visit or having the patient stop by admitting to complete paperwork before surgery if all necessary paperwork has been completed through preregistration).

Figure 17.4 provides a visual perspective of the methodology to move from understanding the overall process to an assessment of value.

Assessment: Findings from the Employee Data Collection

Based on the data collected from employees, Suburban found that of the hospital's total cost associated with the surgical process (salaries only), 40 percent was customer value added (that is, only 40 percent of human resources are spent directly meeting customer needs). A similar amount (37 percent)

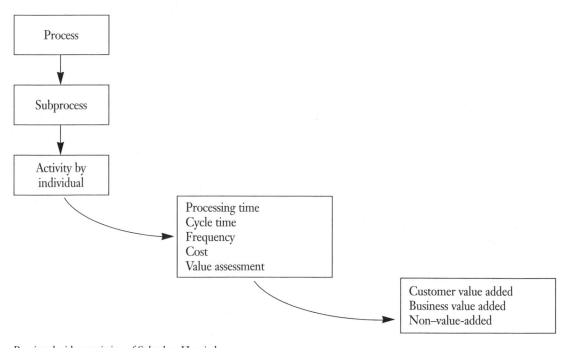

Reprinted with permission of Suburban Hospital.

Figure 17.4. Assessment methodology.

appeared to provide little, if any, value. Of the total time required for an activity to be completed (cycle time), almost 66 percent of employees' time was spent waiting (for supplies, information, approval, specimens, and so on). This did not mean that employees were sitting idle, but rather that employees could not complete their activities as efficiently as they might otherwise have been able to. If employees were waiting, it stood to reason that patients (and other customers) were also waiting.

The details of the data collection also pointed to some major categories where improvement opportunity seemed to frequently occur. The following list details the categories of action verbs that raised red flags because of their high percentage of non–value-added activities.

- Transport
- Receive
- Order
- Call
- Review
- Locate

Assessment: A Score of Measures

Although the employee data collection yielded powerful information regarding how work is done, the core team also used existing data to develop a variety of measures to reflect current performance of the surgical process. In total, the indicators that the team identified for use as the before-and-after scorecard—referred to as key performance indicators (KPIs)—included the following:

Time-based

1. Length of stay (for the top 10 surgical DRGs)
2. Process cycle time (expressed as a percentage of time spent waiting)
3. OR case turnover time

Cost

4. Cost per case

Quality

5. Unplanned returns to OR (for inpatients)
6. Employee turnover rate
7. OR cancellation rate

Other

8. OR volume

The assessment phase findings were important for the core team to develop an understanding of how the process currently was fashioned. The analysis gave the core team and the executive staff powerful organizational ammunition to answer the often-asked question, "Why are we reengineering?" In addition, the scorecard provided a baseline to gauge postredesign improvement. Armed with this information, the core team entered the next phase—design.

Design: Understanding What's Out There

Having immersed themselves in the realities of current practice, the members had to switch gears in the design phase and think about what could be. To focus their thinking for the design phase, the core team members developed a vision statement for the surgical process. This statement provided an underpinning for the redesign activities and served as a communication tool in presentations to stakeholders.

> *The surgical process, part of the continuum of care, will be based on a foundation of partnerships which will facilitate the innovation of dynamic, cost-effective, high-quality integrated services.*

To help the team direct its energies toward achievement of the vision, to build on good ideas that already existed, and to encourage participation from individuals not on the core team, the team identified and then solicited information from a number of managers, staff members, physicians, and the executives about things that had delighted them as both health care and non–health care customers. Simultaneously, the team members conducted an extensive literature search and identified more than 75 articles that they read and discussed. To provide a framework for information gathered, the core team developed the following concept areas.

- Technology
- Specific process changes
- Physical plant and layout
- Organizational structure
- Performance management
- Compensation
- Reward and recognition
- New products and markets

As the information from the interviews and articles was being synthesized, the core team compiled a "short list" of world-class organizations against whom the hospital might benchmark. From the team's research, the organizations—aside from having reputations for quality—were identified because they had multiple areas that interested the team. The team contacted almost a dozen organizations in various parts of the United States, conducting site visits at eight. The core team visited organizations such as Mercy Hospital (California), Stanford, General Health Systems, University of Michigan Hospitals, Mayo Clinic, and Harbor Hospital. A number of the organizations that were not able to host a site visit provided information over the phone or by mail.

The benchmark questions were developed and organized around the concept areas previously listed and, although several organizations were queried on the full set of issues, most of the benchmark organizations were asked questions revolving around their particular area(s) of excellence. One topic that was addressed with virtually all of the organizations was how to implement change. Despite the fact that not all of the organizations had been involved in reengineering per se, all of the organizations were focused on improving their process performance. As such, questions such as the following were asked: "How did you communicate the change?" "How did you reinforce your message?" "How long did it take for employees to acclimate to the new environment?"

Design: What Do the Customers Need?

A system cannot be successfully redesigned without an understanding of customer needs. Although the hospital already had in place several mechanisms to solicit customer feedback (for example, surveys of employees, patients, and physicians administered by the Gallup organization), the team needed more specific information and an opportunity to engage the customer in a dialog. The core team decided to focus on five general groups: (1) patients (including Suburban patients, potential patients, and families of patients); (2) physicians (surgical and medical); (3) physician office managers; (4) payors; and (5) vendors. The core team approached several employees within the hospital who, with some training on how to solicit customer needs and to run focus groups, would be capable of compiling usable customer information and could thus assist with the task.

To obtain good information while minimizing unnecessary effort, Suburban tried to tap into groups of customers who were already meeting (for example, religious groups and support groups run by the hospital), groups for whom access was relatively easy to attain (such as current inpatients), and individuals with existing relationships to the hospital (for example, the medical staff leadership and physicians with high admission and usage rates at Suburban). An effort was also made to solicit ideas and feedback from others who may not use Suburban.

Approximately 75 customers were interviewed. The output required from the Suburban customer focus group leaders was comprised not only of customer needs, but of ideas about how those needs might be met (features). Care was taken to distinguish perceived or stated needs from required benefits. For example, a patient may say he needs the ability to schedule a procedure at any time of the day. Although some patients may require scheduling flexibility, this particular patient, after further questioning, describes his anxiety about missing the procedure time due to bad weather. Specifically, the patient may really need access to afternoon procedure times, or an alternative option such as access to a hospital shuttle service. Figure 17.5 highlights the needs identified for each of the customer groups.

Patients/family
Communications
    Ongoing
    Proactive
    Understandable
Timely response to requests
Little wait time (outpatients)
Caring staff

Physicians and office staff
Quality of staff
    Ability to perform
    Customer service mentality
Timely response to requests
Efficient, easy-to-use process

Payors
Coordination of services
    For patient
    For payor
Communication with the patient
Measurable outcomes

Vendors
Communications
    Business priorities
    Changes in contracts and so on
Cooperative (win-win) approach

Reprinted with permission of Suburban Hospital.

Figure 17.5. Highlights of customer needs.

Design: Developing a New Way of Doing Things

Using the team's research on best practices from interviews with internal hospital sources, the literature review, the information from benchmark organizations, an understanding of customers' needs,
and the data collected during the assessment phase, the team drafted a vision of the ideal process using
flowcharting techniques. Team members concentrated on design concepts—such as technology, specific process changes, and physical plant and layout—to assist them in creating the new process. While
developing the flowcharts for the new process, the team began to record barriers and other impacts
that would require future consideration in order to make the new process a reality. For example, the
team struggled with the preauthorization process currently in place to get approval (and ultimately
payment) from the insurance companies. Under the current system, the physician's office notified the
hospital of a pending patient procedure. The hospital then obtained, from the physician's office, the
details of the procedure and treatment prescribed for the patient. Next, both the hospital and the
physician's office would separately contact the insurance company, each requesting preapproval. To
reduce the number of phone calls (non–value-added work), increase customer service to physicians and
their office, and potentially increase Suburban's business, the team suggested that the hospital personnel work with the payor on behalf of both the hospital and the physician's office to authorize the necessary services. In this example, a potential barrier cited was insurance companies' receptiveness to
consolidation of the approvals.

Because of the scope of the surgical process, development of a draft of the design required the
team to break down the design into manageable pieces. Discussions revolved around desired inputs,
expected outputs, and opportunities for increasing in-process efficiencies and improving levels of service. A first comprehensive draft of the redesign required flowchart after flowchart. Like putting
pieces of a puzzle together, adding each additional piece required the team to revisit the pieces already
in place. This was done to ensure that the team had not compromised any components of the redesign
already identified, as well as to create a common language and understanding about the new process
among the team members. Since core team members were expected to communicate design specifics
to managers, employees, and other stakeholders of the hospital, the common language would prove to
be critical.

Design: Patient Care Delivery and Other Subteams

"The core team does not corner the market on expertise." This phrase was often used during the initiative, articulating the belief that to develop and operationalize the best design possible, the people
most familiar with the issue needed to be involved. As referenced earlier in the chapter, the project
structure was set up with this in mind—to engage others in the design and implementation of the
reengineering recommendations. The first round of teams chartered to fulfill this role was the subteams.

The subteam most integrally tied to design issues was the patient care delivery (PCD) subteam.
Because a significant piece of the reengineering effort involved a fundamental change in the way care
was delivered, the executive staff came to the conclusion that if the appropriate care and service were
given with the expected clinical outcomes and cost results, the inpatient stay was a critical component
to address. To involve staff to the highest degree and to develop a general template that could be modified for each inpatient unit based on patient needs, an initial unit was selected to serve as a pilot. The
unit was one that cared for a large number of surgical patients, had some experience with quality
improvement (via critical pathways), and had solid management personnel. Thus, although the patient

care design initiative at Suburban had its roots in the surgical reengineering effort and adhered to the same conceptual framework, the actual process design was to be created through a separate design sub-team—the PCD subteam. The PCD subteam included staff from a medical/surgical nursing unit (the primary unit for orthopedic cases), key ancillary departments such as physical medicine, several physicians (as consultants), and two members from the surgical reengineering core team (one of whom served as the facilitator). A description of the patient care redesign process and outcomes could alone comprise an entire chapter; however, the highlights of their journey to date are described—along with the other components of the reengineering effort—throughout the rest of this chapter.

The first step in forming all of the subteams was to orient them to the work done so far. For each subteam, the education process encompassed a review of the surgical process design work done so far, global measures of the process, and the case for change resulting from the changing nature of health care. In addition, the PCD subteam also discussed the philosophical underpinnings of the patient care delivery model. To this end, a white paper had been developed prior to the formation of the PCD subteam that outlined the approach the organization was going to pursue in redesigning patient care. Some of key ideas are presented as follows:

Objectives

- Improve clinical scheduling and reduce turnaround time for clinical results
- Bring services to the patient, wherever possible, while avoiding an increase in unit expense—patient-focused care
- Provide the majority of the care on the unit using a small core of staff
- Ensure that the care team has a broad set of skills
- Decentralize and manage the unit-based team within the confines of the major work group (not within each discipline)

Measures

- Customer satisfaction (patient, physician, employee)
- Medication error rate
- Patient falls
- Full-time equivalents (FTEs) providing direct patient care
- Employee turnover
- Operating margin (and cost per unit of service)
- Profitability per FTE (yearly)
- Patient outcomes (SF-12)

The expectation was that the care model would be designed to progress over time, with the unit teams (in their most mature stage) forming interdisciplinary, self-directed work groups. To support this evolution, the patient care (nursing) manager would transition first to a role as facilitator, and then ultimately to outcomes coordinator. Figure 17.6 depicts the current work scenario and the intermediate vision of the team relationships. (The longer-term model—the mature team—will be developed by the teams as they define the work of their unit.) Using these concepts, the PCD subteam drafted a care model for the unit. At the time of this writing, the design is being finalized for implementation.

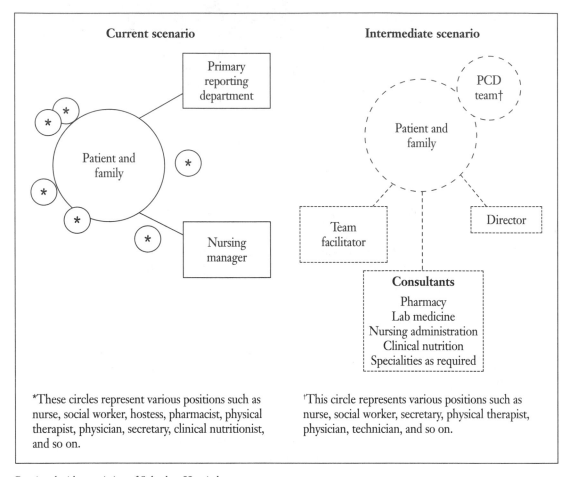

Current scenario

Intermediate scenario

*These circles represent various positions such as nurse, social worker, hostess, pharmacist, physical therapist, physician, secretary, clinical nutritionist, and so on.

†This circle represents various positions such as nurse, social worker, secretary, physical therapist, physician, technician, and so on.

Reprinted with permission of Suburban Hospital.

Figure 17.6. Patient care delivery team.

Wherein the PCD subteam was responsible for developing the unit design, the other three subteams were chartered to critique a draft of the design once it was solidified. All of the subteams were responsible for assisting the core team in developing overall implementation strategies and addressing/developing countermeasures to design barriers. The composition and mission of each team are outlined below.

- Human resources
    - *Responsibilities:* Position descriptions, needs analysis, skills assessment, staffing analysis, skills gap analysis, performance management process review
    - *Composition:* Representatives from compensation and benefits, training and education, admitting, nursing, housekeeping, and core team members
- Technology
    - *Responsibilities:* Technology infrastructure assessment, review of new technologies, strategy for integration of new technology

—*Composition:* Representatives from information services, materials management, surgical services, and core team members

- Finance

  —*Responsibilities:* Cost capturing analysis, cost-benefit analysis

  —*Composition:* Representatives from finance, business office, medical records, and core team members

- Patient care delivery

  —*Responsibilities:* Creation of a template for patient care redesign

  —*Composition:* Staff representatives from the designated pilot medical/surgical nursing unit, key ancillary departments, select physicians, and core team members

The work done by these teams was shared continuously with the core team. As changes to the draft design were made, the information was shared with the implementation teams to be factored into the design. Similarly, as these subteams produced key deliverables, these products were shared with the core team to enhance design strategies.

Design: Planning Teams

In addition to chartering the subteams, once key components of the redesign had been decided, several planning teams were formed to refine the areas that involved significant modification in duties and responsibilities of employees. Unlike the subteams that were primarily composed of managers and supervisors, the composition of the planning teams was that of staff—employees in the areas that were going to be impacted. Also, because the scope of the planning teams was more narrow than the subteams, the planning teams were expected to complete their mission in approximately four meeting sessions. Planning teams were formed for the following concepts.

- *Posting and admitting multifunctional worker:* Improve responsiveness and decrease the handoffs for scheduling surgery and performing preregistration of the patient by utilizing positions that integrate both functions, currently residing in different departments.

- *Pretesting process redesign:* Decrease patient wait time and increase the number of patients who are processed through the hospital's pretesting process prior to surgery by ensuring that process inputs are appropriate and that the process is streamlined.

- *Operating room multifunctional worker:* Decrease the OR turnaround time and increase physician satisfaction with hospital services by developing a position that incorporates technician, housekeeping, supply, and transportation duties.

- *Family waiting room redesign:* Increase patient and family satisfaction with the type and level of communication received before, during, and after operative procedures and increase the comfort and utility of the waiting area. These outcomes are achieved through the institution of a paid family waiting room advocate who can support the current volunteer structure and through the physical renovation of the family waiting room.

In order to manage these teams efficiently and effectively, each team was given an orientation to the ideal design, a mission statement, a list of expected outcomes, tools such as draft job descriptions, and a four-week meeting schedule (including draft agendas).

The output of these teams—suggestions on process changes, insights on possible barriers, and draft job descriptions—was incorporated into revisions of the draft design.

Design: Communicating to Stakeholders

To lay the foundation for reengineering, the case for change had to be built. Although the hospital had been delivering the message about the changing health care environment and the need to be competitive, the Suburban-specific assessment phase data were helpful to bring the communications to a more concrete level by showing Suburban's own opportunity for improvement.

Another important aspect in communicating the ideal design was managing expectations. Because communicating during the six-month design phase meant that the design was still in draft form, the team needed to ensure that the stakeholders involved at that point understood that the design was subject to modification. The strategy for formal communication during the design phase centered around the use of a buddy system. The core team brainstormed a list of key stakeholders, both internal and external. The contents of the list, which comprised both individuals as well as entire departments, was then distributed among the core team members. Each core team member was expected to contact his or her "buddy" on a regular basis to apprise him or her of the initiative's progress, solicit input, and answer questions as necessary. To ensure that all core team members were delivering similar messages, the team synthesized the progress into key points. These messages served as the foundation of a "talking paper" (a high-level, bulleted presentation), which was updated on an ongoing basis. In this way, a copy of an up-to-date outline was always available for team members as needed. (As the team proceeded through the design phase, it began to develop customized sets of the talking paper for different groups of stakeholders.)

The team also relied on the department managers to forward information to their staff. At the monthly department manager meetings, presentations and updates were provided on a regular basis. Handouts were distributed that could be used with staff, and offers were extended by core team members to visit departments to conduct presentations and answer questions.

As expected, informal communications also took place through those stakeholders who were involved in pieces of the redesign process. To assist in managing the "grapevine," the team tried to engage the opinion leaders in the organization, soliciting them for input and making opportunities available to educate and inform.

Existing mechanisms, such as town meetings and the employee newsletter, were used to disseminate general information about the initiative.

Design: Identifying and Quantifying the Vital Few

Improvement ideas, which had originally numbered more than 300, were consolidated to a manageable 75. Barriers were discussed, and countermeasures were strategized. At this stage, the team turned its focus to the development of a cost-benefit analysis. The finance subteam had developed a general framework for the analysis and all the subteams provided any input they could, but the core team was responsible for coordinating the collection of the remaining data. Because the core team was comprised of directors from key departments involved, team input to the analysis was essential. The team prioritized the key concepts to be recommended to the executive team. This helped limit the cost-benefit analysis to 32 items. For each item, the team provided a brief narrative overview, an explanation of assumptions, qualitative costs and benefits, linkages to priority stakeholder needs, and the quantitative impact by period (for three years). Also included was a years-to-payback figure for each concept.

The 32 items were further stratified and the top 13 were analyzed in even further detail, with the results of this analysis submitted to the hospital's budget committee for approval. The detailed cost-benefit analysis developed for these items included a timeline for implementation and a breakdown of capital and operating impacts by month (with detailed statistics at a cost center level). This document estimated the financial impact of the reengineering initiative as $900,000 in capital investment (year one), $860,000 in operating savings (year one), and $1.2 million in annual operating savings (years two and beyond). A synopsis of each of the 13 concepts follows:

- Multifunctional worker in the operating room

  —*Goal:* Centralize tasks to improve efficiency, decrease OR turnaround time, and improve physician satisfaction.

  —*Summary:* Combine duties from housekeepers, anesthesia technicians, and OR ancillary staff into one job description. Assign each worker to an operating room to become part of the OR patient care team.

- Multifunctional worker for posting and admitting

  —*Goal:* Increase ease and accuracy of posting, improve reimbursement, and speed responsiveness.

  —*Summary:* Combine posting, admitting, and financial counseling into one job description. Consolidation of functions should reduce handoffs and allow for the increase in operating hours.

- Patient call/bed-tracking system

  —*Goal:* Improve patient satisfaction and enhance bed availability notification.

  —*Summary:* Install automated system that communicates to all involved parties regarding patient status/patient communication.

- Fax server

  —*Goal:* Reduce time related to information communication, both internally and externally.

  —*Summary:* Install and operationalize direct fax capability from the mainframe system. Provide ability to fax laboratory, radiology, financial reports, and the like to customers directly from terminals.

- Computerized standard orders

  —*Goal:* Decrease patient delays, number of missed tests, and the forms inventory.

  —*Summary:* Develop a computerized library of forms that can be edited and accessed at all terminals. Enable case/physician specific orders (pre- and postoperative) and discharge/teaching tools to be available on demand.

- Intraoperative module

  —*Goal:* Decrease OR delays and inventory and automate manual processes.

  —*Summary:* Expand use of current surgical services software system to move toward an electronic OR record with computers in each OR suite. Provide real-time documentation and billing, just-in-time inventory activities, and access to all patient clinical information.

- Physician office scheduling/order entry

    —*Goal:* Improve physician satisfaction and decrease rework.

    —*Summary:* Provide access to hospital's scheduling software and clinical information from offices. Offer the ability to request OR time, order lab tests, and view patient results.

- Instrument tracking system

    —*Goal:* Decrease OR case delays and enhance instrument availability and maintenance.

    —*Summary:* Automate system that monitors use of instruments to ensure availability through the use of standardized sets, visual display, and computerized reference (for educational purposes and instrument acquisition).

- Sterrad

    —*Goal:* Reduce sterilization and instrument cost, improve staff safety, and decrease turnaround time for sets.

    —*Summary:* Use new gas sterilization technology that eliminates use of ETO (a hazardous chemical) and decreases the time required to sterilize equipment.

- Pneumatic tube system

    —*Goal:* Decrease turnaround time (for lab specimens, pharmacy, and so on) and increase staff availability for patients.

    —*Summary:* Install and operationalize tube system for 13 locations.

- Post-anesthesia recovery unit (PACU)

    —*Goal:* Streamline physical flow of patients, thereby decreasing cycle time and increasing flexibility for staffing and space utilization.

    —*Summary:* Eliminate physical separation of service areas, utilizing one nursing station with cross-trained staff to allow for 24-hour-a-day coverage and insertion of preoperative lines.

- Standard discharge criteria

    —*Goal:* Decrease length of stay, increase patient satisfaction, and improve bed utilization through improved discharge process.

    —*Summary:* Implement a standard discharge policy including time, teaching, and so on.

- Patient care delivery

    —*Goal:* Improve patient satisfaction and outcomes by increasing staff efficiency to allow for increased patient contact, bringing services closer to the patient, and focusing on patient/family education.

    —*Summary:* Redesign the flow of care (and subsequently the positions providing the care and services) by using concepts such as multifunctional workers and developing a work team approach.

Design: More About Patient Care Delivery

Although all 13 of the recommendations cited involve a degree of investment (financially and philosophically), none require more than that of patient care delivery redesign. Touching all of the inpatient nursing units, as well as outpatient areas such as the PACU, this component meant that the reengineering effort would truly impact all major areas. To understand the effect on the patient care units, the highlights of the PCD model are provided as follows.

Use of Two Multifunctional Worker Positions—One Clinical and One Administrative. The design of these positions was the result of synthesizing existing technician positions, clerical roles, and functions acquired from positions that previously had been external to the patient care unit. Examples of functions that are being incorporated into the multifunctional positions are listed here.

Function/service	Traditionally done by . . .	Under the new model done by . . .
Ambulation/ROM	Physical therapy assistant	Patient care technician
Draw blood	Phlebotomist/laboratory	Patient care technician
Daily light cleaning	Housekeeper	Patient care associate
Food to patients	Hostess	Patient care associate

Development of a Unit-Based Team. In addition to the multifunctional workers and those positions found traditionally on the unit (for example, RNs, LPNs, unit secretaries), the PCD template involves the creation of a team(s) that incorporates key professionals from other departments who provide services that are integral to the unit's patient population. Since the pilot unit cares for a high percentage of patients undergoing orthopedic procedures, several physical therapists will serve as unit team members. For other patient services provided, though, caregivers from other departments will serve as consultants to the unit but will not be a part of the unit-level team. For example, although respiratory services may be delivered to patients on the pilot unit, respiratory therapists will not participate as pilot unit team members because these services are not highly utilized by the unit's patient types, but will still be available as needed to provide care. Respiratory therapists may, instead, serve as unit-based team members on other units where respiratory care is critical (for example, the intensive care unit).

Physical Modifications to Facilitate the Flow of Patients and the Delivery of Services on the Unit. Suggestions such as a physical therapy gym on the unit are being considered in an effort to bring services closer to the patient.

Other Improvements Instituted to Improve the System and Infrastructure of the Organization with Resulting Impacts on Care Delivery and Cycle Time. Surgical reengineering concepts such as expansion of the pneumatic tube system (already underway in the emergency department and key ancillary departments) will be extended to include the patient care units. An automated call light/bed-tracking system will be instituted hospitalwide to aid nurses in responding to patient requests as well as patient discharge and bed turnover.

Implementation: Not a Light-Switch Approach

In preparation of approval from the budget committee, the core team began organizing (conceptually) the formation of implementation teams that would be responsible for creating and deploying detailed implementation plans for the design concepts. The implementation teams were to be comprised of staff from highly impacted departments, led by a process owner and facilitated by a member of the core team. To assist the implementation team leaders, the core team developed a package that included a draft agenda for the first meeting, highlights of meeting skills (such as agendas and minute taking), sample ground rules for teams, team member job descriptions, and an implementation planning sheet that included the following information.

Item	Example
Goals/outcome measures	Decrease patient delays
Project steps	Finalize job description; post new position through human resources; develop training curriculum to address any gap in skills
Team membership	Surgeons, staff nurses, housekeeping, unit secretary, technician
Implementation dates	Beginning August 1996 and ending January 1997

Because not all design recommendations were scheduled to begin at the same time, various implementation teams may be at work during the course of the year. The ongoing coordination of these teams remains the responsibility of the core team members. After implementation, the plan is to incorporate the oversight and measurement of the individual design concepts into the departmental quality plans of impacted areas.

Implementation: Expected Results

In addition to the financial impact cited in the cost-benefit analysis, the core team also developed targets for the key performance indicators. These 18-month targets are as follows; target measurement begins 18 months after the implementation date.

Key performance indicator	Target improvement (percent change)
Length of stay (top 10 surgical DRGs)	15 percent
Process cycle time	50 percent
OR case turnover time	50 percent
Cost per case	10 percent
Unplanned returns to OR (inpatients)	25 percent
Employee turnover rate	33 percent to 40 percent
OR cancellation rate	48 percent
OR volume	Maintain at current level

In addition to these macro measures, the implementation team for each design concept was responsible for developing subordinate measures to assess the concept's ability to impact the overall global targets. For example, although process cycle time is targeted to decrease by 50 percent, the implementation of multiple pneumatic tube stations is expected to contribute to the decrease. Thus, the responsibility of the pneumatic tube team is to develop measures relevant to process cycle time that capture changes in components of cycle time attributable to the pneumatic tube.

Lessons Learned

Each step of the reengineering process seemed to yield lessons (both great and small) for the organization. Sometimes the lessons were a recognition of things done well. Many times, though, the most poignant learnings were from things done "not so well." Highlights of both types of lessons are summarized below.

Know What You're Getting Into. The scope of the process requires extensive resources to redesign the process as well as to implement the recommendations. The pain of the process is great for the organization. Be aware of the level of commitment and organizational perseverance required before you start.

Don't Forget the Concept of "Vital Few." The sheer number of ideas can be overwhelming. To avoid being paralyzed, consolidate and prioritize at key steps so that valuable energy is spent on the most important items.

Communicate Desired Goals Up Front. If cost reduction is the primary goal, say so. This message needs to be internalized by the group leading the initiative and then shared with the rest of the organization. If there are quantitative targets (for example, $10 million over two years), the organization should know.

Plan for and Institute a Proactive Communication Strategy. Don't wait until there is something to say before you tackle communications. Begin immediately (even before the initiative) by building the case for change. While one-on-one interactions with key stakeholders (for example, physicians) can be beneficial, avoid hinging the level of communications success solely on the skills or predisposition of individual team members or managers.

Make Reengineering a Strategic Priority and an Organizationwide Team Effort. With the level of activity in the rest of the organization, stakeholders not intimately involved on an ongoing basis may not internalize the importance of the reengineering effort. If reengineering is not placed as a top strategic priority, staff may shuffle projects and slow its progress. Moreover, because a small team is leading the project, those not directly involved may view it as a win/loss for the team leading the initiative, not an organizational win/loss.

Manage Expectations. As teams are formed for brief periods to fulfill specific purposes, ensure that teams are aware of the boundaries of their work (what is negotiable in the redesign and what is not). Also, for those teams that disband before the process has been completed (before implementation), provide follow-up communications so that the members understand how they helped contribute to the ultimate design and implementation.

Beware of Professional Land Mines. As the design begins to take shape, there will be a tendency to "protect the fort." Barriers such as professional licensure may be used as a reason to avoid making changes. All such claims should be researched and reviewed before design change decisions are made and such research shared with all of the professionals impacted.

Secure Executive Ownership Before the Initiative Begins. The executive staff needs not only to buy in to the concept philosophically, but also needs to be prepared to assist on a tactical basis. The more familiar and involved the executives are, the more likely it is that the initiative will be communicated effectively, remain a strategic priority, break down organizational barriers, and fulfill the overall objectives intended for the project.

Don't Underestimate the Value of an Effective Meeting Process. Good meeting skills (timed agendas, minutes), team structure (designated leader, facilitator), and team interaction strategies (consensus building, conflict management) should be incorporated into all activities. Not only will they contribute to efficiency and effectiveness during the assessment and design phases, but they will also help avoid undesirable downstream consequences during implementation.

Summary

Suburban Hospital, having gone through a 17-month initiative to redesign the surgical process, is currently in the midst of implementing recommendations from that undertaking. The experience of the process itself and the approved recommendations yield a number of benefits, both quantitative and qualitative. On the quantitative side, a decrease in operating cost will be enjoyed in the current fiscal year as well as in fiscal years to come. Performance indicators such as process cycle time and operating room cancellation rate are expected to improve significantly. Perhaps as important, however, are the soft benefits experienced by the organization. Things like strengthening of cross-departmental relationships, building participants' skill sets, and ultimately acting out the CQI management philosophy have been important results of the initiative. These benefits do not come without a price. The resources necessary to redesign the process and then implement the recommendations are great. The pain involved is enormous. If the clock were turned back, would Suburban do things differently? Yes. Would the hospital still choose to reengineer? Most definitely.

Questions for Discussion: Senior Management, Executive Council, and Quality Council

- Have you defined a vision for the organization?
- Have you communicated it to the organization?
- Have you established strategic objectives for the organization?
- Have you identified the critical success factors (CSFs) to achieve the strategic objectives?
- Have you prioritized the CSFs for organizational focus for the next two to three years?
- Have you defined and validated the vital few key performance indicators to track the progress toward the strategic objectives?
- Have you defined the value chain for your organization as perceived by your customers?
- Have you defined a flow of the core processes (including management processes) that help you deliver value to customers?
- Have you prioritized the core processes by their degree of impact on your business in the next two to three years?
- Are you willing and ready to go through the reengineering effort in your organization?
- Have you defined the scope of the process(es) to be reengineered?
- Is the size of the proposed process(es) to be reengineered wide and deep enough to significantly impact the organization?

- Do you fully understand the commitment required to go through the proposed change?
- Are you willing to go through the resource investment necessary for such a commitment?
- Have you set performance targets for the redesigned process? Are these targets stretched?
- Are these targets consistent with the organizational performance necessary to achieve the strategic objectives?
- Have you selected the members for the core team that will design the process?
- Are these team members some of the best and brightest in the organization?
- Have you looked at the balance among technical skills, functional expertise, and the personality types of the core team members?
- Is the size of the team optimal?
- Have you considered involvement of an outside resource to assist the team?
- Have you selected a process owner?
- Have you identified an executive sponsor for the project?
- Have you considered the time commitment for the team members for the duration of the project?
- Have you communicated the timeline and the performance objectives to the team?
- Have you communicated with and sought approval of the departmental heads of the selected team members?
- Have you installed a project structure to manage the project's progress?
- Have you developed a case for change for the organization?
- Have you communicated it to the rest of the organization?
- Have you identified the stakeholders that can make or break the project's successful implementation?
- Do you have a communications strategy in place?
- Is there an execution plan for this strategy?
- Are the responsibilities clearly defined for the execution of the communications plan?
- Are the roles and responsibilities, and the necessary time commitment by the senior executives, fully understood?

Questions for Executive Sponsors/Process Owners

- Is the scope of the process clearly defined with boundaries?
- Are there any constraints imposed on the project by the quality council?
- Are these constraints and the scope fully understood by each member of the quality council and the senior leadership?
- Are these constraints freshly reviewed with stakeholders?
- Can they be overcome?
- Is the business case for change communicated and understood?
- Is there an organizational communications plan?

- Is the project structure adequate to resolve issues rapidly when they arise?

- Is the membership of the core team the best possible?

- Are there other people within the organization who can play a critical role in the redesign of the process?

- Have you considered how best to involve these people without increasing the size of the team to an unwieldy level?

- Is the resource commitment adequate to achieve the objectives of the project in the given time frame?

- Have you verified the team members' time commitment to the project with the respective departmental heads?

- Does the team have authority to deal with people who may be affected by the change, both within and outside the organization?

- Is there a formal project plan with clear and measurable goals and objectives; explicitly stated assumptions, tasks, responsibilities, deliverables, schedules, and deadlines; and identified resources?

- Is the team using a methodology to guide the work?

- Is this methodology tailored to the organization's needs?

Questions for Team Members

- Are the project goals and objectives understood? Is the linkage to strategic objectives and the vision understood?

- Is the scope of the project clearly defined and understood?

- Are the roles and responsibilities within the core team defined and understood?

- Do I have all the necessary skills? Can I reinforce my skills by involving somebody else? Do I have a list of these potential resources if needed?

- Is the time commitment for the project understood?

- Is the time commitment realistic? Will I be able to devote the time required for the project?

- How will I manage my time to meet my other responsibilities? How will I prioritize my time?

- How will I prioritize all the things I am responsible for? What will I give up, reprioritize, and delegate?

- Have I presented my plan to my supervisor to obtain approval?

- Do I have any concerns regarding this project? Do I know who to talk to about those? Have I done that?

- Do I understand the implications of the proposed change? Am I willing to go through it? Am I ready to provide leadership for the change?

- Is there a methodology to guide the team and me? Have I been trained or educated in the methodology?

- Do I understand the project timeline, deliverables, deadlines, and so on?
- Have I been trained or am I being trained on the tools and techniques necessary to accomplish the tasks at hand?

Elizabeth H. Dougherty is the quality advisor for Suburban Hospital, serving as a key resource to the organization and its stakeholders regarding continuous quality improvement. Involved in strategic projects such as surgical reengineering and redesign of the patient care delivery system, she facilitates the process and ensures consistency and integration with other hospital initiatives. Prior to working at Suburban in quality, she held consulting and industry positions in the field of human resource management. Dougherty earned a B.A. degree in business and Spanish from the University of Pittsburgh and an M.B.A. degree from the University of Maryland. She is a member of American Society for Quality and GOAL/QPC.

William F. Minogue, M.D., FACP, is the senior vice president for medical affairs of Suburban Hospital, Bethesda, Maryland. He began his career in the private practice of internal medicine and cardiology, became the director of medical education in a large community hospital, and then became vice president for medical affairs. He authored paramedic legislation in New Jersey and served as an EMS medical director in New Jersey for 10 years. From 1985 until 1992, he was at The George Washington University where he was responsible for medical staff, nursing, and house staff, and he served as the chief of staff of the hospital. From 1992 until 1994 he was vice president for clinical affairs for the Bon Secours Health System. He has devoted his career to medical education, quality assurance and improvement, and hospital management. He was a member of the Joint Commission's Task Force on Organization and Management Effectiveness, serving as chairman of the JCAHO Task Force on Quality Improvement. The latter group developed a set of principles that were used to write the 1992–1995 performance improvement standards for all health care organizations surveyed by the Joint Commission.

Minogue was a member of the board of trustees of the Bon Secours Health System and was a trustee of the Educational Commission for Foreign Medical Graduates. He is past president of the Association for Hospital Medical Education and has served on the education committee of the American Hospital Association. He has also served as a member of the Accreditation Council for Continuing Medical Education and was chairman of the Society of Academic Health Centers of the American College of Physician Executives.

Jay B. Mathur is a vice president of Juran Institute and a key industry executive of its Customer and Process Assessment Group.

Before joining the professional staff of Juran Institute, Mathur was employed by an international consulting firm where he held several key leadership positions. He was the national coordinator of its business process reengineering practice and was recognized as the firm's leading business process reengineering expert. He also held positions with Deloitte & Touche and Authur Andersen & Co.

Mathur earned a B.S. degree in physics, chemistry, and mathematics from the University of Delhi, a B.S. degree in polymer technology and chemical engineering from Kanpur University in India, and an MBA degree from Illinois State University. He is a member of various professional organizations and has authored articles and given presentations on a diverse range of quality-related subjects.

Chapter 18

Reengineering in an Integrated Health System

Nancy Henley

In integrated health systems such as group and staff model health maintenance organizations (HMOs), health care is delivered in many settings. The providers who care for one patient may work for several different organizations. The patient's care is generally coordinated by a primary provider. These same facts apply in nonintegrated health care systems. Opportunities for improvements in process and outcomes abound. Distinguishing characteristics of integrated systems include common goals among managers and providers, the ability to control sources of professional and institutional care, and the relatively greater ability to evaluate both clinical and business outcomes. Even components of the system that provide care by contract can be aligned to support the organization's objectives. When a need for improvement is identified, these characteristics enable successful change. Improvement experience across many health care organizations has revealed an absence of existing processes. In these instances, the need is for process engineering (design, quality planning) rather than reengineering. This chapter discusses engineering and reengineering activities in Kaiser Permanente Medical Care Program of North Carolina (KPNC). The initiatives discussed have occurred over the last several years, and many are now in progress.

The organizational setting is described first, Then, the chapter covers KPNC's conceptualization of its clinical work, levels of clinical care, and key support processes. Some specific projects are discussed in the context of levels of care, support systems, facility function, and clinical guidelines.

Organizational Setting

The Kaiser Foundation Health Plan of North Carolina (KFHPNC) is a not-for-profit, historically group model, HMO. It is part of the national Kaiser Permanente organization. The name *Kaiser Permanente* represents a partnership between the medical professionals of The Carolina Permanente Medical Group (TCPMG), PA, and the business professionals of Kaiser Foundation Health Plan of North Carolina. The North Carolina Region was founded in 1985 as an expansion of the national program. TCPMG provides services solely for members of KFHPNC. TCPMG also contracts for all professional services not provided directly by members of TCPMG. Because the region is geographically dispersed and is non–hospital based, specialty care has been provided largely via networks of community specialists. Beginning in 1995, the region added contracted community primary physicians as an option for its members.

Membership. The North Carolina Region includes nearly 127,000 members: 41,000 in Charlotte, 26,000 in Durham/Chapel Hill, and 60,000 in Raleigh.

Geography. There are three clinical service areas as noted; Charlotte is 150 miles from Durham/Chapel Hill and Raleigh.

Organization Structure. The area administrator and area medical director have operational responsibility for all clinical services. They work in partnership with an executive director of health plan who has responsibility for contracting, marketing, and member services.

Providers. Providers include 156 physicians in TCPMG; 60 health care and mental health practitioners; and more than 2000 contract physicians, largely specialists.

Delivery System. KPNC operates nine full-service medical offices. Services include primary care, ob-gyn, some internalized specialty care, laboratory, radiology, and pharmacy. All other specialty and support services (for example, physical therapy, podiatry) are available through contracted community providers. Primary and tertiary hospital care, skilled nursing care, home health/infusion services, and hospice care are contracted from community providers.

History of TQM in the Region. TQM philosophy, methods, and tools were introduced in the region in 1992. Acceptance and usage have waxed and waned since then. For example, the original quality council was established in 1992, decommissioned in favor of a new structure in 1993, and reestablished as a regional quality committee with different responsibilities in 1994. The region continues to refine its methods for setting priorities and for implementation of many innovations. Progress, which has been dramatic in some areas, has been uneven among departments and geographic areas.

Perhaps the most important means of disseminating TQM methods and tools to the organization is quality-in-daily-work (QDW) training. QDW targets executive, middle management, and supervisory personnel and physicians. Since 1994 virtually all managers have participated in the training. This course covers

- Setting the context
- Team meeting leadership
- Establishing the project
- Diagnosing the cause/analyzing symptoms
- Formulating theories, testing theories, and identifying root causes
- Remedying the cause

The training has set common expectations and laid a foundation of common methods and tools. These have enabled significant improvement in use of measurement and in approaches to problems and to new work.

While leaders, physicians, and employees in the region are well-versed in TQM concepts and methods, there has been no formal initiative in reengineering. As well-discussed in the literature, absence of top leadership backing is not optimal for reengineering. However, the concepts of reengineering can be successfully applied, if there is strong leadership in the organizational division and if the cross-functional aspects of the process being reengineered receive concentrated attention. For example, resistance must be carefully managed anticipatorially. Operational owners, in particular, must be consulted frequently, since all of them cannot be on the team.

Another major enabling factor for reengineering, without a full organizat, presence of well-developed clinical support capabilities. In health care, clinical in and health promotion and education capability are two examples of necessary suppo. the following support capabilities have enabled successful reengineering of clinical pro information systems, self-care programs for members, health promotion and edu QRM/case management. Some of these supports are fully operational, and others are in dev opment themselves—work in progress. All of the key supports will be discussed later.

Reconceptualizing the Work

Three High-Level Key Processes

As a first step in conceptualizing the work to be done in revamping care delivery, the organization agreed on three broad processes of care: (1) disease prevention and health promotion, (2) acute care, and (3) chronic care. High-level diagrams of these processes are presented in the chapter appendix. The three processes have a number of common elements. All include information synthesis, documentation, and patient and family education. The flow of information and its synthesis involves assessment of various pieces of information in the development of a plan, implementation of a care plan, and development of a follow-up plan. Disease prevention and health promotion focuses on obtaining risk factor history, physical exam findings, and screening studies in order to develop an individualized preventive care plan. Acute care focuses on triage of the patient and on obtaining information pertinent to that particular illness. Only a few or many components of the delivery system may be involved in caring for an acutely ill patient, depending on severity. The chronic care process assumes an existing history so that all history, physical findings, and diagnostic studies are updating an existing database. Again, many elements of the health care system may be involved, depending of the patient's complexity. The emphasis is on continuity.

Choosing these three familiar categories, admittedly having some overlap, moved us toward restating the goals of health care. Having goals facilitated setting priorities for work, based on the demographics of our population. This done, we could begin assessing the who, what, when, where, how, and especially the why of subprocesses. Of special note here, self-care is of great importance in the care of populations; however, it is viewed as a support to the three key processes, not a key process itself.

Restating the Goals of Health Care

The region's strategic plan for improving health, called for by the region's strategic goal on quality of care, was first approved in 1994. The plan takes a very broad perspective on "health care." Sources for goals include Healthy People 2000, HEDIS, and medical literature. Its five topic areas and goals include the following:

Self-Care. The goal is to support our members in their ability to provide basic care for themselves and their families and in their ability to make well-informed decisions about consulting health professionals.

Screening, Chemoprophylaxis, and Immunization. The goal is to provide efficacious, age-appropriate, risk-appropriate screening, chemoprophylaxis, and immunization services to members.

Wellness and Health Promotion. The goal is to provide our members with:

- Education on risk factor modification and self-screening

- Family planning education and services, with particular attention to the prevention of teenage pregnancies

- Education and support services for lactation

- Education and interventions for prevention of HIV infection and other sexually transmitted diseases

- Education and activities for achieving a healthy lifestyle (examples include nutrition, exercise, and mental health)

Health in the Workplace. The goal is to build health care partnerships with selected Kaiser Permanente employer groups and assist them with workplace interventions to address the following categories.

- Occupational injury prevention

- Occupational illness prevention

- Identification of opportunities for increasing self-care; screening, chemoprophylaxis, and immunization; wellness and health promotion; and appropriate disease-associated care

Disease and Disability-Related Care. The goal is to provide evidence-based, personalized, cost-effective care for members with acute and chronic disease.

Objectives have been developed for each goal. The plan for each objective includes the following:

- Definition of measures

- Action needed

- Responsible persons

- Timeline

- Benchmarks

- Current KPNC measures

Restating our goals significantly broadened our view of the work to be done, allowing us to move beyond the what-happens-in-the-exam-room view of health care.

Distinguishing Levels of Complexity in Clinical Care

Much as physicians approach a particular disease entity via risk stratification, we have analyzed the levels of care delivered in our medical offices. This model describes the medical office, in our well-integrated system, as a central focus to which most other components of the delivery system relate (see Figure 18.1). Our working descriptors for levels of care are

- Disease prevention and health promotion

- Acute illness: Noncomplex

- Acute illness: Severe

- Chronic disease: Amenable to population-based care

- Chronic disease and disability of low incidence/prevalence

- Nonmedical problems

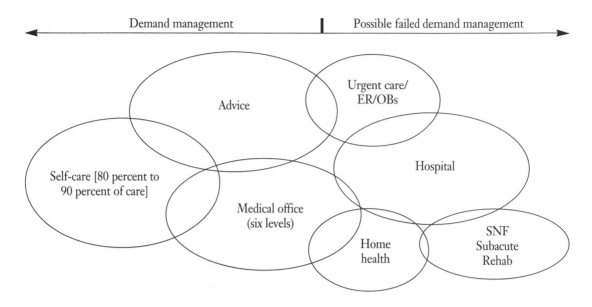

Figure 18.1. The interfaces of the where and who of care.

The levels of care are described later in some detail. Distinguishing levels of complexity has enabled task analysis, utilization of appropriate care provider, and incorporation of support options (for example, health education, home health) needed for the different levels of care. Figure 18.2 contains a sample levels-of-care worksheet.

Understanding Interdependencies

As we mindfully broadened our goals and analyzed levels of care, the interfaces among different providers, facilities, and support systems were highlighted. Thus our systems understanding and thinking have been nurtured. For example, Figure 18.1 illustrates the interfaces in the continuum of care from self-care to hospitalization. Recognizing the multilevel influences of telephone advice services helps operations managers plan for communication with providers who had not previously been considered customers of the call center. The same diagram has been used to illustrate opportunities for demand management across the continuum of care.

Along with such visual representations, customer/supplier analyses have been used to further the understanding of all the systems components involved in any given project. For example, the diabetes care design team, discussed later, used telephone interviews of diabetic members (external customers) and focus groups for several internal customers/suppliers as a key source of information for development of product features.

Levels of Clinical Care

Looking at the work done in our medical offices from the perspectives of severity of illness and intensity of service revealed six levels of clinical care.

1. Disease prevention and health promotion

2. Acute illness: Noncomplex

Provider options				Levels of care in the medical office	Other resource options							
MD	HCP	RN	Skilled clerical		Self-care*	Health promotion and education	Quality resource management*	Choose Health*	Hospital	Specialty physicians	Home health*	Pharmacy
				Acute noncomplex								
				Disease preventive/ health promotion								
				Chronic disease population								
				Severe acute								
				Chronic care ≠ chronic disease								
				Nonmedical illness presenting to medical office								

*Contribute to demand management

Figure 18.2. Levels of primary care and provider and resource options.

3. Acute illness: Severe

4. Chronic disease: Amenable to population-based care

5. Chronic disease and disability of low incidence/prevalence

6. Nonmedical problems

Recognizing these levels and thinking of the medical office as the hub of clinical activity promoted analysis of skills needed in the office (that is, type of personnel) and of supports needed. For example, the most frequent visit type for both adult and pediatric medicine is health maintenance. Most of the tasks related to health maintenance do not require physician skills and training. Many, in fact, could be classified as self-care, once the appropriate teaching has occurred. With this background knowledge, a new member risk assessment was designed and processes for introducing new members to the plan and developing the individual's database were reengineered (Choose Health program). These new processes allow us to integrate new members into the primary care system rapidly. Other components of the preventive care system redesign now in progress include implementation of a self-care book and its supports, automated reporting and reminder systems for selected preventive services, and redesign of preventive services–related processes in clinical modules.

Levels of care are defined as follows. For operational purposes, levels of care have been defined using clinical examples.

Disease prevention and health promotion includes screening, immunization, counseling, and chemoprophylaxis services for the adult and pediatric populations. Interval exams and annual checks for oral contraceptives are in this level.

Acute illness: Noncomplex includes common, non–life–threatening presentations such as upper respiratory illnesses, musculoskeletal complaints, urinary tract infections, and many other minor, generally time-limited illnesses. Such illnesses are often amenable to self-care by a well-informed patient/family member or to management via nursing advice. Nurse practitioners and physician's assistants working with physicians can provide appropriate care, efficiently, for patients who are seen in the medical office.

Acute illness: Severe includes potentially life-threatening presentations such as acute chest pain, severe asthma, severe infections, and complaints that require assessment for possible surgical intervention. Such presentations generally require the care of a physician and may require hospitalization.

Chronic disease: Amenable to population-based care includes such prevalent diseases as diabetes, chronic asthma, and cardiovascular diseases. With a relatively large population of members with a given disease in the plan, it is possible to assess the needs of the members via surveys and focus groups and to risk stratify the population. Programs can be designed to meet the specific needs of the population and address clinical goals. Such programs can focus on prevention, health promotion, and self-care to achieve optimal health outcomes.

Chronic disease and disability of low incidence/prevalence includes diverse chronic medical problems that, by virtue of their low frequency and/or uniqueness, must be managed individually. For example, many malignancies, rheumatologic disorders, multiple trauma cases, complex premature infants, multiple sclerosis, and many other diseases/disabilities require tailored management. Depending on the complexity of the case, a physician along with office support staff may manage the patient, or case management staff may assist. Case management coordinators assess patient and family needs and, under supervision of the provider, develop a care plan for the member. Resources used may include home health care, home infusion, hospice, special equipment, intermittent SNF or subacute care, and various community resources.

ms presenting to the medical office include a broad array of largely psychosocial,
tional problems that require nonmedical intervention. Providers and staff must
ese problems and direct the members to the appropriate resources. Related to
ons are a significant group of patients who have some medical problem with
.... dysfunction that results in personal distress and in inappropriately high utilization of office visits and other resources.

With levels of care as the starting point, physicians and operations staff have begun assessment of needs and redesign of care delivery. Recognition of levels of care has fostered appropriate staffing and training for task needs along with deployment of supports best suited to the patients needs (for example, case management, pharmacy, counseling, and so on). Examples are discussed in the "Reengineering in Action" section.

Key Support Systems

Key support systems are those that cross and integrate multiple levels of care and multiple specialties. They are not the same as key clinical systems, though there is some overlap. Examples of key support systems are the following:

- Information systems: Clinical information systems, disease-specific databases, facility-related databases (for example, hospitals), and preventive care tracking and reminders

- Health promotion and education

- QRM/case management

- Self-care

Information Systems

Presently clinical information supports include automated access to demographics, diagnoses, date and type of visit, provider, laboratory, pharmacy, immunizations, and Pap smear and mammography history. Most of this information also appears on a paper patient visit record at each visit. Case managers also have access to referral and hospitalization history and to durable medical equipment allocation. Tracking and reminder systems are in place or near completion for immunizations, screening and abnormal Pap smears, and abnormal mammograms.

KPNC's electronic clinical information system has been developed to manage member-specific clinical information. This system is currently fully or partially deployed at all medical offices. It gives providers online access to diagnoses, encounter, pharmacy, lab, allergy, immunization, and demographic member data. The system facilitates extraction of meaningful information from the data, by providing filtered and cross-system views. In addition, the system will track diagnostic study results and consultation reports to ensure timely review by the responsible provider. The system augments communication with members through assisted correspondence.

The region maintains numerous other databases for evaluation and planning purposes. Most important among these for clinical purposes are the hospital database and disease-specific databases (such as for diabetes and high-risk obstetrics).

✳Health Promotion and Education

Health promotion and education (HP&E), as a department, has many roles in clinical support. Discrete programs run by the department for high-risk members and high-volume diagnoses include all prenatal and newborn care education, including high-risk obstetrics, lactation support services, diabetes teaching, smoking cessation, and nutritional services. The department also supports the clinical modules through disease-specific training of module nursing staff (for example, low back pain, asthma) and through the CORE health education materials.

The CORE collection of health education pamphlets is intended to assist Kaiser Permanente staff in the delivery of quality care to members in the primary care setting. A needs assessment among providers determined that an efficient, easy-to-use system of ordering up-to-date, quality health education materials is critical to HP&E's mission.

Topics included in CORE were identified using the top 10 diagnoses for inpatient and outpatient visits across the region, the list of pamphlets for which 300 or more were ordered during the past year, the topics required by the National Commission for Quality Assurance, and the most common topics mentioned during the provider needs assessment. Each pamphlet considered was carefully screened for the CORE catalog using the Kaiser Permanente Interregional Handout Evaluation criteria and medical criteria. Pamphlets that met both the educational and medical criteria were selected for CORE. Materials are available in each module according to specialty needs. CORE materials and health education professional support are integral to the Choose Health program.

HP&E also takes an active role in new program development. Examples include adult diabetes care, hypertension management, and lipids management.

QRM/Case Management

QRM/case management, as used here, refers to a wide variety of services provided through the department of quality resource management. The department arranges all outside professional referrals and procedures, home health and infusion services, hospice care, durable medical equipment, prosthetics, orthotics, and supplies. Case management refers to the coordination of these services and liaison with primary care providers and facility services for patients with complex acute and chronic diseases and conditions. Case management coordinators are registered nurses who function as the continuity-of-care "glue" for members who receive care from many providers. Further details on the case management process are included in the "Reengineering in Action" section.

Self-Care

While self-care is clearly a type of care itself, self-care can also be productively thought of as a support system for many levels of care. The goal of self-care is enabling members to make good decisions about caring for themselves and about when to seek professional care (that is, to avoid delays in care). Viewed across the continuum, the same self-care tools and information are used by the patient, family members, providers, office nurses, CMCs, advice nurses, and pharmacists. The complete self-care program was implemented in the region in fall 1996. Staff from each part of the system were trained to give members consistent responses and to support appropriate self-care at every opportunity. Self-care materials can be used for disease prevention and health promotion, all acute illnesses, many chronic illnesses, and for many nonmedical concerns. Many patients with chronic diseases can benefit greatly from well-informed self-care. Self-care for diabetic members, for example, is well-developed and highly valued by patients.

Reengineering in Action

Reengineering methodology has been used in four different types of activities in KPNC. Some projects have been small and others huge. Many are presently in progress. They range from using the methodology to reengineer everything about a new medical office, to designing assimilation of new members, to completely reengineering the organization and use of medical information. Many examples are sketched as follows, and several projects are discussed in detail.

Examples from Levels of Care

Disease Prevention and Health Promotion: New Member Mailing and Risk Assessment. Prior to 1996, new members' contact with Kaiser Permanente (KP) was entirely up to them. From the view of optimizing care and efficient use of resources, this was not a desirable situation. A multidisciplinary work team set out to design a process that would provide information on preventive services to all new members, offer a risk assessment to all new members, and bring new members with significant medical problems into the system quickly. This task had to be accomplished in three months. All of the information received on members had to be forwarded to the appropriate medical office, appointments had to be made, and so on.

The products of this design effort were a brochure on pediatric and adult preventive services, letters to new members, a brief risk assessment questionnaire, and multiple operational linkages. Linkages had to be built among Choose Health, the medical offices, nursing advice, and appointments. Processes for review and routing of questionnaires required coordination among several departments and the clinical agreement of multiple physicians. Figure 18.3 illustrates the linkages.

Choose Health is a comprehensive risk assessment, preventive services, and KP orientation program. The program was initiated in 1989 as a health appraisal program that specialized in providing annual physical exams for members. Care is delivered by nurse practitioners and physicians assistants, with physician backup. An assessment of the function of the existing program in 1994 showed multiple opportunities for improving service to patients, to employers, and to internal customers. In particular, there was significant variation in program components among the areas, which made advertising the program difficult. A team of midlevel providers, medical office administrators, and health educators developed the following goals and redesigned the functions of the program.

- *Mission statement.* Choose Health promotes improvement of individual and population health status through risk appraisal and appropriate preventive medicine screening and intervention including education. In addition, Choose Health promotes member satisfaction and retention through timely orientation and assistance in choice of primary provider.

- *Program components.*

  —Health risk appraisal

  —Screening exam (new or interval)

  —Establishment of patient database

  —Evidence-based health maintenance guidelines

  —Health education and individual goal setting: Group—at HEP; individual—on referral

  —Formal link with Regional Health Promotion and Education

  —Kaiser Permanente orientation

  —Interface with primary care and gynecology: Assistance in choice of primary provider; same health maintenance guidelines; direct referrals to primary care for patients with complex illnesses; direct referrals for disease-related education; treatment of minor illnesses; ongoing interval exams; contraceptive services

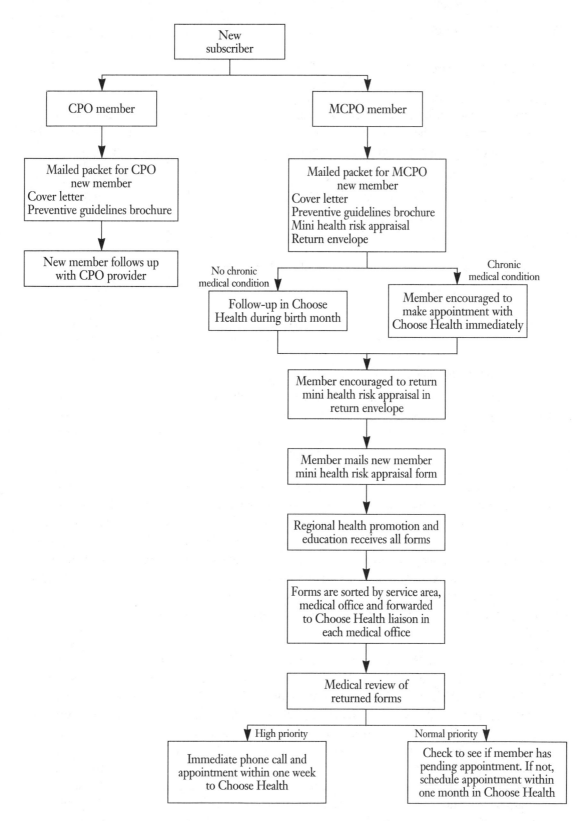

Figure 18.3. Mini health risk appraisal process.

—Self-help resource center

—Evaluation

Internal and external evaluation of the program is now in development and includes the following measures. The revamped health appraisal program is part of the Choose Health (CH) umbrella: Health promotion and education, disease prevention, wellness and self-care, and health appraisal.

- *Internal evaluation components.*

  —No-show rate: Follow-up and new to CH

  —Unscheduled appointments

  —Percent of new members seen in CH

  —Time to mailing of CH letter from member effective date

  —Wait time for appointments

  —Staffing ratio

- *Proposed evaluation of program outcomes:* Utilization (ER, hospital, external), satisfaction with Choose Health, HEDIS with subpopulations for CH, member retention, percentage of members who have had a health risk appraisal

An assessment to date reveals that although Choose Health was redesigned around internal and external customer needs and strong efforts were made to address cross-functional issues, appointment slots are not full. Investigation of causes revealed impact from a new centralized appointment and advice service, scripting about Choose Health for appointments personnel, and inefficient sequencing of appointment screens. Prior to the centralized appointments function, Choose Health booked its own appointments. Moving appointment making to the call center required training of appointments personnel. Unfortunately, the call center has experienced staff instability, so repetitive training has been required. The inefficiency of screen setup contributes to the problem because it is easier for staff to book a check-up with a provider in a primary care module than in Choose Health (staff must move from one screen to another). A theory regarding decreasing new members due to slow membership growth was evaluated. The finding was that, though total membership is not growing rapidly, the plan does have thousands of new members each year. In summary, administrators and providers in charge of the program are in rework mode and are trying to stabilize the situation in the call center and obtain the needed information systems change.

Disease Prevention and Health Promotion: Automated Tracking and Reminders Systems.
KPNC has initiated automation of crucial and tedious tracking and reminders for common preventive services. Effectiveness of automated reminders for both providers and patients is well-documented in the prevention literature. Automated systems are in development for immunizations, Pap smears, and mammograms. The immunization project is discussed here in some detail.

The original immunization process relied on parents/members and providers to recall that an immunization was due and to schedule an appointment. Individual records were kept in the paper record and just finding the whole immunization record could be a challenge. As to reminders, next-immunization-due reminders were given to parents during office visits, and various efforts were made to prompt the whole over-65 population about influenza vaccine. When immunization levels needed to be measured, samples were drawn and individual charts were reviewed. This familiar scenario describes a prime target for reengineering.

The new immunization system, designed by a team of physicians and information systems specialists, targeted automation of every possible aspect of the immunization process. Product features included the following:

- Online entry of immunizations and skin tests
- Online entry of skin test results
- Interface to the patient visit record
- Entry of CDC contraindications
- Next-due guidelines/immunization schedule
- Ability to print an immunization record (on demand)
- Ability to produce patient-specific reminders

An assessment to date reveals that although most of the system was designed and implemented in 1993–94, the mailed patient reminders and provider-specific past due reports have proved to be an implementation challenge. Validity of information on these reports hinged on the complete and correct transfer of prior immunization information from the paper chart to the computer. This task is time-intensive and requires knowledge of both immunizations and medical records for successful completion (that is, operations resources were necessary). In addition, all new immunizations have to be accurately entered. Common processes had to be reengineered at the module level. The region has 16 modules; most accomplished this work for the pediatric population by the end of 1996. Pediatric immunization rates, as defined by HEDIS, have ranged from 83 percent to 87 percent since 1993. The mailed reminders along with efforts to take advantage of every office visit for immunization are expected to boost the rate to more than 90 percent.

Acute Illness, Noncomplex: Point-of-Service Patient Education. Every patient visit requires some type of patient education. The education is often given by the provider, though in most instances it could be delivered by a nonphysician, perhaps more effectively. The quality and quantity of the education can be highly variable, depending on the resources available and the interest and skill of the educator. In addition, health education studies have shown that educating the patient at the time of the encounter is the most effective way to promote behavioral change. For these reasons, one medical office and the department of health promotion and education undertook a pilot project on point-of-service patient education. The goal of the project was integration of health education into the clinic modules via handouts, videotapes, and CD-ROMs. The pilot targeted the top 10 adult diagnoses at that medical office.

Background data for the project included

- Population data for the Cary Medical Office
- Top 10 diagnoses for the Cary Medical Office
- Top 10 pamphlets used in the North Carolina Region
- Pamphlets mandated by regulatory agencies such as NCQA and HCFA
- Provider survey to determine preferred pamphlet titles and location of racks

Population, diagnostic frequency, and current use information was used along with regulatory/accreditation requirements to develop the education collection for the office. Provider survey information was also used in designing the storage method and location of education materials in the medical office. Providers, support staff, and health education personnel worked together to develop protocols for each of the top 10 diagnoses and to chart progress notes for each.

An assessment to date reveals that, after five months of operation, the program was evaluated by providers, clinical staff, and the physician in charge of the facility. This first round of evaluation did not include patients. The subjective findings were as follows; next steps specifically include patient surveys and efforts at quantitative evaluation.

Positive aspects of program	Issues needing to be addressed
Core selection of pamphlets selected that all providers agreed on.	Initial assessment was based on population and top 10 diagnoses—need to also look at diagnoses that take provider time.
Staff is being proactive in placing pamphlets on patient's chart prior to visit.	Some providers have not bought into the program.
Pamphlets are placed in a location that is convenient to providers, staff, and patients.	Staff feels using the protocols slows their work flow and they are worried about getting behind.
Those providers that use the videotapes with their patients like having that source of education available in the module.	Some providers have forgotten they have videotapes for different diagnoses.
	Some protocols are not implemented until after the provider sees the patient, due to time constraints.
	The protocol for sinusitis is not being used because it is titled "Bacterial Sinusitis."

Next steps include the following:

- Survey the providers to determine which visit types/diagnoses take longer to complete.
- Assess why some providers do not follow the program.
- Determine the best point of the visit to implement the health education protocols.
- Develop a list of the available videotapes and include the time length for viewing.
- Determine the best place for patients to view the videotapes (that is, exam room vs. classroom).
- Determine ways to measure the videotapes' effectiveness.

Acute Illness: Severe. Acute severe illness requires the most complex and costly care from both the facility and professional perspectives. For several years, KPNC has had active initiatives to avoid hospitalization and minimize length of stay if hospitalized while maintaining or improving quality of care. The foremost of these are dedicated hospital teams and expansion of home infusion and other home health services. Home care services will be discussed later under case management. Here the development, features, and outcome of one KPNC adult medicine hospital team will be discussed.

Historically, most primary physicians have cared for their patients throughout the continuum of care, referring only when surgical care or tertiary care was needed. This has certainly been true for Permanente physicians in North Carolina who have been dedicated to the full primary care role.

However, in recent years our medical group has been faced with an ever-increasing need for improved efficiency in both the inpatient and outpatient settings. In addition, the complexity of hospital systems and ever-increasing technology have stressed the capabilities of even the most gifted physicians. Due to these factors, the question of whether hospital care could be improved via dedicated hospital physicians was raised. Preservation of continuity of care was the chief concern, though there were many others related to impact on physicians, outpatient panels, and so on.

Physicians tend to discuss only the work of physician team members when talking about hospital care. To move beyond this, a high-level flow diagram of the whole process of care was developed, with hospitalization as one part. The diagram helped those designing the new adult medicine team address all components and handoffs (see Figure 18.4). The hospital team developed a plan for managing admissions, hospitalizations, and transfers through the continuum, and for facilitating high-quality, efficient, and cost-effective care delivery.

- *Purpose of the adult medicine rounding system.* To create a hospital rounding system consisting of four to five physicians that will be stationed in the hospital from 7:00 A.M. to 6:00 P.M., Monday through Friday, with morning rounds on weekends.

- *Operating agreements.* The hospital-based team (HT) will rotate weekly. The HT physician will be responsible for all adult medicine admissions and will be accountable for approving these admissions. The HT physician will

  —Round daily.

  —Cover emergency department encounters as deemed necessary.

  —Conduct medicine consultations.

  —Dictate history, physical, and discharge summaries.

  —Communicate with primary care providers.

The HT physician will work closely with the QRM staff in utilization management.

A verbal report regarding the hospitalized members will be given by the current HT physician rounding on Sunday to the HT physician that begins rotation on Monday. Continuity of care and communication with appropriate caregivers will be handled carefully. Hospitalized members with a primary care physician (PCP) will be managed by the hospital-based physician. The PCP will make "public relations" visits while the member is hospitalized. Upon transfer to an alternate setting or discharge, the hospital-based physician will document all orders for care and to which PCP the member's care will be transferred. The PCP will assume full responsibility for management of care following transfer or discharge.

If the hospitalized member has no PCP, a provider will be selected from a rotating list of providers with less-than-full panels. The selected provider will make "public relations" visits during the hospitalization and will assume care following transfer and/or discharge.

It is imperative that a follow-up appointment be scheduled with the appropriate provider prior to discharge.

- Support and interface needs. The planning process included provision for the following supports and interfaces.

  —Office space, e-mail, Kaiser Permanente computerizing linkage, fax, phone, on-call lists, facility phone directories, courier services

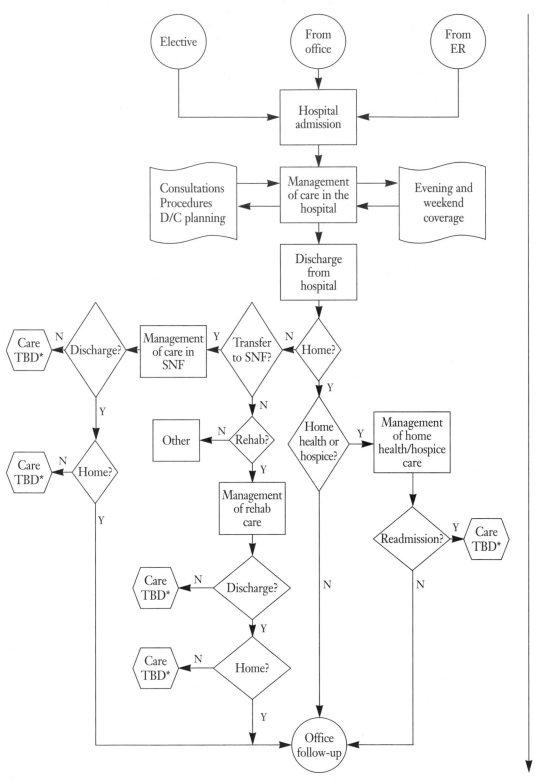

*To be determined

Figure 18.4. Generic process for hospitalization and follow-up care.

—Special phone numbers for obtaining follow-up appointments for members prior to discharge

—A list of receiving providers for unassigned patients

—A communication plan for the hospital, consultants, Kaiser Permanente primary physicians, support staff, and members

An assessment to date reveals that, subjectively, the use of dedicated hospital physicians has led to improved provider skills, greatly increased hospital system familiarity, improved partnership with case management coordinators, and increased use of observation beds for rapid assessment and treatment. For adult medicine, the hospital admission rate has fallen from 13.0 to 12.1; length of stay has fallen from 4.7 to 4.2, giving 50 days per 1000 members for medicine. Though changes in adult surgical utilization are more difficult to attribute directly to the adult medicine team, days per 1000 have fallen from 54 to 39. In addition, the team members have been able to extend their work to care of patients in the subacute facility. Consistent daytime coverage of the hospital by the team has decreased pressure on outpatient providers who previously had to cover hospitalized patients while in clinic.

Chronic Disease, Amenable to Population-Based Care. KPNC began a major design initiative on adult diabetes care in early 1995. This initiative was undertaken with strong organizational support and in the setting of existing regional and area diabetes committees, which had laid the foundation for innovation. A physician and patient-specific diabetes reporting system had been available in the region since 1993. These reports included information on ophthalmology exams, glycosylated hemoglobins, and office visits. They provided ample evidence of variation in processes. The region's diabetic population is increasing as a percent of membership (1.8 percent in 1993 vs. 3.5 percent in 1995, though some of the increase may be due to improved reporting). Evaluation of diabetic population expenditures in 1994 revealed that about 9 percent of KPNC's total budget was spent on this population. Medical office operations managers felt that the management of this large, chronically ill population represented an opportunity to improve clinical quality of patient care, patient and family satisfaction, and office efficiency.

The goal of the design team is to develop a new approach to the management of all adult diabetic patients in the North Carolina region. The new design will decrease variation in practice patterns and improve quality and process of care for patients.

The team sponsors provided the following assumptions.

• Improve patient satisfaction.

• Decrease variation of care.

• Incorporate a comprehensive approach to the care of the diabetic patient.

• Further enable patients to care for themselves.

• Lower the cost of care for these patients.

In the big picture of chronic disease, this project is intended to address "What is the best way to manage chronic diseases?" It is expected to result in a blueprint for design of population-based management of other prevalent chronic diseases. In particular, the issue of management of subpopulations will be addressed.

A quality planning process was used for the project. Once customers were identified, the following customer groups were surveyed.

- Members with diabetes—telephone
- Providers—focus group
- Advice and module RNs—focus group
- Appointments staff—focus group
- Diabetes educators—focus group

These surveys resulted in the identification of internal and external customer needs. The team used this information to develop product features to meet the needs of all customers. The features listed meet more than 80 percent of the identified needs.

- Personal coordinator of care
- Formal team in place
- Clinical information system
- Psychological and behavioral assessment (with feedback loop)
- Patient road map
- Formal training for care team

Patients with diabetes expressed several needs that guided the team to the product feature of personal care coordination (PCC). These attributes of this feature also meshed well with the needs of internal customers. The PCC is an RN/certified diabetes educator who coordinates the individual patient's care among all providers and support staff. The PCC is teamed with an LPN to manage the whole population of diabetics.

The second product feature, establishment of a formal diabetes team, has been interpreted as a multilevel team (see Figure 18.5). Clinical information system (CIS) support needs were delineated as follows:

- Diabetes registry and inquiry screens
- Captures all components of patient care
- Facilitates management of individuals and population: risk management engine
- Automation of protocols
- Generates reminders/tailored messages

Fortunately, the needs of the diabetes care team coincided with the development of CIS. The synergy between these projects has actually speeded the development and implementation of both.

From the beginning of the team's work, psychological factors have been considered paramount in fostering individual patient progress. A psychologist is a member of the team. The fourth product feature has been developed to include the following elements.

- Assessment of mental health status of each individual
- Information built into road map and CIS
- Assists care team and member in developing care plan
- Used to tailor written and verbal messages/feedback to patient

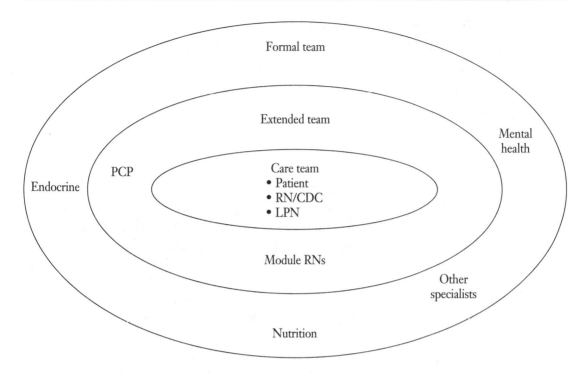

Figure 18.5. Multilevel diabetes care team.

The patient road map synthesizes other product features to address needs of the individual patient. The road map has been conceptualized as follows:

- Individualized care map for each patient
- Goal setting and education based on level of readiness and mental health assessment
- Captured in CIS and updated each visit
- Visual, graphic, and easy to follow (in patient's language)

The concept has been further developed to include specific assessments, data elements, communication tools, and information management by the care team.

The final feature, developed to address needs of all customers, is consistent training for all members of the multilayered, formal team. Training necessary for implementation at each medical office covers these personnel and topics.

- Care teams (PCC/LPN) will receive
  - —Two-month initial orientation/training
  - —Two weeks per year minimum of formal training
- Extended team (PCPs, module nurses):
  - —Orientation to new care model
  - —Orientation of providers and staff
  - —Orientation for call center/module nurses to new care model and protocols

- Formal team (endo, mental health, regional diabetes committee, nutrition, MD liaison, care teams, extended teams):

  —Product features

  —Readiness to change

  —Mental health assessment

  —Basic nutrition principles

  —Low literacy learning

  —Cultural awareness

The diabetes care team established a series of work groups to develop the details of the product features, implementation plans, and evaluation. Though each of the work groups is essential to successful implementation, the work on clinical protocols serves as an excellent example of the reengineering mind-set of this team. The protocols function has standing orders that allow RNs, LPNs, and pharmacists, under the direction of physicians, to provide consistent, state-of-the-art care for KPNC's members with diabetes. Topics covered include initial assessment, activity, nutrition, screening for complications, foot care, insulin and hypoglycemic medication management, aspirin prophylaxis for ASCVD, and management of hyperlipidemia.

Consistent with the degree of change in clinical processes required by the new care design, senior managers, team leaders, and members have devoted a significant amount of time to managing resistance anticipating. From the designation of the team members on, considerable thought has been given to managing resistance. All types of providers and personnel have been involved, and each geographic area has been well represented. Critique from physician opinion leaders in KPNC and from physicians who manage diabetes care programs in other regions has been sought. As the team geared up for implementation in the first service area in July 1996, team leaders worked extensively with operations managers to assure smooth systems interfaces and scheduled kick-off meetings for each office. Diabetes care design is a project with great promise, but still in progress. Measures for evaluation of process and outcome have been developed. KPNC looks forward to reporting the results.

Chronic Disease and Disability. Case management for individual members with significant chronic disease and disability is the key integrative factor for members who require complex care. As in many delivery systems, case management in KPNC began with the discharge planning model—the patient had to be hospitalized to receive case management. Overtime nurses and physicians recognized the potential to improve the care experience and improve outcomes by expanding case management beyond the hospital. Outcomes include patient and family satisfaction, clinical outcomes, functional outcomes, and cost. The evaluation of the outcomes is an ongoing challenge, with much work in progress. Though the redesign of case management has occurred more as evolution (1992 to present) than radical reengineering, many of the same principles apply.

Step one was defining case management. As conceptualized for KPNC, case management is the comprehensive assessment and management of complex patient needs throughout the continuum of care. The management is patient- and family-focused and emphasizes keeping the patient as functional as possible, for as long as possible, using innovative and cost-effective management, within the member's benefits. For patient and family needs that are beyond the scope of medical care and coverage, community referrals are made. An important distinction between case management at KPNC and from many other insurers has to do with "large case" management (the definition of *large* is usually monetary). Case management at KPNC includes large cases, but is in no way limited to them. Consistent with the program's overall emphasis on prevention, case management is intended to identify patients at risk early, so they do not become "large" either by medically catastrophic or monetary definitions.

The early work on definition of the case management function and its customers resulted in changes in the physical location of the case management services. In the discharge planning paradigm, the nurses related to the hospital and physicians working there. They were centrally located in each service area and spent lots of time at the hospital on the telephone. Moving the case management coordinators to each medical office put them close to their physician partners in case management and close to patients and families. This move facilitated early case identification; implementation of safe, effective, efficient alternatives to hospital care; and close case management. For example, as home infusion technology has improved, many opportunities for outpatient management of significant illness have presented themselves. Because the case managers are in the facilities, providers are able to talk directly with them, increasing confidence on the part of the provider and allowing more rapid integration of new technologies.

Delineation of the components of case management was a crucial step in redesigning the processes. They are as follows:

- Ambulatory case identification/screening and management
- Inpatient case identification/screening and management
- Extended care facility placements, management, and monitoring
- Rehabilitation facility placement, management, and monitoring
- Durable medical equipment, acquisition, authorization, and tracking
- Home care services, authorization, and tracking
  —Home health
  —Infusion therapy
  —Hospice
- Transportation
- Social services referrals
- Transplant care management
  —Transportation
  —Lodging
  —Outpatient follow-up care, such as home infusion therapy
- Community agency referrals
- Meals on Wheels
- AIDS coordination
- American Cancer Society
- Hospice

Each component of case management actually has its own set of processes, customers and suppliers, outcomes, and so on. This is the underlying reason that the full redesign of case management has been evolutionary rather then revolutionary! The organization has taken on each of the components in sequence, much like an automotive manufacturer might take on the reengineering of various supplier chains. Of course, reworking all the processes that relate to the CMCs has required changes in the job and its supports.

The core case management team consists of the RN CMC, the patient's primary provider, and other physicians actively involved in the care of the patient (oncologist, neurologist, and so on). The CMC can serve as the communication center and provides continuity for the patient through many settings of care (see Figure 18.6).

An assessment to date reveals that engineering/reengineering has been completed or is in process for DME, home health/home infusion, and transplant management. Reevaluation of the CMC role, staff supports, and information systems supports began in 1996. Opportunities exist to reallocate many tasks to less-skilled personnel and to improve automated supports for documentation, communication, and case tracking.

Examples with Systemwide Impact

Centralization of Appointments and Telephone Advice Services (Call Center). This represents a major reengineering project. The project was given high priority because, for several years, anecdotes and member satisfaction and marketing data had indicated that KPNC was not meeting member expectations regarding telephone access and access to medical office services in the Triangle. This

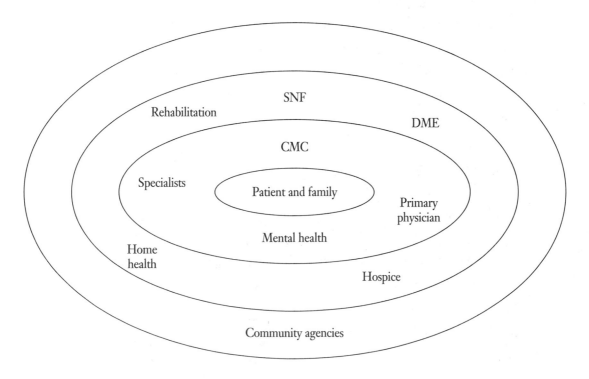

Figure 18.6. Patient-centered case management.

activity was designed to improve call-handling, appointment making, and member satisfaction with access. Though satisfaction levels varied among medical offices, satisfaction with "time on the phone to make an appointment" was less than 50 percent (8–10 on a scale of 10) and less than 60 percent for "days wait for appointments for minor medical problems."

The region assembled a multidisciplinary team to develop and implement a call center for the Triangle, through which members can access appointments and medical advice with one telephone number. Key features are to include the following:

- A single telephone number
- Rapid response time
- Service representatives trained in call management
- Service representatives who follow consistent guidelines for appointment booking and transferring to advice
- Appointment availability in line with member expectations
- Appointment making available on weekdays until 9 P.M. and on weekends from 7 A.M. to 9 P.M.
- A telephone system that supports the activity

The team also had responsibility for planning the schedule-making processes, booking guidelines, advice protocols, staffing, training, telecommunications, information systems, and facilities. Significant, related initiatives included:

- Open access
- Automated advice notes
- Future appointment tracking system
- Telephone network improvement

The call center is the region's largest true reengineering project. As noted at the beginning of this chapter, the region does not have a declared reengineering initiative. Not surprisingly, then, this project has been the richest source of learning about success and failure factors. Many of the factors discussed in the "Lessons Learned" section relate to this project.

An assessment to date reveals that, at the end of 10 months of operation, satisfaction levels are unchanged, measures of call efficiency continue to vary, and operational change has been intense. Operational managers have identified the following needs.

- General
  —Develop a standardized quality assurance program.
  —Provide more supervisor training to improve quality of supervision.
  —Develop continued statistical analysis of performance.
- Appointments
  —Establish pediatric queue to improve service representative handling of pediatric calls.
  —Implement a process and timelines for development, approval, and activation of appointment schedules. The goal is to have appointments available 12 weeks in advance.

- Advice

  —Reformat clinical protocols and advice documentation tool to improve RN triage efficiency.

  —Integrate clinical information system to facilitate nursing assessments.

  —Establish mission and goals for protocol advisory groups to facilitate development of a review process.

  —Provide ongoing training of advice nurses to improve the quality of care provided.

Automated Laboratory Specimen Tracking. The process of shipping specimens to a regional laboratory from the facility laboratories involves many steps and, on occasion, samples have been lost in this process and members have been called back to have specimens recollected. Complaints from the facility laboratories implicating the regional laboratory in losing specimens shipped and complaints from providers when lost samples result in member recollection or test cancellation directed attention to this process.

When a collected sample is in the possession of laboratory services, except for accidental breakage, the loss of a sample in transport is unacceptable. A method was necessary to track the collected specimen from shipping to receiving. Prior to November 1993, microbiological specimens were prioritized as needing a tracking system (most lost specimens were microbiological specimens). Laboratory services first developed a manual tracking system for these specimens.

Occasional loss of laboratory specimens in transit is a problem well-known to health care organizations. In September 1993, a manual system was implemented to track the microbiological specimens. The quality assurance monitor threshold was set at 100 percent; that is, all specimens shipped had to be received. Zero percent of microbiology specimens were lost in transport from the facility to the regional lab during a follow-up study period. At the completion of this study, it was found that the North Carolina regional laboratories were in compliance with the set standard. This manual method proved to be successful in eliminating lost microbiology specimens; however, it was very time-consuming and did not track other samples in the laboratory (such as blood samples).

Based on the success of the manual tracking system for microbiological specimens and its labor intensity, the following plans were made.

- Develop and implement automated specimen tracking via the laboratory computer system (specimen tracking module) to track all microbiological and nonmicrobiological specimens.

- Institute operational changes, including standardization of procedures for shipping and receiving specimens.

- Implement further laboratory computer system enhancements for specimen storage and retrieval to locate specimens received and stored at the regional laboratory.

Elements of the reengineered specimen tracking process, implemented in September 1995, included laboratory computer system enhancements, bar-code scanning for all specimens, standardized procedures for shipping and receiving of all specimens, and retraining of all laboratory staff.

An assessment to date reveals that starting in September 1995, system data reports were reviewed to determine if any loss of specimens was occurring. During the period of September 1 through December 31, 1995, 20,972 microbiological samples were received at the regional laboratory. One hundred percent of the microbiological specimens shipped were received. During this same time period, 55,871 samples were received for other testing (chemistry, serology, and so on). Review of the shipping/receiving manifests indicated no missing samples.

Reengineering Facility Function: Designing and Operationalizing a New Medical Office. In 1994, the decision to open a new medical office presented an opportunity to use quality planning methodology. The goal of the project was to design and build a medical office that would achieve breakthrough levels of performance and service in order to meet or exceed members' needs. Geographic proximity, clinical quality, and service quality all drove the design efforts for the new office. Objectives included managing larger panels of patients per full-time equivalents of staff and providers while improving patient satisfaction with care received and improving staff and provider satisfaction with the workplace.

Baseline satisfaction surveys determined that 86 percent of members were satisfied overall with KP, but only 74 percent were satisfied with access for minor pain or illness. Therefore, access to appointments was important, especially the ability to see a provider on short notice for a minor illness or pain.

The planning team developed solutions focused on improving access. The following are examples of solutions.

- *Physical design.* The office was designed to be divided into two separate six-provider modules, with three exam rooms per provider. The space for extra exam rooms per provider is afforded by storing medical records and hard copies of X-rays off-site and by servicing incoming calls at an off-site call center. The nurses station is situated centrally in the module within visual sight of most of the exam rooms, which enables support staff to give and receive help to each other and to providers/patients as needed. The exam rooms are close to the lab and radiology so that patients can directly access these services without going to the waiting room.

- *Operations.* Simple and consistent operations practices were essential to improve efficiency of operations.

  —Mechanisms to support the absence of on-site advice, on-site storage of medical records, and on-site storage of X-rays

  —Support staff perform phlebotomy services for most labs and exams after the provider visit

  —Small writing surfaces in the hallways whose dual functions are to sort out incoming and outgoing call slips, refill requests, and so on for a provider while affording the provider the ability to write notes and work in the hallways

  —Meticulous but timely preparation of the patient to be seen by the provider

- *Agreements.* Providers and staff made agreements in the following operational areas.

  —Universal set of support staff tasks to adequately prepare patients to be seen by a provider expeditiously

  —Use of a flag-and-order system to convey orders after the provider has concluded the visit with the patient

  —Delegation of callbacks to members to the support staff

  —Sufficient clinical information collected for the provider to be able to answer member requests for advice or test results by phone

  —Standing orders for certain common ailments or health prevention measures that can be carried out by a nurse without a patient having to be seen by a provider

  —Standardized patient education protocols by on-site support staff

—Standardized scheduling of providers in the clinic to avoid having too many or too few providers in the clinic at any time

—Availability of personal computers to assist in managing patient populations

—Integrating mental health services with the primary care team

Implementing these changes required an array of new human resource strategies. Job descriptions for support staff were redefined to include flexibility of roles and responsibilities. Examples include module support staff drawing blood and medical office assistants serving as both receptionists and clinic assistants. Training was developed for staff who had little to no experience with these new functions.

Providers' behaviors were mentored to achieve

- Commitment to managing larger panels of patients

- Managing time well in the clinic

- Cost-effectiveness

- Approachability as a team member by staff and other providers

- Support of open access

- Acceptance of innovative processes

Leadership by the medical office administrator and the physician-in-charge was critical to changing the job descriptions and fostering successful teamwork.

To support the mission, off-hours team-building sessions were developed and implemented. Confidential interviews of all providers and staff provided a candid appraisal of old assumptions that allowed staff and providers to share fears and identify obstacles. This provided an understanding of what team members needed from each other to succeed. Workshops challenged the staff and providers to agree on the following:

- The mission and vision of the clinic

- The measurements for success for the clinic

- Norms of teamwork

- Defining for each other the conditions of satisfaction to complete the job in the clinic

- Mutual dialog on problems to solve to reach goals

- Norms of communication

There are ongoing evaluations of the team-building efforts, which allow the staff and providers to review these issues and renew mutual commitments.

The role of leadership was critical to the success of this project. To change the work culture, senior managers had to articulate a common mission and vision. At each step along the way, systems and strategic thinking was critical. Continuous coaching by management at every level is also critical to ensure ongoing success. The most critical element was supporting team development to implement the strategic changes.

An assessment to date reveals that, after 15 months of operations, the percentage of patients highly satisfied with overall care and service at the facility has been consistently above the North Carolina regional average: for this medical office 90 percent, for the region 87 percent. Satisfaction with "access to medical care when you need it" was 89 percent for this office and 83 percent for the region. The new staff and providers experienced the highest satisfaction with their work environment in the North Carolina region as evidenced with the highest scores for perceived teamwork, which were attained from the employee and provider survey.

Clinical Guidelines: Designing Clinical Care, by Diagnosis. Clinical guidelines provide a mechanism for reengineering clinical care. Usually the work is engineering, not reengineering, because prior to the guidelines each provider, staff person, and module had different processes. The guideline development process used by KPNC has three components (see Figure 18.7). Once physicians have agreed on the clinical algorithm, the multidisciplinary implementation teams develop operational supports and implementation and monitoring plans. (In practice, the work may be concurrent.) KPNC's experience with implementing a guideline for management of acute back pain is described as follows.

- *Purpose.* Low back pain is one of the more common ambulatory problems seen in the primary care setting. Management of this condition is extremely variable, and such variability increases the costs of diagnostic tests and certain therapies that have not been shown to improve the outcomes or satisfaction with the care. This guideline was implemented to improve patient satisfaction, decrease disability time, and decrease referrals related to management of acute low back pain.

- *Methodology.* A common approach for uncomplicated low back pain (herein referred to as "the guideline") was promoted by the guidelines facilitator in December 1994. The guideline adopted for this purpose was developed by Park Nicollett Medical Center, using a continuous quality improvement process. Key steps in the implementation were the following:

—Promotion by the guideline facilitator.

—Provider champions were identified in the internal medicine/family practice departments and in orthopedics.

—The department of internal medicine/family practice agreed to use the flowchart for all acute low back pain.

—In response to providers' requests for training RNs about the guidelines, clinical supervisors were identified to champion the program in their modules.

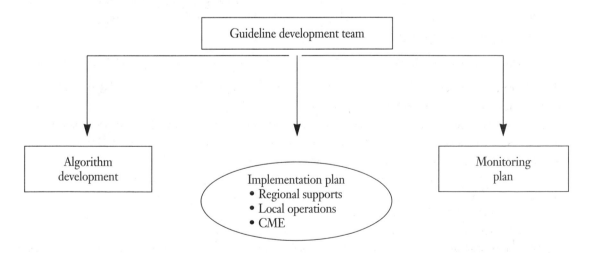

Figure 18.7. Clinical guideline development process.

—The department of patient education identified a training specialist who would promote the guidelines in the form of written handouts and make them available in the primary care clinics.

—The training specialist also developed a program in conjunction with a physical therapist to train primary care clinic nurses to instruct self-care exercises.

Components of acute uncomplicated low back pain management were designed as follows:

—A comprehensive care plan based on the guideline, to be promoted at the first visit for acute low back pain in any primary care setting in KPNC, including urgent care.

—A history/physical resulting in diagnosis of uncomplicated acute low back pain.

—Appropriate expectations set by the provider.

—Self-care activities, including activity prescription, given to the patient either by the nurse on order of the provider or by the provider.

The nursing staff were trained to educate the patient to perform self-care activities for acute low back pain. A brochure outlining the care plan for uncomplicated low back pain was widely promoted and at some facilities a colored progress note in the chart documented that the patient received the brochure. Continued support and sponsorship was given by the department of orthopedics and the senior managers of the region.

An assessment to date reveals that the guidelines were introduced to the departments of internal medicine/family practice during the fourth quarter of 1994. The guideline was implemented gradually during 1995. All of the nurses were trained on self-care activities by the fourth quarter of 1995. Physical therapy referral rates dropped from 6.71/1000/year to 2.92/1000/year by the fourth quarter of 1995. Lumbar laminectomies dropped from 0.28/1000/year to 0.07 by the fourth quarter of 1995. Neuro-surgical referrals for low back pain dropped from 1.48/1000/year to 0.48/1000/year the third quarter of 1995. The rate of MRIs, CT scans, spinal X-rays, and lumbar myleograms did not change significantly. The measure of patient satisfaction will be compared with previous patient satisfaction, which was measured in a retrospective case-controlled study studying the patient satisfaction with low back pain. Data are currently not available and will be collected. These results demonstrate that the promotion and operational support for guidelines used by an undifferentiated large group of primary care providers can be effective in decreasing referrals to physical therapy, laminectomy, and neurosurgery.

The approach taken was innovative from the following standpoints.

• Providers depend heavily on support staff to administer the self-care instructions to patients.

• Clinical practice guidelines that have been traditionally the province of providers are now being promoted by nonproviders.

Continued management will be necessary to maintain the use of these guidelines in primary care. All new providers and staff to the program will need to undergo the same orientation to implement the guidelines.

Lessons Learned: Success Factors and Failure Factors

Success Factors

• A clear charge to the work group: Members need clear statements of what is to be done and why, and of project goals.

- Sponsors must be clearly identified, consistent in support of the team, and advocated for the needs of the project.
- Clear timelines and regular check-ins.
- For clinical projects, a facilitator/leader team composed of a management engineer, health plan leader, and physician leader created powerful leadership synergy.
- Training is needed for the team, in some instances for the sponsors, and for the receiving operations staff and providers.
- Anticipatory management of resistance.
- Assessment of systems interfaces and impacts early in the engineering/reengineering process.
- Soliciting information on related successful practices in other organizations.
- Congruence of the project with organizational goals—improve quality, and cost improvements will follow.

Failure Factors

- Inadequate understanding of systems impacts.
- Uncertain or waffling sponsorship.
- Insufficient or late support from human resources for preparing or revising job descriptions, training new staff, and training interfacing staff.
- A cost-only project focus.
- Insufficient understanding of internal and external customer needs.
- Change readiness of the organization.
- Multiple competing organizational initiatives.
- Operational readiness for handoffs of the reengineered processes.

Questions for a Senior Executives Meeting

1. Are the goals of the proposed project congruent with current organizational goals and objectives?

2. Is the charge to the work group clear? Does the mission statement describe a project that is specific; measurable; agreed on by the sponsors, operations leaders, and team members; and time based?

3. Assess the strength of senior management sponsorship. Do the sponsors understand their roles? Is there evidence of regular meetings with the team leaders, and is that support sufficient to foster expeditious work?

4. At periodic reviews or reports, what is the evidence that the team has a full systems view of the project and that interface issues are being addressed?

5. Is the team meeting its timelines?

6. Has the team identified and addressed the needs of internal and external customers of the process?

7. As the project progresses, what is the evidence that the team is managing resistance anticipatorily?

8. From the senior executives' view, is the organization ready for the degree of change dictated by the project? If not, what can the executive group do to assist?

9. What are other projects and organizational changes that will be competing for operations time and attention? How can the executive team guide implementation schedules in order to avoid organizational overload?

10. Regarding long-term monitoring of the project, are the outcome expectations being met?

Questions for a Governing Body Meeting

1. Are the goals of the proposed project congruent with current organizational goals and objectives?

2. At periodic reviews or reports, what is the evidence that the team has a full systems view of the project and that interface issues are being addressed?

3. Is the team meeting its timelines?

4. Has the team identified and addressed the needs of internal and external customers of the process?

5. What is the evidence that the organization and this team are using appropriate benchmarking for the new processes and for goals?

6. Assess the organization's focus on quality vs. cost projects. Is the organizational target increasing value to customers, $V = Q/P$?

7. Assess the clarity and rigor of the organization's methods for setting priorities.

8. Regarding long-term monitoring of the project, are the outcome expectations being met?

Questions for a Process Owners Meeting

1. Are the right people on the team? Are the necessary operational support areas represented? Geographic representation? Representation of professional groups?

2. Is the charge to the work group clear? Does the mission statement describe a project that is specific; measurable; agreed on by the sponsors, operations leaders, and team members; and time based?

3. At periodic reviews or reports, what is the evidence that the team has a full systems view of the project and that interface issues are being addressed?

4. Is the team meeting its timelines?

5. Has the team identified and addressed the needs of internal and external customers of the process?

6. As the project progresses, what is the evidence that the team is managing resistance anticipatorily?

7. Is the team designing appropriate measures for monitoring processes and outcome?

8. What is the evidence that the team is harvesting best practices from within and outside the organization? Is benchmarking of processes and goals appropriate?

9. Assess the adequacy of the training modules that have been developed for implementation.

Acknowledgments

I would like to thank the leaders of Kaiser Foundation Health Plan of North Carolina and The Carolina Permanente Medical Group for their willingness to share our organization's experiences and lessons learned. Such sharing furthers the work of the greater health care community. In synthesizing our experience with systems thinking and engineering/reengineering, I have drawn heavily on documents developed in the course of our work. These documents were produced by dozens of groups and individuals. While it is not possible to list each individually, I wish to acknowledge the work of each and express my thanks to all.

Nancy Henley, M.D., is associate medical director for quality and research in the North Carolina Region for The Carolina Permanente Medical Group (TCPMG). Henley joined TCPMG in 1985. The scope of her current position includes quality management, utilization management, clinical guidelines, preventive medicine, health promotion and education, and continuing medical education. During her tenure with TCPMG, she has also served as chief of internal medicine and chief of quality assurance and resource management in the Durham service area.

Henley earned an M.D. degree from the University of North Carolina at Chapel Hill. She completed a residency in internal medicine at UNC Hospitals and is board certified. She also earned an M.P.H. degree in health administration from UNC. Prior to pursuing a career in medicine, Henley held several positions in health care administration including serving as regional administrator for a multicounty comprehensive health care program in southern West Virginia.

Appendix: Three High-Level Key Processes
Disease Prevention and Health Promotion

Patient

Patient with appropriate disease prevention and health promotion plan

Obtain risk factor history

Obtain physical exam findings

Obtain screening studies

Order

Report

Information synthesis

Develop plan

Assess risk factors

Document

Implement preventive care plan

Refer

Provide therapy (immunizations etc.)

Follow-up

Educate patient/family

Interval follow-up plan

Acute Care

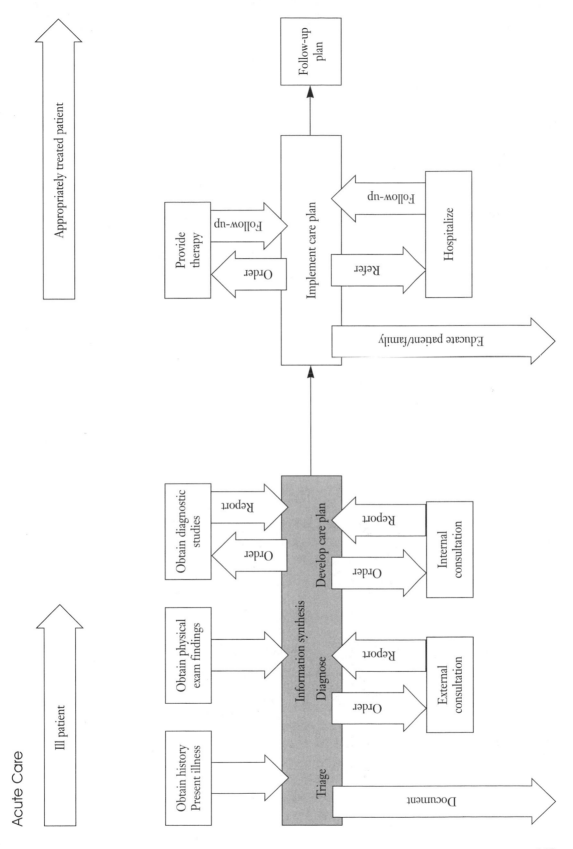

449

Chronic Care

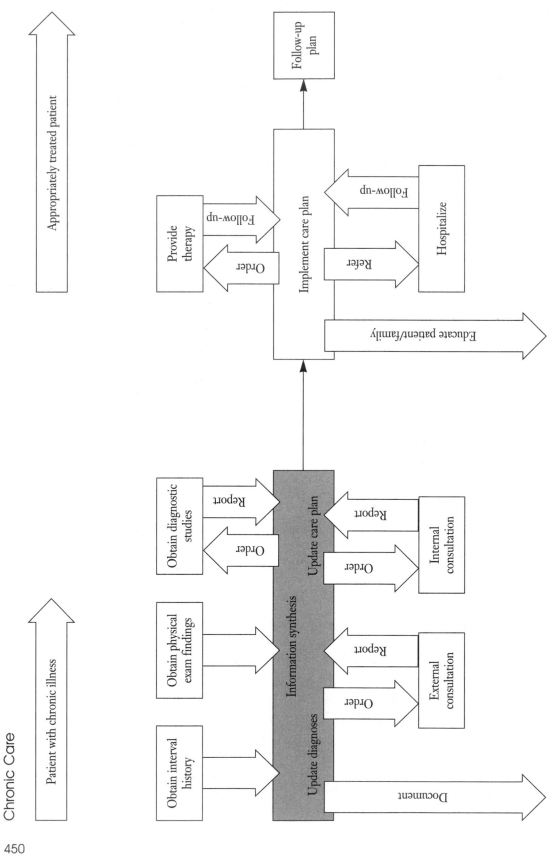

Chapter 19

Quality Management in Academic Health Centers: Using Peer Institutions to Support Practice Improvement

Kimberly J. Rask and Jean Livingston

Recent changes in the health care delivery and academic environments have made it necessary for academic health centers (AHCs) to modify and/or forgo traditional models of teaching, research, and patient care in order to become more responsive to the needs of the marketplace. In this chapter, we describe the nature of the challenges facing AHCs and describe how a consortium of academic health centers is responding to the need to evaluate evolving clinical practices.

This chapter will focus on the clinical enterprises of academic health centers and the universal drive to maximize value within the constraints of each institution's mission. In order to maximize value, academic health centers must identify best practices and benchmark against both external and internal standards. Benchmarking was developed by private corporations as a means of analyzing and comparing practices, products, and services against those of other companies. Benchmarking is a continuous process of adopting or adapting the good features of the best demonstrated practices of other organizations. It has been shown to be an effective tool for identifying and reducing variations in clinical practices and their resulting outcomes.

Some of the unique products of AHCs, such as quaternary care, make finding comparable benchmarks or best practices difficult. The University HealthSystem Consortium (UHC) brings together 70 member institutions to share best practices, benchmark, and identify opportunities for improvement in high-volume or high-cost product lines. By providing member institutions with information about other academic centers with comparable missions, UHC provides quality managers with comparative information that is readily accepted for the quality improvement efforts within their individual institutions.

Challenges Facing Academic Health Centers

Some of the challenges facing academic institutions are similar to those facing all health care organizations. An increasingly competitive marketplace has enhanced the move to managed care, expanding vertical and horizontal integration and new alliances and relationships among insurers, providers, and purchasers. In addition, academic institutions confront unique challenges pertaining to (1) a tripartite mission of teaching, research, and patient care; (2) internal constituencies focused on different aspects of the institution's mission; and (3) the provision of unique products such as quaternary clinical care.

The traditional academic mission of caring for vulnerable populations, conducting research, and training the health care workforce of the future has set AHCs apart from other private institutions. They have historically enjoyed a level of federal subsidy and other cross-subsidies that have allowed them to carry out these functions. Today, as public programs in health and social services are being downsized, reorganized, and privatized, price competition in the private health care markets is driving down the profit margins on AHCs' clinical products.

A recent survey of AHCs found that reported charges were approximately 15 percent to 35 percent above the comparable charges in surrounding community hospitals. A consensus is emerging among AHCs in more advanced markets that, lacking convincing evidence that they provide superior quality of care and care for sicker patients, academic health centers are dependent on the added value of their reputations alone when negotiating higher prices with managed care organizations. These higher prices are anticipated to be substantially less than the current 15 percent to 35 percent differential. All of the AHCs in the survey were engaged in vigorous cost-cutting efforts to reduce operating expenses by an average of 20 percent during the next three to five years.

AHCs are implementing a combination of traditional and nontraditional approaches to cut costs. Most institutions strive to reduce administrative overhead, close beds, decrease associated operating expenses, and obtain better pricing from vendors. More recent methods designed to decrease costs while maintaining quality of care and service include implementation of continuous quality improvement projects, clinical reengineering, and critical pathways. To support these efforts, most institutions are building on a capability for applied outcomes research, clinical epidemiology, and quality improvement.

Quality Management in Academic Health Centers

Effective quality management begins with the identification of the institutional mission. In academic health centers, the mission of the clinical enterprise is intertwined with the educational and research mission. For example, the mission statement of one academic center states that the enterprise is "a comprehensive professional health care organization committed to the delivery of superior medical care, setting the standards for enhancing health through prevention and treatment and furthering knowledge through education and research." Following the mission statement are the institution's developmental goals and its strategies designed to achieve those goals (see Figure 19.1). Given the changing medical marketplace with an increasingly price-based competition, a common strategy for all health care providers—including AHCs—is to optimize clinical operations in order to maximize value. From the strategies follow operational objectives and specific activities designed to optimize business and clinical operations. In many AHCs these operational objectives focus on skills that traditionally have not been high institutional priorities such as way-finding, timeliness, and geographical accessibility. In order to monitor operational objectives that optimize either business operations or clinical operations, one must identify both performance measures and standards in order to set appropriate goals.

Benchmarking is one way to monitor performance measures. Health care providers can benchmark internally using previous performance, continuous quality improvement targets, or similar processes within the same organization. Alternatively, external benchmarks from other health care delivery organizations and/or standards from payors and professional groups can be used. Benchmarks can provide comparisons with the toughest competitors in the local market, with world-class organizations in the same industry, and with similar processes in organizations from different industries. Operational benchmarks for way-finding, waiting times, and business operations in AHCs can be obtained from many sources. However, it is more difficult to locate clinical benchmarks and best practices that will be accepted by academic clinicians. Often AHC staff members are reluctant to

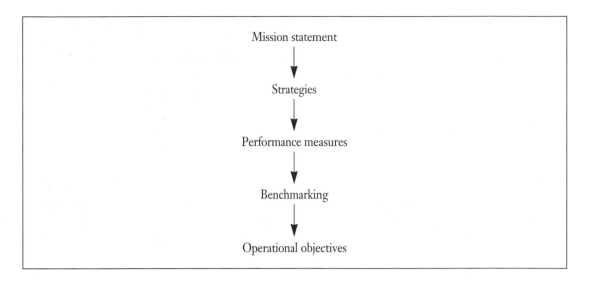

Figure 19.1. Quality management in academic health centers.

compare themselves with nonacademic health care delivery systems because they question the adequacy of current adjustments for severity of illness and because they are producing quaternary medical care or product lines such as bone marrow transplants, which are not performed in most community hospital settings. UHC activities provide an opportunity for clinical benchmarking with other academic institutions that are generally not local competitors.

University HealthSystem Consortium Clinical Benchmarking Program

The University HealthSystem Consortium (formerly the University Hospital Consortium) is a member-driven alliance of academic health centers. Its mission is to strengthen the competitive position of members and their network partners in their respective health care markets. As an idea-generating and information-disseminating enterprise, UHC is designed to pool resources, create economies of scale, improve clinical and operating efficiencies, and influence the direction and delivery of health care. To accomplish these goals, UHC's programs are focused in the areas of supply and services, information resources, value management, and market management. The value management program provides services designed to assist members in their efforts to enhance service, quality, and outcomes while simultaneously reducing costs. The Clinical Practice Advancement Center was established within the value management program to provide practical, scientifically rigorous information in the area of clinical evaluation.

Through its Clinical Practice Advancement Center, UHC has established a clinical process improvement program designed to systematically identify, benchmark, and integrate optimal care by linking defined measures of patient characteristics and linking clinical processes to outcomes. The method uses a two-tiered approach to improving clinical care delivery and reducing costs. The first tier provides compelling comparative information about the variability in care delivery across UHC members and identifies benchmark performers. The second tier involves interpretive statistical analysis of longitudinal, patient-specific, clinical processes of care and outcomes data. Currently, a network of close to 50 benchmarking hospitals with more than 100 clinical teams analyze processes of care in several clinical services (see Table 19.1). Through comparative data and competitive analysis, hospitals can use benchmarking to learn how to surpass their competitors, not merely imitate them. However, in order to be successful, benchmarking requires a sophisticated understanding of one's own processes as well as identifying customer expectations.

UHC benchmarking hospitals have established clinical teams to analyze processes of care in several clinical services including renal transplantation, percutaneous transluminal coronary angioplasty (PTCA), coronary artery bypass graft (CABG) procedure, and hip arthroplasty. Using a collaboratively developed clinical benchmarking model, the teams are comparing pathways and working to understand why they differ.

The UHC clinical benchmarking model (see Figure 19.2) integrates the principles of the industrial benchmarking process model, which expands the tenets of industrial benchmarking to accommodate the complexity of clinical care. One of the keys to understanding the complexities of clinical care is to define the relationship between process and outcome, thus revealing the true cause and effect of clinical processes.

Phase 1: Plan. The organization must decide what to benchmark, then select a team that can understand the organization's own process. Participants and resources are coordinated to create an interdisciplinary clinical team that understands the process.

Phase 2: Collect. The team collects information on the organization's own process, identifies benchmarking partners, and then collects information from these partners. Understanding the process and identifying customer expectations can be accomplished in a variety of ways. For example, flowcharts document processes and can be useful in examining how various steps of a process are related to each other. Hierarchical flowcharts are particularly useful in outlining clinical processes. The interdisciplinary clinical team defines the current process of care and then collects and shares clinical information. A data collection form is created to capture process and outcome information to be used for comparison with benchmarking partners.

Phase 3: Analyze. The different types of clinical information are analyzed and reported. Variation in medication use, laboratory utilization, blood product usage, diagnostic studies, and interventions are

Table 19.1. University HealthSystem Consortium clinical process improvement program.

Current benchmarking projects	Future benchmarking projects
Renal transplantation	Congestive heart failure
Hip arthroplasty	Neonatology
CABG	Liver transplantation
PTCA	Heart transplantation
Ischemic stroke	Ovarian cancer
Bone marrow transplants	Diabetes management
Chest pain and AMI	Hypertension
	Asthma
	Back pain

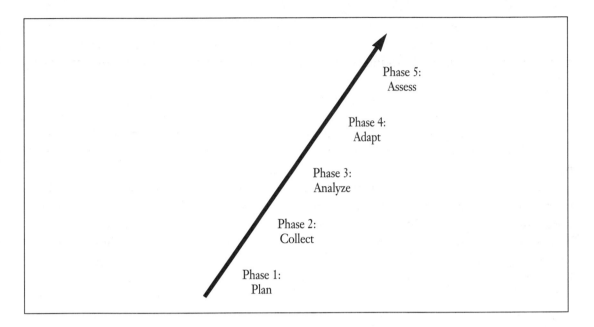

Phase 5:
Assess

Phase 4:
Adapt

Phase 3:
Analyze

Phase 2:
Collect

Phase 1:
Plan

Figure 19.2. UHC clinical benchmarking model.

tracked and reported graphically. Benchmarking participants receive an analysis of the discharge status of each patient along with an analysis of complications, infections, and intensive care unit (ICU) usage that may have contributed to extended length of stay within the institution. These data are combined with risk assessment data to provide hospitals with a risk-adjusted guide to patient outcomes. The team then compares processes and identifies areas for improvement. By identifying characteristics of superior performance, the team determines how to close performance gaps between its institution and its benchmarking partners. Critical or clinical pathways are useful in critically evaluating and modifying processes using comparative information about other processes. Pathways can also be used as a mechanism for changing processes.

Phase 4: Adapt. The clinical team reviews UHC-prepared reports to identify and prioritize institution-specific problems, issues, and opportunities. The team then presents comparative data and findings to its own clinical staff. The team determines improvement goals and finds support for changes in the organization so that performance gaps can be bridged. The clinical team is responsible for selecting local priorities and implementing change through pathway and/or practice protocols.

Phase 5: Assess. The clinical team addresses continuous improvement by evaluating and disseminating the impact of comparative data on process improvement and outcomes.

Case Study of Coronary Artery Bypass Graft

UHC clinical process improvement projects include the preparation of several documents designed to help participants benefit from the experiences of their peers as they work to increase efficiency, reduce costs, and improve quality of care. Case studies, which are produced for each benchmarking project, describe the practices of institutions that have been identified as benchmark performers. Each case study is written by UHC staff members who visit the institution and interview hospital staff members involved in the project so that they may gain a clear understanding of which processes and procedures are successful for that particular institution. Other institutions are encouraged to share their case studies with those responsible for improving their own clinical practice, regarding them as examples of successful practices and, in some cases, evidence that a particular strategy under consideration has been tested and found to be successful.

Potential best-practice institutions are identified from the UHC clinical database, which consists of discharge abstract data from all UHC member institutions. Benchmarking projects are selected based on clinical significance, costs, volume, variation, and member institution interest. A clinical coordinating team of five to six clinicians with resource management perspectives from these best-practice sites are assembled to develop a benchmark questionnaire, a clinical data collection tool, and a case study outline. Invitations are extended to all UHC member institutions to participate in the benchmarking phase, which consists of clinical data set collection and analysis, benchmark question comparisons, and pathway comparisons. A clinician liaison, who will coordinate participation locally, is identified from each participating institution. Next a clinical benchmarking meeting is held, during which clinicians from best-practice institutions present case studies and share clinical variance data. Selected institutions subsequently participate in the collection and sharing of more in-depth, patient-reported outcomes measurement. After the comparative data are distributed to process improvement teams at the participating institutions, a second cycle of data collection, analysis, and reporting is begun to evaluate practice changes resulting from the benchmarking effort.

The CABG benchmarking project was initiated in the fall of 1993 with the goal of identifying best practices. CABG surgery was selected because it had received considerable attention from clinicians, administrators, and payors. As part of the project, 40 academic institutions submitted data for comparative analysis to identify variations in process of care and to benchmark best performance in CABG. The clinician team decided to evaluate the care of consecutive patients who were 20 years of age or older and who were undergoing a first CABG (either elective or urgent) for ischemic coronary disease. The clinical coordinating team met to identify and define the key elements of care to be included in the data collection form. In collaboration with the managers of the Society of Thoracic Surgeons clinical database, the clinical coordinating team completed the final draft and began data collection. Results from the one-time benchmark questionnaires, pathways developed by the member institution, literature reviews, and comparative data from the UHC clinical database were then published and distributed. Subsequently, more than 50 representatives from participating institutions attended a second CABG clinical benchmarking meeting in Chicago.

After the aggregate data were discussed, case studies were presented by three top-performing institutions. A clinician coordinating committee was assembled to serve as a review committee for report development and revision of the data collection form. Analyses of aggregate, institution-specific, and group data were published. The data collection form was reviewed and modified to include greater depth in some processes of care, and a second data collection period was begun with additional participating sites. A third CABG clinical benchmarking meeting was held in Chicago, with case study presentations by top performing institutions.

Emory University Hospital was one of the institutions that presented a case study. The Emory Heart Center has been involved in providing packaged pricing to payors for several years and is currently evaluating a risk-sharing agreement between payors, hospitals, and physicians. If the partners are successful in achieving performance goals set at the beginning of the year, then the physician group will receive a larger percentage of the packaged pricing payment for the following year. The primary performance goal that was determined for this past year was to reduce inpatient length of stay (LOS) for patients undergoing CABG, with the expectation that the hospital would achieve cost reductions as a function of reductions in LOS.

LOS was chosen as the primary performance goal because the institutional LOS was higher than that of many local competitors, a fact that had been noted by payors. By providing cardiovascular professionals with data on their individual performances, the hospital piqued their interest in pathway development. The initial step in accomplishing a reduction in LOS was to have the key players in the cardiovascular program think about these issues and share information with each other. This exercise gave physicians an opportunity to learn about variations in practice and to question why those variations occur. LOS targets were set, with accompanying provisions that quality indicators would not be adversely affected. As a result of the collaborative efforts of physicians and hospital staffs, LOS reductions of more than 35 percent were achieved for CABG and cardiac valve replacement surgery while maintaining patient satisfaction and quality outcomes. The average LOS for CABG was reduced from 11 days to 6.5 days, and from 13.5 days to 8.5 days for valve replacement surgery. The mortality rate for CABG without catheterization decreased from 2.3 percent to 1.3 percent during the same time period. The length of time patients spent in preoperative testing and teaching visits decreased from eight to four hours. Patients are now given patient pathways so that they are aware of the expected timeline of the surgery and the in-hospital recovery time, which helps prevent them from being misled by friends and/or family members who had surgery when LOS was substantially longer. Antibiotic use decreased from an average of seven to an average of three doses with no change in infection rate. The LOS in the ICU dropped substantially, with a significant increase in same-day transfers. In the fourth quarter of 1995, 15 patients were weaned in the recovery room and did not require any ICU admission. Prophylactic beta blocker use decreased the incidence of postoperative atrial fibrillation, overall use of pulmonary artery catheters decreased, and standing orders were revised so that tests and medications were ordered only when specifically needed.

The team currently meets quarterly to review variances and watch for trends while any changes in the pathway are communicated to staff members in a timely manner via a "Clinical Update" memo. The task force focuses on high-priority issues identified by the variance reports and immediately implements strategies to address these issues and make the recommended changes. New performance goals are currently being formulated, and the institution is establishing performance goals for angioplasty and other cardiac procedures as well.

Several lessons have been learned from this project, including the following: (1) physician involvement is crucial to goal setting and outcomes monitoring; (2) appropriate data monitoring systems must be in place; (3) guidelines must be established and followed; (4) cost reduction must be established as a priority, and regular feedback is necessary to assess progress; (5) all members of the multidisciplinary team must have a can-do approach; and (6) initially there will be a steep learning curve for the team, so communication must be open and ongoing.

Several successful strategies to improve outcomes and reduce costs across the participating academic institutions have been identified by the UHC benchmarking projects (see Table 19.2). Physician-led teams were crucial to the development of patient management tools such as protocols, pathways, and algorithms that were implemented and consistently used. Protocols were most effective when they focused on hours rather than days and monitored variance measurements on key events only. Improvements in LOS were achieved by institutions that were able to update staff in a

Table 19.2. CABG clinical process improvement/benchmarking key strategies to improve outcomes and reduce costs that were successfully implemented by UHC members.

General
Physician-led teams as change agents to develop patient management tools
Patient management tools focus on hours rather than days
Variance measurements on key issues only
Patient pathway that corresponds to clinical pathway
UHC comparative data for JCAHO accreditation surveys to illustrate continuous improvement
LOS
Ability to immediately update staff on changes in pathways or processes
Earlier surgical consults for cardiology inpatients
Streamlined preoperative visits
Same-day admission for elective cases
Earlier and more frequent ambulation
Objective and quantifiable criteria for admission, discharge, and transfer
Subacute care for physical and occupational therapy
OR times and costs
More uniform procedure setups and case flow
Reduce costs with vendors
Standardize physician preference for procedure packs, instrument setups, suture, cardioplegia, and supplies
Clinical indication required for invasive monitoring
Criteria-based protocols for use of high-cost pharmaceuticals
Short-acting anesthetics and paralyzers
Prophylactic antibiotics
Protocol for administration
ICU LOS and early extubation
Aggressive monitoring of pre- and postoperative weights, diuretics, and oxygenation
End-tidal CO_2 for weaning
Wean at 36C versus 37C
Protocol for nurses to extubate, remove epicardial wires, chest tubes, and PA catheters
Aggressive atrial fibrillation prophylaxis protocol
Evaluate for transfer out of ICU at least three times a day
Reduced lab testing
Avoid ordering duplicate tests
No "routine" lab tests, EKGs, or CXRs

timely manner on changes in pathways or processes of care. Earlier surgical consults for cardiology inpatients and same-day admissions for elective cases also decreased average LOS. Streamlined preoperative visits included an anesthesia assessment, and pre-procedure tests were ordered on an as-needed basis only, with test results from the prior 30 days accepted from other providers if there had been no change in the patient's clinical status. Earlier ambulation and subacute care for continued physical and occupational therapy also reduced LOS. Establishing objective and quantifiable criteria for admission, discharge, and transfer that were consistently used was also associated with reductions in average LOS.

Operating room (OR) time and costs were reduced through perioperative case management, which facilitated the establishment of more uniform procedure setups and improved the flow of cases. Standardizing physician preferences for procedure packs, instrument setups, sutures, cardioplegia, and supplies increased efficiency and reduced costs, as did the use of clinical indications for invasive monitoring and high-cost pharmaceuticals. The use of short-acting anesthetics and paralyzers facilitated early extubation and early discharge from the ICU. The use of protocols for administering antibiotics by the anesthesiologist prior to the incision were associated with a reduced incidence of wound infections, which again contributed to decreased costs and a lower LOS. Aggressive monitoring of pre- and postoperative weights, diuretic usage, and oxygenation promoted reduced ICU LOS and early extubation. Nurse protocols for extubation and removal of epicardial wires, chest tubes, and PA catheters also decreased average ICU LOS. Aggressive atrial fibrillation prophylaxis protocols, as well as standardized protocols for common events such as pain, shivering, hypotension, blood utilization, and invasive monitoring, were also successful. Evaluating patients for transfer out of the ICU at least three times a day promoted early transfer, and training residents to avoid ordering duplicate tests and daily "routine" lab tests, EKGs, and CXRs also reduced test costs.

Lessons Learned: Success Factors and Failure Factors

Some of the best practices identified by UHC members as being central to the success of benchmarking projects include physician leadership, strong communication among a closely bonded team of clinicians, an enthusiastic attitude toward innovation, and flexibility (see Table 19.3).

UHC benchmarking participants have found that obtaining immediate and long-term improvements in clinical practice and outcomes depends on the work of an interdisciplinary clinical team led by committed, informed physicians who have substantive knowledge of clinical care and a broad understanding of the forces driving the changing health care marketplace. Physician leadership and buy-in are also enhanced by peer group interactions with participating institutions.

Table 19.3. Success and failure factors.

Success factors	Failure factors
Physician leadership for clinical teams	Lack of physical involvement
Physician buy-in through peer group interactions	Direct adoption of another organization's process
Clinical resource management experience	Lack of ongoing commitment
Ongoing support by physician and administrative leadership	Lack of consistent measurement

The following pitfalls should be avoided in order to improve the probability of a successful outcome.

1. Benchmarking cannot be conducted as a one-time event. The process cannot end with the first successful review of outcome indicators. It must be incorporated into the day-to-day routine of the clinical care process, integrated into the decision-making process of the organization, and become one of the quality tools used by the organization.

2. Support and attention from medical staff and administrative leadership must be maintained. If the organization loses this interest and support, then consequently training stops, funding is lost, teams become unable to visit other sites, and recommendations are met with indifference. Any process that facilitates continuous improvement in quality must have continuous support.

3. Adopting the best practices of another organization never works and is not benchmarking. Rather, information obtained from benchmarking partners must be integrated and evaluated in the environment in which it will be used.

4. Benchmarking is a difficult and time-consuming process. Without adequate planning, funding, training, staff time, and resources, the return on investment in such a project will be minimal.

5. In order to allow useful comparisons, data must be collected and defined in a consistent manner.

Summary

Academic health centers face many daunting challenges in the rapidly evolving health care marketplace. In order to obtain and maintain managed care contracts, most AHCs must substantially reduce their operating expenses. As a tool for clinical resource management, benchmarking is an ongoing method of comparing an organization's services, products, or processes with similar ones existing outside of the organization. For institutions in the midst of organizational restructuring, benchmarking is vital to accelerating the rate of improvement. It encourages positive change because it demands involvement and commitment to quality improvement. Benchmarking is not a one-time event, as the best practices of today may well become the minimum standards of tomorrow. When attempting to surpass a best practice, an organization must set challenging but attainable goals and accomplish them by implementing a plan consisting of realistic and efficient activities.

The AHC tripartite mission of teaching, research, and clinical practice makes it difficult to benchmark against community health care providers although they are AHCs' local competitors for managed care contracts. Using peer organizations as benchmark partners promotes physician buy-in, allows for the identification of variations in similar clinical models of practice, and facilitates the identification of clinical champions and opinion leaders. By providing member institutions with information about other academic centers with comparable missions, UHC provides quality managers with comparative information that is readily accepted for quality improvement projects within their individual institutions. Benchmarking involves a continuous search for excellence and innovation.

Discussion Questions for a One-Hour Executive Meeting

1. What strategies can administrators adopt to encourage academic physicians to become clinical champions for clinical resource management?

2. Who are the appropriate benchmark partners for academic health centers—peer organizations or local competitors?

Kimberly J. Rask, M.D., Ph.D., is director of the program in health care system efficiency and quality improvement research, Emory University Center for Clinical Evaluation Sciences; chair of the Medical Outcomes Committee, The Emory Clinic; and Emory representative to the University HealthSystem Consortium Clinical Evaluative Sciences Council, Atlanta, Georgia.

Jean Livingston, R.N., M.S.N. is director of the clinical process improvement program in the Clinical Practice Advancement Center at the University HealthSystem Consortium, Oak Brook, Illinois.

Chapter 20

Community Involvement: The Kingsport Experience

Rob Johnson and Jim Herbert

Some health care quality improvement efforts may be organized more at the community level rather than within a health care provider organization. A community-level approach, driven initially by employers, is ongoing in Kingsport, Tennessee. This chapter describes the journey in Kingsport thus far and the lessons learned.

Background

Setting the Stage

In January 1988, the Midwest Business Group on Health (MBGH), based in Chicago, Illinois, received a grant from the John A. Hartford Foundation to launch a value-managed health care purchasing project. The objectives of the project were to determine the status of health care purchasing and to identify ways that health care purchasers could incorporate more quality-related information in their purchasing decisions. Two advisory panels, composed of representatives from employers, physicians, hospitals, researchers, and consumer groups, were created to review these issues. Consultants were then hired to evaluate eight purchasing models across the country and 18 quality assessment tools available for employer use.

At the end of the study, the consultants and advisory panel members concluded that employers had made great strides in dealing with health care costs, but that very little had been done at that time to improve the quality of health care. Most efforts at that time were focused on quality assessment rather than quality improvement. The advisory panel members identified a number of obstacles that prevented purchasers from making progress in value-managed purchasing, including employers' lack of awareness of the existence of quality problems, lack of top management support, strained provider relations, limited knowledge of quality improvement technology, and a desire for simple solutions.

The panel members believed that changing the focus to a quality improvement process, rather than quality assessment, could help overcome these obstacles. Quality improvement strategies require a high level of commitment, lasting partnerships among employers and providers, and a comprehensive and systematic approach to evaluating quality. Continuous quality improvement (CQI) approaches were being used successfully by many American industries to improve overall quality and their level of competitiveness in the worldwide marketplace. Also, CQI was being implemented by a growing number of health care organizations.

One key aspect of a quality improvement strategy is the supplier improvement process. Employers were using this approach with raw material and service suppliers, but typically not with health care organizations. By extending this approach to health care purchasing, the advisory panel members believed that employers could develop a long-lasting framework for value-managed purchasing that could improve the value received from their health care expenditures.

Kingsport to Be a Player

To test this theory, the John A. Hartford Foundation provided an additional grant to MBGH to fund three demonstration sites. The demonstration sites included a communitywide effort in Kingsport and purchasing groups in Chicago and Milwaukee, Wisconsin.

Kingsport: The Community

The Kingsport demonstration project, which was later named the Kingsport Area Health Improvement Project (KAHIP), was initiated in August 1989. At that time the Kingsport health care system included two acute care hospitals—one not-for-profit community hospital and one Hospital Corporation of America (HCA) hospital—as well as one HCA psychiatric hospital. There was one major managed care organization, John Deere Health Care (JDHC), which had organized an Independent Practice Association (IPA) model health maintenance organization (HMO) in 1987. The one local IPA included most of the local physicians. There was also an active business coalition, the Kingsport Area Business Council on Health Care (KABCHC), whose member companies had approximately 16,000 employees in the Kingsport area.

Kingsport had become somewhat well-known for communitywide quality improvement efforts. Many of the local industries had adopted total quality management (TQM)/CQI principles, and Holston Valley Medical Center (the community hospital) was implementing a quality improvement approach. Northeast State Technical Community College and local industry representatives had established nearby the National Center for Quality (NCQ), which provided TQM/CQI training and consulting services. The level of quality activity in Kingsport was one of the favorable conditions there and was a key reason for its selection as a demonstration site.

Kingsport, incorporated in 1917, is a thriving industrial community of 40,000 people in northeastern Tennessee. The greater Kingsport area has 85,000 people and is part of the 425,000 population in the Tri-Cities metropolitan area, along with Johnson City, Tennessee; Bristol, Tennessee; and Bristol, Virginia.

Kingsport Area Health Improvement Project

The Journey Thus Far

Following are rather succinct descriptions/discussions of a number of items in chronological order pertaining to KAHIP's organization, operation, and improvement projects that collectively describe the journey taken thus far. This information helps portray the special challenges involved in health care quality improvement at the community level.

Original Organization/Operation of KAHIP. KAHIP was first organized with a steering team that would provide overall guidance for the effort and a quality improvement council (QIC) that would identify quality improvement opportunities and charter quality improvement teams (QITs) to work on identified projects. Figure 20.1 illustrates this original organizational structure. The steering team included senior-level executives from two KABCHC member companies, the chief executive officer of each local acute care hospital, and the president of the Kingsport IPA. The QIC included representatives of all of the participating organizations. Eastman Chemical Company, which employs approximately 12,000 people locally, donated the time of internal quality consultants and employee benefits staff personnel to coordinate the administrative activities of KAHIP.

At the start of the project, steering team and QIC members attended two days of intensive CQI training. The training was delivered by nationally recognized quality experts. The training included instruction in many quality improvement techniques like the plan-do-check-act (PDCA) cycle, data-driven decision making, the team process, and so on. During the initial training, the combined steering team and QIC members brainstormed a list of improvement opportunities for the QIC to evaluate. The improvement opportunities fell into two basic categories: (1) care management/utilization issues, and (2) health status issues. Interestingly, the business members of the group focused primarily on care management/utilization issues, which reflected their focus on improvements in efficiency that should lead to cost improvement. The health care provider members, on the other hand, focused almost entirely on health status issues rather than such cost reduction opportunities.

The QIC decided to meet early mornings every other Tuesday for an hour and a half. In its initial meeting, the group finalized the mission statement for the QIC. The QIC mission statement then read: "To improve the health status of Kingsport area residents by applying quality improvement principles to the health care system." Several months later, the mission statement was revised to put more emphasis on clinical process improvement. Figure 20.2 provides this early, but not original, mission statement. The group also decided to establish two subteams: one to work on the list of health status improvement opportunities and the other to focus on care management/utilization issues.

For any broad quality improvement effort to be successful, it is important to have some early successes. This means that initial projects must be doable, otherwise the entire group (organization) may lose interest in a methodical, systematic approach to quality improvement. Also, it is important to use data to identify improvement opportunities and to measure improvement. Both of these important tenets of CQI proved to be difficult to achieve. Both QIC subteams struggled to obtain data that would help them identify improvement opportunities. Also, both groups had difficulty focusing down

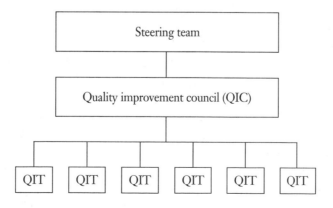

Figure 20.1. KAHIP original organization.

To facilitate Kingsport area hospitals, physicians, employers, and health care insurers in developing a cooperative health care process that assures accessibility to appropriate care for all people and maximizes health care value by focusing on development of data-oriented, quality clinical processes and minimization of cost.

Figure 20.2. KAHIP mission statement.

to projects that could be reasonably accomplished. The tendency was to focus on improvements at a system level (involving multiple processes) rather than at a singular process level.

Initial Quality Improvement Teams. The QIC eventually accepted the fact that existing data sources were far from ideal for its needs. After reviewing hospital discharge data, the group decided to focus its efforts on respiratory disease, the second leading major diagnostic category (MDC) locally, from a cost standpoint. The physician and hospital representatives felt that respiratory disease was a better place to start than circulatory disease, the leading MDC. Respiratory disease is a high-incidence reason for admittance at both hospitals, is the source of a lot of emergency room (ER) visits, and is perhaps less complicated than circulatory disease. QITs were chartered for the following project areas.

1. Reduce the number of readmissions for chronically ill respiratory patients presenting at the emergency room (the assigned team later affectionately dubbed such patients "frequent flyers").

2. Develop a more effective process for transitioning hospital patients to nursing homes.

3. Develop a process to encourage youth to quit or not start smoking.

4. Determine the most appropriate means of conducting third-party utilization reviews.

The QITs were staffed with employees from the participating organizations, and a team leader was designated for each team. For example, the "number of readmissions" team included an ER nurse from Holston Valley Medical Center, the director of cardiopulmonary services at Indian Path Medical Center, and two other health care providers having particular expertise important to the project. In addition, the director of the lung center at Holston Valley was designated as the leader for the team. Other teams were staffed in a similar manner.

The "number of readmissions," "smoking in youth," and "transitioning" teams attended a 60-hour quality improvement (QI) program at Northeast State conducted under the auspices of NCQ. The program was designed to teach teams how to use QI tools and techniques to work through a process improvement project. Typically, the teams attending this QI instructional program were natural unit work teams from local businesses and government entities. These teams would be assigned an improvement project by their employers to use as their case study for the training course. (For example, a team from a local foundry worked on improving the process for making sand castings, a key work process at the foundry.) Classes were held one day every other week and lasted eight hours. The first part of each class was devoted to teaching QI tools and techniques, which participants would then apply to their assigned project. Numerous teams received training in this program and completed improvement projects that saved their respective organizations millions of dollars since the program's inception in 1986.

Because of budget limitations, the "utilization review" team did not participate in the NCQ training program. Instead, this team was led by an Eastman staff person who provided the QI training as needed and led the team through the improvement project process.

The initial four KAHIP quality improvement teams struggled with their assigned projects. The projects were defined too broadly and really focused on a system problem rather than a process. Also, there were little if any data available for the teams to use on their project assignments. Since the NCQ training program focused on improvement of a specific process, the program was not as helpful to the KAHIP teams as it was for regular work teams from industry or government. Also, since the KAHIP team members worked for different employers, they didn't fit together as well as teams composed of members from a single organization that work together daily on a defined work process.

Gallbladder Surgery Project. As a result of these problems, the success of the initial KAHIP teams was limited in spite of much hard work on the part of those teams. But these initial KAHIP projects helped precipitate the next project, which turned out to be significant. Based on the lessons learned through the initial teams, the JDHC and Kingsport IPA representatives involved in the KAHIP effort decided to identify a single hospital care process that would provide a manageable process improvement opportunity. The process for open gallbladder surgery was selected, and a QIT was formed. An Eastman quality consultant was assigned to facilitate the team. In order to keep things simple, the team focused on gallbladder patients who had no comorbidity and no complications with their surgery.

The team reviewed patient charts to identify key process elements for each patient and record the day that each element occurred. The team quickly found that there was no defined process for post-surgical care for gallbladder surgery. Instead, there was significant variation in the lengths of stay for patients of various physicians, as well as variation among the patients of a single surgeon. One surgeon consistently had the lowest post-surgical length of stay (LOS) and the least variation among his patients. This local best practice was documented by the team and adopted by the IPA and the hospitals as a protocol for the community. As a result of this project, the average LOS for such gallbladder surgery was reduced from five days to three days. Figures 20.3 and 20.4 help illustrate some of the project methodology and results.

Although the gallbladder project was not earth-shattering from a dollar savings standpoint, it was in fact a breakthrough for the KAHIP participants because it demonstrated the power of process improvement. The project showed that significant variation existed and that improvements could be made without adversely affecting quality of care. This project drove home one other important point that had hindered success in earlier projects: In many aspects of care delivery, there was not a defined care process. This meant that a process had to be defined before it could be improved. In the case of the gallbladder project, a local best practice was adopted as "the" process of care. Also, the gallbladder project demonstrated that improvement of care processes needs to be driven by the organization or organizations that own the process and work with it on a regular basis. JDHC, the IPA surgeons, and the hospitals worked closely together on the delivery of gallbladder surgical care, so they jointly had ownership of the process and were in the best position to accomplish the process improvement. KAHIP had created the awareness of QI and the desire to use it in improvement of some care processes, but the experience led to or confirmed the conclusion that ongoing process improvement has to be driven within a single organization or by organizations that have well-defined customer/supplier relationships.

Six-Step Quality Improvement Process

1. Why this improvement project?
2. Focus and define the problem.
3. Analyze for root causes.
4. Develop remedies and action plans.
5. Implement, evaluate, and standardize.
6. Review for lessons learned.

Details regarding step 1: Why this improvement project?

- Determine if quality improvement techniques can be used to improve the efficiency of hospital utilization.
- Among the top 20 hospitalizations, gallbladder surgeries rank second in excess days according to national medical audit (NMA) best criteria.
- If the LOS can be reduced by two days, there is an annual potential savings of $194,000.

Details regarding step 2: Focus and define the problem.

What the problem is.

- Reduce the variation in patient care for gallbladder surgeries.
- Reduce hospital LOS for gallbladder surgery patients.
- Includes scheduled surgeries and medical admissions that later result in surgery.

What the problem is not.

- Not an attempt to change physician compensation.
- Not to try to move surgeons to do laser surgery.
- Not to include acute cholecystitis.

Details regarding step 3: Analyze for root causes.

- Flowchart
- Cause-and-effect diagram
- Charts

Data Collected

- LOS by hospital and total
- LOS by age and sex
- LOS elective vs. emergency
- Average LOS by day of week (by hospital and total)
- Pre-surgical days of ER admits
- LOS by employer group
- LOS elective by surgeon
- Individual chart review

Figure 20.3. Gallbladder surgery project: Methodology and results.

Conclusions from Data

- No statistically significant difference in LOS between hospitals for elective cholecystectomy.
- No statistically significant difference in LOS by sex or age.
- No statistically significant difference in LOS by day of week admitted.
- Surgical technique makes a difference in LOS.
- Physician practice patterns make a difference in LOS.

Kingsport Recommended Timetable for Gallbladder Surgery

- *Day 0:* Operating room; IV/IM/PO pain/nausea meds; IV antibiotics; ambulation; IV fluids; ice chips; advance diet as tolerated; drains if needed
- *Day 1:* DC IV fluids or convert to int; advance diet; laxative; increase ambulation; PO pain meds
- *Day 2:* DC drains; DC int; PO pain meds; laxative
- *Day 3:* Patient education for wound care; enema; discharge
- *Goal LOS:* Three days

Note that this recommended timetable is for uncomplicated patients and excludes common bile duct exploration.

Recommendations

- Follow Kingsport recommended practice pattern.
- Use conditional orders.
- Do preplanning and discharge planning.

Figure 20.3. *continued.*

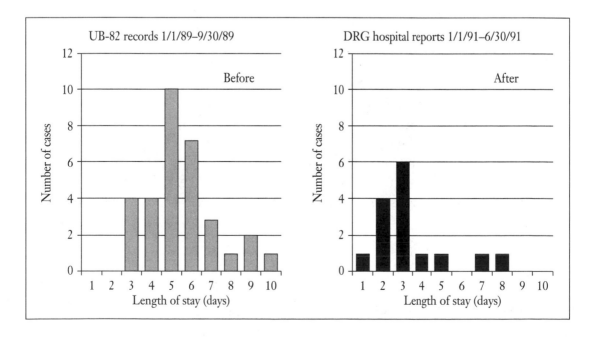

Figure 20.4. Gallbladder surgery project: Length of stay, before and after.

Affiliation with Kingsport Tomorrow. In 1989, independent of the initial KAHIP effort, Kingsport developed a community vision. Community wellness was one of the original 27 goals from the communitywide visioning process that resulted in incorporation of Kingsport Tomorrow, a broad-based citizens' group working to improve the community by citizen participation in determining the path to the community's future. Kingsport Tomorrow, a nonprofit agency, is financed by corporate, governmental, and individual contributions. It takes on some functions that government agencies and chambers of commerce do in other communities. By organizing and nurturing community teams to work on a variety of vision goals, Kingsport Tomorrow was to provide a vehicle for collaborative problem solving and consensus building that has since proven successful in a number of areas of community life. Not wanting to duplicate an existing organization, Kingsport Tomorrow designated KAHIP as its task force on wellness and health.

Reorganization and Change in Operation for KAHIP. By 1992, KAHIP leaders concluded that the so-called steering team for the organization was rather superfluous in that the QIC was actually making the meaningful decisions in directing the effort; in fact, the two leadership groups had some of the same members. Therefore, the first reorganization of KAHIP was elimination of the steering team and establishment of the QIC, with some additional members, as the ultimate guiding body of the KAHIP effort.

The emergence of restricted provider networks during late 1993/early 1994 created a new, more competitive atmosphere within the local health care community. This sense of heightened competition made providers more reluctant to collaborate, and thus contributed to KAHIP losing momentum at that time. KAHIP and Kingsport Tomorrow leaders then began discussing how to best get KAHIP back on track. After much discussion, it was decided that the health care providers might participate more effectively if given more responsibility for leading the effort. The QIC was replaced with a leadership team primarily composed of key provider leaders and a few members representing other community entities with particular interest in health issues. An attorney, specializing in health care law and perceived as a neutral local expert, served as the initial team leader until early 1995 when he decided to leave the area. He was replaced in that role by the industrial representative on the team, the president of a local foundry. Initially the leadership team had 10 members, but now has 18.

Figure 20.5 provides the present KAHIP organization structure, which can be contrasted with the original structure contained in Figure 20.1. KAHIP's latest vision and mission statements are provided in Figure 20.6 and 20.7 respectively. The emphasis within these recent statements is on improving health status within the community as opposed to improving clinical processes.

The leadership team normally meets once a month as a full team, very early in the morning in order to accommodate the physicians on the team. The team's functions are the following:

- To serve as a clearinghouse for prospective community projects related to health issues
- To assist prospective project sponsors and advocates in identifying team members and other potential resources to support the proposed project team
- To monitor progress on projects and provide assistance to teams as needed
- To provide linkage to Kingsport Tomorrow's board and other task forces
- To identify additional needs for the community and form project teams as needed

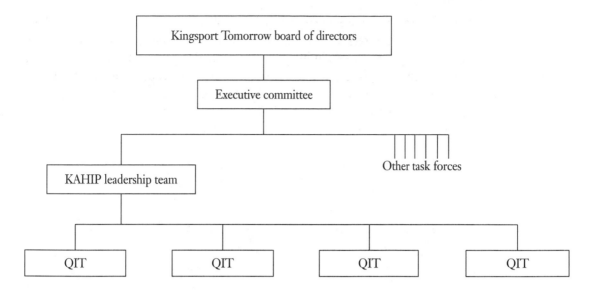

Figure 20.5. KAHIP reorganization.

Kingsport Is a Benchmark for Health Status and Health Care

Residents/Patients

- Health care is available to all residents.

- Residents are made aware of lifestyle factors affecting their health and are taking responsibility for leading healthier lifestyles.

Businesses

- Superior value of health care (high-quality outcomes at optimal cost) helps attract and retain businesses and assists them in maintaining their competitive positions.

- Employees are made aware of factors affecting their health and are taking responsibility for leading healthier lifestyles.

Providers

- A community data system provides facts and data to serve as a resource for improving health care in Kingsport.

- Quality, costs, and scope of services attract patients to Kingsport providers.

Figure 20.6. KAHIP vision.

To facilitate or develop cooperative processes that improve the health status of the people of the community.

Figure 20.7. KAHIP mission statement.

Subteams of the full team meet at other times to carry out various assignments as required. Since September 1995, the leadership team has been using a more defined approach in evaluating prospective projects. Figure 20.8 is a flowchart of this KAHIP project evaluation process. Figure 20.9 contains the KAHIP criteria for project acceptance, recently adopted for use in conjunction with project evaluation. These two documents, along with the list of leadership team functions, collectively provide much insight concerning the current operation of KAHIP.

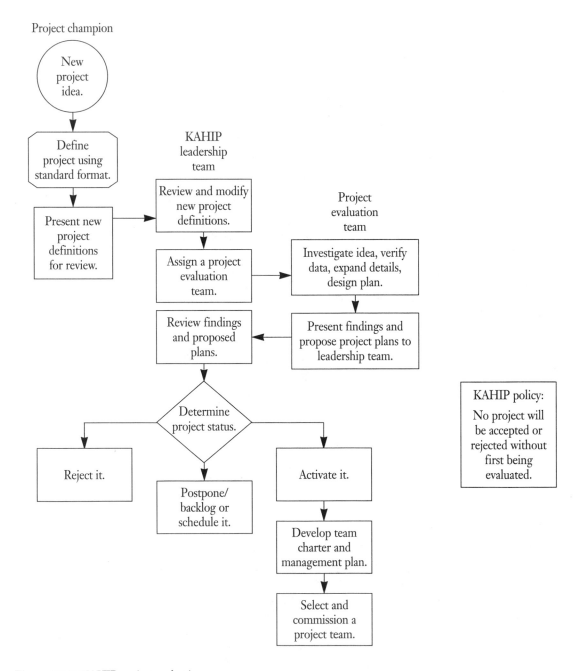

Figure 20.8. KAHIP project evaluation process.

To be eligible for KAHIP support, projects should

- Relate to the KAHIP vision and mission.
- Meet a clearly identified need in our community.
- Be identified and supported with data.
- Have a clear problem statement, objectives, and measurable outcomes.
- Have the commitment of key stakeholders.
- Identify a champion.
- Not duplicate other efforts already adequately addressing the problem.
- Have a high probability of success.
- Be practical from methodology and cost-effectiveness perspectives.
- Have a plan for accessing required resources (financial, human, and so on).
- Have a reasonable time frame with an expected completion date.

All project proposals should proceed through the KAHIP project evaluation process (established in September 1995). Some assistance may be provided to potential worthy projects that do not initially meet all required criteria.

Figure 20.9. KAHIP criteria for project acceptance.

Experience with Later and More Recent Projects. After the four initial projects and later the gall-bladder surgery project, other KAHIP projects were launched. By topic, these are as follows:

- Smoking prevention/cessation (broader outgrowth of the initial smoking project)
- Treatment of simple pneumonia (protocol)
- Knee replacement surgery (protocol)
- Friends-in-Need Health Center
- Learning collaborative
- Early detection of breast cancer

These projects have had varying degrees of success thus far.

- *Smoking prevention/cessation.* The reconstituted smoking prevention/cessation team has continued to function under the leadership of Richard Reed, MD, a true champion for the cause. New people were brought on board from time to time to keep the effort moving. Team members included representatives from the American Cancer Society, the American Heart Association, and the auxiliary of the local medical society. The team's efforts led to a no-smoking policy in the city school system. The team also made requests to the city and county for smoke-free buildings. The city responded by declaring all buildings smoke free except city hall, which still contains a small designated smoking area. The county government has not yet fully responded. In a related effort, the team has facilitated the use of a "Doctors Ought to Care" program by the schools for on-campus health promotions and disease prevention counseling. The smoking prevention/cessation team has also joined the Northeast Tennessee Coalition for Smoking or Health to support regionwide efforts at smoking cessation.

• *Clinical process improvement.* The relatively successful gallbladder surgery project stimulated other such efforts involving development of protocols (treatment guidelines) for certain clinical processes. The simple pneumonia protocol emanating from one improvement project team was fully implemented at Indian Path Medical Center, and thus that project could be considered reasonably successful. The knee replacement surgery protocol project, however, eventually fell victim to the competitive conflicts between the two hospitals, with little accomplished. Another attempt at addressing clinical process improvement needs involved the creation of a special clinical process improvement oversight team. This team included the nursing administrators from both hospitals and representatives from the hospitals' medical staffs, the Kingsport IPA, JDHC, and industry. Team members spent considerable time brainstorming where to concentrate their efforts, given that they could not infringe on the competition between the hospitals. Both hospitals have effective internal CQI processes in place and now perceive those outputs as a competitive weapon against each other. By March 1995, the team agreed that clinical processes within institutions were not going to be legitimate topics in the current competitive climate and agreed to focus on improving the wellness/health status of citizens in future collaborative efforts. Since the leadership team was already guiding such projects through other teams or future teams, the clinical process improvement team was soon thereafter disbanded.

• *Friends-in-Need Health Center.* The Friends-in-Need Health Center project was brought to Kingsport Tomorrow by the community's church groups. The objective is to provide primary health care for the uninsured, underserved working poor. There are a number of people that work and have no health insurance, but are not eligible for Medicaid. The project team, headed by Tom Brock, MD, included representatives from community churches, hospitals, physicians, dentists, pharmacists, the Junior League, family counseling agencies, businesses, and industry. This team's use of the CQI approach has not been as formal as that of some others, but the basic principles have been followed and the team has been highly motivated.

The team established a new community health center, which officially opened July 19, 1995. An executive director, head nurse, and secretary were hired; a building was rented; and a medical director appointed. Staffing is primarily by volunteer health care providers in the community, with the support of lay volunteers from various area churches and civic organizations.

The Friends-in-Need Health Center is effectively meeting a real need in the community and is a shining example of broad-based collaborative project work at its best. KAHIP appropriately "cut the cord" to this project once the Health Center was fully functioning with its own board of directors.

• *Learning collaborative.* Kingsport was one of nine U.S. and Canadian cities selected in 1993 to participate in a communitywide health improvement learning collaborative project, which was jointly sponsored by GOAL/QPC (Methuen, Massachusetts) and the Institute for Healthcare Improvement (Boston, Massachusetts). The objective of the nine individual community projects within the overall project is to determine if applying continuous quality improvement (CQI) in a collaborative fashion within a community can help bring about significant, positive change.

The Kingsport team, working in tandem with a team from Twin Falls, Idaho, decided to focus on reducing preventable injuries to children and adolescents resulting from motor vehicle accidents. Led by Jeanette Blazier, the team has included the Sullivan County sheriff and representatives from private health care and public health providers, education, community and parent groups, and industry.

This team has followed the PDCA model throughout the project, involving a number of large and small PDCA cycles. The team reviewed national data revealing that traffic accidents are the number-one preventable cause of death for youth. The data show that the teenage driving group has four times the accident rate per mile driven of the general population, and that 15% of young drivers have a crash in their first year of driving.

Team members also collected data from the local sheriff's office on juvenile traffic accidents by school for the county's five high schools for the years 1991 through 1993. A Pareto chart of these data was developed. This revealed that improper driving and failure to yield (two out of 11 categories) accounted for 54 percent of the 974 reported crashes. Drinking was blamed in only 6 percent of these cases. A later analysis of broader, additional data indicated that 95 percent of traffic crashes involving 15- to 19-year-olds are caused by lack of driving skill and/or judgment. Contrary to popular public perception, only 3 percent of local traffic crashes for this age group are due to drinking or drug impaired abilities.

Further investigation showed that, while all high school students received classroom instruction, only 40 percent to 50 percent received onroad training, due to a lack of certified instructors, and that this percentage was headed downward. It also became clear that drivers' education classes were under-funded, understaffed, and unstandardized. The use of simulation technology as a more cost-effective alternative to some onroad training wasn't possible due to insufficient funds.

Team members conducted benchmarking efforts and identified model curricula used elsewhere as well as the availability of state-of-the-art driver training simulators. Focus groups were held with students, parents, educators, and community leaders to determine the nature of the problem and the appropriateness of the project objectives selected. The team developed a cause-and-effect diagram and, based on the resultant analysis, decided to improve the quality and reduce the variability among high school drivers' education programs locally and to increase the coverage of those students needing onroad training.

Pilot tests are planned for each of the key interventions, with accompanying evaluation plans. The team implemented a best-practice, standardized drivers' education program, modeled after Washington State's Traffic Safety Education Guide, in one area high school in late 1996. If successful, the program will be replicated in the other four area high schools. The team will measure the program's impact in terms of increased numbers of teens trained and reduced juvenile traffic citations and accidents, as well as accident costs. The team believes a significant savings will occur in terms of health care, public safety resources, court system resources, and property damage, as well as improvement in the quality of life within the community.

The team also plans to purchase an eight-station DORON driving simulator for pilot testing at one high school. If successful, the equipment may be purchased for the other four high schools. Implementation of the pilot for the new program has been delayed temporarily due to a holdup in obtaining necessary funding through a grant.

A second major prong of the project is a program to develop widespread community awareness and understanding to increase participation in addressing the cost and impact of the problem, the limited scope of current driver training programs, and the direct relationship between young drivers' skill levels and motor vehicle crashes. The project was renamed the Drive Smart project, to provide a more recognizable, rallyable designation. Future efforts may include specialized educational materials, organized safe-driving clubs for teens, public service announcements, seminars, a speakers' bureau, regular media features, and special events for students and parents.

• *Early detection of breast cancer.* The team addressing the issue of how to better facilitate early detection of breast cancer has done some good research and analysis of the problem and has made recommendations concerning interventions for improvement needed at the hospitals. One of the two hospitals adopted most of these recommendations, while the other did not. The competitive conflict between the hospitals has reduced the overall effectiveness of this improvement effort, which is now dormant at best. Most people involved believe there is a lot of unrealized potential in such a project. Perhaps it can yet be resurrected if controversies over marketing issues can be put aside.

The Future for KAHIP

In January 1996, the leadership team held a strategic planning workshop to help plan KAHIP's future direction. John O'Brien, chief executive officer of The Cambridge Hospital Community Health Network (Cambridge, Massachusetts), was brought in as the keynote speaker for the workshop. A dynamic speaker, he has achieved national prominence for his work improving health status within a community, and he provided a lot of good ideas and inspiration to the KAHIP group. KAHIP and O'Brien expect to have a continuing collaborative relationship.

The leadership team is now in the process of exploring and developing other opportunities nation-wide for networking and for funding relative to community health improvement. Substantial effort is also being made to secure a regional health database and the services of a critical needs epidemiologist in order to do the best and most efficient job of improving health status in the community.

Summary of Lessons Learned Thus Far

Some basic keys to keeping the KAHIP effort alive have been the following:

1. Strong faith in the CQI approach

2. Commitment to a communitywide change process

3. Willingness to continue to engage in dialog

4. Willingness to try new organizational alliances and structures to revitalize the effort

5. Willingness to address the issues individuals and institutions can agree to work on and set aside those they cannot agree on

Also, the presence of the infrastructure of Kingsport Tomorrow and the prevailing spirit of volunteerism within the community cannot be overestimated in their importance to keeping KAHIP alive. The authors believe that in another community where these things do not exist, it would be difficult to sustain an effort like KAHIP.

The lessons learned in Kingsport about community quality improvement efforts through collaboration include the following:

- Favorable conditions for improvement are not enough. The leadership must be able to deal effectively with the tides of change. Participants' agendas can and do change. When competition is intense in the community, keeping people communicating may become an end in itself.

- Community collaboration on health care issues is a continuous quality journey that is never complete. The forces against collaboration, especially competition, continue to affect what is possible from month to month. It's important in a collaborative project for financial incentives to be properly aligned and thus avoid creating immediate adversarial relationships. A key to the success of the Friends-in-Need Health Center project was that "nobody's ox was getting gored," and therefore it was easy to get buy-in. Projects like this are not easy to find.

- The PDCA cycle is a valuable tool in all phases of a community collaborative effort. It can be applied to the overall effort as well as to individual projects and subunits of projects. However, leaders must elicit cooperation when people are ready, whether or not they are totally committed to formal use of the CQI model. The acceptance of the churches' proposal for the Friends-in-Need Health Center is one such example.

- It is important to carefully determine the focus for each effort before assembling the project team. Improvement efforts need to focus on a *process* rather than on a problem or system. Too many hidden agendas can overwhelm an unclear agenda for a particular effort. KAHIP needed new vision and mission statements to focus community efforts in ways that allowed collaboration, instead of just competition. Developing a common focus is very important and is a constant challenge.

- Community-based collaboration proceeds slowly, much more slowly than many somewhat knowledgeable people would expect. Additional concepts are needed to deal with the special challenges of such an effort, especially when external forces and conditions impinge on it. Extra management leadership and direction are required for multiorganization teams. Otherwise, a project may become "everybody's responsibility and nobody's responsibility." This condition was observed in the early KAHIP projects.

- A changing team membership may also mean revising a team's focus to accommodate changing needs and environmental factors. KAHIP and the IPA had originally focused on collaboration around clinical processes, but now such improvements are seen as competitive weapons by competing hospitals. New areas of collaboration have had to develop. The KAHIP leadership team needed to rethink its structure, mission, and goals to accommodate the climate of increasing competition in the provider community.

- The regionalization of health care payors and providers may call for collaborative improvement efforts to become regional if they are to have any real influence.

- Current data systems are not adequate for communitywide improvement efforts. Developing an appropriate database needs to be a priority. There could be several organizational entities in a region that might profit from such a database, and therefore be willing to help fund its development.

- With all of the financial pressure on businesses and providers today, funding is a major issue for community projects that have little or no immediate return. A lot of other work or potential efforts in a community compete for volunteer resources and money.

- It's important to have some success early in order to keep interest high and maintain momentum. As one project advisor said, "Pick up the fruit laying on the ground before reaching for even the low-hanging fruit on the tree!"

- Due to competition that tends to work against some types of collaboration, improvement of clinical processes probably needs to be driven by marketplace demands involving contractual arrangements between providers, managed care organizations, and businesses.

Discussion Questions for a One-Hour Executive Meeting

1. What are some of the conditions or other things needed to give health care quality improvement at the community level a reasonable chance for success?

2. What are some of the special challenges involved in quality improvement at the community or multiorganization level?

3. What potential, and perhaps unique, benefits can be attained through quality improvement efforts at the community level?

Rob Johnson is a native of Knoxville, Tennessee, and a graduate of the University of Tennessee, where he earned a degree in industrial engineering. He has been employed by Eastman Chemical Company for more than 25 years and has worked in the employee benefits field since 1983. He is currently Eastman's manager of health and welfare plans and is responsible for Eastman's domestic health plan development and administration. He has been active in local, state, and national health care business coalition efforts and is currently a member of the board of directors of the Midwest Business Group on Health.

Jim Herbert is a native of Kingsport, Tennessee, and a graduate of the University of Tennessee, where he earned a degree in industrial engineering. Herbert has been employed by Eastman Chemical Company for more than 34 years and has worked in the employee benefits field since 1989. He is currently a senior employee benefits representative, focusing on health and welfare benefit plan development and administration. He has been very active in community improvement efforts as well as in both business-only and employer-provider coalition efforts to improve health and health care. He currently serves on the board of directors for a number of organizations responsible for these initiatives.

Chapter 21

Directed Creativity and the Management of Quality in Health Care

Paul E. Plsek

Creativity and the Challenges Facing Leaders in Health Care

Today's health care leaders face an imperative for change that, for most, is unprecedented in their careers. Rising consumerism, new health care delivery systems, increased competition, the shift in emphasis from treatment to prevention, and wave after wave of new health care technology are just a few of the many fundamental changes occurring in our industry. Health care leaders instinctively know that their organizations cannot continue to be what they have always been. In these times of change, innovation and creative thinking have become essential, core competencies.[1]

Dilemmas in Tapping Creativity in Organizations. But while the essential need for creative thinking is easy to see, health care leaders face several dilemmas in attempting to stimulate productive innovation within their organizations. Many people (including leaders) are reluctant to even try to be creative because they believe that they lack the creative gift. They believe that truly innovative ideas come only to a chosen few, not to them. However, the research from the field of cognitive science indicates that this is simply not true. (See, for example, works by Perkins,[2] Weisberg,[3] and Plsek.[4,5]) As I will show in this chapter: If you can think, you can think creatively.

Another problem is that many people (again, including leaders) are unaware of the variety of tools they can use to generate creative ideas. They know about brainstorming, but little else. As it turns out, there is a vast literature describing literally hundreds of techniques for stimulating creativity. In this chapter, I will describe several simple tools that anyone can use to go beyond brainstorming to direct their creative thinking when and where they chose.

A final dilemma facing health care leaders is the tension between the need for creative thinking and an organization's affinity or aversion to risk. While there is no easy answer for this dilemma, I will provide some advice regarding leaders' roles in establishing an organizational culture that nurtures new ideas.

Creativity and the Pursuit of Quality in Health Care Organizations. What does all of this have to do with quality management in health care? It might seem that creative thinking and quality management do not mix well. After all, isn't quality management focused on such things as process control and the use of analytical methods, while creativity is about wild ideas that come from out of the blue? Surely quality management and creative thinking have little in common, right?

Wrong. The two disciplines have much in common, and there is much to be gained by exploring the overlap. Quality management is fundamentally related to the success of an organization—and so is innovation and creative thinking. Customer needs drive both the pursuit of quality and the pursuit of innovation. A focus on quality is essential for beating the competition in the marketplace, and so is a focus on innovation. The tools of quality management help us solve problems and redesign processes in order to improve customer satisfaction and reduce waste. The tools of directed creativity can also help us accomplish these goals. And, finally, recall that quality guru W. Edwards Deming called for more "joy in work" to aid the pursuit of higher levels of quality;[6] creative thinking is one way of building that joy.

In this chapter, we will examine the theory and tools of directed creativity and discuss their application in the management of health care quality. I will begin with definitions of terms and a concrete example of directed creativity. In the next section of the chapter we will examine the processes of creative thinking and the mechanics of the mind. Understanding mental processes takes the mystery out of creative thinking and enables us to truly direct it productively in the situations we face in health care quality management. Finally, we will look at some rules of thumb (we will call them *heuristics*) and a process model to guide our creative thinking. These first few sections of the chapter provide good grounding in the essential theory behind directed creativity.

The next sections of the chapter will shift our focus from theory to practical application. We will examine specific tools that support directed creativity. I will outline the three basic principles behind all creative thinking tools, and then demonstrate several of these tools using health care quality examples. This discussion about specific tools will lead naturally to the summary advice in the next section of the chapter regarding four common applications of directed creativity in the pursuit of quality in health care. I will provide guidance on creative problem solving and incremental improvement, creative process design and reengineering, creative customer needs analysis, and creative strategic planning. In the final section of the chapter I will offer some thoughts about organizational structures that impede and support creative thinking.

Defining Creativity and Innovation: The Targets for Our Thinking

Like quality, the terms *creativity* and *innovation* are defined differently by different authors. But, also like quality, there is enough commonality among these definitions to give us a working-level consensus about what people mean when they refer to creativity or innovation.

What Do We Mean by Creativity? Sifting through dozens of definitions of creativity, I have identified several underlying themes that comprise what we commonly mean when we say *creative*.[7] These themes are captured in the following consensus definition of creativity.

> *Creativity is the connecting and rearranging of knowledge—in the minds of people who will allow themselves to think flexibly—to generate new, often surprising ideas that others judge to be useful.*

The recent development of an adhesive to replace sutures in closing surgical wounds is a good illustration of the definition of creativity.[8] Using adhesive to close a wound is a new, useful idea. You probably smiled or expressed some sort of pleasant surprise when you first heard it. In hindsight, we can see that this idea is simply a logical connection of existing knowledge—adhesive as a way of holding things together, and the need to repair the skin following surgery. It makes perfect sense now that we hear it, but coming up with the idea required the mental flexibility and courage to step out of the current paradigm of how surgical wounds should be closed.

Practical Implications from the Definition of Creativity. Understanding what we mean by *creative* is a big step toward directed creativity. Now we know what to direct our thinking toward. That is, when we wish to be creative, we should try to come up with an original idea by making novel associations among what we already know. It may be helpful to explicitly list what we already know to aid this mental process; indeed, many creative thinking techniques begin with listing. It may also be helpful to learn about new concepts simply for the purpose of making them available in the mind for later creative connection. Again, several creative thinking tools are based on this.

Having called to mind what we know, the next practical step suggested by the definition is to search for new connections and be attentive to surprises. This idea of searching for surprising patterns explains why some creativity techniques suggest that we select concepts at random and try our best to combine them into something useful.

The notion of surprise in the definition of creativity has another important practical implication. When you feel yourself laughing or smiling at an idea, pause on that thought and work with it. It is highly likely that it contains the germ of a creative idea. I point this out to contrast it with what usually happens in organizations. When someone expresses an off-the-wall idea in a meeting and everyone laughs at it, rather than pausing to extract the germ of the creative thought, we often simply dismiss it so we can get back to serious business. This works in direct contradiction to what we know from the theory of creativity. Practically speaking, pausing on a laughable thought may be one of the most productive things we can do when we want creativity.

The definition of creativity also provides the practical suggestion that we should cultivate personality characteristics like flexibility and spontaneity in our thinking. If you want to be more creative, purposefully move out of your comfort zone in many small ways on a regular basis. Vary your morning routine, take some paperwork and go sit in the lobby or in a park to work on it, try new restaurants . . . anything that will help you prove to yourself that doing something new is not so bad after all.

Finally, the definition of creativity suggests that we must work hard to develop the practical value of our ideas; creativity is not just about flexible thinking and mental free association. Our analytical and logical thinking abilities are also needed. The ability to practically shape and develop an idea is just as important as the ability to imagine the idea in the first place. Imagination and analysis are equal partners in creativity.

What Do We Mean by Innovation and How Is It Different from Creativity? Having defined creativity, we can now define the related, but different, term *innovation*. Again, various authors in the literature provide various definitions of the term.[9] The consensus definition that I will use here is the following:

> *Innovation is the first, practical, concrete implementation of an idea; done in a way that brings broad-based, extrinsic recognition to an individual or organization.*

An innovation is a step beyond a creative idea. While creativity is about the production of ideas, innovation is about the practical implementation of those ideas. Further, while both creativity and innovation are in the eye of the beholder, innovation involves the significant, formal recognition by others of the idea's value. This extrinsic recognition might take the form of money (sales of product or service), a prize (the Nobel prize, a patent), or notoriety (widespread acknowledgment by others).

I stress this point because it is essential to realize that one can be creative, but fail to be innovative. The difference lies in the hard work of implementing ideas and holding them up to public critique. The practical implications of this distinction for health care organizations are clear. Many people in many health care organizations have had original, creative ideas for process and service innovations. But, being averse to risk, the organization failed to act on the ideas. These organizations have missed the competitive advantage that the innovator enjoys while the followers are working to catch up. Successful organizations and individuals must go beyond the mere production of creative ideas. Real success comes only with the implementation of an idea. Real success comes only with innovation.

**Practical Advice for Creative Thinking from the
Definitions of Creativity and Innovation**

- Try to come up with an original idea by making novel associations among what you already know.

- Be attentive to surprises.

- When you feel yourself laughing or smiling at an idea, pause on the thought and work with it.

- Deliberately cultivate personality characteristics like flexibility and spontaneity in your thinking.

- Work hard to shape your ideas so that others can readily see the value in them.

- Do not be content with merely generating creative ideas. Remember, the rewards of innovation come to the one who takes action on the ideas.

What Is Directed Creativity? I have been using the phrase *directed creativity* without defining it. Let me now clarify and illustrate what I mean by it.

> *Directed creativity is the purposeful production of creative ideas in a given topic area, followed up by deliberate effort to implement some of those ideas.*

Directed creativity is purposeful creative thinking that drives to innovation. When we are faced with a problem, we can employ directed creativity to find a way out. We can decide to use directed creativity when we need to design or redesign health care processes and services. Directed creativity is serious, deliberate, practical thinking aimed at finding new directions for improvement in an organization. Directed creativity does not rely on special gifts or bolts from the blue. Directed creativity is creative thinking for serious people.

To illustrate what we mean by directed creativity, consider the case of the hospital medication process improvement team that I once worked with. This medication quality improvement (QI) team was a model of the scientific approach to quality improvement. Team members had gathered data on the problem, used the Pareto principle to identify the vital few types of medication errors, constructed cause-and-effect diagrams and flowcharts, collected more data, identified root causes, implemented remedial process changes, and measured improvement. The team members were successful with every medication error type they focused on except one: medications not administered on time (late meds).

Interviews with the nurses indicated the primary cause for late meds was simply that the nurses got busy and forgot to give the medications at the prescribed times. As a solution, the team had posted a log sheet at the nurses' station with all of the patients' medication times written in chronological order as a reminder. But as it turned out, the nurses were too busy to look at the log sheet! Unable to secure the resources to relieve the workload burden on the nurses, the team was frustrated and had decided to accept the remaining error rate as simply inevitable.

Here is a team stuck in its thinking. The team had gone down a logical path in its analysis and had come up with a logical solution. The solution should have worked, but it didn't. Team members had put so much analytical effort and logical thought into the work leading up to this point that they were unable to think of anything else to do. Whenever they discussed the matter, they just kept coming back to the same stuck point, rejustifying their analysis, and decrying the lack of resources as the real root cause of the problem. Stuck thinking is a common occurrence in health care QI activities. Directed creativity can be used to relieve stuck thinking.

A directed creativity process for the medication error situation might have proceeded in the following manner.

- Realize that analytical thinking has reached a stuck point, but then resolve to find a creative way beyond it. (The team needed to acknowledge the constraints in the situation, but adopt the attitude that "there has got to be something else we can do.")

- Clarify the focus or concept that requires new thinking. (In this case, "We need a way to remind busy people when a certain time has come.")

- Review the facts. ("We tried to remind them with a time log, but that failed.")

- Look carefully at the current situation to identify elements that could be modified to yield a new approach. ("We tried reminding them visually . . . sight is only one of our senses . . . hearing, touching, tasting, smelling are others. We have used a paper time log . . . a large white board or a computer screen is another option.")

- Restate the focus by modifying an element and looking for an association. ("How could I remind a busy person about time through hearing rather than sight?" The mental association of the concepts of reminding, time, and hearing leads us naturally to identify an alarm clock as a mechanism. We could go on to think of other ways to utilize other senses or modify other elements of the situation.)

- Develop the idea further to meet practical constraints. (For example, it must not cost too much; it must be flexible, portable, and easy to associate with individual patients. One way is to use a stick-on alarm clock—the kind that you can attach to an appliance or car dashboard. They are typically available in the line at the supermarket checkout counter.)

- Express it, develop it, try it out, and see what happens. (The team purchased a few of these stick-on alarm clocks, set them for the appropriate medication times, and stuck them to the appropriate patients' charts. Now, even if the nurses are very busy, when the alarm goes off someone hears it and is reminded that it is time to administer a medication. The implementation of this idea reduced the late meds rate to nearly zero, without the addition of extra staff.)

As we will see in the next section, these processes of directed creativity are based on modern theories of how the mind works. Furthermore, they utilize ordinary thought processes like noticing, associating, remembering, and selecting. No special genius is required. Finally, while the end product of the thinking is creative—a new idea—the thought processes have a logic that makes them appealing even to serious, scientific people (like those that typically work in health care organizations).

While the thinking process outlined here is not a universal sequence that can be applied to all situations, it does illustrate five, basic mental actions that are common to many successful creative thinking endeavors.

Some Basic Mental Actions in Directed Creativity

- Clarify the focus with a broad statement.
- Recognize the concepts in the current situation.
- List alternatives.
- Make mental associations.
- Develop ideas into practical realities.

First, it is often necessary to stop and clarify the focus that requires creative thinking. By stating the focus broadly—I need a way to remind busy people when a certain time has come—we give our minds both a fixed point from which to direct our thinking and a wide space in which to come up with alternatives.

Being clear about the current reality and looking carefully to notice the underlying concepts behind the common things around us is a second critical element in directed creative thinking. Often we fail to pause and consider how or why something works or fails. The medication time log was a good idea, but it failed. If we stop and think about why it failed, we might realize that an underlying assumption was that the nurses would find time to look at it. But what we found was that they were too busy—which, of course, simply brings us back to the original problem. The key insight here is to notice that the failed solution relied on the sense of sight to do the reminding.

Listing alternatives is a third key element in the directed creativity process in this situation. Recognizing that reliance on the sense of sight had failed, directed creativity suggests that we simply list our other senses and consider them as alternative ways of reminding. Careful reflection on this list of senses would lead us to notice that while it is difficult to look at something when you are busy with something else, it is easy to hear something even when you are otherwise occupied. This is not an earth-shaking insight. So why didn't the team members think of it? I believe it is because our minds tend to race quickly past it on the way to the only approach we can think of; that is, the way we remind nurses in a hospital is with a log sheet. So, paradoxically, stuck thinking does not necessarily mean that thinking has stopped. A better metaphor is to say that our thoughts are racing toward a repeated collision with the same brick wall! Listing alternatives helps us slow down our thinking, look around, and find an alternative side street to turn down before we hit that same brick wall again.

Fourth, this example also illustrates the fundamental thinking process of association. When we associate the concepts of reminding, time, and hearing, we come up with the idea of using an alarm clock. Association lies at the core of all creative thought.

Finally, this example illustrates the importance of further refining our ideas in order to make them truly useful. Many good ideas are never implemented because our first impression of them makes them seem unappealing. Since, by definition, a creative idea is a new idea, we cannot be sure what mental model people will conjure up when we first express it. For example, imagine a row of bedside alarm clocks with big brass bells on top going off at various times. This mental picture would certainly lead to immediate rejection of the alarm clock idea as too goofy. But rather than prematurely rejecting the idea, we should consider the alarm clock suggestion merely a seed of an idea that must be further refined. In the development process, we can address practical issues such as cost, fit with the environment, need for flexibility, and so on.

Directed creativity is needed in the pursuit of quality for the simple reason that sometimes creative thinking is useful. When we are stuck in our thinking—whether trying to solve a problem, redesign a process, develop a new service, or delight a customer—it may not do any good to simply think harder. If our analytical thinking has locked us into a particular approach that is unfruitful, thinking harder is analogous to driving faster into the same brick wall in hopes that we will break through it. While there may be a slight chance of success with this brute force approach, wouldn't it be easier to drive around the wall or construct a ramp over it? Driving around or over the walls in our thinking is the creative approach.

Reflecting on the late meds case and other stuck thinking situations like it, we can clearly see that there are limits to traditional analytical thinking when it comes to solving nagging problems or generating breakthrough ideas. What we need is the ability to be analytical when the situation calls for it, and creative when the situation calls for that. Both skills are critical for success in the management of quality.

Some Theory for Directed Creativity: The Mechanics of the Mind

If creative thinking can be directed so easily, then why is it so rare? To answer this question we need to understand the underlying mental processes that go into the production of creative ideas. The bottom line is that creative ideas are relatively rare because our minds are not set up to produce them naturally. Rather, our minds are optimized to store and play back patterns of thought and behavior that we have learned from the past. So while we all possess the capacity for creative thought, creative thought is not automatic. That is why we need *directed* creativity. We must direct our minds to overcome automatic thinking processes and to use creative thinking processes.

While we are far from a full understanding of the mechanics of mind, research over the past 50 years has taught us much about both automatic and creative mental processes. Figure 21.1 provides a high-level systems diagram of these mental processes. (For more details about mental processes and their relationship to creative thinking, see de Bono,[10,11] Osherson and Smith,[12] Perkins,[13] Plsek,[14,15] and Sternberg.[16])

As illustrated in Figure 21.1, our minds take in inputs from the world through the subprocesses of perception. We then retrieve patterns from memory (our past experiences) to make sense of these inputs. Research shows that our perception processes filter out most of what goes on around us and focus our attention toward signals in the environment that fit our existing patterns of how things should be.

While this perception-memory mechanism is efficient for doing routine tasks, it works against creativity. Our automatic mental processes bias our thinking toward existing ways of doing things and cause us to miss observations that could lead us toward a new way. These automatic mental processes were clearly behind the stuck thinking of the medication errors QI team. The team members analyzed the situation and retrieved a past pattern for dealing with it. ("We need a logbook to remind the nurses.") When that solution did not work, the team members were stuck simply repeating the same thought patterns because they failed to observe that the reminder system relied on the sense of sight. They literally did not *see* that they had an option.

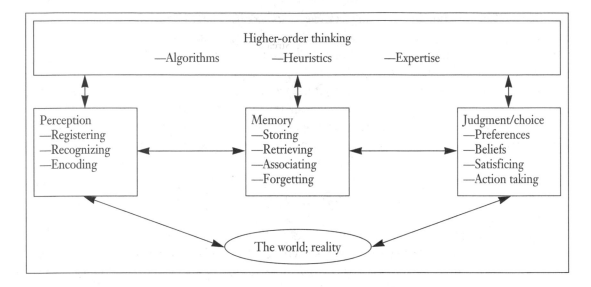

Figure 21.1. A high-level model of the mechanics of mind.

Directed creativity involves slowing down and redirecting our perception and memory retrieval processes. Though it will not be automatic, we can direct our mind to notice things that we do not usually notice and to retrieve different mental patterns (for example, an alarm clock as a reminder mechanism).

Edward de Bono[17,18] supplies the useful model depicted in Figure 21.2 for the mental mechanics of perception and memory. de Bono suggests that we think of the mind as a landscape consisting of high ground (the shaded areas in Figure 21.2), valleys formed between the high ground, and streams where the run-off water collects at the low points of the valleys. In this model, the flow of thought in the mind is analogous to the flow of water. The wide valleys represent the processes of perception. The perception process of *registering* creates a mental impulse that we can depict on this model as a drop of falling rainwater. Perception is channeled toward existing patterns in memory in the same way that a drop of rainwater falling anywhere in a valley is channeled into the stream at the bottom of that valley. de Bono's model is appealing because it corresponds directly to common phrases for mental activity such as *stream of thought* and *mental ruts*.

In this model, memory is a mental rut. When we learn, we carve another rut (valley) into our mental landscape. The more frequently we access that memory, the deeper the rut (like soil erosion). The deeper the rut, the steeper the walls of the valley, the more quickly we access that stream of thought, and the more automatic is our thinking. This explains why habits are so hard to break. Habits lead to frequent access of the same mental patterns—deep ruts and steep valleys that are difficult to escape.

This mental channeling mechanism gives us many useful human abilities that we take for granted. For example, it enables a clinician to make a preliminary diagnosis based on an initial review of the patient's symptoms. The patient's symptoms fall like a raindrop onto the clinician's mental landscape. The clinician has seen the pattern of symptoms before and, therefore, has a well-defined mental valley encoded with the name of the underlying disease. The observation of the symptoms is thereby

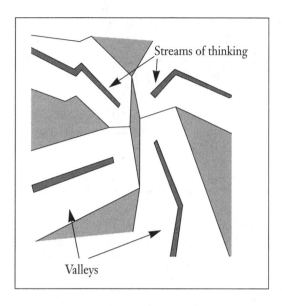

Figure 21.2. Edward de Bono's river and topography model of the mechanics of mind.

translated into a stream of thought that identifies the disease. We call this natural mental ability *experience*. The mental mechanism is the same whether we are preparing a budget, designing a new health care process, or just trying to get out of bed in the morning. We use the past experiences stored in our memory as a guide for how to proceed.

While this self-organizing, channeling system is great for doing the repetitive tasks of daily life, it is clearly not optimal when we want creative ideas. Creative thinking requires that we think in a new direction; away from or beyond our current mental valleys, toward new patterns. Creative thinking involves slowing down and redirecting our perception processes, instead of letting them flow automatically into the usual mental valleys. It involves connecting to and exploring mental valleys that we do not normally access in the context we find ourselves in at the moment.

Therefore, when we need a creative idea, it does little good to tell ourselves and others to just "think harder," simply "suspend judgment" (as in brainstorming), or merely "be playful." While it is indeed helpful to think hard, suspend judgment, and be playful during creative thinking, these simple suggestions fall short by failing to provide a new *direction* for our thinking. If we remain in our current mental valley, we may find that we are only able to come up with small variations on the mental patterns we already have.

While perception and memory mechanisms define our thoughts, judgment and choice are the mental processes that stand between our thoughts and actions (refer to Figure 21.1). Our automatic judgment processes are also channeled toward existing patterns from the past. Research shows that we automatically work to preserve our beliefs, justify our past choices, and avoid taking risks. While we all like to think that we are rational, logical thinkers, research further shows that pure rationality is not possible. So our judgment processes are also mental patterns, but flavored with emotions. Creative thinking involves temporarily—but purposefully—suspending these judgments, abandoning the need to justify our past patterns, and risking the expression of new ideas to see where they take us.

It is important to note that creative thinking does not require that we throw away critical judgment and logical thinking. How could we possibly get to the concrete implementation required to reap the rewards of innovation without critical judgment? Rather, we simply need to hold off judgment a little longer than we are accustomed to when using our automatic mental processes. We can do it. But we must direct our mind to do it.

The box "Mechanics of Mind: Implications for Directed Creativity" summarizes the practical steps that we can take to overcome our automatic mental processes and cultivate our creative thinking abilities.

Mechanics of Mind: Implications for Directed Creativity

Tuning Your Perception

Recognize when your thinking is stuck (that is, hitting the same wall).

Make it a habit to purposely pause and notice things—what works and why.

To perceive something in a new way when you are stuck, try: simply pausing to notice something, defining the current reality, drawing a picture of it, making a slow motion mental movie, explaining it to someone and listening to yourself, imagining the situation as it might be seen by someone else, and so on.

Using Your Memory

Use your perception process to create a store of ideas and concepts in memory.

Try to come up with an original idea by making novel associations among what you already know.

Search for patterns in memory and be attentive to surprises.

Recognize that your streams of thought are not inherently correct or incorrect, they are simply what you think now based primarily on what you have learned in the past.

Look for different mental associations by listening to other people's streams of thought.

Slow down, or back up, in your thinking to identify the intermediate concepts that make up your stream of thought.

Use novel analogies to search for new mental associations. (For example, if nurses were hotel guests, how would we remind them?)

Using Your Judgment

Be aware of the danger of both premature judgment and justification.

Never think that you have arrived at the end of your thinking on a matter; as practical, push yourself to generate more than one good option so that you will not feel so compelled to justify.

Try avoiding the blinders of emotion, judgment, and justification by setting the issue aside for a while and coming back to it later.

Actively seek out the rationality in other people's points of view.

Don't be afraid to try something and then tinker with it.

Heuristics and Models for Directed Creativity

The final element in the system of cognitive processes depicted in Figure 21.1 is generically labeled *higher-order thinking*. Simply put, higher-order thinking is the mental management of repeated acts of perception, memory, and judgment, directed over time toward some goal. Directing our creative thoughts in order to solve a nagging problem or generate a breakthrough idea is an example of higher-order thinking.

Research indicates that heuristics are key to higher-order thinking. (The concept of heuristic thinking is further described in Wallas,[19] Polya,[20] Newell and Simon,[21] and Holyoak.[22]) Perkins defines a heuristic as "a rule of thumb that often helps in solving a certain class of problems, but makes no guarantees."[23] An example of a heuristic in quality management is Juran's advice to "look for the vital few."[24] This is useful advice in that it points us in a potentially productive direction; but, of course, it does not guarantee that we will always be successful.

A variety of researchers have demonstrated that experts in a given area do more effective higher-order thinking primarily because they have better heuristics than novices. (For example, see De Groot,[25] and Holyoak.[26]) Good thinkers do not necessarily think harder, longer, or more exactly; they have simply learned to think in directions that are more likely to be productive. Likewise, in creative thinking, the implications of this research are that we should concentrate on the development and application of heuristics that improve the likelihood of getting beyond incidents of stuck thinking.

The literature on creative thinking offers two types of heuristics; specific lists of advice and models for the process of creative thinking. It should not surprise us that, once again, different authors provide different lists of heuristics and different models. But, again, it is possible to identify common themes after a careful review of the literature. Figures 21.3 and 21.4 present such a list of heuristics and a model for the creative process. (For a thorough explanation of the development of the list and the model described in this chapter, see Plsek.[27])

The heuristic rules of thumb in Figure 21.3 are based on a modern understanding of the mechanics of mind, as well as the practical experience of seasoned creative thinkers. For example, the first heuristic suggests that we make it a habit to purposefully pause and notice things because we know that our automatic perception processes miss a great deal. In other words, if we are currently engaged in

---

1. Make it a habit to purposefully pause and notice things.

2. Focus your creative energies on just a few topic areas that you genuinely care about and work on these purposefully for several weeks or months.

3. Avoid being too narrow in the way you define your problem or topic area; purposefully try broader definitions and see what insights you gain.

4. Try to come up with original and useful ideas by making novel associations among what you already know.

5. When you need creative ideas, remember: attention, escape, and movement.

6. Pause and carefully examine ideas that make you laugh the first time you hear them.

7. Recognize that your streams of thought and patterns of judgment are not inherently right or wrong; they are just what you think now based primarily on patterns from your past.

8. Make a deliberate effort to harvest, develop, and implement at least a few of the ideas you generate.

Figure 21.3. Basic heuristics for getting started in directed creativity.

thinking about a specific topic (for example, the late meds problem), we want to pause and notice something about the situation that we have not noticed before (the log book idea relies on the sense of sight).

The second heuristic—focus, care, and work purposefully—is based on research into the lives of great creators. Creative ideas rarely come "all of a sudden." Good creators work diligently with many ideas, in a specific topic area, over an extended period of time. (For more about research into creative lives, see Wallace and Gruber,[28] Shekerjian,[29] and Weisberg.[30])

We saw an illustration of heuristic number three—define the topic broadly—in the late meds case. Defining the topic as "reminding nurses to administer meds on time" drives our mind quickly and directly into the log book valley. Defining the topic as "reminding busy people that a certain time has come" immediately opens up creative possibilities.

The fourth heuristic—make mental associations—reminds us to take the basic mental action that underlies all creative thought. The fifth heuristic—attention, escape, and movement—further directs our basic mental mechanics. These three mental activities underlie all tools for directed creativity; we will describe them further in the next section of this chapter.

We have already touched on heuristic number six—pause on ideas that make you laugh. Though we are not yet sure, it appears that laughter might be a physiological reaction to a novel connection among neurons in the brain. This explains why we laugh at jokes (the punch line makes a connection we were not expecting) and smile when we finally figure something out. The pause-on-ideas-that-make-you-laugh heuristic calls us to resist the urge to move on when someone suggests a laughable concept. Working with such ideas can be one of the most productive things we can do when we desire innovation.

The seventh heuristic in the set—your judgments are not inherently right or wrong—reminds us that our mental processes of judgment are emotion laden. This heuristic calls us to keep an open mind and cultivate flexibility—essential ingredients in creative thinking. Finally, the last of the heuristics is based on the important distinction between mere creativity and productive innovation. The true innovator is action oriented in approaching things.

These eight basic rules of thumb can be practiced by anyone. No special gift or creative talent is needed. Like the heuristics of quality management—search for the vital few, focus on the customer, the next person in the process is your customer, and so on—the basic heuristics of directed creativity lead to productive expertise. While using the heuristics of either quality management or directed creativity is no guarantee of success, knowing such heuristics shortens the learning curve and raises the chances of success.

Figure 21.4 presents a model for the directed creativity process (analogous to the familiar improvement process models in quality management). Models are a special type of heuristics. In contrast to heuristic statements that provide a focused gem of wise advice, models strive to capture the whole of something in a overall, integrated fashion; showing sequence, interconnection, pattern, flow, and organization. Models and heuristic statements work together to provide scripts to guide higher-order thinking.

The model in Figure 21.4 is a synthesis from among the dozens of models for the creative process that have appeared in the literature since the 1930s. As such, it represents a great deal of accumulated experience in creative thinking and organizational innovation.[31]

Let me walk you through the model, beginning at the 9:00 A.M. position on the circle. We live every day in the same world as everyone else, but creative thinking begins with careful *observation* of that world coupled with thoughtful *analysis* of how things work and fail. These mental processes

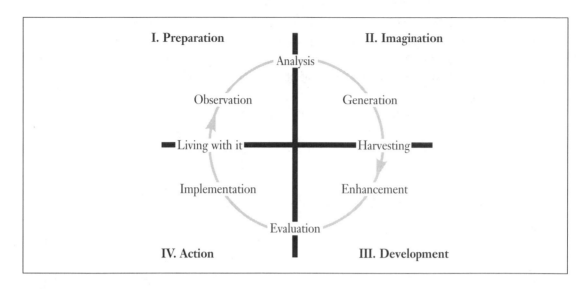

Figure 21.4. A model for the process of directed creativity.

create a store of concepts in our memories. Using this store, we *generate* novel ideas to meet specific needs by actively searching for associations among these concepts. Seeking the balance between creative thinking and critical judgment, we then *harvest* and further *enhance* our ideas before we subject them to a final, practical *evaluation*. But it is not enough just to have creative thoughts; ideas have no value until we put in the work to *implement* them. Every new idea that is put into practice (that is, every innovation) changes the world we live in, which restarts the cycle of observation and analysis. Directed creativity simply means that we make purposeful mental movements to avoid the pitfalls associated with our mental mechanisms at each step of this process of searching for novel and useful ideas.

It is important to note that this model, as well as the writings of many prominent creativity experts, asserts that creativity is *a balance of imagination and analysis*. Our model of the cycle of directed creativity makes it clear that practitioners of quality management need not throw out their traditional strengths in analysis. Quality managers have both a lot to offer and a lot to learn when it comes to creative thinking. But there is clearly a great deal of overlap between the traditions of quality management and those of creative thinking. It is time for us to recognize those overlaps and enhance the field of quality management through yet another acquisition of tools from another discipline.

Three Principles Behind All Tools for Directed Creativity

Just as there are tools that bring the theory and principles of quality management into practical application, there are literally hundreds of tools that help us implement the general advice above in directed creativity. (See, for example, the works of de Bono,[32] Higgins,[33] Koberg and Bagnall,[34] McGartland,[35] Michalko,[36] Plsek,[37] VanGundy,[38] and von Oech.[39,40] These books contain at least 250 tools for creative thinking.) While there are many methods, all such methods are based on three simple principles: *attention*, *escape*, and *movement*.[41,42]

To illustrate these basic principles, imagine a quality improvement team in a primary care physician's office, working to improve the flow of information from specialists when patients are referred. Creative thinking about this problem could begin by paying *attention* to the fact that we usually think that it is the responsibility of the specialist's office to type up consult notes and send these to the primary care physician. We could *escape* this paradigm by asking, "What if they passed a law saying that it was illegal for specialist's offices to do word processing?" If we can turn off the mental processes of judgment that cause us to reject this question out of hand, then we can proceed to creative *movement* in our thinking. For example, if they passed such a law, we could provide a voice mailbox in the primary care physician's office where specialists could dictate consult notes immediately following the encounter with the patient. The primary care physician's office staff could then type up the consult notes, keep a copy for its records, and send a copy to the specialist. In this way, the primary care physician would have immediate access to the results of the specialist consult. As a side benefit, the primary care physician's office staff could even track to make sure that the patient kept the appointment with the specialist. This is a clear quality improvement with important implications for quality of care, especially as we move to capitation and gate-keeping.

The key point here is that we can use the three basic principles of attention, escape, and movement whenever we need to be creative on demand. These three principles suggest that there are a potentially infinite number of ways to direct ourselves toward creative thoughts. Indeed, this explains why there are so many different tools in the literature. Anything that helps us pay *attention* in a different way, *escape* our current mental patterns, and keep *moving* in our thoughts will support our efforts at directed creativity.

Using these principles, we can invent our own methods for directed creativity to fit the various situations we encounter. We can now see how these three simple principles could have aided the late medications QI team. When the team members realized that they were stuck, they could have concocted their own tools to get them unstuck. The principle of attention suggests that they might have begun by listing the elements of the situation and describing to themselves how each element was intended to contribute to the solution to the problem. For example, elements in the log book solution and their intended contributions include the following:

Patient	Passively waits to receive meds
Nurses	Recognize med time and deliver meds
Medical record	Source of information about med times
Physician	Prescribes med timing
Log book	Chronological listing of med times as a reminder to nurses

The principle of escape suggests that the next step would be to provocatively challenge the current elements in the situation. For example,

- How can we get the patient and family more actively involved in remembering medication times?

- What if they passed a law saying the patients had to *give* meds as well as receive them?

- Who else, besides nurses, could take responsibility for remembering meds times?

- Who else has information about meds times, and how can we constructively involve these people in solving the late meds problem?

- How would the people of *Star Trek* deal with this problem?

Listing these questions leads naturally to the next principle, movement. My guess is that you have already generated some ideas just by reading the questions. Simply reading the questions is enough to activate new mental valleys in your memory. Once these are activated, the mind races to make some connection to the mental valley that contains the original problem. While a few connections will occur automatically, deliberate thought can generate even more ideas.

The key barriers to this mental movement are the mental processes of judgment (refer to Figure 21.1). For example, the first escape question immediately made me think that perhaps we could give the medication times list to the patient or family members and ask them to call the nurses' station to request the meds at the appropriate times. But as soon as that idea occurred to me, judgment intervened and told me that some patients would be too sick to do this, there are potential liability issues here, some people would see this as the hospital cutting back on services, and so on. Judgment seeks to squelch mental movement and drive us back into the mental valley from which we came.

So after compiling the list of escape questions, the team should take these and generate as many ideas as possible through mental movement and free association. The rules of brainstorming—no judgment or criticism, go for quantity, build on others' idea—are a useful backdrop. But notice the difference between directed creativity and a standard brainstorming session. Typically, in a brainstorming session, the leader reviews the rules of brainstorming with the group and then simply says, "Okay, so what ideas do you have?" Judgment is suspended and creative ideas are encouraged, *but there is no new direction for thinking.* The modern theory of directed creativity acknowledges the need to first rise out of the current mental valley. This is why there is a purposeful phase of preparation preceding the imagination phase in the directed creativity cycle in Figure 21.4.

Now that we have a better understanding of the mechanics of thinking, we can practice deliberate and focused attention and escape. More importantly, *anyone* can practice deliberate and focused attention and escape. If we then practice flexibility in our thinking, truly suspend judgment, and allow mental movement to take place, *anyone can come up with a creative idea.* Figure 21.5 will serve as a quick memory jogger regarding these key principles.

The mechanics of mind (Figures 21.1 and 21.2), the heuristics of directed creativity (Figure 21.3), the directed creativity cycle (Figure 21.4), and the three basic principles behind all creativity tools (Figure 21.5) form the core theory of directed creativity. In the next portion of this chapter we will examine a few of the many tools for creative thinking and begin applying them to the issues facing mangers in health care today.

Attention	Escape	Movement
To what?	From what?	In what sense?
• Elements in the current reality	• Current mental patterns	• In time or place
• Features, attributes, and categories	• Time and place	• To another point of view
• Assumptions, patterns, and paradigms	• Early judgment	• Free association
• Metaphors and analogies	• Barriers and rules	• Building on ideas
• What works and does not work	• Your past experiences	
• Anything you don't normally pay attention to		

Figure 21.5. The three basic principles behind all methods for directed creativity.

Some Tools for Directed Creativity and Their Application to the Management of Quality in Health Care

Suppose you were asked to set up a clinic in a new medical facility. What are your existing mental patterns associated with the topic of clinic? You are probably imagining an entrance, a receptionist's desk, a waiting area, exam rooms, patients sitting in exam rooms, and so on. Why do you imagine these things? Because they are your *experience* of clinics—quite simply, we have come to believe that these elements actually define what we mean by a clinic. A health care manager asked to design a new clinic might make some incremental improvements in these elements, but it is highly likely that each of them would be present in the final design. Fortunately, our mental pattern matching system is capable of more than just replaying existing patterns with minor variations. And, also fortunately, there are many tools we can use to direct our creative thinking.

Escape the Obvious. Suppose we focused for just a moment on the element of the existing pattern called "the waiting room" (attention) and then asked our minds to step outside of it (escape and movement). While we tend to think that there is an obvious need for a waiting room in a clinic, suppose you could not have a waiting room. What would you do if they passed a law making it illegal to have a waiting room?

Such a question—in the creative thinking literature, it is called a *provocation*[43]—invites our minds to explore, temporarily, a new reality. The astounding truth about the cognitive system we all possess is that, once invited, the mind will make some sense out of an otherwise nonsense suggestion.

For example, in a waiting room–less world we would focus on developing better ways of coordinating the arrival of patients and the availability of clinicians. A practical, yet creative idea might be to issue magnetic strip cards to patients and have them swipe them through a card reader as they enter the parking lot. This would give a few minutes' warning that a specific patient was about to walk in. We could then get the medical record and have a nurse greet patients by name at the door, showing them to an exam room and beginning the work up immediately. A clinic with no waiting room! Try it yourself. Write down three other ways to better coordinate the arrival of patients and the availability of clinicians without a waiting room.

Of course, there will be many practical details to work out with any of the ideas generated (number of exam rooms, staffing levels, and so on). But, the simple mental process of focusing on some portion of our existing mental pattern—a portion we normally take for granted—purposefully escaping that pattern, and then moving on mentally to see what new concepts and possibilities this generates is something that anyone can do. We could proceed in similar fashion to generate a long list of creative ideas for the new clinic by simply focusing on each element in our existing mental pattern of a clinic and escaping from that element.

Be Someone Else. Another tool for stepping outside our existing mental patterns involves approaching the issue as if you were someone with a completely different experience set. For example, what creative improvement ideas (different mental valleys about how things should naturally be) would you bring to the clinic design task if you were . . .

- The manager of a fast-food restaurant? (How about a drive-through clinic?)

- A six-year-old child? (Fun, active things to occupy my mind; so how about a medical information computer that patients can access and learn from?)

- A horse? (Something to munch on, space to exercise; would patient satisfaction improve if we provided these? Could we use these in health promotion?)

- A hotel manager? (Valet service, rapid check-in for frequent guests; maybe we could mimic these in our clinic.)

- A rental car company? (No need to check in, we know you're coming and your car is waiting with the engine running; so why not have the patient walk right into an exam room that has his or her name flashing over the door?)

Again, we will need to develop some of these ideas further to make them practical. But notice that by simply directing our thinking along randomly selected lines—in this case, various occupations—our minds can easily generate creative possibilities.

Element (or Scene) Modification. We can apply another directed creative thinking method by focusing on common scenes in a work process. For example, imagine a patient calling on the phone to schedule an appointment in our new clinic. What are the elements of this scene? There is a patient, a scheduler, providers' schedule books, a telephone, the scheduler's desk, and so on. Now let's systematically change these elements to see what creative possibilities emerge.

- Instead of a phone, substitute a fax machine. Patients could fax in their requests for appointments listing the provider they wish to see, along with preferred dates and times (like faxing in a pizza order). Schedulers could then utilize slow times in the day to respond to these requests.

- Put the providers' calendars on the computer (instead of on paper) and let patients use a modem (instead of a telephone) to schedule their own appointments (thereby substituting for the human scheduler). Or patients could send in their requests via modem, let the scheduler do some screening and matching, and then e-mail the patient with the scheduled date and time. Another way would be to partner with a bank to allow patients to use the bank's automated teller machine network to schedule appointments.

- Why not just eliminate schedules and go to a no-appointment-necessary system?

Random Word. A seemingly bizarre suggestion, but one that makes perfect sense when you understand the flexible, pattern-matching mechanism of the mind, is to use a randomly selected word to provoke creative ideas. If we start our minds thinking down the path normally associated with a topic—we think about *clinics*—and then interject a random word—say, *umbrella*—our minds try to make sense of the connection. For example,

- An umbrella can be opened quickly when you need it. How can we design the clinic such that we can quickly open new exam rooms and staff them instantly to meet the needs of fluctuating demand? If nurses were cross-trained to do other clinic jobs such that every employee in the clinic was also a nurse, we could quickly shift them to nursing roles when needed. We could also design movable partitions to quickly convert all the space in the clinic into temporary exam rooms when needed (for example, a sliding partition covers the filing cabinets and a pad is fitted onto the table to quickly convert the file room to an exam room).

- An umbrella has spokes that come out from a central post. A thought stimulated by the umbrella spokes image is a distributed laboratory system. Drop a blood sample into a device in the exam room, the lab is alerted, the device in the exam room sends information to the lab, and the results quickly appear on a screen in the exam room. No physical movement of the specimen! One could begin to develop such a device by analyzing current lab equipment and separating the parts of the machine that handle the physical specimen (locate these parts in all the exam rooms) from the parts of the machine that process information about the specimen (locate one of these in the lab).

The random word technique works best when the word is a noun that identifies an object. The mental image of the object and the mental pattern of the topic we are focusing on come together in the mind to form combinations that yield novel thoughts. You can select a random word by taking a book, turning to a random page, and placing your finger on random points until it comes to rest on an object noun. There is no way to identify the best random word for a given topic, so don't worry about it. Select four or five random words, list multiple ideas from each, and then step back from the list to harvest and further develop the most promising thoughts.

Concept Fan and Morphological Analysis. When the topic of interest involves a process, the concept fan tool can yield multiple creative possibilities. Of course, organizations that are actively engaged in TQM/CQI will immediately recognize that most work-related topics can be expressed as processes, so this technique has wide potential.

To develop a concept fan, begin with a high-level flowchart of the traditional or current process. The left-hand side of Figure 21.6 depicts this for our clinic process. Now step back from the current process and identify the underlying concepts behind the various steps. As indicated in Figure 21.6, one underlying concept in the clinic process is that the patient and the provider must come together.

Creative possibilities emerge when we note that the current process is only one way of achieving the underlying concept. Are there other ways? Instead of the patient coming to visit the clinician,

- The clinician could travel in a van that comes to the patient.
- The patient could interact with the physician via telemetry equipment at home.
- Patients could be given an algorithm that the clinician has prepared for them. The algorithm becomes a substitute for the presence of the physician. This would eliminate many visits and phone calls; that is, "Come and see me only when certain criteria occur."

We could proceed similarly with the other steps and concepts in the process. The right-hand side of Figure 21.6 represents the beginning of a concept fan. The ideas "fan out" from the various concepts.

With the complete concept fan in hand, our next step would be to run through the fan picking up ideas from each concept to generate a potential creative design for the clinic process. One such creative clinic design scenario would be that cardiac patients are furnished telemetry equipment at home that measures vital signs and blood pressure. At appropriate intervals, the equipment signals the patient that it is time for a check-in. The patient connects the equipment and pushes a button. The home-based equipment accesses the clinic's medical record database (via the telephone line) and uploads the patient's new vital sign information. The clinic computer checks to see if the vital signs are within normal limits for that patient, as established by the physician. If so, the equipment tells the patient that all is well and automatically processes preagreed billing information for the consult. If the vital signs are outside limits, the computer might be programmed to signal the patient to increase the dosage on his or her blood pressure medicine, and then send an e-mail message for the physician to read the following morning. If the values are far outside limits, the computer could check the physician's schedule and give the patient a menu of available appointment times.

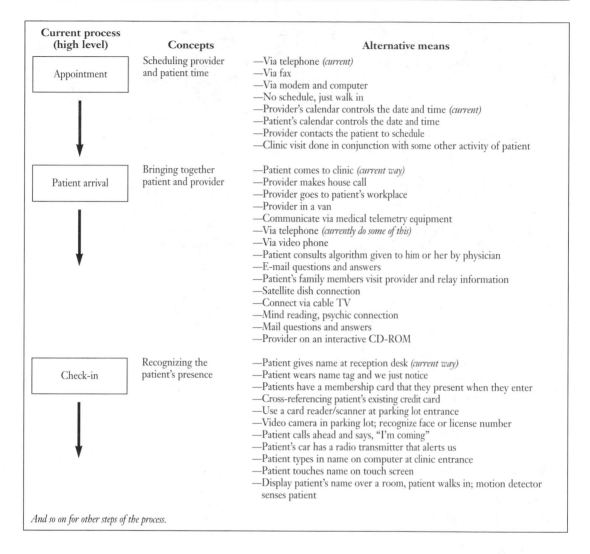

Figure 21.6. Concept fan for clinic design.

On the appointment date, the patient hooks up to the telemetry equipment to get more current readings. The equipment produces a smart card containing the new information that the patient brings to the visit. When the patient arrives at the clinic, a valet swipes the smart card through a reader indicating arrival and then parks the patient's car. The patient enters the clinic lobby, finds his or her name on the TV screen indicating the exam room number and the estimated time of physician contact (like the flight screens at the airport).

The physician enters the exam room and swipes the patient's smart card through a reader, which instantly displays the patient's medical record on a screen. The physician conducts a physical exam. Simple diagnostic tests are done via sample collection equipment in the exam room; the patient never leaves the room. If new medications are indicated, the order is electronically transmitted to the clinic pharmacy, which fills the order and delivers it to the car parking valets. When the visit is over, the physician again swipes the patient's smart card through the reader, initiating the billing process and signaling to the valet that the patient is on the way to pick up the car. The valet puts the medication bag in the car and pulls the car up. The patient exits through the lobby, presents the smart card to the valet to validate identity, gets in the car, and drives away.

All of the technology described is either currently available or well within reach in the next few years. Imagine how such a clinic would revolutionize our concept of what it means to "go to the doctor's office."

This method of developing total design concepts by making multiple runs through lists of independently generated ideas is called *morphological analysis*. It has been used by product designers since the 1950s.[44,45]

These are but a few of the many tools that support the preparation and imagination phases of the directed creativity cycle. The references cited in the Suggestions for Further Reading section at the end of this chapter provide detailed descriptions of these and many other methods. Figure 21.7 provides a brief synopsis of the tools covered in this section and several additional ones.

Harvesting, Developing, and Implementing Creative Ideas: The Bridge Between Mere Creativity and Powerful Innovation

It is important to understand that creative ideas have no value until they are put into action. Without the activities of harvesting, enhancement, and implementation (refer to the directed creativity cycle in Figure 21.4), our ideas are just so many items on a brainstormed list. With these activities, our ideas are transformed into powerful innovations that can bring benefits to those we serve.

Practitioners of quality management have a great deal of experience in implementing change in organizations. We know how to develop and execute plans. We are also familiar with the challenges on the social side of change—resistance to change, the importance of involvement, and so on. There are, however, some special considerations that we should be aware of as we develop and implement truly novel ideas.

The Application of Progressively Critical Judgment. During the imagination phase of the directed creativity cycle, it is important to suspend judgment. Now, in the development and action phases, it is time to apply judgment. Though it is easy to generate dozens (or even hundreds) of novel ideas, these ideas will not all have the same potential value. We need to decide how much additional effort to put into them, and then go on to select just a few for implementation.

So, as a first pass, we can sort our ideas into four categories.

Ready to use	Ideas that we could act on very quickly. They need only a minimum of further study in order to get started on detailed implementation planning (abbreviation: RTU).
Seedlings	Beginnings of a useful idea. A usable concept, but may not be able to do it exactly as stated. The basic idea itself needs more study and development before it is ready (abbreviation: SEED).
Useful directions	A useful broad concept or general idea, but not really fleshed out well enough at this point to evaluate. Could be sent back for more specific idea generation (abbreviation: UD).
Not ready	An idea that is simply unusable at this point in time. Maybe someday, but not anytime soon. Use this category sparingly (abbreviation: NR).

Tool	Synopsis
Escape the obvious	List assumptions, rules, obvious, or taken-for-granted aspects of the current situation. Temporarily escape these (for example, pass a law against them) and free associate to generate novel ideas.
Be someone else	List other people, occupations, animals, and so on, and then imagine what insights or approaches they would bring to your situation.
Element (or scene) modification	Focus on a scene in the current situation. List the elements in that scene; the more mundane the better. Then systematically modify or substitute those elements to see what imaginative insights you get.
Random word	Select a noun at random. Apply to your current situation whatever mental picture you get from thinking about that noun.
Concept fan	Begin with a high-level flowchart of a current process. Identify the concepts that underlie each step on the flowchart. Some steps may have multiple concepts. Now generate alternative ways to achieve each of these concepts. List these next to each concept.
Morphological analysis	Construct multiple creative scenarios by combining several ideas from lists previously generated (for example, from a concept fan). You can do this purposefully or by selecting ideas at random and forcing a coherent connection.
Purpose hierarchy	Write down a statement of the problem, opportunity, or creative challenge that you are facing. Now ask, "Why are we interested in this anyway? What's the purpose or point behind it?" Identify several such purpose statements by repeatedly asking these questions. Arrange these in a rational order; for example, from large to small, strategic to operational, crass to noble—whatever seems to fit your situation. Finally, use each of these statements of purpose as a starting point to generate creative alternatives for accomplishing that purpose. Step back from the list and see what insight you get into your original problem or creative challenge.
Word play	Write down a statement of the problem, opportunity, or creative challenge that you are facing. (You might go on to construct a purpose hierarchy.) Circle key words in your statement. Now select two key words at random and combine them; it is okay if they do not seem to go together. Apply to your current situation whatever mental picture you get from thinking about these randomly selected word pairs. Another type of creative word play involves substituting synonyms and opposites from a thesaurus for the key words. Again, apply to your current situation whatever mental picture you get from thinking about these synonyms and opposites.
Analogies	Adapt concepts, approaches, and ideas from another setting into your context. You can identify an analogy by (1) directly searching for an analogous situation, (2) randomly selecting a setting and forcing yourself to see some analogy, (3) taking a physical or mental excursion to another place looking for insights (for example, a shopping mall, a zoo), or (4) using the be-someone-else tool described above.
Cinematics	Shoot a video, take photographs, act out a role play, mentally imagine, or actually visit the current scene. Explore the scene in slow motion and stop action. Discuss what is going on with others. You are looking for things you have not noticed before about the problem and for novel mental connections.
Reversals	Identify things that you are used to thinking of in one direction only; for example, we always want to decrease costs and raise satisfaction, clinicians care for patients not the other way around. Temporarily reverse the direction and ask "What if . . . ?" Generate several responses to this question. Then practice mental movement from these thoughts to see what insights you gain into the current situation.

Figure 21.7. Some tools for preparation and imagination in the directed creativity cycle.

It is important to note that, with the exception of the not-ready category, we are rating the creative content of the ideas themselves, not our readiness or capability to implement them. A creative idea can be ready to use in the sense that we do not need more large doses of creative thought, but it may still take us several months and lots of detailed work to implement.

This simple sorting and evaluation comprises an initial harvesting. We now know where we can focus our development and action efforts if we want some immediate successes (the RTU items). We also are now in a position to commission some specific feasibility studies (the SEED items). And we can also now set up our final round of idea generation sessions (the UD items).

Following the feasibility studies and the final rounds of idea generation, we will still have many ideas (20 to 100 or more) on our ready-to-use list. Implementing this many ideas would quickly overwhelm the organization. It is important, therefore, to do a final harvesting for the purpose of reducing to a manageable level the number of implementation efforts going on at once.

I recommend harvesting about twice as many ideas as you think you can reasonably expect to implement over the next 12 months. I suggest this because several of the ideas initially selected in the harvest will not make the grade on final evaluation, while other ideas will end up being combined or streamlined. Further, going into the development phase knowing that you will want to eliminate several ideas helps avoid justification and belief preservation. To determine the number of ideas to pass on at this point in your organization, simply ask several people what they think. "Could we implement five ideas in the next year? 10? 15? 20? 25?" and so on, until you identify a consensus comfort level. In subsequent years, you might challenge the organization to continually stretch its capacity to implement innovative change.

Since early involvement aids the implementation of change, it is critically important to get many people involved in the harvesting and evaluation process. The final harvesting might be done by a relatively large group of 12 to 20 or more people. This group should include many of the people that you would want to lead the change efforts, several people who were involved in the preparation and imagination phases of the cycle, and several people whose opinions are representative of key stakeholder groups that will be impacted by the implementation of the innovations.

For the final harvesting, Majaro suggests rating the ideas as high, medium, or low on the attributes of attractiveness and compatibility.[46] *Attractiveness* refers to the idea's impact on customers (both external and internal) or the public at large. Think of this much like Noriaki Kano's notion of attractive quality.[47] Will it get us noticed? Will people like it? *Compatibility* refers to our assessment of the ease with which *we* could implement the idea. In other words, can we do it? Ideas with high-high or high-medium ratings move forward to the next stage of development. A simple multivote would be another way to accomplish this final harvesting.[48,49]

Commissioning Idea Champions. Every idea selected in the final harvesting needs an idea champion to further develop it. This can be an individual or a team. The idea champion may be assigned a single idea or multiple ideas. Use your good judgment, remember that change is hard work, and avoid overloading. Use the same care in selection and the same formality in structure that you would in forming quality teams. Finally, remember that some people who excel at idea generation can be less skilled at handling the details of implementation, and vice versa.

Enhancement. The idea champion's main task is to further develop the idea and get it ready for implementation. Figure 21.8 presents a list of questions, adapted from de Bono,[50] to guide this work. Notice how the questions guide thoughtful analysis aimed at increasing the chances of success. They

Shaping—How can we modify the idea to address objections that would otherwise cause rejection?

Tailoring—Can we modify the idea to even better fit our needs?

Strengthening—How can we increase the power or value of the idea?

Reinforcing—What can we do about weak points?

Looking toward implementation—What can we do to the idea to enhance the probability of implementation? Who must be involved?

Comparison to current—How does the idea compare to what it is replacing? Should we do further enhancement, expand or scale back the idea?

Potential faults or defects—What could possibly go wrong with this idea? What can we do?

Consequences—What are the immediate and long-term consequences of putting the idea into action?

Testability and prototyping—How can we try the idea on a small scale?

Preevaluation—How can we further modify the idea to meet the needs of those who will evaluate it next?

Figure 21.8. An idea enhancement checklist.

guide us to consider emotional and people-related issues, the strengths and weaknesses of the idea, systems effects and consequences, and the need for trials and prototypes. Though the list appears in one-question-at-a-time order, the questions should be taken together. Start anywhere on the list, consider multiple questions at the same time, and be prepared to reevaluate your work on earlier questions as you go along. When you think you are done, go through the list one final time to make sure you have not missed anything.

Expect to spend some time in enhancement. Typically, enhancement involves two to 20 hours of thoughtful work, perhaps spread over several weeks. Short-cutting enhancement is a common pitfall, leading to half-baked ideas that fail. Of course, overdoing enhancement is equally problematic. We will have difficulty in implementation if we load down the idea with too many clever features. The comparison-to-current question in the enhancement checklist suggests that we consider scaling back the idea. It might be helpful to plan a version 1, version 2, and so on to enable us to get the basic idea in place now and then systematically add features over time.

Quality management tools can play an important role in addressing the enhancement questions in Figure 21.8. The concept of multiple customers and the methods of customer needs analysis can help identify potential objections and strong points from others' points of view. Surveys and focus groups might be helpful. We can develop flowcharts of new processes, and requirements documents for new services, as a way to focus our thoughts. Benchmarking visits may enhance our thinking further. Statistical analysis tools can help us choose among alternatives and demonstrate improvements over current practices. We can use failure mode and effects analysis to explore potential faults and defects. We can also use systems diagrams to identify potential unintended consequences. In summary, our traditional strengths in analysis can be very helpful. (For more on these tools of quality management, see chapter 22.)

Enhancement is the meat of the development phase of the directed creativity cycle. The product of our work here is a more well-thought-out idea. While the enhancement questions guide us to critical thinking, we should maintain an overall positive attitude throughout this activity. We want to do everything we can to see the idea accepted by all stakeholders and successfully implemented.

Evaluation. The activities of the development phase of the directed creativity cycle culminate in evaluation. We have been using judgment throughout these activities, but we have been purposefully avoiding final judgment. The time has now come.

The creativity literature provides many suggestions relative to evaluation criteria and processes. Majaro's criteria of attractiveness and compatibility is one approach that we have already examined.[51] If you used this approach for final harvesting, you can simply repeat it here with a more critical eye on the enhanced ideas. LeBoeuf,[52] Michalko,[53] and Parnes[54] suggest additional evaluation criteria:

Effectiveness in achieving original objective	Customer reaction
Cost to implement	Revenue or cost avoidance potential
Uniqueness of the idea	Potential for enabling other innovations
Moral or legal implications	Degree of positive feeling evoked by the idea
Likelihood of success	Freedom from adverse consequences and risk
Ease of implementation	Timeliness of the idea
Availability of technology to carry it out	Match with organizational strengths
Simplicity of the idea	Degree of internal support
Sense of urgency of need	

Evaluation is an activity that should be conducted by the group of organizational leaders who collectively possess the power to allocate resources and should ask for constructive participation by others. Ask the senior leaders in the evaluation group to select criteria from the list above (or develop their own additional criteria) that seem to be a good fit for your specific situation. Then either rank order the ideas with the selected criteria implicitly in mind, or score each idea on a high-medium-low or 1 to 10 scale on each criteria.

Regardless of the method chosen, the products of the development phase of the directed creativity cycle are a few, very well-thought-out creative ideas that have support for implementation.

Implementation. The implementation of creative ideas faces the same challenges encountered in implementing any type of change in an organization. But if you have used the idea enhancement checklist in Figure 21.8, you will have already addressed many implementation issues. In addition to the results of this idea enhancement work, you will need, at a minimum, an action plan, communications plan, training plan, measurement plan, contingency plan, and improvement plan. Depending on the complexity of the innovation, the action plan might be broken down into several subsections covering purchasing, final design, information systems, human resources, and other issues. All these plans should be keyed to an integrated timeline of events.

While implementation involves overcoming some technical and logistical challenges, anyone who has ever participated in the implementation of change will know that the psychological aspects give rise to the greatest problems. Hammer and Stanton[55] advise us to expect resistance to change when implementing innovative ideas. They further suggest that the key mechanisms for overcoming such resistance are the five *I*s: incentives, information, intervention, indoctrination, and involvement.

While we normally focus on overcoming resistance to change in others, we should not overlook the importance of overcoming our own internal fears as idea champions. This is easy to overlook, because it is hard and uncomfortable to reflect on one's own attitudes and beliefs. But because justification and belief preservation are such strong properties of the mechanics of our minds, I strongly urge you to face up to this challenge proactively. Realize that while good inward fear keeps us from doing stupid, inappropriate, or immoral things, unproductive inward fears keep us from stepping out in new, innovative directions. If we think about it, we can usually discern the difference. (See Ryan and Oestreich[56] for interesting research on the effects of fear on creativity in organizations.)

Basdur suggests a number of good techniques for confronting our own fears.[57] Among these are the following:

- Write down the worst thing that could happen. (Often you find that it is not so bad.)

- Ask yourself, "If I wait, how much better will things be?"

- Break down big tasks into smaller pieces and start tackling them.

- Reverse prioritize to say no to less important tasks that you might use as an excuse to avoid pushing ahead with your innovation.

- Set deadlines for yourself and share these commitments with others.

- Use the broccoli-first principle: Do the part you hate most first to get it out of the way.

In addition to these suggestions, I often suggest the circa exercise. *Circa* is a Latin word meaning *about*. It is used in archeology and history to indicate approximate dates of things. Similarly, in the circa exercise we date our existing process concepts. For example, a doctor's waiting room is probably circa 1950. That is about the time when doctors stopped routinely making house calls and started seeing patients almost exclusively in their offices. Except for cosmetic differences, the basic process of handling patients in a doctor's waiting room has not changed much since the 1950s. Identifying the circa date generates energy for change. We do not even need to be exact about it. When we realize that a process has remained conceptually the same for about 40 years, we are likely to react by thinking, "It really is time for a change, isn't it?"

Whatever you choose to do, be proactive and open. Admitting your own fear of the unknown will help others to deal with theirs. Acting frustrated and superior is a common mistake that many change leaders make in implementing creative ideas.

The final implementation of a creative idea completes the directed creativity cycle in Figure 21.4 and fulfills the definition of innovation. But in the excitement of completing a trip through the directed creativity cycle, do not forget to prepare for the next cycle. Foster has documented the sad tales of many successful organizations that rested on their past innovations and lost their imaginations to conservative thinking.[58] Customers are increasingly demanding innovation. Competitors are increasingly supplying innovation. Today, and in the future, *it is the rate of innovation that is decisive.*

Common Applications of Directed Creativity in Health Care Management

We have covered the theory and tools of directed creativity and seen several examples of its use. Table 21.1 provides some specific summary advice on the use of directed creativity in four common applications in health care management. The advice is catalogued according to the four phases of the directed creativity cycle depicted in Figure 21.4. For reference, recall that Figure 21.7 provides synopses of these tools.

Table 21.1. Use of directed creativity in common applications of health care management.

Directed creativity cycle phase	Application			
	Problem solving and incremental improvement	**Process design and reengineering**	**Customer needs analysis**	**Strategic planning**
Preparation (attention, escape)	Tools and methods: List assumptions, rules, obvious things Develop purpose hierarchy List word plays Identify potential analogies Plan for cinematics Identify items for reversals	Tools and methods: List assumptions, rules, obvious things Begin concept fan Identify circa dates for major concepts Develop purpose hierarchy List word plays Identify potential analogies Identify items for reversals	Tools and methods: List assumptions and obvious/nonobvious customers Begin concept fan with underlying dimensions of quality and customer needs drivers as concepts Develop purpose hierarchy List word plays Identify items for reversals	Tools and methods: List assumptions, rules, obvious things Notice circa dates Develop purpose hierarchy List word plays on current mission statement Identify items for reversals Notice customers' world; notice ideas outside health care
Imagination (escape, movement)	Tools and methods: Be someone else Random words Scene modification Escape the obvious Alternatives from fixed concepts, purpose hierarchy, and word plays Explore analogies Cinematics Reversals Involve many people and use rules of brainstorming	Tools and methods: Be someone else Random words Scene modification Escape the obvious Alternatives on concept fan, then morphological analysis Alternatives from purpose hierarchy and word plays Explore analogies Reversals Involve many people and use rules of brainstorming	Tools and methods: Random words Scene modification Escape the obvious Alternatives on concept fan, purpose hierarchy, and word plays Reversals Search for new uses for existing services and elements Focus groups react to prototype/scenario Involve many people and use rules of brainstorming	Tools and methods: Escape the obvious Be someone else; what strategy would other leaders pursue? Alternatives on purpose hierarchy and word plays Reversals Search for new uses for existing services and elements Focus groups reacting to futuristic scenarios Involve many people and use rules of brainstorming
Development (attention to detail, movement to action)	Tools and methods: Harvesting Enhancement checklist Evaluation criteria Involve many people to begin building support for change	Tools and methods: Harvesting Idea champion/team Morphological analysis Enhancement checklist Evaluation criteria Involve many people to begin building support for change	Tools and methods: Harvesting Idea champion/team Morphological analysis Enhancement checklist Evaluation criteria Consider who you must "sell to" to build support	Tools and methods: Harvesting Idea champion/team Morphological analysis Enhancement checklist Evaluation criteria Consider who you must "sell to" to build support
Action (attention to resistance, movement in action)	Expect resistance and deal with it directly Overcommunicate by a factor of three Be prepared to deal with the unexpected	Expect resistance and deal with it directly Overcommunicate by a factor of three Be prepared to deal with the unexpected	Sell the ideas and move on to creative design Overcommunicate by a factor of three Be prepared to deal with the unexpected	Sell the ideas and move on to creative design Overcommunicate by a factor of three Be prepared to deal with the unexpected

While the tools and methods listed under each application are not the only way to succeed, they are a good place to start. Do not be afraid to experiment with other methods, either ones that you have read about or ones that you invented yourself. Anything that you do to provide attention, escape, and movement will help you produce creative ideas.

What Leaders Can Do to Stimulate Creativity in Health Care Organizations

We have seen that creative thinking is a mental ability that everyone possesses. But if creative thinking is as straightforward as it seems, why isn't innovation more commonplace? The answer lies in realizing that innovation is a risky proposition. Even if the traditional approach is poor, at least we know that it is not disastrous. Who can give us such assurances about a new, creative idea? There is simply no way to know until we try.

Affinity or aversion to risk is an element of the cognitive processes of judgment and choice depicted in Figure 21.1. Our orientation toward risk is both an individual personality trait and a product of the organizational culture within which we work. Establishing a climate where taking a risk is rewarded is, therefore, one of the chief challenges for health care leaders who desire higher levels of creativity in their organizations. (For a more comprehensive look at the organizational barriers to creativity, see Adams[59] and Ryan and Oestreich.[60])

One way leaders can signal that risk taking is desired is to establish a creative focus list for the organization. This is a list of topic areas for creative thinking that is widely publicized and clearly endorsed by senior leaders. The focus list is compiled by completing the sentence, "We need creative ideas in the area of . . ." For example, such a list might ask members of the organization to focus their thinking for a predefined time (say, two months) on waiting rooms, meetings, children as customers, reducing wastage of food, and so on. Creative ideas in these areas are submitted to a senior manager, who commits to implement as many of them as practical.

Another mechanism for establishing an organizational culture that values innovation is to set up a pool of resources for pilot testing creative ideas. For example, industrial giant 3M offers seed money and time away from other job responsibilities for employees to develop their creative ideas. Organizations should, of course, establish ground rules about the allocation of such funds, but these guidelines should not be too restrictive. Remember, the goal is to increase risk taking; if the guidelines are too strict, few will bother to apply for fear of being rejected.

A final suggestion for stimulating a creative culture involves increasing the risk associated with *not* taking a risk. If you have an organizational system that provides performance feedback to individuals, make "trying out new ideas" a criteria in that system. The feedback should *not* focus on whether the ideas were successful in the traditional sense; this will only reduce risk taking by driving people to try only those ideas that they are reasonably sure will work (that is, those ideas that are close to the established patterns). Rather, while success is desirable, the focus of the performance feedback should be on the number of ideas tested and the resultant learning from those trials.

These are but a few suggestions for action by senior leaders. Stimulating creativity in an organization is an appropriate topic, itself, for creative thinking.

Conclusion

If you can think, you can think creatively. Directed creativity is the mental process of purposefully altering and linking mental patterns to form new ideas. While the techniques of directed creativity may seem silly or irrational when you first hear them, they make perfect sense when we understand the flexible pattern matching ability of our minds.

Health care organizations are just beginning to experiment with these techniques—and it is not a moment too soon. The demands of the health care marketplace and the pace of change in the industry are combining to make creative thinking an essential competency. The techniques of directed creativity have an important role to play alongside the traditional techniques of quality management as we meet the future.

Suggestions for Further Reading

In the space of a book chapter, we can only touch on the basics of a topic as rich as creative thinking. Readers interested in learning more about the topics covered in this chapter should consult the following references, cited in order of preference. Additional resources are available at the author's Internet web site, http://www.directedcreativity.com.

- Need for creativity: Plsek,[61] and Carr[62]

- Mechanics of mind: de Bono,[63,64] Perkins,[65] Plsek,[66] and Osherson and Smith[67]

- Tools for creativity: Higgins,[68] de Bono,[69] VanGundy,[70] Plsek,[71] Koberg and Bagnall,[72] Michalko[73]

- Application of creativity in work: Plsek,[74] Higgins,[75] Carr[76]

- Management of change in organizations: Beckhard and Harris,[77] Dalziel and Schoonover,[78] Hutton,[79] Kanter, Stein, and Jick,[80] and O'Toole[81]

- Organizational barriers to creativity: Adams,[82] Ryan and Oestreich,[83] and Carr[84]

Discussion Questions for a One-Hour Executive Meeting

1. How important to the future of our organization is our ability to generate creative ideas? Can we succeed with the follower strategy—wait for other organizations to generate innovations and then just replicate them? Be specific in supporting your point of view.

2. List specific creative ideas that have been generated and implemented in our organization in the last two years. How creative were each of these ideas—that is, to what degree were they different from the status quo? To what extent were they truly new ideas versus copies of what others had already done? How risky was it to implement these ideas?

3. What specifically have organizational leaders done to promote creativity in our organization?

4. What topic areas should we include in a creative focus list for our organization?

Notes

1. P. Drucker, "The Information Executives Truly Need," *Harvard Business Review* 73, no. 1 (January-February 1995): 54–62.

2. D. N. Perkins, *The Mind's Best Work* (Cambridge, Mass.: Harvard University Press, 1981).

3. R. W. Weisberg, *Creativity: Beyond the Myth of Genius* (New York: W.H. Freeman, 1993).

4. P. E. Plsek, "Directed Creativity," *Quality Management in Health Care* 2, no. 3 (spring 1994): 62–76.

5. P. E. Plsek, *Creativity, Innovation, and Quality* (Milwaukee: ASQC Quality Press, 1997).

6. W. E. Deming, *The New Economics* (Cambridge, Mass.: MIT Center for Advanced Engineering Study, 1993), 61.

7. Plsek, *Creativity, Innovation, and Quality.*

8. D. Levy, "Medical Glue Sometimes a Cut Above Stitches," *USA Today*, 11 May 1995, D1.

9. Plsek, *Creativity, Innovation, and Quality.*

10. E. de Bono, *Mechanism of Mind* (London: Penguin Books, 1969).

11. E. de Bono, *I Am Right You Are Wrong* (London: Penguin Books, 1990).

12. D. N. Osherson and E. E. Smith, eds., *An Invitation to Cognitive Science: Thinking, Volume 3* (Cambridge, Mass.: MIT Press, 1990).

13. Perkins, *The Mind's Best Work.*

14. Plsek, "Directed Creativity."

15. Plsek, *Creativity, Innovation, and Quality.*

16. R. J. Sternberg, ed., *The Nature of Creativity* (Cambridge: Cambridge University Press, 1988).

17. de Bono, *Mechanism of Mind.*

18. E. de Bono, *Serious Creativity* (New York: HarperCollins Publishers, 1992).

19. G. Wallas, *The Art of Thought* (New York: Harcourt Brace, 1926).

20. G. Polya, *How to Solve It: A New Aspect of Mathematical Method*, 2d ed. (Princeton, N.J.: Princeton University Press, 1957).

21. A. Newell and H. A. Simon, *Human Problem Solving* (Englewood Cliffs, N.J.: Prentice-Hall, 1972).

22. K. J. Holyoak, "Problem Solving," in *An Invitation to Cognitive Science: Thinking, Volume 3*, edited by D. N. Osherson and E. E. Smith (Cambridge, Mass.: MIT Press, 1990).

23. Perkins, *The Mind's Best Work*, 192.

24. J. M. Juran, *Managerial Breakthrough* (New York: McGraw-Hill, 1964), 43.

25. A. D. De Groot, *Thought and Choice in Chess* (The Hague: Mouton, 1965).

26. Holyoak, "Problem Solving."

27. Plsek, *Creativity, Innovation, and Quality.*

28. D. B. Wallace and H. E. Gruber, *Creative People at Work* (New York: Oxford University Press, 1989).

29. D. Shekerjian, *Uncommon Genius: How Great Ideas Are Born* (New York: Penguin Books, 1990).

30. Weisberg, *Creativity: Beyond the Myth of Genius.*

31. Plsek, *Creativity, Innovation, and Quality.*

32. de Bono, *Serious Creativity.*

33. J. M. Higgins, *101 Creative Problem Solving Techniques* (Winter Park, Fla.: New Management Publishing Co., 1994).

34. D. Koberg and J. Bagnall, *The All New Universal Traveler: A Soft-Systems Guide To Creativity, Problem-Solving, and the Process of Reaching Goals* (Los Altos, Calif.: William Kaufmann, 1981).

35. G. McGartland, *Thunderbolt Thinking: Transform Your Insights and Options into Powerful Results* (Austin, Tex.: Bernard-Davis, 1994).

36. M. Michalko, *Thinkertoys: A Handbook of Business Creativity for the 90s* (Berkeley, Calif.: Ten Speed Press, 1991).

37. Plsek, *Creativity, Innovation, and Quality.*

38. A. B. VanGundy, *Idea Power* (New York: American Management Association, 1992).

39. R. von Oech, *A Whack on the Side of the Head* (New York: Warner Books, 1983).

40. R. von Oech, *A Kick in the Seat of the Pants* (New York: Harper Perennial, 1986).

41. P. E. Plsek, "Tapping Creativity in Healthcare Organizations," *The Quality Letter for Healthcare Leaders: CQI Annual 1995* (Rockville, Md.: Bader & Associates).

42. Plsek, *Creativity, Innovation, and Quality.*

43. de Bono, *Serious Creativity.*

44. F. Zwicky, *Discovery, Invention, Research Through the Morphological Approach* (New York: MacMillan, 1966).

45. J. L. Adams, *The Care and Feeding of Ideas* (Reading, Mass.: Addison-Wesley, 1986).

46. S. Majaro, *The Creative Gap: Managing Ideas for Profit* (London: Longman, 1988).

47. N. Kano, N. Seraku, F. Takahashi, and S. Tsuji, "Attractive Quality and Must-Be Quality" *Quality* 14, no. 2 (1984): 39–48.

48. P. R. Scholtes, *The Team Handbook* (Madison, Wis.: Joiner Associates, 1988).

49. Higgins, *101 Creative Problem Solving Techniques.*

50. de Bono, *Serious Creativity.*

51. Majaro, *The Creative Gap.*

52. M. LeBoeuf, *Imagineering: How to Profit from Your Creative Powers* (New York: McGraw-Hill, 1980).

53. Michalko, *Thinkertoys.*

54. S. J. Parnes, *Sourcebook for Creative Problem Solving* (Buffalo, N.Y.: Creative Education Foundation Press, 1992).

55. M. Hammer with S. A. Stanton, *The Reengineering Revolution* (New York: Harper-Collins, 1995).

56. K. D. Ryan and D. K. Oestreich, *Driving Fear Out of the Workplace* (San Francisco: Jossey-Bass, 1991).

57. M. Basdur, *The Power of Innovation: How to Make Innovation a Way of Life and Put Creative Solutions to Work* (London: Pitmann Publishing, 1995), 121–124.

58. R. Foster, *Innovation: The Attacker's Advantage* (New York: Summit Books, 1986).

59. J. L. Adams, *Conceptual Blockbusting* (Reading, Mass.: Addison-Wesley, 1974).

60. Ryan and Oestreich, *Driving Fear Out of the Workplace.*

61. Plsek, *Creativity, Innovation, and Quality.*

62. C. Carr, *The Competitive Power of Constant Creativity* (New York: AMACOM, 1994).

63. de Bono, *Serious Creativity.*

64. de Bono, *Mechanism of Mind.*

65. Perkins, *The Mind's Best Work.*

66. Plsek, "Directed Creativity."

67. Osherson and Smith, *An Invitation to Cognitive Science.*

68. Higgins, *101 Creative Problem Solving Techniques.*

69. de Bono, *Serious Creativity*.

70. VanGundy, *Idea Power*.

71. Plsek, *Creativity, Innovation, and Quality*.

72. Koberg and Bagnall, *The All New Universal Traveler*.

73. Michalko, *Thinkertoys*.

74. Plsek, *Creativity, Innovation, and Quality*.

75. Higgins, *101 Creative Problem Solving Techniques*.

76. Carr, *The Competitive Power of Constant Creativity*.

77. R. Beckhard and R. T. Harris, *Organizational Transitions: Managing Complex Change*, 2d ed. (Reading, Mass.: Addison-Wesley, 1987).

78. M. M. Dalziel and S. C. Schoonover, *Changing Ways: A Practical Tool for Implementing Change Within Organizations* (New York: AMACOM, 1988).

79. D. W. Hutton, *The Change Agent's Handbook: A Survival Guide for Quality Improvement Champions* (Milwaukee: ASQC Quality Press, 1995).

80. R. M. Kanter, B. Stein, and T. Jick, *The Challenge of Organizational Change* (New York: Simon & Schuster, 1992).

81. J. O'Toole, *Leading Change: Overcoming the Ideology of Comfort and the Tyranny of Custom* (San Francisco: Jossey-Bass, 1995).

82. Adams, *Conceptual Blockbusting*.

83. Ryan and Oestreich, *Driving Fear Out of the Workplace*.

84. Carr, *The Competitive Power of Constant Creativity*.

Paul E. Plsek is an independent consultant with 20 years' experience in the field of quality management. He is the former director of AT&T's corporate quality planning. He is widely recognized for his pioneering efforts to bring modern approaches of quality management to health care. Plsek is the author of numerous articles and the two books *Quality Improvement Tools* and *Creativity, Innovation, and Quality*.

Section V
Pilot Changes

Chapter 22

Techniques for the Management of Quality

Paul E. Plsek

The modern approach to the management of quality in health care borrows heavily from the quality management science in use for decades in general industry (see, for example, Berwick,[1] Laffel and Blumenthal,[2] Berwick, Godfrey, and Roessner,[3] Blumenthal,[4] and Gaucher and Coffey[5]). Industrial quality management science—also known as continuous quality improvement (CQI) or total quality management (TQM)—is an eclectic collection of techniques. While some were developed specifically for use in quality management, most are borrowed from the fields of statistics, engineering, operations research, management science, market research, and psychology. In this chapter, I will review a basic collection of techniques using an outline proposed by J. M. Juran, who asserts that quality management science can be understood as comprising techniques for improvement, planning, and measurement (control).[6] For those curious about the definition or meaning of a specific tool or method, a glossary can be found near the end of this chapter.

While Juran's trilogy makes a convenient taxonomy for a review such as this, the classification system proposed here should not be taken as rigid. Tools for improvement can also be used for planning; planning a process can be seen as an improvement; and measurement naturally overlaps with the other two areas. Figure 22.1 describes the elemental tool kit for quality management that I will cover here.

Techniques for Quality Improvement

Quality improvement techniques, specifically those associated with quality improvement projects, have served as a natural point of introduction to modern quality management science in many health care organizations.

Quality Improvement Projects and Teams. A quality improvement project is a focused effort to address a specific improvement opportunity. For example, we might initiate a project to improve waiting times in a clinic or to reduce medication errors in a hospital. In undertaking such a project, senior leaders in an organization charter a quality improvement team, typically consisting of three to nine people who routinely work in the process under investigation. These teams are often multidisciplinary and multilevel in composition, achieving what Juran calls a "breakthrough in organization."[7]

Improvement Methods	Planning Methods

Improvement Methods

Quality improvement project and teams

Models for improvement

Tools for process description
    Flowcharts (chronological description)
    Cause-and-effect diagrams (casual system description)

Tools for data collection
    Check sheets
    Data sheets
    Interviews
    Surveys

Tools for data analysis
    For categorical data
      Pie charts
      Bar charts
      Pareto diagrams
    For continuous data
      Average, median (center)
      Range, standard deviation (spread)
      Histograms (shape)
      Line graphs (sequence)
    To study relationships between variables
      Scatter diagrams
    To determine stability of a process
      Control charts

Advanced tool: Design of experiments

Tools for collaborative work
    Brainstorming
    Boarding
    Multivoting
    Decision matrices
    Composite techniques (for example, nominal group)

Planning Methods

Management and planning tools
    Affinity diagram
    Relations diagram
    Tree diagram
    Process decision program chart
    Failure mode and effects analysis
    Activity network diagram

Models for process design

Critical paths, clinical guidelines, and algorithms

Models for strategic planning
    The annual quality plan
    Hoshin planning/strategic quality management
    Organization-as-a-system exercise

Customer needs analysis
    Dimensions of quality
    Focus groups and surveys
    Moments of truth/critical incident technique

Advanced tool: Quality function deployment

Measurement Methods

Traditional approaches in health care

Framework for a comprehensive measurement system
    Clinical outcomes
    Customer perceptions of quality
    Internal process performance
    Financial performance

Benchmarking
    Internal benchmarking
    Competitive benchmarking
    Functional (or group) benchmarking
    Generic benchmarking

Figure 22.1. A basic, but comprehensive, took kit from the quality management series.

Models for Improvement. To guide the work of these improvement teams, many organizations adopt a quality improvement model. A model provides a high-level road map to remind the team to thoroughly explore the work process under study and to rely on the scientific method to guide decisions. In addition to guiding improvement efforts, these models also establish a common approach and vocabulary for improvement. This enhances both the efficiency of training and the transferability of results across an organization.

    Figure 22.2 shows an example of such a model from the Virginia Mason Medical Center in Seattle. While there are literally dozens of such models in common use, I have shown that all derive from a common set of principles.[8] Chief among these principles are a profound understanding of work processes, involvement of staff, and use of the scientific method. For example, the improvement model in Figure 22.2 reminds the team of these three principles when it suggests "learn and define

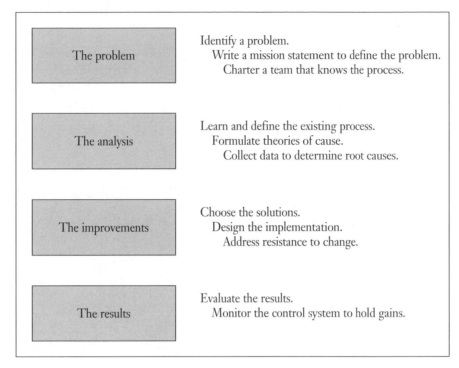

The problem
- Identify a problem.
  - Write a mission statement to define the problem.
    - Charter a team that knows the process.

The analysis
- Learn and define the existing process.
  - Formulate theories of cause.
    - Collect data to determine root causes.

The improvements
- Choose the solutions.
  - Design the implementation.
    - Address resistance to change.

The results
- Evaluate the results.
  - Monitor the control system to hold gains.

Source: Virginia Mason Medical Center, Seattle, Washington.

Figure 22.2. The quality improvement model used to guide project teams at the Virginia Mason Medical Center.

the existing process," "charter a team that knows the process," and "collect data to determine root causes."

Other models also prominently reflect the cycle of divergent and convergent thinking that is critical to effective improvement.[9] Divergent thinking—thinking broadly, exploring various options, and avoiding being locked into traditional approaches—is reflected in improvement models through phrases such as "list opportunities," "form theories of cause," and "develop alternative solutions and controls." Convergent thinking—focusing our efforts, making choices, and getting down to business—is likewise reflected in suggestions to "form a team," "identify root causes," "implement solutions and controls," and "check performance."

Regardless of the specific model used, the work of improvement teams is also aided by a collection of simple engineering and statistical tools. These tools are described fully in a variety of references. (See, for example, Berwick, Godfrey, and Roessner,[10] Gaucher and Coffey,[11] Juran,[12] Wadsworth, Stephens, and Godfrey,[13] Gitlow et al.,[14] Plsek, Onnias, and Early,[15] and Ishikawa.[16]) For classification purposes, we can identify four groups: tools for process description, data collection, data analysis, and collaborative work. These tools are listed in Figure 22.1; some are also schematically displayed in Figure 22.3.

Tools for Process Description. A flowchart graphically depicts the sequence of steps in a work process. It is a chronological description of a process. A flowchart consists of terse descriptions of activities written inside simple symbols (for example, "Take history and physical" or "Is information current?")

Flowchart

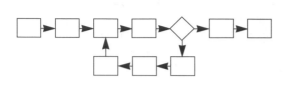

Cause-and-effect diagram

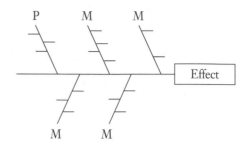

Bar charts

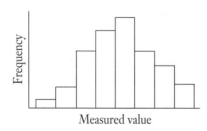

Pareto diagram

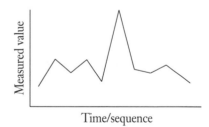

Histogram

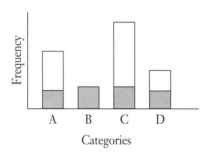

Line graph

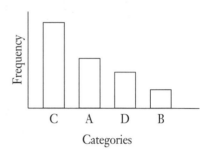

Scatter diagram

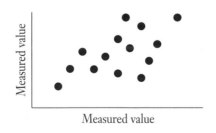

Control chart

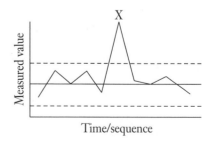

Figure 22.3. Schematic depiction of the graphical tools most commonly used in quality improvement efforts.

These symbols are then connected with arrows to indicate the sequence of events. In health care, flowcharts can be used to describe the flow of patients (the process for admitting), information (the handling of lab orders and test results), materials (the flow of supplies from receiving to the exam rooms), or thought (the clinical algorithm for the treatment of low back pain).

The description of the process can be at any level of detail. Typically, we begin with a high-level conceptual view consisting of three to six major steps, and then get successively more detailed as we focus in on particularly important segments of the process. Sometimes, particularly in early process improvement efforts, the flowchart is the only tool we need. As teams document the sequence of activities, they often uncover redundant steps, wasted effort, and unnecessary complexity. In such cases, improvement can be a simple matter of common sense.

The cause-and-effect diagram is a description of the process at a causal level. Consider, for example, the problem of HMO members being seen by a specialist without their medical record. An improvement team might have a flowchart describing the sequence of events involved in transferring a record from the referring primary care clinic to the specialist, but they are still faced with the question, "What causes missing medical records?" While the natural instinct is to blame people for not doing their jobs properly, quality management theorists point out that work processes are complex causal systems consisting of people, machines, materials, methods, and measurements; the so-called "4 Ms and a P."[17,18,19]

The classic cause-and-effect diagram, depicted schematically in Figure 22.3, embodies this theory by reminding us to think divergently about potential causal factors in each of these categories. Hypothesized theories of cause are written on lines extending from the main categorical spines. When completed, a good diagram is balanced; that is, there are theories associated with each of the categories. For example, in the case of missing medical records, theories of cause might include the following: physicians lose them (people), errors in locator database (machines), ran out of folders (materials), cumbersome transport process (methods), and missing records are actually in file room (measurements).

Such diagrams are referred to in the literature as fishbone diagrams (because they resemble the skeleton of a fish) or Ishikawa diagrams (in honor of their originator, the late Kaoru Ishikawa). Ishikawa also describes several variants of this basic diagram;[20] for example, the process-type diagram where the theories of cause are shown on spines coming off a flowchart at the step in the process where they are likely to occur.

These two tools of process description support divergent thinking and lead naturally to the convergent thinking of the Pareto principle. The Pareto principle states that in any collection of factors that contribute to a common effect, a few of those factors will account for the majority of the effect.[21] In other words, while there may be many steps in the process and many theories about the causes of problems, a focus on the vital few steps or theories will yield the greatest improvement. Furthermore, while there may be various opinions about where to focus, the scientific method calls us to be objective in our thinking. Therefore, after using the tools for process description, improvement teams often turn to the tools for data collection in order to progress to what Juran calls a "breakthrough in knowledge."[22]

Tools for Data Collection. Data collection begins with the formulation of a specific question for which we are seeking an answer.[23] For example, our medical records flow improvement team might now want to know, "What percentage of missing medical records are associated with patients who are referred for an appointment to a specialist later in the same day that they saw their primary care physician?" and "Does that percentage vary significantly according to which primary care clinic was involved?" Note that such questions are much more specific than the vague, "What causes missing records?" This specificity will result in more effective data collection.

Having formed specific questions, the improvement team typically gathers data via one of four methods: check sheets, data sheets, interviews, and surveys. A check sheet is a form for gathering data that enables one to analyze the data directly from the form. In contrast, a data sheet is a form for recording data for which additional processing is required. For example, Figure 22.4 shows both a check sheet and a data sheet for the medical records flow team. The check sheet uses simple tick marks to construct a type of stratified bar chart that focuses our attention immediately on the processes associated with the South Street clinic. But while analysis of this check sheet is easy, notice that along with the simplicity we have lost the ability to explore the situation further. The ubiquitous Xs on the check sheet provide no follow-up information on things like patient demographics, primary care physicians, or diagnostic tests associated with these missing medical records. In contrast, the data sheet in Figure 22.4 does provides the means to dig deeper. In the end, the choice between a check sheet and data sheet depends on the trade-off between desired ease of collection and ease of analysis. Teams often use check sheets early in their efforts to determine simply if there is an opportunity for improvement, switch to a data sheet for more detailed analysis, then switch back to a check sheet to monitor performance after improvements are implemented.

Interviews and surveys are used when the question of interest involves perceptions. While interviews—either one-on-one or in focus groups of multiple participants—are time- and resource-consuming, they do allow us to ask open-ended and follow-up questions that will deepen our understanding. Surveys, on the other hand, allow us to efficiently solicit the perceptions of a large sample of people. With surveys, however, we must carefully select and phrase the questions, since we will be unable to probe deeper on responses. Again, we see a trade-off. I recommend beginning with interviews involving a small number of people. Then, use this information to inform the design of a good survey for administration to a larger group.

Tools for Data Analysis. Data collection leads naturally to data analysis. In the context of organizational quality improvement, it is important that the breakthrough in knowledge generated by the analysis be broad enough to lead to what Juran calls a "breakthrough in cultural patterns."[24] In other words, the analysis must be simple enough for everyone in the work process to understand. Otherwise, they might resist recommendations for changes. So while quality management practitioners do use advanced analytical statistical techniques such as analysis of variance (ANOVA) and tests of hypothesis (for example, t-tests), they would also point out that simple graphical analysis methods can be understood by more people. (For more on advanced statistical techniques, see Duncan,[25] or Snedecor and Cochran.[26]) This need to pay attention to the understandability of statistical analysis is especially acute in health care, where some clinicians and administrators have statistical training while the majority of staff do not. Experience in health care has shown that while the physicians, nurses, and housekeepers on a team might not be equally facile with an analysis of variance table, they can all learn to look for certain departures from the classic bell-shaped curve in a simple histogram.

In some cases, our data fall into categories (for example, number of Medicare bills rejected because of excess charge lines, missing provider ID, and so on). We can graphically display categorical data using a simple pie chart, bar graph, or a special type of bar graph called a Pareto diagram. As the name implies, a Pareto diagram graphically illustrates the Pareto principle. Categories are arranged on the horizontal axis of the graph in the order of decreasing frequency of occurrence. Bars indicate the number of occurrences in each category as read on the vertical axis. (Some practitioners also include a

Missing Medical Records Study

Instructions
- Mark an X at the top of this form for each patient seen.
- Ask, "Were you at the primary care clinic today?"
- If yes, mark the appropriate place in the bottom of this form.

Speciality: Cardiology   **Date:** January 12

Total patients seen today: X X X X X X X X X X X X X X X X X X X X X X X X X X X X X

For same-day appointment patients:

Record present	No record
X	
X	

Edwards Rd. Clinic

Record present	No record
X	
X	
X	
X	X

Edgewood Ave. Clinic

Record present	No record
	X
	X
	X
	X
X	X

South St. Clinic

Check sheet

Missing Medical Records Study

Instructions
- Complete one line of this form for each patient seen.

Speciality: Cardiology   **Date:** January 12

Member number	Specialist	\"Were you at the primary care clinic today?\"			
		Y/N	Primary care clinic	Referring physician	Tests already done

Data sheet

Figure 22.4. Comparison of a check sheet and data sheet to study the problem of missing medical records. Note that while the check sheet can be analyzed with a quick scan, the data sheet provides more detailed information for follow-up.

0 percent to 100 percent scale on a right vertical axis and overlay a line graph showing the cumulative percent of the total as each category is added.) A quick scan of the diagram indicates that the first few categories (the tallest bars) account for the majority of the occurrences (the vital few, 60 percent to 80 percent of the total), while the remainder of the categories have only a little effect (the useful many, 20 percent to 40 percent of the total).

When the data are of a continuously variable nature (for example, time, cost, productive output, or physiological data), other simple data analysis tools are valuable. Continuous data have at least four dimensions, each potentially holding information about the process from which the data comes. The first dimension of the data is the center, which we commonly summarize as an average. For example, we might analyze some data and tell a clinic operations manager that, on average, HMO members waited 33.6 minutes beyond their scheduled appointment times before being seen by a clinician. While this might be useful information, we could be even more helpful by telling the manager about the spread of the values. This second dimension of the data could be reported as the range; the shortest wait was two minutes, while the longest was 77 minutes.

As Figure 22.5 shows, the shape and sequence dimensions reveal even more information. To form the histogram (shape) of the data in Figure 22.5, we have simply tallied the frequency with which waiting times fell within various five-minute intervals. Note that the data fall into three groups; a first group that forms a bell-shaped curve centered at about 12 minutes, a second group with a broader

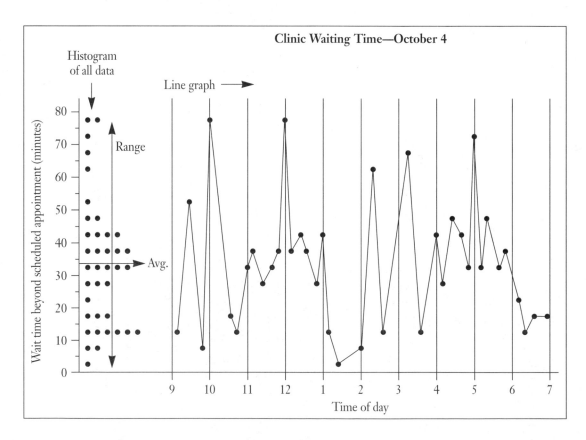

Figure 22.5. Graphical display of the four dimensions of data: center, spread, shape, and sequence. Longer waits occur in the intervals 11 a.m.–1 p.m. and 4 p.m.–6 p.m. Long waits also occur sporadically throughout the day.

bell-shaped distribution centered at around 35 minutes, and a third group of extremely long waits. The line graph (sequence) of the data indicate that the second group is associated with certain time intervals during the day (11 A.M.–1 P.M., and 4 P.M.–6 P.M.), while the extremely long waits seem to occur sporadically throughout the day. This simple graphical analysis naturally leads us to focus our investigation on theories associated with (1) staffing and scheduling policies associated with certain times of the day and (2) how we handle events that occur randomly, such as emergencies.

We can conduct further analyses using two other graphical tools: the scatter diagram and the control chart. A scatter diagram is used to study the relationship between two variables. Continuing with the waiting time example, we might want to examine the relationship between waiting time and number of appointments scheduled. Figure 22.6 shows a scatter diagram for this relationship. Each point on the graph represents paired data for an individual patient. For example, a total of 11 individuals were in the situation of having four other appointments scheduled within 15 minutes of theirs (each such individual is represented by a dot above the 4 on the horizontal axis). The waiting times for these individuals can be read on the vertical axis; it varied from a low of two minutes to a high of 68 minutes. Specifically, consider the case of patient A: There were four other appointments scheduled within 15 minutes of hers, and she waited eight minutes beyond the scheduled appointment time.

The value of the scatter diagram is that it allows us to examine the data as a whole, rather than looking at each piece of data individually. While there are certainly some cases of long waits when there are many simultaneous appointments scheduled in the clinic, the overall pattern in the data indicates that waiting time is not strongly influenced by the number of concurrent appointments. In other

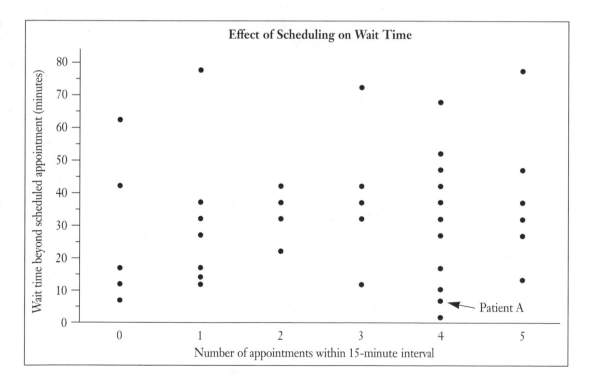

Figure 22.6. Scatter diagram showing that there is only a weak relationship between the number of simultaneous appointments and waiting time in the clinic.

words, even when the number of concurrent appointments is high (say four), the waiting time appears equally likely to be short or long (in this case, ranging from two to 68 minutes).

After the improvement team succeeds in acting on the most influential factors, it can monitor the ongoing stability of the process with a control chart. (See, for example, Carey and Lloyd,[27] Plsek,[28] Wadsworth, Stephens, and Godfrey,[29] Gitlow et al.,[30] Deming,[31] and Shewhart.[32]) A control chart is simply a line graph of the data with superimposed horizontal lines indicating statistically derived upper and lower control limits. These upper and lower limits indicate the range of variability that we would expect if the variation is subject only to small, randomly occurring factors that are inherent in the process (so-called "common cause variation"). If the measured data points fall randomly within the control limits, we say that the process is stable. Stable processes are predictable; performance will continue to fall within the limits as long as the process remains as it is. Furthermore, if the process is stable, we can also assert that further improvements in performance can come about only through fundamental changes in the process itself. Reacting to individual ups and downs in the data within the control limits (for example, "Waiting time was higher today than it was yesterday; I'll speak to the staff and admonish them to do better") is called "tampering" and is likely to be counterproductive.[33,34]

When data values fall outside the control limits or exhibit certain unnatural patterns within the control limits, there is statistical evidence of a so-called "special cause." In other words, the evidence suggests that the variation is not random. We should, therefore, be able to isolate the source of this unnatural variation and remove it from the process.

These basic tools for data analysis are being widely deployed in health care.[35,36,37] But they are not the only statistical and engineering tools for improvement. For example, modern industrial improvement teams commonly employ somewhat more sophisticated techniques for efficient design of experiments (DOE).[38] Using DOE methods, we can determine with statistical confidence, through a minimal set of measurements, the relative impact of the various factors that we believe affect the outcome of the process. Moore has documented an early application of DOE in health care that resulted in improvements in patient satisfaction in the emergency room of the Anderson Area Medical Center (Anderson, South Carolina).[39] I anticipate that the next 10 years will see continued adaptation of analytical improvement techniques into health care from industrial quality management science.

Tools for Collaborative Work. Wide-scale staff involvement in decision making and unprecedented cooperation across traditional departmental boundaries are key principles in the modern approach to quality management. Ferguson, Howell, and Batalden further assert that collaborative work is critical to organizational success because health care is a system of interdependent resources, the functioning of which depends largely on how well we communicate with one another.[40] To support this collaborative work, quality management practitioners have borrowed tools from the work of psychologists and organizational development specialists.[41,42]

The four most commonly used tools for collaborative work are brainstorming, boarding, multivoting, and decision matrices. Brainstorming involves unrestricted, free-wheeling, divergent thinking where group members list options and ideas without detailed discussion or fear of judgment.[43,44] Boarding is simply the visual display of information on easel sheets or other media that all group members can see. Brainstorming and boarding aid collaboration and consensus building by letting everyone know that their ideas are valued.

Multivoting and decision matrices, in contrast, support collaborative convergent thinking. In multivoting, group members review a long list of options, problems, theories, or suggestions and privately select the one-third they feel are most significant.[45] When the votes are tallied, a Pareto distribution typically results. In other words, some items from the divergent thinking list appear on all or nearly all of the group members lists, while other items receive few votes. The feedback to the group of the results of this voting process will either quickly expose an already existing consensus, or pinpoint options that require further discussion and another round of voting in order to build a consensus. While multivoting is useful when the criteria for making a choice are simple, decision matrices can be helpful in situations where the criteria are multidimensional.[46,47] For example, a group might construct a two-dimensional matrix with options listed as row titles down the side and specific criteria listed as column headings across the top. The intersections of the rows and columns are used to capture the group's opinion about how each option rates on the specific criteria. So, in considering optional process changes, the group might agree that option 1 has high desirability in terms of cost, low desirability in terms of potential effectiveness, and medium potential acceptability to the people in the process. A similar analysis of the other options might demonstrate that while no option is perfect, some are better than others. This realization, and the time spent in group discussion, aids consensus building and cross-departmental collaboration.

These four techniques—brainstorming, boarding, multivoting, and decision matrices—are the building blocks for other collaborative methods. For example, the nominal group technique consists of a sequence of boarding the question of interest, silent brainstorming of ideas, boarding those ideas, group discussion, multivoting to prioritize the list, and group discussion to confirm a final decision.[48] Similarly, many other popular group consensus techniques can be decomposed as a sequence of these four elemental techniques.

Tools for Quality Planning

While the graphical and team tools just cited are most often used to improve existing processes, quality management science also includes techniques for planning new processes and services. There is a set of basic planning tools that have been borrowed from various disciplines, models to guide both new process design and strategic planning, and techniques borrowed from the field of market research for determining customer needs.

The Management and Planning Tools. The management and planning tools in the quality management literature aid groups in generating and organizing verbal information (that is, ideas, concepts, intuitions, attributes, descriptions of tasks, and so forth). These tools were adapted from other fields and imported into quality management science by the Japanese in the 1960s and 1970s. These tools are fully described in a variety of references that also provide a host of application examples.[49,50,51] Some of the most commonly used tools are described briefly in the following paragraphs; Figure 22.7 provides a schematic depiction.

The affinity diagram (also known as the K-J method in honor of its developer, Japanese anthropologist Kawakita Jiro) is a group brainstorming and organizing technique. Team members begin by brainstorming freely on a defined topic. (For example, "What are the features of an ideal primary care clinic?") Ideas are written on individual cards or adhesive note papers and arrayed on a surface for everyone to see. After a period of brainstorming, the team then shifts its attention to grouping the ideas into sensible categories. In silence, each team member searches for two cards that he or she feels are related in some way. These cards are then placed together and the process is repeated continuously, with team members finding two new cards that are related or adding additional cards to existing groups. In this process, cards are said to have an "affinity," or attraction, for one another because the individual ideas on them seem related in some way. The silent grouping continues until all cards have

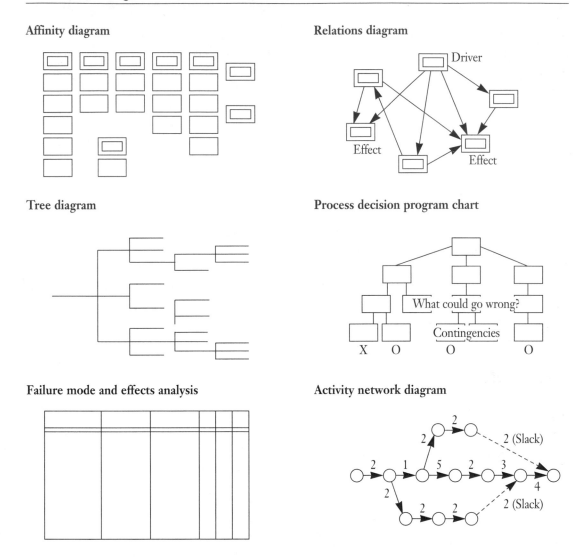

Affinity diagram

Relations diagram

Tree diagram

Process decision program chart

Failure mode and effects analysis

Activity network diagram

Figure 22.7. Schematic depiction of the common planning tools from quality management science.

been placed into six to 10 groups. At this point, the team switches from silent work to discussion mode, examining each group to identify the central theme that ties them all together. This theme is written on a header card, with the individual items arranged under it, to complete the diagram.

The brainstorming allows everyone to participate freely, while the silent grouping allows new patterns of information to emerge by postponing the critical thinking that tends to push information into the mold of preconceived patterns. Finally, the process of naming the group establishes a common understanding among team members as to the central themes reflected in the collection of ideas.

A relations diagram (also known as interrelationship diagraph or ID) documents complex cause-and-effect relationships among items. Again, the construction of the diagram is participatory and verbal. Items are written on individual cards and displayed on a wall or easel sheet. These items might be the themes (header cards) from an earlier affinity diagram. Considering one card at a time, the leader asks the team, "Which other items are driven by or influenced by the factor written on this card?" Based on the discussion, the leader draws arrows from the factor of interest to every other item it influences. This process is repeated for each card in turn until all possible causal relationships have been documented.

The completed diagram gives us a greater appreciation of the system as a whole. Items with many outgoing arrows are key causal factors ("drivers") that, if properly addressed, influence a large number of other items. Identifying these drivers gives the team a sense of priorities, or starting points, in an otherwise overwhelmingly complex situation. Similarly, items with many incoming arrows are key effects. If the team properly addresses the many other driving (causal) factors on the diagram, it should see changes in these key effects as a result. The team might want to track these few items as a way of assessing the ultimate success of the effort, rather than trying to measure each of the causal factors directly.

The tree diagram (also known as the systematic diagram) starts with an end result to be attained, and then describes in increasing detail the full range of tasks or contributors to that result. Graphically, it resembles an organization chart or family tree. To illustrate, suppose that a planning committee in a home health agency has constructed a relations diagram and identified "availability of appropriate staff" as one of the key drivers in the causal system for patient satisfaction. This driver is written on a card and represents the first level of the tree: the problem, objective, or goal statement. In the second level of the tree the group might break "availability of appropriate staff" into four categories of activity: external recruiting, internal transfers, training programs, and retention of existing staff. Note the comprehensive nature of these second-level categories; the team strives to be both complete and increasingly detailed as it moves down the levels of the tree. In the third level, the team takes each second-level item and dissects it further into its component parts or necessary tasks. This dissecting process continues until the team reaches the point where tasks are defined well enough that they can be assigned to someone (typically, this occurs at the third to fifth level of the diagram). The group effort needed to construct the tree diagram ensures that there are no major gaps in our thinking about what needs to be done and that, in the end, the people working on individual tasks will be able to see how what they are doing fits into a bigger picture.

The process decision program chart (PDPC), another of the management and planning tools, maps out conceivable but undesirable events in a plan and indicates appropriate contingencies. Planning teams typically construct PDPCs near the end of their planning efforts, utilizing the collective knowledge of the team to perform a final check of an implementation plan. The team begins as with a tree diagram by defining a goal (level 1) and the high-level steps that contribute to that goal (level 2). Then, instead of breaking down each of the second-level items into more detailed categories or tasks, the team leader takes each second-level item and asks, "What could go wrong with this?" The various failure scenarios—based on data, past experience, or simple hunches—are written on individual cards to form the third level of the tree. Next, the fourth level of the diagram is used to describe various contingencies (countermeasures or preventative actions) that the team could utilize to minimize the impact of each failure scenario. In the fifth and final level of the chart, the team evaluates these contingencies. The symbol X is typically used to mark those that are impractical, while the symbol O is used to mark those that should be implemented (unmarked items are simply held for future consideration).

A failure mode and effects analysis (FMEA) is a slightly more sophisticated version of contingency planning.[52,53] In FMEA, steps, failure scenarios, and contingency plans are typically described in more detail, and the resulting information is displayed in tabular form. The key refinement is that each failure mode is then rated based on likelihood of occurrence and severity. These rating scores follow a Pareto distribution and direct the planning group's attention toward the most likely and most severe potential failures.

A final tool in the basic set of management and planning tools is the activity network diagram (also known as the arrow diagram). This diagram shows the sequence of tasks required to accomplish some objective, along with time estimates for each task. By compiling the time estimates, a team can (1) define start and completion dates, (2) identify the critical path of activities that dictates the minimum total time require to accomplish the objective, (3) manage the slack time in parallel tasks, and (4) monitor progress toward the objective. It is one of the last planning tools that a team might use.

Before leaving this topic, let me emphasize three key points about these tools from the quality management literature. First, it is easy to get carried away with endless detail; we must use common sense and know when to stop. Prudent teams will question the need and set time limits before embarking on the construction of one of these tools. Second, the successful use of the tools depends heavily on team members' commitment and attention to group process skills. Team members must value each other's expertise, be open to active participation by all, and practice good listening. Finally, it is important to understand that while these tools provide a way to make use of verbal information and intuition, they should not be taken as license to ignore the need for data and facts. Planning teams should use the traditional data analysis tools of quality management to confirm the subjective relationships documented in the various management and planning tools.

Models for Process Design. Just as there are models to guide teams seeking incremental improvements in existing processes, various authors have proposed high-level road maps to guide the design (or redesign) of new processes. (See, for example, Plsek,[54,55] Ackoff,[56] Juran,[57] and Hammer and Champy.[58]) While these models differ in their details, there are common threads that run through them all.

The first step typically involves defining the scope and aim of the new process in a way that reflects the needs of the various customers that the process serves. This statement of aim might be derived from an affinity or relations diagram, based on the results of customer focus groups. The various models for process design also stress the importance of involving workers and caregivers directly in design; processes should not be designed by staffers or managers who will never work in the processes themselves. The models typically direct these multidisciplinary design teams to begin by constructing flowcharts of an ideal process to meet customers' needs. These flowcharts lead naturally to focused planning for the internal handoffs between individuals and departments that are often the sources of process breakdowns. Next, the design team reviews the ideal process step by step and plans for realistic contingencies; the PDPC or FMEA tools described previously might be useful here. Finally, the models suggest that the design team plan for the measurements and controls that are needed to ensure quality. It is much easier to design control and feedback systems before the new process is implemented than it is to retrofit them in the climate of defensiveness that may be present after the process is in place and problems have appeared.

Specific Process Planning Methods in Health Care. The importance of process design has led to the development of specific adaptations for health care. Critical paths (also called care paths, clinical paths, care maps, and other names) are multidisciplinary, high-level process design efforts that specify key milestones in the care process for patients in a given diagnostic category. (See, for example, Shoemaker,[59] Mosher et al.,[60] Coffey et al.,[61] and Falconer et al.[62]) These explicit milestones aid coordination of care, help reduce length of stay, improve quality of care, increase patient and family involvement, and enhance cross-departmental cooperation. Similarly, clinical guidelines and algorithms outline the process of clinical decision making and thereby help focus discussion on potentially unnecessary variation in clinical practice.[63,64] Both critical paths and guidelines are used widely in health care, with good initial results.[65,66,67]

Techniques and Models for Strategic Planning. The late W. Edwards Deming, a highly influential thinker in the field of quality management science, stressed the importance of long-term planning in the first of his famous 14 points, "establish constancy of purpose."[68] As a result of this emphasis, quality management practitioners have adapted various techniques from the field of strategic planning.

In the early 1970s, Juran and others recommended that quality goals be given the same prominence in organizations as financial goals. Juran's approach to strategic planning for quality was, therefore, to set up a quality goal-setting system that paralleled the organization's financial budgeting system.[69] The result was an annual quality plan, as formal as the annual budget. A health care organization following Juran's advice (circa 1970 to 1985) might ask each department or service to set specific improvement goals. These would then be categorized and summarized to form organizationwide goals such as "reduce patient waits by 30 percent," "improve physician satisfaction by 50 percent," or "perform mammography screening on 90 percent of at-risk females."

While introducing specific quality goals was a step forward for industrial companies in the 1970s (and would be a step forward for some health care organizations today), practitioners questioned whether such goals were truly strategic in nature and worried that the separateness of the annual quality plan might mean that quality management would never be seen as integrated with day-to-day organizational management. During the decades of the 1970s and 1980s, the Japanese developed a strategic planning system that places quality (in terms of meeting customer needs) firmly at the center of all organizational plans. This method, called hoshin planning, rests on two critical assertions: that (1) the central goal of any organization must be to meet the needs of its customers; and that (2) to be successful, the organization must achieve alignment between its strategic goals and the personal goals of each of its members.[70,71] In hoshin planning, all organizational goals—customer satisfaction, efficiency, financial performance, and so on—emanate from the needs of customers. Senior leaders commission substantial customer research and use this information to develop tentative strategic goals. Then, in order to achieve alignment between organizational and personal goals, these senior leaders personally engage in sharing the tentative strategic plans with subordinates. This process, called *catchball*, is a true negotiation that provides subordinates with a real opportunity to influence the organization's strategic choices. The catchball process continues down the entire organizational hierarchy, with the goals becoming increasingly more detailed at the lower levels. In the end, all departments and workers have clear goals for improvement that are linked to the overall strategic, customer-based goals of the organization.

This approach to planning is so compelling that Juran has incorporated many of its aspects into what he now calls "strategic quality management."[72] Hoshin planning and strategic quality management are now used by many leading U.S. companies and some health care organizations such as the SSM Health Care System (headquartered in St. Louis, Missouri). Unfortunately, implementation of hoshin planning in health care is hindered by confusion over multiple customers, lack of information about the true needs and expectations of these customers, and the tradition of not involving staff in strategic planning. However, there are encouraging signs suggesting that these barriers will be reduced with hard work and good leadership over time.

An approach to strategic planning in health care that reflects the centrality of the customers and also incorporates elements of systems thinking is the organization-as-a-system exercise.[73,74,75] Though not strictly designed for this purpose, health care organizations such as the SSM Health Care System have adapted it as an analysis tool for strategic planning. The exercise—which can be used by a health care system, a stand-alone entity, or a department within an entity—poses a series of questions to be answered by senior leaders based on knowledge of customer and community needs. The first question, "What do we make?" forces leaders to step out of the traditional definitions of hospitals, HMOs, or clinics and define their purpose in broad terms. For example, a hospital leadership team might decide that it makes (among other things) "opportunities for improvement of health." This opens up avenues of strategic thinking that go beyond acute care beds and into such things as community outreach and preventive primary care. The analysis continues with such questions as: Who are our customers? How do they define quality and why? What are the needs of the community? How do we make what we make? What is our vision for the future? What are our general themes for improvement? and What specific processes should we improve, design, or redesign? The end result is a better appreciation of an organization's role in the community and a clearer picture of its strategic vision for the future.

A final word of caution is appropriate in regard to the use of these strategic planning tools. Mintzberg points out that effective strategies can never come solely from analysis. "Strategic thinking," he notes, "is about synthesis; it involves intuition and creativity."[76] The various analytical tools of strategic planning can inform that synthetic thinking process, but they are not a substitute for it.

Customer Needs Analysis. Another major group of quality planning techniques are those borrowed from market research for identifying customer perceptions. (See, for example, Juran,[77] Plsek,[78] Aday,[79] Gerteis et al.,[80] Gustafson et al.[81]) A key insight on which many of these techniques are based is the notion that quality is multidimensional. While Garvin first articulated the concept of dimensions of quality in general industry,[82] the Joint Commission on Accreditation of Healthcare Organizations (JCAHO) has recently brought this concept to health care by noting that quality involves appropriateness, availability, continuity, effectiveness, efficacy, efficiency, respect and caring, safety, and timeliness.[83]

While a list of quality dimensions is helpful, any such list will be too general to guide specific, customer-focused planning. An organization needs to define these dimensions further for each of its services and customers. For example, "accessibility" for walk-in patients to an ER might mean being seen by a clinician within 15 minutes, while "accessibility" for an HMO member might mean being able to schedule a routine appointment within one week. We can develop such specific, measurable definitions for each dimension in conjunction with customers through focus groups and surveys.

Batalden and Nolan have further noted the importance of digging deeper and understanding what drives our customers to define quality in these ways;[84] for example, to ask the question "Why is being seen in 15 minutes or less so important in an ER?" Probing this customer need might lead us to understand that anxiety is the real driver. This insight, in turn, leads us to understand that improvements in ER waiting time must be done in conjunction with efforts to reduce patient anxiety during the wait. If we fail to do this, we might expend resources reducing waiting time but fail to achieve the desired improvements in patient satisfaction.

Other techniques that are helpful in customer needs analysis are the moments-of-truth method,[85] or the related critical incident technique.[86,87] The theory behind these techniques is that quality is a composite of impressions that customers get at various points of contact with our organization. For example, moments of truth for a clinic visit might include entering the parking lot, walking into the building, approaching the receptionist, entering the waiting room, being called back by the nurse, and so on. At each of these moments of truth, HMO members develop an impression about the level of service, attention to customer needs, and ability to provide care. Again, we can use focus groups and surveys to deepen our understanding about what is really important to customers at each of these moments. With this information, we can direct truly strategically focused improvements in areas that customers will really notice, thereby enhancing customer satisfaction and loyalty.

Before leaving the topic of customer needs analysis, let me call your attention to three key points made repeatedly in the quality management literature on this topic. First, it is important to think of the "customer" in very broad terms. Patients, members, families, employees, professional staff, payors, stockholders, boards, regulators, community groups, and others might all be customers. Successful organizations seek to understand and meet the needs of all these customer groups. Second, customers can be internal to the organization as well as external. When you write a memo and hand it to a secretary to type, the secretary is your customer in the transaction. While you are the ultimate customer of the typing, the process will have higher quality in terms of efficiency, accuracy, and ultimate satisfaction if you begin by understanding the needs of the secretary and making that initial handoff as smooth as possible. In this sense, quality management science asserts that every work process is a series of supplier-customer relationships where understanding and meeting needs at every step will ensure higher-quality outcomes.[88,89] Finally, we should understand that analytical market research can never fully identify all customer needs. Noriaki Kano speaks of "surprising quality"—giving customers something they had not thought of before, but that delights them when they experience it.[90] Focus groups and surveys will never uncover such ideas directly; innovative thinking and experimentation is the only way. Gustafson and colleagues have recently documented an approach for uncovering such otherwise unexpressed customer needs in the context of treatment for breast cancer.[91] Their work led to the development of a computer-based bulletin board service that women in one study accessed more than 1600 times for answers to sensitive questions.

Advanced Planning Techniques. Progressive industrial firms and some leading-edge health care organizations are pushing customer-based planning a step further by the use of quality function deployment (QFD). QFD utilizes a series of progressively more detailed matrices to trace specific work process steps and detailed measures back to customer needs. (See, for example, Gaucher and Coffey,[92] Akao,[93] Hauser and Clausing,[94] and Sullivan.[95]) One of the key matrices resembles the silhouette of a house; hence, the technique is also sometimes referred to as *the house of quality*. A comprehensive QFD analysis ensures that we have addressed all customer needs, that everyone who works in the process understands what is important to the customer, and that everyone understands why each performance measure is tracked. An early adopter of this technique in health care is the Bethesda Hospital system in Cincinnati, Ohio.[96]

Techniques for Measurement

Completing Juran's trilogy, the third set of techniques from quality management science are those for measurement. In this final section, I will discuss a framework for a comprehensive measurement system and explain the technique of benchmarking.

Traditional Approaches in Health Care. Let me begin by acknowledging the long tradition of measurement in health care. The work of Donabedian,[97] and the health care quality assurance (QA) practitioners who followed him, led to sets of measures for structure (for example, number of board-certified physicians), process (for example, frequency of use of urinary catheters more than 48 hours following surgery), and outcome (for example, mortality rate). Today, measurements such as these, along with QA committees and chart reviews, are standard practice in nearly every health care organization.

In addition to Donabedian's pioneering work, over the years many contributors have added to our selection of ways to measure the outcomes of health care processes, both technical performance and customer satisfaction.[98,99,100] Recently, various organizations have proposed standardized indicators and data sets to measure performance in health care settings; for example, HEDIS,[101] the Maryland Indicator Project,[102] and JCAHO's IMSystem.[103] The introduction of quality management science in health care organizations should therefore be seen as building on, not tossing out, these past approaches to measurement.

While quality management science builds on the tradition of measurement in health care, it also encourages us to seek three new objectives. First, quality management science encourages us to expand the scope of our thinking about what is important to measure by prominently featuring the perceptions of customers as valid indicators of quality, in addition to technical and professionally based views of performance. Second, quality management science focuses on cross-functional processes and suggests that we view measurements as integrated systems that must be managed by cross-functional teams rather than having one set of measures tracked by medical staff, another set by nursing, and still another by administration. Third, quality management science calls into question the traditional use of measurement as a way of allocating rewards and punishments to individuals. Berwick's seminal article on this topic, in which he described the "search for bad apples" that seems to characterize our traditional approach to measurement,[104] is widely cited as the trigger that initiated the introduction of industrial quality management science into health care.

A Framework for a Comprehensive Measurement System. A system for health care measurement should include measures of clinical outcomes, customer perceptions of quality, internal process performance, and financial performance.[105] Nelson and Batalden further suggest that such systems of measurement be arrayed in a hierarchical fashion, from broad to detailed.[106] At the top of the hierarchy there should be a few, broad summary measures in each category that provide senior leaders with an indication of the overall performance of the organization. These measures are analogous to the meters and warning lights in the cockpit of an airplane or dashboard of an automobile. For example, your car's oil pressure light provides gross performance feedback on your automobile's lubrication system. When the light is off, you can be generally assured that everything is fine, even though you do not have the detailed data to confirm this. In analogous fashion, Group Health Cooperative of Puget Sound's CEO, Henry Berman, describes 13 "dashboard" measurements used by his senior leadership team.[107] These high-level indicators—for example, member retention, hospital days per 1000 members, C-section rate, and appointment waiting time—provide senior leaders with a general overview of organizational performance in the four areas of customer satisfaction, financial performance, clinical outcomes, and internal process performance. Each dashboard measurement is backed up with a set of more detailed measurements, tracked by teams of managers and clinicians throughout the organization, that can be used to quickly pinpoint process difficulties should the dashboard indicators show a problem. The value of this hierarchical approach to measurement is that it avoids the problem of information overload that characterizes many measurement systems. Instead of tracking 40 to 50 indicators as if they were all equally important, senior leaders can focus on about a dozen key measures and trust that other managers are monitoring the details.

Benchmarking. Benchmarking is the process of comparing your performance to that of the best. (See, for example, Tucker, Zivan, and Camp,[108] Camp,[109] Balm,[110] Bader,[111] Flower,[112] and Patrick and Alba.[113]) While not solely a measurement technique, I present it here because it is often thought of as such. In a benchmarking study we begin with measurement, but then go deeper by making site visits to other organizations in order to understand why there are performance differences between seemingly similar processes. Knowing why something is better is the key to improving our own processes.

Balm suggests that there are four types of benchmarking.[114] In internal benchmarking we compare similar processes and services within our organization. For example, we might benchmark (compare) documentation practices on several nursing units in a hospital. While this is a good way to reduce unnecessary variation, we may not uncover substantially better practices simply by looking within our own organization. In competitive benchmarking we compare ourselves with our direct competitors. For example, we might gather information by calling to schedule a routine appointment in our competitors' clinics. Such studies produce strategically important measurement data, but it is often difficult to go to the next step and learn how a competitor achieves better performance.

Functional (or group) benchmarking involves comparing performance against those who are the best in our industry, but not our direct competitors. The absence of direct competition opens up a better channel for detailed sharing across organizations. Group benchmarking is becoming common in health care. For example, 32 hospitals in the Health Care Forum's Quality Improvement Network are sharing information in an effort to streamline their admissions processes.[115] Similarly, SunHealth Alliance, an affiliation of 260 hospitals and other providers, regularly sponsors groups of five to 15 organizations to identify and share best practices in specific areas.[116] Health care organizations are also finding that the group benchmarking concept can be applied to clinical issues as well as administrative processes. The key to success in group benchmarking is identifying the best organizations to form the group. Sponsoring organizations typically accomplish this by surveying specific performance measurements in a number of candidate organizations, and then using that data to identify a smaller number as the best in class.

The phrase *best practices* has touched off a lively debate in health care applications of benchmarking. Because of the strong research tradition in health care, the term *best practices* implies to some that the identified practices are the result of an exhaustive search and rigorous experimental verification (for example, through randomized controlled trials). This is not the intent of benchmarking. Benchmarking is practical and action-oriented in its analysis; it is not a rigorous research methodology. Berwick argues, however, that knowledge gained through the limited and technically nonrigorous observation and measurement associated with benchmarking is knowledge for improvement nonetheless. He suggests that both benchmarking and traditional research methods have their place in advancing the state of the art in health care.[117] To avoid the distracting debate, I suggest the phrase "potentially better practices" as a more apt descriptor of the output from a benchmarking project.[118] Whether the identified practices actually bring about an improvement in performance is a question that every organization must test through its own local implementation of the benchmarking study's results.

Balm's fourth type of benchmarking is generic benchmarking. Here, we make a conscious effort to go outside our industry to find others who excel in a process similar to ours or in a performance dimension that is key to our customers. For example, a hospital admissions department might examine the process of customer intake in an excellent hotel, a home health agency might visit a taxi company to gain insight into the efficient management of mobile resources, or clinic managers might review billing procedures in an excellent company like American Express. In generic benchmarking, quantitative measurement is less important because customer needs and measurement methods necessarily differ across industries. Rather, the keys to success here are open-mindedness, observation skill, and the creativity to adapt ideas for use in our industry. Generic benchmarking is a powerful way to stimulate innovative thinking. There is considerable anecdotal evidence of its use by focused quality improvement project teams in health care, but the traditional feeling that health care is a unique industry has been a barrier to its widespread adoption.

Regardless of the type of benchmarking one employs, it is important to understand that such studies require deep effort to be successful. Garvin notes that "benchmarking is not 'industrial tourism' . . . rather, it is a disciplined process that begins with a thorough search to identify best-practice organizations, continues with careful study of one's own practices and performance, progresses through systematic site visits and interviews, and concludes with analysis of results, development of recommendations, and implementation."[119] Camp underscores these points and goes on to stress the importance of organizationwide communication and top management support.[120] It is this emphasis on applying knowledge and making real changes that takes benchmarking beyond being a simple measurement effort. When properly practiced, benchmarking is an improvement process in the Juranian sense, where breakthroughs in cultural patterns and results (improvement) must follow breakthroughs in knowledge (measurement).[121]

Conclusion

In this chapter, I have briefly surveyed a basic collection of tools and methods from the quality management sciences that can be applied in health care. Consult the liberally supplied references for more information on the various tools mentioned here.

Health care organizations that thoroughly understand and appropriately use the methods outlined in Figure 22.1 are on the leading edge of the modern approach to quality. The pace of adoption of these methods, which have been successfully applied in other industries, into health care over the last 10 years is encouraging. But the field of quality management science is broad, and leading practitioners are continuously developing new tools and applications. The next decade of the evolution of quality management in health care promises to be as exciting as the last.

Glossary

Benchmarking: A structured method for obtaining information on the performance of other organizations in order to drive internal improvements in one's own organization. In one form of benchmarking, organizations exchange data on common performance measures. A more powerful form of benchmarking is when knowledgeable teams visit other organizations to understand in detail how they achieve superior performance levels.

Cause-and-effect diagram: A description of a process at a causal level. The cause-and-effect diagram is used to organize and display the various theories that people have about what might be causing the problem or variation under investigation.

Check sheet: A form for gathering data that enables one to analyze the data directly from the form. For an example, see Figure 22.4.

Common cause variation: Variation in a measurement that is due to small, randomly occurring, difficult-to-control factors that are inherent in a process. Common cause variation is indicated by a pattern of measurements falling randomly within the upper and lower limits on a control chart.

Control chart: A line graph of the data with superimposed horizontal lines indicating statistically derived upper and lower control limits. These upper and lower limits indicate the range of variability that we would expect if the variation is subject only to small, randomly occurring factors that are inherent in the process (so-called "common cause variation"). If the measured data points fall randomly within the control limits, we say that the process is stable.

Customer needs analysis: A set of techniques, such as focus groups and moments-of-truth analysis, that help organizations understand what their customers want and how they define quality in the services they receive from the organization.

Dimensions of quality: A collection of high-level attributes of a process or service that help us understand how customers might define quality. In health care, dimensions of quality include appropriateness, continuity, effectiveness, timeliness, and so on.

Failure mode and effects analysis: A structured process by which a group examines every aspect of a process, product, or service looking for potential failure modes. These failure modes are captured in a table and then scored for their likelihood of occurrence and severity. Analysis of the scores establishes a priority order for improvements that will prevent or reduce the severity of the potential failure modes.

Focus group: A group of people assembled for the purpose of having a detailed, interactive discussion about the performance of an organization, process, product, or service. Typically, the focus group consists of customers or others who could be considered outsiders with regard to the topic under discussion. The information gathered in a focus group is primarily subjective and perceptual in nature and may be either current or future in time perspective.

Histogram: A graphical depiction of the shape in a set of data constructed by dividing the range of the data into six to 12 equal intervals, tallying the number of data values that fall within each interval, and showing the results of this tally as bars arranged along an axis. A single, well-controlled process tends to produce a bell-shaped histogram.

Hoshin planning: A strategic planning system stressing that all organizational goals must be aligned with the needs of customers and the personal goals of all members of the organization.

Line graph: A graphical depiction of the sequence in a set of data. Constructed for the purpose of looking for patterns and trends in the data.

Moments-of-truth analysis (or critical incident technique): Techniques in which we explore detailed customer perceptions and needs at specific moments in time in their interaction with a process, product, or service. The goal is to manage these moments of truth or critical incidents better by understanding more fully what the customer experiences at these times.

Multivoting: A group consensus-building technique where members vote for multiple items on a list (for example, what they believe are the top five most plausible theories of cause on a cause-and-effect diagram). The voting identifies natural consensus, while highlighting for discussion those items where there is important difference of opinion.

Pareto diagram: A graphical depiction of data that illustrates the Pareto principle. Categories are arranged on the horizontal axis of the graph in the order of decreasing frequency of occurrence. Bars indicate the number of occurrences in each category as read on the vertical axis. A quick scan of the diagram indicates that the first few categories account for the majority of the occurrences (the vital few), while the remainder of the categories have only a little effect (the useful many).

Pareto principle: The Pareto principle states that in any collection of factors that contribute to a common effect, a few of those factors will account for the majority of the effect. For example, in an admissions process in a hospital, the majority of patient waiting time might occur in just two of the 23 steps. A focus on the so-called "vital few" provides the biggest return from the investment of our improvement effort.

Quality function deployment: A quality planning technique that utilizes a series of progressively more detailed matrices to trace specific work process steps and detailed measures back to customer needs.

Quality improvement project: A focused effort by a team of knowledgeable members of an organization to address a specific improvement opportunity.

Scatter diagram: A graph used to study the relationship between two variables. For an example, see Figure 22.6.

Special cause variation: Variation in a measurement that is due to unique, assignable causes, resulting in performance that is not considered natural for the process. Special cause variation is indicated by the violation of statistically derived rules on control charts; for example, a point outside the control limits, or two out of three consecutive points more than two standard deviations from the mean.

Tampering: Making changes in a process that are unwarranted. Typically, this occurs when process managers treat random variation (common cause variation) as if it had an assignable cause (special cause variation).

Discussion Questions for a One-Hour Executive Meeting

1. Which of the tools and methods listed in Figure 22.1 have you successfully used in your organization? Give specific examples.

2. Which of the tools and methods listed in Figure 22.2 have been underutilized (or not used at all) in your organization? To what specific issues in your organization might they be applied?

Notes

1. D. M. Berwick, "Continuous Improvement as an Ideal in Health Care," *New England Journal of Medicine* 320 (1989): 53–56.

2. G. Laffel and D. Blumenthal, "The Case for Using Industrial Quality Management Science in Health Care Organizations," *Journal of the American Medical Association* 262, no. 20 (1989): 2869–2873.

3. D. M. Berwick, A. B. Godfrey, and J. Roessner, *Curing Health Care* (San Francisco: Jossey-Bass, 1990).

4. D. Blumenthal, "Total Quality Management and Physicians' Clinical Decisions," *Journal of the American Medical Association* 269, no. 21 (2 June, 1993): 2775–2778.

5. E. J. Gaucher and R. J. Coffey, *Total Quality in Healthcare* (San Francisco: Jossey-Bass, 1993).

6. J. M. Juran, *Juran on Leadership for Quality* (New York: Free Press, 1989).

7. J. M. Juran, *Managerial Breakthrough* (New York: McGraw-Hill, 1964).

8. P. E. Plsek, "Quality Improvement Models," *Quality Management in Health Care* 1, no. 2 (1993): 69–81.

9. Ibid.

10. Berwick, Godfrey, and Roessner, *Curing Health Care*.

11. Gaucher and Coffey, *Total Quality in Healthcare*.

12. J. M. Juran, ed., *Quality Control Handbook*, 4th ed. (New York: McGraw-Hill, 1988).

13. H. M. Wadsworth, K. S. Stephens, and A. B. Godfrey, *Modern Methods for Quality Control and Improvement* (New York: John Wiley & Sons, 1986).

14. H. Gitlow, S. Gitlow, A. Oppenheim, and R. Oppenheim, *Tools and Methods for the Improvement of Quality* (Homewood, Ill.: Irwin, 1989).

15. P. E. Plsek, A. Onnias, and J. F. Early, *Quality Improvement Tools* (Wilton, Conn.: Juran Institute, 1989).

16. K. Ishikawa, *Guide to Quality Control* (New York: UNIPUB, 1985).

17. Berwick, "Continuous Improvement as an Ideal in Health Care."

18. Ishikawa, *Guide to Quality Control*.

19. Plsek, Onnias, and Early, *Quality Improvement Tools*.

20. Ishikawa, *Guide to Quality Control*.

21. Juran, *Managerial Breakthrough*.

22. Ibid.

23. P. E. Plsek, "Planning for Data Collection," *Quality Management in Health Care* 2, no. 2 (1994): 69–81.

24. Juran, *Managerial Breakthrough*.

25. A. J. Duncan, *Quality Control and Industrial Statistics* (Homewood, Ill.: Irwin, 1974).

26. G. Snedecor and W. Cochran, *Statistical Methods*, 8th ed. (Ames, Ia.: Iowa State University Press, 1989).

27. R. G. Carey and R. C. Lloyd, *Measuring Quality Improvement in Healthcare: A Guide to Statistical Process Control Applications* (White Plains, N.Y.: Quality Resources, 1995).

28. P. E. Plsek, "Introduction to Control Charts," *Quality Management in Health Care* 1, no. 1 (1992): 65–74.

29. Wadsworth, Stephens, and Godfrey, *Modern Methods for Quality Control and Improvement*.

30. Gitlow et al., *Tools and Methods for the Improvement of Quality*.

31. W. E. Deming, *Out of the Crisis* (Cambridge, Mass.: MIT Center for Advanced Engineering Study, 1982).

32. W. A. Shewhart, *Economic Control of Quality of Manufactured Product* (New York: D. Van Nostrand Co, 1931).

33. Deming, *Out of the Crisis*.

34. Berwick, "Continuous Improvement as an Ideal in Health Care."

35. Laffel and Blumenthal, "The Case for Using Industrial Quality Management Science . . ."

36. Berwick, Godfrey, and Roessner, *Curing Health Care*.

37. Gaucher and Coffey, *Total Quality in Healthcare*.

38. G. E. P. Box, W. G. Hunter, and J. S. Hunter, *Statistics for Experimenters* (New York: John Wiley & Sons, 1978).

39. C. H. Moore, "Experimental Design in Healthcare." *Quality Management in Health Care* 2, no. 2 (1994).

40. S. Ferguson, T. Howell, and P. Batalden, "Knowledge and Skills Needed for Collaborative Work," *Quality Management in Health Care* 1, no. 2 (1993): 1–11.

41. P. R. Scholtes, *The Team Handbook* (Madison, Wis.: Joiner Associates, 1988).

42. D. Mosel, and M. J. Shamp, "Enhancing Quality Improvement Team Effectiveness," *Quality Management in Health Care* 1, no. 2 (1993): 47–57.

43. Scholtes, *The Team Handbook*.

44. A. Osborn, *Applied Imagination* (New York: Charles Scribner, 1953).

45. Scholtes, *The Team Handbook*.

46. Ibid.

47. J. Grandzol and M. Gershon, "Multiple Criteria Decision Making," *Quality Progress* 27, no. 1 (January 1994): 69–73.

48. A. L. Delbecq, A. H. Van De Ven, and D. H. Gustafson, *Group Techniques for Program Planning* (Chicago: Scott Foresman, 1975).

49. S. Mizuno, ed. *Management for Quality Improvement: The Seven New QC Tools* (Cambridge, Mass.: Productivity Press, 1988).

50. M. Brassard, *The Memory Jogger Plus* (Methuen, Mass.: GOAL/QPC, 1989).

51. P. E. Plsek, "Management and Planning Tools of TQM," *Quality Management in Health Care* 1, no. 3 (spring 1993): 59–72.

52. J. M. Juran, J.M. and F. M. Gryna, *Quality Planning and Analysis: From Product Development Through Use* (New York: McGraw-Hill, 1980).

53. P. E. Plsek, P.E. "FMEA for Process Quality Planning," *Proceedings of the 1989 Annual Quality Congress of the American Society for Quality Control* (Milwaukee: ASQC, 1989).

54. Plsek, "Quality Improvement Models."

55. P. E. Plsek, "Methods for Systematic Process Redesign," *Quality in Health Care* (a companion publication to the *British Medical Journal*).

56. R. L. Ackoff, *Creating the Corporate Future* (New York: John Wiley & Sons, 1978).

57. J. M. Juran, *Juran on Planning for Quality* (New York: Free Press, 1988).

58. M. Hammer and J. Champy, *Reengineering the Corporation* (New York: HarperCollins Publishers, 1993).

59. W. C. Shoemaker, "Critical Path Medicine," *Critical Care Medicine* 2, no. 5 (September-October 1974): 279.

60. C. Mosher et al., "Upgrading Practice with Critical Pathways," *American Journal of Nursing* (January 1992): 41–44.

61. R. J. Coffey, et al., "An Introduction to Critical Paths," *Quality Management in Health Care* 1, no. 1 (1992): 45–54.

62. J. A. Falconer et al., "The Critical Path Method in Stroke Rehabilitation: Lessons from an Experiment in Cost Containment and Outcome Improvement," *Quality Review Bulletin* 19, no. 1 (January 1993): 8–16.

63. K. O. Murrey, L. K. Gottlieb, and S. C. Schoenbaum, "Implementing Clinical Guidelines: A Quality Management Approach to Reminder Systems," *Quality Review Bulletin* 18, no. 12 (December 1992): 423–433.

64. E. Green and J. M. Katz, "Practice Guidelines: A Standard Whose Time Has Come," *Journal of Nursing Care Quality* 8, no. 1 (1993): 23–32.

65. Coffey et al., "An Introduction to Critical Paths."

66. Falconer et al., "The Critical Path Method in Stroke Rehabilitation."

67. Murrey, Gottlieb, and Schoenbaum, "Implementing Clinical Guidelines."

68. Deming, *Out of the Crisis.*

69. Juran and Gryna, *Quality Planning and Analysis.*

70. B. King, *Hoshin Planning: The Developmental Approach* (Methuen, Mass.: GOAL/QPC, 1989).

71. Y. Akao, ed., *Hoshin Kanri Policy Deployment for Successful TQM* (Cambridge, Mass.: Productivity Press, 1991).

72. Juran, *Juran on Leadership for Quality.*

73. P. B. Batalden and T. W. Nolan, "Knowledge for the Leadership of Continual Improvement in Healthcare," in *Manual of Health Services Management,* edited by R. J. Taylor (Gaithersburg, Md.: Aspen, 1993).

74. Deming, *Out of the Crisis.*

75. P. M. Senge, *The Fifth Discipline: The Art and Practice of the Learning Organization* (New York: Doubleday, 1990).

76. H. Mintzberg, "The Fall and Rise of Strategic Planning," *Harvard Business Review* 27, no. 1 (January-February 1994): 107–114.

77. Juran, *Juran on Planning for Quality.*

78. P. E. Plsek, "Defining Quality at the Marketing-Development Interface," *Quality Progress* 20, no. 6 (June 1987): 28–36.

79. L. A. Aday, *Designing and Conducting Health Surveys* (San Francisco: Jossey-Bass, 1989).

80. M. Gerteis, S. Edgman-Levitan, J. Daley, and T. L. Delbanco, eds., *Through the Patient's Eyes: Understanding and Promoting Patient-Centered Care* (San Francisco: Jossey-Bass, 1993).

81. D. H. Gustafson, J. O. Taylor, S. Thompson, and P. Chesney, "Assessing the Needs of Breast Cancer Patients and Their Families," *Quality Management in Health Care* 2, no. 1 (1992): 6–17.

82. D. A. Garvin, *Managing Quality: The Strategic and Competitive Edge* (New York: Free Press, 1988).

83. Joint Commission on the Accreditation of Healthcare Organizations, *The Measurement Mandate* (Oakbrook Terrace, Ill.: JCAHO, 1993).

84. Batalden and Nolan, "Knowledge for the Leadership of Continual Improvement in Healthcare."

85. J. Carlzon, *Moments of Truth* (Cambridge, Mass.: Ballinger, 1987).

86. Gustafson et al., "Assessing the Needs . . ."

87. J. C. Flanagan, "The Critical Incident Technique," *Psychological Bulletin* 51 (1954): 327–358.

88. Ishikawa, *Guide to Quality Control.*

89. Juran, *Juran on Planning for Quality.*

90. N. Kano (1990).

91. Gustafson et al., "Assessing the Needs . . ."

92. Gaucher and Coffey, *Total Quality in Healthcare.*

93. Y. Akao, ed., *Quality Function Deployment: Integrating Customer Requirements Into Product Design* (Cambridge, Mass.: Productivity Press, 1990).

94. J. R. Hauser and D. Clausing, "The House of Quality," *Harvard Business Review* 66, no. 3 (1988): 63–73.

95. L. P. Sullivan, "Policy Management Through Quality Function Deployment," *Quality Progress* 21, no. 6 (June 1988): 18–22.

96. Joint Commission on Accreditation of Healthcare Organizations, *Striving Toward Improvement* (Oakbrook Terrace, Ill.: JCAHO, 1992).

97. A. Donabedian, *Explorations in Quality Assessment and Monitoring, Volumes 1, 2, and 3* (Ann Arbor, Mich.: Health Administration Press, 1985).

98. S. J. Bernstein and L. H. Hilborne, "Clinical Indicators: The Road to Quality Care," *The Joint Commission Journal on Quality Improvement (QRB)* 19, no. 11 (November 1993): 501–509.

99. B. Spiker et al., "Quality of Life Bibliography and Indexes," *Medical Care* 28, supplement (1990): DS3.

100. J. E. Ware and R. Hays, "Methods for Measuring Patient Satisfaction with Specific Medical Encounters," *Medical Care* 26 (1988): 393–402.

101. J. M. Corrigan and D. M. Nielsen, "Toward the Development of Uniform Reporting Standards for Managed Care Organizations: The Health Plan Employer Data and Information Set (HEDIS 2.0)," *The Joint Commission Journal on Quality Improvement (QRB)* 19, no. 12 (December 1993): 566–576.

102. V. A. Kazandjian et al., "Relating Outcomes to Processes of Care: The Maryland Hospital Association's Quality Indicator Project (QI Project®)," *The Joint Commission Journal on Quality Improvement (QRB)* 19, no. 11 (November 1993): 530–538.

103. D. M. Nadzam et al., "Data Driven Performance Improvement in Health Care: The Joint Commission's Indicator Measurement System (IMSystem)," *The Joint Commission Journal on Quality Improvement (QRB)* 19, no. 11 (November 1993): 492–500.

104. Berwick, "Continuous Improvement as an Ideal in Health Care."

105. B. Bader, "A Process for Developing a Board Quality and Performance Report," *The Quality Letter* 5, no. 2 (March 1993): 8–14.

106. E. C. Nelson and P. B. Batalden, "Patient-Based Quality Measurement Systems," *Quality Management in Health Care* 2, no. 1 (1992): 18–30.

107. Bader, "A Process for Developing . . ."

108. F. G. Tucker, S. M. Zivan, and R. Camp, "How to Measure Yourself Against the Best," *Harvard Business Review*, 65, no. 1 (January-February 1987): 8–10.

109. R. C. Camp, *Benchmarking: The Search for Industry Best Practices That Lead to Superior Performance* (Milwaukee: ASQC Quality Press, 1989).

110. G. R. Balm, *Benchmarking: A Practitioner's Guide for Becoming and Staying the Best of the Best* (New York: QPMA Press, 1992).

111. B. Bader, "Benchmarking: A New Tool for Quality Improvement in Healthcare," *The Quality Letter for Healthcare Leaders* 4, no. 7 (September 1992): 1–19.

112. J. Flower, "Benchmarking: Springboard or Buzzword?" *The Healthcare Forum Journal* 36, no. 1 (January 1993): 14–16.

113. M. Patrick and T. Alba, "Healthcare Benchmarking—A Team Approach," *Quality Management in Health Care* 2, no. 2 (winter 1994).

114. Balm, *Benchmarking.*

115. Ibid.

116. Patrick and Alba, "Healthcare Benchmarking."

117. D. M. Berwick, "Harvesting Knowledge from Improvement," *Journal of the American Medical Association* 275, no. 11 (1996): 877–878.

118. P. E. Plsek, "Collaborating Across Organizational Boundaries to Improve the Quality of Care," *American Journal of Infection Control* (1997).

119. D. A. Garvin, "Building a Learning Organization," *Harvard Business Review* 71, no. 4 (July-August 1993): 78–92.

120. Camp, *Benchmarking.*

121. Juran, *Managerial Breakthrough.*

Paul E. Plsek is an independent consultant with 20 years' experience in the field of quality management. He is the former director of AT&T's corporate quality planning. He is widely recognized for his pioneering efforts to bring modern approaches of quality management to health care. Plsek is the author of numerous articles and the two books *Quality Improvement Tools* and *Creativity, Innovation, and Quality.*

Section VI
Implementation

Chapter 23

Managing Change in Health Care

David W. Hutton

To improve is to change; to be perfect is to change frequently.

—Winston Churchill

All improvement involves change, so in a sense this entire book is about change. However, while other chapters map out strategies, processes, and tools that can be used to create useful change, this chapter focuses on the human dimension.

This chapter will help you to understand change as a personal experience and as a social process—and show you how to orchestrate change so that the people affected become part of the solution rather than part of the problem. This topic is important because changes in the workplace affect people profoundly—often more than they realize themselves. When as leaders we do not know how to attend to the human dimensions of change, even our most carefully planned projects are vulnerable to failure because the people who have to carry out the changes no longer care or have "joined the opposition." The symptoms are all too familiar: negative reactions from people at all levels, ranging from foot-dragging and silent resistance to open hostility.

It doesn't have to be that way. The best organizations today—in all sectors—respond successfully to a relentless stream of changes in their environment, such as rapidly changing client needs, scarcity of resources, rapidly evolving new technology, new types of competitive threat, and new legislative and regulatory demands. These organizations are able to adapt swiftly and effectively because they have learned not just how to take their people with them on each step along the road, but how to have their people participate in and drive many of the necessary changes.

I will show how successful organizations think about change and orchestrate the process.

- We will start by considering change as it affects each of us as *individuals*—how we experience the forces of change around us, what we think and feel, and how we react. This will reveal lessons about how to support individuals during change.

- We will then look at how *groups* of people respond to change—the predictable patterns of behavior that we can expect to observe as change unfolds, and how to lead groups through a transition.

- Finally, we will consider the project management aspect of change. We will step through a *formal process for initiating and sustaining change* that can be applied to any situation.

This material may confirm something you already suspected—that there are no easy shortcuts or magic bullets. But you will also find lots of good news. Leadership *does* make a difference—management actions have a major impact (positive or negative) on how organizational change unfolds. Clear strategies, processes, and tools *do* exist that can speed the change process along, make it easier on everyone involved, and greatly improve your chances of success. And these methods are completely consistent with the approaches that you will find set out in other chapters of this handbook.

In fact, the strategies, processes, and tools set out in the other chapters have clearly been *designed* to facilitate change. As we come to better understand the human dimension of change, we discover that there is no need to alter or dilute quality management principles. Rather, we begin to see more clearly why some of these principles—such as seeking to involve everyone and striving for win–win relationships—are not altruistic ideals that are "nice to have," but are practical necessities for success.

Change in Health Care

During the past decade or so, society has been changing at a more rapid pace than ever before in history. As a consequence, organizations of all types—governments, the education system, industry, and commerce—are under pressure to change with the times and to respond to new needs.

Nowhere is this more true than in health care. Everyone understands the vital importance of health care services to our quality of life, yet many stakeholders in the system find the status quo unacceptable or believe that it is not sustainable. A potent combination of circumstances—ballooning costs, more knowledgeable and demanding clients, increasing litigation, spectacular advances in technology, and an aging population—have created intense pressure for reform.

How will reform be achieved? However it is done, it will not be easy. Whatever the solutions, these will involve major changes to the working lives of millions of people who work in our health care system. The ability of the health care system to adapt will depend on the ability of its leaders to adjust and learn new ways—and to help their people do likewise.

Types of Change

This chapter is not about the methods for implementing change that are common practice today—I will call these traditional methods. Typical of these are changes decided on behind closed doors by a few, and then handed out for others to implement unquestioningly; changes implemented through across-the-board budget cuts or staff reductions, without understanding how these changes will affect work processes or the delivery of care; or changes where the preservation of turf has been a major (if undeclared) factor in the decision making.

These traditional methods don't work well enough to meet the needs of health care institutions today. I will be discussing better ways: the application of quality management principles and methods to accomplish purposeful change—for example, to improve patient care and clinical outcomes, to make better use of the talents of everyone involved in the system, and to deliver better value for money to the society we exist to serve.

Of course, these changes will still include budget cuts, staff reductions, and reorganizations. But I will show ways of accomplishing these that enable the institution and its people to emerge stronger and more capable of doing the work, not weakened and demoralized.

There are many types of change that may be sought in any health care setting, such as the following:

- Changes in mission, mandate, or overall strategy
- Changes in organizational structure
- Changes in levels of staffing—either growth or reduction in employment
- Changes in attitudes and behaviors—often referred to as *culture*
- The adoption of new methods and procedures
- The introduction of new technology, tools, equipment, and facilities
- Changes in relationships with stakeholders

All of these changes have something in common: They involve disruption of people's expectations and their lives in the workplace. However, the significance of a change to those involved may vary considerably—and the *organization's* perception of significance may be very different from the *individual's*.

For example, a major capital investment in new technology (which is very significant to the organization) may have little or no impact on the people involved—if it does not materially alter the nature of their jobs or lead to changes in staffing levels. On the other hand, a minor policy or procedure change may have major implications for the people involved. It may change their perceptions of status, risk, reward, or recognition. It may change their working hours, require them to acquire new skills, or place them in new roles where they are not confident of their abilities. It may require them to work with different colleagues in different relationships.

So when contemplating any type of organizational change, the leaders should ask, "What will these changes mean to the people affected?" The greater the impact on people's expectations and their lives in the workplace, the more attention must be paid to the lessons of this chapter.

Note that throughout this chapter I will talk in terms of a major, organizationwide change. For a smaller or more narrowly focused change, the concepts are equally valid, but the reader needs to scale down as appropriate. For example, if the change relates to the introduction of some new technology, then the vision and desired future state defined at the outset would be in terms of the goals for the project, not for the organization as a whole.

Change as a Personal Experience

In order to do a good job of helping others through change, it is essential to understand the nature of change as a personal experience. Let's approach this by recalling a family situation that most of us have experienced at some time. Picture the following scenario: You come home to announce some great news—you have been offered a big promotion into a new, exciting job! There's only one *tiny* fly in the ointment—the job is in a different city, Newville, and you have to give your answer within a week. You rush home to break the news to the family, only to discover that their reactions are not quite the same as yours.

"What about *my* job—I would have to start over at the bottom—*again*."

"Fine, take the job—you can come home on weekends."

"Do you *really* want to do this?"

"What about all my friends at school?"

"Can we take my cat?"

"We've only just got the house fixed up the way we want it!"

"Do they have a McDonald's in Newville?"

"Can I go and play now?"

If you were very lucky, somewhere in there you might also hear this.

"What would your new job be like?"

"Congratulations! They must think a lot of you—and so they should!"

"What kind of place is Newville?"

"Wow, that's where the 'Electric Wombats' live!"

You soon realize that

- Not everyone immediately sees the opportunities or shares your vision of how great life could be in Newville.

- Everyone has a different perspective—different needs and wants, and different concerns about leaving.

- You've been overlooking some of the sacrifices involved—the friendships, routines, and familiar things you will leave behind.

- There's a *lot* to talk about before any kind of decision can be made.

- You need to approach the decision in a way that will enable everyone to buy in.

- If you make the decision on your own, you could find yourself living in Newville on your own.

You also realize that it's going to take some time and lots of discussion to get used to the idea, to review the pros and cons, to gather information, and then to reach a decision. You will need to orchestrate this in such a way that everyone affected has sufficient input to the process—so that their needs can be understood and accommodated, and so that they will buy into the decision.

And all of this is before you even start packing for the move!

Lessons Regarding the Personal Experience of Change

There are some useful lessons that we can glean from this personal experience of change.

Change Triggers Our Emotions. Getting the job offer was an emotional experience—satisfying and exciting, but also scary. But that was nothing compared to the emotional fireworks that took place when the family heard the news. Dealing with all of this emotion—our own and that of others—is no easy task. It is no accident that we use phrases like *working through change*, since coping of this sort is a kind of emotional work.

Change Is Stressful. It may take quite a lot of time and energy to arrive at a decision and to work out an arrangement that all of the family can live with. But the real changes have not even begun—you still have to wind up the old job, start to learn the new one, find new living quarters and schools, relocate the family . . . and so on. Research has consistently shown that the stress associated with high levels of change can affect our health. A classic study by Holmes and Rahe[1] in 1967 examined the correlation between health and levels of change in people's lives, with surprising results. Subsequent research has reinforced these findings.

Holmes and Rahe rated 42 common life events and examined how the incidence of these events affected people's health. For an average person the probability of requiring hospitalization within a two-year period was about 20 percent. However, for people undergoing high levels of change, the probability rose to an astonishing 80 percent.

This study revealed another surprise: While negative changes are obviously stressful, positive and exciting changes can also take their toll. When the degree of stress caused by different life events is analyzed, the death of a spouse easily tops the list (with 100 points), but marriage and retirement are not far behind (with 50 and 45 points respectively).

It Takes Time to Adapt. How much time is needed for our family decision? For most people, one week is not enough! It always takes time to come to grips with changes that affect our lives. The family members may need time to vent and get over their initial emotional reactions—then they need time to reflect and get used to the idea, discuss it at length, and to gather information that will help in making the decision.

Although We Seek Positive Change, We Object to Being Changed. Even though the job promotion scenario looks like a very positive change—most people actively seek promotions and the rewards that go with them—we probably have at least mixed emotions. A lot depends on what we think of the offer and whether we feel that we really have a choice.

The family members' reactions were more negative than ours partly because of a suspicion that they don't really have a say in the decision—that the change was going to be forced on them anyway. With this mind-set they are likely to be resentful of the change, even though it may hold potential benefits for them.

None of this is surprising. We tend to seek changes that benefit us; we don't mind changes that we can control; but we *strongly* resist having changes forced on us. The way that the family members experience change is much the same way that staff members experience change in the workplace, and the same lessons apply. And the consequences of handling the situation badly are also similar.

Phases of Personal Change

We can better understand the personal experience of change by examining the model in Figure 23.1. This shows the three phases of personal change described by William Bridges—endings, transition, and beginnings.[2] Each of these phases is associated with a set of emotions that we are likely to experience. Let's examine each phase in turn.

• *Endings.* The first phase is endings, where we learn to let go of the past. At first sight, it may seem strange to have endings first. But when something significant changes in our lives, even something very positive, then something good (or at least familiar) often has to end to make way for the new.

For example, when we choose to get married, we give up the right to consider only our own needs. When we receive the gift of a child we have to give up some luxuries—sleeping through the night without disturbance or anxiety, going out on an impulse for a meal or a movie, perhaps driving our sporty automobile. So for each new beginning there is usually a corresponding ending—something has to go.

The emotions associated with endings are those of grieving. These include anger, denial, bargaining, a sense of loss—and finally acceptance, which completes the ending phase.

• *Transition.* The next phase is transition, when we search for a new direction. We are in transition when we have accepted that the past is gone, but we have not yet found our future—we have not yet become used to the new ways, or we have not found the new path that we want to pursue.

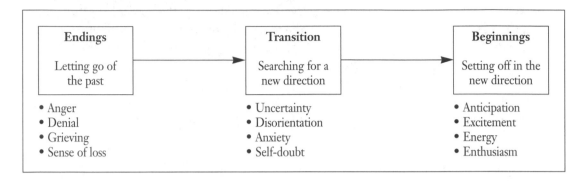

Figure 23.1. Phases of personal change.

The emotions associated with transition are those of confusion and uncertainty. These include disorientation, disenchantment, and anxiety—sometimes low energy and even depression. Transition is an uncomfortable phase, but it can also be one of great personal growth and creativity—with the familiar removed, our minds may be opened up to new possibilities.

• *Beginnings.* The final phase is beginnings, where we embark on our new direction with excitement and enthusiasm. It is easy to recognize this phase—it is the child with a new toy, the adult with a new dream, the learner gaining a sense of proficiency.

The emotions associated with beginnings are easy to relate to: excitement, energy, and enthusiasm as we get back into our stride or find our new goal. We may also feel some anxiety as we forge ahead into new challenges that will surely test our ability.

This model suggests some other learnings about change.

Adaptation to Change Is Not Automatic. Adapting to change (getting used to it, completing the transition) is an internal, largely unconscious process. It is not entirely under the control of the individual, and certainly cannot be commanded by someone else.

Supportive leadership can help people to adapt. But even with such support, some individuals may never accept the need for change, let go of the old ways, or adapt to the new ways. For example, when an institution is trying to adopt a less autocratic style of leadership in order to better harness the talents of its people, some people may find the very idea too threatening to contemplate. When it becomes apparent that many of their colleagues want to go in this direction, these individuals may simply say to themselves "Over my dead body!" and mentally "dig in" for a battle of wills. This is an example of people who are stuck in endings because they cannot let go of the past.

The Internal Process Is Not Synchronized with External Events. The internal process of adaptation may lag behind external events—or it may run ahead of them. For example, consider two people who receive a promotion at work. Person A, who didn't expect this promotion, may take months to come to grips with the loss of the old job—a familiar, low-risk situation where he or she felt in control and knew what to expect. Person A may be stuck in endings for some time.

In contrast, Person B, who had outgrown his or her current job and sought out a promotion, may have gone through the endings and transition phases long before the promotion even came through. Although both individuals may be equally capable and resilient, it is easy to predict that one will find the change much easier to cope with than the other.

This example provides a clue regarding one important way of making change easier on people. We all need time to work through this adaptation process, and providing advance information gives us more time to get used to the idea and to prepare ourselves before we have to deal with the reality.

Dealing with Resistance Versus Helping People Through Change. With these insights into how difficult change can be for those involved, the common phrase *dealing with resistance to change* begins to seem like a mental trap. It tends to convey the idea of people choosing to be difficult by resisting, and management having to deal with this behavior. The image conjured up is of herding people like cattle—someone has to run around threatening the whole herd with a stick and whacking the rumps of lazy laggards and those that are stupidly heading off in the wrong direction.

But the key problem is not that people resist unwelcome changes—it is that coping with change is difficult for most people. Even for those who find it exciting and expect to benefit, it is exhausting and time-consuming. So people need *help*—to come to grips with the changes, to adjust their expectations, and to adapt to new circumstances.

Let's look at some strategies that can be used to help people through change.

Strategies for Helping People Through Change

Figure 23.2 summarizes the needs that everyone has during change and some strategies that address these needs. It also illustrates some common strategies that only make things worse.

Communicate the Need for Change. We will often choose to ignore the prospect of unasked-for change in our lives, hoping that it will just go away. Only when it becomes clear that some kind of change is unavoidable do we begin to come to grips with this reality. Then we begin to think about how to avoid the worst or how to turn the situation to our advantage.

Explaining at an early stage the need for change allows people more time to adjust their expectations and think about how to deal with the changes. Put another way, *people are not in the market for solutions until they recognize that there is a problem.*

Senior managers are often concerned that revealing too much too early (that is, before they have figured out all the answers) will simply cause great anxiety and hence a slump in morale and productivity. This mind-set reveals why senior managers are often part of the problem, because

- The need for change may already be obvious to everyone, not just senior people.

- It is impossible for a few people in senior positions to work out all the answers themselves—the only "revelation" that occurs when a small group tries to plan for everyone else is how naive and inept the resulting plans can be.

- People will take time to adjust regardless. Withholding information simply ensures that all of this emotional turmoil will take place during implementation, rather than some adjustment taking place during the planning phases.

When the University of Alberta Hospital faced the dilemma of how to communicate major changes (including significant job losses), the communications team asked people—physicians, clinical and administrative staff, and patients—what good communications would look like to them. They got answers like "I would like to know before others about decisions that affect me." These answers clarified the needs of each group of participants and were used during the planning of all subsequent communications for each group. This process revealed—and thus prevented—many potential communication problems.

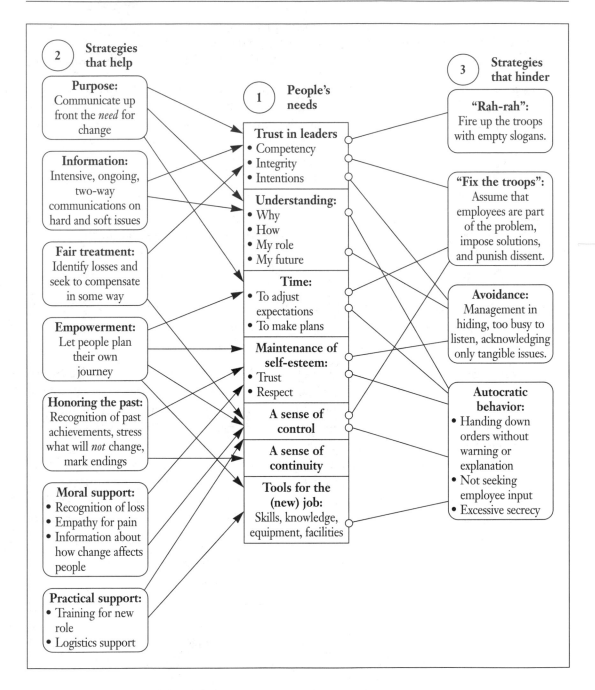

Figure 23.2. Helping people through change.

One of the learnings from this exercise was that people want timely information about bad news, and that they can handle it—if communications are being handled in a way that sustains their trust and confidence in their leaders.

Honor the Past. When an important ending is taking place—wrapping up a military regiment, closing a hospital unit, paying final respects to a loved one—some kind of acknowledgment or ceremony is valuable and appropriate. This allows us to reflect, to relive both the good and the bad moments, to salute the past, to be nostalgic—and most important, to let go.

The special nature of health care—its vocational nature and its social purpose—make this particularly important. The clinic that is threatened with closure is more than a building—and very different from a mere store or factory. To the people who have worked there it has a life of its own—perhaps its hallways seem to echo with the spirits of all those whose lives were touched or changed here. If it has to die, let it be with dignity and respect and some appropriate rites of passage. It is also important to honor what was accomplished. When a unit is closed in an unfeeling or apparently arbitrary manner, long-serving staff often feel a loss of self-worth—a bitter feeling that somehow their life's work didn't matter, and didn't make a difference.

Often, when trying to explain the need for change, leaders fall back on describing what is wrong with the past—for example, "The way we have been doing this is no good." But one of the most threatening and painful experiences for health care practitioners is the advance of medical science—when this reveals that some common practice is somehow inadequate, faulty, or even harmful. What emotions ignite inside someone who is dedicated to helping others when he or she is told that years of effort have been in some way misguided? What a recipe for denial! But the old ways were the best available at the time, and people were helped—even though we didn't know then as much as we do now. The clinical procedure that is now outdated was once the latest thing (and a big improvement over previous methods). Even past failures may have provided invaluable learning experiences that made subsequent successes possible.

Trashing the past is denigrating a part of people's lives. Better to acknowledge the achievements of the past, even if these are no longer sufficient for the future. Better to lead people into the turmoil and uncertainty of change with at least the comfort of knowing that they achieved something and that what they did was valuable.

Identify What Will* Not *Change. It is easy to become preoccupied by what is changing and to lose sight of the continuity that exists—and there is usually some kind of continuity of purpose and values. For example, the fundamental mission and commitment of an institution may remain essentially the same, even though the methods of fulfilling this have to change drastically. The fundamental beliefs that distinguish the organization and guide behavior may remain constant—even though the means of expressing these may have to change. It is important for the leaders to identify and communicate this continuity.

Enable People to "Plan Their Own Journey." Nothing is more certain to provoke resentment—and real, determined resistance—than for management to turn up with detailed plans to rearrange peoples' lives, with no opportunity for people to contribute their ideas or to influence the decision-making process.

Better to turn up with plans that are clearly drafts—and an honest willingness to modify these in the light of suggestions and concerns. Better still to turn up with a few clear goals and a few proposed strategies—and a well-organized process for translating these into plans and fleshing out the details with input from all those affected.

How far the organization can go in seeking involvement depends mostly on the skill of the leadership. Some organizations have successfully implemented visioning and/or planning processes in which everyone contributes to developing the goals and the plans for getting there (and the process is completed relatively quickly). *Policy deployment* and *hoshin planning* are names commonly used to describe a comprehensive planning and implementation system based on quality management principles. Imagine the energy and the human potential unleashed when the organization can achieve such an alignment of individual efforts! Regrettably, other organizations lack the leadership skills and methods to achieve a consensus even among a dozen or so senior executives.

A common concern is that a more participative planning process will become bogged down in lengthy, unnecessary discussions, or become hostage to special interest groups rather than being focused on the goals of the organization. Clearly, a well-designed, well-organized, and disciplined approach is required, and people at all levels need to be taught the skills required for them to participate effectively.

Ensure Intensive, Ongoing, Two-Way Communications. When change is imminent or underway, we want *lots* of information—we want to understand what is going to happen, how we will be affected, what we need to do to prepare ourselves, and so on. Insecurity also makes us paranoid—if we are not getting the information we want from our leaders, we lose trust in them, we turn to the rumor mill, and we see plots and hidden agendas in the most innocent actions.

Intensive, two-way communication is also essential to obtain feedback—to find out how people are coping with the changes, what their concerns are, what their needs are for more information, and so on. Without this feedback, the communications from management begin to feel like megaphone announcements rather than a dialogue.

How can we know if our communications are effective? An excellent practice is to measure this; for example, by regularly conducting a kind of minisurvey.

Identify Losses and Seek to Compensate. Although change may be necessary for the greater well-being of all, there is always breakage. Some people will suffer obvious losses—in compensation, security, even their jobs. And those who are apparently unaffected often have serious concerns that only they can articulate.

For example, consider an organization that has removed a layer of line management in order to shorten the lines of communication, but has retained a few of these skilled and knowledgeable people in staff roles (without loss of job level) to act as coaches and educators. In the eyes of others, these people have lost nothing. But in their eyes (and the eyes of their families), they may have lost status and security. They may keenly feel the loss of a prestigious job title or a large department reporting to them. They may feel that their new job is less important, less valued—perhaps simply a first step in getting rid of them. In this type of situation, these people's confidence and sense of self-worth can be sustained by arranging for them to network as a group, acknowledging their special role, and giving them appropriate recognition.

How can management find out that such concerns exist when people are embarrassed or reluctant to discuss them? Involving participants in the planning process can ensure that many concerns are anticipated and the plans adjusted accordingly. Later, during implementation, suitable feedback mechanisms can be used to identify such soft issues. Many communication forums are intentionally restricted to hard issues—progress against project plans, operational results, and so on. So some other mechanisms may be required, such as a standing team set up explicitly to monitor morale and to surface concerns, or focus groups or minisurveys may need to be set up for the same purpose.

Provide Moral Support. In his book *Emotional Intelligence*, Daniel Goleman outlines a range of abilities that seem to define human intelligence much better than the narrow, academic, IQ definition that has preoccupied us for the past 40 years or so.[3] (We are only just learning how to measure these abilities readily, and unfortunately we don't necessarily look for them when we promote people into management positions.) One of these is the ability to recognize and respond to emotions in others. We usually call this empathy. Most people have this ability to some degree, and hopefully employ it in their family and social lives—but we may not recognize its importance as a leadership skill. Some people may not even consider that providing empathy and moral support is part of a leader's job.

This belief regarding the role of a leader may not have severe consequences in a stable environment. But as we have seen, when the organization starts to mess with people's lives it unleashes a torrent of emotions. Reason does not return until these emotions have been expressed, vented, or somehow dissipated. Leaders who cannot (or won't) deal with this—for example, by revealing their own human side, relating to the feelings of others, and offering appropriate support—are clueless and largely useless in this situation. Like robotic aliens from another planet, they will always be bewildered and taken off-guard by the illogical and unreasonable behavior of earthlings. Given that many managers have the ability to empathize with people and to offer moral support, this ability needs to be legitimized and mobilized to help offset the stressful effects of change.

Another way of providing moral support is to educate people about the effects of change. In 1989, when Mitel, a hi-tech communications company, was going through a wrenching period of reorganization and downsizing, everyone was surprised when a one-day workshop on change became by far the most sought-after educational offering in the company. People signed up for it in droves, on the recommendation of friends and colleagues, until almost everyone (from frontline staff to senior executives) had participated. Why was this? Because people came away understanding that they were not the only ones battling with their feelings, that their experience was universal and normal, and that these feelings would pass. When they went back to work their situation was unchanged—the organization was still in a state of flux, and their jobs were still insecure. What had changed was that they now understood better what was going on and felt better equipped to cope.

Today the value of this type of education is well understood, and many organizations offer similar workshops during times of major change. Some also encourage family members to participate. This is a highly effective approach, which recognizes and involves the invisible workforce—those who support and nurture the stressed-out staff member at home, usually with little understanding of what the family member is going through at work.

Provide Practical Support. This seems a glaringly obvious requirement for successful change, but in practice it is often a serious problem. We have all seen examples: changing processes without providing the necessary tools or logistics, providing new equipment without training in its use, or changing peoples' roles without providing education or coaching.

How can management know what practical support is needed? First by getting input during the planning phase from those affected, then by paying close attention to the feedback mechanisms established. Typical examples of practical support are the following:

- Providing new tools, methods, or procedures that are required—and the training necessary to apply them

- Forming teams that allow people to support each other and to learn new tools and methods together

- Using pilots to test proposed changes on a small scale initially and to learn what works and what doesn't

- Providing human resources supports during redeployment, such as career counseling and aptitude assessment

Change as a Group Process

Once we understand how individuals respond to external changes, we can better understand how groups of people respond. There are more forces at play within a group—the interplay between individuals; the group dynamics; and the various perspectives that arise from people's different roles, different professional training, and different personal experience and attitudes.

The Spectrum of Reactions to Change

Although individual reactions may be unpredictable, the overall pattern of response within any group is very predictable. Here is the typical range of responses that can be expected as proposals for change are discussed and the first steps begin to unfold.

- Enthusiasm and a desire for involvement
- Open opposition and skepticism
- Cynicism—a firm refusal to see any merit
- Apathy and indifference
- Lip service followed by backsliding
- Anger and frustration
- Malicious compliance and sabotage

What can we make of this spectrum of responses? First, it is important to recognize that this type of spread is normal. In fact, if there is unanimous support for a proposed change, then something may be wrong—perhaps many people are afraid to say what they think, perhaps they feel that the proposal is not a serious one, or perhaps they weren't listening carefully!

Reasons for These Reactions

When we think about what the reasons may be for these widely differing reactions, it is not hard to imagine an explanation for every single one. Figure 23.3 suggests just some of the possible causes. Every individual has good reasons (from his or her own perspective) for responding in a certain way. It is usually reasonable to assume that no one is just being difficult, irrational, or stubborn for the sake of it. If we were in their shoes, we might react in just the same way.

But how does this help us? What can we do to get everyone moving in the same direction? Later in this chapter we will discuss the mechanics of a process for building consensus and commitment to change within a group of people, and this will help a lot. However, this process does not eliminate the divergence of attitudes we are looking at—it merely reduces it. So we still need strategies for working with groups that contain diverse attitudes toward the proposed changes.

It may be hard to know initially where people really stand, but once the initial discussions are over and concrete action is called for, this soon becomes clear. Three camps normally emerge.

1. Those who are strongly supporting the changes and getting on with it—typically about 20 percent to 30 percent of the group.

2. Those who are strongly opposed to the changes and whose attitude (whether voiced or held silently) is "over my dead body." Typically, these are people who feel so threatened by the proposed changes that they cannot contemplate accepting them. This camp may account for another 20 percent to 30 percent of the group.

Negative reactions	Positive reactions
• A sense of loss • Threat to job security, satisfaction, prospects, and so on • Fear of loss of control • Uncertainty, insecurity • Mistrust of management motives • Expectation that "this too will pass" • Perceived flaws in the approach	• Opportunity to make a difference • Buy-in to the goal • Challenge • Prospect of personal benefit (for example, job satisfaction) • Dissatisfaction with the status quo

Figure 23.3. Reasons for reactions to change.

3. Those who don't have any strong commitment for or against the changes, but will "go with the flow"—that is, fall in line with the direction that seems likely to prevail. This is often the largest camp.

Strategies for Helping Groups Through Change

Let's return to the analogy of the group that we were tempted to herd along with threats and admonitions to discourage resistance. We have already decided that the main problem is not the willingness of the individuals, but the difficulty of negotiating the swamp of change.

If people are floundering and sinking in this swamp, making threats and punishing a few individuals won't accomplish much. Better to help a few through onto firm ground where they can help encourage and guide others out of the morass. This is a good analogy for the strategy that works best with the three camps that typically develop within a group.

The essence of the strategy is to focus effort where there is the greatest potential for progress. The focus of attention shifts as the group makes progress.

Supporting the Pioneers. The first priority is to support the enthusiasts until they are safely on the way to success. It is a big mistake to assume that these people will succeed simply because they are enthusiastic. Being pioneers, the process will be more difficult for them. They may be better motivated than others, but perhaps no more experienced or able. (Some of those who sign up at the start may be somewhat naive or inexperienced and may not fully understand what they are getting into.) And there is always the risk of sabotage from those who are opposed to the change.

It is most important to consider this: If the pioneers fail, who will step forward to replace them? No one! These individuals *must* be helped to succeed, because if they fail the entire initiative will be dead. The following kinds of support can help ensure that they succeed.

- Suitable training and on-the-job coaching in the new methods

- Appropriate tools for the task

- Expert coaching and facilitation when they work in teams

- Close monitoring by an executive sponsor (and prompt action to remove barriers)

- Moral support

- Recognition for their efforts (whether or not their first attempts are successful)

Encouraging the Undecided. Only when the pioneers are safely on their way should efforts be shifted toward the undecided floating voters. These individuals will be more receptive once they see that others are succeeding and that the changes are going to become the norm. They may now be more motivated, but they will still need the same kind of support as the pioneers did, and it is equally important to ensure—now they are really trying—that they too can succeed. Fortunately, there are now some well-trodden paths to success and more people around who have already made the journey—whose experience can be used to guide others.

Securing the Gains. It is often difficult to decide what to do about entrenched opponents. It may be necessary from the start to run interference, in order to protect the pioneers from being undermined by such opponents. One natural reaction to these individuals is to focus on them and to work extra hard at bringing them on board. This is a common trap for people involved in supporting change. It may feel virtuous to persist, or it may seem an irresistible challenge—but it is usually a waste of precious resources that could be directed to others who actually want help and will benefit from it. It is a pointless waste of scarce resources to keep trying to convert people who clearly can't (or won't) adapt to the new ways.

In the long term, when everyone else is on board, people who have been unable to cope with the transition will be thoroughly uncomfortable with the new status quo. Even before then, once it becomes clear that their view is not going to prevail, these people are likely to start looking for a way out.

Sometimes a situation arises that demands preemptive action at the outset. For example, there may be someone in a senior position who carries so much baggage or is so strongly and visibly opposed to the changes, that this individual must depart before anyone will believe that the leader is serious about the changes. It is in the organization's best interests to help these individuals escape from a no-win situation in which their point of view is at odds with the new direction and their presence represents a constant threat to the continuance of hard-won changes. It is also in the organization's best interests to treat these people with the same consideration as anyone else who is a victim of the changes. These individuals have often served the organization well for many years and made important contributions to its past success. It is their personal misfortune that new times demand new ways that are too difficult for them to accept.

Figure 23.4 portrays the use of these strategies to help a group negotiate major change—in this case referred to as "the swamp."

Change as a Management Process

Adventure is the result of poor planning.

—Colonel Blatchford Snell

Purpose Versus Means

Sometimes the purpose of the change (the why) is forgotten once the actions required (the how) have been devised. Let's recognize the sharp distinction between these—between accomplishing the purpose and completing the planned changes.

For example, an institution experiencing financial difficulties may decide that restructuring and cutting levels of staffing (and hence payroll costs) provides an answer. The leaders may then measure

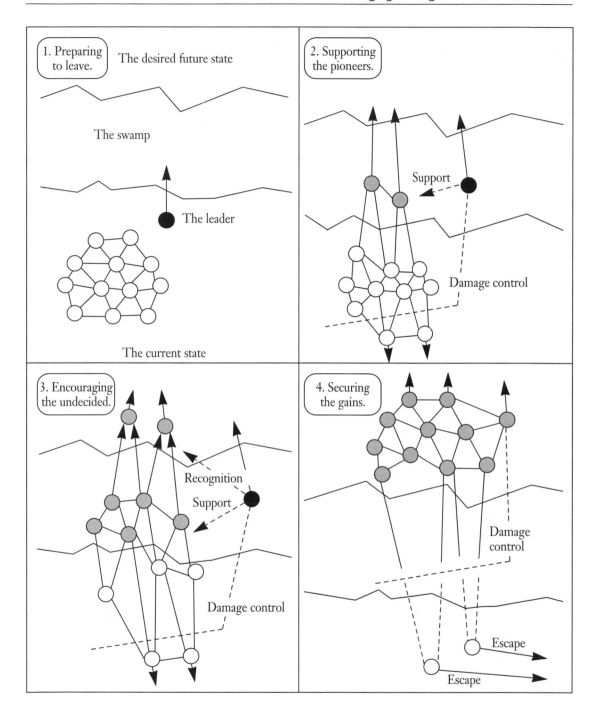

Figure 23.4. How groups work through change.

progress in terms of the mechanics: defining the new organization chart, reassigning people to the new positions, and completing the severance of those who are no longer required. However, *these changes may be completed as planned, yet the purpose not achieved.* The organization may find itself in worse shape financially than before if these changes lead to other unforeseen costs (for example, more oversights, accidents, emergencies, and problems requiring expensive recovery) or put the organization's income at risk (for example, by undermining its reputation or competency in fulfilling its mandate).

Does anyone seriously believe that an institution can become more competent at fulfilling its mandate, add more value, and compete successfully for scarce resources when its people are paralyzed by fear, drowning in personal sorrow, or at war with each other? Of course not; yet these are common consequences of poor leadership and planning, where mere execution of the mechanics was confused with achievement of the purpose.

One important lesson for leaders is to keep achievement of the purpose at the forefront and to be flexible and resourceful in finding means of achieving this. Being clear about the purpose can help prevent short-sighted errors, such as rushing into action impatiently in ways that alienate people, when careful upfront planning and consensus building would be more effective (and quicker in the end).

Another important lesson is not to define the purpose too narrowly, in a way that ignores potential undesirable side effects. For example, it is fairly easy to reduce costs if service to clients can be reduced at the same time. But if the aim is to reduce costs while maintaining or improving service, then this more complete statement of purpose provides a much better foundation for planning and implementing change, and then for measuring success.

The Process

Figure 23.5 shows a generic process for initiating (and sustaining) change. At first sight this model does not look particularly new or unusual—it resembles many standard approaches used for planning and project management. However, although it is not novel, this type of framework is vital—change cannot be accomplished successfully in a haphazard fashion, any more than any other complex project. The discipline of an organized, systematic approach is essential.

What should make the implementation look and feel different from other projects is the attention paid—at every step in the process—to the strategies already described to help people through change. It is this attention to the soft issues that will help management win acceptance and buy-in and make the difference between success and failure. Here is how the phases typically work in practice.

1. Develop a Widely Shared Vision and Desired Future State. The terms *vision* and *desired future state* have meanings here that we should define carefully. The vision is the ultimate goal—often expressed as a distant and perhaps unachievable aim, like a guiding star. The desired future state flows from this vision, but it is a well-defined and not-too-distant goal—it is the next destination on the journey.

The desired future state should be a sharply defined description of what the organization will look like a few years from now, including quantifiable goals. It must be tangible so that people can envision clearly this destination and understand how to measure progress along the way.

With the help of a skilled facilitator, any group of people who work together can develop, within a day or so, a shared vision and a desired future state that they all own. However, all too often the only people who are given this opportunity are senior managers. Their work may then be handed down—rather like tablets from the mountain—for lesser beings to study, venerate, and obey. This may not be the intent, but this is how it often feels to others.

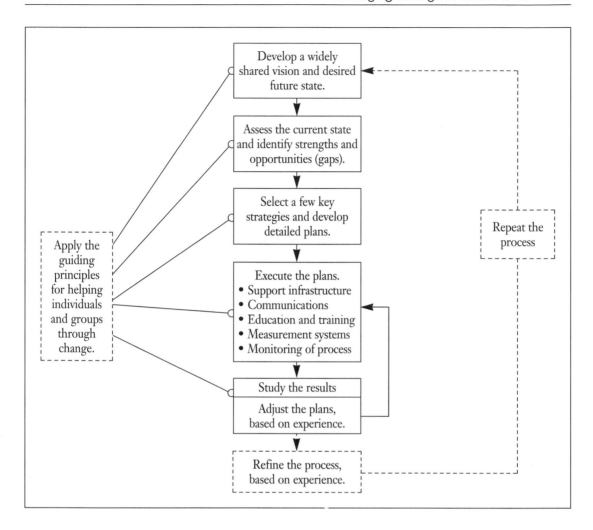

Figure 23.5. Initiating and sustaining change.

As a general rule, the more opportunity that people have to discuss, challenge, and contribute to the process, the more these statements will mean to them. Realizing this, some organizations have developed ways of involving large numbers of people in creating a shared vision for the organization. Figure 23.6 provides a brief description of such a process. Organizations that have used this type of approach have found that the resulting vision is stronger than senior managers could have produced on their own, and the vision is much better understood and more relevant to employees.

Fortunately, vision and mission statements should not change frequently, and it will not be necessary to develop them from scratch every time some organizational change is required. The development and communication of these shared goals is a first step in aligning people's efforts throughout the organization.

2. Assess the Current State and Identify Strengths and Opportunities. A thorough understanding of the current state is essential before any kind of change can be planned. We cannot decide the route to our destination unless we know where we are starting from.

1. A core team is selected, whose job is to orchestrate the visioning process.

2. The team members are trained how to facilitate a visioning session.

3. The target population that is to take part in the visioning exercise is divided into groups.

4. A team member helps each group identify the elements of their vision (for the whole organization).

5. The team assembles all of the vision elements developed by the teams and uses an affinity diagram or similar clustering technique to identify similar ideas.

6. The team drafts a vision statement incorporating the most frequently recurring ideas.

7. The draft vision is distributed for comment and then fine-tuned.

8. The final vision is posted, communicated in various other ways, and incorporated into selected educational offerings, such as the orientation program.

Figure 23.6. Developing a widely shared vision.

This starts with fact finding, which needs to be organized and guided by some type of framework. In its simplest form, a group of executives may conduct a SWOT analysis (strength, weaknesses, opportunities, and threats) using just the information in their heads.

A more thorough and satisfactory approach is to organize systematic fact finding with input from many people. As an example of this, many leading organizations today are conducting a Baldrige–Award style self-assessment as part of their annual planning cycle. This process provides a comprehensive appraisal of the organization's management system, which forms the basis for developing an improvement plan. One of the strengths of this approach is the use of a comprehensive, well-developed, standard framework. The Baldrige Award criteria offer a complete, refined model of a management system that applies to almost any type of organization. A slightly modified version of the Baldrige Award criteria has been developed for health care institutions. In some other countries (Canada and Australia) a single model has been developed for use in all sectors—government, education, health care, and industry.

When considering who to include in the assessment process, the leaders usually recognize several good reasons for involving a wider circle of people during the assessment process.

- The leaders cannot fully understand the current situation without obtaining the perspective of various other groups.

- Involving others builds a wider constituency for the changes, so that the leaders do not have to go out later and sell the plan starting from scratch.

A sound approach is to invite some movers and shakers to form an internal assessment team, to receive training in the approach, and then to conduct the fact-finding phase. During the process, this team develops a keen understanding of the current state and a commitment to the changes required—and becomes a valuable resource to support implementation. This group may then become the core of a transition team that will oversee the execution of the plans.

It is sound practice to interview a cross-section of staff at all levels and in all departments during fact finding, thus ensuring that the day-to-day realities of those in the trenches are properly understood. It is also beneficial to make use of outside experts—particularly during the evaluation phase—to provide perspective and to enhance the credibility and objectivity of the findings.

When organizational changes do not take into account client needs and priorities, there is a risk of undermining the relevance and perceived value of the institution itself. So when contemplating any kind of major change, it is essential to understand the client perspective. If the organization currently lacks client information, then it may be necessary to obtain this information (for example, through surveys and focus groups) during the preparations for change.

The final phase of the assessment is evaluation of the facts—to identify strengths and opportunities (sometimes called gaps), to understand cause-and-effect relationships, and hence to understand the dynamics of the situation. The stage is now set for selecting the key strategies.

3. Select Key Strategies and Develop Detailed Plans. Typically before the planning process is begun, there is a wide divergence of views regarding what needs to be done—but now there is a large measure of agreement. At the outset, each member of the leadership team was focused on departmental and personal goals—now everyone is focusing on the same shared goals (derived from the vision and future desired state). At the outset, each individual had a different, partial understanding of the current situation—now everyone has the same comprehensive understanding.

This leads to a remarkable situation: Everyone has essentially the same view of what needs to be done!

During the next step in the process, this consensus can be demonstrated in various ways, for example,

- By asking individuals to silently list the few top priority actions required to improve the organization and then grouping these using an affinity diagram process

- By returning to the framework used to conduct the self-assessment and asking individuals to choose the few items that offer the greatest opportunity for improving the organization

If the previous work has been done well and an appropriate model used, then this type of exercise will reveal a remarkable convergence of thinking. The key strategies for moving forward are immediately apparent. This consensus energizes the group members and provides confirmation that they have been able to identify the correct levers to pull.

The next step is to translate these selected strategies into detailed implementation plans. These are typically a set of related project plans, each with clear ownership, objectives, schedule and milestones, budget and resources, measures of success, and mechanisms for monitoring progress.

Clearly, the development of these plans has to involve the participants, both to ensure that the plans are well-thought-out and practical and to give people the opportunity to provide their input and to buy in. This is one of the best opportunities for engaging people, before the plans are set in concrete—and effort spent at this stage will be repaid later, when implementation begins. One effective way of doing this is to establish a project team for each objective, with suitably chosen team members. For a major objective, the team often has to represent a cross-section of the organization, championed and supported by an executive sponsor.

Another issue to be considered at the planning stage is that of overload, especially if there are other significant changes underway. Without careful attention to who is doing what, a few particularly talented and knowledgeable individuals may have demands placed on them by several different projects and find themselves in burnout while meeting none of these demands adequately.

4. Execute the Plans. Executing the plans successfully usually means paying attention to the following issues: support infrastructure, communications, education and training, measurement systems, and monitoring of progress. A few of these merit special mention.

- *Support infrastructure.* In assigning responsibilities for execution of the projects, it is typical to employ the normal reporting hierarchy or to set up some kind of project management overlay, and to set up regular reporting to monitor progress. Sometimes a transition team is formed to orchestrate the changes. In an organizationwide change, every member of the senior management team will have some specific responsibilities for the process, as will their direct reports. In this way, the managers responsible direct their people's efforts toward the goal.

This oversight structure is necessary—but usually not sufficient. Regardless of how it is organized, the managers responsible often do not have the time or the skills to help people with methods and tools. Hence the need for additional support—coaching, facilitation, education, and training—and an infrastructure to provide this. Experience has shown that this type of support is a critical success factor, and to be effective it has to be carefully organized.

The individuals who will provide this support are often best organized as a loose, flexible network rather than a monolithic department. This network can include many people who retain their regular jobs and provide this support on a part-time basis. These people acquire special knowledge and skills and bring these to their colleagues. By remaining insiders within their groups, they are uniquely positioned to understand what is going on and to provide timely assistance.

This support is vital and cannot be left to chance. The network needs to be recruited, educated, developed, and led. This requires just as much organization and management skill as operating as a normal department, and some suitably capable (and senior) individual should be assigned this responsibility.

- *Communications.* As we have seen, excellent communications are vital to successful change. The normal channels of communication may not be adequate or even appropriate, and additional mechanisms may be required. This aspect calls for careful planning, assignment of responsibility to a senior person, and allocation of resources—just like any other project within the overall change strategy.

A useful model is to consider communications as a set of processes and to assign a team to design (or redesign) these using process management techniques—for example, starting with customer needs. This approach will result in a well-defined set of communication methods, planned and designed to meet the specific information needs of specific audiences.

- *Education and training.* Most organizational changes call for significant education and training if the process is to be successful, and this is often one of the most significant and costly components of the process. Depending on the nature of the change, education and training may be required in specific job-related skills and/or specific technologies, general-purpose skills such as problem-solving or process management, or leadership skills. During major, widespread change, people also value and appreciate education on coping with change.

- *Measurement systems.* Before the process begins to unfold it should be possible for everyone to answer the question, "How will we know that we have been successful?" The answers to this question will determine what types of high-level measurements need to be put in place, and special systems may be required to gather this information.

The information that most institutions gather is the result of history and happenstance rather than logic. Common failings are the following:

—An excess of internally focused operational and/or financial data (beyond what is useful or cost-effective).

—A corresponding dearth of externally focused measurements (for example, of patient outcomes and levels of client satisfaction).

—A reactive, incident orientation rather than a proactive approach. This reveals itself as an ongoing preoccupation with apparent variances or out-of-line situations, but little or no analysis of trends in the underlying capabilities of the organization. This mind-set also shows up as frequent fire fighting to fix recurring problems, with little effort put into identifying and eliminating the root causes.

If one of the aims is to become more client-focused and prevention-oriented, major changes to the measurement system are generally required—as well as corresponding changes in the way that information is analyzed, presented, and reviewed.

• *Monitoring of process.* Since any change initiative inherently involves more risk than routine operations, the normal management review process may not be sufficient or appropriate. It may be necessary to have a separate review process, a different agenda, and a different set of information and measurements to review.

5. Study the Results and Adjust the Plans Based on Experience. This review process should have a strong focus on learning, not just reacting to out-of-line situations, so that the plans are refined and execution becomes progressively smoother as the initiative unfolds.

There will undoubtedly be some flaws and oversight in the original plans, and many of these will require some kind of recovery action to get projects back on track or back on schedule. The secret of effective execution is to be open to problems so that they are identified early and to make immediate use of the lessons learned. This is common sense, but not common practice. For example, leaders are often instinctively hostile to any suggestion of shortcomings in the plans, feeling that these are attacks on their competence. They may interpret honest concerns as opposition to the goal, shoot the messenger when there is bad news, and underestimate the significance of early signs of trouble. They may unintentionally put great pressure on others to put a positive spin on all that is happening. These all-too-common shortcomings in leadership style virtually guarantee that significant problems will be swept under the carpet until they have grown too big to hide—and too big to deal with.

Clearly, an appropriate leadership style is vital to organizational change and learning. When counterproductive behaviors are common, this is a clear sign that the leaders have not made enough progress in their own personal transition and need to redouble their own efforts. To sustain this effort, it is essential that they have mechanisms (such as upward feedback and opinion surveys) that provide reliable feedback on how they are doing, as well as access to appropriate training and coaching.

Given an appropriate leadership style, an effective review process is the other essential component of the learning cycle. The ingredients of this are the following:

• Use of reliable information to understand what is going on—both good and bad

• A practice of searching for the causes of problems rather than casting blame on the individuals concerned

• Consciously creating an environment in which participants are encouraged to voice concerns rather than being punished in some way for doing so

• Going beyond mere recovery of out-of-line situations—digesting the lessons from past problems and successes, and using these to adjust current and future plans

This last point is an important one. Past overachievements may reveal approaches that are particularly effective and should be reinforced during the remainder of the project. Past problems often reveal shortcomings in the plans (or the basic approach) that can and should be quickly corrected.

6. Refine the Process, Based on Experience. In the past, much thinking about change has been built around the mental model of a one-time change—hence models with phases called *unfreezing, transition,* and *refreezing.* The insights gained from this thinking are still valid, but change today is often an ongoing process rather than a step function.

Most organizations, in order to secure their future, need to be engaged in improving operations and refining strategies all the time. Only the focus and priorities vary from year to year; that is, *where* these efforts are directed (as progress is made and as the external environment changes) and the *intensity* of effort that is required (and can be afforded) at any given time.

In this environment some proven, routine approach to change is extremely valuable. Rather than waiting for change to become a glaring necessity (and then reinvent the wheel in implementation), why not develop a system for identifying necessary changes early and implementing them smoothly in a practiced fashion? Why not develop a system for doing this that can become part of the fabric of the organization and be studied and fine-tuned over time?

Many leading organizations are doing exactly this. At a tactical level, their application of quality principles and methods greatly enhances their ability to change rapidly, by putting the tools for change (improvement) in the hands of their staff and by empowering people to initiate action consistent with a well-understood overall plan. At a strategic level, they are building mechanisms to drive continuous improvement through the corporate planning process. This typically takes the form of a formal, comprehensive assessment of the organization's management system as a precursor to developing the annual plan.

In order to reflect this emerging practice, this change model shows an additional loop—refining the organization's approach to change and returning to the start of the process to plan for the next cycle.

Avoiding Unnecessary Change

> *We trained hard—but every time we were beginning to form up into teams, we would be reorganized. I was to learn later in life that we tend to meet new situations by reorganizing . . . and a wonderful method it can be for creating the illusion of progress while producing confusion, inefficiency, and demoralization.*
>
> —Petronius Arbiter

We have already observed how costly any type of change can be—not just in dollars and labor-hours, but also in its demands on people's energy, motivation, and goodwill toward the organization. However, unnecessary or inappropriate change is deadly to morale and efficiency.

Petronius Arbiter observed almost 2000 years ago, during the Roman Empire, how leaders under pressure often feel compelled to do something and resort to changes that have dubious value—such as seemingly arbitrary changes in personnel or in organizational structure. They may feel that they are shaking up the organization or removing dead wood. (W. Edwards Deming was once asked about the best way of removing dead wood. He responded with a question: "Did you buy it that way, or did you kill it yourself?")

Another trap is to pin hopes on centralization ("to improve efficiency") or decentralization ("to remove bottlenecks"). Often such changes merely perpetuate the power struggle between the center and the periphery of the organization, without addressing the fundamental causes of conflict.

So change is sometimes a substitute for a properly thought out strategy; a blunt instrument that causes huge disruption but does nothing to improve fundamental organizational competencies such as

- Identifying client needs accurately and developing services that meet these needs.
- Organizing the flow of work to deliver these services efficiently and reliably.
- Harnessing the talents of people.

At the same time, we observe that high-performing institutions are in a state of constant change and thrive on this. The difference is that, through enlightened leadership practices, they have greatly increased their capacity to absorb change and their ability to pick their targets. Rather than squandering effort on changes that may not contribute to improved performance, they systematically identify opportunities for useful change, prioritize, and focus their energies on the areas that offer the greatest leverage. And they routinely implement change in ways that enable their people to be a part of it—to understand the reasons, to influence decisions, to get involved, and to make a contribution to success.

The Key Success Factors

All of the lessons that we have learned from our study of change can be summarized under a few headings: providing leadership, engaging people, project management, and change support strategies. These are the key success factors for creating organizational change, as shown in Figure 23.7.

To know and not act is not to know.

—Wang Yang-min

When we look at the needs of health care practitioners trying to cope with change, it is striking how these mirror the needs of patients trying to cope with illness: trust in the competence and integrity of others, an understanding of what is happening and why, a sense of control, and maintenance of their dignity and self-esteem. Why shouldn't this be so? We are all cut from the same cloth.

When we look at the fulfillment of these needs today, there also seems to be a parallel: a tendency toward dehumanization of both medical practice and management practice. This may be an unintended side effect of large doses of scientific and technological progress. One of the common concerns of patients today is a feeling that the care has been taken out of health care—that they are processed as medical cases rather than treated as human beings. This often causes them considerable unnecessary anxiety and distress.

It has been amply demonstrated that attending to patients' nonmedical needs—such as their needs for information, control, and preservation of their dignity—can have a major impact on clinical outcomes. But health care practitioners cannot give their best to patients—and cannot truly be there for patients who need moral support and empathy—when their own emotions are in turmoil and their own needs for support are unmet.

Just as medical practice must recognize the whole person in order to deliver effective health care to clients, management practice must recognize the needs of the whole person in order to deliver effective leadership to health care practitioners. In times of major change, such leadership will be essential if the changes are to achieve the goal—not simply to complete the mechanics of restructuring, reorganizing, and rebudgeting, but to help people in our society lead healthy lives and make best possible use of the scarce resources allotted to this important work.

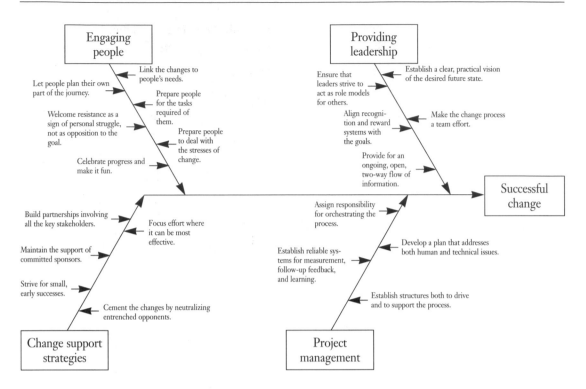

Figure 23.7. Key success factors for organizational change.

The good news is that we already know how to do this. The challenge for leaders is to grasp this knowledge and to apply it to the task at hand.

Discussion Questions for a One-Hour Executive Meeting

1. Explain the purpose of the session, for example, "to review our approach to orchestrating change in our institution."

2. Provide a copy of the key success factors in Figure 23.7 (the fishbone diagram), and lead a short discussion on interpretation—to ensure that everyone understands what these short phrases mean. Ask if there is anything on the diagram that needs to be changed or added.

3. Assign the participants to four small groups, each to work on one arm of the fishbone diagram. Ask them to discuss what the institution is doing regarding each success factor and to identify *strengths* and *areas for improvement*. Suggest 20 minutes to complete the discussion and be ready to report back to the large group.

4. Ask each of the small groups to report their conclusions in five minutes or less, and take questions from the others.

5. Facilitate a wrap-up discussion, perhaps around questions such as: Was the exercise useful? What did we learn? Are there any areas where we don't have enough information? What are the next steps *for this group* that we should consider? Would it be helpful for any other groups to go through this exercise?

This workshop normally requires a meeting venue that will allow the participants to work in four small groups of about three to six people.

Consider the following variations for different situations.

Situation	Action
Group is large (say, >20 people).	Have more small groups, some working in parallel on the same topic. Debrief only one group on each topic—others can comment only on differences.
Group is small (say, <12 people).	Assign participants to work in pairs.
Participants are not used to small group work.	Provide careful guidance regarding small group process and roles.
	Orchestrate assignments so that each group contains someone with facilitation skills.
The group is new to these concepts or may be overwhelmed or have misgivings about these ideas or this process.	Provide some prework reading. Discuss objectives, roles, and possible reactions with the group leader beforehand. Engage an external facilitator.

Acknowledgments

The following individuals generously gave their time to review drafts of this chapter and to offer valuable comments and suggestions: Doug Bell, Lynn Cook, Ken DeVane, Elma Heidemann, Pat Henderson, and Rita Mulroney-Leitch.

Notes

1. Thomas Holmes and Richard Rahe, "Holmes-Rahe Social Readjustment Rating Scale," *The Journal of Psychosomatic Research* 11 (1967): 213–18.

2. William Bridges, *Transitions: Making Sense of Life's Changes* (Don Mills, Ontario: Addison Wesley, 1980).

3. Daniel Goleman, *Emotional Intelligence* (New York: Bantam Books, 1995).

David W. Hutton is a quality practitioner with extensive practical experience gained by applying quality management methods throughout his career as an engineer, manager, and senior executive. Since establishing his consulting practice in 1990 he has focused on two key aspects of quality management: (1) organizational assessment as a tool for planning and driving continuous improvement; and (2) the human dimension of change. Hutton is also the author of the best-selling ASQC Quality Press book *The Change Agents' Handbook: A Survival Guide for Quality Improvement Champions.* He lives with his family in Ottawa, Canada.

Chapter 24

Clinical Path Success Factors

Robert B. Halder and Jackie Lobien

The primary impediment to the maturation of clinical improvement efforts is the failure of physicians to participate in the various quality activities such as improvement teams, reengineering teams, and benchmarking projects, to name a few. Various reasons are given, but the significant time required to participate on such teams and the failure of physicians to see the immediate benefits for their patients and themselves are the main factors for nonparticipation. Because of this, hospital executives and their quality councils have become increasingly frustrated. They realize that significant efficiencies can be realized only if they tackle clinical issues—that only by reducing unwanted, unintended, unnecessary practice variations can they realize the promised results of continuous improvement. In many instances, this situation has led to polarization within the organization and a propensity to blame the doctors for failed quality initiatives.

Yet one quality tool, above all others, has genuinely captured the attention of physicians and has not only brought them to the table but, in many instances, has provided them an opportunity to take the lead in their institutions' quality initiatives. This tool of quality is the clinical path. Known synonymously as the clinical pathway or critical pathway, this quality application works on the premise that if you expose the same people to improved processes, improved outcomes will be achieved.

Same people + Improved process = Improved outcomes

It works on the premise that public display of performance and process will lead to improvement. In addition, the clinical path relies on measurement. In fact, data integration and data dissemination are prerequisites for success in pathway design and implementation. And finally, this approach to practice variation reduction is a clear example of the application of systems knowledge in the health care setting.

This chapter will stress the factors that have been shown to contribute to successful development, implementation, utilization, and improvement of clinical paths. The case study—from Suburban Hospital in Bethesda, Maryland—will show how success has been achieved in pathway utilization in a large, tertiary hospital.

Understanding Clinical Quality

The drivers of change in our health care system are myriad, and with increased management and capitation schemes the strategies for survival are becoming increasingly complex and dependent on physician participation. Payors believe that capitation will drive increased levels of accountability, teamwork, information sharing, financial rewards, efficiency, and value. They believe that physicians will be forced to manage the care and thereby manage the costs; that there will be a significant move to design high-performing clinical processes that maintain acceptable quality while reducing the waste associated with undesirable variation in practice and process; and that this will result in the customers of the health care system being more satisfied and a reduction in malpractice suits, awards, and premiums. If these assumptions have any merit, then it is incumbent for clinicians to respond by defining process improvement in terms that have the greatest benefits for them and their patients. Clinical paths represent such a response.

To be successfully utilized, clinical paths should be part of a health care organization's total quality management (TQM) or continuous quality improvement (CQI) strategy. As can be seen in Figure 24.1, the results of CQI—delighted customers, empowered employees, higher revenue, and lower costs—must be understood. Pathways are designed to achieve these results. Because pathways are models of quality design (quality planning), utilize measures and goals of performance (quality control), and, once designed, are continuously improved (quality improvement), they reflect clear application of the trilogy of quality.

The infrastructure necessary to support pathway activities includes a quality system featuring a quality council of senior clinical and administrative leaders. Customer-supplier partnerships between physicians, nurses, and ancillary personnel must be strong; the entire organization should be engaged in quality activities even if this only means that everyone measures those indicators of performance of the key processes that support their most important customers; strong information/measurement systems are needed to support pathway design, implementation, utilization, and improvement; and education and training concerning facets of this quality tool are likewise vital.

The foundations of CQI will optimize pathway performance. Clinical paths are a way to successfully deploy the strategic plan (strategic quality management). The organization's vision and key strategies will become reality when actionable areas can be identified. For example, to support a key strategy concerning excellence in the provision of cardiac care, the development of clinical paths targeting those few DRGs/procedures accounting for 80 percent to 90 percent of the cardiac bed days will ensure that the global strategy becomes a reality.

Clinical paths can reach their full potential only in organizations where executive leaders (especially physicians) support such activities and where customer focus on issues important to patients, nurses, and doctors is pervasive.

Understanding the drivers for change and working in a mature CQI climate establishes fertile ground for pathway proliferation. For example, an eye care outpatient surgical center evaluates an adverse outcome involving a juvenile diabetic who is evaluated preoperatively by an internist and is scheduled as first case. Because of a delayed start, this patient enters the postoperative care environment late and—despite the best intentions of highly trained, skilled professionals—the patient develops ketoacidosis requiring transfer to an acute care facility. Evaluation of this care reveals errors of communication and the failure of the system to accommodate for the late start. Review of aggregate data reveals that similar episodes have occurred in the recent past. A multidisciplinary team is formed consisting of an ophthalmologist, internist, surgical center nurse, social service provider, and dietician. Together they design a pathway of care for vitrectomy patients with juvenile diabetes. Because this

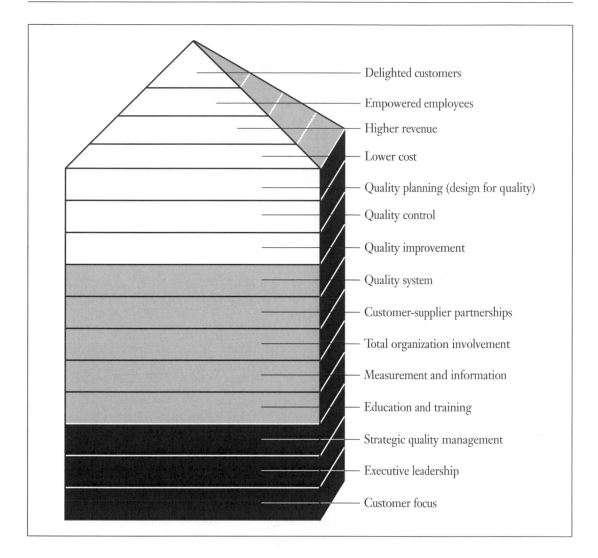

Figure 24.1. TQM/CQI strategy.

represents a sizeable number of their surgical center patients, they know that using this clinical path will reduce the chance of unwelcomed outcomes. Understanding the need to effect this positive change in practice and practicing in a climate indicative of strong CQI maturation allows this team to quickly achieve desired outcomes using the pathway tool.

Preconditions for Pathway Development

Hospitals that have successfully integrated severity adjustment systems into their operations will often use these systems to ensure that the appropriate patients are placed on the pathways and that physicians will agree that these patients and their pathway outcomes truly represent apples-to-apples comparisons. In the absence of such severity systems, most of which have some shortcomings, hospitals/clinics can use consensus-based inclusion and exclusion criteria to ensure that the patients on the pathway represent a homogenous population—a population for which process and outcome measures are, by agreement, apples-to-apples comparisons. In fact, excluding patients from pathways whose known or suspected comorbidity impact may cause the patient to leave the pathway will still leave the vast majority of patients, including those with comorbidities under control, on the pathway with a high degree of confidence that they will stay on the pathway throughout its duration.

Other preconditions include an understanding of need: What factors of health care reform can best be addressed by using pathways? Usually the realization of the need to reduce unnecessary, unwanted, and unintended variation stimulates physicians to use the pathway tool. In addition, in order to create a pathway, the team needs to understand how care for this particular diagnosis has been traditionally provided. Much, if not most, of traditional practice by doctors, nurses, and ancillary support personnel will be carried over into the pathway design.

It is also necessary that a culture of cooperation exist before pathways can be developed. Optimally, doctors and other staff should be practicing in a climate of collegiality where respect for each provider's professionalism is high. Also, properly managing and massaging egos is necessary so that, during pathway development and use, areas of sensitivity are recognized and addressed. Physicians recognize that they are part of a team—a team whose best consensus-based approach to a diagnosis or procedure is reflected in the clinical pathway; nurses confront the fact that the ultimate pathway replaces the chart. Ego management is a must.

The organization should also be comfortable with the concept of case management, because the pathway represents just that. The critical interventions directed by the pathway will be required seven days a week. If a patient cannot be extubated on Sunday because the provider is not available, one unnecessary day has just been added to the pathway.

Selecting Pathway Topics

Critical to the success of pathways is the selection of the right diagnoses and procedures. Selection criteria include high frequency (volume), high cost, high risk, high provider/payor interest, high known variation in provider/practice options, high comorbidity impact, and high levels of patient homogeneity. The hospital's first pathway usually meets most of these criteria. The confidence gained by knowing what others have reported as successful pathway topics will likewise contribute to the selection process. The proliferation of total hip/knee replacement pathways clearly reflects these criteria.

Figure 24.2 represents a matrix that can be used with a numerical weighting system to select pathway candidates.

Pathway Development Methodologies

The best clinical pathways are developed by integrating expert opinion, evidence-based literature review, and practice panel consensus. This applies to each pathway team member community. For the total hip replacement pathway, the orthopedic surgeons have gathered the best practices in the literature and have networked with the recognized leaders in the field. In addition, they have reached consensus among their own practice panel as to which of their own current practices reflect the best approach to this procedure. The clinical nurses have done the same, as have the social workers, the physical therapists, and the dieticians. Each team member brings to the table the best identified practices that represent consensus among the community of providers who will be using this pathway. In addition, examples of pathways used at respected hospitals and clinics by trusted peers can be used to stimulate and accelerate the pathway development process, fully realizing that the final product will be "our" pathway. Only then will buy-in be achieved.

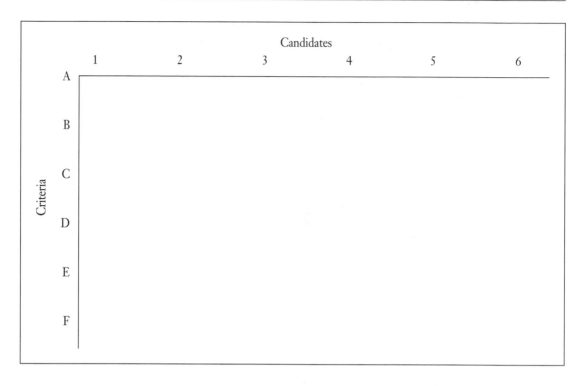

Figure 24.2. Selecting pathway topics.

Pathway Creation/Road Map

Pathways can be nominated by physicians, nurses, payors, administrators, and others. They may be identified as a result of quality improvement activities, medicolegal reviews, and utilization reviews. Figure 24.3 shows a review of a specific severity-adjusted DRG wherein provider variation from the average length of stay and patient bill variations led to the creation of a clinical pathway. The physicians with 130 cases, 49 cases, and 108 cases provided especially valuable input toward the design of the ultimate process of care reflected in the new pathway. Using the criteria and selection matrix described earlier will simplify the selection process.

Next a team of providers—physicians, nurses, support, and ancillary personnel—closest to the process is chosen. Those on the team are those who actually provide the care. This multidisciplinary team uses an agreed-upon model to develop the pathway. This model has perhaps been designed by a standing pathway support group using input from clinicians and others. This model is based on what others have done and how that best can be adapted/adopted into the user organization's culture. The degree of complexity and sophistication of the tool represents consensus and compromise; it is also planned that, with experience, the model may change to meet the user's emerging needs. Standardization means that all users will be familiar with the instrument—its cover sheet, exclusion criteria, variance sheet, standing orders, patient version, and main pathway format—even though the diagnosis or procedure around which the pathway is built will vary. In this way, nurses floating to a new ward will recognize the instrument; it will be user-friendly, even though on one ward it is used to treat orthopedic diagnoses, on another ward pediatric diagnoses. Everyone will be familiar with the selected model.

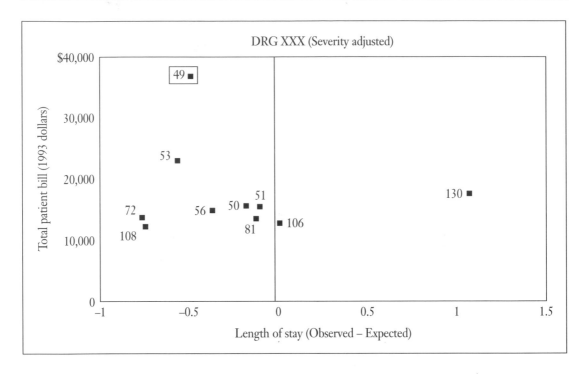

Figure 24.3. Total patient cost vs. length of stay.

The pathway team members will be trained on how to develop the tool. During their deliberations they may require consultation with non–team members such as an information systems specialist or epidemiologist.

Those authorizing the pathway will have identified its goals. These traditionally include goals related to length of stay, cost, patient satisfaction, and functional outcome. In addition, the boundaries of the pathway will be established. These include prehospital activities as well as postdischarge critical events.

Next the team maps, by provider community, the critical steps of care and builds offline consensus among its practice groups that these community-specific activities reflect best practice. For example, the physical therapists agree on ambulation/therapy interventions throughout the pathway. The team then sequences these community-specific activities to ensure that they are complementary. At this point the team selects the pathway measures.

The importance of selecting and designing the right measures into the pathway cannot be overstated. One cannot manage what one cannot measure. Therefore, the selection of the right pathway metrics is critical.

Process measures include compliance rates by physician and by patient, variance rates, utilization rates, fall-off (drop-off) rates, and appropriateness rates. These are measured to ensure that the path is being used as intended and that nonutilization can be analyzed for trending so that interventions can be conducted. For example, variance analysis may show that a sizeable number of total hip replacement pathway patients are not being switched from IV to oral antibiotics on day 2. Analysis of the reasons for this variance may indicate that many patients are slightly febrile or exhibiting excessive incisional hyperemia. Further review may show that even though these patients are not developing wound infections, the physicians are concerned. The knowledge imparted by this variance may stimulate the physicians to look to a new antibiotic or consider an additional day of IV antibiotic therapy. Without variance documentation and analysis, this opportunity may be missed.

Pathway outcome measures include measures of milestones such as extubation, ambulation, length of stay, cost per episode of care, patient satisfaction, functional outcomes (for example, ability to climb stairs or to return to full premorbid activity), and recidivism (readmission) rates. These outcome measures, as well as the process measures, should be developed in collaboration with the information management specialists. As a rule of thumb, select only those measures on which clinical decisions will be made. These, by definition, will cover critical events along the pathway.

Select measures that can be extracted and analyzed using the existing data systems or by working with the data specialists to design the software necessary to track previously unmeasurable metrics. And because measurement requires input, extraction, analysis, and decisions, nurses and physicians in particular will want to take ownership of the measurement issues related to the pathway. Most data entry will be performed by nurses and most analysis by physicians and nurses. Making the measurements user-friendly will go a long way to ensure success.

Following creation of the draft version of the pathway, the team then conducts stakeholder review to ensure buy-in and further consensus. This step likewise enhances the quality of the pathway. Offline discussion within user groups will refine the pathway.

Next comes the development of an implementation plan. Where will the path be tested? By which physicians will it be used, and when? Will it be used on all wards, or initially just one ward? Addressing these issues ensures a smooth transition to path utilization. Likewise, cultural issues as well as resistances need to be identified and confronted at this stage. Hopefully, the participation and preparation of stakeholders throughout the development process will preclude the emergence of significant resistance. When it occurs, it can often be dealt with using negotiation or consensus building. Engaging the recognized leaders or opinion-shapers in the organization can assist in removing barriers. Finding pathway champions can make implementation easier.

As the pathway is implemented, the need for adjustments/modifications will be obvious and should be effected immediately. Continued literature review, new technologies, and new methodologies will stimulate pathway improvement. Most important, because the pathway is designed to stabilize the variation in critical process steps, it affords the opportunity to test new approaches to care.

For example, a member of the orthopedic practice attends a conference at which a paper is presented suggesting that earlier ambulation for postoperative total hip replacement patients shortens length of stay without increasing the rate of recognized complications (for example, wound infections or prosthesis dislocation). This surgeon brings this information to the practice group. The group members decide to test this theory on a group of pathway patients. They enjoy the same results as reported at the conference. The total hip replacement pathway is modified to reflect this new methodology. The use of the path as a bedside research tool is one of its strengths.

The final step of pathway development is a final step common to all improvement/design activities: Look for opportunities to replicate what has been learned. A total hip replacement pathway can be used to accelerate the development of a total knee replacement pathway. Likewise, a pathway for major depression can contribute to the development of a clinical path for schizophrenia.

Identifying and Overcoming Barriers

Barriers commonly encountered in pathway use include concerns about cookbook medicine intended by administrators only as a cost-reduction tool, worries about litigation, pathways creating more documentation, pathways withholding care, physician nonparticipation, pathways replacing individual case management, inflexibility, and focusing on the wrong outcomes.

Because pathways are related to standing orders and algorithms, they are not a new concept. In fact, many of the textbooks of medical care (especially pediatrics) have traditionally used the pathway model to ensure the reliability and quality of multidisciplinary care with respect to a specific diagnosis or procedure.

As previously stated, when developed by consensus with expert (including literature) input, pathways will reduce undesirable variation and contribute to optimal outcomes for populations of patients (as well as individuals). They are preemptive and provide a warning approach. Proper user education ensures optimal pathway performance. Effective measurement and analysis provide opportunity to improve the processes of care and, thereby, the outcomes of care. They are nonjudgmental and are designed to be user-friendly. Most important, they should *never* be used to replace sound clinical judgment.

Pathways and Litigation

The jury is not yet in on the issue of pathways and litigation (pun intended). Anecdotes can be found to support both sides of the issue.

The factors that influence malpractice determinations include confusing practice standards, sympathy, medical record inaccuracies, and 20/20 hindsight, just to name a few. Pathways demonstrate the intentional choice of best-practice options; they represent coordinated care; they help create clarity of the medical record; and they build in a fail-safe mechanism to preclude missing a critical intervention. They are also a powerful patient communication tool. The lay version, with patient-friendly language and icons, is a wonderful education tool for both patients and family members. It lays out the anticipated timeline for major events in the episode of care and creates an expectation of patient participation. The pathway also reassures patients that there is a plan for their care.

Pathways not only improve patient and provider communication but in a court of law can be effective representations of care that is planned, based on best specialty practices, flexible to the needs of the individual, and well-documented. Pathways reflect logic in clinical decision making. Of course, poorly designed or inappropriately used pathways do not reduce vulnerability in malpractice cases; but when designed and implemented well, measured as planned, and improved as indicated, they are an effective advocate of well-intended, well-documented care. Again, they are designed to support the provision of care, not to replace sound clinical judgment.

Case Examples/Results

Scripps Memorial Hospital in La Jolla, California, developed a pathway to manage cardiac surgery patients. It reported the following results:[1]

- A 22 percent reduction in length of stay

- A 12 percent decrease in patient charges

- A 50 percent decrease in physician paperwork

The Medical Center of Vermont created a pathway for ICU pain control that resulted in a 30 percent decrease in hours of intubation and ICU length of stay, a 50 percent reduction in reintubation rates, and savings of $1 million per year.[2]

Figure 24.4 shows the result of Forbes Health System's severe pneumonia pathway. Note the mortality rate reduction.

Medical literature is replete with the results of pathway utilization. Medical conferences are featuring pathway workshops with increasing frequency.

Variable	Before	After
ER blood cultures	36%	96%
ER sputum cultures	53%	86%
Antibiotics <4 hours	42%	87%
Mortality rate	10.2%	6.8%
Average LOS (days)	10.4	9.1

Source: Quality Review Bulletin 19, no. 5 (1993): 124–130.

Figure 24.4. Forbes Health System: Critical pathway for severe pneumonia (DRG 89).

Lessons Learned

The main opportunity for improving the efficiency of health care systems resides in the reduction of unwanted, unnecessary, and unintended practice variation. Real benefits result from a decline in these variations and with the stabilization of process that allows measurement of process capabilities (outcomes). If pathways are to be effective, they must be driven by the desire to improve the quality of care. Physicians must take the lead in their development, utilization, measurement, and improvement.

Finally, if pathways represent *added* work, especially added documentation, they will fail. The quid pro quo must include a transition from the standard medical record to the pathway tool as the documentation source for care. This represents a challenge to the old documentation paradigm, especially for nurses. But to the degree that the pathway can incorporate such features as exclusion criteria, variance tracking sheets, signature pages, supporting standing orders, algorithms, lay versions, patient education packets, nursing assessment forms, and the like, the transition from old charting to pathway charting will be easier.

The following case study from Suburban Hospital in Bethesda, Maryland, well illustrates those factors contributing to clinical path success.

Case Study: Suburban Hospital Hip Replacement Critical Pathway Development Process

Suburban Hospital is a 250-bed, community-owned, not-for-profit hospital that has been serving Montgomery County, Maryland, since 1943. An acute care, adult medical/surgical hospital, Suburban is the county-designated shock trauma center.

In 1993, the board of trustees conducted a retreat to develop a new vision for reducing costs while maintaining a high level of quality. With the assistance of the Juran Institute, the hospital began its initiative toward cultural change into continuous quality improvement. Merging quality activities, a strategic plan, quality improvement teams, reengineering, critical pathway development, and continuous improvement training began.

Establishing the Project

The quality council, comprised of executive staff, made the decision to form multidisciplinary, quality improvement teams to develop critical pathways—maps of care to increase attractiveness to managed care organizations and accelerate the quality improvement initiative. The objective in forming in-house teams to develop the pathways was to enhance communication, break down departmental silos, and provide a means for increased collaboration. In addition, clinical and nonclinical processes would be evaluated. Developing the pathways internally provided the ability to customize the data essential to gaining physician acceptance.

When the quality management department began reviewing severity adjusted data (received from Iameter Inc.) and sharing the results with the physicians, variability was apparent in every DRG. There was high variation in length of stay and patients' charges even though acuity levels were similar. Sharing this data with the physicians was the initiative to getting them involved with the critical pathway development. Quantifying variation focused the physicians and staff on variation reduction, outcomes management, and systems thinking.

Using a selection matrix, hip procedures (DRG 209.81.51–81.53) were identified as the first critical pathway to be addressed (see Figure 24.5). Criteria of high volume, high clinical practice variation, a homogeneous patient population, and a primary focus of the hospital strategic initiative were all met. In addition, the orthopedic surgeons were enthusiastic and agreed to be the champions for the initiation of critical pathways into the organization.

A brainstorming exercise was conducted by the quality council to identify and verify a team that had representation from each of the most affected parts of the organization. The manager of the orthopedic nursing unit was identified as the process owner and team leader. Other members of the team were from care management, utilization management, discharge planning, physical medicine and rehabilitation, nursing, and the skilled nursing facility. Two orthopedic physicians also served as team members, with their role to consult with the physicians of the orthopedic subsection. The chief financial officer, although not an official team member, served as the quality council sponsor. The

Figure 24.5. Selection matrix.

facilitator for the team was an individual formally trained in the quality improvement process, team interaction skills, and the use of quality improvement tools.

Based on a review of initial length of stay data, the quality council prepared a mission statement:

> *The team will develop a critical pathway beginning with preadmission and ending with a postoperative follow-up to decrease length of stay from 8.3 days to 6 days for DRG 209 (hip procedures).*

The team was given a goal by the quality council to accomplish this mission within three months. To achieve this goal, team members decided to meet weekly for an hour and a half.

At the first meeting, team members verified that membership did in fact represent the appropriate parts of the organization. Those departments not represented on the team and not acutely involved with the patients were identified as consultants. They were notified that they would be called if additional information was needed. The mission statement received from the quality council was reviewed. The team agreed that it could meet the objective set forth by the council.

Diagnosing the Cause

The team decided first to complete a high-level flow diagram of a hip replacement admission. It began with the patient's visit to the physician's office and ended with the inpatient discharge (see Figure 24.6). The discussion during the formulation of the flow diagram was an important part of the process. It helped establish open channels of communication and a sense of teamwork. Team members began to have a clearer understanding of the roles of each department and opened up valuable dialog. Several office managers from large orthopedic groups were interviewed to discuss the role of the physician and their office staff in scheduling surgery and giving preoperative education. Managers from departments not represented on the team were consulted by a team member to identify that the flow diagram accurately reflected all elements of a patient's stay.

Although the flow diagram provided the logic of the process and the procedures involved in a hip replacement, the team members felt they needed additional, detailed data to identify causes of the variation in length of stay. The team spent the next meeting reviewing severity-adjusted data to determine the key clinical contributors to increased length of stay. Once these were identified, a detailed medical record review form was developed by the team. Using the severity-adjusted database, members of the team reviewed 56 medical records to compare best demonstrated (most efficient) to high utilization (least efficient) cases.

The analysis of the medical record review revealed to the team variation in the ordering and frequency of all ancillary services provided during the patient's hospital stay (see Figure 24.7). Specifically, variations in discharge planning and physical therapy were highlighted. The team theorized that there may be a delay in the time between when these services were ordered to when they were initiated. This is important since the day (that is, admission day vs. postoperative days 1–4) that discharge planning and physical therapy were ordered appeared to impact the length of stay. To validate their theory, team members completed a second review that focused on the days service was ordered and initiated. The results from the second review demonstrated that there were no delays between the day the order was written and the implementation day for both discharge planning and physical therapy. There was, however, a one-day difference in length of stay when physical therapy was ordered on admission day (in PACU) versus postoperative days 1–4 (see Figure 24.8). This information validated the need to order services early in the admission phase.

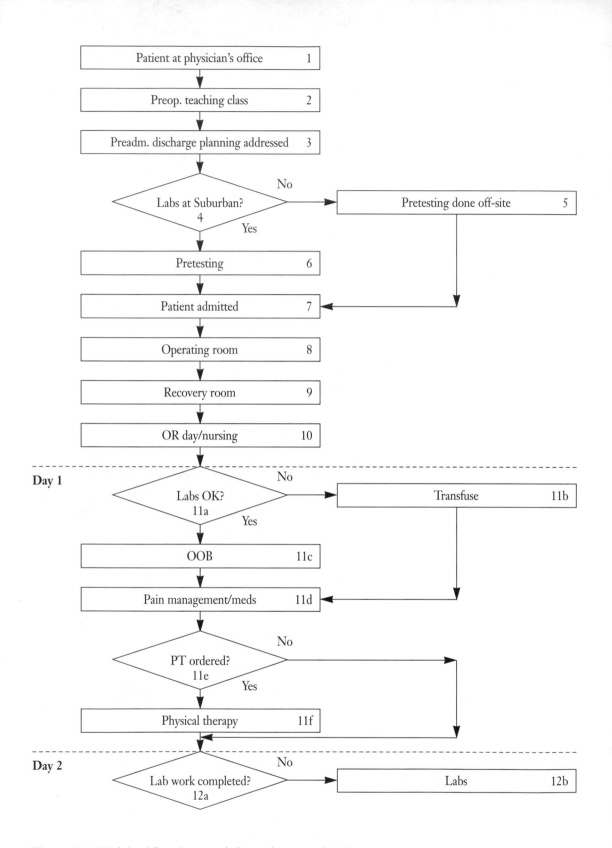

Figure 24.6. High-level flow diagram of a hip replacement admission.

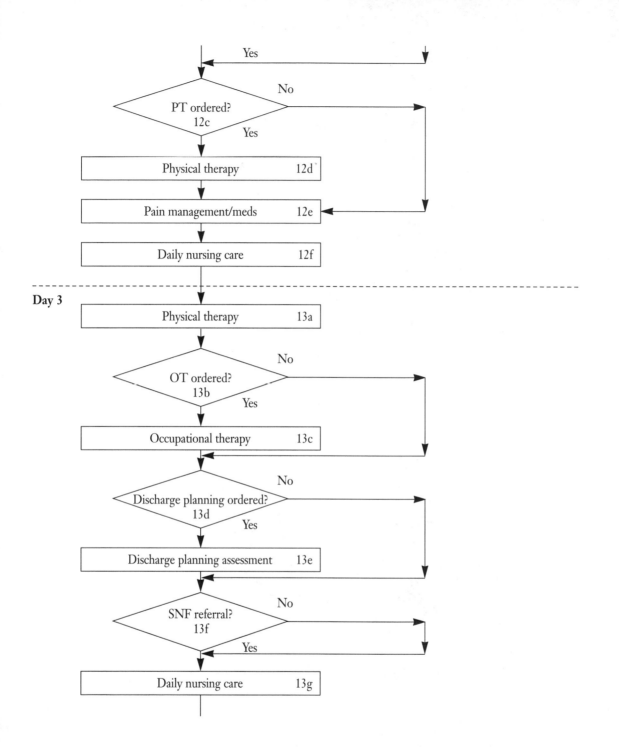

Day 3

Figure 24.6. *Continued.*

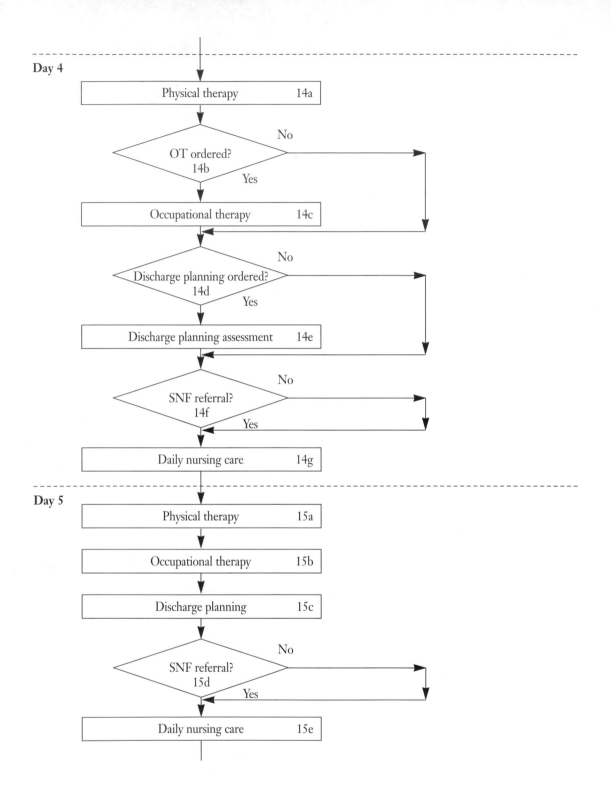

Figure 24.6. *Continued.*

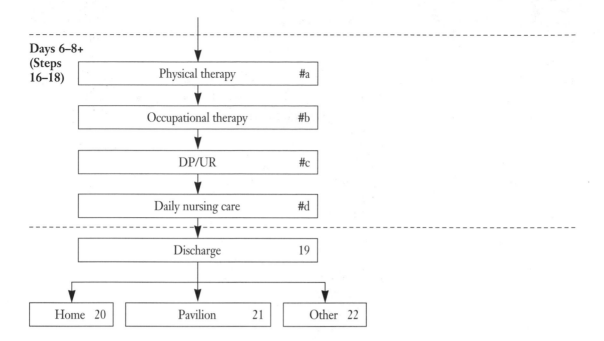

Days 6–8+ (Steps 16–18)

Physical therapy	#a
Occupational therapy	#b
DP/UR	#c
Daily nursing care	#d
Discharge	19

| Home 20 | Pavilion 21 | Other 22 |

Figure 24.6. *Continued.*

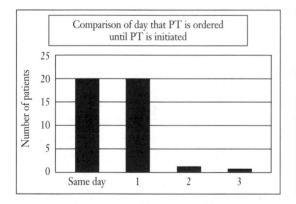

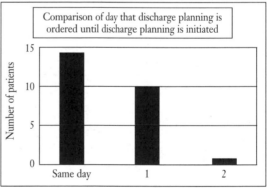

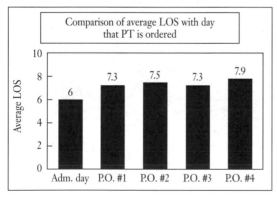

Figure 24.7. Results of the medical record review.

Designing the Pathway

The team members reviewed articles on pathway design and specific pathways on hip replacements that were available in the literature. Also, information was obtained from insurance companies regarding guidelines for physical therapy (once a day vs. twice a day). The team discussed the need to have

	Surgery	Postop #1	Postop #2	Postop #3
Labwork				
CBC	100%	88%	80%	56%
ELR	4%	24%	8%	8%
PT	20%	32%	28%	24%
PTT	20%	12%	12%	8%
Activity				
Bedrest	100%	12%	0%	0%
OOB/chair	0%	88%	60%	70%
OOB/walker	0%	0%	40%	30%
Meds/IV				
Antibiotic (IV)	90%	48%	24%	0%
IV	82%	80%	52%	20%
PCA	85%	78%	40%	12%
Heparin	12%	12%	12%	8%
Coumadin	28%	28%	20%	16%
Lovenox	0%	0%	0%	0%
IM pain med	15%	22%	20%	12%
PO pain med	0%	15%	40%	50%
Respiratory care				
Oxygen	32%	16%		
Incentive spirometer	95%			
PT/OT				
PT	0%	72%	100%	100%
OT	0%	0%	12%	12%
Miscellaneous				
Abduction pillow	60%			
Venodynes	100%			
Foley	24%			
D/C planning	0%	12%	16%	12%

Summary of days 4–6
Three patients had labwork ordered
All patients continued progressing in activity to OOB with walker/crutches
No IV antibiotics/IV/PCA given
Patients placed on PO pain meds
PT and OT (when ordered) continued until discharge
D/C planning completed when ordered

Figure 24.8. Total hip medical record review analysis: 25 best demonstrated medical records reviewed.

its own hospital/physician data to drive the pathway. In order to convince physicians to modify their clinical practice, it was imperative that they be presented with a data-driven analysis. Specifically, they needed to be shown how their performance compared to the best-demonstrated patients.

A review form was developed by the team to analyze clinical data day by day from the top 25 best-demonstrated records. Figure 24.9 shows the results of that review. These data were used to design the pathway by validating the rationale for each step of the pathway. Discussion ensued during the team meeting regarding the intradepartmental system issues that would need to be resolved prior to the initiation of the pathway. The physical medicine and rehabilitation department needed to review its

---

Preoperative Consult for Care Manager (Community Outreach)

1. The orthopedic unit manager will obtain the operative schedule for total hip procedures.
2. The orthopedic unit manager will call those patients and inquire if he/she will attend total joint class.
3. If the patient cannot attend the class, the patient's name will be forwarded to the care manager.
4. The care manager will contact the patient and arrange for a home visit.
   a. The discharge planner's name and phone number will be given to the patient.
   b. The care manager will review the plan of care to include
      1. Surgery date
      2. Critical path review
      3. Home care/PAV/SNF
      4. DME
      5. Handouts and information shared at total joint class
   c. The care manager will complete a home assessment to include
      1. Medications
      2. Safety home evaluation
      3. Health assessment
      4. Gait/balance assessment
      5. ADL evaluation
      6. Mini mental exam
      7. Identify social supports
5. The care manager will document the assessment and provide a copy to the discharge planner.
6. The discharge planner will place the assessment on the medical record (UR D/P section).

Postoperative Follow-Up Completed by Care Manager (Community Outreach)

1. The discharge planner will notify the care manager with discharge plan to include
   a. Agency name for home care
   b. SNF name
   c. DME company
   d. Medication list
   e. Social supports
2. Care manager will call the patient at home and ask the checklist of questions. Based on the response to the questions, the care manager will determine appropriate follow-up.
3. For follow-up months (2–6), the care manager will call the patient and provide phone consultation as needed.

Figure 24.9. Review form developed from clinical data analysis of best-demonstrated records.

staffing patterns to ensure that physical therapy would occur seven days a week, twice a day. The orthopedic nursing unit needed to discuss how it would utilize its staff to be certain that all patients were out of bed on postoperative day 1. Discharge planning and care management needed to address pre- and postoperative evaluations/outcomes. Similarly, team members and consultants reviewed the pathway with their respective departments. Expert opinion provided by the physician consultants was integrated.

Once the team felt comfortable that all departments involved would be able to meet the desired clinical steps of the pathway, the draft was shared with the entire orthopedic subsection. A team member presented the draft along with the data to back up the rationale for each piece of the pathway. The presentation of data to formulate the pathway was an important step. When physicians questioned certain clinical criteria—for example, use of patient-controlled analgesic versus IM pain medication—the team was able to provide data to validate that 85 percent of the best-demonstrated patients had used the patient-controlled analgesic. The subsection then agreed to keep it on the pathway.

Physicians were also concerned about patient outcomes with a shorter length of stay. Did the team provide mechanisms to monitor readmission rates, functional status, and patient satisfaction?

The hospital provides a total joint class monthly, with multidisciplinary participation. At this class, patients would be shown the pathway and given a functional health status evaluation. If they did not attend the class, a member of the care management department would call each patient, review the pathway, and conduct the functional health status evaluation. If discharge planning needs were identified during the class or phone call, the discharge planning department would be notified. Postoperatively, all patients would receive a follow-up phone call and again receive the functional health status evaluation. The utilization management department will provide readmission data. Once the care manager plan was developed (see Figure 24.10) in conjunction with the total joint class, the physicians felt comfortable that these mechanisms addressed their concerns regarding monitoring patient outcomes.

Once the pathway was approved by the orthopedic subsection, the hospital information systems department became an integral piece of the process. Using the hospital-based computer system, the pathway and variance tracking sheet were automated (see Figure 24.11). To achieve accountability and continue with the multidisciplinary approach, the decision was made by the team and approved by the quality council to have each department concurrently record its own variances (variances would be recorded by exception only).

The team was now ready to embark on hospitalwide education. Each department was given an in-service session on the development of the pathway, use of the pathway in the computer, and variance tracking. The pathway would be piloted for three months.

Measurement

During the three-month pilot, 14 patients were placed on the hip pathway. This represented 85 percent of patients under DRG 209.8151–8153. The 15 percent not on the pathway had high acuity levels and were not appropriate pathway candidates. The average length of stay decreased from a prepilot LOS of 8.3 days to a postpilot LOS of 4.6 days (see Figure 24.12). The team met again to review the variances and to determine, based on the number and type of variances, if changes needed to be made to the pathway. At this time, the team members felt that the pathway needed no changes.

Once additional patients were placed on the pathway, specific departmental variances were analyzed. The physical therapy and rehabilitation department, for example, reviewed the number of variances for patients receiving physical therapy twice a day. The department related this information

Total Hip Replacement
Critical Pathway: LOS 5 Days w/Variance Keys

Account #:   Unit #:   Status: ADM IN

Admit Date: Patient: Age/Sex: Rm:

	Preop	Surgery day	Postop Day 1	Postop Day 2	Postop Day 3	Postop Day 4
Consults D/C plan	• Preop Class • If no Case Mgmt or Social Svc Consult	• Discharge Plan Consult • RT Consult for Incent. Spirometer Teach	• Bedside D/C Plan Visit • PAV Referral • Home Care Consult	• Identify PAV/SNF Placement vs. Home Care	• Identify PAV Accept Data • Case Management F/u	• PAV/SNF Transf or D/C w/Home Care • Notify Pt re: QM F/u call/visit 1–6 times
Lab tests	• T&S • PT • CBC • EKG • CXR • UA • ELR	• CBC • PT (if on anticoagulant)	• CBC • PT (if on anticoagulant)	• CBC • PT (if on anticoagulant)	• CBC • PT (if on anticoagulant)	• PT (if on anticoagulant)
PT/OT		• Order PT (Use Blue Orthopedic Prescript.) • Order OT	• To PT in Geri Chair	• PT AM • PT PM • OT Evaluation	• PT AM • PT PM • OT	• PT AM • PT PM • OT
Activity		• Bedrest on Air Mattress	• OOB to Chair • Walker in Room	• OOB to Chair AM • OOB to Chair PM • Progress to OOB w/Walker	• OOB to Chair AM • OOB to Chair PM • OOB w/Walker	• OOB
Nursing Tx's	• Review treatments in preop class	• Trapeze • Abduction Pillow • Leg Lifter • Venodynes • I & O • Diet as Tolerated • IV Fluids • Incentive Spirometer	• D/C Abduct Pillow in PM • Pillow Between Legs in Bed • Venodynes • I & O • Diet as Tol until D/C • IV Fluids • Incentive Spirometer • Reinforce Hip Drsng PR	• Pillow Between Legs in Bed • Venodynes • I & O • Assess Bowel Function • D/C Foley if Present • Change IV to Hep Lock • Incentive Spirometer • Change Hip Dressing • Bedside Commode in Rm	• Pillow Between Legs in Bed • Venodynes • D/C I & O • D/C Hep Lock • Assess Bowel Function • Change Hip Dressing	• Pillow Between Legs in Bed • Check Incision, if no drain, staples open to air • Ambulate to BR w/Walker (elevate toilet seat) • D/C Venodynes
Meds		• PCA • Anticoagulant • IV Antibiotic • Laxative PRN	• PCA • Anticoagulant • IV Fluids • Laxative PRN	• PCA/IM Pain Medication • Anticoagulant • Laxative of Choice PRN	• P.O. Pain Management • Anticoagulant	• PO Pain Medicine • Anticoagulant • Home RX on chart
Patient educ		• Review Clinical Path • Review Nurs. Treatments	• Review Clinical Path	• Review/Reinforce Prev. Learning	• Review/Reinforce Prev. Learning	• Review D/C Instr Activity; Precaut. Meds, Home Care Agency, Med Equip Referral

System/Other:

9.   10.

11.   12.

13.   AA.

Practitioner/Other:

32.   33.

34.   35.

36.   BB.

Patient/Family Other:

50.   51.

52.   53.

54.   CC.

Figure 24.10. Care manager plan for total hip replacement.

Critical Pathway—Variance Key

Account #:	Unit #:	Patient:	Room/Bed:
Admit Date:	Attending:	Age/Sex:	

System

1. Nursing/rehab bed not available
2. Delay completing test
3. Equipment mission/not available
4. Insurance-related problems
5. Test results not available
6. Test not completed
7. Delay transfer; no beds available
8. Department closed on weekend

Other

9. _____
10. _____
11. _____
12. _____
13. _____

Practitioner

21. Procedure not completed
22. Consult not done in 24 hours
23. Failure to contact appropriate consult
24. Incomplete documentation
25. Intervention not ordered
26. Difficulty contacting physician
27. Incomplete records
28. Consensus needed among team
29. Transcription error
30. MD preference
31. MD preference/discharge

Other

32. _____
33. _____
34. _____
35. _____
36. _____

Patient/family

41. Complication R/T DX, not infection
42. Family unavailable for consult
43. Delay decision making
44. Complication not R/T DX, not infection
45. Noncompliance with treatment plan
46. PT refused procedure
47. Inability to learn self-care skills
48. Inadequate social support at home
49. Suspected/confirmed infection

Other

50. _____
51. _____
52. _____
53. _____
54. _____

Figure 24.10. *Continued.*

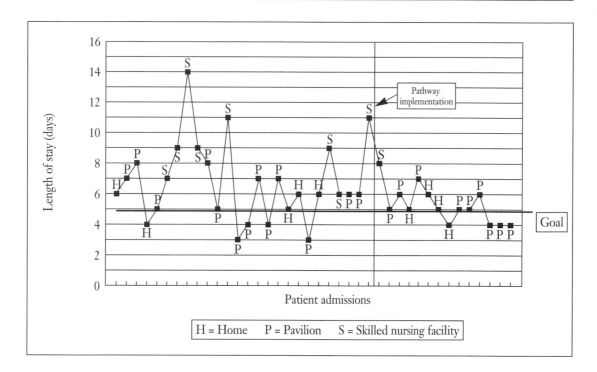

Figure 24.11. Pathway and variance tracking sheet.

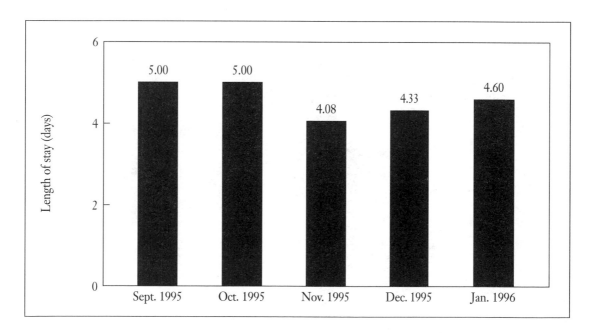

Figure 24.12. Hip replacement length of stay.

to an LOS comparison (see Figure 24.13). This department, as well as others, began to use collected variance data to integrate the pathways into quality control activities. Department staff reviewed the measures, discussing them at staff meetings to determine any necessary remedial actions required. By reviewing the length of stay data and supporting literature for physical therapy twice a day versus once a day the department began quality planning to design care processes to accommodate the increased volume in the department.

Length of stay (see Figure 24.14) and resource utilization data were shared with the orthopedic physicians. Process measurements of compliance, readmission rates, fall-off-rates (patients who were initially placed on the pathway but due to high acuity levels did not remain on it), and overall variances were reviewed.

Holding the Gains

The team met again after six months to review pathway compliance and length of stay data. The length of stay remained below the five-day goal (see Figure 24.12) with the increase for November and December due to higher-acuity patients. Because the compliance for pathway usage remained between 85 percent and 90 percent and the readmission rate was zero, the team identified the clinical criteria on the pathway impacting length of stay (activity, discharge planning, physical therapy). Only exceptions to these criteria would be indicated as variances.

Information from the six-month review was shared with the orthopedic physicians, fostering buy-in from the subsection. The orthopedic physicians were so supportive that they requested building another pathway, for total knee replacements.

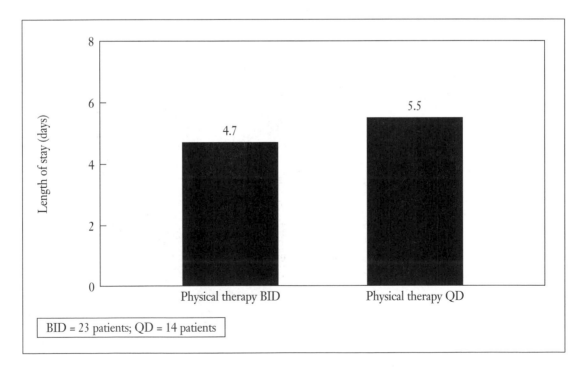

Figure 24.13. Hip critical pathway review: Average LOS, physical therapy BID vs. QD (postop day 2).

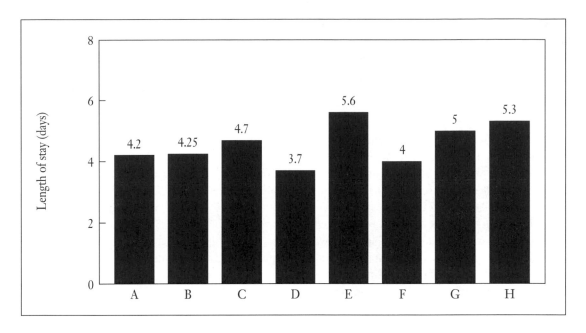

Figure 24.14. Hip replacement average LOS by physician.

Conclusion/Lessons Learned

In retrospect, several lessons were learned throughout this journey. The first was the need for an implementation infrastructure. Once the pathway was completed, the infrastructure was not yet in place to support it. The pathway team had to develop its own guidelines for implementation. Concerns were raised regarding the need for consistency with the implementation of future pathways. A committee was then formed to develop policies to address this issue.

The second lesson learned was the need for ongoing education about pathways. Staff were educated initially during the process, but new employees joining the staff did not consistently receive the computer training needed to implement the pathways. A plan is now being developed to provide education to new employees at orientation.

Our experience supports the notion that multidisciplinary quality improvement teams are valuable in the implementation of critical pathways. Equipped with the understanding of the methods of quality improvement and use of related tools, team members met the quality council's initial objectives to enhance communication, break down departmental "silos," and increase collaboration. In addition, processes were evaluated and departmental system issues impacting length of stay were resolved. Physicians are now engaged and eager to participate in new critical pathway teams. The pathways were integrated into the continuous quality improvement process.

Notes

1. *The Quality Letter* 5 (1993): 2–4.
2. *Quality Connection Storyboard* (IHI) 2, no. 3 (1993): 8–9.

Robert B. Halder, M.D., Rear Admiral, Medical Corps, U.S. Navy, Retired, is senior vice president of Juran Institute, Inc. At the Institute, Halder works closely with the senior management of major health care clients to develop and implement TQM systems. He also provides leadership in health care quality activities on a national and international level.

Halder had a distinguished career in the Navy as a senior executive and practicing ophthalmologist. He has been an outstanding leader in the National Demonstration Project Quality Management Network and a much-in-demand speaker on health care quality.

Halder earned a B.A. degree from the State University of New York, Harpur College in 1964. He has an M.D. degree from the State University of New York Upstate Medical School in Syracuse. He served as a surgical intern at the State University of California, University Hospital, San Diego. Halder entered the U.S. Navy in 1969 as a student flight surgeon. He entered the Ophthalmology Postgraduate Training Program at Naval Hospital, San Diego, in 1971 and became board certified in 1974. In 1985 Bob assumed command of the U.S. Naval Hospital, Naples, Italy, and was promoted to Rear Admiral in June 1988 when he was assigned as Commander, Naval Medical Command, Southwest Region. In May 1989, he assumed command of Naval Hospital, San Diego, the Navy's largest tertiary and teaching hospital. He was promoted to the two-star rank in 1990 and retired from a distinguished military career in June 1992. Upon his retirement, Halder was awarded the Distinguished Service Medal, the highest peacetime military award.

Halder is licensed to practice in the State of California and is a Diplomat of the American Academy of Ophthalmology, a member of the American College of Physician Executives, and a member of the American Medical Association.

Jackie Lobien, RN, is an adjunct faculty consultant with Juran Institute and is a member of its Healthcare Team. She brings to the team expertise in the development and implementation of critical pathways. She also directs the clinical efficiency functions at Suburban Hospital in Bethesda, Maryland, where her primary roles are medical staff–related resource use and practice analysis and clinical cost accounting. She oversees the clinical improvement efforts related to critical pathways. Lobien has held positions at Suburban Hospital that include manager of two medical/surgical nursing units and director of admissions and surgical pretesting. She earned a B.S. degree at Valparaiso University and is a certified nursing administrator.

Chapter 25

Success Factors in Reducing Cost in Hospital Organizations

Ijaz M. Bokhari and David A. Farson

An Industry Undergoing Change

The traumatic upheaval in the health care industry during the mid-1990s has been well documented. Both health care business and professional society publications during this time period reported on the extent of the changes, which affected how health care was provided in most markets throughout the nation. The most significant developments included health care reforms, significant growth in managed care, and industry mergers and acquisitions.

Health Care Reforms

During the first two years of Bill Clinton's presidency, the major domestic program was health care reform. Hillary Rodham Clinton headed a White House task force whose goal was to propose reforms to ensure that all Americans would have access to affordable health care. Based on her findings, President Clinton proposed a national health plan that provided universal coverage for all Americans. This plan did not gain Congressional approval. Although President Clinton was unable to pass major health care reform, his initiative to have a government-mandated overhaul of the health care industry did highlight major problems within the existing health care delivery system and spurred the industry to continue to accelerate its own reform.

Significant Growth in Managed Care

Instead of the federal government forcing change through legislation, the market is the driving force behind pivotal health care changes that are occurring in almost every region throughout the United States, particularly in terms of how health care is delivered.

Since the implementation of Medicare and Medicaid programs during the mid-1960s, health care providers have been the beneficiaries of a lucrative delivery model. Providers were reimbursed for patient care based on a fee-for-service arrangement in which the majority of the bill was paid by a third-party payor, the federal and state governments (for Medicare and Medicaid patients respectively) and indemnity insurers (for people who receive health care benefits through employment). Obviously, the financial incentive under this arrangement was to provide services. In 1965, health care represented 6 percent of the gross domestic product; in 1994, it represented 14 percent.[1]

Prior to the mid-1990s, however, there were many indications that the significant growth rate in health care costs could not be sustained by the American economy. During the late 1980s, with the annual growth rate in health care costs far outpacing the inflation rate, large corporations joined small business owners in sounding the alarm bells. Large corporations complained that they would not be able to compete in an increasingly competitive global market if health care costs for their employees continued to increase at annual double-digit rates. Small business owners complained that health care costs were making it increasingly difficult for them to just stay in business.

With health care costs spiraling out of control, American businesses became much more aggressive in seeking out alternatives to the existing delivery model. This led to a significant growth rate in the percentage of American employees who are covered under a managed health care plan.

In just the three-year period from 1992 to 1994, national employee enrollment in managed care plans has increased from 48 percent to 63 percent. Total HMO enrollment grew from 40,388,000 in 1991 to 56,850,000 in 1994.[2]

Mergers and Acquisitions

The shift from the fee-for-service arrangement provided by traditional indemnity insurers to capitated payment plans provided by HMOs has created serious challenges for hospitals. Under the fee-for-service arrangement, hospitals were financially motivated to build and expand their services as well as purchase expensive, state-of-the-art diagnostic and therapeutic equipment. Favorable reimbursement rates enabled many community hospitals to acquire the financial resources to provide a full range of health services like MRI, cancer treatment programs, and cardiovascular services. However, the shift to the managed care environment brought about a new focus for payors. Managed care companies provide services to their patient populations under capitated payment plans; therefore, they must effectively manage the cost of providing care in order to make a profit. The financial incentive under capitation is *not* to provide services. This has resulted in a steady decrease in the utilization of hospital services, particularly inpatient stays.

National statistics show the extent of the problem. The United States has 5000 acute hospitals and more than 1 million beds.[3] National occupancy rates for community hospitals average between 55 percent and 60 percent. In addition to the shift to managed care, there are other reasons for this excess capacity; two in particular stand out.

1. New clinical approaches that enable patients to be treated on an outpatient basis

2. Decrease in length of patient stay

In addition to declining utilization of services, hospitals have also experienced declining reimbursement rates from managed care companies. As their patient populations have grown, managed care companies have greater clout in the health care market. They use this clout to obtain discounted rates from hospital(s) by offering exclusive contractual arrangements with them in return. Hospitals that are not willing or not able to provide the discounts demanded by the managed care companies are excluded from their business. Hospitals that provide the discounts hope that there will be economies in scale through the increased utilization of their services, which will enable them to make a profit.

Faced with both decreasing utilization of services and declining reimbursement rates, hospitals throughout the nation are feeling the financial squeeze. Hospital administrators and boards of directors are faced with the difficult task of preparing their institutions for a continually worsening financial picture. Many realize that continued competition among community hospitals within a declining health care market jeopardizes each organization's long-term survival. A number of community, not-for-profit institutions have reached the conclusion that the long-term outlook is not very promising for a stand-alone institution.

This has led to a significant increase in the number of mergers of community not-for-profit hospitals that are joining together to form a health system within a regional market. Through mergers, duplicative services can be eliminated and operations streamlined to maximize profitability. It has also resulted in an extraordinary increase in the number of community not-for-profit hospitals being acquired by for-profit investor-owned hospital chains. The numbers speak for themselves.

- "Roughly one in five U.S. community hospitals changed hands" during the two-year period of 1994 and 1995.

- In 1995, "445 community hospitals were involved in 224" merger and acquisition deals; in 1994, "301 hospitals were involved in 176" such deals.

- In 1995, 48 community not-for-profit hospitals either changed their status or were planning to change their status to for-profit. On the other hand, only "eight hospitals were sold by for-profit owners to not-for-profit corporations."[4]

Clearly, the health care industry is experiencing a tremendous amount of change. What is the underlying reason for all this change? It can be summarized in one word: *cost*. Any health care organization aspiring to flourish in today's environment must develop an effective cost containment strategy.

History of Cost Containment Methodologies

There have been many attempts over the years to control health care costs. Each approach has made its impact on the health care industry, particularly in terms of focusing attention on the financial implications of the existing health care delivery model. However, when reviewing the impact each approach has made in terms of the total cost to provide health care to Americans, the overall effectiveness of each approach is open to debate. A summary of the top eight cost containment methodologies is provided here.

Diagnosis-Related Groupings

During the early 1980s, the federal government sounded the alarm bells concerning the rising cost to provide health care services. Because it represented the largest purchaser of health care (paying for services provided to Medicare recipients), it was in a position to make changes in order to reduce its cost. The federal government decided that in order to keep costs under control, a fundamental change needed to be made in the health care reimbursement structure. In 1984 it began to implement a complete overhaul of the payment system with its introduction of diagnosis-related groupings (DRGs).

As indicated by the name of the program, the payment structure changed from one that reimbursed hospitals for all services rendered based on their charges for each service to one that reimbursed hospitals for all services rendered based on a flat fee amount determined by the patient's diagnosis. The hospital received the same reimbursement amount regardless of whether the patient stayed for 5 or 10 days or had 10 or 20 ancillary service tests (such as labs or radiology) performed. The federal government was not dictating to doctors or hospitals a treatment protocol for each diagnosis; the federal government was, however, discouraging the excessive utilization of hospital services by fixing the reimbursement amount. Obviously, the goal of this program was to motivate hospitals to care for Medicare patients in an efficient manner.

The one drawback of this program, at least from a hospital's perspective, is that the doctor—not the hospital—determines the care the patient receives. Since doctors are typically not employees of the hospital, hospitals do not have the authority to control doctors or alter their patient care practice patterns. In fact, hospitals are typically very careful in terms of how they approach their physician community to resolve problems, because hospitals rely on physicians to bring in business. Typically, the most hospitals can do is make physicians aware of the financial implications of their patient care protocols and encourage them to choose treatment options that are the most cost-effective. The physician, however, always makes the final decision in terms of the utilization of hospital services.

Did American health care become more efficient in treating patient ailments as a result of the DRG reimbursement program? Did DRGs reduce the total U.S. health care cost? There is certainly no argument that it reduced the cost for the federal government. However, when hospitals starting losing money on Medicare patients, they simply increased their rates for other patients. This practice is known as cost shifting. It should come as no surprise that, not long after this program was implemented, American businesses complained that they could not afford the spiraling increases in health care insurance costs for their employees.

Management Engineering Studies, Productivity Reporting Systems, and Benchmarking

Some hospitals, like most other American industries, utilize traditional industrial engineering (IE) approaches to provide cost-effective services. Until recently, the utilization of IE tools and techniques within health care has neither been as widely accepted as in other U.S. industries, particularly manufacturing, nor has it enjoyed the same level of success. There are many reasons for this; three in particular stand out.

1. Lack of resources committed to IE work

2. Lack of a systems approach

3. Lack of IE authority within the hospital organization

Lack of Resources Committed to IE Work. Most hospitals do not have industrial engineering staffs. When hospital administrators have operational problems arise that they are unable to resolve or when productivity measurement systems need to be developed for departmental operations, they hire a consultant to perform the work.

When a hospital does have an IE staff, the department tends to be small, with typically less than five people. In addition to size, experience level is also an issue in many IE departments. Introductory/junior level IEs or administrative assistants who lack an IE background many times comprise the small IE staff. This is unfortunate, because a hospital is a very challenging environment for an IE, and experience can make a difference in terms of the successes achieved. It can take years for an IE to gain a full understanding of hospital operations, because patient care tends to require a significant level of coordination of services among a large number of diverse, centralized departments that oftentimes have complicated internal operating systems. Unfortunately, in most hospitals so few experienced IE bodies are available that there simply is not enough time to make a difference in all areas within the hospital that need it.

Lack of a Systems Approach. IEs have focused too much of their attention on making incremental gains in individual departmental operations. For example, many hospitals utilize an internal productivity monitoring system and/or an external comparative database report (for benchmarking purposes) to measure the performance level of each hospital department. Obviously, when the management reporting tools focus on departmental performance, the IE project work performed also tends to focus on departmental performance, particularly optimizing operations. This type of management engineering approach suboptimizes hospital performance and has resulted in many management engineering (ME) departments not achieving significant, noticeable gains hospitalwide.

As core business processes run across many departments and functional silos, a high-impact ME project has to be cross-functional in nature. In order to achieve more significant gains in performance, MEs should look at the big picture across functional lines (optimizing entire operating systems).

Lack of IE Authority Within the Hospital Organization. The other issue IEs face within health care is the lack of authority to implement their work or expand their scope beyond departmental silos. Since IEs are not medical or nursing staff personnel, IE work tends to be viewed as that of a consultant—even if the IE is part of an in-house staff. Typically IEs do not have the authority within the organizational structure to implement their recommendations from project studies. Good IE work can be blocked by organizational politics or by the lack of commitment to positive change on the part of those given the authority to make it.

For most hospitals that have utilized the work of IEs, only a marginal difference has been made in the organization's *total* cost to provide patient care. However, those few hospitals that have committed the resources necessary to have a strong, in-house management systems department (such as the University of Michigan Hospital, the Henry Ford Health System, and Alexandria Hospital) have reaped significant benefits.

Total Quality Management

The focus of total quality management (TQM) is to improve quality. Cost reduction is achieved through the elimination of work processes that are described as the cost of poor quality. TQM is a structured, data-driven problem-solving process that emphasizes customer satisfaction and problem prevention. Problem solving is accomplished in employee work teams. Before teamwork begins, employees receive training in TQM tools such as flowcharting and Pareto analysis. Employees are then guided through the process by a facilitator, an employee who has received more intensive TQM training. This approach to cost containment began to take hold during the late 1980s. It is widely utilized within hospitals because the Joint Commission for the Accreditation of Healthcare Organizations (JCAHO)—the accrediting body for hospitals—has endorsed TQM, and JCAHO expects hospitals to demonstrate TQM success stories during its certification process.

Although TQM is widely accepted and utilized within health care, it does have its drawbacks. The two most significant problems are the following:

1. The time required to complete project work

2. The maintenance cost of the program

TQM represents a cultural change within health care, because most hospital decision making is not based on a problem-solving process that is analytical and data driven. Many of the TQM tools and techniques are challenging for hospital personnel to learn and utilize appropriately. With many TQM projects taking six months to a year (or longer) to complete, the labor cost of the program many times outweighs its savings. A review of TQM's effectiveness (within both health care and non–health care organizations) shows that "there is very little organization-level data to substantiate a conclusion that its benefits outweigh its substantial costs of implementation and ongoing maintenance."[5] The TQM cultural change within hospitals is not keeping pace with the rapid changes occurring within the health care market environment.

Reengineering

Michael Hammer and James Champy introduced this cost containment strategy, which (like TQM) is focused on process improvement. What is the difference between the two approaches? According to Hammer and Champy, the difference is that TQM focuses on making incremental gains in an existing process, whereas reengineering focuses on making dramatic improvements by completely changing the existing process.[6]

A small number of hospitals have implemented the reengineering approach in order to radically change their operations. These attempts are also known as *patient-focused care* (PFC) *design*. The promise of reengineering is that dramatic cost reduction occurs through dramatic changes in operational processes. At this point in time, the results of reengineering are mixed. Reengineering does bring dramatic changes; if not planned properly, these dramatic changes can result in significant problems, of which two in particular stand out.

1. The cost to the organization to cross-train employees in order to transform them from specialists to generalists

2. Dissatisfied employees who feel a loss of professional identify

Utilization Review Activities

Most hospitals have a utilization review (UR) staff. Hospitals had hoped that UR would save them money on inpatient care by reducing the overall average length of stay (ALOS). For this reason, the focus of the UR staff is on discharge planning. The UR functionality has helped hospitals reduce their ALOS; however, the reduced ALOS has not translated into a reduction in cost to provide care to inpatients. The cost of care has not changed because patients are still receiving the same level of services (such as lab tests and radiology exams); the only thing that has changed is that service delivery has been compressed into a shorter time period.

Short-Term Approaches Such as an Arbitrary Across-the-Board Reduction in Workforce

This is an easy solution that will result in a short-term gain. However, this approach rarely holds up over the long term. Typically the costs come back, and sometimes the costs come back with a vengeance. The following analogy explains why.

> *A statistician (who did not know how to swim) drowned in a lake that had an average depth of four feet. The statistician assumed, since he was six feet tall, that he could walk across the lake safely.*

When an across-the-board labor cost reduction (such as 5 percent) is implemented within a hospital, the assumption is that every department within the hospital has at least 5 percent fat. This assumption is not true for every department.

Use of Consultants as Cost Reduction Gurus

If not utilized properly, consultants can many times have the same effect as an across-the-board workforce reduction.

- Cost reduction that is initially significant
- Cost reduction that is not sustained over the long term

The problem with consultants is that many times they utilize off-the-shelf programs. The source of information for their recommendations comes from how other hospitals function, such as through the use of hospital comparative database reports. If a consultant does not take the time to understand the uniqueness of a hospital and its operating environment, its recommendations are many times not well received by the hospital employees. If employees do not accept the changes being implemented, the changes will not likely be sustained over the long term. Once the consultant leaves, the former processes creep back along with their costs.

Employee Suggestion Programs

The focus of this program is to ask the real experts, the line staff who perform the work every day, how to contain costs without compromising quality. Typically, the potential gains from this type of program are significantly larger than the successes actually achieved. The problem is not with the quality of ideas submitted by employees; Japanese firms provide good examples of the type of successes that can be achieved through active employee participation. The problem is typically with the infrastructure of the program. When the infrastructure of the program is not designed to provide a timely response to each employee who submits an idea (either accepting and implementing the idea or providing the employee with a legitimate reason why the idea was denied), employees lose faith and interest in the program and then stop participating in it.

Success Factors

Most of these just-described strategies have had a moderate to significant impact in achieving short-term cost containment. However, in order to achieve meaningful, long-term results, our experience has shown that an effective strategy has certain success factors associated with it, which are presented in the next section as follows:

- Cases for action
- Relative priority of the organization
- Fact-based decision making
- Sense of urgency
- Magnitude defined
- Employee participation
- Commitment
- Risk assessment/preparedness
- Cohesive strategy
- Infrastructure
- Communication
- Rewards and recognition

Cases for Action

A Powerful Business Case. One may argue that a powerful business case for action can be made based solely on the reasoning that it represents long-term survival. Clearly, this motivates many organizations to implement a cost containment initiative. However, it is important to keep in mind that any cost containment initiative selected will create changes within an organization, and these changes typically create problems for staff. It is not enough for an organization to implement a cost containment initiative based on the fact that it appears to be the right thing to do or that competitors are doing it. In order for staff to be motivated to overcome the problems that result from cost containment, executive management must articulate a business reason that is relevant to the organization. Executive management must explain to its staff

- Why a cost containment initiative needs to be implemented

- How cost containment relates to the organization's business strategy

There are many business reasons for why hospitals develop cost containment initiatives. The following are most often indicated.

- *Mergers and acquisitions.* As mergers and acquisitions increasingly become the option of choice, it is imperative that a community hospital be fiscally sound, particularly when a for-profit chain is looking to acquire it. Most community hospitals have mission statements that make a commitment to serving their communities. For-profit hospitals have mission statements to provide health care services within their communities. The major difference between these competing systems is that for-profit hospitals pay taxes, which means they are not required to provide charity care. Therefore, for-profit hospitals restrict (as much as possible) their health care services to only those residents within the community who can afford to pay for it. Also, unlike community hospitals, their profit is not fully invested into the hospital because they have a financial commitment to their shareholders.

If a community not-for-profit hospital is being acquired by a for-profit chain, its mission to provide health care services to all residents within its community may be in jeopardy. A fiscally sound community hospital, however, greatly increases its likelihood to continue to meet its mission, because it will be in a stronger negotiating position with the for-profit chain. The hospital will be much more likely (than a hospital that is in financial trouble) to obtain the sale price that it wants. The money from the proceeds of the sale could be used to establish a charitable foundation.

- *Future changes in payor mix and reimbursement levels.* Due to budgetary problems within both federal and state governments, both Medicare and Medicaid reimbursement levels are likely to decrease. Hospitals cannot continue to cost shift to patients who have insurance coverage due to the continued growth in HMO companies. HMO companies are likely to make further inroads within the employer-sponsored health care insurance market. As their size and market share increases, so does their ability to force hospitals to offer larger discounts. Hospitals should expect more of the same shrinking revenue with increasing cost. For most hospitals, strong action is needed today to avoid negative operating margins within the next two to five years.

- *Capital needs.* Every hospital, regardless of whether it is for-profit or not-for-profit, must make money in order to have the capital necessary to meet the basic, continuing needs of a health care organization. The hospital building deteriorates over time and must be refurbished; equipment eventually becomes too old and/or outdated for use and must be replaced. If a hospital is located in a market in which physicians have a number of choices as to where to send their patients, the hospital must invest in state-of-the-art equipment and facilities in order to attract business.

Capital is also necessary for a hospital to respond to changing market needs. A hospital that has the resources to grow and add new services—such as a sleep lab, an in-vitro fertilization program, or the latest cancer treatment programs—will attract business to its facility.

At times a hospital needs to borrow money, regardless of the reason (new facility, new equipment, information systems, renovations, and so on), and the hospital's bond rating influences the type of note the hospital receives. The stronger the fiscal health of an organization, the better the bond rating. The better the bond rating, the lower the interest rate on the note.

A Convincing Case. Most people in any organization are familiar with the old routine. At the beginning of the fiscal year, a new cost containment program is introduced to employees. Given the successes achieved by other organizations that have followed this path, there is much excitement on the part of executive management about the program's potential. With bells and whistles blaring, the organization goes full steam ahead.

By midyear, the mood within the organization is quite different. Unexpected problems have cropped up and have slowed the program's pace. The program no longer enjoys the same level of attention it had at the beginning of the year, and there seems to be little momentum to overcome the obstacles that are preventing the organization from achieving its goals.

By the end of the fiscal year, the program is dead. At best, only some of the initial goals were achieved. The disappointment is short lived, though, because a brand new program that is touted to achieve the turnaround the organization needs is about to be introduced to employees.

It is no wonder that employees are not always enthusiastic about the potential benefits of a new program from the latest management guru. If this scenario has occurred frequently within your organization, management should plan a strategy for overcoming the initial inertia that will inevitably be there.

In order for a cost containment initiative to stand any chance of achieving its primary goals, every group within the organization (physicians, board members, employees, and particularly the entire executive management) must be convinced of the program's merits and its importance to the organization. It cannot simply be lip service, particularly on the part of executive management; there must be full commitment to achieving program successes and sustaining the accomplishments over the long term. In order to obtain people's cooperation and participation within the organization, there must be a common and shared understanding of why (the case for action) this program is necessary and what (specifically) must be achieved in order for the organization to meet its business goals.

A Timely Case. One of the problems of a TQM program is that project work takes too long to complete. Since TQM represents a fundamental change in the method by which problem solving occurs, a long learning curve is typically associated. This typically results in a vague time frame being established for achieving TQM program goals (reaping the real benefits of a TQM environment), such as "over the next three to five years." There is a significant disadvantage, however, when specific and realistic time frames are not established to achieve program goals. Health care employees constantly have to reprioritize their schedules to juggle a wide array of competing priorities. For most employees, the squeaky wheel gets the most oil. Work that can be delayed until later probably will be. In order for a program to get off to a good start and maintain momentum, a timetable identifying specific dates for the achievement of specific goals should be established that covers the entire program process.

Relative Priority of the Organization

After establishing cost containment as a business case for action, executive management must determine where it falls within the goals of the organization. In order to determine its priority relative to that of other organizational goals, one must first identify the organization's critical success measures.

According to Chip Caldwell in *Mentoring Strategic Change in Health Care*, each organization should identify six or seven factors that are critical to its success. The importance of each factor must then be assessed relative to the organization's current operating environment and market competition. Based on this assessment, each success factor can then be placed into a rank order of priority.[7] If cost containment is not one of the organization's top priorities, do not pursue it.

Fact-Based Decision Making

Hospitals, like all organizations, have limited resources. Many different types of resources are required to operate effectively within the health care environment, such as the following:

- Human resources
- Supplies
- Equipment
- Space
- Information systems

Decisions are made every day about how best to distribute these limited resources throughout the organization.

An important question that every organization needs to address is, how are these decisions made? Do resources tend to be distributed based on political considerations? Do influential physician specialists or powerful managers manipulate the decision-making process in order to get exactly what they want? If so, do certain groups within the hospital routinely receive more than what they really need, while others typically go without and make do with the few resources they are given to function?

During the former fee-for-service reimbursement arrangement, cost considerations were not critical to an organization's success. Therefore, executive management did not rely heavily on decision support systems that were data driven. Health care organizations emerged to be political powerhouses, where power was measured by how many resources an individual controlled. More often than not, people in power made decisions based on political correctness.

This type of decision making can be very dangerous for an organization. When decision making is not data driven or fact based, it tends to be inconsistent. When influential people within an organization spot inconsistencies, they can use it to their advantage. They can argue for additional resources not based on need, but based on the fact that unfair preferences to others have been made in the past. When decision making is based on the politics of "If you can find the resources for them, than you certainly can provide me with the resources that I am requesting," costs can quickly spiral out of control.

There is a saying that "sacred cows make the best hamburgers; eat them first." "Sacred cows" are those people within an organization that have the most political power and influence. Since their decision making in particular can create significant barriers to achieving a cost containment environment within an organization, their power and control must be addressed first.

An organization can create a paradigm shift toward cost containment by requiring its managers to provide supporting documentation for their decisions. Supporting documentation requires managers to collect data. It forces them out of a familiar and comfortable decision-making style in which decisions are based on a gut feel for a situation, which many times is derived from their years of experience. Change is occurring so rapidly within health care that it is becoming increasingly difficult to make management decisions based on previous experience. Consequently, in the absence of data and relevant facts about a situation, a poor decision is much more likely to occur. This can be very costly to an organization.

Sense of Urgency

Decision making that is data driven/fact based is critical to achieving a cost containment environment within an organization. In order to be successful within this environment, executive management must establish a sense of urgency.

Many good initiative ideas fail simply because there is no impetus for change. Change involves giving up a familiar routine with which staff feels comfortable. A complacent attitude among staff can be difficult to overcome. This is particularly true for health care organizations, because most are not-for-profit and typically do not make rapid changes, even when major changes are occurring within their markets. Quality care, not profit, has always been the main focal point. Therefore, health care employees do not have the mind-set to seek out opportunities for change, particularly change that involves reducing cost and/or making more money.

This resistance to change must be overcome in order for the organization to be successful. The best way to overcome this initial inertia on the part of staff is to create a sense of urgency. As anyone who has watched the hit NBC television drama series "ER" will tell you, people respond differently in emergency situations. During an emergency people move quickly, work together as a team, and are totally focused on achieving a singular goal. Nothing distracts them from the task at hand. When people are aware that it is an emergency situation and this is their one and only chance to effect a change, the level of high-quality work accomplished in a short period of time is absolutely amazing.

How do you create a sense of urgency within an organization, particularly one related to cost containment? It's not as if health care employees are not aware of the current environment. Most know that a number of hospitals throughout the United States have had to downsize in response to cost pressures. In fact, national surveys of hospital employees indicate that morale is very low, in large part because employees are aware that the grass is not greener somewhere else. There is no geographic cure to this situation. Yet all this knowledge has not translated into emergency action.

In order to create a sense of urgency, executive management must create a scenario for employees that the hospital has a closing window of opportunity to achieve its cost containment goals. Hospital staff must be aware that this situation requires an emergency response. If the goal is not achieved, the opportunity is lost and more drastic measures may need to be taken.

Magnitude Defined

In order for staff to have an emergency-level response, there must be a clear understanding of what the goal is. Executive management should not simply state that cost containment is the goal, because this statement does not convey anything specific to the hospital staff. Even a statement such as reducing cost by $5 million can be confusing to staff. Some staff may interpret this to mean cost avoidance—not to request capital purchases in order to hold down the hospital's annual inflation rate.

In order for hospital staff to be mobilized to take specific action, executive management must state a goal relating to a specific performance measure that has a clearly understood meaning to all staff. For example,

- Achieve a $10 million cost reduction from the approved budget.

- Decrease the total cost per adjusted discharge by 10 percent, which is equal to $500 per adjusted discharge.

Combining a specific, attainable goal within a short, yet achievable time frame should produce a focused and energetic response from employees that produces significant results.

Employee Participation

The employees' response is critical to success, because an organization cannot implement a cost containment environment without the full cooperation and support of its employees. Seven key elements must be present in order for employee participation to be laser focused within an organization.

1. *Awareness:* As stated, employees must be aware of the business case for action. Any cost containment strategy that is implemented within an organization will cause changes, and people do not generally respond well to changes. Particularly in today's health care market with job security being such a concern, employees may be unusually suspicious of the "real" purpose for a new program and therefore create obstacles to block its implementation.

Frequent and consistent communication is key to success. Employees must understand

- Why changes have to be made
- What the specific goal is, stated in terms of a performance measure that is understandable to everyone
- How much time they have to achieve the goal
- The approach executive management has established to achieve the goal

2. *Education/training:* Employee education and training are key elements in achieving program success. They are also key elements for executive management to consider when selecting a cost containment program. Health care organizations are comprised largely of individuals who have strong clinical, not analytical, skills. For the most part, health care employees do not have the educational background or experience that enables them to learn and understand program tools that are mathematical in nature, such as Pareto charts (creating them) or histograms (interpreting them). Even a straightforward task, such as drawing a flowchart that accurately illustrates a process, can be problematic for clinicians.

Since employees must understand and be able to apply program tools in order for the program's approach to succeed, the tools must be relatively easy to learn. Program tools that require skill or experience to master can spell trouble within the health care environment.

3. *Ownership:* Employees must take ownership of the program process. It is sometimes easy for employees who work for community hospitals to forget for whom they work. They are not hospital employees; they are community employees. An effective cost containment program should focus every employee's attention on that fact. Employee ownership means that every employee takes personal responsibility to fulfill the hospital's mission. Employees simply cannot be permitted to have an attitude that "this is not my job." It is the responsibility of every employee to provide high-quality and affordable health care for the residents of the community that they serve.

4. *Motivation:* What is the best way to motivate employees to make changes? How do you convince employees to give up their comfortable and familiar routines? How do you address employees who are skeptical that this approach will really work?

One possible way to motivate health care employees is to focus their attention on why they entered the health care field. Most hospital employees entered the health care field because they enjoy helping and caring for others. They want to make a real difference in other peoples' lives.

A cost containment strategy that can tap into what naturally motivates employees should be successful. Health care employees know that a patient is made well due to the efforts of a team of health care professionals. Teamwork can make a real difference in peoples' lives, particularly when it is focused on accomplishing a singular goal.

An effective cost containment strategy can also provide employees with the same type of positive and productive feelings that they receive when helping their patients get well. Health care employees typically achieve their patient goal within a relatively short amount of time; the average length of stay in hospitals is approximately five days. Health care employees can be motivated to achieve cost containment if they can see real success stories within a reasonable time frame. It is far more difficult to motivate employees to embrace the cost containment environment if it takes years to plan the program's implementation and/or plow through a learning curve.

5. *Empowerment:* Simply motivating employees is not enough. Executive management must also empower employees to make things happen. Empowerment is much more than granting employees authority to implement the changes they deem necessary. In order for employees to be empowered, they must understand who their customers are and what those customers expect in terms of service.

Employees typically know exactly what their employer expects of them. Most employees are accustomed to receiving at least an annual evaluation that identifies for them how well they are doing in terms of performing their job duties. Employees are motivated to perform their job duties well in order to receive a favorable evaluation. A good performance evaluation may translate into a higher percentage increase in annual salary.

However, what do the employees' customers think about the job duties being performed? Employees may be surprised to learn that some duties they perform very well may be perceived as of little or no value by their customers. Therefore, in order for employees to be empowered to make changes, they must receive meaningful feedback from *all* their customers.

6. *Customer focus:* How much time is spent every day by employees who perform job functions that are not designed to meet or exceed customer expectations? Studies have shown that hospital employees spend

- 40 percent of their time on non–value-added functions
- 40 percent of their time on business value-added functions
- 20 percent of their time on customer value-added functions

The majority of the work functions being performed are not customer value added, and many times these are the same work functions that irritate the staff. It should come as no surprise that it is the staff members who many times have the best ideas for how to resolve problems affecting the quality of service provided to their customers. They are the experts, because they do the work every day. By including them in the problem-solving process, an organization places itself in a position to not only meet but consistently exceed customer expectations. This not only improves quality, but can also reduce cost, as wasteful and unproductive tasks are reduced or eliminated.

7. *Recognition:* One proven way to motivate people to take action is to have an incentive system in place that recognizes their work accomplishments. It is important to keep in mind that not every person is motivated by the same incentive. For example, hospital employees who are financially secure may not be motivated by money. A combination of incentives may be the best solution.

All incentive systems can be placed into one of two distinct categories: intrinsic awards and extrinsic awards. An incentive system is intrinsic if employees are motivated by an internal desire to perform at their best. Intrinsic awards include letters of thanks, plaques, or public recognition (such as an article in the hospital's newsletter). An incentive system is extrinsic if employees are motivated by a desire to receive an external award in exchange for their extra effort. Extrinsic awards include money, gifts, or a promotion.

Commitment

A hospital must have more than just laser-focused employee participation to successfully create a cost containment environment. The hospital must also have a laser-focused commitment to achieving this goal. This commitment must be specific in the form of a philosophical buy-in at every level throughout the organization.

- Hospital board
- Executive management
- Middle management
- Staff
- Physicians

Each one of these groups represents a distinct entity within the hospital, and each one's commitment is vitally important if the hospital is to achieve a cost containment environment. Each group must understand the hospital's case for action and be strongly committed to the cost containment strategy as the best approach to achieving the hospital's business goals.

When an organization makes a commitment to achieving business goals, individual members must be held accountable for their actions, specifically the chief executive officer (CEO). The hospital board should hold the CEO accountable for achieving the stated goal.

- What is to be achieved? (The cost reduction goal should be stated in the form of a specific performance measure that has a clearly understood meaning to all staff.)
- How much time does the organization have to achieve this goal? (The CEO should create a closing window of opportunity.)

The organization must be committed not only to the cost containment strategy, but also to the proper allocation of resources to provide the best chance for success. Decisions on how best to allocate valuable resources should be based on data-driven analysis. In addition to staffing, other key hospital resources that should be considered within such an analysis include equipment, information technology, and facilities. Sometimes an analysis may indicate that a financial investment is needed in order to achieve long-term cost reduction. If this occurs, do not allow conventional management tools such as the hospital's budget to prevent the implementation of ideas that make sound business sense.

Risk Assessment/Preparedness

In order for an organization to be fully committed to a program, it must assess the program's risks. It's very easy to fall into the trap, particularly when evaluating a highly touted new program, of focusing predominantly on the upside of program implementation. When other health care organizations report significant success stories through utilization of the program's approach, an evaluation of the program's impact may focus too much on the probability of achieving various performance goals. However, the organization should also carefully consider what the possible negative outcomes may be.

Any change implemented in an organization will likely cause at least some negative responses. People may dislike a program because

- They feel threatened by it.
- They do not see potential benefits from implementation.
- They fear that it will only disrupt their familiar, comfortable routine.

An organization must plan for repercussions such as the following:

- People may try to create obstacles that prevent program initiatives from being implemented.
- Implemented initiatives may result in a decrease in staff morale.
- Influential people, such as key physicians and/or staff members, may threaten to leave.
- Employees may threaten to unionize.

By planning for repercussions, the organization will not abort the program at the first signs of trouble. When a problem occurs, the appropriate change management strategy can be deployed. Contingency planning will ensure commitment to achieving the organization's goals.

Cohesive Strategy

Because every organization is unique (to some degree) in terms of both its operating environment and its business goals, the cost containment strategy that is being considered for implementation should also (to some degree) be unique to that organization. The cost containment strategy should be customized to meet the specific needs of the organization's current environment. Prior to implementation, a business analysis should be conducted to make a determination about the approach. If the analysis determines that implementing the proposed cost containment environment is just an incremental step in a process to enable the organization to achieve its business goals, the strategy (when implemented) will not likely make a significant or long-term impact on the organization due to lack of impetus from executive management. On the other hand, if the analysis reveals that cost containment can be established as a relevant business strategy, significant results are much more likely to be achieved.

After making a commitment to implementing a cost reduction environment and fully assessing all the risks associated with program implementation, an implementation strategy must be developed. The key questions that must be answered before a strategy can be developed is, "What is the objective to be achieved? How large a cost reduction is needed in order for the organization to achieve its business goal? How long does the organization have to achieve its goal?" This is vitally important in determining which cost reduction approach is right for the organization, particularly in today's health care environment.

Keep in mind that some cost reduction approaches require a lengthy time period for staff to work through the learning curve and/or develop the program's implementation plan. If an organization needs to achieve cost reduction today, not tomorrow, several options are available depending on how much cost reduction needs to be achieved.

- A grassroots cost containment drive involving employees to participate actively in identifying low-hanging opportunities and empowering them to implement change
- Formal teams chartered throughout the organization working continuously on process improvement in order to reduce costs
- Two to three drastic change initiatives, commissioned by the executive management, to implement significant cost reduction

Once a decision is made concerning how large an impact is needed and/or how soon the impact needs to happen, then a decision must be made as to whether there is sufficient in-house expertise to implement the cost reduction environment. If there is not, outside consultants will need to be hired. Most organizations have had both good and not-so-good experiences with consultants. When properly used, consultants can provide valuable services that greatly assist an organization to achieve its goals. Some important points to remember when dealing with consultants are as follows:

- The organization must manage the consultants; do not allow the consultants to manage the organization.

- Consultants should be partners with the organization and, as such, should be held responsible for the work being performed. A risk-sharing arrangement should be developed with the consulting group being utilized.

- Consultants must tailor the cost reduction program to the organization's environment. Every organization is unique. Off-the-shelf approaches do not always lead to the best results, because they do not take into account the psychosocial needs of the organization, such as the level of change the organization is able to take on or the readiness of the organization to implement that change level.

- The executive management must present to the organization the consultant's recommendations as being their own. Hospital staff must see cost reduction as being an in-house initiative for which executive management is taking full responsibility.

Infrastructure

In order to implement a cost reduction environment, an organization must develop the proper infrastructure to support it. Since an effective cost reduction environment will lead to many changes, an organization should designate at least one person within each work area to facilitate this process by acting as a change champion. Change champions should be employees who are viewed by their coworkers as creative people who have both leadership ability and a positive outlook. The change champions should be trained on how best to support the implementation strategy within their areas and should be held accountable for achieving specific results.

In addition to change champions, the organization's information systems (IS) department must be ready to support changes. Since the completion of so many work processes within health care relies on information system support, how successful an organization is in implementing a cost reduction environment may depend on how proficient the IS department is in supporting the operational changes being implemented.

Communication

An organization's cost reduction strategy must have a sound plan of action. In order for staff to support fully and participate in a program, they must know

- What the priorities of the organization are

- How these priorities were established

- What the goal is (stated in terms of a performance measure that has a clearly defined meaning to everyone)

- How much time the organization has to achieve its goal

Health care employees, in particular, are aware of the downsizing occurring nationally within their industry. Therefore, they may be particularly suspicious about any new program, particularly one that focuses on cost reduction. Executive management should communicate to staff on a frequent basis in order to eliminate speculation and rumors concerning the real purpose for implementing the cost reduction program.

Frequent communication with staff can be accomplished in many ways; the following are some examples.

- Memos from the CEO
- Bulletin boards
- Departmental meetings
- Videotapes
- Brochures
- Round-the-clock employee meetings

In addition to communicating on a frequent basis, executive management must also send staff a consistent message. Mixed messages (inconsistencies within executive management's verbal communications and/or actions) can result in reduced staff support and participation in the cost reduction program. Some examples of mixed messages are as follows:

- The organization has a healthy bottom line, yet executive management speaks of the need to cut costs. Employees do not understand why.
- Executive management explains the financial pressures being placed on the organization today and outlines a continually worsening financial picture, yet employees see that millions of dollars are being spent on renovations and/or new medical equipment.

A cost reduction environment can be implemented within an organization only if (for the most part) everyone comes on board. In order for this to occur, there must be open and honest communication. A we-versus-they culture cannot exist. If employees perceive that executive management is not withholding vital information from them, they are more likely to work toward achieving the organization's business goals. The bottom line is that staff must trust executive management; when they do, they are more likely to take on personal responsibility because they believe that they are an integral part of the process.

Rewards and Recognition

In today's cost-conscious times, health care employees have been hit in their pocketbooks. Many have experienced at least one of the following:

- No annual increase in pay or cost-of-living allowance
- Some reduction in benefits
- Demotion in position grade and/or salary
- Organization layoff

Morale within hospitals nationally is low. Employees may need some form of incentive for hospitals to win their support. Employees are being asked to provide more services with less resources, yet (for the most part) they are not given any financial compensation for their extra efforts. A financial bonus program is an excellent form of enticement. The financial bonus does not have to be large. A small dollar amount can be appreciated by staff members because (at the very least) it is an acknowledgment of their hard work and participation.

In addition to financial compensation, public recognition and thanks can also be an excellent motivator.

Most of the success factors described here are exemplified by the following case study of the Alexandria Hospital in Alexandria, Virginia.

Cost Containment: A Success Story at the Alexandria Hospital

There are many different approaches being utilized by hospitals nationwide to control or reduce costs. Published accounts of these approaches typically provide only a limited amount of information in terms of what successes have actually been achieved (particularly long term). A number of questions may therefore arise, such as the following, which were asked by administrators and managers at the Alexandria Hospital, a 379-bed community hospital in Alexandria, Virginia.

- Which approach is right for the institution?

- What decisive actions can be taken to reduce costs without creating an opposite reaction within the institution, such as lower quality patient care, physician and/or patient dissatisfaction, or low employee morale?

- Can a strategy be developed that provides both short-term success and long-term viability?

Alexandria Hospital began to focus intently on cost issues during the late 1980s and early 1990s for two primary reasons.

1. It had unfavorable financial trends during that time period, such as the following:

   —A 12 percent yearly growth in total expenses measured in cost per adjusted discharge.

   —A 19 percent yearly increase in charges just to cover the growth in expenses. Note that the higher increase in charges was necessary due to uncollectible revenue from government programs (Medicare and Medicaid), uninsured patients who were unable to pay, and managed care contracts.

2. The health care trends that occurred during that time period in its local market, the Washington, D.C. metropolitan area, included

   —Fierce competition to win managed care contracts

   —Employee layoffs at several area hospitals

   —Closures of several neighboring hospitals

It was clear that Alexandria Hospital needed to develop a strategy to address the high yearly growth in cost so that the negative outcomes experienced by its competitors could be avoided.

Fortunately, the Alexandria Hospital has a corporate culture with a long history of being progressive in terms of being receptive to change. During the late 1980s and early 1990s, cost-control changes were implemented that were identified through the following cost management strategies.

1. *Flexible budgeting:* The budget for each department and nursing unit is adjusted each accounting period based on the actual volume of work performed. For example, more resources (for both labor and supplies) are provided in the budget if the actual volume of work performed is more than the budgeted amount; conversely, less resources are provided if the volume is less than the budgeted amount.

2. *Management systems engineering:* Problem solving is accomplished by performing studies that utilize scientific methodologies (instead of basing decisions on the intuitive feelings or experience of middle managers or administrators). Scientific studies are performed in order to determine which course of action will optimize operational efficiency.

3. *Productivity monitoring system:* This management tool provides feedback to both directors and administrators on how well each department and nursing unit manages its labor resources. For example, if a nursing unit's productivity is low, the daily staffing patterns are examined and adjustments are made.

4. *Benchmarking through hospital comparative database reporting:* This is also a management tool, which provides feedback to directors and administrators on how efficiently departments and inpatient nursing units utilize their resources (for both labor and supplies) in comparison to their peers.

5. *Quality assurance/utilization review:* This structured program examines operational performance from a clinical point of view. For example, if a clinical outcome is inconsistent with the expected level, practice patterns are reviewed, which may result in changes in clinical protocol.

6. *Use of outside consultants:* This has been done on a limited basis for selected projects in which a consultant (who has either the expertise or the technology) is needed to accomplish a specific goal that cannot be performed by in-house staff.

These cost management strategies were instrumental in terms of providing a framework to control costs, yet only marginally successful in terms of achieving cost reduction. However, without cost reduction, the future viability of the Alexandria Hospital was uncertain, due both to limiting reimbursements from its primary third-party payors and increasing competition to win managed care contracts.

A hospitalwide cost reduction strategy was needed. Prior to any work being performed in terms of the development of a strategic plan, administration determined the major objectives to be achieved by the hospital. The following three were identified.

1. Compete successfully in a managed care environment.

2. Reduce significantly the yearly growth rate in total expenses as measured by cost per adjusted discharge.

3. Reduce costs while maintaining or improving the high quality in patient care services.

Based on these strategic objectives, criteria for hospitalwide cost reduction were established by the chief financial officer, the vice president of professional and ambulatory care services, and the director of management engineering.

1. *No employees are to be laid off.* Layoffs are not an option to be considered due to its effect on employee morale, retention of good employees, and hiring.

2. *The strategic plan must be politically viable.* In order for the plan to be successful within the political framework of a medium-sized health care institution, two key components must be present.

—All administrators must fully support the plan.

—The plan must create an environment of teamwork and cooperation: The plan is unlikely to succeed if conditions are created in which employees, departments, and/or divisions are pitted against each other; and the focus of each employee's efforts must be on what is good for the hospital (not what is good for the employee, the department, or the division).

3. *Employees must have a positive perception about the purpose for the strategic goals and the criterion established to meet them.* The plan must be nonthreatening to employees, as well as to physicians and administrators. It must be seen as a positive drive within the hospital that creates minimal organizational stress/shock.

4. *Employees need to participate actively in the plan.* Line employees who perform the work on a daily basis are likely to identify more ideas and better ideas for work improvement than either middle management or administration. Employees are likely to be much more enthusiastic about implementing and supporting changes that they participate in creating.

5. *Tangible employee incentives need to be provided.* Employees, particularly those who have been at Alexandria Hospital for more than five years, have seen a number of programs come and go. In order to stimulate enthusiasm for the strategic plan in this type of environment, incentives (recognition, gifts, or financial rewards) need to be provided to make the plan highly visible within the institution and to stimulate employee participation and support.

6. *Ground rules must be established to determine whether any initiative idea submitted is acceptable for implementation.* The quality of services cannot deteriorate in order to achieve cost reduction. Also, the cost to provide services cannot increase in order to achieve quality improvement.

7. *There should be a minimal use of outside consultants.* Based on research conducted by Alexandria Hospital, outside consultants who have implemented cost reduction programs for hospitals typically achieve only short-term, not long-term, gains. These findings seem to indicate that in order to hold gains over the long term, employees (particularly middle managers) must support and commit themselves to the changes that are implemented. Internal changes that are employee driven are therefore more likely to hold gains over the long term than externally driven changes.

These criteria were carefully thought out to ensure that the hospitalwide strategic plan that is developed will have the desired result (cost reduction) without creating a whole host of new problems to solve, such as poor-quality service, patient and physician dissatisfaction, low employee morale, and so on—in short, "kill the snake without breaking the stick."

The Strategic Plan

The Alexandria Hospital addressed its cost issues by developing an integrated approach to hospitalwide cost reduction. This approach integrated the efforts of three separate programs, with each one having a distinct focus in terms of the type of cost reduction to be achieved.

1. *Work improvement initiative program.* The focus of this program is to obtain active employee participation in a hospitalwide effort to improve performance. The program provides a structure to implement changes that are employee driven. All initiatives that result in any type of work improvement are acceptable, such as ideas to reduce both salary and nonsalary expenses, improve quality, increase worker productivity, and so on.

2. *Position evaluation panel.* The focus of this program is to review each vacant position and determine whether it needs to be filled or can be eliminated. This program is designed to address one cost that is highly visible to administrators—new employees—whereas the work improvement initiative program is designed to address cost issues that may not be visible to administrators but are visible to either middle managers or line employees.

3. *Value analysis committee.* The focus of this program is to reduce all non-salary expenditures, particularly the cost for supplies. An outside consultant was utilized to assist in this effort.

WII Program

The first program developed was the hospitalwide work improvement initiative (WII) program, which was designed to be implemented in two stages.

1. *Stage 1:* Obtain the participation of middle managers. Hospital administrators felt that middle managers could implement many good ideas to improve performance if the proper structure was provided in which to work. Therefore, no financial investment was made in terms of costly educational or training programs for middle managers on how to identify and implement initiative improvements. Middle managers generated their own ideas based on their experience and intuitive feelings of how work should be performed within their departments.

2. *Stage 2:* Obtain the participation of all employees. Financial incentives are provided to employees to participate in cost reduction. Employees are empowered to implement their ideas as a result of significantly reducing the tiers of bureaucracy that previously had been required to obtain permission to implement change. Administrators felt that many marginal successes could be achieved in this manner, with the end result being a significant hospitalwide cost reduction.

In accordance with the criteria of the strategic plan, the first stage of the WII program was designed with five key features.

1. *Accountability.* Each manager and supervisor is required to implement at least one work improvement initiative each year. This requirement was included in the performance guidelines for the annual evaluation of all midlevel managers.

2. *Acceptability of any type of initiative that results in a work improvement.* Ideas that improve quality or productivity are as important as ideas that reduce cost.

3. *No judgment as to whether a work improvement actually occurred.* Although it is tempting to challenge questionable achievements, it is very important not to discourage people who are just beginning the process of actively looking for ways to improve performance. There is nothing that kills the creative brainstorming process faster than negative comments. Although negative feedback should be avoided, all midlevel managers should be made aware of the level of effort, creativity, and commitment required to achieve significant results.

4. *Recognition of outstanding achievement.* This program was designed to recognize and honor the people who submitted the best initiatives. In the program's first year, the outstanding achievers were honored at a roundtable meeting attended by all managers throughout the hospital. Their initiative improvements were presented as examples for the entire group.

5. *Publication of all initiatives.* All initiatives submitted throughout the hospital were compiled into one publication. Each manager received a copy and was encouraged to read it. By honoring individuals who made outstanding achievements and by publishing all initiatives, managers

made their own judgment as to the quality of their initiative(s). This created an internal drive to improve performance. The initiatives that were submitted during the program's second year were far better than during the first year.

During its first year, administration promoted the WII program throughout the hospital, and management engineering developed and then presented at departmental meetings a simple eight-step process that all employees could follow or use as a guideline to help them identify and implement effective work improvement initiatives. (Note that from the inception of the WII program, all employees were invited and encouraged to participate; however, only middle managers were required to participate.)

The goal of stage 2 was to obtain the active participation of all hospital employees. In order to obtain employee enthusiasm and involvement in the WII program, two significant modifications were made.

1. Financial incentives were offered to employees to reduce costs.

2. Work improvement teams were formed.

There was considerable discussion among administrators concerning how a financial incentive should be distributed to employees and how large the financial incentive should be. Administration finally determined that financial incentives should be distributed to all employees (instead of only to the employee(s) who originated and submitted the idea) for the following reasons.

1. Individual employees identify cost reduction ideas; however, the support and cooperation of a team of employees (either intra- or interdepartmental) is needed in order to implement the idea. To obtain the support necessary to implement positive changes and to hold the gains achieved over the long term, incentives must also be provided to all employees who participate in this process.

2. When an employee works alone to solve a problem, the idea presented is typically very good in terms of resolving the problem encountered by the employee who originated the idea but unfortunately may create new problems for employees in other work areas. Teamwork is therefore needed to generate ideas that are workable for all employees.

3. If money is given only to the employee(s) who originated a cost savings idea, there is the potential that employee conflicts will arise in terms of who actually originated the idea. By giving the financial award to all employees, there will be no such disputes to settle.

Administration also determined the amount of the financial distribution to employees, which is calculated as follows:

1. For each implemented initiative that results in a cost savings from the approved budget, the amount of the savings realized is placed into a hospitalwide gain-sharing pool.

2. At the end of each fiscal year, 25 percent of the pool money is distributed to all eligible employees if the following two conditions are met: (1) the hospital must maintain its very high quality standard in patient care services (high quality patient care is being maintained if at least 90 percent of patients respond yes to the survey question, "Would you return to Alexandria Hospital for future health care needs?"; (2) the hospital must achieve its target financial bottom-line goal.

One-quarter of the money in the gain-sharing pool will be distributed equally among all eligible full-time hospital employees, and part-time employees will receive a percentage of the award amount based on the number of hours worked during the fiscal year.

The second major modification made to the WII program was the creation of work improvement teams that are empowered to implement change. Administration has given the green light to work improvement teams to implement ideas that do not violate the ground-rule criteria: The quality of services cannot deteriorate (in order to achieve cost reduction) and the cost to provide services cannot increase (in order to achieve quality improvement). The bureaucracy that had previously been required to obtain approval to implement an idea is significantly reduced. Only approval of the work improvement team (not middle managers or administrators) is needed. Administration is trusting the judgment of employees to implement positive change in this bottom-up approach to cost reduction. An organizational diagram of the WII program is shown as Figure 25.1.

More than 50 hospital teams, both departmental and ad hoc (created to solve a specific problem) have been formed and are responsible for performing three primary functions.

1. Generating work improvement initiative ideas

2. Analyzing submitted ideas (generated by both team members and nonteam members) that affect the operation of the team's department in order to determine whether the idea is acceptable for implementation

3. Implementing all acceptable ideas that do not decrease quality or increase cost

WII is a straightforward process that is easy for employees to understand. Since the structure of this program is not complicated or intimidating—that is, employees do not have to "jump through a series of hoops" to make the changes they want—hospitalwide employee participation has been high. Also, employees have seen real change implemented and, as a result, a team spirit and camaraderie has been established in which employees build on the ideas of their colleagues to create an environment of continual work improvement.

The following is a summary of the successes achieved by the WII program during each of its four years.

Stage 1

1991

    Total number of implemented ideas = 236

    Total cost savings achieved = $1.12 million

    Cash payment enhancement realized = $694,000

1992

    Total number of implemented ideas = 218

    Total cost savings achieved = $1.57 million

1993

    Total number of implemented ideas = 242

    Total cost savings achieved = $1.23 million

Stage 2

1994

    Total number of implemented ideas = 175

    Total cost savings achieved = $1.15 million

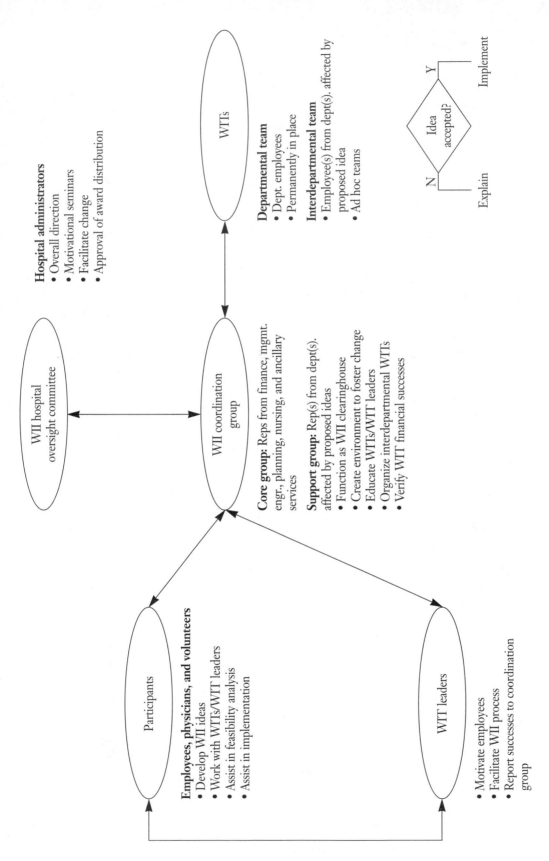

Figure 25.1. Organization of the WII program.

This program, so far, has yielded numerous success stories. One such story has been the work of the emergency department (ED) work redesign team.

ED Work Redesign Team. Due to closure of a neighboring hospital, the number of ED visits increased by 19.2 percent from 1991 to 1994. This growth could have justified a similar growth in the ED budget. However, the ED viewed the increased volume as an opportunity to reengineer its processes. An ED work redesign team was formed to focus on staffing/scheduling issues that had a negative impact on the workload within the department. The ED team began by collecting data that identified the average ED census for each hour of each day of the week. Data analysis revealed that staffing patterns needed to be adjusted in order to ensure adequate staffing to meet the workload during typically busy periods, as well as to eliminate overstaffing during typically slow periods. The team then specifically defined the role or work duties of the nurse and the technician to ensure that the ED staffing pattern has the proper skill-level mix.

Based on these adjustments in the staffing pattern and skill-level mix (which were implemented in February 1993), a significant cost reduction was realized, as shown in Figure 25.2. Especially note the following items.

1. The actual salary cost per visit decreased by 14.6 percent.

2. The total ED salary cost increased by 1.8 percent over four years; however, this figure includes annual salary rate increases of 3 percent.

Top-Down Approach to Achieve Cost Reduction. In addition to establishing an employee-driven program to implement change, the Alexandria Hospital also developed two programs that achieve cost reduction through the traditional top-down management approach. In order to take advantage of every opportunity to reduce costs, administration created the position evaluation panel (PEP), focused on salary expenses; and the value analysis committee (VAC), focused on nonsalary expenses. Like WII, both programs provide a simple, straightforward process that enables administrators and managers to implement change quickly when opportunities are presented to reduce costs.

Position Evaluation Panel: Hospitalwide Reduction in Total Salary Expense

PEP's mission is to reduce labor expense by eliminating unnecessary vacant positions. The reason why PEP was formed was to reduce the likelihood that the hospital would one day be put into a financial position in which current employees must be laid off.

PEP is an interdisciplinary team that is headed by the president of the hospital. In order to accomplish its mission, PEP developed criteria to evaluate all vacant positions. PEP asks all directors to look first for opportunities to improve departmental productivity before submitting a request to fill a vacant position. If a director still needs a position filled, PEP reviews the request by utilizing internal productivity reports, the comparative database report, information obtained from the director (during an in-depth interview), and information obtained on departmental operations in order to determine whether to fill or eliminate the vacant position. If the vacant position needs to be filled, PEP then determines whether the position can be filled by transferring a current hospital employee or by hiring a new employee.

PEP established its own turnaround time standard for evaluating requests for vacant positions, which is to make a decision within the same week that a director submitted the request. When first formed, PEP had a standing meeting once a week and met on an ad hoc basis to meet its turnaround time standard.

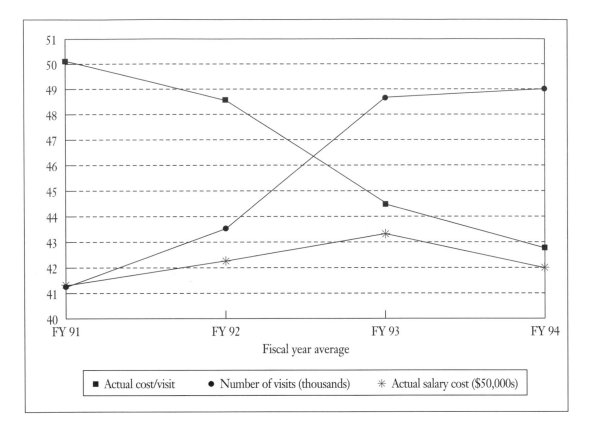

Figure 25.2. Emergency department redesign: A success story in cost containment.

PEP achieved a labor cost savings of $731,128 in one fiscal year. In addition to the quantifiable labor savings, PEP has had a significant impact within the hospital because directors are aware that they must be prepared to justify filling a vacant position; it is no longer automatic. Each vacancy creates an opportunity to redesign work functions with a goal to improve productivity and reduce cost.

Value Analysis Committee: A Hospitalwide Reduction in Total Nonsalary Expense

VAC's mission is to reduce nonsalary expenses, particularly supply costs. Alexandria Hospital hired a consultant to assist in this effort. The consultant provided information on alternative supplies that are cheaper yet provide the same quality as the present inventory. Employees reviewed the consultant's supply recommendations and implemented supply changes that were acceptable to them.

Since this program focuses strictly on nonsalary expenses, employees are in no way threatened by this cost reduction drive. Although employee participation is not a mandatory requirement, a number of employees have submitted their own ideas on how to reduce nonsalary expenditures, and many employee-recommended changes were received well after the consultant completed the study.

The following is a summary of the successes achieved by VAC.

- Total number of implemented supply changes = 118 (of which 75 were recommended by employees)
- Total cost savings achieved = $1.43 million

Results of Integrated Hospitalwide Cost Reduction

In order to measure the total impact of this integrated approach to hospitalwide cost reduction, the Alexandria Hospital administration selected one financial statistical indicator to track performance. The indicator, cost per adjusted discharge, was selected because it is a comprehensive statistic that is computed on a workload measure (adjusted discharges) that is a solid number and accurately reported throughout the health care industry.

The success of Alexandria Hospital's integrated cost reduction effort is shown in Figure 25.3. (In addition to the three separate programs discussed, Alexandria Hospital also achieved cost reduction by lowering the rate of annual salary increases given to all employees.)

In Figure 25.3, CAD means projected the projected cost per adjusted discharge (PCAD) if none of the cost reduction programs were implemented (including the salary adjustment measure). Salary-adjusted PCAD means the projected cost per adjusted discharge if none of the cost reduction programs were implemented except the salary adjustment measure. Note especially the following items.

- CAD grew at a rate of approximately 12 percent a year from 1988 to 1991; at 8 percent from 1991 to 1992; and then at a rate of 1 percent or less per year from 1992 to 1994.

- Note when each cost reduction program began: WII in 1991, and VAC and PEP in 1992.

- The projected expenditures without cost reduction measures are $32.6 million (which includes the labor cost if the hospital continued to provide its employees with annual salary rate increases

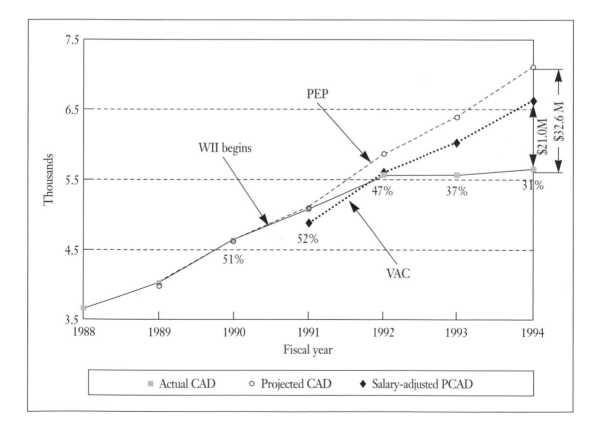

Figure 25.3. A success story in integrated hospitalwide cost reduction.

at the historical level) and $21.0 million (which identifies the total savings with employees receiving annual salary rate increases at the actual, lower rate).

- Among all Veterans Health Administration hospitals with 301 to 400 beds, Alexandria Hospital reduced its ranking for cost per adjusted discharge from the 51st percentile (prior to the integrated program) to the 31st percentile (by the end of fiscal year 1994).

The Future

Alexandria Hospital has achieved success by developing its own programs to reduce costs and improve quality. All of its programs are informal in that no substantial financial investment was required (for administrative or employee education and training) and the promotion of these programs, particularly WII, was not overdone (that is, no lofty expectations were made or fanfare given in order to obtain employee interest and enthusiasm).

Many of the cost reduction opportunities that can be described as "low-hanging fruit" have been realized. Now more intensive effort is needed to achieve further cost reduction. The Alexandria Hospital is providing its employees with a formalized education program in order to explore the next generation of cost reduction opportunities.

Discussion Questions for a One-Hour and a Two-Hour Executive Meeting

1. Ask the executive management to identify major cost containment initiatives implemented in the past and then review each initiative to determine how many of the 12 success factors described within this chapter were in place. This exercise should take approximately one hour to accomplish.

—Five minutes to discuss the logistics of the exercise

—20 minutes to identify previous initiatives

—20 minutes to identify how many success factors were in place

—15 minutes to discuss the success of each initiative as it relates to this diagram

Number of success factors in place		
	High Low	High High
	Review success factors again	
	Low Low	Low High
		Publish your success story

Impact of cost containment

2. Ask the executive management to modify one of the cost containment initiatives discussed in item 1 so that it incorporates the success factors discussed within this chapter. This exercise should take approximately two hours to accomplish.

—10 minutes to have the facilitator discuss the logistics of the exercise

—30 minutes to split into six groups so that each group discusses how to incorporate two of the 12 success factors described within this chapter into the cost containment initiative

—60 minutes to reconvene and allow each group 10 minutes to share its findings

—15 minutes to wrap up

Notes

1. Phillip A. Newbold, "Benchmarking in Health Care—Paradigms, Culture and Change," *Quality Management in Health Care* 3, no. 3 (1995): 73.

2. Carol Sardinha, ed., *Managed Care Outlook* 8, no. 1 (January 13, 1995) and 8, no. 4 (February 24, 1995).

3. "Will Reengineering Save Us All?" *Integrated Healthcare Report* (May 1995): 40.

4. Sandy Lutz, "Mergers and Acquisitions Report—1995: A Record Year for Hospital Deals," *Modern Healthcare* (December 18–25, 1995): 40.

5. Loyd Eskildom, "Questioning Cost/Benefit Value of 'Pure' TQM in Healthcare Organizations," *Strategies for Healthcare Excellence* (April 1996): 9.

6. Tim Weddle, "Are TQM and Reengineering Really Different?" *The Journal of the Healthcare Information and Management Systems Society* 8, no. 4:12.

7. Chip Caldwell, *Mentoring Strategic Change in Health Care* (Milwaukee: ASQC Quality Press, 1995).

Ijaz M. Bokhari is the Mid-Atlantic Regional Director of Performance Improvement & Measures at Kaiser Permanente. He has 14 years of health care management system consulting experience in teaching and non-teaching hospitals and in an HMO environment. Bokhari has successfully developed and implemented cost reduction programs that have achieved national recognition in various publications. He has also developed a number of quality/productivity improvement programs and has received, on behalf of the Alexandria Hospital, awards from the U.S. Senate recognizing outstanding productivity and quality achievement for two consecutive years. He has published numerous papers on a variety of topics related to health care management systems engineering. Bokhari earned a bachelor's degree in mechanical engineering from the University of Engineering and Technology, Lahore, Pakistan, and a master's degree in engineering administration from the George Washington University. He is a fellow member of the Healthcare Information and Management Systems Society (HIMSS) and an adjunct faculty member of the Juran Institute.

David A. Farson is a management engineer with eight years of experience at the Alexandria Hospital, a community nonteaching facility located in Alexandria, Virginia. He is the past president of the National Capital Area Chapter of the Healthcare Information and Management Systems Society (HIMSS). He has presented Alexandria Hospital's management engineering success stories at numerous conferences, including the 1993 HIMSS national conference and the VHA Quality Celebration Day II. Farson earned a bachelor's degree in industrial engineering and operations research from Virginia Polytechnic Institute & State University.

Chapter 26

Physician Leadership in Developing Systems of Care

Kimberly E. Sangari and Gene Beyt

The Role of the Physician Executive

The role of the physician executive, in today's evolutionary environment, may not be suitable for those who are motivated by corporate olympics and the Wall Street mind-set of the past decade. It is a role for those who want to fulfill a mission. It is more about philosophy and intrinsic value than about competitive business strategy. This is not to say that business principles should not be employed, but to say that the framework from which they are developed and deployed should spring from a foundation that is solidly aligned with personal values and a shared vision centered on community health. This calls for rethinking the rationale for what we do and how we do it. The issue is not whether we create a system that is profitable or operates like a business, for these must exist to ensure viability. The issue is whether service and community health are the core reasons for existence and whether these values are the central drivers in day-to-day decision making.

Health care reform, global economics, and industry evolution are redefining the relationships of those involved in the system of care. Within the care delivery components—institutions, physicians, purchasers, and patients—there are radical shifts in every aspect. For the delivery of care to operate effectively (for example, produce improved health for the community) and efficiently (that is, in a manner that is value-added and economically viable), systemization must occur. Integrating the physicians and the components of care delivery will take a clinical architect. Enter the physician executive.

But the charge goes beyond merging clinical and administrative structures. The call is to build a seamless system, not just patch together the current structures. What is called for is reengineering—from the inside and the outside; a real system transformation, not just a merger of existing components. The physician executive plays a critical role in reestablishing the legitimacy of who we serve, what we make for them, and how we make it, and in clarifying the purpose and the focus as to *why*. This calls for courage in leading the industry on a pilgrimage to get back in touch with values centered on community, creating health, and societal responsibility.

The role of the physician executive in today's environment is filled with opportunities to leave a legacy for future generations and to make lasting contributions within the industry and on the health of the community. Most physicians become doctors because of humanitarian values. The physician executive, if he or she demonstrates the courage to pioneer the needed changes, has the opportunity to realize these personal values in much greater magnitude than could be realized in the traditional patient-doctor relationship. The charge of this role is to

- Build a bridge between key physician constituents, administration, and community through shared vision and alignment of incentives.

- Develop systems of care centered on the health of the community; that is, an integrated delivery system (IDS).

Assessing the Fit: Checklist of Key Considerations

Embracing the role of the physician executive should begin with clarity of purpose and a defined framework of expectations. To create and understand this new role in the context of current challenges, a checklist of key considerations is provided.

Personal Profile

- Committed to the greater good, above and beyond personal reward and affirmation
- Strong, unwavering commitment to community and ideals of health
- Risk taker with courage to break new ground
- Patience and perseverance
- Comfortable with not having a local peer group, comfortable with being his or her own person
- Visionary who is thirsty for innovation that leads to realization of ideals
- Values trust and dialogue
- Values learning and creating new knowledge and is quality driven
- Ability to see bigger picture, with the ability to reconfigure the pieces to create yet even a different picture
- Generative with ethical integrity
- Systems thinker, who understands causality, leverage, and delays

Tool Kit for Change Mastery

- Actively charts a new course, often undefined and uncomfortable
- Overcomes defensive routines and obstacles through understanding, process management, and rechanneling energies
- Creates a new vision, not just renewing or improving the current reality
- Creates the dynamics for change to occur
  - —Tension for change between current reality and a desired future state
  - —Shared vision for future
  - —Strategies, structures, and interdependencies that will serve as the framework for deploying the new vision into reality

- Skillfully uses dialogue as the central tool for seeking the truth

  —Change is often linked to discussion with the recognized chain of events leading to action: Perception > Memory > Emotion > Action.

  —Dialogue for the purpose of balancing truth with advocacy can be achieved through constantly bringing thought and intellect back into the conversation. Preconceived emotions typically interfere with logic and breakthrough possibilities and erode trust. Dialogue should let the meaning pass between, rather than be an exercise of heaving ideas. The goal is to understand the frame of reference tied to preconceived emotions. Redirect the chain of events leading to action: Perception > Thought and Intellect > Action.

Dual Responsibilities as Clinical and Institutional Leadership

- Clinical responsibilities

  —Steward for the overall health of the community

  —Develop and integrate the continuum of care

- Organizational responsibilities

  —Manage administrative issues that keep the physician constituents evolving into a more integrated model

  —Develop the clinical leaders and empower them to fulfill their charge

Implicit Responsibilities as Bridge Builder and Boundary Spanner (Within and Beyond the IDS)

- Integrate and cross-pollinate the issues, perspectives, and resources.

- Merge clinical and organizational perspectives as a foundation to springboard the creation of a new reality. The new reality should maximize the value of the whole, not that of each component.

- Direct the focus on a nontraditional system, not just improving what we already have. Create a new system that operates differently, with clarity of purpose, producing measurable outcomes of health and satisfaction of key stakeholders.

- Grasp the big picture and help others to understand the global charge.

- Develop road maps for integrating the clinical and organizational components within the IDS.

Overall Charge to Create True Partnership

- Serve as the catalyst for joint problem solving.

- Create a win-win environment focused on higher ideals that links intrinsic value with action.

- Develop pluralistic partnerships with an overriding goal of creating health and value for the community.

- Create a culture of partnerships and collaboration: among physicians, between physicians and the organization or a virtual IDS, and between the IDS and the community served.

Physician Executive Leadership

Much of our understanding of leadership applies directly to the physician executive. Leaders have been defined as people who, by word or example, markedly influence the behavior, thoughts, and/or feelings of a significant number of others who elect to be followers. It also seems clear that leadership is a subject that can be mastered and a role that can be achieved by understanding the personal traits and the core competencies that have been discussed. Leadership occurs at all levels of the organization in the clinical and managerial ranks. The leaders' words or actions can have a direct or indirect influence through ordinary day-to-day events or can encompass innovative or visionary approaches, creating tension for the preferred future state. As a physician executive creates a shared vision of a system of care (one which progresses through continual improvements to bear risk, reduce cost, and increase health of the population), his or her leadership role will alternate between a steward of the community resources, a designer of systems of care, and a teacher leading and creating learning opportunities to measure and foster redesign.

Physician executives may approach their role emphasizing dominant themes. For instance, in a direct and visionary way the approach might be focused on strategy and change, while some who emphasize the clinical knowledge and architectural proclivity for system redesign may utilize an approach centered in the expertise of clinical medicine. Other physician executives may approach the role as a people person—emphasizing, developing, and empowering the human capabilities of the organization.

All of these approaches share specific themes of the unfolding story within the organizational and community arenas. It is a story with a framework of delivering health care services in a manner that holds more value based on the community's needs. The physician leader surfaces as a leading change agent who must embody the principles, values, and ethics in the story. Through direct evidence of the physician executive's intent and actions, he or she must remain true to the story while demonstrating competence as a clinical manager. In a cognitive sense, the leader characterizes resolve for the importance of health status and clinical efficiency. This resolve will act in parallel for the system redesign that is necessary for the IDS to develop.

An exemplary physician executive needs to be a high-energy resource individual who has good listening and communication skills. The individual's central concern with moral issues focuses the activity to attain the articulated aims, and when necessary, take risks. Central to this action is the ability of the physician executive to create increasing circles of relationships that are nurtured and maintained. The shared story is adjusted for the appropriate audiences but remains true.

The physician executive must be a credible clinician, which includes the completion of the necessary apprenticeship and track record in clinical medicine. He or she needs the clinical frame of reference and credibility to relate to the clinicians, and the first-hand knowledge base to be able to effectively understand and redesign the system of care. Concurrently, the physician executive must be able to share administrative experiences and the viewpoint of management in general. As previously noted, he or she must have a perception of the larger picture outside of the events of the day and understanding the important role of systems thinking and personal mastery.

An effective physician executive is often an individual who can create balance. Through a constancy of purpose and the ability to anticipate and synthesize major trends and changes in environment, the effective leader must recognize and manage the paradoxes and the possibilities. On a real-time, day-to-day basis, the physician executive must balance the following:

- Individual agendas with group and organizational aims

- Knowledge of clinical medicine with the language needed to communicate health-related issues for the population in general

- Anecdotal stories of individual care with the health of the population

- Development of a broad-based consensus among physicians in management versus the intact command and control structure

- Stories (for example, messages and themes) that are rational based on health and well-being versus those founded on mental models of power and control

The physician executive must recognize that he or she, like all leaders, will fail. Leaders are limited as to what they can accomplish and will hit obstacles they cannot overcome. Every defeat must be constructed as an opportunity, changing the circumstances and adjusting while remaining true to the core convictions and the core vision. It is key in this process that the organization, as well as the physician executive, learn as the shared experience influences and molds the story and the action in both leader and follower. In this sense, through failure there is learning and change, and thus ultimately success.

The physician executive, through the utilization of the core competencies discussed, develops a leadership role whose boundary spans between clinical medicine and health systems management, physician and managers, and the organization and the community. This leadership evolution is based on continued learning and experience through application. This leadership is an absolute necessity if systems of care are going to improve the health of the populations served.

Tools of the Trade: Shared Vision and Alignment of Incentives

Health care organizations have traditionally been constituted with two segregated, yet somewhat parallel, streams of consciousness: clinical and institutional. Institutional lines of authority were seen as business caretakers and facility managers. Clinical lines of authority were seen as a consortium of autonomous, independent agents. The tension for change, driven primarily by market forces, continues to influence shifts in their structures and processes. These shifts must eventually integrate the clinical and institutional elements. This transformation will enable the new IDS, comprised of both institutions and physicians, to more effectively manage care, bear risk, and demonstrate better value to the communities served.

The physician component may be the most difficult part of integration. Most physicians are nervous about health care reform, industry changes, and organizational shifts. Physicians don't trust institutions. As the evolution of health care continues, there is immediate risk for physicians to personally suffer economic consequence and diminished independence. Real market disciplines will be imposed on physicians going forward that have not been historically evident. Leaders will face the challenge of helping physicians to *understand* the tension for change—where the future is headed and how that differs from the current reality. The next stage is helping physicians *accept* the responsibility of change, then to embrace it and help to *create* it.

The physician executive's role in this process is to help persuade physicians to, rather than fight the tide of change, work together to direct it. A culture of cooperation and shared equity—whether tangible or virtual—needs to be fostered. The approach for accomplishing this is twofold.

1. Shared vision in a culture of dialogue and trust

2. Alignment of incentives with the goal of improving the health of the community

Shared vision is a force that mobilizes people to achieve common goals. It is a powerful unseen hand that guides and directs individual action leading to a realization of the bigger picture. Shared vision is the vehicle for thinking globally and acting locally. It begins with personal values and personal vision and transforms these to a higher level of action that focuses on the greater good. The physician executive serves as the catalyst for galvanizing the intrinsic values of key physician stakeholders with the core values shared by the institution. The ability to transform values and personal vision to that of a shared vision may determine the success and credibility of the physician executive.

While shared vision inspires action and sets the direction, alignment of incentives removes the obstacles and fuels the journey. The leverage point for making the IDS components truly merge into an effective system is aligned incentives. The role of the physician executive in the development and deployment of aligned incentives is on two levels.

1. Link the physician and institutional components to aid in the functional development of the IDS.

2. Link the IDS with the community to form an interactive health partnership that promotes health and value.

Even if the shared vision is compelling, there has to be overriding tension for change and incentives that work to overcome the natural resistance to change. Furthermore, for true alignment of incentives to exist it has to include financial and operational mechanisms, but must expand to also encompass intrinsic drivers such as the degree of autonomy, sense of belonging, and support for a level of personal and professional competency. Thus shared vision and alignment of incentives are often most effective when in coexistence.

There is a continuum for alignment of incentives with physicians, from shared rewards on clinical quality improvement goals to full alignment based on IDS equity. The culture of equity can also be created through virtual alliances, in which the institutional elements and the clinical elements enter into joint risk sharing and contracting for covered lives.

Alignment of incentives is also related to a population at risk, or a defined community, and requires buy-in from purchasers and customers on health promotion and treatment partnerships. A current example is that demand management is being supported with financial incentives such as decreased insurance premiums for prevention or wellness activities. Another trend is that healthy lifestyles are valued in corporate culture, with resources directed toward employee participation in health fairs and exercise programs. Communities have begun to develop collaboratives that create learning experiments linking health and neighborhood safety. Interest and motivation builds as the creativity of a community occurs jointly with public reflection. The role of the physician executive is to leverage and integrate these initiatives with the IDS for a collaborative health partnership that will springboard the redesign of the "sick care" system to a "health care" system.

The Physician Executive in Action: Creating Systems of Care

New challenges to the way health care decisions are made, both clinically and administratively, is producing real shifts in the focus.

From	To
• Responsibility for a person each time he or she presents him- or herself as a patient	• Responsibility for a defined population over a period of time, whether or not the individual ever becomes a patient
• Patient lives or dies	• Functional outcome and well-being

- Treating illness and disease

- Doctor-centered treatment and medical intervention

- Set payment per procedure

- Hospitals, physicians, and other medical providers as revenue centers

- Improvements based on medical knowledge alone

- Health care at all costs

- Health status of community with increased focus on prevention and demand management

- Patient-centered and family-centered choices from a continuum of care alternatives through a clinical team approach

- Set payment for health, per member per month, regardless of expenditures or lack thereof

- Hospitals, physicians, and other medical providers as cost centers

- Improvements based on system redesign innovation that leverages new knowledge

- Balance of health with value and other dimensions of life

As the focus shifts, so does the structure. There is significant movement in the health care industry toward the formation of the IDS. The current provider industry has evolved to fragments patched together to accommodate the needs of providers more than the needs of patients. This evolutionary period offers a window of opportunity for not only redesigning the structures and how they operate as a system, but also in redefining the core purpose. The core purpose should start with the community's health needs and build the systems of care accordingly, not vice versa. This charge largely defines the architectural role of the physician executive in developing the IDS.

IDS development should be approached with the clear articulation of benefit and purpose or the process will take on a life of its own and fall short of its potential. IDS formation is a turning point that goes beyond being the next business maneuver, but a transformation to becoming a true partner with the community. The premise for forming an IDS should be that it creates better value. Value, within the context of IDS development, can be defined in three dimensions.

1. Contributing to health and positive patient outcomes

2. Contributing in a manner that is economically viable

3. User-friendly—seamless systems and free from deficiencies and rework

The redefinition of purpose will transform and elevate the industry movement beyond merely being an improvement to existing structures. A new design is called for that integrates care delivery along the continuum of care. To be effective, the system of care must assume risk for, measure, and improve the health of the community.

System models can be constructed with specific detail and unique considerations; however, even a general model serves as a framework to address redesign and management of the continuum. The high-level system model is useful in identifying the leverage points of assumption of risk, alignment of incentives, development of care paths, management of demand, and the measurement and redesign of clinical processes.

The continuum of care is a system of health-related processes beginning before birth and ending with death. It is useful to think of the continuum of care as having discreet access points that correlate in a general way with most health delivery systems' institutional groupings. The continuum of care should be developed collaboratively between management and physicians, based on community need. A high-level model of the continuum of care is shown in Figure 26.1.

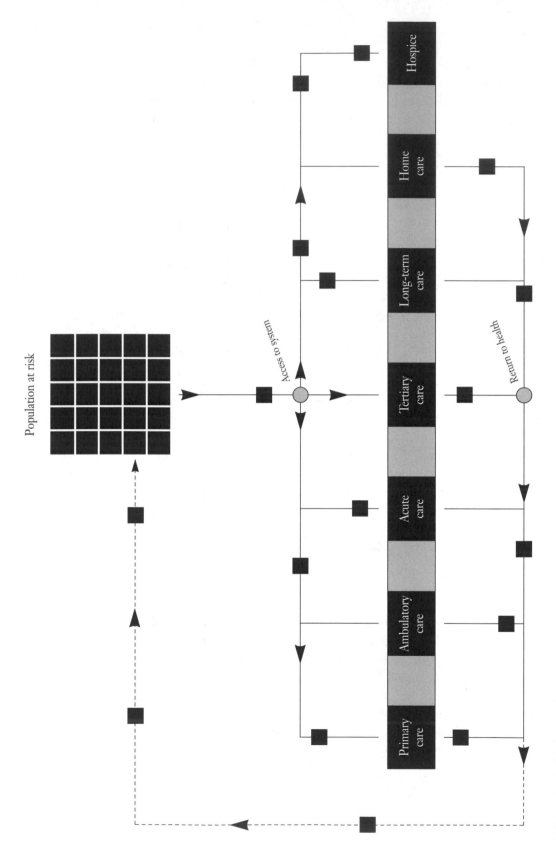

Figure 26.1. Continuum of care.

As the structural components begin to integrate and the continuum of care begins to function systemically, the management of care becomes more critical. Management of care is driven from within by the industry evolution—as this is the next stage of integration—but also by other forces such as health care reform, declines in reimbursement, and promulgation of financing mechanisms that require providers (clinicians and institutions) to share risk.

The management of care could reside with the physician, case manager, and patient—a triad of health partners. The role of the physician executive is to develop models and facilitate decision making so that the management of care develops as a system within the IDS.

Figure 26.2 represents one proposed model to serve as a care management tool. The community served can be divided into two populations at risk: (1) the healthy and (2) those needing or receiving intervention for chronic illnesses.

Models of care become essential as individuals move between health and intervention, and of particular importance during intervention to make sure the patient receives the "right care, in the right setting, at the right time."

This stage is where the IDS and the community become more interactive in understanding and learning more about each other. Physicians and case managers should profile the health of the population at risk to gain an understanding of health status. Health status of the community will enable the IDS to target resources and proactively promote health, prevent illness, and manage an efficient return to health for those needing intervention.

For an IDS to emerge, certainly the structural components must exist; but the strength will be realized in the coordination of the components in a system that produces value. Depending on the health needs of the community, resources can be allocated and systems developed that target specific health improvements or clinical aims.

The role of the physician executive is to create learning experiments that foster the process and knowledge related to value chains that achieve the defined clinical aims. In this process, aims should be established as well as agreement on the necessary measures to ensure that the aim has been reached, and a cycle of learning implemented and facilitated by the physician executive. Clinical aims have been published that incorporate measures and can be used to seed the process. The following is an example of one of the clinical aims to be achieved.

Sample Clinical Aim: Cardiovascular Disease

Early intervention: Establish a process for early identification of high-risk patients within a defined population, focusing on serum cholesterol and blood pressure screenings, with a resulting 10 percent improvement in treatment, compliance, and follow-up.

Acute management: Redesign the process of care for treatment of heart disease that results in a 10 percent to 20 percent reduction in cost and variation, without compromising the clinical and functional outcome of the patient.

Chronic management: Establish a clinical pathway of care addressing the chronicity of congestive heart failure that improves the patient's perception of personal health, reducing readmissions and cost by 40 percent, without compromising clinical outcomes.

The physician executive can create a culture of learning through implementation of clinical aims, such as in this example. Clinical aims can be customized and developed based on community need or

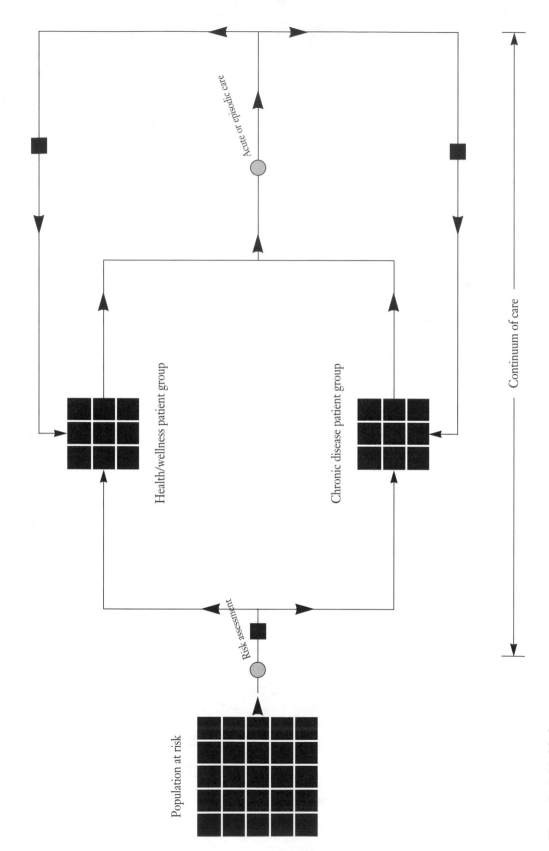

Figure 26.2. Model of care.

high-volume procedures with wide clinical and cost variation. Figure 26.3 is a sample value chain for a clinical aim. This model can serve as a learning tool with a multidisciplinary team in efforts to establish and conduct clinical quality experiments with corresponding measurements of value.

Figures 26.1, 26.2, and 26.3 depict merely an evolution of possible means to an end. Stage one evolution facilitates a systems approach to better organizing the health care processes and resources for more coordinated and seamless webs of care. Stage one is about integrating the components and the intellectual property to form an integrated continuum of care (see Figure 26.1).

Stage two of the evolution is the demonstration of measurable improvements in patient outcomes and community health as the flow of patients is managed. Stage two (see Figures 26.2 and 26.3) is an efficient system, still primarily focused on "sick care" with the goal being a return to health, not a vicious cycle of self-perpetuating clinical intervention.

The real breakthrough is in the transformation from a "sick care" system to a "health care" system, which occurs in stage three after the other stages have been enacted. Stage three is the realization of better value in terms of both cost efficiencies and increased health status. Figure 26.4 illustrates the system dynamics of a redesigned "health care" system. In this model, the rate of illness and the number of patients needing intervention are lowered through preventive care. Concurrently, investments in quality improvement efforts act to lower the cost of care and accelerate the rate of return to health. The model becomes virtuous as the decreases in costs and increases in financial resources accumulate with each cycle, which can then be invested in additional preventive care and quality improvement initiatives. Figure 26.4 maps the leverage points for system transformation from "sick care" to a "health care" IDS.

This system of care develops with stages of integration and system redesign through learning experiments. The physician executive's role is not to lead the experiments, but to facilitate and deploy them while concurrently developing other physician leaders as clinical champions. One vehicle that may serve the physician executive is the development of a clinical quality council, comprised of key clinician leaders. This forum can serve as a think tank, while concurrently spawning physician champions and ownership of clinical redesign.

This is merely a suggested approach; many other approaches and techniques can be employed. The keys here are learning and deploying through dialogue, systems thinking, experiments, empowerment, and innovation—creating a system of lean production. The end result should be a higher-quality health care system that is designed around meeting health needs and producing better value, as defined by the community served.

Summary

Selecting a physician executive, or accepting the responsibility to fulfill the mission of the physician executive, should be predicated upon a fit between personal values and the challenges of this role. The personal profile, mastery of certain tools, championship of integration, and clinical redesign are elements that warrant consideration in finding a mutually beneficial fit between professional and profession.

This role is about creating a new system in which people, processes, and structures are integrated to form a greater whole. The foundation for this should be developed first from the alignment of personal, organizational, and community values. Then, once the alignment of values occurs, shared vision can emerge. Shared vision, when coupled with the alignment of incentives (financial and operational), sets the stage for real transformation from a "sick care" system to a "health care" IDS.

634

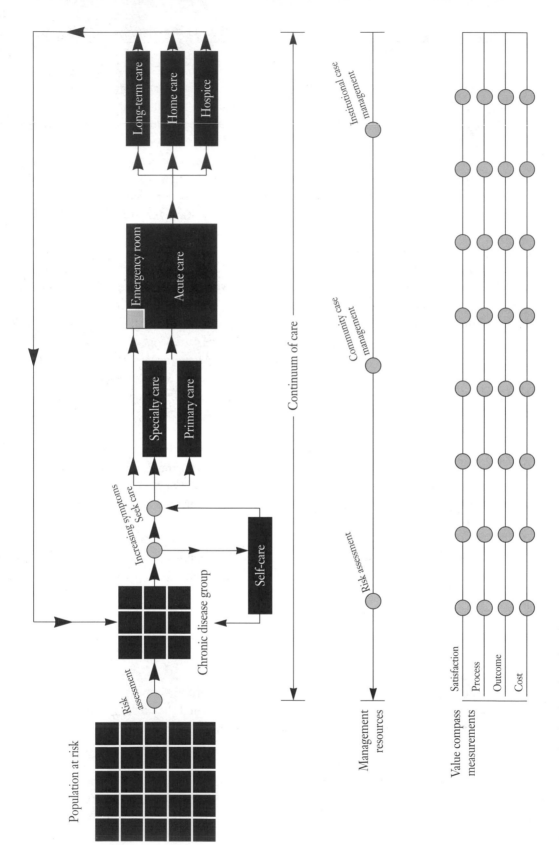

Figure 26.3. Sample value chain for a clinical aim.

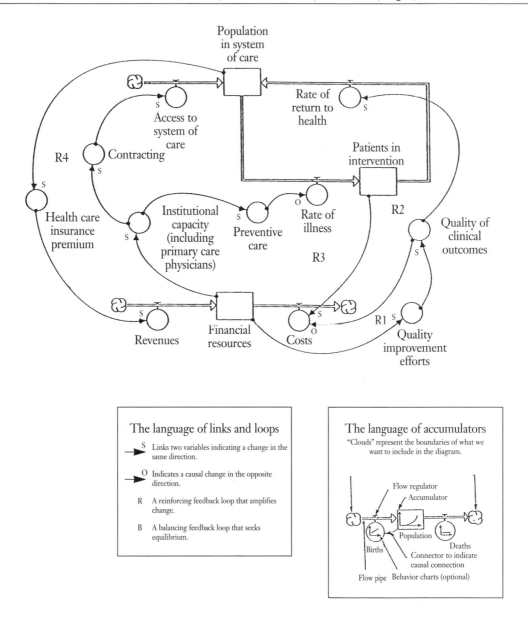

Figure 26.4. Redesigned health care system.

In the development of the IDS, the physician executive's role is to facilitate the design of the new system of care. This system begins with the needs of the community, in terms of both the healthy and those requiring clinical intervention. The approach of facilitation can be divided into creating a culture of learning and clinical experiments and fostering physician champions and physician ownership of clinical redesign.

Physician leadership is the propelling force in the integration of clinical and institutional elements, which is a cornerstone for IDS development. This new era calls for physician executives to emerge who are dynamic leaders, both clinically and organizationally. So, when trying to create, influence, and understand the future of health care, envision both a new delivery system and a new wave of leadership. If we think the way we have thought, we will get what we got. Start with the community, and work backward.

Questions for Personal Exploration and Team Learning

1. What are my/our core values?

2. What is my/our personal vision?

3. How do these relate to our corporate values and vision?

4. Who do we serve? Who are our customers?

5. What are our customers' needs?

6. What do we make?

7. Why do we make it?

8. How do we make it?

9. How do we improve it?

10. What are the leverage points and barriers for system integration?

11. What is learning? What do we learn?

12. What are the forces that have driven the need for the physician executive?

13. What are the tasks and responsibilities of the physician executive?

14. How do we measure accomplishment and monitor progress?

15. What are the core competencies of the physician executive?

16. How will these core competencies be acquired and developed?

17. What are our aims?

18. How do we know if we have reached them?

19. What are the learning experiences we need to improve our system of care so that we can reach our aims?

Kimberly E. Sangari is a vice president with Pitts Management Associates, Inc. PMA is a consulting and strategic advisory firm specializing in strategy development, mergers, and consolidations in the health care industry. Her health care experience includes strategic and financial planning, operations development, and partnering and alliance development.

Before joining PMA, she worked for five years as a senior-level director with General Health System in Baton Rouge, Louisiana, a $450 million provider-insurer, organized as a regional integrated delivery system, with an HMO, care delivery components comprising the full continuum of care, and strategic alliances with physicians.

Prior to working with General Health, Sangari was a senior consultant with Price Waterhouse in Houston, Texas. She specialized in management consulting related to financial and operational issues. She performed financial and business analysis and due diligence associated with money center bank financings, bond offerings, corporate strategy development, corporate recovery, business development ventures, and litigation matters.

Sangari holds a master's degree in health care administration from the University of Houston-Clear Lake and a bachelor's degree in business administration from the University of Texas at Austin.

Gene Beyt, M.D., M.S., is a clinical associate professor of public health in the Medical Management Program at Tulane University's Department of Health Systems Management, where he teaches physician executive leadership. He previously served as chief clinical officer and senior vice president of medical affairs for an integrated system of care that included acute care facilities, primary care group practices, a managed care organization, and ambulatory, home, and long-term care services. He is an AOA graduate of the LSU School of Medicine, and finished his internal medicine and infectious diseases training at Barnes Hospital and Washington University School of Medicine in St. Louis. Beyt completed his M.S. degree in preventive and administrative medicine at the University of Wisconsin in Madison, is board certified in internal medicine, infectious diseases, and medical management, and is a Fellow in the American College of Physicians. He previously served as an associate professor of medicine and program director in internal medicine for LSU, and maintained a private practice in infectious diseases.

Chapter 27

Emerging Concepts: Self-Managed Teams

Lisa Ethier and Marian Furlong

The power of teamwork in health care settings has been demonstrated time and again by organizations that have embraced total quality management. As a result, more health care executives are becoming interested in advanced methods to engage employees and physicians in joint decision making. The health care industry is also experiencing a need to function with flatter organizations while increasing or at least maintaining current levels of quality. In production-related industries, self-managed teams have been shown to be an effective vehicle for improving quality, flexibility, productivity, and efficiency while maintaining leaner management structures.

A *self-managed team* is defined as a highly trained group of employees who have day-to-day responsibility for themselves and the work they do. They have access to more resources than other types of teams, are cross-trained in a variety of skills, have more information available to them, and have a high degree of decision-making authority.[1] Other characteristics of a self-managed team include sharing equal responsibility for a defined segment of work and regular meetings to discuss work assignments, problem solving, and personnel issues. A plethora of literature is available on self-managed teams (see, for example, Cohen,[2] Fisher,[3] Lawler,[4] Mohrman, Cohen, and Mohrman,[5] Orsburn,[6] and Wellins, Byham, and Wilson[7]). Companies such as Hewlett Packard, Xerox, Procter & Gamble, General Electric, General Mills, and Federal Express, to name a few, have used self-managed teams for a number of years with varying degrees of success.

Until recently, self-managed teams have been popular in industries other than health care. The concept of employee empowerment, however, is not new to health care. The three major forces that have shaped employee participation in health care are shared governance, total quality management, and patient-focused care. Shared governance for nurses is the closest that health care has come to implementing dramatic increases in decision-making authority at the staff level. Historically, nurse executives have embraced the tenets and infrastructure of shared governance as a way to advance their belief in empowerment. An elaborate council structure with by-laws is oftentimes the vehicle used to engage the nursing staff in making decisions about myriad topics. Nursing practice is usually the core of the council structure.

Shared governance has been effective for nursing, but the infrastructure rarely involves the rest of the organization in a meaningful way. As Perley and Raab point out, "While shared governance enhances professional practice, it is limited in its ability to change operational processes that often hinder nursing care."[8] Furthermore, once the initiative is well established, shared governance can be difficult to expand outside of nursing. Other disciplines might reject involvement because it is viewed as "a nursing thing." Blancett claims that "functional-hierarchical issues" interfere with successful restructuring in health care.[9] Strong allegiance to one's own professional discipline, to the exclusion of others, is not uncommon in health care settings. This phenomena explains why shared governance has rarely gone beyond the realm of nursing and why strategic planning for self-managed teams must occur at a cross-functional, executive level to ensure more widespread acceptance and ultimate success.

Process improvement methodologies have also played an important role in shaping employee involvement in health care, and they are important to the overall functioning of self-managed teams. Temporary teams that are chartered to resolve chronic problems have been extremely effective in driving out waste and rework in business and clinical processes. Typically, these teams are empowered to carry out an implementation plan to achieve the recommended improvements, then they disband. Often their empowerment does not extend into everyday work. Process improvement teams can be viewed as special project teams, but are not self-managing per se. Team members are empowered only during their tenure as a process improvement team. Self-managed teams, on the other hand, must know how to effectively use process improvement tools and techniques in everyday work. That is why organizations that have embraced total quality management find self-managing teams a logical extension of what they have been doing all along.

Patient-focused care and other forms of reengineering in health care have also served to increase the interest in self-managed teams. Patient-focused care models often stipulate a small team of people, such as a patient care trio, who must work together to meet patient and family needs and desires. A hospital in Pennsylvania, as well as many others, is expanding its patient-focused care initiatives to incorporate self-managed team characteristics. It seems incongruous to spend a lot of time, energy, and dollars on reengineering without considering the use of self-managed teams within the newly designed processes. Designing work to allow people to respond quickly and decisively to customer needs while directly managing problems along the way is a cornerstone characteristic of self-managed teams that also fits well with the purpose of patient-focused care and reengineering. Patient-focused care methodologies provide the clinical focus, and self-managed teams provide the infrastructure and methodology for further empowering staff.

A combination of other forces has also created increased interest in teams. The extremely competitive marketplace makes the use of self-managed teams a natural choice for health care organizations. One might say that, in our current environment, consideration of self-managed teams is an ethical imperative. Delayering the organization without providing new skills, expectations, support, and resources for managers and employees is a formula for trouble. Two parallel and undesirable scenarios can unfold. First, the remaining managers become overloaded and burnt out because they are performing the work of several managers; and second, employees have less supervision, but have not been given the opportunity to learn new skills to make them successful. Both managers and employees are burdened with working in old, outdated processes while taking on expanded responsibilities for which they are not prepared. The personal and professional toll it takes on managers and employees is great and, not least of all, the customer ultimately suffers. While using self-managed teams is not a quick fix, it is a potential long-term solution for an organization that wants to remain competitive, flexible, and state-of-the-art in both its human and technical systems. As executives are challenged to cut expenses and run leaner operations, they are turning to self-managed teams as an ethical and effective way to more meaningfully involve staff in day-to-day decision making.

A review of the literature indicates a wide range of implementation strategies for self-managed teams in health care (see, for example, Blancett,[10] Constantinides et al.,[11] Jannotta and Maldonado,[12] Maurer,[13] McHenry,[14] Thyen, Theis, and Tebbitt,[15] and Wurstner and Koch[16]). Several authors record their organization's journey toward self-managed teams. Frequently, the journey began with shared governance for nurses and expanded to the wider enterprise,[17] or it was implemented department by department with or without the benefit of overall organizational planning. Jannotta and Maldonado reported on a remarkable 80-hour training program called "Basics of Collaborative Management."[18] The course included topics such as schedule development, performance evaluation, interviewing skills, quality management, and budgeting. The course offered professional education units and a comprehensive new employee orientation. One article outlined a process to turn a group of managers into their own self-managing team.[19] Like many self-managed team initiatives, this one was borne from the departure of a key leader. Rather than fill the position, this group chose to redefine roles and responsibilities to work within a flatter organizational structure. Results such as improved perceptions of staff autonomy, increased ability to manage crises, increased effectiveness of the group, getting more work done with fewer people, increased collegiality between disciplines, increased individual responsibility, better decision making, heightened personal satisfaction and growth, productive competition, improved turnaround times, and decreased workload have been reported (see, for example, Constantinides et al.,[20] Gustin and Fellows,[21] Inkson, et al.,[22] and Wurstner and Koch[23]).

In this chapter, we report on a study of self-managed teams conducted by Premier and Sharp HealthCare. Premier is the largest voluntary health care alliance in the United States, with more than 250 owner systems that own or operate 700 institutions and have affiliations with another 1100 hospitals. Premier resulted from a merger in 1995 between Premier Health Alliance, American Healthcare Systems, and SunHealth Alliance. Sharp HealthCare is an integrated health care delivery system located in San Diego, California. A survey developed jointly by Development Dimensions International (DDI), Association for Quality and Participation (AQP), and *Industry Week* was adapted for use in a health care setting.[24] That study focused on manufacturing companies. Comparisons between our findings in health care and that study are made.

Data Collection

A survey was mailed to 250 chief operating officers of Premier's owner hospitals and health care organizations. A brief, preliminary survey was attached to the more intensive survey. The brief survey asked whether the organization was involved in self-managed teams (SMTs) based on a definition provided. If their effort matched the definition, they were requested to complete the more in-depth survey. If it did not, they were asked to circle no and return the survey to acknowledge a lack of involvement with SMTs. We received 141 responses; therefore, the response rate was 56 percent. Of those that responded, 27 reported that they were involved with self-managed teams and completed the in-depth survey. Several people contacted us to determine whether their initiative met the definition provided. Typically, their efforts included a limited version of patient-focused care or shared governance that did not qualify, for the purposes of this study, as true self-managed teams. The results reported in this chapter are from the 27 organizations that said their initiative matched the definition we provided. The respondents represent 16 states throughout the United States.

Results

Background

Our respondents were midsized to large health care organizations. The majority (76 percent) of the sample had 1000 to more than 3500 employees (see Figure 27.1). That the concept of SMTs in health care is relatively new is evidenced in our finding that more than 70 percent of the respondents have been involved with SMTs for one year or less (see Figure 27.2). Based on our experience, initiatives such as total quality management, shared governance, and patient-focused care have taken the lead in health care organizations.

Improving quality, improving productivity, and reducing costs were the most popular motivations for undertaking SMTs (see Figure 27.3). Historically, organizations were interested in the concept of

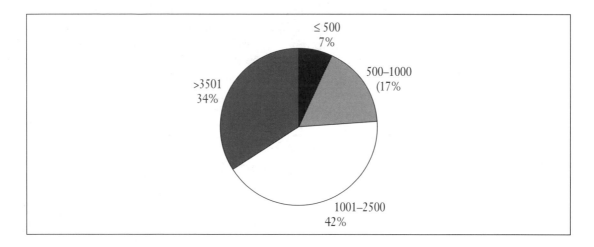

Figure 27.1. Number of employees in the respondent organizations.

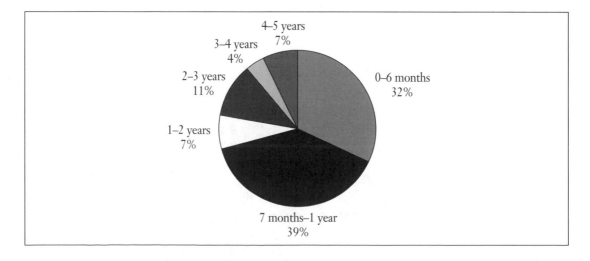

Figure 27.2. Length of involvement with SMTs.

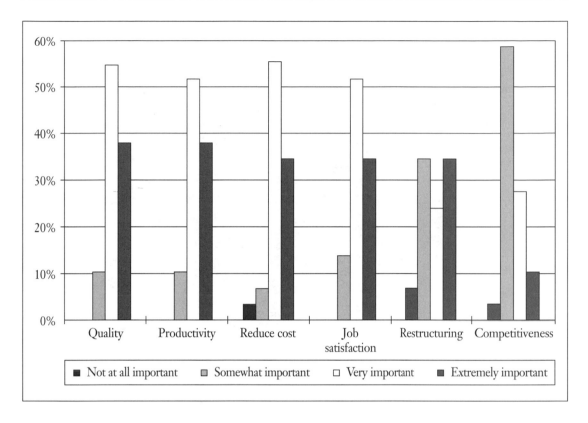

Figure 27.3. Motivation for implementing SMTs.

teams for the purpose of increasing employee morale and satisfaction; the teams were an end in themselves rather than a means to a greater outcome. Today, the focus has shifted to the perception of teams as a vehicle for improved bottom-line results.

Planning for SMTs

Figure 27.4 reflects the planning strategies used by the respondents. The data indicate that planning and implementing teams is not necessarily a linear process. Typically, a cycle of planning and implementation occurs over time. Slightly more than 5 percent approached planning on an organizationwide basis and have reached the pilot phase, while 45 percent reported that they planned on a department-by-department basis. Approximately 40 percent said that they have already implemented teams. The written responses indicated that less than half of the respondents reported using a classic infrastructure for creating major organizational change that includes a steering council to create the vision and foundation and employee design teams to draft an implementation plan. When they did use design teams, they tended to be cross functional, and the use of pilot sites was mentioned in only four cases. One respondent's comment summarizes what appears to be a common practice of planning for teams in health care: "Each department has used its own preference for design. Some have had the managers design the teams; others have used a design team of employees; others have used 100 percent employees in making design decisions."

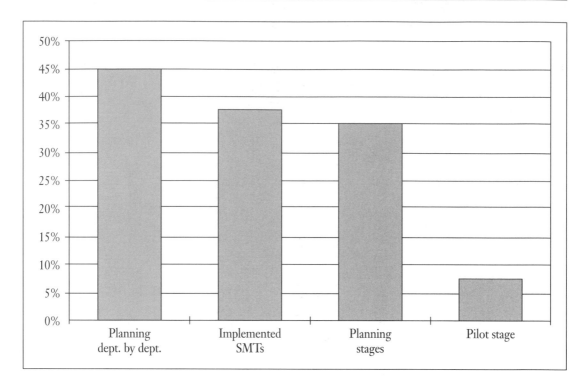

Figure 27.4. Stages of planning and implementing SMTs.

Planning and Implementation Responsibilities

The majority of the people who completed the survey served as internal consultants to the self-managed team initiative and had been involved with it for less than a year. When it came to the level of involvement of the various management and clinical and nonclinical groups, the first-line supervisors were the most involved (86 percent), then middle managers (82 percent) and clinical staff (77 percent). As expected, the board of directors and physicians were the least involved. The clinical staff was generally more involved than the nonclinical staff (see Figure 27.5). As with any major organizational change initiative, the first-line and midlevel managers have the most to lose from self-managed teams; therefore, it is not surprising that they were the most involved.

Of the 27 responses that we received, one respondent reported a negative experience with self-managed teams after a two- to three-year implementation. Upon analysis of the returned survey, it appears that the root cause of this particular failure related to a lack of adequate planning and stakeholder involvement. Executives were the only group that was rated as involved in planning "to a great extent." All other groups were either not involved at all or were involved very little. It was also reported that while there were some demonstrated positive impacts such as the ability to operate with fewer managers, the lack of departmental direction and problems in getting teams of people to discipline one another outweighed any benefits that might have been achieved.

Physician Involvement

Most of the respondents reported a general lack of physician involvement. When physicians were involved, they tended to be key physician leaders, then the chief of staff and medical directors (see

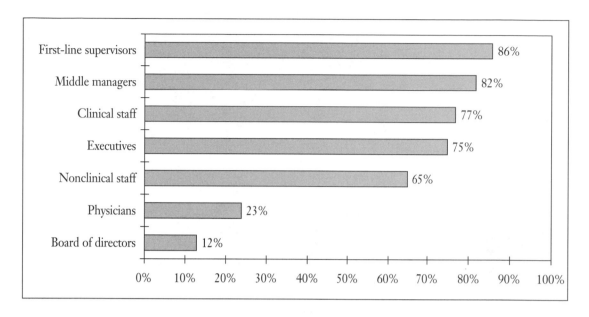

Figure 27.5. Extent of involvement in planning for SMTs.

Figure 27.6). Key physician leaders were defined as either formal or informal leaders. They were most likely to serve as ad hoc consultants rather than as members of a steering committee or design team (see Figure 27.7). Physician involvement is a unique and challenging issue for the development of teams in health care settings, and it appears that most of the respondents are struggling with this issue. When asked to describe successful and unsuccessful strategies for involving physicians, respondents suggested visiting medical staff meetings to "tell the story;" written publications; one-on-one discussions; focusing on improvements in patient care—the case management approach; creating a medical advisory committee of informal and formal leaders; choosing a few key physicians who would inform the rest of the staff; and holding regular, bimonthly meetings with department chiefs.

When asked how physicians viewed the SMT initiative, 62 percent said that physicians were generally uninformed. Twenty-four percent said they believed physicians viewed SMTs as somewhat valuable, and 9 percent as somewhat unsuccessful. Some of the comments about physician involvement and perceptions were: "Many of our physicians are traditional in the sense that they look for traditional structure (head nurse/director) to take their issues to;" "The physicians with patients on the [self-managed team] units are more interested. If it's not their unit . . . they are uninformed;" "Medical staff is small and not interested in these activities;" and "Physicians were not involved in the planning for SMTs. Their response was somewhat skeptical. [Their] early commitment and input would have helped."

Union Involvement

Only three organizations reported that they were unionized and, of those organizations, two reported that the union was against SMTs. Industrial case studies demonstrate that union representatives typically do not support the concept of self-managed teams. Union representatives believe that teams usurp their authority by encouraging team members to become more loyal to the team and, therefore, the company rather than the union. Additionally, union leaders spend a lot of time protecting jobs and specific job descriptions, and the sheer nature of self-managed teams threatens both. Organizations

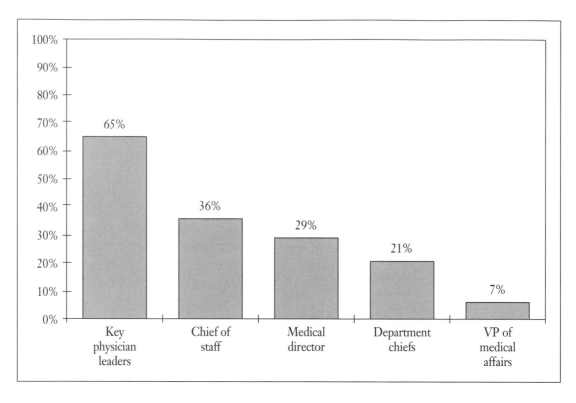

Figure 27.6. The percentage of time physicians were involved in planning and implementing SMTs.

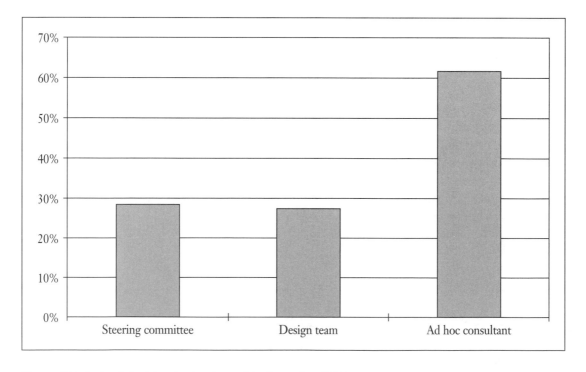

Figure 27.7. Role of physicians in planning and implementing SMTs.

with mature self-managed teams can function effectively with fewer people because they have more employees who can perform a variety of tasks.

Integration with Other Initiatives

It is not uncommon for SMTs to occur as either an extension of or in parallel with other organizational initiatives. In our sample, 82 percent of respondents are actively involved with total quality management, 78 percent with reengineering, 74 percent with cost reductions, and 59 percent with customer service training (see Figure 27.8). To maximize the effectiveness of teams, teams must be linked in a meaningful way to other initiatives in the organization. In most cases, SMTs are a natural extension of other well-established efforts. When asked how the connection is made between SMTs and other activities, the respondents said "SMTs are the ultimate in shared governance;" "Should be the result of a successful reengineering process;" "SMTs can do their own ongoing reengineering. They address cost reduction, customer service, and possibly downsizing. We're using our SMTs on patient-focused care units;" "With difficulty;" "Very consistent with TQM and cost reduction;" "Very compatible and will enhance overall benefits of other initiatives;" "SMTs may prove to be integral in their [service lines, TQM, and so on] success;" and "Patient-focused care will be designed using SMTs, and SMTs will be used to integrate the other initiatives."

Management, Team, and Physician Roles and Responsibilities

More than half of the respondents said that the SMTs report to either a supervisor or manager for their daily work activities or to someone designated as a team leader. It is rare that organizations completely

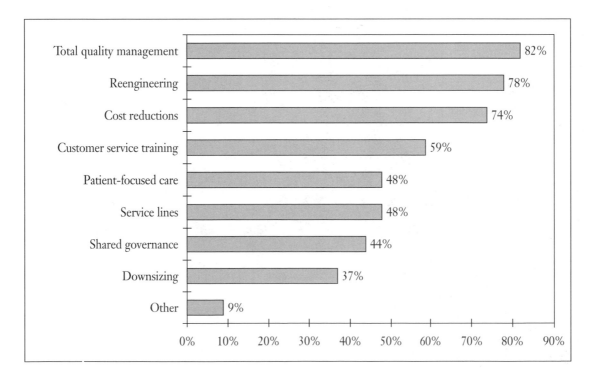

Figure 27.8. Other organizational initiatives underway in addition to SMTs.

eliminate manager positions, and even rarer to design teams without a formal team leader role. Blancett notes that in the case of nurses, there is a definite trend toward redefining rather than eliminating the nurse manager role.[25]

Orsburn et al. estimate that it takes two or more years for teams to become fully self-managed.[26] There are five stages to team development (start-up, state of confusion, leader-centered teams, tightly formed teams, and self-managed teams), and over time the role of the manager decreases while the decision-making authority of the team dramatically increases. Mohrman, Cohen, and Mohrman point to several new roles and demands of managers in team-based organizations such as designing team structures, developing teams, being a team member, managing team performance, and crafting large-scale change.[27] Kerfoot suggests that health care break out of its "blue-collar industrial military model" by adopting self-managed teams as the new model for leadership.[28] Eighty-two percent of respondents said that they are operating with fewer managers, and 94 percent said that the impact has been a positive one. The positive effects of working with fewer traditional managers increases over time as the teams become more mature and autonomous and as managers learn new skills and broaden their responsibilities for running the business.

Figure 27.9 demonstrates that team members tend to have the most responsibility for assigning daily tasks, equipment maintenance, safety and housekeeping, and working with internal customers

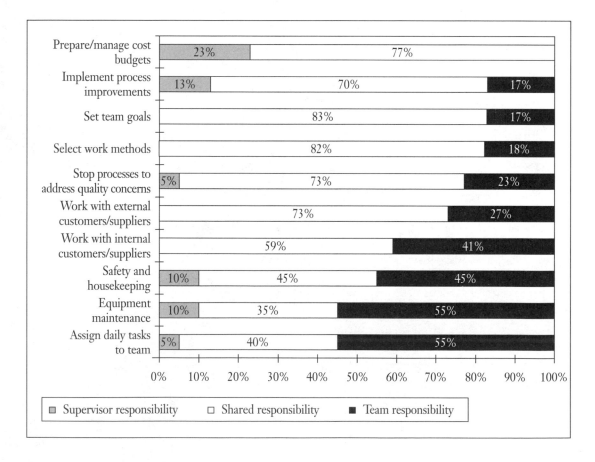

Figure 27.9. Responsibility for tasks.

and suppliers. Preparing and managing budgets, implementing process improvements, setting team goals, selecting work methods, addressing quality concerns, and working with external customers and suppliers were tasks that tended to be shared among supervisors and team members. Supervisors tended to be more involved with personnel functions relating to compensation decisions and selection; however, the majority of tasks in this category are shared (see Figure 27.10).

When it comes to selecting the team leader, 41 percent of the respondents said that management makes the decision, 21 percent said that the team members interview candidates and management makes the final decision, and 38 percent said that the team members make their own decision (see Figure 27.11). Fifty-two percent said that the role of the team leader rotates.

When asked how successful certain groups of people have been in adjusting to their new roles in an SMT environment, the respondents reported all groups have been largely successful. While 69 percent of the executives were rated as successful in adjusting to their new roles, 19 percent of the respondents felt that this group was unsuccessful (Figure 27.12). Personal experience indicates that executives are prone to segregating themselves from what is going on in the rest of the organization, even when they are the initiators. Many do not understand the importance of forming their own self-managing team and fundamentally changing their own behavior and practices.

Morhman et al. suggest a strong role for executives.

> *The executive management team is responsible for creating the context within which team-based business units can operate effectively. This means providing overall business direction and leadership in developing organizational capabilities for team effectiveness and fostering lateral integration across teams and business units. The importance of leadership from this team cannot be overestimated. Unless the macro context is brought into alignment with the team approach, organizational members will be caught in the tension between the new and old ways of operating.*[29]

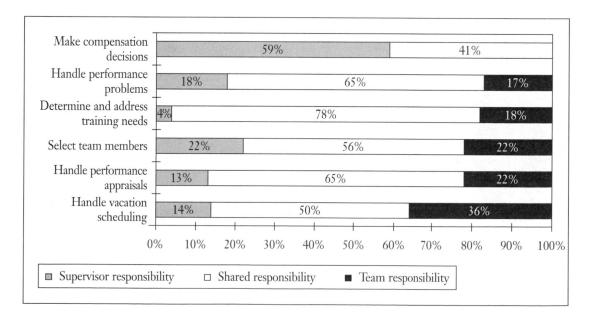

Figure 27.10. Responsibility for personnel functions.

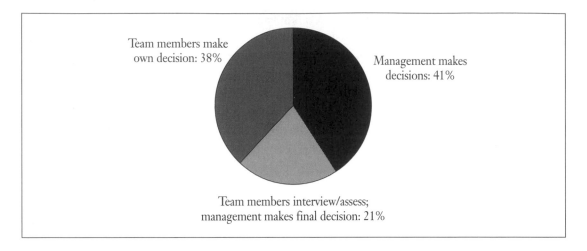

Figure 27.11. Team leader selection responsibilities.

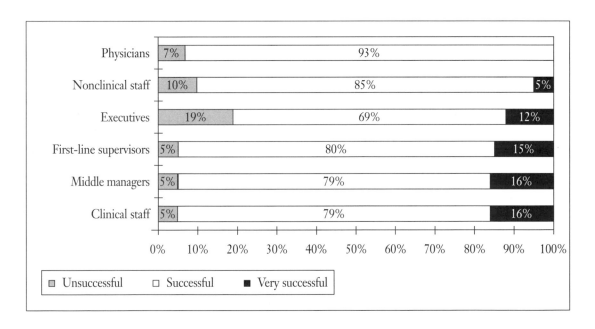

Figure 27.12. Success in adjusting to new roles in an SMT environment.

Decentralization

A key characteristic of self-managed teams is decentralization of various functions. The idea is to col-locate people who interface on a regular basis to produce a defined segment of work. An example is the manufacturing process for Volvo automobiles. Employees in a Volvo plant work in teams and together as they build a car. This arrangement naturally creates an environment where employees have greater accountability for quality, cost, and productivity. An added benefit is that morale and interest in the work is sustained because employees are involved with an entire output, rather than pieces of a total output that may lose meaning over time outside of the larger context. Galbraith points to the evidence that collocation increases communication and fosters productive relationships.[30]

Partial decentralization of support departments occurred in 46 percent of the sample, while 54 percent had not decentralized at all. Complete decentralization was reported in the areas of utilization review and phlebotomy. Of those that were partially decentralized, dietary was most frequently affected (28 percent), followed by housekeeping (22 percent), laboratory (19 percent), and pharmacy (16 percent). Very little decentralization has occurred in the areas of materials management, transportation, social work, EKG, IV team, and maintenance (see Figure 27.13). Perhaps the relatively low rate of decentralization in our sample relates to the newness of self-managed teams in the organizations represented. Some of the comments relating to decentralization were "Dietary is having problems with thermalization on the units;" "Phlebotomy has been completely decentralized and picked up by the nursing staff;" "Coordinating decentralized functions with central functions [has been difficult];" and "The only issue we have is in having the teams support each other in the pharmacy as well as support the service line department they are aligned with."

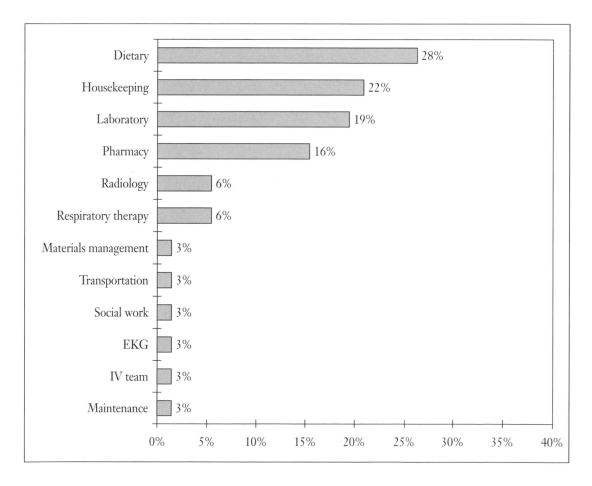

Figure 27.13. Percentage of the time support departments were found to be partially decentralized.

Job Rotation and Multiskilling

Job rotation is another important characteristic of self-managed teams. Galbraith calls interdepartmental rotation "the most powerful tool of the organization designer for creating voluntary lateral processes.[31] He goes on to say that job rotation goes beyond teaching people specific skills; it also teaches people how to learn and become flexible. Flexibility allows team members to be more efficient and customer focused. It also provides job enrichment for employees who enjoy a broad scope of responsibilities. Multiskilling is particularly challenging in health care settings for two related reasons. First, most health care workers are knowledge workers, and knowledge is time-consuming and potentially costly to transfer from person to person. Second, the rules and regulations pertaining to professional licensure create barriers to cross-training individuals.

Many organizations have successfully tackled the issue of job rotation and multiskilling through their patient-focused care initiatives. In our sample, 41 percent reported that members rotated jobs to some extent, while 21 percent reported that team members rotated jobs very little or not at all (see Figure 27.14). More than 80 percent reported that the members of their teams are already multiskilled. One respondent said, "[We have had a lot of] interaction with state boards and legal departments to determine the appropriateness [of our plans] prior to any implementation." Multiskilling is usually an integral component to patient-focused care models and, therefore, is not a new concept in health care.

When asked whether professional licensure requirements posed a barrier, 81 percent said that it did not. It seems that many health care organizations are finding appropriate and efficient ways to institute job rotation and multiskilling. Another factor that may explain this finding is that since most of the organizations in the sample are relatively new at SMTs, they might not yet have progressed to the point of multiskilling their workforce. Organizations may wait until the second year before instituting multiskilling because it is a training- and cost-intensive task.

Team Training

The single most costly aspect of transitioning to self-managed teams relates to training. Employees must be given new skills to function successfully in a team environment as well as skills to perform multiple, new tasks. Orsburn et al. consider training a core activity not only in the early stages of self-managed team development, but also to sustain teams over the long haul. They say that "companies

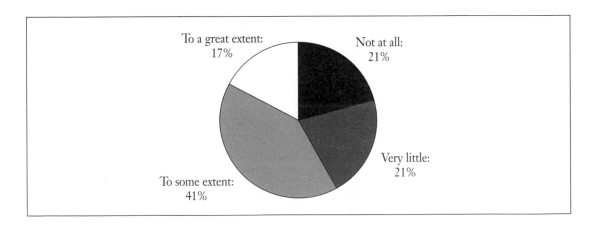

Figure 27.14. Extent to which members rotate jobs within SMTs.

that reap continuing rewards through their teams—Procter & Gamble, Corning, TRW, and Digital—recognize and act on one of the most fundamental facts of self-direction: Training and reinforcement, like food and oxygen, are forever required by teams and their managers.[32]

Figure 27.15 depicts the types of training offered by respondents. More than half the sample said that their organizations provided training in self-managed team roles and responsibilities, handling conflict, group problem solving, running effective meetings, work redesign, and communication skills. Presentation skills, influencing others, and budgeting were offered less frequently. Training in selecting team members and evaluating performance will probably be offered by more organizations as they mature in their self-managed team initiatives.

Compensation

Compensation systems are rarely modified during the first year of SMT implementation, which explains the finding that 72 percent of the respondents reported continued use of individual merit increases rather than skill-based pay or gain sharing. Only 20 percent reported using skill-based pay, and 16 percent reported the use of bonuses. Several industrial examples point to the effectiveness of skill-based pay in encouraging and rewarding multiskilling, but current compensation trends in health

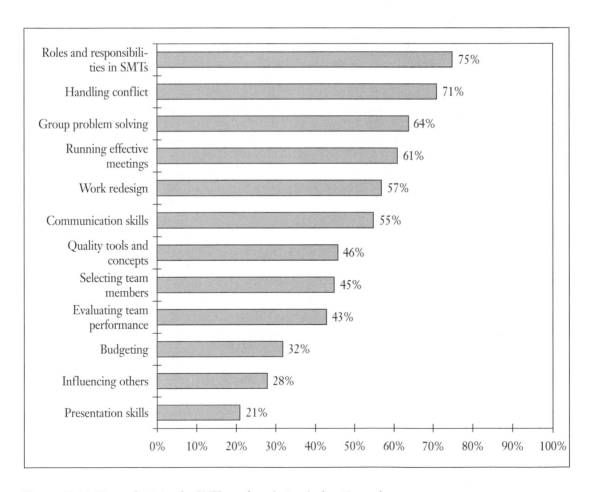

Figure 27.15. Types of training for SMT members during the last 12 months.

care indicate that gain sharing is a more popular alternative pay system. Regardless of the type of pay structure chosen, it appears that health care in general views compensation as a lag system rather than a lead system—that is, compensation systems are changed *after* rather than before or in parallel to other fundamental changes in the organization. Lawler cautions that if pay systems do not catch up quickly enough, this can prevent institutionalization of desired changes.[33] Furthermore, maintaining the old ways may inadvertently reward people for behavior that is the antithesis of what is expected in the new organizational culture.

Implementation Barriers

All organizations face certain barriers when implementing major change. The transition to self-managed teams affects almost every aspect of the human and technical components of an organization and, therefore, it is only natural to encounter problems along the way, especially if careful planning did not occur. In our survey, we asked respondents to rate the various barriers they have encountered in their roll-out of self-managed teams. The largest barrier by far was no time given to get adjusted to new roles (87 percent), then insufficient training (44 percent), and lack of autonomy/latitude in making decisions (41 percent) (see Figure 27.16).

Given the current environment and the dwindling health care dollar, we specifically asked respondents whether their organization was financially challenged at any point during planning or implementing SMTs. The financial health of an organization plays an obvious role in implementing a major change such as self-managed teams, especially when considering the extent of planning and training that must occur. Thirty-seven percent of our sample said that their organizations experienced financial difficulties during either the planning or implementation stages for self-managed teams. Of those that said yes, 55 percent said that the financial situation did not impact the SMT initiative. Written comments included, "The RIF (reduction in force) actually drew the team together and led them to increased reliance between team members;" "We require the teams to develop and function within a

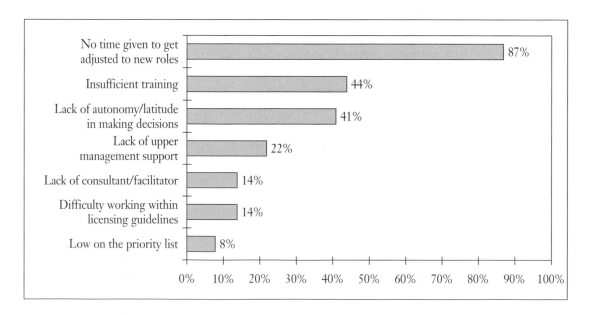

Figure 27.16. Barriers encountered while implementing SMTs.

budget;" and "The potential for loss of revenue based on reimbursement only strengthens the resolve for the coordination and roll-out for more SMTs. They are highly responsive to customer needs."

Impact of SMTs

The respondents reported very positive results of their SMT initiatives, even though many are in the very early stages of implementation. Some of the more positive impacts on team members include an increased opportunity to demonstrate leadership, better communication with coworkers, and increased enthusiasm and spirit (see Figure 27.17). It is not uncommon for people who work in a self-managed team environment to experience these positive effects.[34] Many say that they would never want to go back to working in a traditional, hierarchical management structure.

On an organizational level, respondents reported the greatest benefits in the areas of improved quality (85 percent), improved productivity (75 percent), and heightened morale (67 percent). Improved levels of service, lower labor costs, and decreased absenteeism and turnover were also rated as benefits (see Figure 27.18), but to a lesser extent. Other benefits cited include improvements in patient satisfaction; increased amount of nurse and patient interactions; financial savings by hiring line workers in place of supervisors; reductions in delays and length of stay; high morale of team members; improved organizational communication; the feeling of more control; empowering staff to make difficult decisions; increased employee satisfaction ratings; learning by team members; and increased self-esteem of team members.

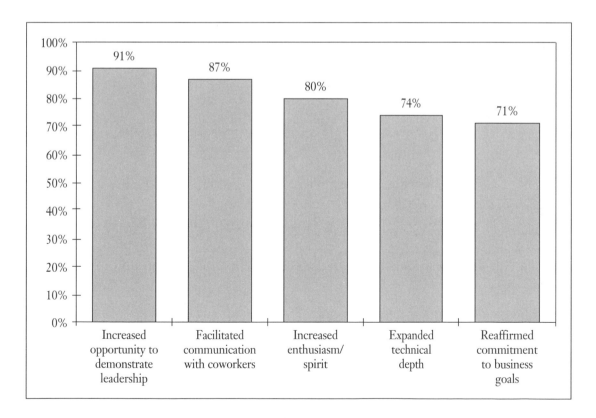

Figure 27.17. Positive impact of SMTs on team members.

Improved quality: 85%

Improved productivity: 75%

Heightened morale: 67%

Improved levels of service: 60%

Lower labor costs: 50%

Decreased turnover: 47%

Lower absenteeism: 42%

Figure 27.18. Top benefits that hospitals have derived from SMTs.

When asked to report on the most negative aspects of SMTs, respondents said, "Increased time for decision making;" "Other department's [lack of] ability to understand when relating to the team versus a manager;" "Difficulty of managers taking on the role of a 'coach;'" "Staff perception that they are required to do more with less money;" "Frightened of change;" "Personality conflicts between team members;" "Acceptance by operations supervisors;" "Fear of failure;" "The time element of getting everyone trained;" "Communication;" and "Time-consuming."

Lessons Learned

The respondents were the most prolific when asked to record their lessons learned. Most of the responses centered on the need for careful change management. Senior leader and middle manager buy-in was frequently mentioned, as was the need for awareness, education, training, and communication. Some comments were, "Include everyone that is impacted; teach the skills needed for SMT roles;" "More buy-in throughout the house. More visible and verbal executive support;" "Get buy-in from senior management first;" "Plan, plan, plan;" "You cannot communicate too much;" "It takes a lot of resources, particularly education, to get started;" "[Leaders should] be ready for some negative feedback;" and "Give parameters for teams to make decisions with boundaries, guidance, and expectations."

The Future of SMTs

Understanding an organization's future plans for SMTs is a good indicator of the level of organizational commitment and perceptions of success with teams overall. Figure 27.19 shows what the respondents plan to do with SMTs in the way of expansion or contraction. More than 70 percent plan to either increase the presence of SMTs in selected areas or across the entire organization, while 19 percent plan to remain stable and 8 percent will decrease SMT activity in selected areas and across the board.

Comparison of Health Care and Other Industry Practices

There are both similarities and dissimilarities between the findings reported in this chapter and those of the DDI/AQP/*Industry Week* study that was based on industries other than health care. One-fourth of the respondents in the other study were from companies with 20,000 to 75,000 employees,

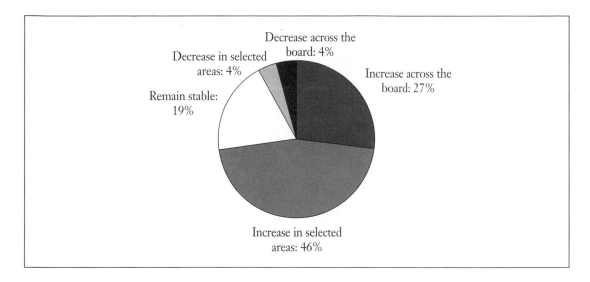

Figure 27.19. The future scope of SMTs.

compared to our respondents predominately from companies with 1000 to 3500 employees. The size of the organization does not necessarily make the roll-out of self-managed teams more or less difficult, just more time-consuming if yours is a large operation. In 1990, the time of the DDI study, more than half of the respondents had two years' experience or less with SMTs, while more than 70 percent of our sample had one year or less of experience with teams. This finding reinforces the notion that compared to other industries, health care is behind when it comes to implementing empowering work structures.

We also saw some significant differences between the health care sample and the other study's sample regarding responsibility for certain key tasks, including personnel functions. The health care respondents reported significantly higher shared responsibility for all tasks except equipment maintenance than the manufacturing respondents. They also reported across-the-board lower levels of responsibility held by teams only. This finding could reflect the relatively early stages of SMT implementation in the health care study. Typically, managers begin to hand off a significant number of tasks during the second year of SMT implementation.

In the manufacturing study, each of the tasks listed had a certain percentage of respondents who said that the supervisor was solely responsible; however, in the health care study, there were four tasks for which there was no sole supervisory responsibility: setting goals, selecting work methods, and working with internal and external customers. It seems that, where possible, managers in health care have taken a hands-off approach in certain important areas early in the implementation process. This can be explained by two factors that may be unique to health care. First, employees in health care settings tend to be highly trained individuals who are accustomed to making high-level decisions on a daily basis. Second, shared governance practices have been popular in health care, which means that managers have been sharing responsibility for certain tasks for a long time. Finally, in the manufacturing study, all of the tasks listed had some level of team-only responsibility, and in the health care study, all but preparing and managing cost budgets and making compensation decisions had some level of team-only responsibility. Again, it is likely that the health care companies represented in this sample have not progressed to the point where they are turning over to self-managed teams what might be considered the last bastion of supervisory responsibility.

The similarities between the findings in our study and the other study were extensive. First, both studies found that the top motivation for implementing self-managed teams was to improve quality and productivity. The top four training offerings in both studies included roles and responsibilities, handling conflict, group problem solving, and running effective meetings. This finding clearly points to the fact that all teams, no matter what industry they work in, need the same basic skills to become successful.

The level of team leader rotation was almost identical (50 percent manufacturing vs. 52 percent health care) as was the extent of job rotation between team members (41 percent manufacturing vs. 42 percent health care). Merit-based pay was the most prevalent compensation system reported in both studies. A top barrier reported by respondents from the manufacturing and health care studies was the difficulty managers experienced in adjusting to their new roles. Finally, both studies reported improvements in quality and productivity.

The differences between the manufacturing study and our study are probably based more on the maturity level of the teams in the various organizations rather than on the differences inherent in each of the settings. While health care companies do have some unique characteristics that may require different strategic and tactical considerations, many of the planning and implementation steps for teams will be the same across industries.

Challenges for Health Care

Since the Industrial Revolution, industries—including health care—have faced challenges and concerns that have fostered uniqueness in personnel management, definitions of the core business, and work processes. These unique qualities now present real and/or imaginary barriers to the realization of new concepts, including self-managed teams. As more and more health care organizations explore the concept of self-managed teams, they are challenged to creatively confront these barriers. The unique challenges that we face in health care when planning and implementing self-managed teams are fivefold.

1. The physician as customer, supplier, and team member
2. Professional licensing requirements
3. The high skill level of health care workers
4. The nature of the work itself
5. The unstable market environment

Physicians are integral to health care delivery, and it is important that they become meaningfully involved with the teams. Self-managed teams impact physicians in their workshop and in the hospital. The challenge is in getting physicians to fully participate in a team-based environment that may not be comfortable for them at first. Like all of us, physicians tend to view SMTs from their own frame of reference as a result of their education, participation in organized medical staff committees, and independent office practice settings.

Physician education is scientifically based with clear definitions of right and wrong, legal accountability, and responsibility for life and death. The concept of multidisciplinary teams, at first glance, conflicts with these basic tenets. The Hippocratic oath dictates physician responsibility for quality patient care in their workshop, with or without SMTs. The hospital-organized medical staff is hierarchical and political, not participative, and it is governed via by-laws and department rules and regulations. Traditional medical staff governance processes are seeped in due process, multiple committee reviews, and politics, all of which can bottleneck the work of self-managed teams. Professional practice and boundaries gleaned from the traditional medical staff model must be considered and integrated where possible.

While physicians themselves form a type of homogeneous team in that they have access to key resources and a high degree of decision-making authority, it is crucial that they expand their definition of "team" and be willing to include others from all disciplines and educational backgrounds. In contrast to the time physicians spend in hospitals, health care leaders and staff spend the majority of their day in the health care facility. One physician/client faced with the prospect of working as part of a team said, "I am kidding myself if I think that I am the only decision maker involved in the care of my patients. Out of a day, I spend five to 10 minutes with each patient, and the hospital staff spends 23 hours and 55 minutes with them. They, not me, are making the bulk of the decisions. I have no choice but to become part of the team."

A key issue with physicians and teams is the lack of an identified person to go to for information and general communication. They become frustrated and thus dissatisfied with the amount of time they must spend trying to identify individuals who can address a given issue. Physicians must become part of the planning process, and their unique perspectives and needs considered when defining the roles, responsibilities, and work structures of the teams. Ideally, the organization will find viable vehicles for involving physicians in decision making about these topics. Clear communication, including active listening and creative leadership, is important in addressing physician resistance to SMTs. Additionally, organizations may have to pay physicians for their time while serving on steering committees and design teams. Written expectations and performance standards for paid medical director positions that are aligned with SMT philosophies and practices will also reinforce the physician-team link.

The second unique challenge faced by health care organizations that are interested in forming SMTs relates to multiskilling and the associated competency and licensing requirements. Unlike a manufacturing setting, employees cannot be cross-trained at will. Health care core business activities are often dependent on licensing boards and national and state organizations for professional standards. Health care leaders must be poised to work with these boards to review and evaluate their current standards in light of self-managed team requirements. Incorporating the various boards and licensing organizations as key stakeholders will ensure a smoother roll-out for teams.

A third challenge relates to the high skill level of the average health care worker. Health care workers are knowledge workers. They are well educated and committed to certain philosophies and practices. Mohrman et al. point out that the application of self-managed teamwork designs in a knowledge-based setting requires a different strategic and tactical focus than in a manufacturing setting. We can transfer a great deal from our learnings about teams in factories, but some of their practices do not translate well to a knowledge-based work environment. The authors write,

> Knowledge work involves multiple, specialized knowledge bases, is frequently performed by specialists who expect professional autonomy (but are often embedded in highly interdependent work networks), is nonroutine, and requires judgment, interpretation, and

the creation of knowledge. Multiple concurrent organizational processes influence one another in organizations involved in knowledge work. . . . For these subprocesses to be coordinated, individuals with different worldviews have to integrate their work. Furthermore, the environment is dynamic, contributing an inherent uncertainty to decision making that already entails contention because of multiple perspectives. The dynamics of teams in a knowledge-work setting are affected by this uncertainty, contention, and complexity. In the midst of all this, they must be able to establish sufficient shared understanding to allow them to proceed with their work.[35]

Steering councils and design teams for self-management must fully understand the implications of designing teams in a knowledge-based setting where the level of technical skills is already high and the resistance to transferring these skills may also be high. Additionally, a focus on the soft skills such as managing conflict, communication, consensus decision making, and running effective meetings is imperative to round out the technical expertise that is already present.

The profound nature of the work in health care also poses a unique challenge to organizations that are interested in implementing SMTs. Working with the lives of human beings is very different than producing widgets or selling advertising. In health care, planning and implementation schedules must often be delayed based on fluctuations in volume and the critical nature of the services provided. Hospitals are constantly challenged with emergency and urgent situations that cannot be planned, but take precedence over everything else. One of the questions most often asked by health care executives who are considering teams is, "How do people who deal with lives every moment of the day find the time to meet to discuss team issues?" The underlying assumption to this question is that employees are engaged in hands-on patient care and do not have the luxury to gain consensus on each and every decision.

The answer to this dilemma is twofold. First, once the teams have been designed and established, they can do much of their work as individuals or in smaller subgroups. A person or small group of people can take responsibility for specific tasks that relate to both the technical and social aspects of the work, such as performance appraisals. One group might be responsible for coordinating performance evaluations one quarter, and another group responsible for developing algorithms. The key is in the design work. It must be based on an accurate representation of the work and all of the associated customer needs and wants. Only when sound work redesign methodologies are used can a design team understand task interdependencies and the degree to which teams should become self-managing.

The second part of the answer relates to the extent to which people in health care organizations traditionally meet. In conducting an evaluation of the number of committees in the nursing area of a midsized hospital, for example, one author found that there were more than 200 ongoing committees. The department manager and vice president were flabbergasted by the amount of duplication and non–value-added work that was in progress. The organization was forming committee upon committee, without a unified objective or time limitation. To add insult to injury, typical meetings in health care include 20 or more people. The amount of time away from patients and the amount of money it costs to have that many people attend that many meetings is mind boggling. The bottom line is that people in health care settings are already finding the time to meet, and leadership must spearhead the alignment of priorities, expectations, work structures, and processes to better meet the organization's vision and strategic goals.

The last challenge that health care organizations that are interested in teams must face is based on economics and the marketplace. The current health care climate is characterized by merger and affiliation mania, unstable leadership, lack of job security, and market consolidation. The emphasis on operational efficiencies including cost, quality, and service has increased dramatically. Timing is pivotal in any major change; therefore, it is important that SMTs are positioned as a strategic initiative that fits into the overall scheme of what is happening within and outside the organization. It is important to avoid the perception by physicians and employees that SMTs are a pet project or a work structure that will go away with the next affiliation or merger. Boards and executives must be willing to sponsor teams just as they would a new, far-reaching information system or a reengineering initiative. SMTs, when positioned properly, can become a strategic tool that will make organizations more robust in the currently turbulent economic environment.

Limitations of the Study

Our sample size was relatively small; therefore, it may not be representative of the general health care organization population. Another limitation, similar to the manufacturing study, was the definition of self-managed teams provided. Some of the organizations might not be involved with self-managed teams per se, but with another form of teams. A third limitation relates to the relative newness of SMTs in our sample. The majority of respondents had been using teams for a year or less; therefore, it is difficult to draw conclusions regarding the effects that teams are having on quality, cost, and satisfaction. The final limitation, also similar to the other study, relates to who the respondents were. The fact that they were primarily internal consultants with a vested interest in the success of the teams may have biased their responses.

How to Get Started

Any organization seriously considering teams must first begin the journey by understanding its own culture, management style, work processes, and commitment to training. Laying the groundwork for teams is an intensive task that requires at least 40 hours of work by a steering council composed of executives and other key players in the organization. Finding an experienced consultant who can lead the steering council through the phases of developing self-managed teams will help the organization avoid certain pitfalls.

Some of the foundational activities include the following:

- *Define the level of involvement that best fits the work.* Orsburn et al. outline eight levels of employee involvement from autocratic to self-management: information sharing, dialogue, special problem solving, intragroup problem solving, intergroup problem solving, focused problem solving, limited self-direction, and total self-direction.[36] The steering council should define its vision for self-management and use the agreed-upon level of empowerment to drive all strategic and operational plans for self-management.

- *Determine readiness for a change as dramatic as self-management.* A change readiness assessment can, among other things, highlight the organization's historical strengths and weaknesses in managing major change; determine how feasible teams are given the nature of the work now and in the future; uncover the organization's culture and performance management systems and the relevant characteristics that are blockers and drivers for self-management; and determine how personally ready major stakeholders are for self-managed teams.

- *Align vision, mission, and values with self-managed teams.* Teams must be strategically aligned with what the organization is today and where it is headed in the future. Alignment discussions can also become the content for early communication about why executives have chosen to implement self-managed teams.

- *Benchmark.* Visit other organizations that have adopted self-managed teams, both within and outside of health care. Seeing what other companies have done and understanding their lessons learned creates a sense of direction and resolve around teams.

- *Define overall organizational goals for self-management.* To help drive the design and implementation of teams, goals should be defined for the length of time it will take to fully implement teams and the expected outcomes teams will have on specific quality and other indicators.

- *Define a supporting infrastructure for teams, with roles and responsibilities.* A recommended planning infrastructure for self-managed teams is a steering council with representatives from all levels of management including *all* of the executives, one or more design teams, implementation teams, and a pilot site, then finally full organization roll-out. Design and implementation teams should have team leaders and facilitators. Members of the steering council should serve as design team liaisons to keep informed about specific resource and other needs of the team.

- *Integrate current initiatives with self-managed teams.* Conner says that people can absorb just so much change at any given time.[37] All types of organizations are famous for concurrently introducing myriad projects and initiatives without defining how they all fit—or do not fit—together. When people see how things are linked they can make better sense of them, and therefore they have a greater capacity to become meaningfully involved in making certain things happen. Effective integration often requires the steering council to halt or eliminate certain projects that are either duplicative or out of sync with self-managed teams.

- *Define the organization's downsizing stance.* Just mention "self-management" or "multiskilling," and people become fearful for their jobs. The steering council should define early on what the organization's stance will be regarding increased efficiencies as a result of teams, then communicate this stance. Associating layoffs with self-managed teams sends a two-sided message that is hard for people to reconcile: "This initiative will either empower you or put you on the street." Orsburn et al. does not recommend moving forward with teams if layoffs are inevitable.[38] If possible it is best to deal with increased efficiencies that result from self-managed teams through attrition rather than layoffs. The steering council should also preliminarily define the role of managers and how they will be trained for success in the new environment.

- *Define design parameters for design teams.* All design teams need to know what to design around. The level of employee involvement in self-managed teams that was selected early in the process will define the boundaries of the design teams. If the organization decides to go to fully self-managing teams, then the design teams will need to redesign performance management systems and management structure as well as the way the clinical and nonclinical work is performed.

- *Develop a stakeholder commitment plan.* As with any major change, it is the job of the steering council to define who has a stake in the success or failure of self-managed teams. Major players should be identified and communicated. Developing and working a viable stakeholder commitment plan is one of the most crucial responsibilities of a steering council.

- *Develop a communication plan.* The steering council must also strategize how it will c̲̅
  cate about this initiative. Newsletters, town hall meetings, leadership meetings, books, a̲̅
  and speakers are options for keeping everyone informed.

- *Evaluate and manage organizational symbols.* The steering council should take a hard look at the
  unspoken messages the organization sends others. Practices, policies, and procedures should be
  scrutinized with a microscope to determine whether they are aligned with self-managed teams.
  For example, a cornerstone philosophy of self-management is that everyone in the organization
  is a valued and equal contributor and that preferential treatment should not be given to certain
  members of the organization based on title. An age-old tradition in many organizations is preferential parking for executives. Special parking spaces for executives establishes a class system
  that directly contradicts an important tenet of self-management. Finding and killing contradictory symbols will send the message that management is serious about building a new organizational culture.

- *Define high-level obstacles for the implementation of teams.* Inherent in any major change initiative are the things that will drive the project and things that will block it. Define both the
  drivers and blockers, and develop actions to strengthen the former and weaken the latter.

- *Define design team charters, member selection criteria, member selection strategies, and rewards and
  recognition.* The business of forming and nurturing design teams is also a central focus of the
  steering council. Clear charters, selection methods, and sound strategies for keeping the teams
  motivated will ensure a more successful design and implementation phase.

- *Create a preliminary staff, manager, and physician training plan.* Begin to look at the desired
  characteristics of staff, managers, and physicians in a self-managed team environment and
  appropriate training resources.

- *Define an evaluation strategy.* The design teams, in conjunction with the steering council,
  should identify how the initiative will be evaluated. The initial goals established by the steering
  council can be augmented by the design teams.

Conclusion

Joseph M. Juran laments the onset of the Taylor system of scientific management and its impact on
quality and the people who produce products and services of all kinds. From a historical perspective,
he believes that the United States made a grave error in abandoning the European practice of the
craftsmanship concept in favor of the Taylor system.[39] The latter was designed for mass production;
planning and execution became separate tasks, and upper management became detached from the
process of managing for quality. People no longer worked on whole products or services; they lost contact with customers and the overall control over quality diminished. The concept of self-managed
teams harkens back to the craftsman era where people had direct control over their work, direct contact with the customer, and full responsibility for quality. The concepts of multiskilling, collocation,
and flattening the hierarchy are directly linked to the need to get back to simplicity and ownership in
the way work is done. It is about being efficient and making the most of resources while giving people
an opportunity to become meaningfully engaged in their work, an activity that consumes at least 50
percent of our waking hours in a given work week. Self-managed teams are not for every organization,

and to some extent the methodologies are applicable to every work situa-
owerful vehicle for restructuring care delivery in our current competitive

for an Executive Meeting

led by an internal organization development representative or an outside consultant.

1. What is our motivation for exploring self-managed teams? Are they viewed as a quick fix, or as a long-term vehicle to improve quality, productivity, and satisfaction?

2. How do we want to define self-managed teams? What is appropriate for our organization? How do they fit with our vision, mission, and values.

3. Are we committed to the time and dollars it will take to strategically and tactically plan and implement teams? What have we done in the past to prepare for a major change? How effective were we in following up with plans? Are we willing to expand our training budget, if necessary, to teach everyone new skills?

4. Can our executives and managers be successful in a self-managing work environment?

5. Do our physicians buy into the team concept? How successful have we been in including them in our total quality management initiative? How well have they received other similar initiatives?

Notes

1. J. D. Orsburn, L. Moran, E. Musselwhite, and J. H. Zenger, *Self-Directed Work Teams: The New American Challenge* (Homewood, Ill.: Business One Irwin, 1990).

2. S. G. Cohen, "Designing Effective Self-Managing Work Teams," in *Advances in Interdisciplinary Studies of Work Teams*, edited by M. Beyerlein. *Vol. 1: Self-Managed Work Teams* (Greenwich, Conn.: JAI Press, 1994).

3. K. Fisher, *Leading Self-Directing Work Teams: A Guide to Developing New Team Leadership Skills* (New York: McGraw-Hill, 1993).

4. E. E. Lawler III, *The Ultimate Advantage: Creating the High-Involvement Organization* (San Francisco: Jossey-Bass, 1992).

5. S. A. Mohrman, S. G. Cohen, and A. M. Mohrman Jr., *Designing Team-Based Organizations* (San Francisco: Jossey-Bass, 1995).

6. Orsburn et al., *Self-Directed Work Teams.*

7. R. S. Wellins, W. C. Byham, and J. M. Wilson, *Empowered Teams* (San Francisco: Jossey-Bass, 1991).

8. M. J. Perley and A. Raab, "Beyond Shared Governance: Restructuring Care Delivery for Self-Managing Work Teams," *Nursing Administration* 19, no. 1 (1994): 12–20.

9. S. S. Blancett, "Self-Managed Teams: The Reality and the Promise," *Health Care Supervision* 12, no. 4 (1994): 48–55.

10. Ibid.

11. G. H. Constantinides, D. Tscharner, D. Kalpowsky, and R. Baker-Priebe, "Increasing Autonomy: A Self-Directed MICU," *Nursing Management* 25, no. 1 (1994): 32C, 32H.

12. M. Jannotta and T. Maldonado, "Self-Management for Nurses," *Journal of Nursing Administration* 22, no. 6 (May 1992): 59–63.

13. G. M. Maurer, "True Empowerment: From Shared Governance to Self-Managed Work Groups on a Patient Care Unit," *Journal of Shared Governance* 1, no. 1 (1995): 25–27.

14. L. McHenry, "Implementing Self-Directed Teams," *Critical Care Management* 23, no. 3 (1994): 80I–80J, 80L.

15. M. N. Thyen, R. Theis, and B. Volk Tebbitt, "Organizational Empowerment Through Self-Governed Teams," *Journal of Nursing Administration* 23, no. 1 (1993): 24–26.

16. J. Wurstner and F. Koch, "Role Redesign in Perioperative Settings," *AORN Journal* 61, no. 5 (May 1995): 834–838, 840, 843–844.

17. Mauer, "True Empowerment."

18. Jannotta and Maldonato, "Self-Management for Nurses."

19. T. Inkson, G. Latham, C. Mather, D. Prokopczak, and E. Smits, "CHUM: Collaborative Healthcare Utilization Model—An Example of a Self-Directed Team in a Hospital Setting," *Canadian Journal of Nursing Administration* 7, no. 2 (1994): 50–68.

20. Constantinides et al., "Increasing Autonomy."

21. T. J. Gustin and K. Fellows, "A Self-Managed Work Group in Nursing Management," *Journal of Shared Governance* 1, no. 1 (1995): 17–20.

22. Inkson et al., "CHUM."

23. Wurstner and Koch, "Role Redesign in Perioperative Settings."

24. R. S. Wellins, J. Wilson, A. J. Katz, P. Laughlin, C. R. Day Jr., and D. Price, *Self-Directed Teams: A Study of Current Practice* (Development Dimensions International, Association for Quality and Participation, and *Industry Week*, 1990).

25. Blancett, "Self-Managed Teams."

26. Orsburn et al., *Self-Directed Work Teams.*

27. Mohrman, Cohen, and Mohrman, *Designing Team-Based Organizations.*

28. K. Kerfoot, "Nursing Management Considerations," *Nursing Economics* 9, no. 2 (March-April 1991): 121, 125.

29. Mohrman, Cohen, and Mohrman, *Designing Team-Based Organizations*, 263.

30. J. R. Galbraith, *Designing Organizations* (San Francisco: Jossey-Bass, 1995).

31. Ibid., 50.

32. Orsburn et al., *Self-Directed Work Teams*, 144.

33. E. E. Lawler III, *Pay and Organization Development* (Reading, Mass.: Addison-Wesley, 1983).

34. Orsburn et al., *Self-Directed Work Teams.*

35. Mohrman, Cohen, and Mohrman, *Designing Team-Based Organizations*, 51.

36. Orsburn et al., *Self-Directed Work Teams.*

37. D. Conner, *Managing at the Speed of Change* (New York: Villard Books, 1993).

38. Orsburn et al., *Self-Directed Work Teams.*

39. J. M. Juran, *Juran on Leadership for Quality: An Executive Handbook* (New York: Free Press, 1989).

Lisa Ethier, Ph.D., is a senior associate for Premier, based in Charlotte, North Carolina. She provides organizational effectiveness and reengineering training and consulting services to Premier owners. She has assisted alliance owners in creating and sustaining large-scale organizational change including reengineering, self-managed teams, and total quality management.

Previously, Ethier was a senior consultant for Sharp HealthCare, a multihospital system in San Diego. In that capacity, she was the principal consultant for Grossmont Hospital in a major reengineering project involving self-managed teams. She was also Sharp HealthCare's total quality management coordinator.

Prior to joining Sharp HealthCare, Ethier was director of organization development for General Dynamics. She created the company's first organizational development department, serving all levels of managers in the division. She has also provided extensive external consulting to a variety of organizations in government, manufacturing, education, and mental health.

Ethier earned a doctorate in industrial and organizational psychology from the California School of Professional Psychology and a master's degree in counseling psychology from Colgate University.

Marian Furlong, R.N., BAN, MBA, CHE, has extensive health care leadership experience in two of the nation's largest managed care markets. As vice president of institutional care for Sharp Healthcare in San Diego, California, she was responsible for a variety of hospital and patient care functions. She provided the sponsorship for Grossmont Hospital's self-managed team initiative, as well as other large-scale change projects such as service line development. Prior to 1991, she worked in Minneapolis. She currently provides independent consulting services on a national level.

Furlong is an alumnus of Johnson and Johnson/Wharton Fellows Program in Management for nurse executives. She is a member of several health care organizations such as American College of Healthcare Executives and the American Organization of Nurse Executives.

Section VII

The Need for Speed

Chapter 28

Accelerated Replication Approaches

Chip Caldwell

In the 1995 movie *Speed*, a former cop gone bad, played by Dennis Hopper, jury-rigged a fully loaded city bus so that if the speed dropped below 60 mph at any time a bomb locked onto the chassis would explode and kill all the passengers aboard. A take-charge, saucy passenger, played by Sandra Bullock, found herself in the driver's seat after the assigned driver suffered an injury. She struggles throughout the entire movie to keep the bus at or above 60 mph while a never-say-die detective attempts 900 times to defuse the bomb. For two hours, viewers sit on the edge of their seats while the bus encounters one after another seemingly hopeless situation. Sandra Bullock first must make a tight, 60 mph lefthand turn, only to find herself heading the wrong way down a one-way street into heavy traffic. Later, after being directed by police helicopters onto a would-be safe and nearly completed expressway extension, she notices that a mile ahead the expressway overpass remains uncompleted; determining no other plan, she and the detective decide to increase their speed to 100 mph in order to hurdle the uncompleted section. The bus teeters through the air, lands wobbling on the other side, then finally emerging intact and on the road again. One after another after another impossible situation faces the two travellers in charge until, finally, the bomb is defused.

Imagine what it would be like if our reengineering teams, clinical path teams, and quality improvement teams faced the same critical requirement—you must engage the project at breakneck speed and, regardless of the impossible barriers encountered, you must never slow down at the risk of peril to yourselves and the organization.

The Need for Speed

It seems that institutional leaders and senior strategists are, in fact, beginning to express "the need for speed." In research conducted last year by the Juran Institute, and independently by American Society for Quality, top leaders feel three compelling pressures. First, the necessity to dramatically reduce costs without negatively impacting clinical outcomes and customer satisfaction is accelerating and intensifying. Second, there exists the need to reduce these costs faster and faster. Third, organizations must incorporate the expanded integrated delivery system components into strategic improvement efforts, including primary care physicians, specialists, and extended care providers.

These three compelling needs are driving strategic and operating plans in every health care organization, from health maintenance organizations to medical centers, physician practices, physician-hospital organizations (PHOs), and insurers.

The Importance of Cost of Poor Quality

There is reason, however, for optimism. The health care industry lags other industries in regard to the understanding and management of the cost of poor quality (COPQ)—those costs unassociated with delivering value to the customer, such as inspection. We can, thus, take lessons from other industries' experiences. Most manufacturing companies have recognized the need to aggressively remove costs while improving the quality of their goods and services due to the increasing global market. And they have crafted methods to effectively remove these unwarranted costs. The notion of COPQ has been a long-standing strategic concern for manufacturing executives. Since as far back as 1951, Joseph M. Juran and others have been enlightening leaders regarding the drain on the value of a company's goods and services as a result of COPQ, comprised of needless inspection; internal and external failures causing rework, work around, and malpractice costs; and waste.[1] In addition, these unnecessary costs certainly warrant management attention, comprising more than 20 percent of sales in the average company.[2] Several curious and enlightened health care leaders have asked themselves if this COPQ burden was present in their organizations and found that, indeed, COPQ exists in health care and may even surpass the rate of waste found in manufacturing companies. One health care organization found that nearly 30 percent of its operating budget went down the drain as COPQ.[3] Don Berwick, president of the Institute for Healthcare Improvement and one of the three founders of the modern quality movement in health care, documented that the efficacy of as many as 40 percent of clinical procedures could not be substantiated through published clinical research.[4]

Many have taken heed, developing effective methods to effectively reduce COPQ. In a study presented at Georgia Tech of 50 manufacturing companies, the average reduction of COPQ using TQM methods in the first year topped 21 percent, followed by 18 percent in the second year, 12 percent in the third, and 8 percent in the fourth year.[5] These companies were rewarded with a substantial return on their TQM project investments.

Consider the average medical center managing a $200 million operating budget. This typical organization suffers from a COPQ of more than $40 million. Assuming a comparable success rate at COPQ reduction as those in the referenced study, the organization could recoup $23.6 million over four years! This reduction of COPQ also has the impact of improving quality, as shown by Juran, as a result of decreases in waiting time due to rework and work around.[6]

Strategic Intent

Before any organization embarks upon a COPQ reduction plan, the organization's leaders should ensure the presence of a strategic measurement set at the quality council and/or CEO level to track the cumulative impact of projects and initiatives. I was consulted by one organization adamant that it had removed more than $40 million in cost, representing about 5 percent of its budget, through reengineering. Among the data I requested was operating cost per discharge; amazingly, cost per discharge had increased 8 percent during the same period that the reengineering program was completed. The organization's leaders were stunned. Moreover, aggressive cost reduction—particularly the across-the-board budget cuts so popular today—can produce unforeseen negative consequences on customer satisfaction and clinical outcomes without an effective strategic measurement set. Figure 28.1 illustrates a simple approach for the quality council to ensure, on a month-by-month basis, that projects are meeting the intended targets. The cost graph shows, in six-month increments represented by the dotted line, the expected decline in cost per discharge or cost per member per month; the solid line reflects the actual trend by month. The customer satisfaction and clinical outcome graphs signal the "repel" points below which remedial action should be immediately chartered. The dotted line highlights the repel zone. The organization shown here is progressing nicely along its cost reduction path, but has in the last month failed to meet customer satisfaction goals; in this case, immediate remedial action is required. A helpful tool would be a fully deployed strategic measurement set from the quality council through the vice president level to every clinical and administrative department in the organization.[7] For additional suggestions on the deployment of strategic measures, refer to chapter 3 in this handbook and *Mentoring Strategic Change in Health Care*.[8]

Once senior leaders have articulated the desired strategic intent and deployed a strategic measurement set to analyze the effectiveness of projects and initiatives, the chartering and deployment of projects can be assessed against known criteria. Successful results depend on the linkage of projects—the way work gets done—with tracking the effectiveness of projects—the strategic measurement set. However, all too often in our zeal to "get on with it," we jump immediately to the creation of tactical action plans and projects without first establishing the measurement set. This premature tactical planning can lead to the situation just described. Projects are completed on time, but unforeseen events throw the cumulative results off target; without some weekly or monthly trending, the organization can be caught off guard. It is my opinion that naysayers of TQM often cite TQM's failures on this phenomenon rather than any inherent weakness of organizations' implementation tracking processes;

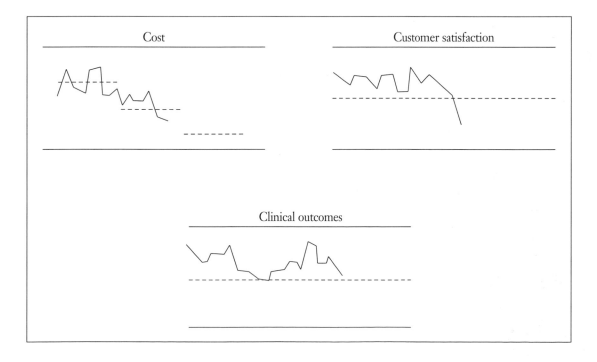

Figure 28.1. Cost strategic intent.

casting such doubt upon the customer-focused, data-driven logic of TQM not only is a disservice to statistical thinkers, it also masks the true underlying symptoms present in such organizations.

Establishing a logical cascade of strategies, goals, subgoals, and annual goals to projects, as illustrated in Figure 28.2, enables the quality council and senior leaders to create a proven and trackable plan to achieve strategic goals and to ensure that the current number of projects will indeed achieve the desired results. Often strategists move directly to the tactical plan, for example, "purchase 10 primary care practices," without quantifying the strategic impact of each tactic on its underlying strategy. Using the deployment method described in Figure 28.2 allows strategists to link the strategy "increase delivery system referrals by $8 million per year for the next three years" to the tactic "purchase 10 primary care practices to add 450 referrals per month." In this way, strategists can apply the concepts of "necessary" and "sufficient" to each project considered. As each project is nominated—either by the quality council, senior leaders, or department managers—the quality council or its designee can assess, first, the necessity of the project as measured against strategic goals; if a project is nominated, but it cannot be secured somewhere in Figure 28.2, then the quality council should question whether resources should be assigned to charter the nomination.

After all nominations are completed, the second test to be applied by the quality council or its designee is the "sufficient" concept. By quantifying all projects, like the primary care practice acquisition project suggested previously, the organization can determine if it will achieve its strategic goals. For example, as diagrammed in Figure 28.3, one integrated delivery system I mentor determined that

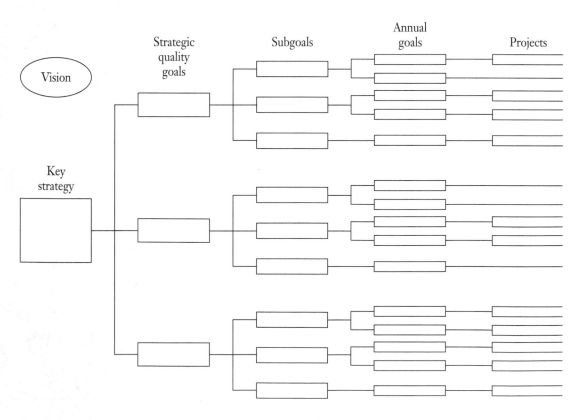

Figure 28.2. Strategy deployment.

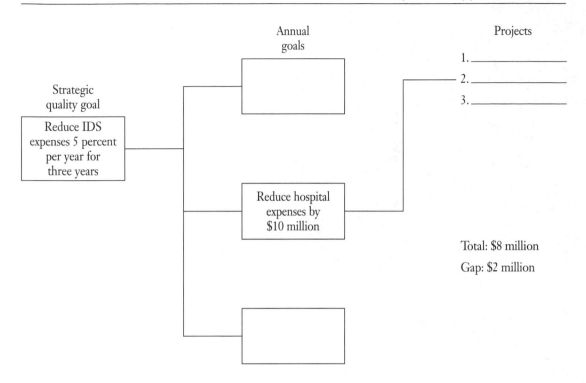

Annual
goals

Projects

1._____

2._____

3._____

Strategic
quality goal

Reduce IDS
expenses 5 percent
per year for
three years

Reduce hospital
expenses by
$10 million

Total: $8 million

Gap: $2 million

Figure 28.3. Necessary and sufficient.

in order to achieve the payor customers' needs, it must reduce operating expenses 5 percent per year in each of the next three years. One of the hospitals, by extension, was assigned the annual goal of reducing cost per discharge from approximately $6600 to $6300, representing a required savings of $10 million. Upon completion of its project nomination, evaluation, and quantification process, all projects were summed to determine if the "sufficient" test would be met. The organization fell short by 20 percent. It is this discipline of strategic deployment of quality that should consume at least 50 percent of the quality council's time, leaving the quality resource group, medical director, and quality director to invest up to 70 percent of their time ensuring that quality improvement methods are properly applied by teams.[9]

Diagnosing Project Delays

Why is it that project teams, including quality improvement teams, often require nine to 12 months to achieve results? In a study of 20 projects in 10 organizations representing five different industries (see Figure 28.4), John Early, chief operating officer of the Juran Institute, found that more than 60 percent of teams' time investment was COPQ; of the excess time, two-thirds was a result of management and one-third a result of the teams' inefficiencies.[10] Assuming that an average team consumes $15,000 in resources, this equates to more than $9000 per team. For an organization hosting 30 project teams during the course of a year, COPQ exceeds $270,000 in the quality department alone! And this cost does not account for the cost of delays in implementing process improvements, which further drives up the cost of poor quality. Of this excess time, 45 percent occurred in identifying and establishing the project,[11] the domain of the quality council.

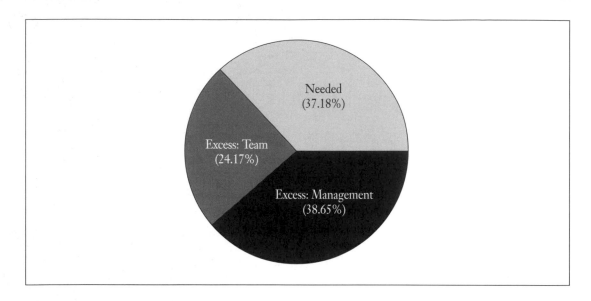

Figure 28.4. Project cost of poor quality.

Early further diagnosed the specific causes of project COPQ and the impact, in weeks, of these delays. They were the following:[12]

COPQ	Average lost time (weeks)
Limited time dedicated to the project	5.7
Executives delay confronting resistance	5.5
No preexisting process measure	5.3
Vague, debatable mission statement	4.4
Not sticking with the vital few root causes	3.6
Too much flow diagramming	3.1
Inadequate team training on time and project management	2.6
Jumping to remedy prematurely	2.2
Poor implementation plans	2.0

Several of these deserve further discussion. In my own experience, one of the greatest inhibitors of fast team cycle time remains the failure of senior leaders to ensure that adequate time is devoted to strategic project teams; the research supports that this was indeed the number-one deterrent to speed, costing 5.7 weeks of delay. A further observation, albeit anecdotal, is that teams increase their probability of success if the frequency of meetings is at least once per week and their duration is at least 90 minutes. The logic for these criteria are applicable to other meetings as well. Consider those meetings you attend with only a monthly frequency; the first 15 minutes of each meeting is invested in recalling the events and discussion from the last meeting. For a one-hour meeting, this is a 25 percent cost of poor quality. Consider also the impact of meeting duration. For a one-hour meeting with the first 15 minutes devoted to rehashing the last meeting's events, the team is just getting into the creative mode when it is time to adjourn. This moment of creativity is lost forever. It is no wonder that it takes so long to complete a project.

If a project team's mission is truly linked to the organization's ability to achieve its strategic plan, as deployed in Figures 28.2 and 28.3, then by extension it is vital; therefore, all members' participation should be ensured before they are placed on the team. This requires coordination with each team member's supervisor and each physician nominee to ensure that other priorities will not inhibit their ability to attend each team meeting. It also requires that the team leader consider attendance as a factor in setting the team meeting time.

The second most common time waster, costing 5.5 weeks in this study, is the failure to confront resistance early on in the process. This is probably the most critical for the long-term success of projects, but also the most difficult to manage. This is true because the management of resistance cannot be managed project by project; overcoming individual resistance is an organization culture issue and requires the intense and constant attention of the CEO and senior leaders. Management of resistance is more a factor of the presence of strong trust among physicians (both individually and collectively), senior management, middle management, and employees.

However, there are some actions that individual teams can take. First, it is important to anticipate sources of and reasons for resistance. Team members, rather than attempting to overcome resistance by piling on all the reasons to accept the change, are perhaps better served by first attempting to understand the underlying reasons for the resistance. Understanding requires opening channels of communication between all parties in a constructive and collaborative way. Many teams attempt to address resistance by thinking of the resistors as oddballs and thinking that simply overwhelming them with data supporting the change will sway them. This approach sometimes works, but it often causes even deeper entrenchment of the parties. Making a genuine attempt to understand the viewpoint of resistors before launching into resolving the resistance first enables us to appreciate the logic of the thinking, but also serves as an encouragement for the resistors to attempt to understand the team's viewpoint. As a result, sometimes the team and the resistors arrive at a mutually agreeable, and perhaps innovative, alternative. As the organization gains a reputation for approaching resistors in this way, a culture of trust is fostered that can carry over into other arenas. Likewise, an organization that attempts to resolve resistance through applying pressure tactics on resistors often finds itself debating and arguing over the simplest of issues.

A second tactic that teams can apply to overcome resistance, after first analyzing the sources and logic of resistance, is to recruit one or more respected champions to support the desired process change. This is particularly helpful in an organization that has in the past damaged the trust of the medical staff due to application of strong-arm tactics.

Accelerated Replication Approaches

The idea of replication is certainly not new; in fact, it is the last step of the Juran six-step process.[13] What is new is the creativity that can be applied to the replication process as a result of the maturing of the Information Age. Organizations desiring to engage in accelerated replication generally choose from among three approaches: replicating outcomes or outputs, replicating subprocesses linked to outcomes (more commonly called benchmarking), and replicating theories about outcomes or outputs.

At this juncture, an operational definition becomes necessary. *Benchmarking* is a term that continues to be used widely in the field and can mean anything from simply comparing outcomes, like length of stay, to extensive flowcharting of an identified best practice to look for subprocesses driving the best practice. For the purpose of this chapter, the more rigorous definition applies. Comparing the length of stay for hip replacement to our own performance for our purposes will be called comparative outcome analysis; we simply wish to know how our C-section rate relates to a comparative group's results. Benchmarking will be used to describe an extensive process, used by us in reengineering, to flowchart our own process, collecting data on our outcome and on eight to 10 of our subprocesses; at this point, we would identify the best outcome and visit up to five sites to flowchart and collect data on their outcomes and subprocesses. Using this benchmarking process, for example, could lead us to uncover that in those health plans or hospitals with a four-day average length of stay for hip replacement, 78 percent of patients ambulated on the first postoperative day while only 33 percent of patients ambulated on the first postoperative day in the patient group with a seven-day length of stay. Using a data-driven benchmarking process has proven to be effective for many organizations.

Each of the three replication approaches has its strengths and weaknesses. The first approach, replicating outcomes, is the least sophisticated of the three and still requires the project team to analyze its own subprocesses and generate creative interventions to move closer to the comparative performance. This method is also the most common. The University Hospital Consortium (the focus of chapter 19), Voluntary Hospitals of America, Premier, and other coalitions provide their members with comparative data on selected performance indicators like length of stay, charge per DRG, and labor productivity by department; members can use this high-level comparative data to set improvement priorities. Its weakness is that if organizations knew how to decrease length of stay or improve productivity, they would have already done so. Therefore, these data are most often used to convince process owners and physicians that change is needed. For example, in an initiative chartered by Don Hutton of the Morgan Group, Gar Fritts, and me, to decrease the C-section rate in Atlanta's hospitals, extensive run charts were provided to each of the 15 participating hospitals, but no underlying subprocess data were provided. The effect of publishing these data internally among the hospitals led to a significant decrease in the average C-section rate; however, specific subprocess changes leading to these improvements were left to the individual hospitals and their obstetricians.

The second method, replicating subprocesses linked to outcomes, is known as benchmarking and was briefly described. Extensive data collection, site visits, and interviews are required to identify the specific subprocess variation between the host organization and the best-practice organization. Continuing the example of hip replacement benchmarking, we might expect that our data further revealed that a four-day length of stay was also statistically tied to two other subprocesses: explaining the four-day clinical path to the patient and family at least two days prior to admission, and the use of automated pain management like a PCA pump versus PRN. Therefore, the host organization could implement these three subprocesses in the benchmarking project and follow up to determine any impact on length of stay. The obvious advantage of this method is that the team is relying on statistically validated subprocess analysis. The disadvantage is cost and time. The typical cost for a benchmarking project, including travel, can easily exceed $100,000, and at a minimum requires four to six months. However, the organization must also realize that it is making this investment to ensure that results begin immediately, whereas in the other two methods we must assume, fine-tune, and validate more frequently. Therefore, for those processes in which great potential exists, traditional benchmarking provides a strong return on investment; it is for this reason that benchmarking became so popular among manufacturers.

The third method, replicating theories about outcomes, is the preferred method for accelerated replication. First, we avoid the expense and delay of benchmarking, but we also benefit from detailed subprocess analysis of best-practice process owners. In this method, the sources of theories or change concepts are an expert panel, literature research, Internet research, and/or consulting and actuarial companies.

Types of Accelerated Replication Initiatives

There are two types of accelerated replication initiatives: interorganization accelerated replication collaboratives and intraorganization accelerated replication teams. Both types involve the creation of a process to identify change concepts, implement them, and follow up to determine the rate of improvement. Initiatives can last as long as a year, or as short as six months; however, both require participants to commit to implement change concepts in as little as five days but no longer than 90 days. Failure to implement within the specified time period can result in a participant being excused from the project. Accelerated replication initiatives should not, however, be confused with networking and training coalitions like the Institute for Healthcare Improvement's Quality Management Network or Premier's Quality Roundtables; these are important educational functions, but are not intended to be as focused as accelerated replication initiatives.

Interorganization Accelerated Replication Collaboratives

Accelerated replication collaboratives, created by the Institute for Healthcare Improvement for its Breakthrough Series[14] and the Juran Institute for the National Antibiotic Collaborative and Health Care Financing Administration Diabetic Outcomes Improvement Collaborative, are distinguished by five characteristics. First, collaboratives study a homogenous process, like maternal health, diabetes, hip replacement, or hospital nursing labor productivity.

Second, participants number from 12 to 50 and come from a variety of backgrounds, regions, ownership, and so on; therefore, the audience is usually diverse.

Third, an expert panel is convened to generate a change concepts manual for testing by participants. For example, in the National Antibiotic Collaborative, the Centers for Disease Control and Prevention had previously convened an international group of experts in antibiotic use and nosocomial infection for a three-day retreat. The recommendations from this group consisted of a set of six strategies to reduce the use of antibiotics and decrease nosocomial infections in hospitals. These six strategies, like " reduce the empiric use of antibiotics," were further supplemented by about 10 change concepts per strategy, or 60 change concepts in all. For example, one change concept under the strategy "reduce the empiric use of antibiotics" was to implement a standing order for the administration of prophylactic antibiotics two hours prior to surgery and terminate at 24 hours after surgery unless changed by the surgeon. Participants studied these change concepts and determined which would be appropriate for implementation in their organizations. Therefore, as mentioned, the approach for the generation of ideas in accelerated replication collaboratives does not require the extensive analysis of benchmarking site visits, but relies on a group of experts whose experience, previous research, and/or extrapolation from their knowledge of research can produce a usable set of theories that can be quickly tested.

Fourth, since participants are not collocated, multiple communication vehicles must be established. The collaborative is kicked off at a one- to two-hour meeting at which participants receive and are briefed on the change concept manual, are educated about accelerated replication, and leave with a road map for implementation the first day they return to their respective organizations. Participants are also able to communicate with each other and with some members of the expert panel via Internet user groups; this vehicle of communication allows members to discuss implementation in a real-time mode. For example, in the National Antibiotic Collaborative, some members experienced resistance in such change concepts as substitution of Ancef for Vancomycin in coronary artery bypass, and the Internet user group allowed for rapid mentoring and feedback. However, as common and popular as electronic communication has become, many individuals remain uncomfortable on the "Net" and this vehicle cannot be expected to meet the needs of all participants. Another vehicle for communication is the conduct of a quarterly or semiannual miniconference in which participants share the change concepts they have implemented and work to further accelerate implementation. The final vehicle of communication provides for a monthly two-hour conference call among participants to discuss issues; to be maximally effective, we have found that establishing a process in which members fax their specific inquiries a week in advance to the collaborative facilitator improves quality of the responses, as well as causes participants to give their inquiries greater thought.

Fifth, participants are asked to follow the discipline of completing an accelerated replication journal for each change concept implemented. The purpose of the journal, a 10-question document, is to ensure that participants follow the logic of all strong quality improvement projects and avoid the implementation of poorly thought out change concepts. The journal asks participants to complete a high-level flowchart of the process containing the change concept, to identify the measure of success including the baseline measurement, and to identify sources of resistance and plans for resolution. The journal is important for documenting the work of the participant over the course of the collaborative, as well as a resource that can be utilized by other participants. However, keeping the journal simple and effective is also important; completion time should be less than one hour.

Figure 28.5 provides a detailed example of an accelerated replication collaborative, in this case the Juran Institute National Antibiotic Collaborative.

Intraorganization Accelerated Replication Team

The major difference between intraorganization accelerated replication teams and interorganization accelerated replication collaboratives is the absence of the design team to create the list of change concepts. In intraorganization accelerated replication teams, process owners must utilize various techniques to come up with their own ideas. However, this has not proven as difficult as it might sound at first. A single radiology process owner armed with a PC, modem, and Internet browser can identify as many as 100,000 articles regarding cost reductions in the field of radiology in less than three minutes and can further refine the offering to the vital few in less than an hour. The problem in intraorganization accelerated replication is not a scarcity of published ideas; it is culling the ideas to a manageable few.

Building on Tom Nolan's work,[15] replication first requires the establishment of the aim of the change, which must be logically linked to the organization's strategic intent. Each project in a COPQ strategic intent, like the strategic intent portrayed in Figure 28.3, begins with the purpose or aim of the idea to be replicated. The accelerated replication team process, illustrated in Figure 28.6, begins with the aim and includes three subprocesses. Contrasted to traditional quality improvement teams in which members first diagnose the root cause of a process problem and then generate creative alternatives to remedy the root cause, the accelerated replication process begins with process owners culling available literature, the Internet, and other sources for ideas to replicate. These ideas are evaluated for the best fit and then implemented in short cycle times. Some ideas not requiring changes in policy or extensive training can be implemented in five days. One New York hospital changed the way in which biohazardous material was handled in the operating room over a weekend and saved an estimated $75,000 annually. The final subprocess, and one so often lacking in traditional quality improvement

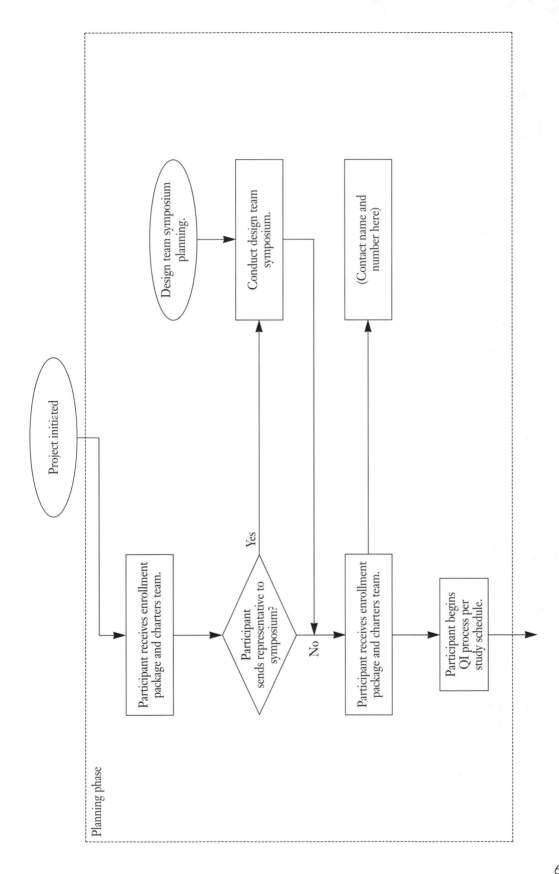

Figure 28.5. Accelerated replication collaborative process example: Antibiotic Collaborative.

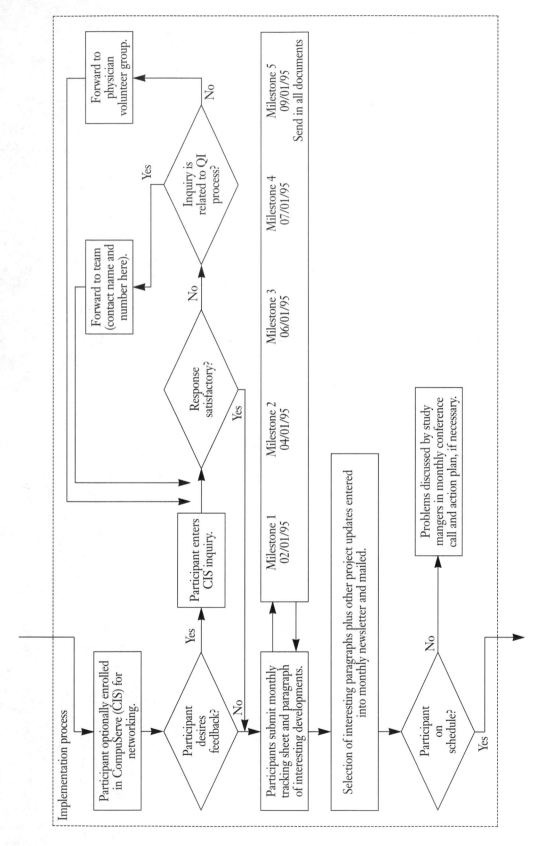

Figure 28.5. *Continued.*

Chapter 29

A Quality Planning Blitz Team: Developing a Medical Record in 15 Days

Kimberly Blake, Julie O'Shaughnessy, and Peggy Schroeder

New Hanover Regional Medical Center's (NHRMC) quality efforts began with the initiation of quality improvement teams. While these teams achieved good results, the time to complete the process ranged from six to 24 months. As the initiative progressed, the quality council recognized that the quality planning process would address several of the organization's strategic objectives. The council was reluctant, however, to utilize quality planning teams because of past experiences with the quality improvement team cycle time and the sense of urgency to address the organization's strategic objectives. Other organizations were utilizing an accelerated approach with quality improvement teams to achieve quicker results. These "blitz teams" were identifying root causes in one week and completing the quality improvement process within six weeks. Since the blitz approach was proven to be effective in reducing the improvement cycle time, the quality council initiated the first blitz team as a quality planning team with a mission to develop and implement an integrated patient care documentation system.

This chapter describes our experience with the organization's first blitz team, the Chart CHIMPS, from concept identification of a blitz team to the implementation of the new medical record. Our objective is to share our collective experiences as the quality administrator, team facilitator, and team leader with other organizations who choose to initiate quality planning blitz teams.

Why a Dedicated Team?

NHRMC's quality council was formed in December 1993. As an organization that chose to utilize the Juran Trilogy for its quality methodology, the council's early efforts focused on education and the chartering of several quality improvement teams. The individuals selected to serve as facilitators at NHRMC received 40 hours of training on the Juran quality improvement process, quality tools, and facilitation skills. On completion of this training, two facilitators were assigned to each quality improvement team. By the end of the first year, each facilitator had a minimum of six months' experience working with a pilot team. None of the quality improvement teams chartered during this year was close to completing the process. Therefore, the feedback facilitators provided to the quality council was timely and based on their actual experience in facilitating teams at NHRMC.

On completion of the first year of the initiative, the quality council conducted an assessment that included feedback from the facilitators to the organization's pilot quality improvement teams. As part of the annual assessment process, the quality council met to review and discuss this feedback and identify mechanisms to address the opportunities for improvement. The facilitators' feedback included the following areas of concern.

- Time required to be a team member
- Mission statements that lack data to support the direction a team should take
- Selection process for facilitators, team leaders, and team members
- Team attendance
- Team members not completing assignments
- Duplication of efforts
- Lack of facilitator recognition
- Team members unwilling to contribute to the team's discussion when superiors are present
- Inefficient use of team time
- Poor group dynamics
- Inconsistency in excusing individuals from team assignments
- Lack of belief that the quality council will support team decisions
- Time for team leaders to prepare for team meetings
- Lack of recognition from department managers for participation on a team
- Lack of knowledge of teams and quality initiative
- Members of the same team trained at different times
- Untrained team members

This list includes only barriers and no enablers, yet it represents the only feedback the facilitators provided to the quality council. In fact, this feedback was valuable information that identified multiple opportunities for improving the process. The communication of this feedback to the quality council presented a challenge for the quality administrator. A major concern was keeping the group focused on the identification of strategies to address the barriers rather than allowing the discussion to disintegrate to challenging the validity of the information or dismissing the feedback as one group's opinion.

The quality council held a day-long retreat to assess progress for the first year and to develop objectives and identify critical milestones for the next year. The agenda for this meeting included the facilitators' feedback just described and a status report on the progress of the current quality teams from each quality council liaison. The facilitators' feedback and the fact that no team had completed its mission over the past year initiated a discussion on how the quality council could address the facilitator concerns and achieve results from the quality teams. Multiple strategies were identified that day, including an idea to allow teams to work full-time on a project until completion. This strategy was discussed at length in relationship to the concerns voiced by the facilitators and was identified as a method to address nine of the concerns (see Figure 29.1).

Quality Council Support

Another issue discussed at length during this retreat was the quality council's commitment to the process. As an organization in the infancy of its quality initiative, it was apparent that the quality

Facilitator concerns	Addressed by a blitz team
Time required to be a team member	X
Mission statements that lack data to support the direction a team should take	
Selection process for facilitators, team leaders, and team members	
Team attendance	X
Team members not completing assignments	X
Duplication of efforts	X
Lack of facilitator recognition	
Team members unwilling to contribute to the team's discussion when superiors are present	
Inefficient use of team time	X
Poor group dynamics	
Inconsistency in excusing individuals from team assignments	X
Lack of belief that the quality council will support team decisions	
Time for team leaders to prepare for team meetings	X
Lack of recognition from department managers for participation on a team	
Lack of knowledge of teams and quality initiative	
Members of the same team trained at different times	X
Untrained team members	X

Figure 29.1. Facilitator concerns that were addressed by a blitz team.

council members believed the initiation of 10 teams and regular attendance at quality council meetings demonstrated their commitment and support to the process. However, discussions that occurred during the monthly facilitator support group meetings indicated a different perception. The members and facilitators of the quality teams did not believe that the quality council members were supportive of the process and did not "walk the talk." One example relates to the quality council's role as liaisons to the quality teams. At NHRMC, each quality team is assigned a quality council liaison whose role can be described as one of an enabler to the team and includes the following responsibilities.

- Being informed of the team's progress
- Coordinating the team's work with key individuals not represented on the team
- Informing the quality council of the team's progress
- Removing any barriers the team may encounter during the quality process

These responsibilities were fulfilled in a variety of ways by the members of the quality council. Some attended most of the team's meetings and participated as a member, including completing assignments. In one case, this included the liaison arriving to work at 5:00 A.M. for one week and collecting blood samples with a team member to validate a remedy. If other quality council members attended a team meeting, they had to be introduced to the team members because they weren't recognized. In the worst case, the liaison met the team members when they presented their results to the quality council. While some teams preferred for the liaison to attend only when needed, most of the facilitators agreed that this depended on the combination of the team composition and the individual liaison assigned. This feedback allowed the quality administrator to make appropriate assignments for quality council liaisons to future quality teams and was a key consideration during the chartering of NHRMC's first blitz team.

The result of the quality council's retreat was the identification of strategies to focus on during the next year. Each strategy was assigned a champion for development and implementation and a target completion date. One of these strategies was to "pilot a dedicated quality team by September 1995." This time frame was selected for two reasons. First, it would allow the current teams to complete the process, and second, an experienced facilitator would be available to facilitate the blitz team.

The meeting evaluations from the quality council retreat included appreciation for the facilitators' feedback as well as recognition of valuable lessons learned. In light of our experiences during the first year, the quality council also made a commitment that day to focus on not making the same mistakes twice.

Integrated Documentation

Another one of the quality council's strategies during the second year (1995) was to prepare the organization for the next triennial Joint Commission for Accreditation of Healthcare Organizations (JCAHO) survey, which would occur in the spring of 1996. This strategy was accomplished through the development of a JCAHO work group that included a representative for each of the 11 JCAHO functions (see Figure 29.2). The responsibility of the JCAHO work group was to coordinate the organization's preparations for the survey.

Each member of the JCAHO work group was also responsible for facilitating a function work group, composed of representatives from all the departments impacted by the JCAHO standards. The responsibility of the function work groups was to assess compliance with the standards for their function and develop and monitor an action plan to address any compliance issues.

JCAHO function	Job title
Patient rights and organizational ethics	Vice president—operations
Assessment of patients	Director of ambulatory care I.S.
Treatment of patients	Administrator—surgical nursing Coordinator—clinical epidemiology
Education	Director of ambulatory care I.S.
Continuum of care	Administrator—surgical nursing
Improving organizational performance	Administrator—quality management
Leadership	Administrative resident
Environment of care	Director—facilities services Safety officer
Human resources	Director—compensation and benefits
Information management	Director—information services Director—medical records
Infection control	Coordinator—clinical epidemiology

Figure 29.2. JCAHO work group composition.

At the same time, the clinical staff in the quality resources department was conducting a closed medical record review to assess the organization's compliance with all the JCAHO standards that could be evaluated with a medical record. This review included a sample of 100 medical records and their compliance with 127 standards. The results of the review revealed that for some standards the records were compliant with the standards 100 percent of the time and that for other standards the records were compliant 0 percent of the time. A score of 3, 4, or 5 on any standard could result in a Type I or supplemental recommendation by the JCAHO surveyors. The opportunities for improvement generated from this review included the following:

- The medical record should demonstrate evidence of interdisciplinary planning for patient care from admission through discharge.

- The medical record should demonstrate evidence of the communication of pertinent information among disciplines, with appropriate collaborative efforts to manage patients and enhance the continuity of care.

- The medical record should demonstrate evidence of continuous communication with the patients and/or families regarding the plans for treatment and their involvement in decisions.

- Nursing documentation would benefit from the development of a comprehensive, user-friendly form that would facilitate the consistency and uniformity of documentation.

The JCAHO work group met to review the results of each function work group's assessment of compliance with the 1995 standards, review the results of the medical record review, and prioritize the action plans. As the meeting progressed, the group became overwhelmed. Part of the group's frustration was based on the impact that the current documentation system would have on the JCAHO survey outcome. Considering mechanisms that were available and feasible to address this issue in the seven months that remained until the survey, the group members felt defeated.

They discussed at length traditional approaches to addressing the documentation issue, and the only option that seemed feasible was to engage a consultant to complete the medical record redesign. After a lengthy discussion, this option was eliminated because of the limited opportunity to customize any product to meet the organization's specific needs. As the end of the meeting approached with no solution identified to address the documentation issue, the group discussed the impact that doing nothing would have on the JCAHO survey outcome. At that point, one of the members commented that if it weren't for the time constraint, the ideal solution would be to form a quality team. This comment prompted the quality administrator to inform the group of the quality council's objective to pilot a blitz team. After explaining the concept of a blitz team to the group, the group discussed the feasibility of a quality blitz team to address the documentation problems. Several members of the group who had had positive experiences using the quality problem-solving process and tools voiced their enthusiastic support of this solution.

However, two key individuals in the documentation process—the directors of medical records and information services—expressed concerns regarding the commitment of resources from their respective departments to a blitz team. The vice president of operations, who served on the JCAHO work group and the quality council, voiced her support of the concept and commented that she believed the quality council would support the concept as well. The meeting ended with the JCAHO work group agreeing that a quality blitz team was the appropriate mechanism to address the documentation issues. The recommendation for a quality blitz team became one of the key components of the presentation to the quality council on the prioritization of the function work group action plans.

Selling the Concept: Behind the Scenes

After the JCAHO work group meeting, it was clear that the blitz team concept could work but there would also be resistance. This realization quickly became apparent when the nursing administration representative on the JCAHO work group discussed the idea with her peers and received a less-than-positive response. The comments from the nursing administrators ranged from "There isn't a documentation problem" to "This isn't a problem for a quality team to address." This feedback indicated to the quality administrator that it would be a challenge to gain the quality council's approval to initiate a quality blitz team to address the documentation issue.

The quality administrator's efforts to garner support for a blitz team began with a meeting with the chief executive officer (CEO). During this meeting the results of the JCAHO assessment and medical record review were highlighted, as well as the other alternatives the JCAHO work group had considered and the rationale for pursuing a quality blitz team. The decision to start with the CEO was made for the following reasons: First, he served as the chair of the quality council, which had the final authority to charter the team; second, the response from nursing administration and the chief nurse executive to the concept was less than enthusiastic; and consideration of the reporting relationship of the other areas identified as potential resisters (information services and medical records) to the CEO. Information services reported directly to the CEO, and medical records reported to the chief financial officer. The result of this meeting was the full commitment and support of the CEO to utilize a quality planning blitz team to redesign the medical record and the development of a strategy to ensure approval by the quality council.

The strategy developed by the quality administrator and CEO included the following components.

- The quality administrator meeting with every member of the quality council prior to the JCAHO work group's presentation to quality council

- The identification of the "right" people to serve on the team

- The assignment of the facilitator and quality council liaison to the team

The easiest part of this strategy was completed first: the assignment of the facilitator and quality council liaison. The facilitator chosen was Peggy Schroeder, who was employed as the organization's quality coordinator. Besides serving as a facilitator to numerous quality teams, Peggy also serves as a resource to other teams and facilitators and is responsible for educating departmental quality teams. Peggy had also completed the Juran Institute's "Facilitating Quality Planning Teams" 40-hour course and was working with another quality planning team at NHRMC to design a chest pain center. The quality council liaison chosen was Anne Patterson, vice president of operations. Anne was regarded as one of the "liaisons of choice" by the facilitators based on her interactions with current teams. Anne also served on the JCAHO work group, so she was familiar with the standards and the complexity of the task the team would be chartered to accomplish.

Since the composition of the team was a critical success factor, the quality administrator and quality coordinator identified the individuals who would be "ideal" members for the team. The quality administrator and coordinator made these selections based on their interactions with individuals who had previously been involved in the quality initiative as team facilitators, team leaders, and team members. An additional consideration was individuals who had been trained as quality resource facilitators (QRFs). A QRF is an employee who has received 40 hours of training in the Juran quality improvement process, quality tools, and facilitation skills. The individuals selected to be QRFs were identified by their director and vice president as people who are committed to the organization and have strong analytical and communication skills. The step of identifying individuals to participate on the team preceded the individual meetings with the quality council members. This allowed the quality administrator to make the vice presidents aware of the preferred individuals to serve on the team from their division. As previously mentioned, the director of medical records, who served on the JCAHO work group, was resistant to the blitz concept. Since the individual identified to be the ideal team member from medical records was the assistant director and resistance from the director for this representative was expected, the decision was made to gain support from the director's vice president during his individual briefing. Other ingredients for success in securing the right individuals for the team included obtaining feedback from the quality council members who were quality zealots, calling in favors with vice presidents, and using the support of the CEO to elicit support from other vice presidents.

Equipped with the results of the JCAHO assessment and medical record review, the support of the CEO, and the identification of ideal individuals to serve on the team, the quality administrator met with each quality council member. The purpose of these meetings was to discuss the significance of the problem and to inform the quality council member of the forthcoming JCAHO work group recommendation. Also discussed during these meetings was the importance of having the individuals who had been identified as ideal to be selected by the department directors. Meetings were held with every member of the quality council, with the exception of the chief nurse executive (CNE). Since resistance had already been voiced by this individual, the CEO agreed to personally discuss the concept with the CNE.

Quality Council Presentation

On August 2, 1995, the JCAHO work group recommended that the quality council approve the initiation of a quality planning blitz team to address caregiver documentation in the medical record. The JCAHO work group's rationale for recommending this approach included the following:

- The current format of the medical record did not demonstrate the intent of JCAHO's requirement for the integration of providing patient care among all disciplines.

- Documentation is a crucial component for the scoring of multiple standards.

- Noncompliance would result in multiple Type I recommendations.

- The only alternative given the time constraints would be to hire an external consultant to implement a turnkey system.

- No group currently existed that could resolve the problem.

- The quality council objective to pilot a dedicated quality team would be met.

The JCAHO work group proposed the following to the quality council.

Mission: Develop and implement an integrated patient care documentation system for non-physician disciplines

Goals:

- Develop by 10/1/95
- Implement by 12/1/95
- Consistent with the plan for the provision of patient care
- Consistent with the outcomes management program
- Compliant with JCAHO standards

Team composition:

>   Medical records
>   Nursing representatives
>   Clinical nutritionist
>   Rehabilitation therapist
>   Discharge planning nurse
>   Respiratory care

Ad-hoc members:

>   JCAHO work group representative
>   Information services
>   Chairman of the medical records committee

Leader: Pending selection of team members

Facilitator: Peggy Schroeder, quality resources

Liaison: Anne Patterson, vice president of operations

Start date: September 11, 1995

Completion date: September 29, 1995

Presentation to quality council: October 4, 1995

The quality council approved the JCAHO work group's recommendation, and NHRMC's first blitz team was chartered to apply the Juran quality planning methodology (see Figure 29.3) to the mission and goals identified.

Team Membership

Team members' roles and actions will be described throughout the rest of this chapter. While at the beginning of the process the personalities and roles each member would play were unknown, a brief description will facilitate the reader's understanding of group dynamics and the team process. The team's story is told here from the perspective of the facilitator and leader.

The facilitator recognized the importance of identifying a leader and other team member roles as quickly as possible; however, the process of identifying roles took about three days. Subsequently, the team lacked a leader at kickoff and had no minutes of its first meeting. However, this strategy still proved to be successful. Selecting the right person for each role, most importantly the team leader, should not be rushed. The impact of the leader on the team's success cannot be underestimated. The facilitator was acquainted with some of the individuals selected to serve on the team and knew that she would have to expedite the development of the leader's skills quickly enough to meet the needs of the team. By the end of the third day, the facilitator had identified the best person for each role.

Opting for the quiet voice of reason, Kim Blake, clinical nurse specialist at the Coastal Rehabilitation Hospital, was approached by the facilitator. Kim graciously accepted the responsibility of team leader. Kim was experienced in developing clinical documentation systems and had been trained as a QRF. Kim provided a sensible and objective perspective coupled with a wide knowledge base. Although this team would be using the quality planning methodology, the additional training Kim had received as a QRF would be an asset to her as a team leader.

The team leader was pleased to have the opportunity to serve the team. She thought she would be able to fulfill the role, but had only been with the organization for one year and was concerned about

1. **Establish project**
   - Identify project
   - Establish mission
   - Establish team
   - Verify mission
   - Plan the project

2. **Identify customers**
   - Construct high-level flow diagram
   - Create list of all external customers
   - Create list of all internal customers
   - Prioritize customer lists

3. **Discover customer needs**
   - Plan to collect customers' needs
   - Collect list of customers' needs in *their* language
   - Examine and prioritize customers' needs
   - Translate their needs into your language
   - Establish units of measurement and sensors

4. **Develop product**
   - Group together related customers' needs
   - Determine methods for identifying product features
   - Select high-level product features and goals
   - Develop detailed product features and goals
   - Optimize product features and goals
   - Set and publish final product design

5. **Develop process**
   - Review product goals
   - Identify operating conditions
   - Collect known information on alternative processes
   - Select general process design
   - Identify high-level process features and goals
   - Identify detailed process features and goals
   - Design for critical factors and human error
   - Optimize process features and goals
   - Establish process capability
   - Set and publish final process features and goals
   - Set and publish final process design

6. **Develop process controls/transfer to operations**
   - Identify controls needed
   - Design feedback loop
   - Optimize self-control and self-inspection
   - Establish audit
   - Demonstrate process capability and controllability
   - Plan for transfer to operations
   - Implement plan, and validate transfer

Source: Juran Institute, *Quality Planning Ready Reference* (Wilton, Conn.: Juran Institute, 1994), 5, 9, 15, 21, 29, 41.

Figure 29.3. The Juran quality planning process.

her familiarity with the corporate culture and the needs of the entire facility. Since Kim had worked with the facilitator before and was very comfortable with Peggy's "enthusiastic, move ahead, get the job done style" and thought they would be a good team, Kim agreed to be the team leader. Of course in the beginning, neither the facilitator nor the leader realized how many after-hours they would be spending together, planning the team's next moves.

John Long, coronary care unit staff nurse, seemed to thrive at the task of team recorder. The role that is often the least desirable found a willing volunteer. Using a tip from the director of his unit that John enjoyed working with a computer, he was provided with a laptop computer and proceeded to type the minutes while the meetings were in progress. John prepared, printed, and copied the minutes each day and provided each member with a copy before the start of each meeting.

Wendy Fletcher-Hardee, medical-surgical staff nurse, served as the team's timekeeper throughout the project. By the end of day 2, most team members were comfortable voicing opinions, and taking part in discussions, so the anecdotes began—stories to go with every thought and idea. Timekeeping emerged as essential. The meeting evaluations at the end of Wendy's first day as timekeeper confirmed the expected benefits and proved to serve the team well throughout difficult discussions. Wendy's role as timekeeper was repeatedly useful to help the team get back on schedule and stay focused.

Celeste Beal, respiratory therapist, initially played the role of "flipper" (NHRMC's term for the person taking responsibility for recording information on a flip chart during meetings). Celeste is also a QRF and is responsible for facilitating quality activities within her department; she is very organized, thoughtful, and a self-proclaimed compulsive. Celeste made sure that we had all the details. Celeste was also willing to take a chance when her thoughts were different from the direction in which the team was going. She described it as "going out on a limb," and as time went on it became a joke and stress reliever for the team, going so far as becoming "going out on a twig."

Ray Nestler, clinical nutritionist, demonstrated an inclination for getting consensus on the definition of terms to facilitate the discussions and keep things moving. This ability landed Ray the role of glossary keeper. Ray also became a key player in ensuring that the team was listening to what the customers wanted. He earned the nickname "voice of the people."

Evelyn Bowden, discharge planning nurse, was not comfortable allowing the team to miss an occasion to thank or recognize people outside the team for any assistance they had provided. Consequently, Evelyn created a role never before defined for teams at NHRMC: etiquette director. In spite of the levity with which one might initially regard such a team role, it proved to be an important responsibility, providing positive recognition for the team.

Roxanne Brammer, women's and childrens' staff nurse, over time served the team well as the sounding board and barometer for emotions and frustrations. By nature she is a quiet person, very dedicated to whatever she is doing, and very approachable. Team members were comfortable sharing things with her that needed to be addressed. Roxanne's department, the labor and delivery unit, was selected as a pilot location. During this time she excelled as a staff facilitator. Her drive and skills helped her to grow and be recognized for her abilities and later be selected to oversee long-term implementation of the product.

Beth Layman, assistant director of medical records, acted as the voice of reason by quizzing the team on its decisions. Beth is also highly regarded by physicians and other key individuals as practical and someone who meets their needs. This reputation assisted the team to gain support and respect.

Karen Marchbanks, coordinator of clinical epidemiology, and Dee Lammers, information services project specialist, served as ad hoc members of the team. Dee's role was to inform the team of the status of the organization's effort in acquiring an electronic medical record system and an overview of what these systems can and cannot do. Her input was valuable to help the team publicize the link between preparing the documentation system and the implementation of an electronic medical record. Karen's role was integral to the success of the project in providing a comfortable familiarization with the JCAHO standards regarding documentation. Karen reviewed the standards with the team and discussed how NHRMC had failed and succeeded in the past relative to those standards.

Kathy Helak, responsible for the outcomes management program at NHRMC, informed the team of the status of this initiative. She also provided invaluable support to the team by serving as a consultant and cheerleader. Kathy was ultimately named as the management sponsor for housewide implementation of the medical record. (Also see the chapter appendix.)

Informing the Group of Expectations

Team members received a memo from the CEO prior to their first meeting. This memo explained that each member's sole responsibility as employees of NHRMC would be to participate on this team from September 11–29, 1995. However, as part of an organization still in the infancy of its quality initiative, the facilitator suspected that most team members would not fully understand from a memo the particulars of being on a quality team, no less a blitz team. Since the memo had informed participants that the team would be a full-time job, it was important to explain what this full-time job would entail. This explanation was provided to the team at a preliminary meeting held one week in advance of the team's first day. Team members were instructed that their voice mail messages were to be changed to reflect that they were on a special assignment and not available for three weeks, and that they should not check electronic mail or even appear in their offices for the duration of the project. Outside of that meeting, supervisors and directors were also informed that no work was to be assigned to these individuals during the time period. The logistics of a blitz team were explained and discussed. Few questions were raised at that point. The mission statement was also reviewed, with a brief discussion of the purpose of the team. In spite of the magnitude of the project on which the members were about to embark, there was no problem finishing the meeting in just one hour. Had they all been so well informed that no questions remained? Actually, at that point in time, the members were in sync with the quality council in not knowing what to expect.

Preparation

With a keen awareness of entering uncharted waters, any consistency the facilitator could provide would be a benefit. As later proven by meeting evaluations, consistency in meeting rooms would be an appreciated entity. Securing a meeting room for three weeks at NHRMC was impossible. Thus, it was necessary to find an off-site location for the first week's meetings. This meant that, in addition to planning for 40 hours worth of consecutive meeting time, every detail of the meetings had to be thought out in advance to ensure that the team would have everything it needed from pens, pads, and Post-its to getting team members' paychecks to the off-site location on payday. Probably the most interesting assortment of supplies included maps, push pins, suckers, compact discs, shiny pennies, and more; all for the various icebreakers planned.

Being given three weeks to develop the product meant that time was of the essence. Detailed agendas were prepared in advance for the first five days. These agendas included introductions, icebreakers, establishing ground rules, training, and study times. Meeting evaluations were also prepared. These evaluations would be used as a key indicator for measuring the momentum of the team as well as planning daily strategies.

Day One: Getting Started

Physical separation from the medical center was conducive to the team building necessary for the team's success. The team arrived to a new world and would learn much the first day. The first morning began with introductions and an icebreaker followed by two hours dedicated to discussing the process for chartering the team. Team members did not recognize the importance of this discussion at the time, because they were anxious to get on with the business of being a team and creating the product. However, without realizing it, the members needed that discussion time, and later conversations revealed that it had been beneficial.

As noted previously, a comfortable familiarization with outcomes management and JCAHO standards regarding documentation was integral to the success of the project. Subsequently, the afternoon of the first day was spent with Karen Marchbanks reviewing 62 of the JCAHO standards. Karen also reviewed NHRMC's past performance relative to those standards. Poring over the JCAHO standards for hours was tedious. However, the team persevered, recognizing the importance of this exercise. At the end of the first day, a routine that would bring each day to a close was begun: completion of a meeting evaluation form.

Day Two

Prior to training the team in the quality planning methodology, the facilitator reviewed the Juran Trilogy to ensure an understanding of the difference between quality planning and quality improvement. Then the facilitator provided a basic overview of the quality planning process. Even though the facilitator had completed 40 hours of training in quality planning, the team spent just four hours on it to provide enough background to move forward. The key concepts of customers, customers' needs, and creativity were highlighted as essential to the quality planning process. Meeting evaluations for the second day reflected that an understanding of the methodology increased the team's confidence to successfully complete the project.

Also important was the establishment of ground rules (see Figure 29.4). The team identified its rules and faithfully utilized them to stay on track. Throughout the process, team members could be heard calling "number 4!" to each other, signifying the fourth ground rule: stay focused.

Team members were given a Juran Institute *Quality Planning Ready Reference* for their personal use,[1] as well as a three-ring binder. The binder contained the list of team members and their phone numbers, the mission and goals, and dividers. The notebooks proved indispensable in helping team members stay organized as the work progressed.

```
1. No blame
2. Confidentiality
3. Start on time
4. Stay focused
5. 100 percent attendance
6. Complete assignments
7. One speaker at a time
```

Figure 29.4. Chart CHIMPS ground rules.

The team then reviewed and verified the mission statement using the SMART criteria (see Figure 29.5). The team determined that cost had been overlooked and decided to add "benefits will exceed the cost" to the list of goals (see Figure 29.6). The established process for the endorsement of a mission statement modification at NHRMC involves the reporting of the change to the quality council liaison, and the liaison reporting it to the quality council to obtain approval. A blitz team however, could not wait for the quality council to meet and approve the change. The team needed to have approval and proceed. Therefore, the change was shared with and approved by the quality council liaison on the same day.

That afternoon Kathy Helak, the individual responsible for the outcomes management program at NHRMC, reviewed the principles of outcomes management with the team. Potential applications and associations of outcomes for documentation were explained.

Finally, brainstorming was used to come up with a team name (process detailed in group dynamics section). The team became known as the Chart CHIMPS, an acronym for "**c**ollaborative **h**olistic **i**ntegrated **m**edical **p**atient documentation **s**ystem."

Product Development

Once the team members had been trained in the quality planning process, they were more anxious than ever to get to the work of product development. A discussion ensued from which the basis of the work plan emerged. When a global idea of the work plan was defined, team members armed with Post-its and markers moved to a long folding table in another part of the room. The team members wrote every possible task that they thought they would need to complete to get through the *identifying customer needs* step of the process. It became evident that this task would not require eight people, so a few of the members began drafting a letter to the physicians. Physician input and buy-in had been identified early on as a necessary ingredient to the success of the project. This first letter would apprise physicians of the team's existence and mission and ask for their suggestions. That small initiative demonstrated the value in having good team members; they recognized a need and promptly acted on it.

Meanwhile, back at the work plan table, Post-its with such tasks as developing interview questions, grouping customers into like areas, starting a benchmarking search, arranging meeting places for interviews, and obtaining a list of forms were organized chronologically to create the schedule for the next few days of team meetings. The development of this work plan proved to be one of the most satisfying activities early in the team's tenure. It helped the team identify and clarify its objectives.

---

1. Goals should be **S**pecific: cover the what, when, and how of a situation.
2. Goals should be **M**easurable: cover areas such as quantity, quality, costs, and/or time.
3. Goals should be **A**greed upon: agreement that the end result is desirable and achievable.
4. Goals should be **R**ealistic: cover areas such as practicality, available resources, control over variables, and authority.
5. Goals should be **T**ime-phased: completed within the needed time frame.

Source: Juran Institute, *Designs for World-Class Quality, Step 1* (Wilton, Conn.: Juran Institute, 1994), 25.

Figure 29.5. SMART criteria.

Original Mission Statement (Developed by the Quality Council)

Develop and implement an integrated patient care documentation system for nonphysician disciplines.

Goals:
- Develop by 10/1
- Implement by 12/1
- Consistent with plan for the provision of patient care
- Consistent with outcomes management program
- Compliant with JCAHO standards
- Compatible with an electronic medical record format

First Revision Made by Team After Verifying Mission According to SMART Criteria

Develop and implement an integrated patient care documentation system for nonphysician disciplines.

Goals:
- Develop by 10/1
- Implement by 12/1
- Consistent with plan for the provision of patient care
- Consistent with outcomes management program
- Compliant with JCAHO standards
- Compatible with an electronic medical record format
- *Benefits will exceed the cost*

Second Revision Made by Team Based on Customer Needs

Develop and implement an integrated patient care documentation system for nonphysician disciplines.

Goals:
- Develop by 10/1
- Implement by 12/1
- Consistent with plan for the provision of patient care
- Consistent with outcomes management program
- Compliant with JCAHO standards
- Compatible with an electronic medical record format
- Benefits will exceed the cost
- *Meets the following customer needs*
  - *—Not redundant*
  - *—Quick*
  - *—Streamlined*
  - *—Cost-effective*
  - *—Standardized*
  - *—Timely*
  - *—Serve as a physician communication tool*

Figure 29.6. Quality blitz team mission statement.

Meeting evaluations that afternoon demonstrated a sense of satisfaction. Members now felt they were on their way. Although at the end of the three-week period some members suggested that things could have progressed more rapidly if the work plan had been developed prior to team kickoff, the team building resulting from that task was well worth the time spent. Buy-in on a project for which one has identified the work to be done will often be greater than for a task for which the assignments are dictated.

The team decided that the best method for receiving input from chart customers was to hold a series of focus groups. The team did not want its focus groups confused with other focus groups conducted at NHRMC, so the team's focus groups were called *chart talks*.

The creation of the customer list for chart talks was a true challenge. It was the number-one item on the work plan, so the team performed that task the afternoon of the same day that the work plan had been developed. In a medical center with 3000 employees, identifying the customers of the patient documentation system was complicated. The team members had a difficult time leaving any customer out. Documentation by any position in the medical center was regarded as significant to the care of the patient. While this is true, for the team's success it was imperative to prioritize the list.

The team designed the chart talks around the five JCAHO patient-focused functions of patient rights, assessment, treatment, education, and continuum of care. This provided a method for the team to identify which customers of the patient's chart were truly more significant contributors, thereby narrowing and prioritizing the customer list.

Discussion ensued on the best approach for getting people to attend the chart talks. Putting the task in the hands of department directors meant explaining to each director the purpose of the chart talks, waiting to hear back from that director, and then contacting the person. The team knew that the department directors had been instructed to respond to team requests in a timely manner. If the team relied on the directors to identify individuals to attend chart talks, it would probably not occur in the team's time frame. The team instead chose to identify as many individuals who not only held named positions, but had the desire to effect positive change in the organization. The value of teamwork emerged again and again in many facets of the project; however, when planning the chart talks, the team's knowledge of the medical center's staff was impressive. The team identified 75 individuals from the identified positions, called each one personally, and managed to get almost 100 percent attendance with no more than two days' notice.

Between 10 and 30 people were invited to each of the series of five chart talks to answer key questions. Attendees were also asked to bring any and all forms they were currently using in their areas in the medical record. Three broad and five specific questions were developed for each chart talk. At each session, team members recorded responses, complaints, suggestions, and comments on a flip chart. A timekeeper ensured that all questions would be addressed in the hour allotted, and a facilitator led the discussion. Again, the completion of this task was a milestone that left the team with a true sense of accomplishment. The chart talks were a great success. Attendees were given a banana as a token of the team's appreciation for their help, and Chart CHIMPS became a household name.

This methodology was not the only one by which customers' needs were identified. As stated earlier, a letter was sent out to each physician. Although the mission statement specified that the team was not to address physician documentation, members recognized the impact any change would have on the physicians' use of the chart and, therefore, the importance of involving them from the beginning. The letter explained the mission of the team, asked what the physicians liked and disliked about the current charting system, their thoughts on what could make it easier, and which parts of the chart they used. Unfortunately, while the information obtained here was valuable, the response rate was low.

The team also identified the informal leaders of each physician department and personally contacted them, conducting in-person or telephone interviews to get their contributions. Separate meetings were arranged with the president of the medical staff and the chairman of the medical records committee, who both gave their full support to the team. The chairman of the medical records committee, after understanding the team's true mission, proclaimed himself a CHIMP; this was an undeniable morale booster for the team.

Additional interviews were conducted with a variety of individuals in the organization representing medical records, education, psychiatry, and quality review, to name a few. The team became adept at showing its appreciation for a presenter's time and information, as well as letting the person know when the time allotted had been used, by giving a drum roll on the table. Keeping things moving was always a priority.

After each interview session the CHIMPS would debrief, discussing what each member thought was pertinent and consolidating the interview or presentation into a few key points on a flip chart. When combined with the consolidated lists from the chart talks, the team further consolidated and prioritized the information to arrive at its hybrid list of customer needs. The customer needs for a new patient documentation system included

- Quick
- Streamlined
- Physician communication tool
- Not redundant
- Meets JCAHO standards
- Timely
- Cost-effective
- Standardized

All new needs were added to the goals of the mission and, again, presented to and approved by the quality council liaison.

Until this point the team had been involved in a flurry of activity, and now it was finally time to settle down to the work of developing the product features. Although this activity was the process for which the team had been longing, it quickly emerged as a challenge for the facilitator. (See the Group Dynamics: Storming section later in this chapter).

Once that challenge was met, the team quickly got back on track and prepared to begin product development. In an effort to drive home the team's mission as quality planning rather than improvement, the facilitator recognized that something must be done to demonstrate this point. The team members had been working with the existing system for quite some time, so they needed to be reminded that their mission was to develop a new product.

To illustrate this point, a medical record that was about to be destroyed and a wicker basket were obtained. The team was instructed to stand around the medical record and the basket at a table and to start tearing. Most of the team members were hesitant at first, but they all indulged themselves. As they shredded, the facilitator spoke of the end of the medical record as they knew it. The facilitator reminded the team of its mission to develop a new system based on the customers' needs. The basket remained in the center of the table as a graphic representation of the mission as the brainstorming sessions began to generate ideas for product features.

Suggestions continued to be communicated to the CHIMPS about various aspects of the chart. This information was compiled, considered, incorporated, or reserved for future reference as appropriate. However, what the team was really interested in was still not available: benchmarking information. Numerous organizations in North Carolina as well as across the United States had been contacted, but the people with whom the team members needed to speak were typically not available and when they were, the information that was promised would not arrive. Waiting for return phone calls and faxes became an increasing disappointment.

Since time was of the essence, the team had to move forward. The final blitz week was dedicated to the development of the overall concept of the new patient documentation system. By Wednesday of the final week, the team began to melt down and time had to be taken to achieve a comfort zone for the team. Members began to feel that completion of the task before them was impossible by the end of that week. Discussion centered on requesting a fourth week for completion of the product. Members discussed the various reasons for proposing the request. The team determined that the principal reason they did not want to finish by the end of the week was mainly because they were aiming for perfection. The team finally agreed that it would present to the quality council the overall concept of the product. Once the quality council approved the concept, the team would develop the detailed product for implementation.

The final day of blitz team time was a marathon of finalizing the product design and developing an implementation timeline. The implementation timeline included piloting the product, refining the product, and—the final step of the quality planning methodology—transferring to operations. Some of the team members developed the timeline, while the remainder of the team worked on the final pieces of the product. By 5:00 that afternoon, everyone was exhausted. The room where the team had worked for the past eight days was a muddle of flip charts, stress-reduction toys, medical record forms, and more. The room walls were not only lined with pages of flip charts, but the charts were multilayered. It truly reflected the work that had been accomplished.

The team had decided that the presentation to the quality council would be shared by the team leader and team facilitator. The team leader would review the product that had been developed. The facilitator would review the application of the quality planning methodology, logistics, and the lessons learned. The leader and facilitator made arrangements to meet and organize their presentation, never suspecting the impact this meeting would have on the team (See the Group Dynamics: Storming Again section later in this chapter.)

The presentation was a success. The quality council approved moving forward, and each quality council member accepted responsibility to champion a defined objective. The CHIMPS would henceforth meet weekly to advance product implementation.

Group Dynamics

Managing group dynamics is a principal ingredient in keeping team productivity high. As teams develop and function, they go through several phases that include the following:[2]

- *Forming:* In this stage, members cautiously explore the boundaries of acceptable group behavior. This is a stage of transition from individual to member status and of testing the leader's guidance both formally and informally.

- *Storming:* In this stage, team members realize their task is different and more difficult than they imagined. As a result, the team members become testy, blameful, or overzealous. This makes it the most difficult stage for the team.

- *Norming:* In this stage, members reconcile competing loyalties and responsibilities. They accept the team, team rules, their role on the team, and the individuality of fellow members.

- *Performing:* In this stage, the team has settled its relationships and expectations. Team members have discovered and accepted each other's strengths and weaknesses and learned what their roles are. The team is able to complete its task.

The group dynamics of the Chart CHIMPS may have been the key to the success of this team.

Forming

One of the purposes of the preliminary one-hour meeting, which took place the Wednesday prior to the team's full-time dedicated effort, was to provide an opportunity to increase the comfort level for arrival on that first day. In an organization with approximately 3000 employees, few team members knew each other and most had never set eyes on each other. Apprehension was high as the team members introduced themselves. During this time, the facilitator assessed the group dynamics and variety of cultural backgrounds to which she would need to be sensitive.

Although the memo received by the participants had informed them that the team would be a full-time job, the responses of the individuals selected was an indication of the eventual team personality that would emerge. One member asked if she could still attend other committee meetings and complete work if it did not interfere with the team's meeting time. The people who are ideal team members, the exceptional employees, are the same people who are dedicated to their work and find it very difficult to let go. Sensitivity to this dedication and the need to be sure that members didn't take on too much became a responsibility of the facilitator that day and continued throughout the duration of the three-week process.

Of course, the most pressing need at the onset was team building, and a variety of icebreakers were used to accomplish this process. The quality administrator attended the team's meeting on the first day, and most of the team members did not know her. Each team member was given a slip of paper with a fact about her that was not widely known. When she arrived and the time came to introduce her to the team, the facilitator suggested that perhaps some of the team members could help in the introduction. Each team member offered the hidden information in a very casual manner. This activity not only surprised the quality administrator and gave the team a few laughs, but it immediately put the team members "in cahoots" with each other and the team building began.

The team's favorite icebreaker came unexpectedly. On the third morning, a weird news story was broadcast on the radio. It involved an obscure medical condition and the resulting surgery that most found hard to believe. The team decided then that team members should report any "news of the weird" at the beginning of the next day's meeting. It became a cornerstone as the first agenda item for all subsequent meetings.

Meeting off-site for the first five days provided team members the opportunity to separate themselves not only physically, but mentally, from their customary job assignments. Perhaps more importantly, it demonstrated the importance of the task to which they were now assigned, as well as establishing a level of personal comfort with each other in a short amount of time.

The first event that provided a lot of laughs and a sense of camaraderie for the team was giving itself a name. The team used brainstorming, which was an excellent opportunity for practicing the use of that tool while providing everyone the chance to suggest any name, no matter how silly. When the flip chart page was full of suggestions, the team began narrowing to the name by which they would be known. As the team worked to narrow down the list, one team member quietly worked on her pad and, just as the team thought it had its name, she suggested that perhaps the team would like to reconsider the name Chart CHIMPS since she had worked it out as an acronym. The members all immediately called for a vote on just that name, and it was unanimous: The Chart CHIMPS were born.

The time spent naming the team was well worth it, for little did anyone know at the time how much that name would affect the team. The members immediately began to call themselves chimps. Each week the team submitted a "swinging update" to the hospital newsletter. The hospital was referred to as the jungle. Bananas became a standard part of the team's diet. One team member inadvertently named the CEO the "chief chimp," and it stuck. Another team member wore a gorilla suit to a presentation to gain attention to the process. The quality council gave the team members a Barrel of Monkeys game after their presentation. Another member purchased chimp cards for advertising. Another team member made banana bread for key members of the organization, and another team member made chimp pins. All of these activities can be tied to the team's name and demonstrate how a seemingly unimportant activity can be a key to team building.

Meeting evaluations were a routine that brought each day to a close. No matter how hectic the day had been, no one left without completing an evaluation. These evaluations were essential to the leader and facilitator in planning the next meeting. A simple form was used throughout the project (see Figure 29.7). All evaluations were anonymous, and team members took a variety of approaches in completing them. The second day and each day thereafter, each team member was given a copy of the compilation of all the comments from the previous day's evaluation. In that way, everyone knew what everyone else was thinking about how the meetings were progressing. The team recognized that the evaluation form was not only a method for communicating with the facilitator, but with each other. Team members began to use it as a formal method of recognizing one another for special accomplishments, and it should also be noted that after a while at least one team member used it as an avenue for pure humor. A sample of the comments are included in Figure 29.8.

Even during the first week, when the agendas had all been planned well in advance, feedback from the meeting evaluation forms was taken into account in revising the agenda and rearranging the meeting in any way possible to accommodate the team members. One might expect that the most helpful comments would appear under "two things I would change about today's meeting." However, the section on "what was liked" provided valuable information about how to keep the group happy and high functioning.

Storming

This team went quickly from forming to norming and then performing, with barely noticeable storming. However, there was a constant undercurrent of two concerns: that the organization might not support the team's product, and that the task was too great to complete in three weeks. Addressing those on a regular basis—sometimes briefly, sometimes at length—the facilitator was able to hold those concerns at bay and encourage the team to move forward.

Norming and Performing

Meeting eight hours a day meant that the team was in the norming and then performing phase rather quickly. Before the end of the first week, the team was a high-functioning group committed to its mission. This vitality can be attributed to several things. First, the people chosen for this team were truly the "cream of the crop." Second, the team members were committed to the project. This commitment was a result of their personalities and work ethics, coupled with the commitment of the quality council through its allocation of resources to the project.

This commitment made the leader's and facilitator's jobs easier as team members offered to take on assignments and readily suggested directions in which the team should move. From the development of

Chart CHIMPS Quality Planning Team
September 11, 1995
8:30 A.M.–5:00 P.M.
Meeting Evaluation

Please evaluate the meeting on a scale of 1 to 5, with 5 being positive and effective and 1 being negative and a waste of time.

1	2	3	4	5

What two things did you like about this meeting?

_____

_____

_____

_____

What two things would you change about this meeting?

_____

_____

_____

_____

Additional thoughts or comments:

_____

_____

_____

_____

Figure 29.7. Meeting evaluation form.

Two things I liked about today's meeting
• Active involvement
• Started and ended on time!
• I enjoy group exercises to prove a point
• Using the timer was very helpful
• Getting things done
• Roxanne took a risk
• Division of labor
• Sufficient time to work on our assignments
• The brainstorming on our feet
• Celeste "stepping on a twig"
• The special appearance and support of Jim Hobbs was a great morale booster
Two things I would change about today's meeting
• More focused vs. "war stories"
• We need to keep breaks to a minimum
• Needed more breaks today
• Sometimes we agree to agree too much—agree, then move on
• Phone access is not sufficient for our communication needs
• Less discussion about terms (won't happen—unrealistic)
• Let 24 chickens loose in team room while meeting is in progress and two red foxes (day 8)
• Fish tank in meeting room with goldfish—whoever talks out of turn must ingest live fish (day 13)
Additional comments
• Thanks for your positive approach
• I think you picked a good group of people
• Thanks for all your preparation
• Good second wind from Peggy (facilitator) helped keep us going even when she was tired too
• Thank you Wendy and Evelyn for all the goodies you brought
• What a great team
• Big kudos to John for excellent minutes, task list, etc. . . . Thanks

Figure 29.8. Meeting evaluation examples.

the work plan through the identification of customers to the identification and prioritization of needs, the team remained a high-functioning work group. Using the work plan and agenda as their guides, team members took initiative and pushed forward.

However, once those well-defined tasks were completed, the team began to melt down. A new avenue of thought was necessary, and it was difficult for the team members to make the shift. While the team members had barely stormed prior to entering the norming and performing stages, at this point they returned to the storming phase.

Storming Again

Storming is the most difficult stage for any team. Team members begin debating issues boldly and questioning the process. The Chart CHIMPS were no exception, since they had two storming experiences.

Although the team had been longing to begin product development, the task quickly emerged as a challenge. Team members lost focus and became disheartened, as if they had hit a wall. They felt as if they were falling apart as a team, and a rapid recovery was critical. As a strategy to overcome this phenomenon, the facilitator spent some time describing the fundamental dynamics of working in a group, using the forming, storming, norming, and performing framework.

Using comments from the daily meeting evaluations, the facilitator identified the phases through which the team had already passed. The team realized that it had gone through all four phases and had become a well-organized, high-functioning team. Now that a series of tasks to identify customer needs had been completed, the team needed to focus on a new task: product development. Shifting focus threw them for a loop. The facilitator explained to the team members how they had been working as a team with a strong sense of purpose. Reaching a milestone was wonderful and provided an opportunity to congratulate themselves. However, this could not be confused with completion. Recognizing that only one step in a major project had been completed detracted from the pleasure accompanying that milestone. Needing to start anew was a disappointment. Many team members returned to the forming phase, requiring a need for clarity and the definition of objectives. However, a simple understanding of the phases of group dynamics allowed team members to identify their feelings individually and place themselves somewhere in the continuum. Subsequently, team members realized their feelings and behaviors were expected, which afforded them the confidence that they could and would move forward.

The team's second storming experience occurred when it completed the development stage. The team had decided that the leader and facilitator would present the product to the quality council. The leader and facilitator decided to meet and rehearse their presentation apart from the team to save time and allow the team to focus on other needs. Because the leader and facilitator were trying to ensure the team was fully prepared, they identified potential questions the members of the quality council might raise.

This approach produced a more detailed implementation plan. The leader and facilitator worked diligently, ready to change any part of the plan with which the team might disagree. Training needs, potential for marketing the chart, piloting schedules, and the review and revision of policies were identified as items to include in the implementation plan. Each activity was assigned a team member as the responsible party and, in most cases, a quality council champion to ensure that any barriers to the implementation would be removed. The leader and facilitator were unaware that they were bringing forth the document that would create the most conflict the team would experience.

Team dissatisfaction with the facilitator and leader for completing the timeline started as a slight tremor because no one wanted to cause an earthquake, but it soon erupted into one. The team members felt insulted and angry that so much work had been done without them. Each one sincerely said that he or she would have gladly come in on Sunday to work on the timeline. The team members felt their work had been undermined. They didn't want a break; their dedication to this project went beyond any work schedule—it was the team's baby, and they didn't want to be left out of any piece. The damage was done. It was recovery time again, but it wouldn't be so easy this time. The leader and facilitator met with each team member individually to offer a sincere apology and to explain how the detailed timeline had emerged. This time it took more than a week before the team returned to its normal state of congeniality.

Lessons Learned

Overall, the Chart CHIMP project was a most rewarding team experience. But no experience is complete unless you learn something from it, and this one was no different. The following are the lessons learned from this experience.

1. Administrative support is vital.

2. Choose the right team members.

3. Define the role of ad hoc members.

4. The meeting location needs to support the team's needs.

5. Avoid multiple meeting rooms.

6. Train the team at the beginning of the process.

7. Plan agendas to match tasks with the appropriate part of the day.

8. Conduct and prepare for presentations judiciously.

9. Initiate benchmarking activities prior to the team meetings.

10. The scope of the project should determine the timeline.

Lesson 1: Administrative Support Is Vital

It is crucial to the success of a team that administrators play a supportive role in quality planning teams. Initially, team members received notification by memo from the CEO that they had been selected as a member of a dedicated quality planning team. The CEO took a personal interest in the team by visiting some of the team's meetings and talking about his belief in the process and in this particular team. This interaction made a big difference in the team's confidence and ability to take a risk. Team members were also supported along the way by the quality council through the liaison. Anne was always available to review the progress of the group and to assist in removing barriers to success. The quality administrator advocated for the quality process and the team specifically as needed, working closely with the team facilitator, leader, and liaison. She made sure that the work was noticed by the right people within the organization. This administrative support was critical and cannot be overemphasized in quality planning.

Lesson 2: Choose the Right Team Members

Our organization had learned this lesson from experiences with teams chartered prior to the Chart CHIMPS, but had not had the opportunity to test the solution. Team members for our first blitz team were chosen carefully. The individuals chosen to be CHIMPS had consistently demonstrated a commitment to the organization and a desire to be involved in making NHRMC the best medical center it could be, rather than selecting individuals who were available and willing (as had been done in the past). The individuals selected as CHIMPS had also demonstrated achievements in their own fields. The team was stacked with the best players, and the results the team achieved proved that the individuals who serve on the team make the difference.

Creating buy-in for team selection was a feat accomplished by the quality administrator. As an administrator, she had the clout to pay personal visits to the individual vice presidents and get their attention. She requested that the vice presidents commit the key employees(s) from their divisions who would make the perfect CHIMP. This approach proved to be well worth the effort.

Lesson 3: Define the Role of Ad Hoc Members

Prior to the team kickoff, there was no doubt about the roles of the team members: Their responsibilities had been made clear. However, the ad hoc members' responsibilities were not clear at all. As a result, when the team needed their input, the ad hoc members were frequently not available. Ad hoc members on future teams are advised more clearly on the importance of their immediate availability to the team.

Lesson 4: The Meeting Location Needs to Support the Team's Needs

Communication was problematic while the team was meeting off-site for the first week. As employees who had become accustomed to the convenience of electronic mail and voice mail, having only one telephone line available was an obstacle. As the team began trying to contact customers for focus groups and others for interviews, the problem became more evident. While meeting off-site has it advantages, be aware of the items that are taken for granted when working within the organization.

Lesson 5: Avoid Multiple Meeting Rooms

When the team returned to the medical center for weeks two and three, it initially had to use different rooms. Using a variety of rooms meant getting all settled and then having to pack up and move to a new location. While it may sound trivial, anyone who saw the rooms in which this team worked would understand. Multiple flip chart pages were the most evident. However, when team members spend 40 hours a week in the same room with the same group of people, they start getting comfortable. Information one might become accustomed to finding in the same spot would now be somewhere else as a result of the move. The problem became evident rather quickly. The facilitator did her best to shift other in-house meetings around and, after a couple of days, the team was able to be in one room for the final eight days of the blitz.

Lesson 6: Train the Team at the Beginning of the Process

When in the team process the quality planning training occurs is an element of timing. The meeting evaluations led the facilitator to conclude that the team would have benefited from receiving training in the quality planning methodology on the first day. Although it was not a clear detriment that the training was conducted on the second day, the members clearly attained a good level of comfort with an understanding of how the project would be approached.

Lesson 7: Plan Agendas to Match Tasks with the Appropriate Part of the Day

Mornings were consistently the most productive time for the team, thus planning accordingly for this phenomena proved to make a difference in the group dynamics. Afternoon discussions were arduous, requiring the use of more creative facilitation techniques such as breaks, standing up to think and work, using small group work, or giving assignments requiring the need to utilize another location.

Lesson 8: Conduct and Prepare for Presentations Judiciously

The Chart CHIMPS were very creative and had a lot of fun preparing a presentation for the organization's management council during the second week of the project. However, this preparation required valuable time away from the team's work. The facilitator cannot clearly say whether this should or should not have been done. The presentation was beneficial as an informational update to the council, and certainly should have occurred at some point. However, taking time away from the three weeks allotted for the blitz needs to be weighed against the stress relief and team building provided through this creative outlet. In making such a determination, one must consider the culture of the organization and the relative necessity of such presentations.

When the group completed the product development stage, it was time to present the product to the quality council. Staying true to form, the CHIMPS spent hours preparing a detailed report that would cover every question the council might raise, when in fact an executive summary was all the quality council members required. Don't overwhelm executives with details—get to the point.

Lesson 9: Initiate Benchmarking Activities Prior to the Team Meetings

The team was constantly frustrated by its benchmarking experiences. Trying to gather pertinent information from other organizations in less than two weeks was not successful. This is not to imply that the time constraint was the only problem. The principal problem is that benchmarking is a time-consuming and often arduous process. In anticipation of the project, benchmarking data from other organizations were requested, and to this day they have not been received. Even now, team members joke about continuing to wait for the data to arrive.

Another problem with this process is the time required to analyze benchmarking information. Often the information that was received was not necessarily what was needed, or was so detailed that the team had to assign a member the role of research analyst to glean what was valuable. Therefore, it is clear that plenty of advance work on benchmarking with someone devoting the time necessary to gather pertinent data would be the logical solution.

Lesson 10: The Scope of the Project Should Determine the Timeline

Developing a new system for patient documentation is a tremendous undertaking. While the quality council supported this project because of its importance and scope, efficiency in producing the multifaceted product might have been improved through the chartering of multiple implementation teams, thereby allowing the team to focus on concept development instead of minutiae.

Summary

Our objective was to share our collective experiences as the quality administrator, team facilitator, and team leader with the organization's first quality planning blitz team. As of March 1, 1996, the new charting system has been implemented for these distinct patient populations: orthopedics, neurology, labor and delivery, postpartum, and newborns. The implementation plan outlined by the CHIMPS identified December 31, 1996, as the date that housewide inpatient implementation would be complete. In July 1996, a quality planning team addressing the outpatient documentation system, including a goal to incorporate the new inpatient system, will be initiated.

In retrospect, our experiences have taught us what works and what doesn't when using a blitz team.

Barriers	Enablers
Commitment of resources	**C**ommitted team members
Hindrance to change	**H**onesty and humor
Usual thinking (in the box)	**I**nnovative thinking
Management unsupportive	**M**aterials
Pessimism	**P**riority projects
Scheduling	**S**upport of key players

If you have these enablers in your organization, you too can overcome these common barriers and have a successful blitz team. Don't be a CHUMP, be a CHIMP!

Discussion Exercise for a One-Hour Quality Council Meeting

1. List the lessons learned identified in this chapter on a flip chart.

2. Engage the quality council members to brainstorm additional lessons learned.

3. Identify and discuss strategies that address each lesson learned.

4. Assign a champion from the quality council to each strategy that has been identified. The responsibility of the champion is to ensure that the lesson learned is addressed for future blitz teams chartered by the quality council. It may be necessary to assign the champion role to an individual who is not a member of the quality council. If this is true, a quality council member should be assigned as the sponsor to the champion that is identified.

Discussion Exercise for a Two-Hour Department Manager Meeting

1. Assign a member of the quality council to facilitate this session. Other council members should be available to help facilitate small group discussions.

2. Organize participants in groups of six to eight people and provide a flip chart to each group.

3. The facilitator introduces the mission statement for a quality planning blitz team that is being chartered by the quality council to the group.

4. Each small group identifies barriers to the team achieving their mission in the stated time frame.

5. Members of the quality council facilitate each small group, identifying strategies to address the barriers.

6. Each small group presents the barriers and enablers to the entire group.

7. The quality council member facilitating the exercise (preferably the liaison for the project) reviews the common barriers and enablers and solicits support from the large group to address all the barriers to ensure the team's success.

Discussion Exercise for a 90-Minute Quality Facilitator Meeting

The objectives are to gain support for the blitz team concept and to provide facilitators for quality blitz teams keys for success. This session, if possible, should be facilitated by an individual who has facilitated a traditional quality team *and* a blitz team.

1. Prior to the meeting, ask each participant to submit a list of barriers he or she has encountered while facilitating a quality team.

2. The facilitator for this exercise reviews the list of barriers to determine which ones can be addressed by a blitz team.

3. The facilitator identifies barriers to a blitz team achieving its mission in a timely manner (see the Lessons Learned section).

4. The facilitator reviews the barriers identified by the group, indicating which ones can be addressed with a blitz format. If there are barriers that can't be addressed by a blitz team, have the group brainstorm enablers.

5. The facilitator presents the barriers to a blitz team achieving its mission, based on the experiences.

6. The group identifies and discusses strategies to overcome the barriers.

Appendix: Chart CHIMPS at NHRMC

Team Members

Member's name	Title	Department	Role
Celeste Beal	Respiratory therapist	Respiratory care	Flipper
Kim Blake	Clinical nurse specialist	Coastal Rehabilitation Hospital	Leader
Evelyn Bowden	Discharge planning nurse	Patient care resources	Etiquette director
Roxanne Brammer	Staff nurse	Birthplace	
Wendy Fletcher-Hardee	Staff nurse	Medical/surgical	Timekeeper
Beth Layman	Assistant director	Medical records	
John Long	Staff nurse	Coronary care unit	Recorder
Ray Nestler	Clinical nutritionist	Food and nutrition	Glossary keeper

Team Consultants

Consultant's name	Title	Department	Role
Kathy Helak	Administrator	Surgical nursing services	Outcomes management champion
Dee Lammers	Project specialist	Information services	Electronic medical record
Karen Marchbanks	Coordinator of clinical epidemiology	Quality management	JCAHO standards

Support

Name	Title	Department	Role
Julie O'Shaughnessy	Administrator	Quality management	Advocate
Anne Patterson	Vice president	Operations	Quality council liaison
Peggy Schroeder	Quality coordinator	Quality resources	Facilitator

Notes

1. Juran Institute, *Quality Planning Ready Reference* (Wilton, Conn.: Juran Institute, 1994).

2. Peter R. Scholtes, *The Team Handbook* (Madison, Wis.: Joiner Associates, 1988), 6-4–6-7.

Kimberly Blake is the manager of the stroke, brain injury, day hospital programs, and case management services at Coastal Rehabilitation Services of New Hanover Regional Medical Center. She has diverse experiences as a quality resource facilitator and team leader for the medical center. Her responsibilities include the overall design, development, and monitoring of the quality processes and performance improvement activities for the rehabilitation services product line. Blake earned an M.S.N. degree from the University of Missouri at Columbia; a B.S.N. degree from Central Methodist College, Fayette, Missouri; and a degree from Massillon Community Hospital in Massillon, Ohio.

Julie O'Shaughnessy, director of performance improvement at New Hanover Regional Medical Center, serves as a key resource to the organization regarding quality management. Her responsibilities include the overall design, development, and monitoring of the organization's quality processes and performance improvement activities. In addition, she is responsible for the direct operation of the management engineering, discharge planning, infection control, risk management, social work, quality resources, and utilization review functions. She is a Certified Professional in Healthcare Quality (CPHQ) and belongs to a variety of professional organizations, such as the National Association for Healthcare Quality, the American College of Healthcare Executives, American Society for Quality, and the North Carolina Association for Healthcare Quality. O'Shaughnessy earned an M.H.A. degree from Duke University and a B.S. degree from Cornell University.

Peggy Schroeder is the quality educator/facilitator in the performance improvement department at New Hanover Regional Medical Center (NHRMC). She has extensive experience facilitating quality improvement and quality planning teams for the medical center. Her current responsibilities involve overall design and coordination of education and development of programs for managers and employees in the medical center's quality initiative, which includes week-long facilitator and team training. In addition, she is responsible for mentoring the more than 75 quality improvement and planning teams currently in place at NHRMC. Schroeder belongs to the National Association for Healthcare Quality and the North Carolina Association for Healthcare Quality. She earned a B.A. degree in philosophy from the University of North Carolina at Wilmington and is a member of *Who's Who Among Students in American Universities and Colleges* and the Honor Society of Phi Kappa Phi.

Index

READER FEEDBACK

Fax to ASQ Quality Press Acquisitions: 414-272-1734

Comments and Areas for Improvement:
The Handbook for Managing Change in Health Care

Please give us your comments, feedback, and suggestions for making this book more useful. We believe in the importance of continuous improvement and in meeting your needs. Your comments will help determine what improvements can be made in all ASQ Quality Press books.

Please share your opinion by circling the number below:

Ratings of the book	Needs Work		Satisfactory		Excellent	Comments
Stucture, flow, and logic	1	2	3	4	5	
Content, ideas, and information	1	2	3	4	5	
Style, clarity, ease of reading	1	2	3	4	5	
Held my interest	1	2	3	4	5	
Met my overall expectations	1	2	3	4	5	

I read the book because:

The best part of the book was:

The least satisfactory part of the book was:

Other suggestions for improvement:

General comments:

Thank you for your feedback. If you do not have access to a fax machine, please mail this form to:
ASQ Quality Press, 611 East Wisconsin Avenue, P.O. Box 3005, Milwaukee, WI 53201-3005   Phone: 414-272-8575